SIXTH EDITION

STRATEGIC MARKETING FOR NONPROFIT ORGANIZATIONS

Alan R. Andreasen

Georgetown University

Philip Kotler

Northwestern University

Upper Saddle River, New Jersey 07458

Library of Congress Cataloging-in-Publication Data

Andreasen, Alan R., 1934-
    Strategic marketing for nonprofit organizations / Alan R. Andreasen, Philip Kotler.—
6th ed.
        p. cm.
    Rev. ed. of: Strategic marketing for nonprofit organizations / Philip Kotler, Alan R.
Andreasen. 1996.
    Includes bibliographical references and index.
    ISBN 0-13-041977-X
    1. Nonprofit organizations—Marketing. I. Kotler, Philip. II. Kotler, Philip. Strategic
marketing for nonprofit organizations. III. Title.

HF5415 .A622 2002
658.8—dc21   2002027440

Senior Editor: Wendy Craven
Editor-in-Chief: Jeff Shelstad
Assistant Editor: Melissa Pellerano
Editorial Assistant: Danielle Rose Serra
Marketing Manager: Michelle O'Brien
Marketing Assistant: Amanda Fisher
Managing Editor (Production): John Roberts
Production Editor: Renata Butera
Production Assistant: Joe DeProspero
Permissions Coordinator: Suzanne Grappi
Associate Director, Manufacturing: Vincent Scelta
Production Manager: Arnold Vila
Manufacturing Buyer: Michelle Klein
Cover Design: Joseph Sengotta
Cover Illustration/Photo: The Art Institute of Chicago; Photographer Mike Peters
Composition: Carlisle Communications, Ltd.
Full-Service Project Management: Carlisle Communications, Ltd.
Printer/Binder: R.R. Donnelly

Pearson Education LTD.
Pearson Education Australia PTY, Limited
Pearson Education Singapore, Pte. Ltd.
Pearson Education North Asia Ltd.
Pearson Education, Canada, Ltd.
Pearson Educación de México, S.A. de C.V.
Pearson Education—Japan
Pearson Education Malaysia, Pte. Ltd.

10 9 8 7 6 5 4 3 2 1
ISBN 0-13-041977-X

Contents

Preface

This sixth edition of *Strategic Marketing for Nonprofit Organizations* comes at a time when nonprofit marketing is poised to have a much greater impact on the field of nonprofit management and on the growing intersection between that sector and the business world. The first two editions of this book served to legitimize marketing as a distinct career and a distinct educational discipline, while the third edition focused less on *whether* one should carry out nonprofit marketing and more on *how* one should do it well. The fourth edition shifted its emphasis to focus more closely on strategic planning. As the fourth edition noted, "The major need of the nonprofit sector now is not so much for techniques to implement marketing, but for assistance in strategic planning. Many nonprofits face significant declines in traditional sources of revenue, dramatic changes in their customer mix, and bold new competition. They need help rethinking where they are going and what broad strategies they should be using to get there."

The fifth edition strongly reflected the growing sophistication of the field and its cadre of skilled practitioners by incorporating their insights into the text and examples. It also emphasized the growing importance of social marketing, the application of marketing concepts not just to *organizations* but to *programs* designed to bring about social change. It tiptoed into the international arena where the nonprofit sector was beginning to have a significant impact and sought to reflect the blurring of the previously distinct lines between nonprofit and commercial marketing.

This sixth edition marks a major change in the way in which nonprofit marketing is conceived and applied. First of all, much more strongly than in previous editions, it seeks to position marketing as among the most critical—if not *the* most critical—disciplines needed for nonprofit success. It argues that success ultimately requires the influencing of the behavior in a wide range of key target markets—clients, funders, policy makers, volunteers, and the media, as well as the nonprofit's own staff. This is the province of marketing because marketing is the "behavioral influence business." The book positions marketing as central to top management's achievement of the organization's mission. Implicit in this volume is the notion that everyone in nonprofit management—including the CEO—ought to have a thorough grounding in marketing and what it does and can do.

Second, this edition reflects the breaking down of three kinds of boundaries that heretofore limited the field. First, it removes the conception of nonprofit marketing as primarily a North American phenomenon. As we will show in several places in the book, nonprofit enterprise is flourishing everywhere in the world, including Asian countries with a tradition of family self-help and formerly communist countries with a tradition of state social service. We recognize that we have much to learn—as well as contribute—as we broaden our compass to include these new environments.

The sixth edition also removes the assumption that the target audience for a text on nonprofit marketing is only present and future practitioners in nonprofit organizations. It is a growing reality that both the government and for-profit sectors have a growing interest in "social enterprise." Many government agencies have missions highly similar to nonprofits and are often major players in the field of social marketing. At the same time, corporations are increasingly becoming involved in the social sector through venture philanthropy, cause marketing, and corporate volunteerism programs. Managers—and future managers—in both the government and corporate domains need to appreciate the concepts and tools described here and understand the nonprofit environment and what it is like to try to bring about change within it.

Finally, consistent with its behavioral focus, this edition organizes much of the discussion of strategic and tactical options around two central behavioral science models, what we call "the Stages of Change" and "the BCOS drivers." These models guide our thinking about how to influence behavior in many different contexts. They provide a powerful portable framework for nonprofit practitioners to use to be successful in this challenging environment

ACKNOWLEDGMENTS

The first edition of this book was the result of a happy association of Philip Kotler with extremely creative and valued colleagues and students in the marketing department of the J. L. Kellogg Graduate School of Management at Northwestern University. The second edition benefited from dialogues with members of the marketing department: Bobby J. Calder, Richard M. Clewett, Jehoshua Eliashberg, Trudy Kehret, Lakshmanan Krishnamurthi, Stephen A. LaTour, Sidney J. Levy, Api Ruzdic, Louis W. Stern, Brian Sternthal, Alice M. Tybout, and Andris A. Zoltners, as well as reviews by Paul Bloom (University of North Carolina); Roberta N. Clarke (Boston University); and Karen F. A. Fox (University of Santa Clara).

The third, fourth, and fifth editions, in which Alan Andreasen participated, have reflected the input of many additional academics and nonprofit practitioners. Particularly valuable have been the insights of Jean Manning, now of the U.S. Senate; William Smith of the Academy for Educational Development; Mary Debus and Michael Ramah of Porter/Novelli; Bill Novelli of AARP; Tony Meyer of the U.S. Agency for International Development; and Robert Hornik and Martin Fishbein of the University of Pennsylvania.

The sixth edition reflects insights from practitioners such as Cynthia Currence of the American Cancer Society, Susan Kirby formerly of the Centers for Disease Control and Prevention, Kurt Aschermann of the Boys & Girls Clubs of America, Tom Reis of the Kellogg Foundation, Sharyn Sutton of Sutton Social Marketing, James Austin of the Harvard Business School, and Christine Letts of the Hauser Center at Harvard University. Thanks must be given to the more than 50 participants in three Nonprofit Marketing Managers Summits held in 2000 under the auspices of the Social Marketing Institute for their wisdom and experience. Many of them are represented by the comments, vignettes, and graphics in the chapters to follow.

The assistance of Frank Bracken in preparing the end-of-chapter questions is also gratefully acknowledged.

SECTION I

Developing a Customer Orientation

CHAPTER 1

The Growth and Development of Nonprofit Marketing

CHAPTER 2

Developing a Customer-Centered Mindset

CHAPTER 1

The Growth and Development of Nonprofit Marketing

The nonprofit world in the 21st Century is using technology in imaginative new ways. An example is the extensive use of Personal Digital Assistants or PDAs. In Nicaragua, Microsoft's Disaster Assistance Technology Program is helping Save the Children manage disaster relief efforts in remote locations using PDAs. A critical problem after a hurricane is to determine where help is needed and this, in turn, requires field workers to survey villages to find out their condition, the type of assistance needed, and any likely impediments to providing relief (e.g., washed-out bridges). In the past, this work would have had to be done by hand with paper forms and faxes to headquarters. Now, light, easily portable PDAs can be used to collect the data in a standardized form, download it back to a laptop at the hotel, and e-mail it to a central office. (Soon, even more advanced technology will permit the PDAs to transmit the details themselves.)

PDAs are also used by social workers in Atlanta to enter data about homeless people while encountering them on the street and, in many cases, instantly hooking them up with programs that can help them. (It is often impossible to get a homeless person to come to the office to fill in forms.) In San Francisco, HIV/AIDS workers keep track of intravenous drug users' needle usage and demographic characteristics. This easily recorded information is used to track shifts in risky behaviors and tie any trends to various at-risk groups. Such data can then lead to quicker interventions to deflect a possible outburst of infection in the community.

The ability of PDAs to present images on their screens has allowed imaginative conservationists in the Kalahari Desert of Africa to get native Bushmen to record their findings as they trek the bush. The trekkers, who are illiterate, select icons from the screen to record their observations in some detail, including how many animals of what types were observed, their gender, what they were doing, and what they were eating. Global Positioning System software built into the PDAs allows the researchers to match the trekkers' sightings with specific geographic locations . This CyberTracker system allows mapping of animal movements and helps anticipate potential problems. The system has already been used to study the reintroduction of the black rhinoceros into the Karoo National Park in South Africa and to track forest elephants in the Odzala National Park in the Congo. The future will see digital cameras added to the PDAs to record visually what is actually being observed and recorded. The applications then will be even more imaginative.

Source: Adapted from Nicole Wallace, "Good Works in the Palm of a Hand," *The Chronicle of Philanthropy,* September 20, 2001, pp. 41–43.

SOME MYTHS ABOUT THE NONPROFIT WORLD

In the world of business management, it is not uncommon to find otherwise knowledgeable individuals dismissing the nonprofit sector as a rather minor, not very serious corner of society. Among the canards one hears are the following:

- While nonprofits address important problems in nooks and crannies, the sector is not a very significant component of the overall output of society.
- While nonprofits may have some importance in North America, in the global economy they are very minor players.
- With a few rare exceptions, nonprofit organizations are relatively small, local enterprises specializing in narrow domains.
- Nonprofits tend to be populated with—and run by—"do-gooders" who have limited interest in efficient management and a dismissive attitude toward those who do.
- While the missions of nonprofits may be socially very important, the management challenges they face are relatively mundane in comparison to the really hard problems that businesses address routinely.
- Working in the nonprofit sector is a poor career move for those who wish to make "Big Money" and be major players in the national and international scenes.
- Businesses need to have only token involvement in the nonprofit world in order to maintain good public relations or to produce short-term marketing gains.

In this and succeeding chapters of this book, we shall demonstrate that all of the previous statements are myths and, indeed, that the nonprofit sector is a large, growing, important, challenging sector that is relevant to business and businesspeople in ways they may not have appreciated, for example:

- Nonprofits comprise about 7 percent of the entire paid labor force in the United States and, if one adds an appropriate value to the 200 million hours of unpaid volunteer service performed by over 100 million volunteers, this amounts to almost 11 percent of the workforce in this country. (If one then adds in the government sector, this figure increases to almost one-third.)

- The nonprofit sector has at times been growing faster than most sectors of business (excepting technology).

- Internationally, the nonprofit sector is often as important in countries such as the United Kingdom and Scandinavia as it is in North America and, in parts of the world such as Central and Eastern Europe, it is growing at an extremely rapid pace.[1]

- The sector has now developed a number of very large, very sophisticated organizations. The top five nonprofits took in $2.4 *billion* each in 2000.[2]

• Some nonprofits are small and still controlled by charismatic founders who often have limited management experience. However, the sector now has a large number of very complex multi-site—often international—organizations. Further, the field is increasingly populated with well-trained MBAs and ex-businesspeople. The recent growth of venture philanthropy is expected to have further positive effects on nonprofit management effectiveness.

• While the "difficulty" of one's management challenges may be a matter of opinion, very few corporate chieftains would think it easier to increase their market share 2 percent than to reduce the number of AIDS cases in an African country with volunteer workers, an antagonistic government, countervailing religious and cultural norms, rampant customer illiteracy, and crumbling public infrastructure.

• While nonprofit managers clearly earn less than equivalent for-profit managers (who can get dramatic stock bonuses in addition to salaries), there is still "real" money to be made. A recent survey by *The Chronicle of Philanthropy* listed 30 leaders of major nonprofit organizations and foundations with salaries over $400,000 and several over $1 million.[3]

• Sophisticated businesspeople have learned that there are dramatic benefits from involvement in the nonprofit sector that go beyond routine charity and occasional cause-marketing ventures. In 2000, Sears committed to a million hours of volunteering because it learned of the significant impact this kind of social activity has on employee morale. Timberland is deeply involved in the work of City Year for the same reasons and because this helps the firm define and differentiate itself from competitors.[4]

Why Study Nonprofit Marketing?

This is a book designed for both present and future managers. It is about marketing, specifically marketing in nonprofit organizations. But it is not just about the challenges facing marketing managers in nonprofit organizations. Why is that? First, marketing is a discipline that applies whenever one has the challenge of influencing the behavior of others. In the private sector, this means influencing customers to eat at your fast-food chain and not at rival eateries or at home. It means influencing retailers to stock your merchandise and, through *internal marketing,* making sure that the frontline staff of service organizations really deliver exceptional customer service. Private sector managers at all levels, right up to the CEO and COO, know that marketing and a customer-centered marketing mindset are crucial to their success.

The same is true in the nonprofit world, and it is also true in many parts of the public sector. Managers in these worlds also realize that their missions involve influencing donors to give, volunteers to come forward, clients to seek help, staff to be client-friendly, and so on. Therefore, marketing and the marketing mindset are critical to their success as well.

Finally, players outside the nonprofit world are increasingly being called upon to interact with the nonprofit sector.[5] Government agencies such as the National Cancer Institute or the Centers for Disease Control and Prevention partner with organizations like the American Cancer Society or the Campaign for Tobacco-Free Kids to achieve mutual objectives. Corporations increasingly partner with nonprofits to achieve corporate objectives. Cause-related marketing is a $7 billion sector with corporations like Nike and Coca-Cola actively engaged with Boys & Girls Clubs of America in achieving each organization's objectives as well as the objectives they have in common. And, of course, a great many corporate managers and marketers at some time in their careers volunteer for nonprofit organizations and/or serve on their boards.

Thus, managers in all three sectors need to understand marketing and how marketing is—and ought to be—used in the nonprofit environment. Nonprofit managers need to know how to be better at influencing all of the different publics whose behaviors determine the nonprofit's success. Government managers need to know about marketing techniques in the nonprofit world because they might be useful in parallel settings in their own environments and because they need to know how nonprofit marketers think and act so that they can work effectively with them. Finally, corporate marketers need to understand nonprofit marketers and the special world in which they operate if they are going to partner effectively with them.

Thus, this book is really about influencing behavior in a special environment. It is important to stress that, while we believe the concepts and tools outlined in this book are in some sense generic and fundamental and, thus, apply to all kinds of behaviors (including getting a date, a job, or a promotion), we know that the nonprofit world is different in important ways. This is a final reason why managers in many environments need to study nonprofit marketing. First, they need to understand how the nonprofit environment is different so that they can work effectively within it. But, understanding these differences has a very valuable secondary benefit. It can be a very "stretching" undertaking to think about ways in which basic marketing concepts and tools that are used to sell burgers and airplane seats can be applied to obstinate problems like getting New Zealand fathers not to slap their children as a "natural" form of discipline. One of the great rewards that have come to commercial marketers who have carried their skills into this new environment is that they come away invigorated with new insights and a more profound appreciation for the robustness of their armamentarium.[6]

This last sentiment is very much reflected in a watershed article by management guru Peter Drucker. In the *Harvard Business Review* in the summer of 1989, Drucker argued that nonprofit organizations are becoming America's management leaders, especially in the areas of strategy and the effective use of boards of directors. Drucker claims, "They are practicing what most American businesses only preach." Drucker continues:

> Twenty years ago, management was a dirty word for those involved in nonprofit organizations. It meant business, and nonprofits prided themselves on being free of the taint of commercialism and above such sordid considerations as the bottom line. Now most of them have learned that nonprofits need management even more than business does, precisely because they lack the discipline of the bottom line. The nonprofits are, of course, still dedicated to "doing good." But they also realize that good intentions are no substitute for organization and leadership, for accountability, performance, and results. Those require management and that, in turn, begins with the organization's mission.[7]

More recently, Rosabeth Moss Kanter has argued that nonprofits may be the "beta site" for new management innovations in the twenty-first century.[8]

History of an Idea

The idea of applying marketing to nonprofit organizations had its "birth" in a series of articles by Kotler and Levy,[9] Kotler and Zaltman,[10] and Shapiro[11] between 1969 and 1973. These articles argued that

> Marketing is a pervasive societal activity that goes considerably beyond the selling of toothpaste, soap, and steel. Political contests remind us that candidates are marketed as well as soap; student recruitment in colleges reminds us that higher education is marketed; and fundraising reminds us that "causes" are marketed. . . . [Yet no] attempt is made to examine whether the principles of "good" marketing in traditional product areas are transferable to the marketing of services, persons, and ideas.[12]

The 1970s and 1980s saw the growth period of this philosophy and a dramatically steep rise in its acceptance. As Andreasen has noted, adoption of marketing concepts and tools occurred most rapidly in those areas most like the private sector in terms of the organizational environment and the kinds of transactions involved.[13] Early applications were in service marketing areas like education, health care, recreation, transportation, libraries, and the arts, as well as in product sales like contraceptive social marketing.[14] This early work stimulated scholars excited at the prospect of expanding the horizons of the discipline and testing the robustness of its concepts and tools. These scholars included both those inside academic marketing, such as the present authors and such people as Christopher Lovelock,[15] Charles Weinberg,[16] Michael Rothschild,[17] Paul Bloom,[18] Gerald Zaltman,[19] and numerous others, but also those outside the traditional field, such as Robin MacStravic in health care[20] and John Crompton in leisure and recreation.[21]

In the late 1980s, the nonprofit marketing idea extended itself into new organizational environments such as government agencies and new kinds of transactions where, for example, no products or services were involved (child abuse) and no money changed hands. The excitement inherent in this widening of the purview of the field was reflected in several general textbooks that became available,[22] as well as trade books and textbooks in specific subcategories such as the marketing of health care,[23] education,[24] religion,[25] places,[26] countries,[27] and social issues.[28] Specialized readers, conference proceedings, collections,[29] and casebooks[30] abounded. The period also saw the beginnings of *social marketing,* which saw texts by Manoff appear in 1985[31] and by Kotler and Roberto in 1989.[32]

The 1980s also saw a number of nonacademic publications appearing that summarized experiences from practicing nonprofit marketers. Prominent among these was a series of reports on contraceptive social marketing from the Population Information Program at Johns Hopkins University,[33] a marketing planning workbook from the United Way of America,[34] handbooks for conducting focus group research[35] and carrying out communications programs for child survival[36] from the Academy for Educational Development, and a planner's guide on health communications from the Office of Cancer Communications in the U.S. Department of Health and Human Services.[37] These were supplemented by speeches and articles from a wide array of thoughtful practitioners, such as William Novelli, Mary Debus, and William Smith, writing and lecturing about their experiences in applying marketing in the nonprofit sector.[38]

In addition to a growing array of articles on nonprofits in traditional and not-so-traditional journals, several new journals appeared, including the *Journal of Health Care Marketing,* the *Health Marketing Quarterly,* the *Praeger Series in Public and Nonprofit Sector Marketing,* the *Journal of Public Policy and Marketing, Health Marketing, Hospital Public Relations,* the *Journal of Marketing for Higher Education,* the *Journal of Marketing for Mental Health, Nonprofit and Voluntary Sector Marketing,* and the *Journal of Marketing Management for Professionals.* Journals in such diverse fields as library science, art history, leisure studies, occupational therapy, and hospital management joined the marketing bandwagon. In 2002, over 240 universities were offering courses in nonprofit management, a tripling of the number found in 1995.[39]

In the field, marketing specialists in nonprofit organizations were no longer a rarity. Although the content of their jobs still varies widely, they no longer have to hide behind deceptive job titles like director of development, education coordinator, or patient liaison officer. A wide range of consulting organizations sprang up in major centers, especially around Washington, D.C., to offer their services as marketing specialists in the nonprofit sector. To meet this new competition, the major traditional consulting, advertising, and public relations firms found that they had to have special divisions or individuals dedicated to providing nonprofit marketing assistance. The growth of cause-marketing in the 1990s accelerated this pace.

The Millennium

The last decade of the twentieth century saw four important developments in the field. First, there was a significant acceleration in the growth of **social marketing.**[40] Once a tiny subset of the field of nonprofit marketing that focused on the applications of private sector marketing to improve social welfare, social marketing has grown dramatically in the last 20 years. Major international and domestic behavior change programs now routinely have social marketing components.[41] Individuals with titles such as "manager of social marketing" can now be found in private consulting organizations. Social marketing centers have been established at the University of South Florida in Tampa, the University of Strathclyde in Scotland, and in Warsaw, Poland. Publications abound. In addition to books by Kotler and Roberto and by Manoff that appeared in the previous decade, social marketing has spawned a teaching note at Harvard by Rangun,[42] a book of commissioned chapters edited by Fine,[43] and new books by Andreasen[44] and Kotler, Roberto, and Lee.[45] A Social Marketing Institute has been established and three annual conferences are held in Clearwater, Sacramento, and Washington. There is now a journal, the *Social Marketing Quarterly,* and a range of articles in mainstream journals and papers at mainstream marketing conferences.

The second major change in the 1990s was the growing attention being paid to the **international dimensions** of nonprofit marketing.[46] Much that has been written about nonprofit marketing in the preceding 20 years was about experiences in the United States. Although some handbooks have been written overseas,[47] as well as selected articles and cases,[48] most insights reflected American experience and management. However, it has long been known that there is a vigorous nonprofit sector in other Western developed countries and in the Third World. As is documented in the following pages, interest in nonprofit enterprises in these cultures has grown dramatically in recent years as a result of three forces. First, many governments that were once the primary source of social support for their citizens are now cutting back and leaving private nonprofit organizations to shoulder the burden.[49] Second, many international social agencies, such as the World Bank and the U.S. Agency for International Development, have had to rely on local and international nonprofits to carry out, and then sustain, major social interventions. Finally, the emergence of many new countries, first from "behind the Iron Curtain" and more recently from within the former Soviet Union, has dramatically increased the interest in nonprofits and what they might do to replace programs of defunct socialist states.[50] Many nonprofits have already recognized the importance of international markets and have developed international partnerships; for example, Goodwill Industries of America changed its name to Goodwill Industries International, Inc. This reflected what its chairman said is "the global influence of our organization in providing training to those in need." Goodwill Industries is the largest network of privately operated vocational rehabilitation programs.[51]

The third major change was the growth in importance of **corporate involvement in the nonprofit sector.** As nonprofits found themselves in greater and greater need of outside support, they turned to private sector partnerships for assistance. In cause-related marketing, Frito-Lay agrees to contribute to an anti-drug program for every bag of potato chips sold, for example, or General Foods gives 10 cents to Mothers Against Drunk Driving for every Tang proof of purchase submitted. Corporations have found that these and other public sector activities not only improve their public image but also contribute to their bottom line.[52] Although these liaisons raise a number of difficult questions for nonprofit managers,[53] there is no doubt that they have dramatically increased in number and scope. Cone Communications estimates that cause-marketing generated over $9 billion for charities at the turn of the century.

Corporations have also increased their attention to company volunteer programs. One of the largest growth areas for the Points of Light Foundation, a nonprofit committed to stimulating volunteering, has been in the corporate sector. Corporations have found that, in addition to building corporate reputations and improving local and national political and social connections, company volunteerism can have a major impact on employee morale.

Part of the pressure on corporations to get involved with the nonprofit sector is growing criticism of corporate practices that are deemed to be socially irresponsible. The fact that stellar corporations such as Nike and Wal-Mart have been criticized for allegedly condoning sweatshop labor has put enormous pressure on companies to change the nature of their interactions with the "social sector."[54] Accelerating this pressure has been a relatively new stock market trend (and corporations pay close attention to the stock market these days). This trend has been the emergence of "social" mutual funds that are based on careful screening of corporate social performance. A recent study showed that many of these funds have outperformed that market and are now major market players. In the early 1990s, Amy Domini developed a "Domini 400 Social Index" to rate corporations. The Domini Social Equity Fund based on it has over $1.8 billion in assets and in mid-2000 was ranked the 15th fastest-growing fund in the United States.[55]

The fourth major development was the growth of concern about the **ethics** of the nonprofit field. There have always been scams in the charity field, from the individual drunk asking for money for "food" to Jim Bakker asking for donations for the ministry he grossly mismanaged. More recently, concerns have grown in a number of other areas. First, as business organizations have become more involved in social and charitable activities, a number of observers have become particularly concerned about the ethics of both the corporations and the nonprofits that participate with these ventures.[56] Second, as marketing techniques are increasingly employed in trying to bring about changes with regard to highly volatile social issues such as AIDS, abortion, abuse, and so on, marketers have been forced to ask themselves questions about when and how they should be using their powerful technologies.[57] Finally, marketers have recognized that many approaches that they have used in the nonprofit world might not be justifiable in other contexts.[58] They have asked whether political advertising should be held to the same standards as corporate advertising, whether market research techniques should probe subjects that are taboo in certain ethnic and religious cultures, or whether the importance of certain ends might justify means that we might ordinarily not condone. The first book on the topic, *Ethics in Social Marketing,* appeared in 2001.[59]

THIS BOOK

We shall revisit all of these issues throughout this book; however, the book has more fundamental objectives. It provides a motivated audience of students and practitioners with the concepts, techniques, and illustrations needed to make them first-rate nonprofit marketing managers. The book, therefore, is decidedly not introductory in the sense of acquainting the naïve reader with marketing and its possibilities and motivating him or her to begin to use marketing in the day-to-day management of a nonprofit organization. Instead, the book assumes that the reader is *already* motivated and knows a little about marketing and what it might do but wants to know how to actually carry out marketing programs more extensively and more effectively.

As will be demonstrated repeatedly in the chapters to follow, this book is rooted in two basic premises. First, it posits that marketing goes on everywhere in a nonprofit environment (and the private and government sectors, too) and everyone needs to be good at marketing because he or she must *influence behavior* to achieve success. Second, we believe that a first-rate marketer (whether a "marketing manager" or a CEO or an HR director) is one who has acquired (1) an ingrained appreciation of the mindset of marketing, (2) a comprehensive and practical process for solving marketing problems, and (3) an awareness and understanding of the latest tools and techniques that can be used to make effective marketing decisions in specific areas. The book is organized around these premises.

It is also a book specifically designed around the unique nonprofit environment. The "nonprofit" distinction is not just an academic exercise. If there were not factors that were unique to the nonprofit context, there would be no point to a book like this; any of the many excellent general marketing texts would be perfectly satisfactory. But nonprofit marketing is not the same as for-profit marketing. The student and practitioner must appreciate the differences because they have major effects on what one can and cannot do as a marketer. We begin by considering the evolution of this new sector and the significantly increased role for marketing.

Before proceeding, one caveat must be stated. Although the book focuses primarily on "nonprofits," an organizational form that, as we shall see, has a relatively strict and clear definition, we will from time to time employ examples and lessons involving organizations in the public sector, such as the Office of Cancer Communications of the National Cancer Institute, or the Centers for Disease Control and Prevention. It is our view that the missions and environments of such entities are not significantly different from those found in the nonprofit sector.

EVOLUTION OF NONPROFIT ORGANIZATIONS

Nelson Rosenbaum has proposed that since the American Revolution, the role of non-profit organizations in society has evolved through four stages. The earliest stage con-forms to what he terms a *voluntary/civic model.*[60] In Pilgrim times through the beginning of the twentieth century, services that were not available from the government and were beyond the means of individual citizens were often provided for each other by neighbors. Thus, in those times—and in some suburban and rural areas and some fundamentalist religious communities today—citizens would band together to operate the volunteer fire department or to help a needy family build a barn. Such a model was (and in some cases, still is) appropriate to a world with homogeneous interests, personal philosophies based on sharing, and a generally low level of economic welfare.

As the country prospered, the industrial revolution concentrated great wealth in the hands of a few families. Whether out of a sense of social responsibility or plain guilt, extremely rich families like the Morgans, Rockefellers, and Carnegies developed a pattern of what Rosenbaum calls *philanthropic patronage.* This patronage signifi-cantly benefited major U.S. educational and cultural institutions during the early part of the twentieth century. It finds its remnants today in the large foundations that play a prominent role in funding many nonprofits and also play a prominent role in shaping the national agenda in the areas of education, health care, political reform, and the environment. This role is not without its critics.[61]

Following the onset of the Great Depression and the rapid growth of government-supported social institutions and programs, America in the 1940s and 1950s turned to a nonprofit model based on *rights and entitlements.* Many groups argued that they were entitled to at least some share of public taxation funds for their work, their institutions, or both, in part because they served the general social interest.

The final stage is the one in which we presently find ourselves in the United States and parts of the developing world—the *competitive/market* stage. In the earlier three stages, nonprofits relied for support on (1) individual willingness to share, (2) the gen-erosity of the wealthy, or (3) the largess of federal, state, and municipal governments and the major foundations. Today, nonprofits cannot rely on automatic continuation of traditional sources of support. Further, as they turn increasingly to the marketplace for this support, they find other nonprofits there searching for the same subsistence. The consequence in the twenty-first century is that the greatest challenges facing nonprofit managers are *competitive* challenges. This means that marketing and marketing skills inevitably must play a more central role.

An important manifestation of this change is the shift in the source of nonprofit organization revenues. In an important recent volume called *To Profit or Not to Profit: The Commercial Transformation of the Nonprofit Sector*, economist Burton Weisbrod notes:

> Massive change is occurring in the nonprofit sector. Seemingly isolated events touching the lives of virtually everyone are, in fact, parts of a pattern

that is little recognized but has enormous impact; it is a pattern of growing commercialization of nonprofit organizations.[62]

He points to the hospitals that are getting into the fitness business,[63] museums generating vast incomes from shops and catalogues,[64] and universities entering profitable research alliances with business[65] and forming for-profit subsidiaries to generate major levels of revenue.[66]

This shift toward commercialism in the nonprofit sector is not without its critics. Peter Dobkin Hall, for example, argues that, except for some faith-based entities, nonprofits are no longer the kinds of voluntary associations that De Toqueville noted were among the new colony's greatest strengths.[67] Authors like Robert Putnam mourn the loss of social capital, that we have become a nation of individuals "bowling alone."[68] Hall believes that the so-called independent sector is at a moral crisis point and needs to rethink its place and purpose. He proposes a number of "central contradictions" in our understanding of nonprofit enterprise. Among them are the following:

- How can nonprofits be defended as an "independent sector" when so many are dependent on direct and indirect government support?
- How can nonprofits be defended as donor-supported when so many of them are sustained by government grants and earned income?
- How can nonprofits be defended as voluntary entities when they are increasingly run by professional managers and when managerial professionalization . . . has become so central to efforts to make them more efficient and effective?
- How can defenders of nonprofits claim a distinctive role as guardians of the public interest when they have been so resistant to efforts to assess the social benefits they provide and have been, in many instances, such poor corporate citizens (i.e., [seeking] local tax exemption)?[69]

There are many reasons why nonprofits have been subject to criticism. As Hall implies, many citizens feel that nonprofits have become too large and too bureaucratic. There have been a number of major scandals implicating poor nonprofit management ranging from scandals at the United Way involving its former president, William Aramony, to the recent embezzlement of $7 million from a Midwest chapter of the American Cancer Society. Criticism over the American Red Cross's handling of donations around the September 11, 2001, attack on the World Trade Center and Pentagon has led many organizations to rethink what they do and how they do it. Paul Light points to the increased call for a "watchful eye" to keep the sector in line and meet society's needs.[70]

At the same time, other pressures are generating other "tides" of reform. First, many nonprofits are becoming extremely large. For example, excluding universities and health care systems, the annual revenues in 2000 of the 15 largest nonprofits exceeded $625 million, with the largest, Lutheran Services, generating over $6.9 *billion* which would put it around 271 in the Fortune 500, above such private sector giants as Unisys and Campbell Soup. (It should be noted that the largest fundraising organization is not listed in the table on page 13. The United Way system is a collection of individual local United Ways. If its fundraising for 2000–2001 were added together, this would amount to $3.9 billion.)

Top 15 Nonacademic Nonprofits	2000 Revenues (000)
Lutheran Services of America	$6,909,131
YMCA of the USA	3,987,476
Salvation Army	2,792,816
American Red Cross	2,492,418
Catholic Charities USA	2,342,189
Goodwill Industries International	1,852,900
Fidelity Investments Charitable Fund	1,260,525
Boys & Girls Club of America	984,916
American Cancer Society	812,297
The Nature Conservancy	784,264
Boy Scouts of America	692,600
Girl Scouts of the USA	665,995
YWCA of the USA	657,972
Planned Parenthood Federation	627,200
United Cerebral Palsy Association	625,688

Source: The Chronicle of Philanthropy, November 1, 2001, p. 37.

Such large organizations are under significant internal pressure to introduce much better, more sophisticated management. That is also the case for the largest individual U.S. universities. Income for each of the top five exceeded $3 billion in 2000:[71]

Harvard University	$5,967,156,304
University of Michigan	$4,609,275,000
Stanford University	$3,780,956,626
Yale	$3,081,904,467
MIT	$3,062,308,000

For these large organizations, and many others, pressure for improved management is also increasing from external sources. A major influence is the new breed of "venture philanthropists" like Mario Marino. These entrepreneurs have made fortunes in the expanding high-tech environment and want to apply their management and financial skills to their charitable giving. They are forming venture capital funds for nonprofits but are demanding great attention to sound management on the part of their grantees.[72]

Paul Light sees these pressures as leading to three "tides," pressures for (1) scientific management, based on best practices; (2) war on waste, based on increasing efficiencies; and (3) liberation management, based on superior outcomes no matter how they are achieved.[73] Clearly, increased attention to effective marketing can advance all three tides. However, a future major role for marketing thinking in nonprofit organizations would be problematic if many nonprofit observers, managers, and board members feel that "managerial professionalization" is not desirable. It is our view that a marketing perspective is essential to effective nonprofit management no matter whether the organization focuses heavily on a mission of voluntary association or focuses more closely on effective management. In any case, the empirical evidence suggests that the problem may not be as serious as Hall believes. A recently published study by Galaskiewicz and Bielefeld traced the extent to which 229 nonprofit organizations in the Minneapolis–St. Paul area shifted in the use of their "business" or "charitable" model between 1980 and 1994. They found for many organizations that "The application of business techniques by nonprofits were essential in order to compete for clients and donations." However, they did not find "wholesale application of business and commercial practices." More importantly, they concluded that "nonprofits experienced no obvious detrimental organizational effects if they adopted business-like tactics or relied on commercial income."[74]

IMPORTANCE OF THE NONPROFIT SECTOR

The United States

An important reason to study the nonprofit sector is that it is surprisingly large and, in many years and in many countries, it has grown faster than the private sector. In the United States, the Independent Sector regularly estimates the size and scope of the nonprofit sector. In its most recent study, it found that, in the United States in 1998, there were 1,626,000 private nonprofit organizations and government entities and that, since 1987, the number of organizations in the independent sector has grown much faster (35.6 percent) than the total number of U.S. organizations (26.5 percent). The distribution across categories and over time is noted in Table 1-1.

An alternative method of estimating the size of the nonprofit sector—one that we shall see is more useful internationally—is in terms of employment. The sector is highly labor-intensive, but a significant portion of its labor force is volunteer and therefore difficult to count. The Independent Sector estimates that about 109.4 million Americans 18 years or older volunteered an average of 3.5 hours per week in 1998.[75] Not all of this was *formal* volunteering with a specific commitment to an organization. The latter represented 15.8 billion hours in 1998, which is equivalent to 9.3 million employees with an estimated equivalent labor value of $225.9 billion. The Independent Sector estimates that there were 16.6 million people employed in the independent sector, full-time, part-time, and volunteers. This comprised 10.8 percent of all U.S. employment. This figure is a significant increase over 1982 when it was 9.7 percent.

Despite their growth, nonprofits of all kinds in the United States face significant challenges that can be attacked with more effective marketing. For example, the audience for the arts is growing old at a very rapid rate and must be significantly augmented by new, excited young people who want to experience the arts and do so outside the confines of their own family rooms.[76] Another problem is in the religious sector. As noted in Table 1-2, the number of religious organizations has increased scarcely at all since 1992. The proportion of U.S. households giving to religious organizations fell from 53.2 percent in 1989 to 45.2 percent. There has also been some shift in relative importance in the sector away from education and toward social and legal services as shown in Table 1-2.

The Nonprofit Sector Around the World

Of course, the United States is not unique in having a thriving nonprofit sector. Nonprofit organizations and voluntary participation have a long history in other parts

TABLE 1-1   Number of Private Nonprofit Organizations in the United States 1982–1998 (in thousands)

	1998	1997	1992	1987	1982
Number of organizations in U.S.	27,692	27,586	24,468	21,867	18,209
Independent sector organizations	1,228	1,188	1,030	907	793
Percent of total organizations	4.4%	4.3%	4.2%	4.1%	4.4%
501(c)3 organizations	734	693	546	422	322
501(c)4 organizations	140	142	143	139	132
Church congregations	354	353	341	346	339
Other tax-exempt organizations (not included above)	399	398	396	378	387
Total nonprofit organizations	1,627	1,586	1,426	1,285	1,180
National income (including value of volunteer time)	$7,300,000	$6,900,000	$5,200,000	$3,800,000	$2,700,000
Percentage attributed to all nonprofits	6.7%	6.7%	6.8%	6.5%	6.4%
Percentage attributed to independent sector	6.1%	6.1%	6.3%	5.7%	5.8%

Source: Used with permission. Independent Sector, www.independentsector.org

TABLE 1-2   Distribution of Operating Expenditures Across Sectors in the United States by Year

	1997	1992	1987	1982
Operating expenditures (billions)	$551.6	$435.8	$272.7	$172.3
Health services	53.9%	54.5%	50.3%	51.4%
Education/Research	18.3%	19.4%	22.89%	23.5%
Religious organizations	9.7%	9.4%	11.0%	9.3%
Social and legal services	12.0%	11.1%	10.1%	9.8%
Civic, social, and fraternal	3.0%	3.1%	3.2%	3.3%
Arts and culture	2.2%	1.8%	1.9%	1.9%
Foundations	0.9%	0.7%	0.7%	0.8%

Source: Used with permission. Independent Sector, www.independentsector.org

of the world. A nonprofit sector is slowly growing in additional parts of the world and is even emerging in the former communist countries of Eastern Europe and China. The world is well aware of the work that nonprofits are doing in the developing world, particularly to combat the spread of HIV/AIDS.

The most comprehensive portrait of the nonprofit sector outside the United States is that being developed by Lester Salamon and his colleagues at the Center for Civil Society Studies (CCSS) at Johns Hopkins University's Institute for Policy Studies (http://www.jhu.edu/~cnp). By mid-2001, data had been collected in 24 countries, primarily in Western countries and Japan. Additional work is ongoing in Asia and Africa.[77]

The CCSS data indicate that the nonprofit sector is a very significant economic factor in the 24 countries studied. They employ over 19.7 million full-time equivalent (FTE) paid workers plus 11.3 million FTE volunteer workers generating $1.2 trillion in economic expenditures. In four countries (The Netherlands, Ireland, Belgium, and Israel), the nonprofit sector is larger (as measured by paid employment as a share of the total labor force) than in the United States (see also Chapter 9). A distribution of the nonprofit share of total non-agricultural employment is given in Table 1-3.

TABLE 1-3   Nonprofit Share of Total Non-Agricultural Employment in 26 Countries, 1995

Country	Paid	Volunteer	Total
The Netherlands	12.6%	6.1%	18.7%
Ireland	11.5	2.6	14.2
Belgium	10.5	2.5	13.0
Israel	9.2	1.8	11.0
United States	7.8	4.0	11.9
Australia	7.2	2.9	10.1
United Kingdom	6.2	4.4	10.6
Germany	4.9	3.1	8.0
France	4.9	4.7	9.6
Spain	4.5	2.2	6.8
Austria	4.5	1.2	5.7
Argentina	3.7	2.3	6.0
Norway	3.5	5.5	9.1
Japan	3.5	1.1	4.6
Finland	3.0	3.3	6.3
Sweden	2.6	7.4	10.0
Peru	2.4	1.4	3.9
Colombia	2.2	0.7	3.1
Brazil	1.9	0.3	2.5
Italy	1.2	1.2	3.2
Czech Republic	0.9	0.9	2.7
Slovakia	0.9	0.4	1.2
Hungary	0.6	0.3	1.6
Romania	0.6	0.7	1.3
Mexico	0.4	0.2	0.7
Poland	0.3	0.3	1.5
Average	4.4	2.4	6.8

Source: Lester M. Salamon and Associates, *Global Civil Society At-a-Glance.* Institute for Policy Studies, Center for Civil Society Studies, Johns Hopkins University, 2001. Reproduced with permission.

The sector appears to be growing more rapidly internationally than in the United States. In eight countries where the project has data from 1990 and 1995, the CCSS project found growth of 24.4 percent versus 8.1 percent growth for the eight countries overall. About two-thirds of nonprofit sector activity is in three areas: education, health, and social services. However, this pattern varies by region as indicated in Table 1-4.

The sources of funding for the nonprofit sector also vary significantly across the four regions, with much more support in Latin America from fees, whereas the United States and Western Europe rely more on public sector support. The relevant figures are these:

	Public Sector	Philanthropy	Fees
Other (Incl. United States)	42.7%	8.0%	49.3%
Western Europe	50.4	7.1	42.5
Latin America	15.3	10.3	74.4
Eastern Europe	31.5	19.5	49.0

TABLE 1-4 Percentage Distribution of Nonprofit Paid Employment in 26 countries, 1995

	Other (incl. United States)	Western Europe	Latin America	Eastern Europe	All 26 Countries
Education	29.4%	27.4%	44.0%	18.9%	29.3%
Health	34.8	18.7	12.2	8.1	17.9
Social services	15.3	26.7	10.3	13.1	19.1
Culture	8.2	11.5	10.6	34.3	15.2
Professional	3.5	5.4	12.6	10.8	7.5
Development	4.6	5.2	6.9	5.3	5.5
Environment/Advocacy	1.8	3.4	1.2	5.4	3.1
Other	2.5	1.8	2.1	4.1	2.4

Source: Lester M. Salamon and Associates, *Global Civil Society At-a-Glance.* Institute for Policy Studies, Center for Civil Society Studies, Johns Hopkins University, 2001. Reproduced with permission.

Explanation of Cross-Country Differences

Salamon and Sokolowski propose that the patterns reflected in Table 1-3 could possibly be explained by three sets of hypotheses.[78] One possibility suggested by Weisbrod[79] is subsumed under what they call "macro-structural" arguments, namely that the size of the nonprofit sector is determined by *market or government failure.* Citizens in all countries have need for and desire for a range of goods and services that, for economic reasons, will not be provided by the private sector (market failure). Theoretically, these needs could be met by government (education, old-age security, and so on). However, societies differ in their willingness to support public sector provision of these goods and services. Nonprofits then step in to meet this "government failure." This leads these authors to predict that the size of the nonprofit sector will vary with:

a. The heterogeneity of the population—The greater the ethnic and religious diversity, the more controversy there will be about what the government should do and therefore the greater the role for nonprofits.
b. The size of government—The more the government does, the less the need for a nonprofit sector.
c. The proportion of nonprofit funding that is from charitable donations—The more individuals want what government and the market do not deliver, the more they are likely to be willing to pay for it.

Salamon and Sokolowski test these hypotheses with data from 22 of their countries and find that heterogeneity does not predict the size of the sector. The exact opposite is true for the other two hypotheses; a larger nonprofit sector was associated with a *larger* government role and a *smaller* funding role for private charity. In search of an explanation, the authors then turn to hypotheses that follow a line of reasoning that suggests that the nonprofit sector is not competitive with government but, in fact, is more often cooperative with it to meet needs in which societies believe strongly. This would explain the positive relationship between the size of the government and the nonprofit sectors previously noted. The authors further predict that sector interdependency would predict both higher proportions of nonprofit funding from the government and greater levels of nonprofit activity in areas where government is already active, namely health and social services. Both the latter hypotheses are strongly supported by the data.[80]

The results of their analyses allow the authors to categorize countries according to the "regime" in which nonprofits operate. They partition countries on whether their government spending on welfare is low or high and whether the scale of nonprofit activity is small or large. The resulting four categories are the following:

Government Social Welfare Spending	Nonprofit Scale	
	Small	*Large*
Low	Statist	Liberal
High	Social Democratic	Corporatist

- **Statist regimes** reflect a government role that looks to the needs of elites and not the middle or lower classes as in the social democratic regimes and, perhaps as a consequence, the nonprofit sector is not powerful (e.g., Japan, Brazil).
- **Liberal regimes** are generally hostile to government programs and enthusiastic about private volunteerism (e.g., the United Kingdom to some extent).
- **Social democratic regimes** believe in government provision of public services and not the volunteer sector (e.g., Austria, Finland).
- **Corporatist regimes** involve a strong role for government, but one in partnerships with a strong role for nonprofits (e.g., Germany, France, Belgium).

Their data give good support for this model.

Cross-Sector Confusion

Implicit in the preceding section is a recognition that the performance of the nonprofit sector is not independent from the other two sectors of the economy (the public and commercial sectors). These sectors both compete and cooperate. The following are just some examples in the U.S. context:

1. The nonprofit and commercial sectors.
   a. *Competition.* Historically, organizations in these two sectors have competed vigorously. Private and nonprofit hospitals battle over patients. Performing arts centers compete with Broadway and the movies. And, as we will discuss in later chapters, many nonprofits now have sales divisions that are major sources of revenues such as the hundreds of millions of dollars that the Girl Scouts of the United States generates annually in cookie sales. While commercial firms have often criticized these efforts on the part of tax-free nonprofits, they have increasingly found it profitable to enter domains that were once thought the sole province of nonprofits, such as Lockheed Martin's ventures into job training for the unemployed.[81] Nonprofits have been losing market share in many domains they once thought were their preserves. For example, hospice care for the elderly or children with serious disabilities was thought to be the province of the charitable sector. In 1992, there were fewer than 200 for-profit hospice centers and in 1999 there were 593. While the number of nonprofit hospice organizations has grown as well, their numbers grew only 43 percent compared to 293 percent for their commercial competitors.[82] Increased competition has also occurred when some nonprofits have

been lured by the prospect of self-sufficiency to cross over and become for-profit, as did QuitNet, a service to help people quit smoking, in 2000.[83]

   b. *Cooperation.* As we will discuss in Chapter 9, one of the most promising areas of growth in marketing in the nonprofit sector has been so-called "cause-marketing" partnerships between nonprofits and corporations large and small. Corporations have seen that they can meet important strategic needs by helping nonprofits raise funds or otherwise carry out their missions. Nonprofits have found huge new streams of revenue and areas of expertise in their commercial partnerships.

2. The nonprofit and public sectors.
   a. *Competition.* Again, historically, the conventional view is that these two sectors ought to cooperate and not get in each other's way. They are all working for the same social ends—so the argument goes. But many nonprofits have found important market niches for themselves *in between* the public and commercial sectors. Perhaps the best example of this is found in family planning programs around the world. Organizations like the Futures Group and Population Services International have had major success by positioning their condoms and pills above the free public sector goods and well below the prices charged in the commercial sector. As Philip Harvey has recently pointed out, they have found that by effective branding and promotion they have increased the overall size of the market and had a major impact on population growth rates around the world.[84]

   b. *Cooperation.* As noted, the traditional view is for the nonprofit sector to step in either when the economics of the market make a social issue unattractive to the private sector ("market failure") or when government programs are inadequate or nonexistent (e.g., opera in the United States or AIDS programs in some African countries). In many of these cases, the government cooperates by funding the activities and granting special privileges to the nonprofit sector, such as tax breaks and special mailing rates.

3. The public and commercial sectors.
   a. *Competition.* Although these sectors have traditionally been quite separate, in recent years competition has grown from two sources. First, as part of the "reinventing government" movement, federal, state, and local agencies have found that they can decrease costs and improve public service by contracting out such services as waste collection or prison management to the private sector.[85] Second, enterprising commercial firms decided that there is money to be made in areas like public education in the United States that were heretofore thought to be the sole preserve of state and local governments.

   b. *Cooperation.* One of the areas in which cooperation between governments and business is manifested is in economic and community growth projects in developing countries. Local governments often give special treatment to firms that will help build roads or fiber optic links. In turn, many firms are willing to give special help to government programs and interests because this can lead to favorable treatment of the firm's commercial interests at some later time.[86]

4. All three sectors.
   a. *Competition.* There are certain domains in which competition among all three exists. Government-supported museums like the Smithsonian have gift shops that compete with businesses and nonprofit catalogues. Education for special education students is often delivered by all three sectors. And, of course, in many parts of the world, health care services are available from all three sectors—although the providers would argue that they are addressing different markets.
   b. *Cooperation.* Many of the areas previously described as "competitive," especially those in developing countries, are in many respects cooperative. That is, government agencies may subsidize nonprofits to provide health care in rural areas which may use products for patients discounted by generous commercial marketers.

Classification of Nonprofit Organizations

It is often difficult to distinguish various kinds of nonprofit organizations from each other. One very important classification dimension is the legal one. One may always ask whether the organization is, in fact, a legally defined nonprofit. Section 501 of the Internal Revenue Code grants tax-exempt status to 24 different categories of organizations. About half are covered under Section 501(c)(3), which includes the traditional charitable, religious, scientific, and educational institutions. Organizations in this category may not use their resources to lobby. Section 501(c)(4) of the Tax Code includes social welfare groups, and this category does allow lobbying. Section 501(c)(6) includes business leagues, and Section 501(c)(7) contains social clubs.

It is essential that nonprofit managers obtain a formal designation as a nonprofit since many benefits are available to such enterprises. For example, U.S. nonprofits receive the following special treatments or exemptions:

- exemption from federal, state, and local income taxes,
- exemption from local property taxes in most cases,
- exemption from unemployment insurance payments in some areas,
- lower bulk postage rates,
- exemption from the Robinson-Patman Act,
- possible lower charges or none at all for federal services,
- exemption from tort liability under common law,
- hospitals and some other organizations can issue tax-exempt bonds,
- charitable, educational, scientific, and certain other organizations can receive donations, gifts, and bequests that permit tax deductions for the giver,
- access to donated space and air time from media.

Two rationales are typically offered for the special tax status of nonprofits. The most common is the "public goods" rationale, which argues that nonprofits provide services such as health care, education, and basic research that would not be provided were it not for the tax subsidy offered by the government. The second rationale, called the "quality assurance" rationale, argues that nonprofits provide services in areas in which consumers are ordinarily ill-equipped to judge quality, such as health care and education. Having these services performed by tax-exempt nonprofits supposedly ensures the public of quality and protection in situations where for-profit firms might charge excessive prices for inferior services.

In the past, government was relatively generous in granting special benefits to nonprofits. Ironically, however, the recent successes of marketing in the nonprofit sector have caused a major shift in federal thinking about nonprofits. As we shall note throughout this volume, many nonprofits have become extremely entrepreneurial, taking advantage of opportunities for direct revenue generation to supplement donative sources of funding.[87]

The reason nonprofits have "gotten away" with these "business" activities is that the IRS looks at the overall purpose of the organization, not at individual ventures, to define nonprofit status. In 1950, however, Congress determined that nonprofits must pay taxes on proceeds of "unrelated" business activities. Thus, even when an organization has been designated a nonprofit, the government still pays very close attention to its individual activities. The government's position is that any revenue-generating activity that is *unrelated* to the organization's basic mission must be taxed as would a for-profit enterprise. Thus, a marketing manager must clearly understand whether any present or proposed ventures for which marketing plans are to be developed will be officially classified by the IRS as unrelated business activities. In some cases, it may be desirable to spin off an operation into a for-profit subsidiary.[88] Above all, managers should be extremely careful that the amount of unrelated, taxable activity does not grow to comprise too large a percentage of overall revenue. Hopkins has suggested that if this percentage rises above 35 percent, the organization should be concerned that it may lose its overall tax-exempt status.[89] The IRS will permit most kinds of unrelated business but will be very attentive to the *total* quantity of such ventures.

National Taxonomy of Tax-Exempt Entities

The problem of classifying nonprofits is important not only to tax collectors, but also to those who wish to track the performance of the nonprofit sector. One solution to this dilemma is the general taxonomy developed by the National Center for Charitable Statistics (NCCS). Their "National Taxonomy of Exempt Entities" was developed in the 1980s to classify all non-business and nongovernmental organizations in the United States with an emphasis on the philanthropic sector.[90] In response to conversations with the Internal Revenue Service, the taxonomy was simplified in 1999 to comprise the new National Taxonomy of Tax-Exempt Entities–Core Codes (or NTEE–CC). The new system reduced the number of categories from 645 to about 400 under 10 broad headings.

Arts, Culture, and Humanities
Education
Environment and Animals
Health
Human Services
International, Foreign Affairs
Public, Societal Benefit
Religion Related

Mutual/Membership Benefit

Unknown, Unclassified

Recent data on the number of organizations in each category are available at www.nccs. urban.org.

MANAGERIALLY RELEVANT CLASSIFICATION

Although the NTEE–CC taxonomy may be useful for outside observers evaluating the nonprofit sector, it is of limited usefulness to *managers* of nonprofit enterprises. Managers need to know "To what extent does the *type* of nonprofit I have to manage affect what I can do strategically?" Experience has shown that there are two key dimensions that affect what a manager can do in a nonprofit: (1) the nature of the relationship between the nonprofit and its regulatory and support environment and (2) the nature of the basic exchanges the organization is trying to create.

Nature of the Organization's Environment

Five key questions help define the organization's environment:

- Does the organization rely on donations in whole or in part?
- Is the organization's performance likely to be subject to public scrutiny?
- Is marketing seen as undesirable from the standpoint of some or all members of the organization or its major sponsors or reviewers?
- Does the organization rely extensively on volunteers?
- Is performance largely judged by nonmarketing measures?

We shall consider each of these questions before turning to distinctions associated with the specific *activities* a nonprofit might perform.

Is the Organization Donative?

If the proposed activity or the organization as a whole is funded through private philanthropy or government grants, how one *can* market and *ought* to market is influenced in two major ways. First, outside funding agencies may establish restrictions on what can be done. In such cases, the least bothersome problem (but nonetheless an important source of irritation) is procedural restrictions that formally specify the steps to be taken, the forms to be filled out, the individuals with whom one must "touch base," or all three. To cite a typical example, many U.S. government contracts put a substantial hurdle before nonprofit marketers who wish to carry out research by requiring that questionnaires be approved by the Office of Management and Budget before being taken into the field.

More troublesome are outright restrictions on certain activities. Donors may require that a funded program target specific audiences, even though this may be an inefficient and ineffective use of the nonprofit's resources in the short run. They may proscribe certain media, prevent the hiring of particular specialist staff members, or require that some products be used where better choices are available elsewhere.

One problem of government sponsorship is that nonprofit marketers may not be allowed to choose the segments to which they will market. In some situations they may not be permitted to segment at all, as when the postal service must charge the same price for a first-class letter between any sender and receiver no matter what the costs of the service or the ability or willingness of either party to pay for the service.

In some cases, nonprofit marketers are required by sponsors to tackle segments that are very difficult to reach and influence in comparison with other segments on which limited resources might be more efficiently spent. Contraceptive marketing programs in many developing countries, for example, must be directed at consumers with low literacy and limited awareness of the birth control issue in villages where conventional distribution facilities are nonexistent or primitive. Agencies that would prefer in the short run to build marketing skills and develop a stable revenue base by marketing to more sophisticated (but still needy) urban target audiences are often effectively barred (or at least discouraged) from doing so by sponsoring agencies.

The second consequence of an organization's donative status is that the marketing task is doubled. Not only do marketers have to plan programs aimed at final consumers, but they must also consciously plan strategies to ensure continued—and preferably increased—outside support. This problem of having to market to multiple publics is not strictly unique to nonprofits. For-profit corporations must market to stockholders, investment specialists, regulatory agencies, town councils, and even labor unions. But in the private sector, these are typically relatively minor problems. Indeed, the interests of many of these secondary publics (for example, investors and town councils) are well served simply if the corporation's main customer marketing task is successful. More sales revenue means more profits, more jobs, and more taxes. However, it must be remembered that nonprofits get a substantial proportion of their revenues from donations and grants. Support publics are therefore not at all minor concerns. Thus, nonprofits must arrange marketing strategies for *resource attraction* as well as *resource allocation* in a rapidly changing environment.[91]

Is There Public Scrutiny?

Nonprofits may find their marketing options severely restricted if they are subjected to constant public scrutiny. The kinds of problems that can occur are well illustrated by a situation involving the government of Canada many years ago. At one point, the Canadian government actively sought public support for its newly proposed constitution. To achieve this goal, the government decided to undertake a major advertising campaign at a cost of about $6 million. The campaign raised all sorts of questions about whether the government was doing "too much" marketing. Routine ads for agricultural products and job openings were quite acceptable, but government marketing of highly visible and controversial campaigns like that for the Constitution raised a number of public protests. At the time, total promotional expenditures were $160 million or about $6.66 for each Canadian citizen. This compared to 65 cents per person in the United States at the time. The Canadian federal government was the country's largest advertiser, which received extensive public criticism from both industry leaders and individual citizens. J. L. Foley, chairman of the Institute of canadian Advertising, said that the growth in government advertising constitutes a threat to free speech, a waste of taxpayers' money, and "a further emasculation of Parliament and parliamentary democracy." A reader of Toronto's *Globe and Mail* put it more simply: "Good government needs no advertising. It speaks for itself."[92]

The fact that a nonprofit organization is publicly accountable has other restrictive features. One consequence is that nonprofits feel they should ignore certain competitors or not compete with them. Bloom and Novelli distinguish between friendly and unfriendly competitors as follows:

> Social marketers must also be concerned about the impact of a type of competition that commercial marketers rarely face—the friendly competition provided by other social organizations fighting for the same cause. Thus, in developing a marketing plan for the smoking cessation program of the National Cancer Institute, it becomes necessary to consider the potential actions of the National Heart, Lung and Blood Institute, the U.S. Office of Smoking and Health, the American Cancer Society, the American Lung Association, the American Heart Association, and a host of others. Friendly competitors can help the social marketer in many ways, but they can also create fragmented efforts, funding problems, and other difficulties.[93]

Is Marketing Seen as Undesirable?

Over the years, marketing has had difficulty in gaining acceptance in a number of nonprofit organizations. One hindrance was the view that marketing really wasn't necessary. It was argued, for example, that good health does not need to be sold, that hospitals don't need to be marketed, that lawful behavior is simply a social requirement, and that one shouldn't have to advertise to drivers to get them not to speed.

Fortunately, the view that marketing is undesirable because it is unnecessary has faded away, in part because nonprofit managers and their supporters have learned the potential of marketing and in part because they have been starkly confronted with the *need* for it.

More vexing and more lasting is the sometimes not-so-subconscious opinion that, at base, marketing is *evil*. This opinion manifests itself in three views:

Marketing Is Seen as Wasting the Public's Money   As we have seen in the Canadian government case, a frequent criticism of marketing activities is that they are too expensive. Many people carefully watch the administrative and marketing expenses of charitable organizations to make sure that they do not get out of line with the organization's mission and the amount of money being raised. The Better Business Bureau's charity watchdog (www.give.org/standards/cbbbstds.asp) judges charities on the basis of whether expenditures on these two categories are "reasonable" and defines this as follows:

> Reasonable use of funds requires that a) at least 50 percent of total income from all sources be spent on programs and activities directly related to the organization's purposes; b) at least 50 percent of public contributions be spent on the programs and activities described in solicitations, in accordance with donor expectations; c) fund raising costs not exceed 35 percent of related contributions; and d) total fund raising and administrative costs not exceed 50 percent of total income.

Marketing Activities Are Seen as Intrusive   A second objection to marketing is that it often intrudes into people's personal lives. Marketing researchers go into homes and ask people about their likes and dislikes, their beliefs, their attitudes, their incomes, and other personal matters. There is a widespread concern that if various government agencies started doing a lot of marketing research, the information might eventually be used against individual citizens or in mass propaganda. Citizens also dislike the fact that their tax money is being spent to do the research.

Ironically, marketing research is primarily carried out to learn about the needs and wants of people and their attitudes toward the organization's current products so that the organization can deliver greater satisfaction to its target publics. At the same time, organizations must show a sensitivity to the public's feelings for privacy.[94]

Marketing Is Seen as Manipulative A third criticism is that organizations will use marketing to manipulate the target market. Many smokers resent the anti-smoking ads put out by the American Legacy Foundation. Image ads by police departments are seen by some citizens as manipulative.

Administrators should be sensitive to the possible charge of manipulation when they implement a marketing program. In the majority of cases, the nonprofit organization is seeking some public good for which there is widespread consensus, and it is using proper means. In other cases, the charge of manipulation may be justified and such efforts, unless they are checked, will bring a "black eye" to the organization and to marketing.

Does the Organization Rely Heavily on Volunteers?

A significant proportion of nonprofit organizations rely upon unpaid volunteers for clerical assistance, fundraising, stuffing envelopes, conducting tours, and even attracting other volunteers. This can create two types of problems for the nonprofit manager. First, the need for a steady influx of volunteers means that a third "public" is added to those to whom the manager must market. Programs must be designed to attract and retain paid personnel, while a watchful eye must be kept on possible ramifications of proposed programs on existing volunteers. Directors of blood donation programs who rely heavily on volunteers, for example, often find that plans for extending collection hours or expanding into new, marginal, and sometimes unsavory neighborhoods meet with strong resistance from the volunteer segments of their staffs. Blood program managers have succeeded in these needed outreach efforts when they have first marketed the program and its benefits to the volunteers.

The second problem with volunteers involves day-to-day management. A universal complaint of managers who have to work with volunteers is that they are unreliable. One manager has what he calls a "rule of thirds" for volunteers. According to his experience, one-third of all volunteers will be highly motivated, eager to help out, and highly responsive to superiors' directions. At the other extreme is the third who seem to want little more than to tell their friends that they volunteered. They seldom appear at all for work. Their promises of assistance are rarely kept, and when they do appear, they resist directions to do anything they don't *really* feel like doing. The third in the middle is the group that can make or break the organization. The ability to effectively motivate and direct this group is the true test of a nonprofit managers' interpersonal skills. Although, as we shall outline in Chapter 9, many of the principal techniques of personnel management in the private sector can and ought to be applied in nonprofit organizations, the simple fact that a manager doesn't have the "carrot" of a salary or the "stick" of potential firing to use to motivate and direct the people needed to make the marketing program successful is often a crucial hindrance in carrying out an effective and fast-moving marketing program.

Is Performance Judged Primarily by Nonmarketing Standards?

Those who judge marketing performance in nonprofit organizations (e.g., boards or funding agencies) have often been trained in other disciplines and have only a crude appreciation of the realities of day-to-day management. This can seriously affect the kinds of marketing goals that are set for the nonprofit marketer.

Expectations for success, for example, can often be highly exaggerated. Those who evaluate nonprofit programs often want "everyone" to wear seat belts or to stop smoking or to give to their charity. As Peter Drucker notes, "To obtain its budget, [the nonprofit] needs the approval, or at least the acquiescence, of practically everybody who remotely could be considered a 'constituent.' Where a market share of 22 percent might be perfectly satisfactory to a business, a 'rejection' by 78 percent of its 'constituents' . . . would be fatal to a budget-based institution."[95]

A second problem with nonprofit marketing objectives is that accomplishments may be very difficult to detect because of their intangibility. How does one *know,* for example, that museum visits or symphony attendance have become "more educational" or that they "improve the quality of life in the community?" Yet these are often set as the marketing goals of nonprofit institutions. They are perfectly legitimate goals; they just present serious measurement problems. Unfortunately, the combination of that measurement difficulty and the glare of public accountability that faces many nonprofits leads managers too often to seek to achieve what is *measurable* rather than what is important. There is a serious danger, for example, that the nonprofit organization will become a budget maximizer. As Peter Drucker has noted:

> Being paid out of a budget allocation changes what is meant by "performance" or "results." *"Results" in the budget-based institution means a larger budget. "Performance" is the ability to maintain or increase one's budget. . . .* Not to spend the budget to the hilt will only convince the budget-maker that the budget for the next fiscal period can safely be cut.[96] (Italics in original.)

As we shall see, this is one of the many distortions in planning and performance to which the peculiar status of the nonprofit marketing task can give rise.

Nature of the Exchanges the Organization Is Attempting to Influence

In addition to the differences in organizational milieu just described, nonprofit marketers' options are often affected considerably by the things they are attempting to market. The major *organizational* mission of a church or a synagogue involves the promulgation of religious values, whereas the major organizational mission of museums involves cultural education. But some of the specific *activities* of these two institutions could be virtually identical from a marketing standpoint—both, for example, seek members, conduct fundraising lotteries, and sell goods such as Christmas cards or posters. However, the *way* identical marketing activities are carried out may be affected by the type of organization. A church, for example, might feel it had to be relatively dignified in promoting its lottery or its Christmas cards, a museum might feel it should have a relatively "classy" promotion, and a neighborhood youth group might feel that its image required a more trendy style.

As we will discuss further in Chapter 4, the behavior that the nonprofit marketer is trying to influence can be thought of as the result of an *exchange*. Target audience members are asked to exchange something they value for something beneficial provided by the nonprofit organization. As seen from the target consumer's perspective, he or she is being "asked" to incur costs or to make some sacrifices (that is, to give up something valuable) in return for some promised benefits. In the main, the kinds of costs consumers are usually asked to "pay" by nonprofit marketers are any of four types:

1. *Economic costs*—for example, to give up money or goods to a charity, or simply to buy a product or service.
2. *Sacrifices of old ideas, values, or views of the world*—for example, to give up believing that the world is flat, that women are inferior, that one is not getting senile, or that one is not hooked on drugs.
3. *Sacrifices of old patterns of behavior*—for example, to start to wear seat belts or to let someone else meet some of your physical or psychological needs.
4. *Sacrifices of time and energy*—for example, to perform a voluntary service or give blood to a hospital or the Red Cross.

In return for these kinds of sacrifices, consumers in nonprofit enterprises receive benefits of three basic kinds: economic (both goods and services), social, and psychological. The combination of these kinds of sacrifices and benefits yields the matrix outlined in Table 1-5. Here we see that it is only the first two cells in the top left corner of the matrix that we typically identify as the domain of the profit sector—although, as we've noted, some nonprofits such as hospitals and schools also promote these transactions as their primary objective. It is the other 14 cells that are truly in the nonprofit domain, since *by definition* they cannot generate a profit. What does it mean to be responsible for transactions in these 14 cells?

TABLE 1-5 Cost/Benefit Matrix for the Profit/Nonprofit Sector

	BENEFITS			
Costs	*A Product*	*A Service*	*Social*	*Psychological*
Give up economic assets	Buy a poster	Pay for surgery or an education	Donate to alma mater	Donate to charity
Give up old ideas, values, opinions	Receive free Goodwill clothing	Support neighborhood vigilantes	Support Republicans	Oppose abortion
Give up old behaviors, undertake or learn new behaviors	Practice birth control and receive a radio	Undertake drug detoxification treatment	Go to geriatric group once a week	Wear seat belts
Give up time or energy	Participate in a study and receive a coffeemaker	Attend a free concert	Volunteer for Junior League	Give blood

THE UNIQUENESS OF NONPROFIT MARKETING

It is important to emphasize that, while nonprofit marketing does make extensive use of commercial marketing concepts, marketing in this special environment is not the same and, indeed, is *much harder!* In a landmark article, Michael Rothschild implicitly raised this question: What difference does it make *from a marketing management standpoint* to be involved in activities surrounding exchanges other than those where the consumer makes economic sacrifices for economic benefits? Rothschild asks this: Why is it so hard to sell brotherhood like soap?[97] Among the answers that he and other authors[98] have developed are the following:

1. There is usually very little good secondary data available to the nonprofit marketer about consumer characteristics, behaviors, media preferences, perceptions, attitudes, and the like compared to what is available in commercial markets. Although studies are sometimes available in the general social science literature, they seldom address key marketing issues, although this situation is improving.

2. Because the sacrifices consumers are asked to make often involve very central ego needs as well as attitudes and behaviors with respect to controversial or taboo topics, it is often very difficult to secure reliable research data from consumers to serve as the basis for marketing decisions. As Bloom and Novelli point out, "While people are generally willing to be interviewed about these topics, they are more likely to give inaccurate, self-serving, or socially desirable answers to such questions than to questions about cake mixes, soft drinks, or cereals."[99]

3. Very often consumers are being asked to make sacrifices where they are often largely indifferent about the issue. (For example, who really worried about water conservation or the effects of speeding on a country's energy consumption before we were told about it?) This means, as previously noted, that marketers will have a serious development marketing problem, which can be extremely costly.

4. Consumers are often asked to make 180-degree shifts in attitudes or behaviors. In the private sector, a marketer simply tries to get consumers to value a product or service *more* than they used to (or at least more than they value competitors' offerings). Seldom does the marketer have a mandate to convert those who are *against* the product to favor it. Yet nonprofit marketers are asked to do this all the time. They must try to entice "macho men" into wearing seat belts, timid souls into giving blood or taking medication around which swirl rumors about devastating effects on sexual potency, or aging citizens to finally admit they are infirm or otherwise need assistance.

5. In the private sector it is often possible to modify an offering to meet consumer needs and wants better, but this is often difficult in the nonprofit sector. There is only one way to obtain blood, for example. Pills must be taken if one is to control high blood pressure. So many notes must be played by an organized set of musicians in order to perform Beethoven's Fifth Symphony. However, as will be noted in later chapters, the fact that some basic physical or behavioral aspects of the transaction cannot be changed does not mean that other elements of the marketing mix cannot. One can give blood in a great many different, often very attractive physical environments and social settings, for example. Most emphatically, even though the basic offering cannot be changed to meet consumers' needs and wants, other elements of the marketing mix (such as how the offering is described and promoted) can be very responsive to consumer needs and wants.

6.   Because the issues with which nonprofits deal involve very complex behaviors and attitudes, especially in areas like health care or conservation, large amounts of information must be communicated to consumers. For example, to get consumers in developing countries to use oral rehydration therapy (ORT) correctly and regularly to keep their fragile offspring from dying from the loss of fluids and electrolytes during prolonged and severe bouts of diarrhea, they must learn (a) that dehydration per se is life-threatening for the child, (b) that ORT will solve the problem, (c) that the benefits of use exceed the costs, (d) that they must use it properly or else it will not be effective or, indeed, may cause more problems than it cures, and (e) that there are specific places where the salts can be obtained and that it will cost x units of the local currency.

7.   Very often the benefits resulting from the sacrifice are not evident. If ORT is used properly and in time—that is, *before* the child becomes dehydrated—the mother will *not see* any benefits due to the action she took. A similar problem is faced by those trying to market high blood pressure control programs. High blood pressure is a health problem with no overt symptoms, and treatment with appropriate therapy does not result in immediately visible effects for its victims. As Rothschild points out, "In order to establish and maintain a behavior, there must be a positive reinforcer. . . . In many non-business cases, neither positive nor negative reinforcements are perceivable."[100]

8.   Another distinction in nonprofit marketing is that for some sacrifices, the benefits accrue to others and the individual making the sacrifice benefits little or not at all. A case in point is imposed speed limits in times of energy crises. Drivers are asked to change their behavior in return for energy savings that would benefit the government, that would possibly keep prices for everyone down to some degree, and that would improve the bargaining position and perhaps the profits of U.S. oil companies. It is understandable that many drivers are not very responsive to marketing programs designed to get them to obey such a new law.

9.   Because many of the changes to be marketed involve intangible social and psychological benefits, it is often difficult to portray the offering in media presentations. Just how does one describe a symphony concert or the benefits of energy conservation? If a physical object is involved, its portrayal (for example, showing an orchestra or an army tank) simply does not capture the real benefits one is trying to communicate. Indeed, the product may simply carry the wrong connotations (for example, an orchestra in white tie and tails may connote an intimidating formal occasion; a tank may connote skill training that may not seem useful outside of an army setting).

ETHICAL CHALLENGES IN THE NONPROFIT SECTOR

A final dimension that makes the nonprofit sector different is the ethical challenges it faces. As Salamon and Sokolowski point out, nonprofits are challenged to meet important social service and value-expressive needs of communities and nations that are not met by the other two sectors.[101] To help them meet their challenges, the government

---

EXHIBIT 1-1

SOME ETHICAL ISSUES
FOR NONPROFIT MARKETERS

1. Is it ethical to use marketing strategies and tactics for *any* social problem? Is the Ku Klux Klan a nonprofit? Can it use nonprofit marketing techniques? Should a nonprofit marketer work for the Klan?

2. Should nonprofit techniques that are successful in one culture be applied to other cultures? For example, should condom advertising be used in Muslim countries?

3. Do the ends of nonprofit marketing justify any means? Is deception acceptable if one is trying to induce a person to give up harmful drugs? Should radios be given

out as an incentive for men to get vasectomies in countries with excessive population growth?

4. Should a nonprofit marketer with *proven* strategies overpromise outcomes in order to be allowed to work on a new social problem where he or she *knows* nonprofit marketing can be very effective?

5. Does the involvement of Girl Scouts selling cookies as their major fundraising activity change Girl Scout members into salespeople? Is this good for the girls?

---

gives them special rights, privileges, and financial support while the citizenry contributes its own time and money to further these ends.

However, this special status comes with special obligations. All organizations and all citizens have the responsibility to pursue their missions and goals in a responsible and ethical manner. But in our opinion, nonprofits have a higher standard to meet. Nonprofits do not operate mainly to advance the interests of their own supporters—they use society's resources and goodwill to meet society's needs. Thus, they owe that society careful attention to the ends it seeks and the methods it uses.[102] Some of the ethical issues that we can raise are suggested in Exhibit 1-1. We shall return to many of these issues in succeeding chapters.

SUMMARY

Marketing is no longer considered a radical approach to solving the problems of public and nonprofit organizations. It is well accepted as an effective management tool. Economic and social changes and a proven rate of success have led to rapidly broadened and deepened applications. In the twenty-first century, increased privatization of public programs, increased voluntarism, and decreased support from traditional sources have converged to dramatically expand the importance of nonprofit marketing. Dramatic growth is seen in social marketing, international growth of the nonprofit sector, cause-related marketing, and concern about the ethical implications of nonprofit marketing strategies and tactics.

This sixth-edition text focuses on approaches and techniques that can significantly improve the practice of marketing management in the nonprofit sector on the part of existing and future managers. It emphasizes the development of (1) a proper *philosophy* of marketing, (2) a *systematic approach* to solving marketing problems, and (3) an awareness and ability to use the very latest *concepts and techniques* from the private sector.

The starting point for consideration of strategic marketing in nonprofit organizations is a clear perception and understanding of the unique environment in which they operate. Nonprofit organizations can be defined legally, but it is more crucial to understand the organization's environment and the specific marketing activities that constitute its mission. The major factors affecting the organization's environment are (1) whether it is a donative or commercial organization, (2) whether its performance is subject to public scrutiny, (3) whether marketing is perceived to be undesirable, (4) whether the organization is largely volunteer, and (5) whether marketing is judged by nonmarketing standards.

The missions of nonprofit organizations differ depending on the type of demand they seek to influence and the type of activity in which they are engaged. The organization's type of activity can be defined in terms of the key concept of exchange. On the one hand, target customers are asked to "pay" economic costs; sacrifice old ideas, values, and views of the world; sacrifice old patterns of behavior; or sacrifice time and energy. In return, they can expect products, services, social or psychological benefits, or some combination of these. Although some nonprofits seek to influence exchanges of money for goods and services just like for-profit organizations, what makes them unique is their concentration on exchanges involving nonmonetary costs on the one hand and social and psychological benefits on the other. Influencing such exchanges requires different perspectives and modified techniques. Peculiarities of the present state of the nonprofit world make it hard to "sell brotherhood" like soap. They also raise important ethical issues with which each nonprofit marketer must grapple.

QUESTIONS

1. What are the primary drivers for applying for-profit marketing strategies to the nonprofit sector? Do you agree that for-profit marketing strategies can be successfully applied to the nonprofit sector? Identify two cases in which this would not be appropriate.
2. Why are there a growing number of nonprofit firms in the United States and other countries? Would you expect this growth trend to continue? Why?
3. Why should a nonprofit organization ensure that it has secured appropriate legal status in the United States? What are the benefits of being registered as a nonprofit organization in the United States? How does this legal status help, and hurt, the marketer?
4. What is meant by the author when he writes that "a nonprofit organization's marketing task is doubled"? What impact does this have on the nonprofit marketing manager?
5. In nonprofit organization/consumer "exchanges," what are the four types of costs that consumers are asked to pay? What are the three basic types of benefits consumers receive?

NOTES

1. Lester M. Salamon, et al., *Global Civil Society: Dimension of the Nonprofit Sector* (Baltimore: The Johns Hopkins Center for Civil Society Studies, 1999).
2. "NPT 100," *The Nonprofit Times,* November 1, 2001, pp. 34–41.
3. Harvey Lipman, "Pay for Leaders at Biggest Charities Rises 6.2 Percent Chronicle Survey Find," *The Chronicle of Philanthropy,* September 21, 2000, pp. 38–48; M. Gibelman, "What's All the Fuss About? Executive Salaries in the Nonprofit Sector," *Administration and Social Work,* Vol. 24. No. 4 (2000), pp. 59–74.
4. James E. Austin and Jan Elias, "Timberland and Community Involvement," Harvard Business School Case No. 9-796-156, Boston, MA: Harvard Business School Publishing, 1996. Also, James E. Austin, *The Collaboration Challenge* (San Francisco: Jossey-Bass, 2000). See also: Dwight F. Burlingame and Dennis R. Young (Eds.), *Corporate Philanthropy at the Crossroads* (Bloomington: Indiana University Press, 1996); Michael E. Porter and Mark R. Kramer, "Philanthropy's New Agenda: Creating Value," *Harvard Business Review,* November-December 1999, pp. 121–130.
5. Shirley Sagawa and Eli Segal, *Common Interest, Common Good: Creating Value Through Business and Social Sector Partnerships* (Boston: Harvard Business School Press, 2000); Joseph Galaskiewicz and Wolfgang Bielefeld, *Nonprofits in an Age of Uncertainty: A Study in Organizational Change* (Hawthorne, New York: Aldine de Gruyter, 1998). (Summarized in *The Independent Sector, Facts and Findings,* Vol. 2, No. 1 (summer 2000), pp. 1–4.)
6. Alan R. Andreasen, "Intersector Transfer of Marketing Knowledge" in Paul N. Boom and Gregory T. Gundlach (Eds.), *Handbook of Marketing and Society* (Thousand Oaks, CA: Sage Publications, Ltd., 2001), pp. 80–104.
7. Peter F. Drucker, "What Business Can Learn from Nonprofits," *Harvard Business Review,* July–August 1989, pp. 88–93.
8. Rosabeth Moss Kanter, "From Spare Change to Real Change: The Social Sector as Beta Site for Business Innovation," *Harvard Business Review,* May–June 1999, pp. 122–132; Robin J. B. Ritchie, Sanjeev Swami, and Charles B. Weinberg, "A Brand New World for Nonprofits," *Journal of Nonprofit and Voluntary Sector Marketing,* Vol. 4, No. 1, (1999) pp. 29–42.
9. Philip Kotler and Sidney J. Levy, "Broadening the Concept of Marketing," *Journal of Marketing,* January 1969, pp. 10–15.
10. Philip Kotler and Gerald Zaltman, "Social Marketing: An Approach to Planned Social Change," *Journal of Marketing,* July 1971, pp. 3–12
11. Benson Shapiro, "Marketing for Nonprofit Organizations," *Harvard Business Review,* September–October, 1973, pp. 223–232.
12. Kotler and Levy, "Broadening the Concept of Marketing."
13. Andreasen, "Intersector Transfer of Marketing Knowledge."
14. Philip D. Harvey, *Let Every Child Be Wanted: How Social Marketing Is Revolutionizing Contraceptive Use Around the World* (Westport, Conn.: Auburn House, 1999); Christopher H. Lovelock, "A Market Segmentation Approach to Transit Planning, Modeling and Management," in *Proceedings of the Sixteenth Annual Meeting of the Transportation Research Forum,* 1975, pp. 247–258.
15. Ibid.
16. See, for example, Charles Weinberg, "Marketing Mix Decision Rules for Nonprofit Organizations," in Jagdish Sheth (Ed.), *Research in Marketing,* Vol. 3 (Greenwich, Conn.: JAI Press, 1980), pp. 191–234.
17. See, for example, Michael L. Rothschild, *An Incomplete Bibliography of Works Relating to Marketing for Public Sector and Nonprofit Organizations,* 3rd ed. (Madison: Bureau of Business Research and Services, University of Wisconsin, 1981).
18. See, for example, Paul N. Bloom, "Evaluating Social Marketing Programs:

Problems and Prospect," *1980 Educators Conference Proceedings* (Chicago: American Marketing Association).

19. Kotler and Zaltman, "Social Marketing."

20. Robin E. MacStravic, *Marketing Health Care* (Germantown, Md.: Aspen Systems Corporation, 1977).

21. See, for example, John L. Compton, "Public Services—To Charge or Not to Charge," *Business,* March–April 1980, pp. 31–38.

22. In addition to the first five editions of the present volume, there are now the following: Christopher H. Lovelock and Charles B. Weinberg, *Marketing for Public and Nonprofit Managers,* 2nd ed. (Redwood City, Calif.: The Scientific Press, 1989); David Rados, *Marketing for Non-Profit Organizations* (Boston: Auburn House Publishing Company, 1981); Armand Lauffer, *Strategic Marketing for Not-for-Profit Organizations* (New York: The Free Press, 1984); Larry L. Coffman, *Public Sector Marketing* (New York: John Wiley, 1986); Douglas Herron, *Marketing Nonprofit Programs and Services: Proven and Practical Strategies to Get More Customers, Members, and Donors* (San Francisco: Jossey-Bass, 1997); Janel M. Radtke, *Strategic Communications for Nonprofit Organizations: Seven Steps to Creating a Successful Plan* (San Francisco: Jossey-Bass, 1998); Adrian Sargeant, *Marketing Management for Nonprofit Organizations* (Oxford: Oxford University Press, 1999).

23. Philip Kotler and Roberta N. Clarke, *Marketing for Health Care Organizations* (Englewood Cliffs, N.J.: Prentice-Hall, 1986).

24. Philip Kotler and Karen F. A. Fox, *Strategic Marketing for Educational Organizations* (Englewood Cliffs, N.J.: Prentice-Hall, 1985).

25. Robert E. Stearns, *Marketing for Churches and Ministries* (New York: The Haworth Press, 1992).

26. Philip Kotler, Donald H. Haider, and Irving Rein, *Marketing Places* (New York: The Free Press, 1993).

27. Philip Kotler, Somkid Jatusripitak, and Suvit Maesincee, *The Marketing of Nations: A Strategic Approach to Building National Wealth* (New York: The Free Press, 1997).

28. Seymour H. Fine, *The Marketing of Ideas and Social Issues* (New York: Praeger, 1981).

29. For example, Ralph M. Gaedeke (Ed.), *Marketing in Private and Public and Nonprofit Organizations: Perspectives and Illustrations* (Santa Monica, Calif.: Goodyear, 1977); Michael P. Mokwa, William D. Dawson, and E. Arthur Priere (Eds.), *Marketing the Arts* (New York: Praeger, 1980); Michael P. Mokwa and Steven E. Permut, *Government Marketing* (New York: Praeger, 1981); Philip D. Cooper, *Health Care Marketing: Issues and Trends* (Germantown, Md.: Aspen Systems Corporation, 1979); Russell W. Belk (Ed.), *Advances in Nonprofit Marketing* (Greenwich, Conn.: JAI Press, 1985, 1990); Lee W. Frederiksen, Laura J. Solomon, and Kathleen A. Brehony, Eds., *Marketing Health Behavior* (New York: Plenum, 1984).

30. Christopher H. Lovelock and Charles B. Weinberg, *Public & Nonprofit Marketing: Readings & Cases,* 2nd ed. (South San Francisco, Calif.: The Scientific Press, 1990); Philip Kotler, O. C. Ferrell, and Charles Lamb (Eds.), *Strategic Marketing for Nonprofit Organizations: Cases and Readings* (Englewood Cliffs, N.J.: Prentice-Hall, 1987).

31. Richard K. Manoff, *Social Marketing* (New York: Praeger, 1985).

32. Philip Kotler and Eduardo L. Roberto, *Social Marketing: Strategies for Changing Public Behavior* (New York: The Free Press, 1989).

33. For example, *Populations Reports, Contraceptive Social Marketing: Lessons from Experience* (Series J, No. 30, July–August 1985); *Operations Research: Lessons for Policy and Programs* (Series J, No. 31, May– June 1986); and *AIDS Education—A Beginning* (Series L, No. 8, September 1989).

34. *The Marketing Planning Workbook* (Alexandria, Va.: United Way of America, 1989).

35. Mary Debus, *Handbook for Excellence in Focus Group Research* (Washington, D.C.: Academy for Educational Development, n.d.).

36. Mark R. Rasmuson, Renata E. Seidel, William A. Smith, and Elizabeth Mills

Booth, *Communications for Child Survival* (Washington, D.C.: Academy for Educational Development, June 1988).

37. *Making Health Communications Work: A Planner's Guide* (Washington, D.C.: Office of Cancer Communications, U.S. Department of Health and Human Services, April 1989).

38. For example, William D. Novelli, "Can We Really Market Public Health? Evidence of Efficacy," paper presented to the Third National Conference on Chronic Disease Prevention and Control, Denver, Colorado, October 19–21, 1988; Mary Debus, "Lessons Learned from the Dualima Condom Test Market," SOMARC Occasional Paper, September 1987; and William Smith, "A Consumer Strategy for Health, Nutrition and Population," Academy for Educational Development, 1989.

39. Roseanne Mirabella and Naomi B. Wish, "Nonprofit Management Education: Current Offerings in University Based Programs" at http://pirate.shu.edu/~mirabero/Kellogg. html; Roseanne Mirabella and Naomi B. Wish, "Educational Impact of Graduate Nonprofit Degree Programs: Perspectives of Multiple Stakeholders," *Nonprofit Management & Leadership,* Vol. 9, No. 3 (2000), pp. 329–340; Dennis R. Young, "Nonprofit Management Studies in the United States: Current Developments and Future Prospects, *Journal of Public Affairs Education,* Vol. 5 (1999), pp. 13–23.

40. B. J. Elliott, *A Re-examination of the Social Marketing Concept* (Sydney: Elliott & Shanahan Research, 1991).

41. William A. Smith, *Lifestyles for Survival: The Role of Social Marketing in Mass Education.* (Washington, D.C.: Academy for Educational Development, October 1989); Michael Ramah, "Social Marketing and the Prevention of AIDS," Washington, D.C.: Academy for Educational Development AIDSCOM Project, 1992.

42. V. K. Rangun and S. Karim, *Teaching Note: Focusing the Causes of Public and Nonprofit Agencies* (Boston: Allyn & Bacon, 1990).

43. Seymour Fine (Eds.), *Social Marketing: Promoting the Causes of Public and Nonprofit Agencies* (Boston: Allyn & Bacon, 1990).

44. Alan R. Andreasen, *Marketing Social Change* (San Francisco: Jossey-Bass, 1995).

45. Philip Kotler, Eduardo Roberto, and Nancy Lee, *Social Marketing: Strategies for Changing Public Behavior* (Thousand Oaks, Calif.: Sage Publications, 2002).

46. Lester M. Salamon, et al., *Global Civil Society: Dimension of the Nonprofit Sector.*

47. Peter Davies and Keith Scribbens, *Marketing Further and Higher Education* (Bath, England: Further Education Staff College, 1985).

48. Christopher Lovelock, "An International Perspective on Public Sector Marketing," in Mokwa and Permut, *Government Marketing,* pp. 114–143.

49. David Osborne and Ted Gaebler, *Reinventing Government* (New York: Plume, 1993).

50. Miklós Marschall, "The Nonprofit Sector in a Centrally Planned Economy," in Helmut K. Anheier and Wolfgang Seibel (Eds.), *The Third Sector: Comparative Studies of Nonprofit Organizations* (Berlin: Walter de Gruyter, 1990), pp. 277–291.

51. "Goodwill Changes Name to Reflect 'Global Influence,'" *The Nonprofit Times* (December 1993), p. 41.

52. Curt Weeden, *Corporate Social Investing* (San Francisco: Berrett-Koehler Publishers, Inc. 1998); Richard Steckel, Robin Simons, Jeffrey Simons, and Norman Tanen, *Making Money While Making a Difference: How to Profit with a Nonprofit Partner* (Homewood, Il.: High Tide Press, 1999); John M. Hood, *The Heroic Enterprise* (New York: The Free Press, 1996); Sue Adkins, *Cause-Related Marketing: Who Cares Wins* (Oxford: Butterworth-Heinemann, 1999); Richard Earle, *The Art of Cause Marketing* (Chicago: NTC Books, 2000).

53. Burton A. Weisbrod (Eds.), *To Profit or Not to Profit: The Commercialization of the Nonprofit Sector* (Cambridge: Harvard University Press, 1998); F. McLean, "Corporate Identity: What Does It Mean for Museums?" *Journal of Nonprofit and Voluntary Sector Marketing,* Vol. 3, No. 1 (1998), pp. 11–21.

54. Kelvin Shawn Sealey, Jerr Boschee, Jed Emerson, and Wendy A. Sealy, *A Reader in Social Enterprise* (Boston: Pearson Custom Publishing, 2000); Bernard Avishai, "What's Business's Social Contract?", *Harvard Business Review,* January–February 1994.

55. Richard Williamson, "Investors See Profits Flow Through Green Screens," *The Nonprofit Times,* June 15, 2000, pp. 1,4. b

56. Kathleen M. O'Regan and Sharon M. Oster, "Nonprofit and For-Profit Partnerships: Rationale and Challenges of Cross-Sector Contracting," *Nonprofit and Voluntary Sector Quarterly,* Vol. 29, No. 1 (2000), pp. 120–140; Alan R. Andreasen and Minette E. Drumwright, "Alliances and Ethics in Social Marketing" in Alan R. Andreasen (Ed.), *Ethics in Social Marketing* (Washington, D.C.: Georgetown University Press, 2001), pp. 95–124.

57. M. Lindenberg, "Are We at the Cutting Edge or the Blunt Edge? Improving NGO Organizational Performance with Private and Public Sector Strategic Management Frameworks," *Nonprofit Management & Leadership,* Vol. 11 (2001), pp. 247–270.

58. Patrick E. Murphy and Paul N. Bloom, "Ethical Issues in Social Marketing," in Seymour Fine (Ed.), *Social Marketing: Promoting the Causes of Public and Nonprofit Agencies* (Boston: Allyn & Bacon, 1990), pp. 68–78.

59. Alan R. Andreasen (Ed.), *Ethics in Social Marketing.*

60. Nelson Rosenbaum, "The Competitive Market Model: Emerging Strategy for Nonprofits," *The Nonprofit Executive,* July 1984, pp. 4–5.

61. Mark Dowie, *American Foundations* (Cambridge, Mass.: The MIT Press, 2001).

62. Burton A. Weisbrod (Ed.), *To Profit or Not to Profit,* p. 1.

63. Brad Stone, "R$_x$ Thirty Minutes of Stairmaster Twice Weekly: Hospitals Court the Sweaty Set with Health Clubs," *Newsweek,* March 17, 1997, p. 46 (cited in Burton A. Weisbrod (Eds.), *To Profit or Not to Profit*).

64. Judith Dobrzynski, "Art (?) To Go: Museum Shops Broaden Wares at a Profit," *New York Times,* December 10, 1997,

pp. A1, A16 (cited in Burton A. Weisbrod (Ed.), *To Profit or Not to Profit*).

65. Gina Kolata, "Safeguards Urged for Researchers: Aim Is to Keep Vested Interests from Suppressing Discoveries," *New York Times,* April 17, 1997, p. A13 (cited in Burton A. Weisbrod [Ed.], *To Profit or Not to Profit*).

66. Reed Abelson, "Charities Use For-Profit Units to Avoid Disclosing Finances," *New York Times,* February 9, 1998, pp. A1–A12 (cited in Burton A. Weisbrod [Ed.], *To Profit or Not to Profit*).

67. Peter Dobkin Hall, "Philanthropy, Public Welfare, and the Politics of Knowledge: Acquiring Knowledge by Taking Risks," in Deborah S. Gardner (Ed.), *Vision and Values: Rethinking the Nonprofit Sector in America* (New York: The Nathan Cummings Foundation, 1998), pp. 11–27.

68. Robert D. Putnam, *Bowling Alone: The Collapse and Revival of American Community* (New York: Simon & Schuster, 2000).

69. Peter Dobkin Hall, "Philanthropy, Public Welfare, and the Politics of Knowledge."

70. Paul Light, *Making Nonprofits Work* (Washington, D.C.: The Aspen Institute, 2000).

71. *The Chronicle of Philanthropy,* November 1, 2001, p. 37

72. Jed Emerson and Fay Twersky (Eds.), *New Social Entrepreneurs: The Success, Challenge and Lessons of Nonprofit Enterprise Creation* (San Francisco: The Roberts Foundation, 1996); C. T. Clotfelter and T. Ehrlich (Eds.), *Philanthropy and the Nonprofit Sector in a Changing America* (Bloomington Indiana University Press, 1999); Christine W. Letts, William P. Ryan, and Allen Grossman, *High Performance Nonprofit Organizations* (New York: John Wiley and Sons, Inc., 1999).

73. Paul Light, *Making Nonprofits Work.*

74. Joseph Galaskiewicz and Wolfgang Bielefeld, *Nonprofits in an Age of Uncertainty.*

75. *Giving and Volunteering 1999.* Washington, DC: The Independent Sector, 2001.

76. Philip Kotler and Joanne Scheff, *Standing Room Only* (Boston: Harvard Business School Press, 1997); Neil Kotler and Philip

Kotler, *Museum Strategy and Marketing* (San Francisco: Jossey-Bass Publisher, 1998).

77. Lester A. Salamon and Wojciech Sokolowski, "Volunteering in Cross-National Perspective: Evidence from 26 Countries," Working Paper, The Johns Hopkins Comparative Nonprofit Sector Project, 2001.

78. Ibid.

79. Burton A Weisbrod, *The Voluntary Independent Sector* (Lexington, KY.: Lexington Books, 1978).

80. Lester A. Salamon and Wojciech Sokolowski, "Volunteering in Cross-National Perspective."

81. William P. Ryan, "The New Landscape for Nonprofits," *Harvard Business Review,* January–February 1999, pp. 127–136.

82. Robert Davis, "The Painful Truth of Hospice Care," *USA Today,* August 20, 2001, pp. D1–D2.

83. "Charity's Anti-Smoking Site Turns For-Profit," *The Chronicle of Philanthropy,* May 3, 2001, p. 44.

84. Philip D. Harvey, *Let Every Child Be Wanted.*

85. David Osborne and Ted Gaebler, *Reinventing Government.*

86. Neill McKee, *Social Mobilization and Social Marketing in Developing Communities* (Penang: Southbound 1992).

87. *Unfair Competition by Nonprofit Organizations with Small Business: An Issue for the 1980s* (Washington, D.C.: Office of Advocacy, U.S. Small Business Administration, November 1983); Robert D. Herman and Denise Rendina, "Donor Reaction to Commercial Activities of Nonprofit Organizations: An American Case Study," *Voluntas: International Journal of Voluntary and Nonprofit Organizations,* Vol. 12, No. 2 (June 2001), pp. 157–169.

88. Bruce R. Hopkins, "The Tax Implications of Profit-Making Ventures," *The*

Grantsmanship Center News, March–April 1982, pp. 38–41.

89. Bruce R. Hopkins, *The Law of Tax-Exempt Organizations,* 3rd ed. (New York: John Wiley, 1979).

90. National Center for Charitable Statistics, *National Taxonomy of Exempt Entities* (Washington, D.C.: The Independent Sector, March 14, 1987).

91. Margaret M. Maxwell (Ed.), *Marketing the Nonprofit: The Challenge of Fundraising in a Consumer Culture* (San Francisco: Jossey-Bass Publisher, 1997).

92. Andrew H. Malcolm, "Ottawa Runs Into Protests Over Its Huge Advertising Costs," *New York Times,* November 1, 1980, p. 10.

93. Paul Bloom and William D. Novelli, "Problems and Challenges in Social Marketing," *Journal of Marketing,* Spring 1981, p. 80.

94. See, for example, the American Marketing Association code of ethics for marketing research at www.marketingpower.com.

95. Peter Drucker, "Managing the Public Service Institution," *The Public Interest,* Vol. 33 (Fall 1973), pp. 43–60.

96. Ibid., p. 50.

97. Michael L. Rothschild, "Marketing Communications in Nonbusiness Situations or Why It's So Hard to Sell Brotherhood Like Soap," *Journal of Marketing,* Spring 1979, pp. 11–20.

98. Alan R. Andreasen, *Marketing Social Change.*

99. Bloom and Novelli, "Problems and Challenges."

100. Michael L. Rothschild, "Marketing Communications."

101. Lester A. Salamon and Wojciech Sokolowski, "Volunteering in Cross-National Perspective."

102. Alan R. Andreasen (Ed.), *Ethics in Social Marketing.*

CHAPTER 2

Developing a Customer-Centered Mindset

Nonprofit marketers are fanatical about making behavior change their major focus. To improve the health and welfare of children at risk in developing countries, three key players—the BASICS project, USAID, and the Centers for Disease Control and Prevention, decided in 1997 to use this focus to coordinate their efforts and concentrate on prevention programs that would have the largest potential payoff.

A starting point was the recognition that five medical conditions are the cause of at least 70 percent of childhood mortality. These are diarrheal diseases, acute lower respiratory tract infections, malnutrition, malaria, and measles. Further, these organizations and agencies realized that, because at-risk children often have multiple illness conditions, they ought not to focus on only one or two of the five conditions. What they recognized was that the key to prevention and effective treatment of these children was to figure out a manageable set of behaviors on the part of caregivers that, if influenced by their marketing programs and those of many others concerned about children's lives, could have a major impact on the five problem areas.

As a result of extensive research and consultation, the team came up with 16 emphasis behaviors that met five criteria. Put in simple terms, the behavior has to:

1. Have an impact on multiple diseases.
2. Be known to lead to serious illness and death.
3. Impact the most important health problems in each country in which a program is working.
4. Be measurable.
5. Be subject to influence through public health programs that are not prohibitively costly.

The emphasis behaviors were grouped into five broad areas. The first involves family planning and prenatal care. The second focuses on breastfeeding and other early feeding practices, and the third encourages timely immunizations. The fourth set of emphasis behaviors involves in-home preventive and curative health practices, such as hand washing, use of insecticide-treated bednets, consumption of Vitamin A and iodine, and, when the child is ill, properly feeding the child and using oral rehydration solution and any prescribed medications. The final behavior is taking the sick child to appropriate health care facilities when he or she is clearly ill.

Source: Adapted from John Murray, Gabriella Newes Adeyi, Judith Graeff, Rebecca Fields, Mark Rasmuson, Rene Salgado, and Tina Sanghi, *Emphasis Behaviors in Maternal and Child Health: Focusing on Caretaker Behaviors to Develop Maternal and Child Health Programs in Communities* (Washington, D.C.: BASICS Technical Report, 1997).

It is the central tenet of this book that one can be a successful marketer only if one has adopted the proper *marketing mindset*. This means having a clear appreciation for what marketing comprises and what it can do for the organization. More important, it means developing a philosophy of marketing that *puts the customer at the center of everything one does*. We would argue that much of what is unattractive about marketing practice today is the result of a lack of appreciation of the proper way to go about *doing* marketing.

Marketing is not intimidation or coercion. It is not "hard selling" and deceptive advertising. It is a sound, effective technology for creating exchanges and influencing behavior that, when properly applied, *must be* socially beneficent because its major premise is responding to customer needs and wants. In the wrong hands (i.e., in the hands of those without the proper mindset), what is called "marketing" can be manipulative and intrusive, and an embarrassment to those of us who use marketing as it ought to be used.

A major objective of this book is to develop this proper marketing mindset in the reader to the extent that it will become second nature in his or her future day-to-day marketing practice.

THE BOUNDARIES OF MARKETING

One of the reasons for the rapidly growing interest in marketing is that it applies to such a wide range of situations in individuals' professional and personal lives. We would argue that *all* the following represent instances of *marketing:*

- McDonald's says, "You deserve the best today."
- Safeway supermarkets claims it has "lower prices overall."
- You (or your son or daughter) ask someone for a date to go to the movies.
- A subordinate asks for a raise in pay.
- You ask a co-worker to join you as a volunteer in the upcoming United Way fund drive.
- You approach a foundation for a major grant.
- You seek government approval of a new social venture in a developing country.
- You petition a Senator for a new law.
- Your local public TV station holds a pledge drive.
- You try to convince your sister to stop smoking.
- You request that a supplier give you an additional 3 percent discount if you commit to a larger order.
- You send a press release to a local TV station urging coverage of an upcoming workshop on the homeless.

What is common to all of these situations is that someone (a marketer) is attempting to influence the behavior of someone else (a target market). Marketing is not just something that an organization such as Procter & Gamble or Pepsi-Cola does. It is something nonprofits and government agencies do and something we do daily in our individual personal lives. And, given that all these situations involve marketing, they can all benefit from the application of the very best marketing management techniques.

We define marketing management as follows:

Marketing management is the process of planning and executing programs designed to influence the behavior of target audiences by creating and maintaining beneficial exchanges for the purposes of satisfying individual and organizational objectives.

An important feature of this definition is *that it focuses on exchanges.* Marketers are in the profession of creating, building, and maintaining *exchanges.* For example, I give you 79 cents and you give me a bar of sweet-smelling soap; or I walk two hours to get to the doctor's office, wait there three more hours, and worry that my house and children are being neglected, and the doctor gives my baby an immunization which protects her from measles. Because exchanges only take place when a target audience member takes an action, *the ultimate objective of marketing is to influence behavior.*

This definition permits us to distinguish marketing from several things it is *not.* Marketing's objectives are not *ultimately* either to educate or to change values or attitudes. It may seek to do so as *a means* of influencing behavior. However, if someone has a final goal of imparting information or knowledge, that person is in the education profession, not marketing. Further, if someone has a final goal of changing attitudes or values, that person may be described as a propagandist, a lobbyist, or perhaps an artist, but not a marketer. While marketing may use the tools of the educator or the propagandist, its critical distinguishing feature is that its ultimate goal is to influence behavior (either changing it or keeping it the same in the face of other pressures).

Unfortunately, however, many of those who *could* use marketing principles do not do so because they do not see the relevance of marketing to their tasks. But we would argue that, in nonprofit organizations, public relations specialists, fundraisers, volunteer recruiters, and employee supervisors are all marketers at one time or another. And, as such, they can all benefit from understanding the philosophy and approach to marketing outlined in this book.

However, there are many nonprofit organizations (as well as some in the private sector) who *think* they are marketers but who go about it the wrong way because they do not really understand what proper marketing is all about. Consider the following examples:[1]

• The director of an urban art museum describes her marketing strategy as "an educational task. I assemble the best works available and then display them grouped by period and style so that the museum-goer can readily see the similarities and differences between, say, a Braque and a Picasso or between a Brancusi and an Arp. Our catalogues and lecture programs are carefully coordinated with this approach to complete our marketing mix."

• The public relations manager of a social service agency claims, "We are very marketing oriented. We research our target markets extensively and hire top-flight creative people with strong marketing backgrounds to prepare brochures. They tell our story with a sense of style and graphic innovation that has won us several awards."

• A marketing vice-president for a charitable foundation ascribes his success to careful, marketing-oriented planning. "Once a year we plan the entire year's series of messages, events, and door-to-door solicitation. We emphasize the fine humanitarian work we do, showing and telling potential donors about the real people who have benefited from donations to us. Hardly a week goes by without some human-interest story appearing in the local press about our work. The donors just love it!"

Each of these executives *thinks* he or she understands what marketing is all about. *They do not.* A study of museum directors showed that, as compared to marketing practitioners, museum directors were the following:

- Less likely to have secured "information from [their] customers regarding what they would like [the museum] to offer."
- More likely to see their product as desirable for everyone rather than as targeted at specific segments.
- Less interested in changing prices to increase revenues.
- Less willing to change their distribution strategy.
- Less willing in the future to "change the nature of the products and services [they] offer [their] customers."

Despite this confusion about marketing, it is not uncommon for these managers to sprinkle their planning documents and casual conversations with terms like "benefit segmentation," "product positioning," "message strategies," "marketing mix," and so forth. But if one were to pay careful attention to the subtle nuances of these managers' attitudes toward their customers and toward what they are offering them, it would become strikingly clear that their approach to marketing resembles what one would have found 30 years ago in the private sector. This approach is very different from that permeating today's modern marketing management.

THE EVOLUTION OF MARKETING PHILOSOPHY

To understand modern marketing management, it is useful to trace the evolution of different business orientations toward marketing in the private sector over the last hundred years, in part because examples of all of them exist today. Three orientations can be distinguished.

The Product Mindset

When marketing first emerged as a distinct managerial function around the turn of the century, it found itself in an era that venerated industrial innovation in the design of new products. It was a period that saw the development of the radio, the automobile, and the electric light. In this first period, marketing also was decidedly *product oriented*. The belief was that to be an effective marketer, you simply had to "build a better mousetrap," and, in effect, customers would beat a pathway to your door.

Even today, many organizations are in love with their product. They believe strongly in its value even if their publics are having second thoughts. They strongly resist modifying it even if this would increase its appeal to others. Thus, colleges continue to require their students to study a foreign language even though few ever learn the language and most students report the whole experience as a waste of time and money. Museums feature certain works of art year after year even though they attract the attention or interest of virtually no one. And many churches present the same dull Sunday morning sermons year after year as a matter of tradition, ignoring the changing interests of churchgoers and the steadily declining attendance. We define a product mindset as follows:

A product mindset toward marketing holds that success will come to those organizations that bring to market goods and services they are convinced will be good for the public.

The Sales Mindset

The Great Depression of the 1930s dealt a fatal blow to those product-centered marketers who defined successful marketing in terms of their attractive offerings. Building ingenious products, producing them cheaply, and distributing them as widely as possible was a reasonable way to be a successful marketer as long as there were customers out there to buy them. But with the Depression, demand shrank dramatically and both factories and distribution systems found themselves with large volumes of excess capacity. In response to this turn of events, marketers reconceived their objectives in competitive terms. The problem was no longer how to grind out masses of low-cost, inventive products and distribute them broadly. Now the challenge seemed to be to convince consumers that (1) they should give up their hard-earned money for things other than the bare necessities and (2) when they did, they should choose the marketer's offering over anyone else's. The key was to persuade consumers that the marketer's offering was *better* than buying nothing or buying competitors' products or services. This new orientation led to significant increases in the role of advertising and personal selling in the marketing mix. "Salesmanship" became a byword of successful marketing. In the 1930s, salesmen and the denizens of Madison Avenue achieved a central role in American folklore. Willy Loman and the "Man in the Grey Flannel Suit" became important symbols of the new business culture.

The selling orientation also continues to be pervasive today. Some organizations believe they can substantially increase the size of their market by increasing their selling effort. Rather than change their offerings to make them more attractive, these organizations increase the budget for advertising, personal selling, sales promotion, and other demand-stimulating activities. A sales mindset is defined as follows:

A sales mindset toward marketing holds that success will come to those organizations that best persuade customers to accept their offerings rather than competitors' or rather than no offering at all.

The Customer Mindset

The orientations that characterized the two earliest stages in marketing's historical development had one thing in common: They began marketing planning with the *organization* and *what it wanted to offer*. In the first stage, it was expected that grateful customers would come to the organization that had the best or the cheapest offerings. In the "selling" era, the task was somewhat different. The organization was forced to go out and convince customers that they had a really good—perhaps superior—offering. As the economy rebounded after the Great Depression, however, consumers became wealthier and more sophisticated. Consumers became pickier, more responsive to custom-tailored options, and less willing to settle for just anything the market tried to persuade them to buy.

At that point, a number of leading marketers came to a very important realization: They had the marketing equation turned backward. They had been trying to *change consumers to fit what the organization had to offer,* but truly the customer was sovereign. Whatever he or she chose to buy determined the organization's success. Consumers ultimately decided what transactions were to be made—not the marketer. And if this was so, then *marketing planning must begin with the consumer, not with the organization. Outside–inside marketing must replace inside–outside marketing.*

This simple idea is the essence of the modern approach to marketing. It is, in fact, the philosophy that will guide this volume. We shall see that, for the organization, a marketing mindset of "customer-centeredness" requires that the organization systematically study customers' needs, wants, perceptions, preferences, and satisfaction through using surveys, focus groups, and other means. The organization must constantly act on this information to improve its offerings to meet its customers' needs better. The employees must be well selected and trained to feel that they are working for the customer (rather than the boss). A customer orientation will express itself in the friendliness with which the organization's telephone operators answer the phone and the helpfulness of various employees in solving customer problems. The employees in a customer-oriented organization will work as a team to meet the needs of the specific target markets that are to be served. Their focus will not be just on individual transactions, but on making customers for life.

A customer mindset toward marketing holds that success will come to that organization that best determines the perceptions, needs, and wants of target markets and continually satisfies them through the design, communication, pricing, and delivery of appropriate and competitively viable offerings.

This proper philosophic orientation has a great many implications for the way a nonprofit marketing program ought to be run. As we shall see, adopting a customer orientation does not, as many nonprofit managers fear, mean that the organization must cater to every consumer whim and fancy. It doesn't mean that a symphony conductor or theater manager must give up his or her artistic integrity. Nor does it mean that health care institutions must abandon their professional standards or that college professors must become classroom song-and-dance performers. Those who argue that these consequences will befall the organization if the devil (marketing) is let in the door simply misunderstand what a customer orientation truly means. To restate: It means that marketing planning must *start* with customer perceptions, needs, and wants. It means that, even if an organization can't or ought not change certain aspects of the offering, the highest volume of exchange will always be generated if the way the organization's offering is described, "priced," "packaged," and delivered is fully responsive to what is referred to in the current jargon as "where the customer is coming from."

Consider two small examples. For years, the Buffalo Philharmonic, like many other symphonies, had a serious problem in trying to broaden its audience. It was willing to change its program somewhat, but ultimately it felt that Mozart is Mozart and somehow customers must be made to change *their* attitudes and behavior. Then, in the early 1970s, a modest university research project revealed that many consumers who indicated that they thought they *might* like to attend a concert did not do so because they expected the occasion to be very formal. As these potential target consumers put it, "We can't go because we don't have the proper clothes. We would feel really uncomfortable around all those fancy-dressed people." The orchestra itself was seen as distant, formal, and forbidding. Once the Philharmonic realized that this was where these potential customers were "coming from," they took great pains to humanize the orchestra and the concert-going experience. Orchestra section members began playing shirt-sleeve chamber music programs at neighborhood art fairs and other local outdoor events. Contact was made with local primary and secondary schools. The orchestra itself even performed at halftime at a Buffalo Bills football game!

A new conductor, Michael Tilson Thomas, began appearing on local television and giving brief informal talks to audiences at specific concerts. Concert-going never again had the sense of formality that was clearly keeping many potential patrons away, and attendance figures clearly reflected this new customer-centered orientation.

Another example is national in scope. For years, organizations committed to reducing the incidence of smoking in the United States believed that the major reason individuals did not quit was that they did not realize the consequences of continued smoking, or if they did, they were not frightened enough of these consequences to take action. As a result the marketing programs focused almost exclusively on communicating the very real dangers of smoking to target smokers. In a sense, they were trying to *sell* the stop-smoking idea to what they thought was an ignorant and reluctant audience.

It was only after an extensive review of a large number of consumer studies that organizations like the National Cancer Institute (NCI) realized that the "product" they were trying to sell—that smoking is bad for you—had already been sold. Seven out of eight smokers reported that they either wanted to quit smoking or had tried to quit several times in the past. Further analysis revealed that these consumers perceived two extremely significant barriers to quitting. First, they felt they did not really know a technique for quitting that would be effective for them. Second, even in cases where they were vaguely aware of a method that might work, they were reluctant to try to quit because they expected to fail. They had either heard of many who had failed, or had failed themselves many times in the past. For these very reasons, they tended to "turn off" most antismoking commercials, since they saw these commercials as, in effect, asking them to fail again.

Once the cancer-fighting organizations finally understood this consumer perspective, the marketing efforts of NCI and its sister nonprofits changed dramatically. Warnings of the dangers of smoking were, of course, continued to deter new, young potential smokers. At the same time, a major new marketing thrust was developed along two fronts. First, efforts were made to develop and get into the field a wide range of quitting techniques. Second, NCI and the American Cancer Society worked to persuade physicians and other health care workers to help smokers implement the newly available techniques and, just as important, to cope with smokers' often desperate fears of failing. The effects on cigarette consumption of this new customer-centered campaign have been considerable.

CUSTOMER-CENTERED ORGANIZATIONS

The Buffalo Philharmonic and NCI cases are dramatic examples of the way individual marketing programs can be developed to respond to consumers' needs, wants, and perceptions, and not just to the organization's own needs. But why, one must ask, did these organizations not develop these solutions sooner? The answer—and it is a crucial one—is that the organizations had not (and many still have not) developed a true customer-centered *mindset* that had seeped into the consciousness of every member of the organization who had any managerial responsibility or contact of any kind with potential target customers. We define a customer-centered organization as follows:

A customer-centered organization is one that makes every effort to sense, serve, and satisfy the needs and wants of its clients and publics within the constraints of its budget.

One result of a customer-centered orientation is that the people who come in contact with such organizations report high personal satisfaction. They make such comments as "This is the best church I ever belonged to"; "My college was terrific—the professors really taught well and cared about the students"; "I think this hospital is fine—the nurses are cheerful, the food is good, and the room is clean." These consumers become the best advertisement for these institutions. Their goodwill and favorable word of mouth reach other ears and make it easy for the organization to attract and serve more people; they become supporters for life! The organizations are effective because they are customer-centered.

Most organizations are not highly customer-centered.[2] They fall into one of three groups. The first group would like to be more customer-centered but lacks the needed resources or power over employees. The organization's budget may be insufficient to hire, train, and motivate good employees and to monitor their performance. Or management may lack the power to require employees to give good service, as when the employees are under civil service regulations or are volunteers and cannot be disciplined or fired for being insensitive to customers. One inner-city high school principal complained that his problem was not poor students but poor teachers, many of whom were "burned out" in the classroom and uncooperative but who could not be removed.

A second group of organizations is not customer-centered simply because it prefers to concentrate on things other than customer satisfaction. Thus, many museums are more interested in collecting antiquarian material than in making the material relevant or interesting to museum-goers. The U.S. Internal Revenue Service may be more interested in the number of people it processes per hour than in how much help each one really receives. When these organizations are mandated to exist or are without competition, they usually behave bureaucratically toward their clients.

Finally, there are always a few organizations that intentionally act unresponsively to the publics they are supposed to serve. In the 1980s, a local newspaper exposed that one food stamp office chose to be inaccessible in order to minimize the public's use of its service: "There is no sign on the building indicating that the food stamp office is inside . . . there also was no sign anywhere in the building directing applicants to the basement, no sign on the door leading to the stairs, and no sign on the door to the office itself. The only indication that a food stamp office is located in the building is a small, handwritten sign on the door at the top of the stairs. Adding to the inconvenience, the food stamp office was closed from March 10 to April 8."[3]

DETECTING AN ORGANIZATION-CENTERED ORIENTATION[4]

Conversations with nonprofit managers such as those quoted earlier make it abundantly clear that they *wish* to be customer-centered and, in virtually all cases, truly believe they already are. In most cases, they are not. Fortunately, a number of "clues" exist that tend to give away an organization's *organization-centered* marketing philosophy. These clues, simply stated, are these:

1. The organization's offering is seen as inherently desirable.
2. Lack of organizational success is attributed to customer ignorance, absence of motivation, or both.
3. A minor role is afforded customer research.
4. Marketing is defined primarily as promotion.
5. One "best" marketing strategy is typically employed in approaching the market.
6. Generic competition tends to be ignored.

Understanding and recognizing these clues is essential if a nonprofit organization is to adopt the appropriate customer-centered mindset and not deceive itself about its true orientation.

Clue No. 1: The Offer Is Seen as Inherently Desirable

The very nature of the offerings promoted in the nonprofit sector often leads their sponsors to have an extremely high opinion of the value of their offerings. They simply see the behavior they are promoting as inherently desirable. They find it hard to believe that anyone would turn them down!

Committed theater managers find it hard to believe that right-thinking people wouldn't wish to attend a well-acted play; charitable organizations cannot accept a consumer's unwillingness to give; and those who head up nonprofit social issues groups often can't see why people won't vote for, say, cleaner air or prison reform. One organization that overcame the notion that its offerings were inherently desirable is the NCI. Most women, NCI discovered, agreed that practicing breast self-examination was a good way to ensure early detection of breast cancer, and many knew how to do it. Yet the majority were not practicing breast self-examination, or did so at best only rarely. What was the problem? It turned out that among women who practiced self-examination, the discovery that there was no problem led to a sense of relief the first few times, but eventually the women became bored and stopped the procedure. At the same time, the prospect of finding a problem was so frightening to most other women that they never even tried self-examination. It was only when NCI understood the barriers perceived by the target audience to an obviously beneficial practice that it began to develop more user-oriented marketing programs. NCI's new stance, which was based on assuring women that lumps are often nonmalignant and that progress is being made in the fight against breast cancer, resulted in significant increases in breast self-examination practices among American women.

Clue No. 2: Customer Ignorance and Lack of Motivation Are Seen as the Barriers to Success

It is, of course, not surprising to find that if a manager believes that wearing seat belts or giving to the United Way is something everyone should do, then if someone does *not* respond to a specific marketing effort, there are really only two explanations. Either potential customers do not *truly* understand the offering (that is, do not share the organization's inherent belief in it), or they are simply not motivated enough to take action. Managers conclude that they simply haven't yet found the right way to communicate the benefits of the offering or they just haven't found the right incentives to get target customers to overcome their "natural" inertia.

These managers have a relatively benign view of consumers. There is, however, a very large number of nonprofit managers who feel—often unconsciously—much hostility toward customers. Their basic perception is that customers are really *enemies*. The managers feel that it is these recalcitrant customers who are standing in the way of the organization's becoming more successful. Such views manifest themselves in the organization's treatment of consumers at the box office, on the telephone, in the field, or in any other personal encounter. They are evident in the disapproving look of the health worker confronted by an impoverished family unwilling to get proper immunization for their children. They are apparent in the resentful faces of fundraisers turned down by those who are "uninterested" or "too busy" and in the sarcastic voices of box office people trying to explain ticket availability to confused telephone customers.

It is not hard for the consuming public to sense in these encounters the organization's true colors and to perhaps respond in kind. And if they do, of course, they only convince the managers that they were right about consumers in the first place.

A key strategic assumption of managers in organizations with this attitude seems to be that the task of marketing is to get the customer to change to fit the organization rather than the other way around. They do not realize that (1) in a great many nonprofit marketing situations, customers are very hard to change, while the organization is not; (2) the organization is under the manager's control and the consumer is not; (3) changing the organization to accommodate customers, if fully carried out, ensures that consumer needs and wants will be carefully monitored and followed.

Clue No. 3: A Minor Role Is Given to Consumer Research

Customer ignorance or lack of motivation is not always the key problem in causing an organization's lack of success. This was obvious in the NCI smoking example discussed earlier. However, many organization-centered marketing managers are unlikely to discover this through consumer research. Because they attribute their lack of success to customers, their opinions about what research is needed is very straightforward. Since part of the problem is that too many consumers are too ignorant about the organization's offering, they believe one kind of study that is needed is to research into the nature and extent of consumer ignorance and into the characteristics of who is ignorant. Further, since motivation is a major problem, research may also be needed to try to map the attitudes of those who are knowledgeable to show why they are so negative and unmotivated. Such research, it is hoped, will yield clues as to how to motivate them to take action.

In the main, however, customer research is too often absent in nonprofit organizations. As we point out in Chapter 5, there are a number of reasons for this. Many nonprofit managers think that research is too expensive, or they think it is needed only for major decisions. Some managers associate research with statistics and computers that can be intimidating. Often these managers argue that research typically tells managers what they already knew. These myths all get in the way of effective use of key consumer information.

Despite the low level of research activity, the potential can be dramatic. As most profit-sector marketers will attest, research can challenge some managers' most fundamental assumptions about their customers. The example of the antismoking groups' assumptions about consumer ignorance of the dangers of smoking is a classic case in point.

Clue No. 4: Marketing Is Defined as Promotion

If one seeks the marketing challenge as one of eliminating ignorance and increasing motivation, then it is inevitable that the tool one will focus on is better communication. Managers will see the need for the following:

- a better copywriter and better copywriting
- a better brochure
- a new image
- better salespeople with better sales presentations
- more posters in more places
- ads placed in prime time rather than in public service announcement (PSA) "media ghettos"
- more and better press releases
- better relations with newspapers and TV news departments
- a new advertising agency

Other elements of the marketing mix pricing, offer redesign, and better distribution, such as are seen as "not really the problem."

A good example of the consequences of viewing marketing problems as stemming from consumer ignorance and lack of motivation is found in the efforts to secure blood donations. Many blood-collection agency heads believe that the best way to encourage donations is to tell consumers about the good things that a donor's blood can do or to stress that giving blood is a civic duty. They believe that people hold back from giving because they don't appreciate the "gift's" virtues or because they are afraid. Thus, agency heads reason, the marketing task is to tell consumers as dramatically and convincingly as possible about the benefits to society of giving blood and to assure them that the costs are trivial; indeed, giving is not really such a "big deal."

While these messages work for some people, important segments respond to very different approaches that are not based on impersonal media. Many donation programs, for example, have become more successful by simply changing the distribution strategy and going to major customer groups rather than insisting that they come to the agency, or having the hours of service convenient for potential donors, not just for the medical staff. In some cases, men can be motivated by challenges to their masculinity. Contrary to the view of the typical donor, the macho man who can brag to his co-workers that he is a 20-gallon donor is really responding to benefits he sees for himself. He may care relatively little about "society." Even more perversely, it may be that the higher the costs of giving, the greater the pain and suffering in the process of giving, the greater the rewards! Thus, campaigns in factories that publicize individuals' giving records (bar charts or 10- and 20-gallon lapel pins) and that (contrary to the usual program) don't downplay the possible psychological and physical costs of giving can be highly effective. In such situations, informal group pressure, rather than persuasion, is the key marketing tool.

However, social, fraternal, and church group members can be motivated to give blood by the let's-all-participate aspects of a bloodmobile visit. They will respond to messages about camaraderie, about "feeling left out if you don't join in," or about letting the group down if you don't go. Messages of this sort have little to say about the occasion for the get-together or its value to society, recognizing that for these potential donors the key distinction is also selfish: the desire to be wanted and loved by other members of a group. Here again, rather than brochures and advertisements, it is within-group word of mouth stimulated by key opinion leaders that does the job.

Clue No. 5: One Really Good Strategy Is Seen as All You Need

Since the nonprofit administrator is not often in as close touch with the market as a customer-oriented marketer would be, he or she may view the market as monolithic or at least as having only a few crudely defined market segments. Subtle distinctions are ignored or played down. As a consequence, most nonprofits tend to see the need for only one or two marketing strategies aimed at the most obvious market segments (e.g., young people, families, and the elderly). This climate of managerial certainty precludes experimentation either with alternative strategies or with variations across a number of subtle market subsegments. In this view, the problem is to inform and motivate, and the challenge is about the same for every target customer.

Also encouraging this approach is the fact that nonprofit managers often come from nonbusiness backgrounds and may fear taking risks. Personal job survival and slow aggrandizement of the budget and staff are often their paramount objectives. And since such administrators are typically responsible only to a volunteer board which meets irregularly and sometimes prefers to know little about day-to-day operations, they do their best to keep a low profile and avoid causing waves. Simple, consistent strategies that imply well-thought-out analysis are the best choice for career safety. Too much change, too much variation, and too much experimentation may seem to imply that one really isn't too sure about what to do. Such a low-profile, risk-averting strategy is, of course, tactically sound if one's organization happens to make up any losses with fundraising or government allocations. In such cases, aggressive marketing strategies are not really necessary.

Clue No. 6: There Is Assumed to Be No Generic Competition

In the private sector, organizations compete at many different levels, from interbrand competition all the way back to competition at the generic or basic desire levels. In the nonprofit sector, while many organizations do, in fact, compete—the Heart Fund with the American Cancer Society, the Metropolitan Museum of Art with the Whitney Museum or the Museum of Modern Art—many institutions don't have clear competitors because their services or so-called products are intangible or stress unique behavior changes. The competitors faced by those marketing, say, blood donations or forest-fire prevention are not immediately apparent. Therefore, it's not surprising that marketers ignore competition at more basic levels. But at the product level, blood banks, for example, undoubtedly compete with other charities (who seek dollars, not blood) for donors. Even institutions with easily identifiable organizational competitors often face product competition from unlikely quarters. Thus, art museums compete with aquariums for family outings, with books and educational TV for art appreciation, and with movies and restaurants as places to socialize.

Probably the most serious competition that nonprofit marketers face is the status quo. Marketing is typically about behavior change. Existing behavior patterns provide consumers with important rewards, or they wouldn't be doing them. Naïve marketers seem to think that simply promoting the new behavior will be enough. But, in reality, their biggest challenge will be to "unsell" or at least replace the old behavior. A program that simply urges a teenager to stop using drugs because he or she will be healthier, less likely to be imprisoned, and so on is likely to be much less successful than a program that recognizes that "doing drugs" provides important satisfactions to the user: It may contribute to a sense of belonging (to a gang or a group); it may help the person define himself or herself (e.g., as being unique or "not like mom or dad"); it may relieve boredom or dull the pain and anguish of a dreadful home life. In such cases, the motivations to maintain the status quo will be very powerful. To be effective, marketers must clearly find ways to show that the recommended course of action will meet the same needs that the target audience member has. Simply to say that youngsters "shouldn't" do drugs to escape the reality of their painful lives is naïve in the extreme.

CHARACTERISTICS OF CUSTOMER-CENTERED MARKETING MANAGEMENT

The preceding sections have held up a mirror to the organization-centered nonprofit organization. We have learned what a true marketing organization is *not*. What, then, are the characteristics that one observes in a nonprofit organization that has fully adopted a modern marketing orientation? It will have the following characteristics:

- It will focus on behavior as the "bottom line" of much of what it does.
- It will be customer-centered.
- It will rely heavily on research.
- It will have a bias toward segmentation.
- It will define competition broadly.
- It will have strategies using all elements of the "marketing mix," not just communication.

Behavioral Bottom Line

Customer-centered marketers recognize that their success is ultimately achieved when people act. This is why an understanding of people and why and how they behave is the place where they start in thinking about any new marketing challenge. In well-planned marketing approaches, a considerable amount of time is spent just defining the behaviors that will be the focus and that will let the marketer brag about his or her success. An example of such a definition is the set of 16 critical "emphasis behaviors" defined by a coalition of health promoters for worldwide family health programs outlined in Exhibit 2-1.

EXHIBIT 2-1

EMPHASIS BEHAVIORS
FOR FAMILY HEALTH PROGRAMS

Reproductive Health Practices: Women of reproductive age need to practice family planning and seek antenatal care when they are pregnant.

1. For all women of reproductive age, delay the first pregnancy, practice birth spacing, and limit family size.

2. For all pregnant women, seek antenatal care at least two times during the pregnancy.

3. For all pregnant women, take iron tablets.

Infant and Child Feeding Practices: Mothers need to give age-appropriate foods and fluids.

4. Breastfeed exclusively for about 6 months.

5. From about 6 months, provide appropriate complementary feeding and continue breastfeeding until 24 months.

Immunization Practices: Infants need to receive a full course of vaccinations; women of childbearing age need to receive an appropriate course of tetanus vaccinations.

6. Take infant for measles immunization as soon as possible after the age of 9 months.

7. Take infant for immunization even when he or she is sick. Allow sick infant to be immunized during visit for curative care.

8. For pregnant women and women of childbearing age, seek tetanus toxoid vaccine at every opportunity.

Home Health Practices: Caretakers need to implement appropriate behaviors to prevent childhood illnesses and to treat them when they do occur.

Prevention

9. Use and maintain insecticide-treated bednets.

10. Wash hands with soap at appropriate times.

11. For all infants and children, consume enough vitamin A.

12. For all families, use iodized salt.

Treatment

13. Continue feeding and increase fluids during illness; increase feeding immediately after illness.

14. Mix and administer ORS, or appropriate home-available fluid, correctly.

15. Administer treatment and medications according to instruction (amount and duration).

Care-Seeking Practices: Caretakers need to recognize a sick infant or child and need to know when to take the infant or child to a health worker or health facility.

16. Seek appropriate care when infant or child is recognized as being sick (i.e., looks unwell, not playing, not eating or drinking, lethargic or change in consciousness, vomiting everything, high fever, fast or difficult breathing).

Source: Adapted from: John Murray, Gabriella Newes Adeyi, Judith Graeff, Rebecca Fields, Mark Rasmuson, Rene Salgado, and Tina Sanghi, *Emphasis Behaviors in Maternal and Child Health: Focusing on Caretaker Behaviors to Develop Maternal and Child Health Programs in Communities* (Washington, D.C.: BASICS Technical Report, 1997).

Customer-Centeredness

In a sophisticated marketing organization, all marketing analysis and planning begin and end with the *customer*. A customer-centered organization always asks the following:

- To whom are we planning to market?
- Where are they and what are they like?
- What are their current perceptions, needs, and wants?
- Will these perceptions, needs, and wants be different in the future when our strategy is to be implemented?
- How satisfied are our customers with our offering?

Reliance on Research

Because the customer is central, management realizes that it must have a profound understanding of consumer perceptions, needs, and wants and must constantly track changes in them so that the organization can respond to subtle shifts as quickly as they occur. Better still, to ensure that it is not merely reactive but *proactive* in its strategic planning, an alert market-oriented management will have in place a forecasting capability that can *anticipate* changes in customer needs, wants, and perceptions.

This is not to say that a consistent reliance on research need be expensive. As we shall outline in Chapter 5, there are a great many techniques by which high-quality and clearly useful research can be carried out by imaginative managements at relatively modest cost. The critical requirement for achieving these benefits, however, is the proper mindset. The truly customer-centered manager must continually "think research." The manager should assume that what he or she "believes" is not necessarily what is true. Intuition, casual observation, or "just common sense" do not constitute the ideal bedrock on which to build social marketing strategies and sound tactical decisions.

Take the case of the Midwestern hospital marketer who believed he had a "foreign doctor" problem. The marketer knew that his hospital had more foreign doctors than major competitors in nearby cities. In part, this situation resulted from the fact that there was a major veteran's hospital nearby and many foreign doctors came there to do their residencies or to carry out a public service obligation. After such service, the doctors, many of whom had begun to develop modest practices in the area, quite naturally decided to stay in the city permanently.

The marketing manager "knew" that their presence in his hospital constituted a serious problem. After all, he knew the hospital was statistically different in its physician profile. And, besides, he saw these doctors regularly in the building. He had heard patients and staff both complain about having difficulty understanding their "foreign doctors." Finally, the one major malpractice issue the hospital had recently faced had involved a foreign doctor. Thus, the manager *knew* he had a problem.

To cope with this "problem," hospital management began to develop strategies both to change the mix of doctors in the community (and therefore the hospital) and to change patient and staff perceptions about the "foreign doctor problem." Fortunately, at about this time the hospital decided to carry out a field study with about 500 past and potential patients. Among the other valuable insights gained from this study was the information that the marketing manager's presumption about consumer perceptions of his foreign doctors was entirely wrong! Consumers were indeed aware that there were many foreign doctors at the hospital, and a few acknowledged that communicating with these doctors was sometimes difficult. But on the whole, they did not see this as a serious problem. In fact, many in the patient sample felt that the foreign doctors were more conscientious and more caring for their patients than were some of their golf-playing, blasé U.S. counterparts. Several respondents said that they thought that cultural and language differences simply made the foreign doctors more conscientious about clearly understanding exactly what the patient really meant and what he or she needed. For many patients, then, the foreign doctors were not a problem but a boon to the hospital.

The lesson, of course, is that for a few thousand dollars (much of which was spent for information serving a wide range of other planning needs), the organization saved itself the cost of an extensive communication and recruitment project that could well have boomeranged.[5]

A Predilection for Segmentation

Just as the customer-centered manager routinely thinks of the consumer and of the possible need for research before planning programs, so, too, should he or she habitually "think segmentation." That is, in designing any particular marketing program, the nonprofit manager should routinely assume, until shown otherwise, that the market ought best be thought of as a combination of a great many smaller subsegments that may deserve separate marketing programs.

Of course, many nonprofit marketing managers do think of segmentation from time to time, but in our experience, only in the most general terms. Managers of symphony organizations, for example, are well aware that their prospects are better in high- than in low-income households, among women than among men, among the well educated rather than the less educated, and among the young or old rather than the middle-aged. And this understanding does affect where they concentrate their budgets. But all too often these budgets are spent on a single "best" program, usually aimed at upscale households. (This, of course, stems from the familiar ignorance-and-motivation definition of the marketing "problem.")

Yet even within this market, many possibilities for more subtle segmentation exist and are all too often passed by. A study for the National Endowment for the Arts, for example, revealed that, despite wide industry "intuition" to the contrary, the best predictors of likely symphony attendance were not at all the traditional demographic characteristics like income and education but lifestyle factors, attitudes toward actual attendance, past experience, and childhood training.[6] Considering only the lifestyle measure, the study clearly showed that there were not just one but *two* major lifestyle groups interested in symphony attendance. One group was the "traditional" Cultural Lifestyle Group. This group made cultural events the center of their leisure pursuits. They tended to patronize the theater, opera, and museums, as well as the symphony. They were very much interested in the program content and artists at specific performances and tended to be swayed less by atmospherics and prices. They attended largely for the cultural experience it provided. This group is undoubtedly the one that many theater and symphony marketers have in mind when they design their "one best" strategy.

The research, however, identified a very different lifestyle group that also included excellent prospects for the symphony. The members of this Socially Active Group were very outgoing in their lifestyles. They went out a lot, not only to the symphony but to all sorts of nonclassical events. They liked to give parties and dinners and attend those of their friends. For this group, symphony attendance was largely a social experience. It was an opportunity to meet and talk with their friends. It was an occasion to plan a dinner beforehand and, perhaps, dessert or cocktails afterward. *Going out* was the thing. What was actually on the program was of less interest than who among their friends were going, what restaurants might be worth trying before the concert, and so forth.

Clearly, the appropriate strategies to reach these two groups are very different. More importantly, a strategy designed to appeal to one group might very well turn off the other. Suppose, for example, that a symphony manager designed a typical "one best," nonsegmented strategy stressing program elements. Print ads, public relations releases, and interviews by guest artists and the symphony staff would emphasize the works to be performed—perhaps highlighting a first performance locally of a particular composition, the debut of a precocious youngster, the innovativeness or difficulty of a particular program selection, or the conductor's mastery of the works of the composer featured at the concert. All this would be very appealing to those in the Cultural Lifestyle Group. At the same time, it might have just the opposite effect on the Socially Active Group. The latter might see the event as formal and stuffy, a program for the aficionados and definitely not one that they would understand and enjoy. Certainly it would not seem to them to be something that their friends would attend. The group, then, would be very much turned off by this "best" strategy.

Nonetheless, a marketing strategy could be chosen that emphasized the informality of the audience and the event, described the possibilities of making "an evening" of the occasion, talked about the ease of parking, and implied that "just about everyone" would be there. The Socially Active potential attendees might well be very attracted by such a prospect. At the same time, the Cultural Group may find this set of appeals vaguely distasteful. The marketing program might signal to them that the concert program would not be very challenging or, perhaps, even particularly well performed. Even worse, the campaign might suggest to the cultural sophisticates that all those untutored, unsophisticated social types would be in attendance, over-dressed, and applauding in all the wrong places.

The lesson from this and similar lifestyle studies[7] is obvious. Markets can usually be segmented much further and in much more sophisticated ways than the naïve marketer usually imagines. However, only if the marketer has a customer- and segmentation-oriented philosophy clearly in mind is he or she likely to look for these potentials. As this extended example shows, ignoring segmentation possibilities can mean not only missing chances for attracting new customers whom one is not now reaching, but driving away important audiences to whom one may have considerable appeal.

A Richer Conceptualization of Competition

An organization-centered marketer naturally defines the competition as "other organizations like us." Yet if one begins with customers, the definition of competition can become very different. Competition, in its most basic sense, really becomes whatever the *customer* thinks it is. Thus, if certain customer segments are considering treating a

At 4:00 my kid will be at _____

If you can't fill in the blank, you need to start asking. It's a proven way to steer kids clear of drugs. It's not pestering. It's parenting.

ASK: WHO? WHAT? WHEN? WHERE?
QUESTIONS. THE ANTI-DRUG.

For ideas on questions to ask, contact us. 1-800-788-2800 • www.theantidrug.com • www.drugfreeamerica.org

FIGURE 2-1   Competition for the Anti-Drug

Source: Partnership for Drug Free America. Reproduced with permission.

particular medical problem *themselves,* then *that* is a hospital or clinic's competition. If a potential donor thinks that money given to the American Red Cross is money that could have gone for a "needed" weekend ski vacation, then that vacation is the competition. If going to the symphony competes with working in the garden or having friends over for pizza in front of the TV, then those activities are the competition. If giving up drugs appears to mean giving up "the gang life," this must be addressed (see Figure 2-1).

Using the Full Marketing Mix

In contrast to those who conceive of marketing largely in terms of communications strategies designed to change customers to fit the organization's offering, sophisticated marketers view the marketing function as more diverse and the marketing objective as, above all, responding to customer needs and wants. A diverse marketing program pays attention not only to communication but also to the nature of the offering, its cost to target audience members, and the channels through which it is made available. The true marketer's mindset considers that it is the organization that must be willing to adapt its offering to the customer, and not vice versa. This necessarily means not just a willingness to talk about the offering in different terms but actually to change it (within the constraints set by artistic and professional standards and the organization's capabilities). The marketer must be willing to change the offering *itself* to which it wishes the customer to respond. For instance, skilled political infighters in any legislature—federal, state or local—are well schooled in the need to adjust proposed bills or regulations to fit the needs and wants of specific legislators with whom they are trying to make an exchange. It is not usually effective to take the stance that one knows one's position is *right.* Often one must compromise. Compromising may be seen simply as adaptive marketing.

The marketers must also be willing to change the cost of the offering or the place of performance. The marketing director of the Mass Transit District in Champaign–Urbana found that by offering free or minimal-cost bus service on the very coldest, snowiest days, he could induce auto owners who were averse to using buses (but who are perhaps *more* averse to driving and parking their own cars in terrible weather) to try using the bus. The director also cleverly put extra emphasis on on-time performance at every stop on these nasty days, with the reasonable expectation that customers would believe that punctual performance under such terrible circumstances surely would predict excellent service on normal days. Clearly, this nonprofit marketer had learned well that effective marketing is a lot more than just good advertising. It is the right offerings in the right place at the right time and at the right price.

INTRODUCING A CUSTOMER-CENTERED MINDSET

If marketing is to take its rightful place in nonprofit organizations, management must not only understand and accept its function, but also take care to introduce it effectively.[8] When seeking to introduce marketing formally to an organization, remember the following:

1. Marketing should not be positioned as a substitute for organizational management.
2. Other pressures on the organization should be recognized (for example, the need to maintain artistic or professional integrity, to secure major government subsidies, and so on).
3. Limited understanding of marketing by present organization members should be accommodated.
4. The translation of for-profit marketing to the specific nonprofit context should not be done mechanically.
5. It should be granted that the organization is already doing many things that are "marketing." Marketing will be accepted more rapidly if one adopts the existing language, at least initially, rather than trying to change the organization's accustomed language to fit current marketing jargon.

6. Recognize that many nonprofit managers have come to their positions from non-business backgrounds and may be defensive about their naïveté (although not necessarily hostile to marketing).

7. There should be a careful selection of early marketing projects. Lovelock and Weinberg suggest that five criteria should be met by such programs:

   - They should be evaluated by explicit performance measures.

   - They should be completed within a short to medium time period.

   - They should use a limited portion of available resources.

   - They should be neither peripheral nor central to the organization.

   - Their results should be obvious to key decision makers within the organization.[9]

8. In the final analysis, getting marketing accepted in an ongoing organization is much more a *political* activity than a simple attempt to market marketing through persuasion. Allies must be sought—most particularly the chief executive officer. "Enemies" whose view of the organization and of their own turf as being threatened by the new approach (e.g., those in public relations or communications) should be assumed to exist, whether visible or not, and dealt with directly.

9. Setbacks will occur and compromises will have to be made.

The issue of achieving organizational change is a subject beyond the scope of this book. Interested readers may wish to read the works of Argyris and Schon,[10] Quinn,[11] or Weick.[12] How the marketing function should eventually be structured in order to be effective in an ongoing, nonprofit organization will be discussed further in Chapter 10.

HOW FAR TO GO IN ADOPTING A CUSTOMER ORIENTATION

We have argued in this chapter that marketing can be successful only if it tailors the organization's offering to customer needs and wants. But many professionals in nonprofit organizations fear that such an approach, taken to the extreme, would mean that anything goes to "please the masses." They fear that the basic mission of their hospital, museum, child-care program, or university will be compromised. As Lewin notes,

> Many doctors are worried that a hospital's success may come to depend more on the quality of its marketing efforts than on the quality of the health care. "The whole thing turns my stomach," said one doctor at a New York hospital with an active marketing department. "I cringe every time I see one of our ads. The administrators here tell me it's important, but I think hospitals ought to be striving for clinical excellence, not publicity."[13]

Similarly, the Archbishop of Canterbury, William Carey, stated in 1992, "If a charity director is too eager to tell me about the budget, the number of staff he manages, and the size of the donor list, a warning light starts to flash. If the sector as a whole ceases to be a moral force, it loses its relevance."[14]

We too share these concerns. Ultimately, we view marketing's role as one of supporting the organization in achieving its goals. It does this best by devising strategies that start with the customer and not with the organization. But note that marketing is designated as a *means* to achieve the *organization's* goal. It is a tool—really a process and set of tools wrapped in a philosophy—for helping the organization do what *it* wants to do. Using marketing and being customer-oriented should *never* be thought of as goals; they are ways to achieve goals.

Marketing is a subarea of management, and not necessarily at the top of the organization. Clearly and importantly, top management has a responsibility to decide what role it will allocate to marketing. *Management* must decide which goals marketing can help achieve and how. It is management's prerogative to say that certain decisions will be made with little or no attention to marketing concerns. Thus, the management of a theater company may decide that it will choose the season's program on the basis of the interests of its directors who, in turn, will consider both past programming and the availability of acting and production talent in choosing specific plays and performers. Marketing may *then* be assigned the task of maximizing audience revenues for that given program. It is important to realize, however, that this does not mean that marketing should fall back upon a selling mindset. It means that marketing planning must simply start with customers in deciding how to describe, package, price, and distribute a given behavior change program. Marketers must merely recognize that the specific program cannot be changed. But, there are many ways to market *Othello!*

At the other extreme, a theater manager may decide to be very customer-driven. He or she may very carefully survey the potential audience, consider past revenues and audience reactions, and consider what artist and plays are available to maximize future attendance. This organization would then establish an offering that limits attention to achieving artistic objectives but that maximizes sales. Note that the two approaches were equally customer-oriented. They simply differ in the management goals they were designed to achieve.

Many institutions, by their very nature, may have more or less latitude in the extent to which offerings are customer driven. At one extreme are organizations that seemingly ought to give marketing a very central role because achieving "sales" is virtually their only objective. This would apply to a great many charitable organizations, alumni associations, and other groups that have as their major objective getting customers to give funds, time, and other resources to the marketer. At the other extreme are organizations that cannot change many elements of their basic offering at all because these elements very much define who they are. Included in this group would be most religious organizations and research institutions.

To repeat, then, the question of "how far marketing should go" is really a variable always under the control of management. Since marketing is merely a means to other ends, those who wish to protect those other ends need not fear marketing. At the same time, it is very important to stress that management should not allow the fears of artists and professionals to compromise marketing's legitimate place. As we shall indicate throughout this volume, marketing can make major contributions to nonprofit success in areas where it is appropriate. It must be controlled by management but not hamstrung by those who are suspicious of it if it is to be truly effective.

SUMMARY

The starting point for an effective marketing strategy is the proper marketing mindset. Historically, marketing has passed through three stages: a product mindset stage, a selling mindset stage, and, finally, a customer mindset stage. The first two stages are characterized by management putting the organization's own needs and desires at the center of the strategic process. It is only when management realizes that it is the customer who truly determines the long-run success of any strategy that the nonprofit firm can join the ranks of the sophisticated customer-centered marketing strategists typically found in the private sector.

Several clues can be used to identify nonprofits that are still mired in an organization-centered perspective. They see their offerings as inherently desirable. They see the ignorance or lack of motivation of their customers as the major barrier to the organization's success. Research plays a minor role in strategy formulation. Marketing tends to be defined as synonymous with promotion. A "one best" strategy is typically used in approaching the market, and generic competition is typically ignored in the process.

By contrast, customer-centered strategies begin with the customer and the customer's needs and wants. They rely heavily on research findings about their customers. They routinely assume—unless shown otherwise—that their markets ought to be segmented. Since they adopt the customer's perspective, they inevitably define competition as coming from widely diverse sources, not just from similar products or services. Finally, they use all elements of the marketing mix (design of the offering, cost reduction, distribution, and promotion), not just communication.

Indoctrinating a nonprofit organization from top to bottom with the proper marketing mindset is not an easy task. The experience of those who have successfully achieved this objective suggests such strategies as recognizing the limited understanding of others about what marketing really is; allowing for other pressures on the organization that may temporarily mandate noncustomer-oriented approaches; picking visible, short-term projects for the first marketing applications; and recognizing that the introduction of a new mindset is as much a political exercise as a matter of logic and persuasion. Allies must be sought and enemies deflected. Above all, it is essential to secure a top-management commitment to the new way of thinking. Without it, a true marketing orientation will not be achieved and customer-centered thrusts in one area will inevitably run afoul of organization-mindedness elsewhere.

QUESTIONS

1. Examine a nonprofit organization that you know well. Does it seem to have a customer-centered mindset? Why or why not? What would you recommend the organization's managers do to make it more customer-centered?
2. How does segmentation affect marketing strategy? How might a marketer justify multiple marketing strategies when serving several segments?
3. Does consumer segmentation apply equally to resource attraction and resource allocation? How might a marketer segment the market for resource attraction in order to help homeless victims?

4. Consider a local hospital that you know. Is marketing important to this hospital? What other management functions are important to the hospital? When might marketing's importance increase for this hospital?
5. If hired as the marketing director for a nonprofit youth club in an urban city, how might you use market research to develop your marketing strategy? What key questions would you want to answer with your market research?

NOTES

1. Alan R. Andreasen, "Nonprofits: Check Your Attention to Customers," *Harvard Business Review,* May-June 1982, pp. 105–110.
2. Chris T. Allen and Charles D. Schewe, "An Empirical Assessment of the Relative Marketing Orientations of Museum Directors and Marketing Practitioners," Working Paper 81-14, School of Business Administration, University of Massachusetts, Amherst.
3. Bill Gray, "This Food Stamp Office Is Hiding," *Chicago Tribune,* May 22, 1980.
4. Much of the material in this section was first presented in Andreasen, "Nonprofits."
5. For other approaches to health care marketing, see Michael Siegel and Lynne Doner, *Marketing Public Health* (Gaithersburg, Md.: Aspen Publishers, Inc., 1998).
6. Alan R. Andreasen and Russell W. Belk, "Predictors of Attendance at the Performing Arts," *Journal of Consumer Research,* September 1980, pp. 112–120.
7. Sarah Todd and Rob Lawson, "Lifestyle Segmentation and Museum/Gallery Visiting Behaviour," *International Journal of Nonprofit and Voluntary Sector Marketing,* 6, 3 (2001), pp. 269–277.
8. See Philip Kotler, "Strategies for Introducing Marketing into Nonprofit Organizations," *Journal of Marketing,* Vol. 43 (January 1979), pp. 37–44; William R. George and Fran Compton, "How to Initiate a Marketing Perspective in a Health Care Organization," *Journal of Health Care Marketing,* Vol. 5, No. 1 (winter 1985), pp. 29–37.
9. Christopher H. Lovelock and Charles B. Weinberg, *Marketing for Public and Nonprofit Managers* (New York: John Wiley, 1984), p. 561.
10. Chris Argyris and Donald A. Schon, *Organizational Learning: A Theory of Action Perspective* (Reading, Mass.: Addison-Wesley, 1978).
11. James Brian Quinn, *Strategies for Change: Logical Incrementation* (Homewood, Ill.: Richard D. Irwin, 1980).
12. Karl E. Weick, *The Social Psychology of Organizing* (Reading, Mass.: Addison-Wesley, 1969).
13. Tamar Lewin, "Hospitals Pitch Harder for Patients," *New York Times,* May 10, 1987, Section 3, pp. 1, 28.
14. Sonya Freedman Cohen, "Working in Europe: A Nonprofit Perspective," *Nonprofit Times,* February 1993.

SECTION II

Strategic Planning and Organization

CHAPTER 3

Strategic Marketing Planning

Wendy Kopp had a great idea. In 1989, in her senior year at Princeton, she wrote a business plan for a new charity. Her idea was simple: Take bright, socially conscious college graduates—like herself—who didn't want to rush into the cutthroat "real world" and put them to work for two years teaching in poor urban and rural schools. The graduates would get a great experience and the schools would get a significant influx of bright, committed—if a bit untrained—new teachers.

By 2001, the charity she started, Teach for America, had grown to the point where it was placing 1,600 teachers around the country and had 120 employees and a budget of $10 million. The program made a real impact on both the schools and the new teachers. Of the 5,000 people who have gone through the program, 60 percent ended up in teaching careers or working elsewhere in education, while an additional 4 percent work for other charitable organizations. Teach for America alumni have started programs like America Scores to bring soccer to poor areas, the Learning Project that creates new schools, Credit Where Credit Is Due that sets up credit unions in poor New York City neighborhoods, and KIPP academies that improve academic performance of poor minority students through a method called the *Knowledge Is Power Program*.

However, this success did not come about without a serious crisis that required a rethinking and refocusing of what the organization was all about. Like many great ideas, Teach for America got off to an impressive start and more or less coasted for its first four years on its initial grants. Ms. Kopp then confronted a reality faced by many nonprofit start-ups—namely, that foundations love to launch ventures but few want to support them long term or help them grow.

Teach for America also faced critics who questioned its basic mission, saying that it was foisting untrained teachers onto grateful but unsuspecting schoolchildren to the latter's detriment. This further frightened potential donors.

It was at this point that Wendy Kopp brought together her key foundation supporters for advice, cut her budget by a third, and set aside new ventures that were not part of the core mission. She decided to create decentralized boards of trustees in each of the organization's 13 regions who, in turn, built strong ties to the local educational community and to key local political and business leaders. The local boards currently generate about one-half of Teach for America's annual budget, while a further 12 percent comes from

AmeriCorps, a government program to promote community service. Additional significant funding comes from the new venture philanthropists who appreciate risk-takers and are more likely to stay for the long haul.

Teach for America now has a tight management system, has fixed its funding and training problems, and is broadening its scope to convert its experience into programs to help stressed school districts find and train new teachers.

Source: Adapted from Meg Sommerfeld, "A Lesson in Charity Survival," *The Chronicle of Philanthropy,* November 2, 2000, pp. 69–73.

Once management believes that it has understood and internalized the customer-oriented marketing mindset, the next critical step in becoming an effective marketer is to develop *systematic processes* for actually doing marketing. In this edition, we make a distinction between two kinds of planning. First, organizations need to develop longer-range marketing plans. These consider where the organization wishes to go in various marketplaces where marketing experts should have their impact. Among the questions the organization must ask are these:

- What customers or clients do we wish to serve?
- Where will we get our resources?
- How do we attract volunteers?
- How do we position ourselves against similar or competitive organizations?
- What approaches will we use to reach target audiences?
- (Most important) where and how will "marketing thinking" fit within our organization—especially at the top management level?

We shall refer to the process by which these questions are addressed as *Organizational Marketing Planning* or OMP.

Organizations with—or without—a sound organizational marketing plan spend a great deal of their time and energy carrying out specific campaigns. These can range from relatively long-term efforts, such as the Academy for Educational Development's program to increase the number of girls getting advanced schooling in Bangladesh, to short-term ventures, such as a six-month collaboration with a retail chain to generate new contributions and volunteers. We shall refer to this level of marketing thinking as *Campaign Marketing Planning* or CMP.

In the chapters to follow in Section II of this book, we focus on fundamental concepts and issues that apply to the strategy formulation process at both the organizational and campaign levels. In the present chapter, we present an overview of the processes at each level. Chapter 4 then focuses in greater depth on the starting point of all marketing: the customer. Chapter 5 describes approaches to developing and using marketing research and other information that is crucial to sound planning. Chapter 6 then turns to the two key problems in strategy formulation at both levels: segmentation and positioning.

Section III of the book then focuses on a subset of issues that are particularly important in organizational planning (although they often apply with equal force in specific campaigns). In particular, we discuss the problems of developing and organizing various kinds of resources to carry out the strategic plan and how one evaluates and controls these activities. Section IV then turns to the myriad issues involved in putting together powerful and effective campaigns. This includes making decisions on organizational offerings, communications, "pricing" (which we shall see does not necessarily involve currency), and issues of accessibility and distribution.

ORGANIZATIONAL MARKETING PLANNING

The approach we advocate for carrying out strategic planning in marketing at the organizational level is what we shall call the organizational marketing planning process (OMPP). The OMPP, as outlined in Figure 3-1, is organized into three central components or stages. First, the marketing manager must carry out an analysis of the two broad environments in which the organization must operate. This involves looking inside the organization—at its goals, objectives, culture, and at the strengths and weaknesses it brings to its marketing challenges. Analysis also involves looking outside the organization at the market environment it faces, particularly the publics it will target and its competition. Long-range planning will also require analysis of trends in the organization's macroenvironment, including social, political, technical, and economic components.

The next stage of the OMPP is developing the broad *strategy* that will guide the organization's overall marketing effort and its many details. There are two parts to this, first setting marketing goals and objectives and then specifying what we will call *the core marketing strategy*. The latter consists of specific market targets, competitive positioning, and key elements of the marketing mix. This guiding core strategy will be the framework within which various campaigns will be developed over the years.

For effective marketing at both the organizational and campaign level to be carried out, an appropriate and effective structure must be created and a measurement and control system put in place. This is the final stage of the OMPP.

ANALYZING ORGANIZATIONAL MISSION, OBJECTIVES, AND GOALS

An organization-level marketing planning program is not developed in a vacuum. It must adjust to both internal and external realities. The principal internal reality is where the organization as a whole wishes to go. If the organization is mature and well managed, it should have already completed an organization-wide strategic planning process that will "fill in the blanks" of many of the boxes in Figure 3-1. In this case, strategic marketing planning can be seen as nested within organization-level strategic planning. Further, if the organization is large enough, the same kind of strategic planning can be carried out by subunits *within* the marketing function. In general, the further down the planning hierarchy, the more detailed the planning and the shorter the planning horizons.

Plan formulation involves the organization in determining an appropriate mission, objectives, and goals for the current or expected environment. The three terms are distinguished as follows:

- *Mission:* the basic purpose of an organization, that is, what it is trying to accomplish.
- *Objective:* a major variable that the organization will emphasize, such as social impact, market share, growth, or reputation.

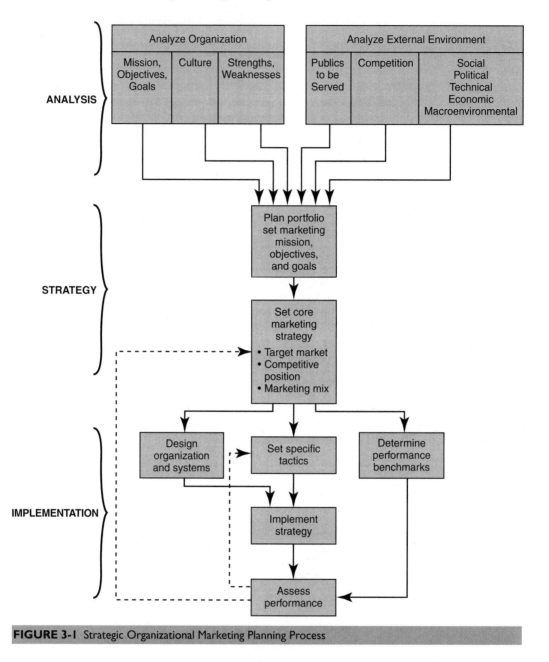

FIGURE 3-1 Strategic Organizational Marketing Planning Process

- *Goal:* an objective of the organization that is made specific with respect to magnitude, time, and responsibility.

Mission

Every organization starts with a mission. To paraphrase Peter Drucker, in setting out its mission an organization needs to answer the following questions: What is our purpose?

Who are our customers? What value can/should we offer to these customers? Although the first question—"What is our purpose?"—sounds simple, it is really the most profound question an organization can ask. Here the customer-centered mindset has a very useful role to play. Marketers would argue that an organization should define its purpose as meeting a specific set of needs or a specific set of customers. Thus, a church should not define its purpose by listing the particular services it offers; it should identify the underlying need that it is trying to serve. The church might decide that it is in the "feeling good" business, that is, helping people feel better about themselves and the world. Or it might decide that it is in the "hope" business, that is, helping people feel that they will eventually experience joy and fulfillment, either in this life or in the next. Ultimately, the church, or any nonprofit organization, has to decide what its mission is so as not to confuse itself with a lot of intermediate goals and services that it might provide.

An organization should strive for a mission that is *feasible, motivating,* and *distinctive.* In terms of being feasible, the organization should avoid a "mission impossible." The United Way of America set its mission to double its level of volunteers and financial support in the 1990s, but it has discovered this to be infeasible. United Way staff and volunteers must believe in the feasibility of this goal if they are to lend their support. An institution should always reach high, but not so high as to produce incredulity in its publics.

The mission should also be motivating. Those working for the organization should feel they are worthwhile members of a worthwhile organization. A church whose mission includes "helping the poor" is likely to inspire more support than one whose mission is "meeting the social, cultural, and aesthetic needs of its current members." The mission should be something that enriches people's lives.

A mission works better when it is distinctive. If all churches resembled each other, there would be little basis for pride in one's particular church. People take pride in belonging to an institution that "does it differently" or "does it better." By cultivating a distinctive mission and personality, an organization stands out more and attracts a more loyal group of members.

Following are some mission statements for major nonprofits:

- "The mission of Mothers Against Drunk Driving is to stop drunk driving, support the victims of this violent crime and prevent underage drinking." —*Mothers Against Drunk Driving* (www.madd.org)

- "The American Red Cross, a humanitarian organization led by volunteers, guided by its Congressional Charter and the Fundamental Principles of the International Red Cross Movement, will provide relief to victims of disasters and help people prevent, prepare for, and respond to emergencies."—*The American Red Cross* (www.redcross.org)

- "The American Marketing Association is an international professional organization for people involved in the practice, study and teaching of marketing. Our principal roles are:
    - To always understand and satisfy the needs of marketers so as to provide them with products and services that will help them be better marketers.
    - To empower marketers through information, education, relationships, and resources that will enrich their professional development and careers.
    - To advance the thought, application and ethical practice of marketing."
      —*The American Marketing Association* (www.marketingpower.com)

- "The V Foundation is a charitable organization dedicated to saving lives by helping to find a cure for cancer. The Foundation seeks to make a difference by generating broad-based support for cancer research and by creating an urgent awareness among all Americans of the importance of the war against cancer. The Foundation performs these dual roles through advocacy, education, fundraising, and philanthropy."—*The V Foundation* (www.thevfoundation.org)
- "The YMCA of San Diego County is dedicated to improving the quality of human life and to helping all people realize their fullest potential as children of God through development of the spirit, mind, and body."—*The YMCA of San Diego County (California)* (www.ymca.org)
- "The American Cancer Society is the nationwide community-based voluntary health organization dedicated to eliminating cancer as a major health problem by preventing cancer, saving lives, and diminishing suffering from cancer, through research, education, advocacy, and service."—*The American Cancer Society* (www.cancer.org)
- "IRI conducts programs outside the United States to promote democracy and strengthen free markets and the rule of law. The programs are tailored to the needs of pro-democracy activists in over 30 countries and training, judicial reform, and election monitoring."—*International Republican Institute* (www.iri.org)
- "To promote and foster the highest ethical relationship between businesses and the public . . . through voluntary self-regulation, consumer and business education, and service excellence."—*Better Business Bureau* (www.bbb.org)

Often, organizational advertising helps communicate a mission to various publics. The Nature Conservancy does this effectively (Figure 3-2).

Objectives

The mission of an institution suggests more about where that institution is coming from than where it is going. It describes what the institution is about rather than the specific objectives and goals it will pursue in the coming period. Objectives state the broad direction; goals then operationalize that direction, numerically if possible.

For every type of institution, there is always a potential set of relevant objectives, and the institution's task is to make choices among them. For example, the objectives of interest to a college might be increased national reputation, improved classroom teaching, higher enrollment, higher-quality students, increased efficiency, larger endowment, improved student social life, improved physical plant, lower operating deficit, and so on. A college cannot successfully pursue all these objectives simultaneously because of a limited budget and because some of them are incompatible, such as increased cost efficiency and improved classroom teaching. In any given year, therefore, institutions will choose to emphasize certain objectives and either ignore others or treat them as constraints. Thus, an institution's major obstacles can vary from year to year depending on the administration's perception of the major problems that the institution must address at that time.

Goals

The chosen objectives must be restated in an operational and measurable form called *goals* which then can be tracked through the organization's evaluation and control sys-

FIGURE 3-2 The Nature Conservancy

Source: The Nature Conservancy. Reproduced with Permission.

tem. Without such goals, it will be impossible for the organization to know how it is progressing, who should be rewarded for progress, and where change is needed. For a school, the objective of "increased enrollment" must be turned into a goal, such as "a 15 percent enrollment increase in next year's fall class." A number of questions may arise: Is a 15 percent enrollment increase feasible? What resources would it take? What activities would have to be carried out? Who would be responsible and accountable? How will we track achievement? All of these critical questions must be answered when deciding whether to adopt a proposed goal.

When the marketing manager looks carefully at the organization's goals, he or she may discover that what the organization *says* its goals are and what they *actually* are constitute two very different things. There are two implications of this fact. First, marketing managers must be aware that many organizations will, in practice, turn out to be schizophrenic in their goal setting, speaking and acting in different ways. Sometimes this is intentional. It is not so important to the marketing manager to know the true explanation, only that he or she be able to read the proper signals and either respond to what management *really* wants or, if the marketing manager believes management is misguided in what it is doing, try to bring the organization's real goals more in line with its stated goals.

Goals should have people "attached" to them. It should be clear who is assigned responsibility for goal achievement.

Philip Harvey and James Snyder point out that clear goal definition is relatively rare in nonprofit organizations for six reasons:

1. Many nonprofit managers fear accountability. They come to the job, in part, because they expect to have limited surveillance.
2. Many projects continue even when they no longer serve an organization's mission and no one wants to look hard at these projects' performance.
3. Nonprofits often undertake projects simply because there is money available for doing them.
4. Some nonprofit managers fear that management science will replace humanitarian concerns.
5. Nonprofit managers often equate busyness with doing something worthwhile.
6. Nonprofits seldom have financial report cards to tell them how they are doing.[1]

ANALYZING ORGANIZATIONAL CULTURE

A number of students of management have pointed out that the "organizational culture"[2] of an institution may be the single most important determinant of what the organization can achieve and what will be expected of those (such as the marketing manager) who are challenged to achieve it.

Peters and Waterman stress the central contribution of *culture* to the success of "best-run" organizations:

> Without exception, the dominance and coherence of culture proved to be an essential quality of the excellent companies. Moreover, the stronger the culture and the more it was directed toward the marketplace, the less need was there for policy manuals, organization charts, or detailed procedures and rules. In these companies, people way down the line know what they are supposed to do in most situations because the handful of guiding values is crystal clear.[3]

The success of organizations like Ben & Jerry's, Coca-Cola, and Domino's Pizza reflects the impact of a clear, customer-centered, pervasive culture. Cultures in many nonprofit organizations are set by charismatic leaders who very much make the institution in their own image. This includes the Boys & Girls Clubs of America under Rick

Goings, the Girl Scouts under Frances Hesselbein, and the Metropolitan Museum of Art under Thomas Hoving.[4] The danger of allowing a single individual to dominate an organization is that if the charismatic leader falls from grace, the organization can undergo periods of considerable turmoil. This was the case of the National Association for the Advancement of Colored People after the departure of Ben Chavis in 1994 and the United Way after the departure of William Aramony in 1992.

Culture Conflict

Many organizations in the nonprofit area appear to suffer from a significant, perhaps inherent, *culture conflict*. At a minimum, this conflict severely inhibits nonprofit marketers' abilities to be effective in the marketplace and, at worst, threatens to tear their organizations apart through internal dissension.

The problem is often caused by normal growth dynamics. A significant number of nonprofit programs and institutions were begun by individuals or ad hoc groups committed to doing something positive about an aspect of a society's well-being. Examples include hospitals such as the Mayo Clinic, the current "Just Say No" antidrug campaign of the Reagan era, and many AIDS-prevention and breast cancer organizations.

The early life of most of these organizations is typically dominated by what might be called a *social service culture*. Health care organizations adopting this perspective see their mission as one of maximizing some aspect of the public's health status by "improving health" rather than by "being efficient." The organization is willing to overlook waste and misdirection in the short run as long as the effort is a case of "doing good." Senior managers, and most if not all of the staff, are recruited from basic health care disciplines such as medicine, social work, or public health. They see themselves as professionals with strict codes of ethics and feel that they should serve everyone possible within the limits of time and economic resources. Camaraderie pervades the organization, in part because it is small, its members share the same training and goals, and there is a zeal to "have a real impact." In many respects, the organization and participation in it are ends in themselves to those involved.

A social service culture is ideal for such organizations in their beginning years. Often they lack resources, and employees must endure low salaries, inadequate equipment, limited staff assistance, and so on. Without the vision of significant social service payoffs, such deprivations might be "killing." The vision builds a close sense of camaraderie in the organization and helps members defend themselves from early critics and doomsayers.

The social service culture can survive for years for two reasons. First, the organization is undertaking something the public truly needs at a time of great pent-up demand and little competition. Many wasteful and misdirected approaches are tolerated because most work. Even if they do not, the culture tends to accept any "good-hearted" efforts as long as they are intended to have a social impact. Second, the organization is largely free to "do its own thing" because of a lack of outside supervision. Support is usually from a few individuals or small grants, often with few strings attached. The lack of competition reinforces a sense of freedom to pursue what organizational members personally believe is the right course of action.

Marketers and other managers are often brought in from the business world as such organizations grow and meet challenges. This can produce problems because they come from a *corporate culture*. This culture is significantly different from the social service culture and, to the extent the nonprofit organization is serious about becoming marketing oriented, a severe clash of cultures is inevitable. In the corporate culture, competitors are not viewed as benign and cooperative. Staff are expected to produce results and are not coddled as long as "their heart is in the right place." Strategic thinking replaces uncoordinated programs, resources are husbanded carefully, and ineffective programs that may be the personal fiefdoms of staff members are routinely called into question. Short-term tactics become equal in importance to long-term programs, and the organization is seen as a means to *achieving* ends, not an end in itself.

When nonprofit organizations bring these two cultures together, signs of culture conflict soon appear in subtle and not-so-subtle forms. The marketer is "shocked" by the extent of mismanagement in the organization and suspicious of pet projects lacking clear purposes. Questions are raised about costs and about the "fit" of tactics to general strategies. Concurrently, the founding professionals are equally "shocked" by the marketer's seeming lack of commitment to the organization's "real purposes." The professionals are suspicious of the corporate culture and scrutinize the marketer's every action for signs of the unethical, expedient, and manipulative behavior they are sure this alien culture promotes. The marketer, in turn, sees professionals as having "their heads in the sand," not recognizing the realities of today's marketplace. The marketer will, indeed, accept the long-run mission of the organization, but will not understand why the specialists fail to realize that unless the organization becomes more effective and uses its resources better in the short run, there will be no long run.

Solutions

The most serious consequence of culture conflict is that the organization becomes schizophrenic. People are not sure what direction it is taking. Ill feelings and distrust develop among co-workers who have allegiances to different values. The organization vacillates between "giving in" to the marketers for a while and then "coming back to the (social service) basics."

In the private sector, cultural conflict is usually transitional. Stockholders eventually rebel and force some resolution or the company simply fails and goes out of business or is absorbed by others. In contrast, in the nonprofit field a number of market characteristics can prolong this period of conflict—perhaps interminably. For example, the bottom line is often not clear, no tough-minded board of directors or outside funders intervene, or no clear competitors move into the market vacuum.

Part of the problem is that top managers in nonprofit organizations are likely to be part of the conflict. They do not recognize it or see its implications for the organization and those allied with it. The first step in correcting any problem is to recognize its symptoms and face them squarely. The next step is to resolve the problem, which is not an easy task. Several suggestions can be offered.

1. Key members of the organization must learn to recognize the symptoms and then *admit* that, indeed, cultural conflict is present within the organization and that its effects are personally and professionally debilitating.
2. Specific time should be set aside for beginning to resolve the conflict, with the understanding that full resolution will probably (a) take a long time to be effectuated and (b) lead to some resignations.

3. Initial discussions should be guided by the assumption that unless one culture dominates, and those adhering to its rival accommodate themselves to that dominance, the organization is doomed at worst to failure or at best to continuing friction and a generally unpleasant working environment.

4. Because all parties are too close (both perceptually and emotionally) to the crisis, resolution can be achieved only under the guidance of an outside catalyst sensitive to the issues and skillful enough to help the participants face and resolve them.

5. Resolution is most likely if all key organizational members can be brought to articulate for themselves and others (a) what they feel the basic mission of the organization should be, (b) what they feel are the best means of achieving that mission, (c) what they feel are *inappropriate* means for the organization to use (on the grounds of either ethics or efficiency), and, most important, (d) what they *personally* wish to achieve through their participation in the organization.

6. Once these perceptions, wishes, and hopes are "on the table," there should be a mutual exploration, with minimal guidance, of how both the participants and the organization can maximize their goals. In the process, the exploration will inevitably lead to heightened empathy for others' dreams and aspirations and an open consideration of who will have to compromise or resign if the organization is to survive and grow. The participants also will recognize that, unless the latter goal is achieved, individual dreams are unlikely to be fulfilled.

7. The eventual outcome of this process will be not only a resolution of the cultural conflict, but also, through the consideration of the values of participants, a bonding of the remaining co-workers in a more empathetic and productive personal and organizational relationship.

ANALYZING ORGANIZATIONAL STRENGTHS AND WEAKNESSES

A third aspect of the internal analysis is a cold-blooded review of the organization's strengths and weaknesses, especially as they will impact the marketing program. Clearly, an organization cannot think about tackling a great opportunity if it does not have—and is unlikely to develop—the needed capabilities. On the other hand, an opportunity may be ideal if it fits well with the organization's core competencies.

Weaknesses come in two forms. First, there are weaknesses that are environmental or organizational constraints on what the organization is *allowed* to do. For example, Georgetown University's McDonough School of Business may see a major opportunity to do significant management research on Internet privacy issues. However, a major program of high-quality research would require staffing by doctoral students who carry out much of the work, generate papers, and perhaps help train visiting businesspeople. Unfortunately, the Georgetown School of Business does not offer a Ph.D. in business.

Many other nonprofits suffer similar restrictions. As noted in Chapter 1, the U.S. Internal Revenue Service sets implicit bounds on how much nonprofits can generate revenue from unrelated activities. Similarly, donors may set limits on what may be done with their money. Physicians may effectively limit what a hospital may do in the area of preventive care or holistic health. And governments in developing countries may tell private voluntary organizations (PVOs) that they cannot duplicate activities carried out in the public sector and that they cannot engage in tactics that are offensive to the culture (e.g., advertising on television).

A second form of weakness is more correctable. There are aspects of the organization's structure, strategy, and tactics that are just not very good. Not surprisingly, many managers are blind to these deficiencies. For this reason, it is important that management from time to time have an outside *audit* of the total organization, including the marketing function. A thorough audit typically covers both the external and internal environments. Thus, it can serve as a major vehicle for carrying out both internal and external analyses of nonprofit environments as part of the OMPP.[5]

ANALYZING EXTERNAL THREATS AND OPPORTUNITIES

A marketer operates in an external environment that is constantly changing. The internal environment tells the marketers what is *desired* and what is *permissible.* The external market tells the marketer what is *possible.* The external environment has three components:

1. The *public environment,* consisting of groups and organizations that take an interest in the activities of the focal organization. The public environment consists of local publics, activist publics, the general public, media publics, and regulatory agencies whose actions can affect the welfare of the focal organization.
2. The *competitive environment,* consisting of groups and organizations that compete for attention and loyalty from the audiences of the focal organization. The competitive environment includes desire competitors, generic competitors, form competitors, and enterprise competitors.
3. The *macroenvironment,* consisting of large-scale fundamental forces that shape opportunities and pose threats to the focal organization. The main macroenvironmental forces that have to be watched are the demographic, economic, technological, political, and social forces. These forces largely represent "uncontrollables" in the organization's future situation to which it has to adapt.

We shall consider each of these environmental components in turn.

The Public Environment

When marketing managers turn to examining the external environment, they realize that it contains several publics, and the organization has to market to most or all of them. This is an important difference between for-profit and nonprofit organizations. We define a public in the following way:

A public is a distinct group of people, organizations, or both whose actual or potential needs must in some sense be served.

It is fairly easy to identify the key publics that surround a particular organization. Consider the American Cancer Society. Figure 3-3 shows 16 of the major publics with which the society deals and whose needs it must consider.

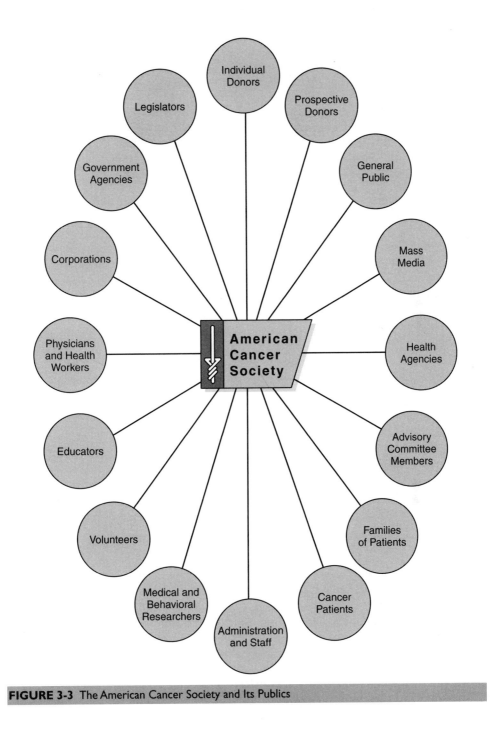

FIGURE 3-3 The American Cancer Society and Its Publics

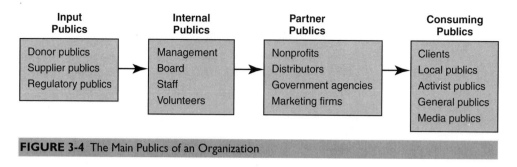

FIGURE 3-4 The Main Publics of an Organization

Not all publics are equally active or important to an organization. Publics come about because the organization's activities and policies can draw support or criticism from outside groups. Publics can be classified by their functional relation to the organization. Figure 3-4 presents such a classification. An organization is viewed as a resource-conversion machine in which certain *input publics* supply resources that are converted by *internal publics* into useful goods, services, and programs that are carried by *partner publics* to designated *consuming publics.* Here we will look at the various publics more closely.

Input Publics

Input publics mainly supply original resources and constraints to the organization, and as such consist of donors, suppliers, and regulatory publics.

Internal Publics

It has been argued that it is often as important to do effective internal marketing as external marketing. The internal publics of an organization define, refine, and carry out the organization's strategy. Thus, as we noted earlier, if marketing is to be effective, these internal publics must understand and internalize the marketing mindset. They must also help carry out the marketing strategy. This applies to all four of the key internal publics of the organization: management, board of directors, staff, and volunteers. (Public agencies often lack volunteers and may have a government agency or a legislative committee as a "board of directors.") We have already considered the requirement that marketing managers be responsive to those above them in the organization hierarchy, that is, top management and the board of directors. Marketing managers must also be responsive to those below them in the organization.

Partner Publics

To be successful in environments with daunting objectives and limited resources, a nonprofit organization must recruit many partner organizations to help it achieve its mission. These can be other nonprofits, commercial distributors, government agencies, and advertising and marketing research agencies. As we will note in Chapter 9, private sector partnerships are one of the most important developments in nonprofit marketing the last years of the twentieth century.

Consuming Publics

Various groups have interests in the output of an organization, and in varying senses have needs the marketing manager must meet. These are customers, local residents, activists, the general public, and the media.

The Competitive Environment

As we noted in Chapter 1, an increasingly significant characteristic of the nonprofit marketplace in the twenty-first century is the extent of competition. Unfortunately, many nonprofit organizations still deny the existence of such competition, feeling that this is only characteristic of private-sector markets. However, as we will note throughout this book, competition is a reality at two levels. First, there is competition between organizations for resources, customers, and volunteers. This kind of competition is most relevant to Organizational Marketing Planning, but it is also critical to recognize that there is competition at what might be called "the behavioral level." This is especially important for Campaign Marketing Planning.

Organization-Level Competition

Hospitals until the 1980s did not like to think of other hospitals as competitors, museums tended to ignore other museums, and the Red Cross saw other blood banks as all seeking the same general public goal. They preferred to think of their sister organizations as simply helping provide social services and not competing. Yet the reality of competition is driven home when one hospital starts attracting doctors and patients from another hospital, blood banks lose donors, or YMCAs see members joining local racquetball clubs and gymnasiums.

By contrast, there are also nonprofits which recognize the existence of potential competitors but seem to think that competing is "not nice." They feel that since all nonprofits, in some sense, are attempting to achieve the same (obviously desirable) social goals, any attention to competition would divert energies from what each competitor should *really* be doing. Sometimes nonprofit marketers are rudely awakened when a competitor doesn't "play fair." A major concern of the American Cancer Society in the 1990s was so-called "look-alike" cancer fundraisers which used similar names and took money that donors intended for the American Cancer Society.

What many sophisticated nonprofits recognize is that competition may *help* rather than hurt the nonprofit marketers' performance in two important ways. First, the existence of two competitors in the marketplace, clamoring for attention, spending two advertising budgets, and commanding even more customer attention or media interest, can stimulate increases in *the size of the total market.* Thus, it is entirely possible that with more competition, an organization might lose market share but discover that, because the entire market grows more than its share loss, total organizational impact may be higher.

The second way in which competition can benefit the nonprofit is that it can sharpen the competitive skills of the embattled marketers. It is a serious danger in the nonprofit domain that marketers will become fat and happy by observing growing sales and pretending there is no competition. There is nothing like the effect of new competitive activity to give complacent managers the needed slap to the side of the head. To compete, they have to rethink how their organization is positioned. They have to look to their customers more carefully to see if there are better ways to meet their

TABLE 3-1   Sources of Intelligence on Competitors

From Competitors Themselves	*From Outside Observers*
Annual reports	Suppliers
Newsletters	Trade associations
Planning documents	Other competitors
Marketing brochures	Newspaper articles
Advertisements	Magazine articles
Speeches and public	Stock market analyses (Moodys, D & B)
statements	Court records
Reports to regulatory	Distribution channels
agencies	Advertising agencies
Want ads	Financial institutions
	Former employees of competitors

From One's Own Organization	*From Competitors' Customers*
Customer contact people	Market research
Personnel department	Interviews
Economic or market	Focus groups
researchers	Surveys

needs and wants. They have to consider the possibility of changing offerings, price, and advertising. This reevaluation and the continuing close attention to marketing details can only help the marketer's overall performance.

Nonprofit marketers must understand who their competitors are and what strengths and weaknesses each has. Information on competitors can be gained from sources such as those described in Table 3-1. Much of this information is now readily available on the Internet or from syndicated services.

Behavior-Level Competition

Campaigns are focused on getting people to do things—or in some cases, to stop doing them. This means that alternative behaviors or the status quo are important competition that must be addressed. At the behavioral level, a marketer can face up to four major types of competitors in trying to serve a target market:

1. *Desire competitors*—other immediate desires that the consumer might want to satisfy.
2. *Generic competitors*—other basic ways in which the consumer can satisfy a particular desire.
3. *Service form competitors*—other service forms that can satisfy the consumer's particular desire.
4. *Enterprise competitors*—other enterprises offering the same service form that can satisfy the consumer's particular desire.

We will illustrate these four types of competitors as they were faced by a New York theater, the Palace, offering the musical *Aida* by Elton John and Tim Rice in the spring of 2001. Consider a young professional woman in New York deciding what to do on a particular evening. Suppose her options were evaluated as shown in Figure 3-5. She realizes that she has several desires she could satisfy—finishing a project at work, get-

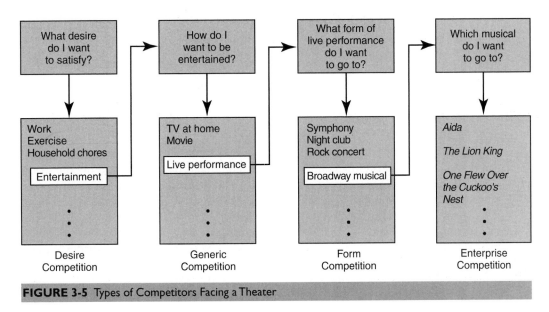

FIGURE 3-5 Types of Competitors Facing a Theater

ting some exercise, meeting several household responsibilities, or being entertained. Once she determines that the *desire* she will satisfy is to be entertained, she has to consider various *generic* competitors, including TV at home, a movie, or a live performance. Choosing to be entertained by a live performance, she has to consider various *forms* of live entertainment—a symphony, a nightclub performance, a rock concert, or a Broadway musical. Finally, after settling on a musical, she has to choose among the offerings of various *enterprises*—*Aida* at the Palace, *The Lion King* at the New Amsterdam, or *One Flew Over the Cuckoo's Nest* at the Royale.

If the Palace Theater is experiencing poor sales, the causes may be a poor marketing campaign strategy at *any or all* of the four levels of competition. The Palace may have chosen a poor offering and so loses out to other *enterprise competitors.* Or the musical may be terrific, but too many consumers may be choosing to go to other *form competitors* such as nightclubs or rock concerts. In the latter case, the marketing manager's challenge would be to focus on those who like live entertainment and convince them that a Broadway musical is a better alternative. This could involve research into why the theater is losing out to other forms. It may be that competitors in other forms have discovered better ways to meet consumer needs that the theater might wish to copy (for example, reducing prices, selling popcorn or liquor). Or it might be that more people would choose the theater except for certain disincentives ("costs") that the marketer could correct. For instance, potential customers could fear for their safety in downtown parking lots (the marketer could build a new structure, put in stronger lights, or hire a bus service to bring fearful people up to the door from a distant, safe lot). Or they could feel their friends might not want to come. In that case, the marketers could offer two-for-one ticket bargains or a "bring-a-friend-free" promotion.

At the next level of behavioral competition, if the manager found that too many promising customers were not choosing live entertainment as the preferred generic form of entertainment, the theater manager might consider joint campaigns with its generic comrades (symphony managers, rock concert promoters, nightclub owners) to get people out to "the live world of entertainment." However, if the problem is at the *desire level* of competition, joint promotion by those in the entertainment industry (live performance promoters, movie house owners, TV station managers) could compete with other desires by promoting the theme that "in this stressful, work-conscious world, you need more entertainment to relax, to replenish, to grow."

The Macroenvironment

Organizational Marketing Planning has its consequences in the future. Thus, it is crucial that nonprofit marketing managers understand the broad forces creating the world in which they must operate. These broad forces can be divided into demographic, economic, technological, political–legal, and social–cultural categories. The nature of these forces varies, of course, by the country in which the nonprofit markets, and within a given country their relative impact varies significantly by region, city, and nonprofit sector. Demographic and political–legal trends are very important for strategic planning in social service agencies. Economic trends are important to charities, technological trends to hospitals and libraries, demographic and economic trends to the armed forces, and social–cultural trends to parks, recreation services, and the performing arts.

There are many sources of data on such trends. Many are discussed in Chapter 5 and are available online. Many nonprofits, such as the United Way, consider macroenvironmental forecasting to be so important that the firm creates high-powered committees to carry out this activity on a regular basis.

PORTFOLIO PLANNING

The information from the analysis stage provides a basis for updating the organization's mission, objectives and goals. This, however, must be based on portfolio planning, a systematic "big picture" consideration of the alternatives. Most nonprofits are involved in many offerings and many markets. They must make strategic decisions about where to grow, where to retrench, and where to change marketing programs. In effect, the marketing manager has a portfolio of options—and potential options, not unlike an investor. As Kearns and others have pointed out,[6] a useful framework for thinking about these decisions is the Offer/Market Opportunity Matrix outlined in Figure 3-6. Originally a two-by-two matrix proposed by Ansoff,[7] it is here expanded into a three-by-three matrix. Markets are listed at the left and offerings along the top.

Each cell in Figure 3-6 has a name. Potential opportunities—in this case, for a college—are listed in small letters. The choice depends in part on the organization's strengths—its offerings or its market knowledge and experience. The administration should first consider cell 1, *market penetration*. This cell deepens its penetration into its existing markets with its existing offerings.

Cell 2, *geographical expansion*, would involve the college expanding into new geographical markets with its existing offerings. The college could open a branch in another part of the city, or in a new city, or start a new campus in another country. Southern Methodist of Dallas has offered courses in its M.B.A. program in Houston. Similarly, Notre Dame now grants an M.B.A. in London, and Antioch operates campuses in several countries.

Offerings

	Existing	Modified	New
Existing	1. Market Penetration	4. Offer Modification • short courses • evening programs • weekend programs • new delivery system	7. Offer Innovation • new courses • new departments • new schools
Geographical	2. Geographical Expansion • new areas of city • new cities • foreign	5. Modification for Dispersed Markets • programs offered on military bases or at U.S.-based firms abroad	8. Geographical Innovation • distance learning

New	3. New Markets
	A. Individual
	  • senior citizens
	  • homemakers
	  • ethnic minorites
	B. Institutional
	  • business firms
	  • social agencies
		6. Modification for New Markets
		A. Individual
		  • senior citizens
		  • homemakers
		  • ethnic minorities
		B. Institutional
		  • business
		  • government
			9. Total Innovation
			• new courses
			• new departments
			• new schools

(left axis label: **Markets**)

FIGURE 3-6 Offer/Market Opportunity Matrix

Another possibility is cell 3, *new markets,* where one can consider offering a strong portfolio of existing programs to new individual and institutional markets. Colleges are increasingly recruiting nontraditional student groups such as senior citizens, homemakers, and ethnic minorities. Iowa State University, for instance, has instituted "Eldercollege," a program for retired and older adults, which meets once a week for two months. In addition, colleges are trying to interest business firms, social service agencies, and other organizations in buying educational and training programs to be delivered on their premises or through distance learning.

Next the marketing manager can consider whether the organization should engage in *offer modification* to attract more of an existing market that it knows well (cell 4). Standard courses can be shortened in the evening or on weekends. For example, Alverno College, a private women's school in Milwaukee, instituted a weekend college and drew large numbers of housewives and employed women. Some colleges are beginning to offer courses in the very late evening or very early morning, having discovered a number of working people for whom these hours would be more convenient. The Internet is also being used to grant more options for learning.

Cell 5 is *modification for dispersed markets.* The University of Maryland, for example, offers modified programs for members of the armed forces both domestically and abroad.

Modification for new markets (cell 6) may be a more realistic growth approach for colleges and universities. To penetrate the senior citizens market, for example, may require a modification of standard courses. Specifically, the time period might need to be shorter and less reading might be required, with more comfortable seats and probably books with larger print. *Offer innovation* (cell 7) involves developing new courses, departments, or schools for existing markets. A business school, for example, might develop a new program in managing nonprofit organizations to offer to its students. *Geographical innovation* (cell 8) involves finding new ways to serve new geographical areas. With the advent of the Internet, home computers, interactive television, and other new media technologies, it is possible to offer courses to national and international audiences through "distance learning."

The final category, *total innovation,* refers to developing new offerings for new markets. The "university without walls" college where learning takes place away from a campus is an example.

The offer/market opportunity matrix helps the administration imagine an array of new opportunities in a systematic way. These opportunities are evaluated and the better ones are pursued.

CORE MARKETING STRATEGY

The single most important stage in the OMPP is determining the organization's *core marketing strategy.* A core marketing strategy comprises the basic thrust an organization wishes to take over an extended period of time to achieve the marketing objectives it has set for itself. This longer view then provides the framework within which detailed tactical elements are created and specific year-to-year programs are formulated. It is the "skeleton" of the entire marketing program. The core marketing strategy has three elements:

- Selection of one or more *specific target markets.*
- A clearly defined *competitive position.*
- A carefully designed and coordinated *marketing mix* to meet the needs of the target markets with a positioning strategy that differentiates the marketer from major competitors, including generic and desire competitors.

An organization's core marketing strategy should flow naturally from the earlier stages of the strategic marketing planning process. There will already have been a careful assessment of the organization's mission and goals, trends in the market environment, characteristics of target customers, and the organization's present strengths and weaknesses. Marketing management will have begun to define marketing's own objectives and goals. The difficult part is translating all this insight and information into a basic strategy that will guide the marketing effort over 3, 5, or 10 years. The core strategy is so important because it is the statement or set of statements that sets out just how the organization will tackle the market challenges.

IBM, Dell, and Apple are all in the personal computer business, but the ways in which they approach customers, advertise themselves, position and price their products and services, and work through distributors are very different. It is these elements of substance and style that make the organizations very different. CBS's approach to the news is different from CNN's. Sears tackles the retail market differently from Nordstrom, and both are different from Macy's. Yale is not MIT, and Carnegie Hall is not Radio City Music Hall. There are many nondescript me-too organizations in every marketplace. What makes successful organizations stand out is that each has a unique view of itself and its role in the marketplace that has the following characteristics:

1. It is *customer-centered*. It has as its principal focus meeting the needs and wants of its target audiences. It tailors offerings and communications to those it wishes to influence.
2. It is *visionary*. It articulates a future for the organization that offers a clear sense of where the organization is going, what the "new" enterprise will look like, and what it will achieve when it meets with its offerings.
3. It *differentiates* the organization from its key rivals. The marketer stands out; it offers target markets unique reasons to prefer its offerings.
4. It is *sustainable* for the long run and in the face of likely competitors' reactions.
5. It is *easily communicated*. The central elements of the strategy are simple and clear so that both target audiences and the marketer's own staff have an unambiguous understanding of just what the strategy is and why it should be supported.
6. It is *motivating*. A successful strategy has the enthusiastic commitment of those who will carry it out.
7. It is *flexible*. It is sufficiently broad that it allows for diversity in the ways that individual staffers implement it and not so rigid and uncompromising that it is not adaptable to unforeseen contingencies.

Michael Porter, in his book, *Competitive Strategy*,[8] has proposed three basic core strategies an organization can adopt:

1. *Differentiation*. This approach means offering something that no or few other competitors can offer. Differentiation can be in terms of *real differences* in the products and/or services offered or in the distribution systems through which they are offered or *perceived differences* created primarily through promotion. Thus, a hospital might differentiate itself by:
    a. offering live-in facilities for expecting fathers; gourmet meals, cable television, fax machines, and computers for long-term business patients and visitors; and so on (offer differentiation).
    b. offering "Doc-in-the-box" neighborhood emergency care or physical therapy in the home (place differentiation).
    c. promoting the hospital as the most technologically advanced, the most experimental, or the most patient-friendly hospital (image differentiation).
2. *Cost Leadership*. This approach involves marketing the lowest-cost offerings in the marketplace. In an industry where overhead costs often run 50 to 80 percent of donations, the United Way can typically boast that it keeps its administrative costs below 15 percent.

3. *Focus.* This approach involves selecting a limited segment of the market—typically one not served by anyone else—and concentrating on uniquely serving it. Thus, a program for the homeless might focus on a particular neighborhood, such as the homeless on the riverfront, a particular customer group, such as American Samoan homeless, or a particular kind of offering, such as emergency mental care.

Notice that each of these approaches involves a unique combination of the three elements of the core marketing strategy: choice of market segments, positioning, and marketing mix. Porter argues that organizations should not attempt to carry out more than one core strategy at the same time. Furthermore, the choice of core strategy should be based on evaluations of the organization's internal and external environments and should recognize that each type of core strategy will require a different type of organization and often a different organizational culture and leadership style.

CAMPAIGN MARKETING PLANNING

Broad organizational marketing strategies inevitably must be translated into specific campaigns to achieve specific behavioral goals.[9] These goals can target clients, volunteers, commercial partners, donors, or government agencies. But, true to the essence of marketing, the bottom line at the campaign level must always be influencing behavior. This fundamental objective reinforces the principle outlined in the previous chapter that the customer has ultimate control over the success or failure of any campaign efforts. Thus, the process of effective Campaign Marketing Planning must constantly keep the customer as the central focus of this effort.

The structure of the Campaign Marketing Planning Process is outlined in Figures 3-7 and 3-8. As Figure 3-7 makes clear, the process begins with the target customer (listening) and constantly returns to that customer to assess how the campaign is likely to be received (pretesting) and then actually received (monitoring). As shown in Figure 3-8, this

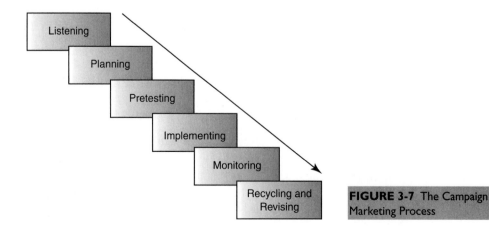

Listening

Planning

Pretesting

Implementing

Monitoring

Recycling and Revising

FIGURE 3-7 The Campaign Marketing Process

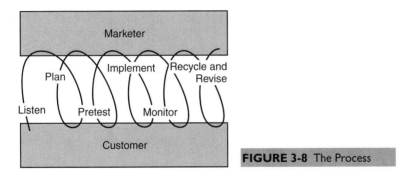

FIGURE 3-8 The Process

amounts to a constant recycling process, going again and again to the people who will govern campaign success. The six steps are as follows:

1. *Listening.* Campaigns must begin with a thorough understanding of the target audience they seek to influence, whether these are factory workers who might give blood, college students who might volunteer at a soup kitchen once a week, or educated homeowners who might attend the city's symphony concerts during the upcoming season. Effective campaign planning must start with a thorough understanding of "where the audience is coming from"—what do they think of the offer implicit in the campaign, what do they see as the benefits and costs, what do their friends think, and do they think they can actually carry out the behavior that's being recommended? This type of research is often called *formative research.* It has been our experience that one of the most common causes of marketing campaign failures in the nonprofit world is inadequate "listening" to the target audience. We shall outline in Chapter 4 some basic frameworks that will help us understand target audiences, and in Chapter 5 show how one can carry out formal research at this "listening" stage.

2. *Planning.* At this stage, campaign planners must translate their learnings about customers into concrete programs of action. These programs typically will involve crafting an "offer" that will contain motivating benefits appealing to the target audience, a sense of minimized costs (both monetary and non-monetary) that could inhibit behavior, communications that "talk" effectively to target audiences about the offer, and a contact system that will make it feasible and easy for the audience to act. Planning will also entail setting goals, timelines, and responsibilities, and making sure that systems are in place and coalitions formed to actually carry out the effort.

3. *Pretesting.* Probably the second biggest mistake in campaign planning and implementation is not pretesting key elements of the plan with the target audience. Planners often think that they have learned enough at the listening stage and are clever enough to translate those insights into an effective program. But customers are the ones who will decide a program's fate, and they very often will not have the reactions to program elements that the planners expected. A vivid example of this is the campaign of a major U.S. government agency that sought to increase the number of women getting mammograms by telling them about the factors that heighten a woman's risk of getting breast cancer. The campaign planners neglected the pretesting step and were puzzled when the campaign resulted in a *decrease* in the desired behavior. An evaluation study carried out *after* considerable time and funds had been spent revealed that (a) the target women learned the risk factors well (i.e., the campaign was a great *educational* success) and (b) many women intending to get a mammogram did not have the risk factors and decided not to go ahead even though the risk factors accounted for only 10 percent of all breast cancer cases. Clearly, if the campaign managers had only done a few simple pretest interviews using their campaign materials, they would have quickly learned of the folly of their approach and saved themselves significant amounts of time, money, and embarrassment.

4. *Implementation.* Once adjustments have been made based on the pretest results, the next step is to actually launch the campaign, putting in place all of the 4 Ps (product, price, place, and promotion) that marketers in the private sector emphasize. A key variable here is making sure that responsibilities are clearly assigned and performance deadlines set. Without such controls, campaigns can wander off target, elements can be neglected or underutilized, and goals can be missed.

5. *Monitoring.* Campaigns (as well as organization-level marketing programs) never turn out as planned. Competition doesn't stand still. Customers change, often as a result of early elements of the campaign. The environment has a tendency to toss in unexpected hurdles like an economic downturn or a health scare. For these reasons, it is essential that campaigns have a clear tracking system to monitor program performance along most of the key dimensions. Is the right audience being reached? Are they acting as intended—or at least moving toward action? Are they being reached by the program? How are they responding to elements of the program—is the offer understood and valued? Answers to all of these questions provide the critical clues that tell campaign managers what needs to be done at the next step.

6. *Recycling and revising.* Monitoring data may suggest a return either to the Listening or Planning stages. It may be that the data show that key customer segments are not "getting" the message—they don't see the benefits that the campaign intended them to value. They think behavior is too costly. Or they are somewhat interested in the behavior but just aren't acting. All of these findings suggest that management has failed to really understand the target audiences and that they must go back to "deep" listening if they are to succeed. However, new listening may not be necessary if the problem is mostly a matter of coordinating campaign elements so they reinforce each other and don't conflict. Or the problem may be a matter of emphasis: Some markets are getting too much attention and other markets too little. In these cases, management needs to go back to the Planning stage. It is important to note that whether the recycling is back to Listening or Planning, the campaign managers must still remember to *pretest* their new ideas. Once a campaign is well under way, there is a natural tendency for campaign staff to think that they really, really know customers and "are sure" how they will react. Too many horror stories from the field have convinced us that such an attitude can effectively sabotage an otherwise well-planned campaign—one that would have benefited considerably from greater attention to mid-campaign program pretesting.

MARKETING EVALUATION AND CONTROL

As we have suggested, to ensure that strategic marketing at both the organizational and campaign levels achieves its goals in a timely and efficient manner, the nonprofit manager must develop and put in place effective control systems for these plans. The data from such systems are important for strategic purposes and are also important in providing data for outside evaluators and funders. The latter role is much more important in the twenty-first century due to the increasing involvement of "venture philanthropists" in nonprofit funding.[10] Because of their importance, we shall return to these issues at greater length in Chapter 20.

SUMMARY

Once the marketer and his or her staff have developed the appropriate marketing mindset, they must determine the basic direction the organization will take over the strategic planning horizon. The means by which this is carried out is called the strategic marketing planning process. This takes place at both the organizational and campaign level. At the organizational level, the first step in this process is to identify the organization's overall mission, objectives, and specific goals and to understand the nature of its basic culture.

The next step is to analyze the strengths and weaknesses that the organization brings to the marketplace. A marketing audit is an effective tool for this purpose. This should be followed by a careful analysis of the organization's external environment. First, management must identify and understand the key publics it must consider in its planning. Publics can be input publics (donors, suppliers, and regulatory organizations), internal publics (management, board, staff, and volunteers), intermediary publics (merchants, agents, facilitators, and marketing firms), and consuming publics (customers, local residents, the general public, and the media).

The second major environmental component is competition. Here, with respect to specific customer behaviors, the organization must recognize that it has competitors on four levels: desire, generic, service form, and enterprise. It may be required to consider all four of them in its planning. The third component is the macroenvironment. The organization must understand major trends taking place in its social, political, technological, and economic environments. Many nonprofits conduct environmental scanning exercises with private-sector assistance for this purpose.

Once the internal and external environments have been analyzed, organizational planners take the information and develop specific objectives and goals for the marketing department. Objectives set out the broad "destinations" for the marketing strategy over the planning horizon. Goals specify numeric milestones for each objective. Goals should give direction to the organization's staff and describe pathways to its future. They should offer benchmarks for measuring progress and provide triggers for contingency plans. Goals should be motivating for staff and provide a basis for assessing future performance. Finally, goals should communicate the organization's direction to the outside world and indicate needs for developing marketing tracking information systems.

Strategic planning at the campaign level involves six steps. First, the organization conducts formative research to deeply understand its target market. This is followed by planning and pretesting. Implementation is the next step, leading to routine performance monitoring and necessary recycling and revision. As with all marketing, the campaign planning process begins and ends with the customer.

Effective organizations develop formal evaluation systems, which are becoming increasingly important as more formal business tools are brought to the nonprofit sector.

QUESTIONS

1. Refer to Figure 3-6. Develop an Offer/Market Opportunity Matrix for a technical trade school that helps displaced automotive workers. Its core service (offer) is a computer training course offered in Detroit, Michigan.
2. Student "U." is a public university on the East Coast of the United States. The dean of the school has appointed you as marketing director and asked you to help "increase the enrollment." Using the OMPP, what are the first steps you would undertake to impress the dean?
3. Refer to the situation in Question 2. Select three performance measures, besides enrollment, that you will use to help you measure the progress in meeting the dean's directive. Why did you select these measures?
4. The American Lung Association is a powerful non-smoking advocate. What consumer behaviors should it be monitoring in order to help it determine whether its cause is being advanced?
5. The chapter refers to different levels of competition a nonprofit marketer might face. What levels of competition does an AIDS awareness group face? Assume its primary objective is to reduce risky behaviors by the target audience that increase the risk of AIDS. How would your strategy planning be altered by the competition you identified?

NOTES

1. Philip D. Harvey and James D. Snyder, "Charities Need a Bottom Line Too," *Harvard Business Review,* Vol. 66, No. 1 (January–February 1987), p. 14.
2. The material in this section is drawn from Alan R. Andreasen and Jean M. Manning, "Culture Conflict in Health Care Marketing," *Journal of Health Care Marketing,* Vol. 7, No. 1 (March 1987), pp. 2–8.
3. Thomas J. Peters and Robert H. Waterman, Jr., *In Search of Excellence* (New York: Harper & Row, 1982).
4. See Thomas Hoving, *Making Mummies Dance: Inside the Metropolitan Museum of Art* (New York: Simon & Schuster, 1993).
5. For a marketing audit guide for social service organizations, see Douglas B. Herron, "Developing a Marketing Audit for Social Service Organizations," in Charles B. Weinberg and Christopher H. Lovelock (eds.), *Reading in Public and Nonprofit Marketing* (Palo Alto, Calif.: Scientific Press, 1978), pp. 269–271. For arts organizations, see Tom Horwitz, *Arts Administration* (Chicago: Review Press, 1978), pp. 81–85. For hospitals, see Eric N. Berkowitz and William A. Flexner, "The Marketing Audit: A Tool for Health Service Organizations," *HCM Review,* Fall 1978, pp. 55–56.
6. Kevin P. Kearns, *Private Sector Strategies for Social Sector Success* (San Francisco: Jossey-Bass Publisher, 2000).

7. H. Igor Ansoff, "Strategies for Diversification," *Harvard Business Review,* September–October 1957, pp. 1,123–1,124.

8. Michael E. Porter, *Competitive Strategy: Techniques for Analyzing Industries and Competitors* (New York: The Free Press, 1980); see also Michael E. Porter, "What is Strategy?" *Harvard Business Review,* November–December 1996, pp. 61–78.

9. Some of these ideas were developed earlier in Alan R. Andreasen, *Marketing Social Change* (San Francisco: Jossey-Bass Publisher, 1995).

10. Christine W. Letts, William P. Ryan, and Allan Grossman, *High Performance Nonprofit Organizations* (New York: Wiley, 1998).

CHAPTER 4

Understanding Target Audience Behavior

Life for poor young men in Zambia is depressing and discouraging. Many have migrated to major cities to find work and build enough of a "nest egg" to be able to someday go back home to the life they grew up with and, perhaps, to the girl they left behind. Days are spent working, and the prospect of returning each evening to a dingy, crowded room only makes the time in the unfamiliar big city drag on longer. So, many young men simply congregate at the open-air nightclubs that are common in the big cities in that part of the world.

Early in the evening, one finds many young men in similar circumstances, and their principal activity is drinking beer. Beer helps the time pass and the pain subside. But, as Dr. Kwasi Nimo, a health advisor for World Vision Zambia, argues, beer is one of the leading contributors to the AIDS epidemic that is sweeping that part of the world. The connection is both obvious and subtle. Drinking beer clearly affects a person's judgment, but it also affects the likelihood of being in a situation when good judgment might save one's life.

At the outdoor nightclubs, later in the evening the young men are joined by young girls, many of them sex workers. The sex workers are clever profit maximizers who wait until the young men have had a few drinks. That's when they get them out on the dance floor and negotiate the price for a sexual encounter. The subtle effect is that their strategy virtually ensures that the young men are far from sober when they have sex. The lack of sobriety when coupled with loneliness severely diminishes the likelihood that they will use a condom or otherwise protect themselves. This is true even if the men are educated and aware of AIDS and its method of transmission.

How has the Zambian government responded to this crisis? They reduced the price of beer! This means that behavior change programs addressing the AIDS problem in Zambia now have a dual problem. How do they influence people to protect themselves when they do have sex and how do they decrease the chance they will be in situations where "protection knowledge" is both essential and, often fatally, not put into practice? Francis Mulenga of Youth Alive in Zambia says that many young men consider abstinence to be unrealistic. Therefore, widespread availability of low-cost beer is a major contributor to the HIV/AIDS epidemic in that part of the world. That must be the first priority.

Source: Adapted from: *Young Men and HIV: Culture, Poverty and Sexual Risk* (London: Joint United Nations Programme on HIV/AIDS (UNAIDS), 2001/ The Panos Institute, 2001, pp. 16–17).

In our view, the bottom line of all marketing strategy and tactics is to influence behavior. Sometimes this necessitates changing ideas and thoughts first, but in the end, it is behavior change we are after. This is an absolutely crucial point. Some nonprofit marketers may think they are in the "business" of changing *ideas,* but it can legitimately be asked why they should bother if such changes do not lead to action—that is, why bother changing whites' attitudes toward blacks unless it leads to fair treatment socially and in the workplace? Is marketing really successful if the attitudes of a specific white population (for example, teenage boys in a given neighborhood) are made more positive while their behaviors continue to be prejudicial? If one argues that attitude change alone really does represent success because *eventually* behavior will change, one is simply reinforcing our fundamental position that the bottom line of nonprofit marketing really is—or ought to be— *behavior change.*

If the end product of a particular program is *only* a change in a mental state, this should more properly be called *educating* or *propagandizing.* It is not really marketing. Our definition still leaves a very wide area for the application of marketing principles. Indeed, there are scholars like Bartels and Luck who believe that the arena for marketing is defined too broadly.[1] Nonetheless, marketing concepts and principles can be applied to all of the following kinds of behavioral objectives:

- Inducing people to buy products and services.
- Inducing people to give up undesirable behaviors, such as smoking and drug use.
- Inducing people to adopt new desirable behaviors, such as exercising or taking high blood pressure medication.
- Inducing people to donate time or money.
- Inducing staff people or volunteers to carry out specific actions.
- Inducing legislators to vote for certain desirable laws or to fund specific programs.
- Inducing members of the media to report certain stories.

BEHAVIORAL DRIVERS

Why do people behave in ways that a marketer desires? The obvious answer is that behavior is driven by a vast complex of factors both internal and external to the individual actor. In the present volume, we adopt a framework first proposed by Andreasen in 1995[2] that focuses on four key drivers which we call the BCOS factors.

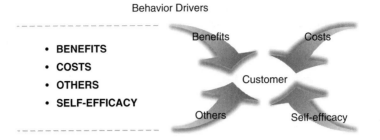

The first two factors are the ones that are the most frequent focus of marketing texts in that they emphasize the role of exchange with the consumer. As we shall consider below, one way to think of the behaviors that are critical to nonprofit success (and the success of most for-profit firms) is that they involve the buyer making a trade-off—or exchange—between *benefits* and *costs*. They have to give up some costs and, in return, get some benefits. In the private sector, the costs are typically money and time, but in the nonprofit world they can include pain (in inoculation, blood donation, or drug withdrawal), embarrassment or loss of self-respect (getting tested for Alzheimer's), guilt (reporting a suspected child abuser), and many other complex decision inputs. The challenge to the nonprofit marketer is to create a compelling package of benefits to overcome these important costs. This can be a daunting challenge.

However, behavior is not driven solely by the benefits and costs that comprise exchanges—although attention to these components alone may be sufficient to bring about considerable success. Behaviors can be—and are—strongly influenced by *others* in the target audience's environment. We all know of occasions when we made our own benefit/cost calculation and came up with the best choice for us and then did something entirely different because someone else wanted us to do so. The force of interpersonal or social pressure can be very powerful influences both for and against the nonprofit marketer's campaign. Many large donors give to nonprofits because their peers are giving and have asked them to join them. However, many wives and mothers in developing countries do not adopt better health practices for themselves and their children because their mother-in-law opposes them. Therefore, the "Other" factor can work for or against a marketer. Clever marketers learn to bring social pressure to bear when it helps and minimize it when it hurts.

Even if the benefits of a particular behavior exceed the costs and even if social pressures are strongly favorable, target audience members may still not act. Considerable experience has shown that the missing factor is what Albert Bandura refers to as *self-efficacy*.[3] Self-efficacy is simply the individual's belief that he or she can actually make the behavior happen. This is easiest to see in the case of smoking and dieting. A significant proportion of all smokers and obese individuals (at least in developing countries) are quite convinced that the benefits of quitting smoking or dieting well exceed the costs. Further, they know that others who are important to them (e.g., their children) want them to "do the right thing." But they don't act because—sometimes from experience—they think they simply cannot succeed. For the marketer in these cases to add another benefit or to "shout louder" through a clever communications program will simply not succeed. The individual's sense of self-efficacy must be addressed if the program is to be successful.

We will return again and again to these BCOS factors as we discuss how one researches audiences and how one develops elements of successful programs. In the sections to follow, we will also introduce other factors that impinge on audience behavior. However, we have found that the BCOS framework itself comprises a simple, portable model that is useful in a wide range of behavior change situations.

THE CENTRAL ROLE OF EXCHANGE

When someone buys a Big Mac, he or she pays $2.09 or 38,000 yen and, in exchange, gets a burger. At the simplest level, it is an exchange of money for food. A customer engages in the transaction because he or she believes that the ratio of benefits to costs is better than alternative actions to meet his or her hunger needs. In the same sense, a reporter for a TV station covers a fundraising event at a nonprofit organization's headquarters because he or she believes the ratio of benefits (either personal or organizational) to costs in time and equipment is greater than any other alternative at the time of the event.

Similarly, the potential volunteer compares the joys of helping with the time involved; the staffer compares the benefits of working hard on some management directive against the costs in time and stress of doing so; or the man with high blood pressure compares the benefits of better health against the annoyance of having to exercise and take medication. In each case, there is a mental calculation of trade-offs to be made. For the marketer to be successful, the customer must believe that the exchange that the marketer is promoting is better than any reasonable alternative—including doing nothing. Thus, in the simplest sense, the basic challenge of marketing is, for each customer, *maximizing the perceived benefits and minimizing the perceived costs* of whatever it is the marketer wants done.

Further, it should be noted that each of the benefits that a customer might derive from the transaction represents a cost to the marketer (of providing it), and many of the costs that the consumer pays (e.g., effort expended, money paid, blood given, and so on) represent benefits to the marketer.

Types of Exchanges

Exchanges can vary in whether they are *two party* or *multiple party* and whether they lead to transactions that are *continuing* or of *fixed duration*. Multiple-party exchanges occur in a number of contexts: the "additional" party can be (1) *allied with the customer*—for example, other family members, other members of the neighborhood, or other members of a buying group; (2) *allied with the marketer*—for example, an advertising agency or distribution channel member; (3) *independent* of either prime transactor but necessary to *facilitate* the transaction—for example, a credit card company; (4) *independent* of either party but *seeking to influence* the existence or content of an exchange—for example, a bystander urging a teenager not to take an offered cigarette or a national politician urging citizens to be sure to vote.[4]

"Continuing transactions" are transactions in which one or more parties must perform some continuing behavior as their part of the exchange agreement. "Fixed duration transactions" are, most commonly, specific one-time behaviors like inoculations or sales. Some transactions, such as renting a car or a motel room for several days or weeks, take place over time but are of fixed duration. A great many of the transactions sought in the nonprofit sector, however, require the target consumer to change for a long time some behavior or set of behaviors. Examples include campaigns to induce children to brush their teeth regularly, teenagers to avoid drugs, adults to stop smoking, and couples to prevent HIV/AIDS. Implicit in continuing transactions—and therefore crucial to marketers—is the fact that marketing does not stop and *should not stop* with the parties' agreement to the transaction or when the exchange is first performed under the terms of the transaction. Marketers must continue to influence (i.e., reinforce) the desired behavior. In the private sector, this is often called Customer Relationship Management (CRM).[5]

LEVELS OF UNDERSTANDING OF CONSUMER BEHAVIOR

As noted in Chapter 3, the marketing manager for a nonprofit organization must understand consumer behavior because the organization's success depends on it. There are four broad classes of management decisions for which an understanding of consumers is especially crucial. The decisions will determine the following:

1. *How to aggregate consumers into similar groupings for purposes of marketing planning.* This is the issue of *segmentation,* which is taken up in Chapter 6.
2. *How to market to each chosen segment, if at all.* These are the *marketing mix* decisions taken up in Section IV of this book. The marketer must decide what to offer in benefits and costs (offer and "pricing" decisions), how to communicate these (promotion decisions), and how to make them available and easy to accomplish (distribution decisions).
3. *How much to market to each segment.* These strategic allocation decisions involve questions about how many dollars in investment and operating budget to put into a particular market, how much personnel to use, and how much to use of one of the scarcest organizational resources—management's own time.
4. *When to apply the marketing efforts to the segment.* These timing decisions are also critical strategic choices. They involve allocations of resources over time as well as sequencing decisions for various tactics within a given strategy.

There are also four levels at which a manager may wish to understand consumer behavior so as to make these decisions better:

1. *Descriptive understanding.* At the simplest level, the manager may wish to profile the characteristics of the market at a given point in time. How many buyers of what age, sex, and occupational status are in market A, creating how many exchanges of type B, in month Y, costing X marketing dollars, and so on? At a more sophisticated level, the manager may wish to categorize consumers in terms of complex indexes such as their social class or family life cycle or their psychographic profile.

2. *Understanding of associations.* At this level, the manager may desire to know what behaviors or characteristics in the profile are associated with what other behaviors or characteristics at a certain point in time. Thus, the manager may wish to know whether museum attendance is associated with occupation, theater attendance with gender, and attendance at both with age and family composition.

3. *Understanding of causation.* If a curvilinear association between family life cycle and arts attendance is found, a manager may wish to know whether getting older and

having children *leads* to less performing arts attendance or whether the two sets of factors just happen to occur together for other reasons. This level of understanding moves beyond association to show determinacy. Such information is particularly valuable if the "cause" at issue is a marketing intervention the manager can control.

4. *Ability to explain causation.* Ideally, a manager would like to move beyond knowing that A causes B to know *why* this is so. That is, the manager may "know" that arts attendance has a curvilinear association with age and that the appearance of children *causes* a decline in attendance. However, the manager may only have hypotheses as to why this is so. It is possible, for example, that the explanation is that the appearance of children puts a strain on budgets that precludes former luxuries like arts attendance (an economic explanation). Alternatively, it may be that younger family members put pressure on adult consumers to *not* attend the performing arts (a sociological explanation). Or, the appearance of children may change the consumer's personal priorities. He or she may decide to devote more time to being with the children or more time working to build a firm economic future for the family, which leaves no room for attending the performing arts (a psychological explanation). Quite obviously, what a performing-arts marketer should do to win back families with new children—or whether one should do anything at all—depends on which of these explanations is the most valid.

Developing a sophisticated understanding of various consumer markets is, of course, not easy. It comes with time, experience, and the careful use of the formal and informal research approaches discussed in Chapter 5 to accumulate facts, understand relationships, and slowly form patterns from them. But personal observation and formal research are both likely to be much more effective if they are based on a sound conceptualization or model of consumer behavior. The remainder of this chapter will offer such a conceptualization centered on the BCOS model. We will focus on individual behavior although we recognize that, in some cases, the focus of the marketer may be on groups of individuals (e.g., inducing a corporation or other nonprofit to cooperate in a strategy) or even entire communities.

INDIVIDUAL BEHAVIORS

Individual behaviors that a marketer can influence require consumers to decide to act. Decisions about actions vary in two important dimensions: involvement and complexity.

Involvement and Complexity

While it is obviously a continuum, consumer behavior theorists make a distinction between *low-involvement* and *high-involvement* exchanges. They believe this difference affects the amount of cognition or problem solving a consumer will undertake during and after the exchange process. As defined by Engel and Blackwell, with respect to products and services,

Involvement is the activation of extended problem-solving behavior when the act of purchase or consumption is seen by the decision maker as having high personal importance or relevance.[6]

TABLE 4-1   A Taxonomy of Consumer Decision-Making Approaches

	Degree of Personal Involvement	
Experience	*High*	*Low*
None	Extensive decision making	Simplified decision making
Some	Simplified decision making	No observable decision making
Much	Routinized decision making	No observable decision making

High personal involvement has been found to occur when one or more of the following conditions are operative:

1. The behavior required of the consumer will reflect upon his or her self-image.
2. The economic and personal costs of behaving "incorrectly" are perceived as high.
3. The personal or social risks of a "wrong" decision are perceived as high.
4. Outside (nonmarketer) reference group pressures to act in a particular way are strong and the target consumer's motivation to comply is strong.

Thus, exchanges can vary in the extent to which they are personally involving. They can also vary in their complexity for the decision maker. Complexity varies with involvement and the degree of newness of the decision. There are, of course, exchanges made for the first time and exchanges made after years and years of experience. Thus, we might expect very complex decision making to occur for exchanges that are highly involving and that are being made for the first time. As the consumer gains experience, however, decisions will be simplified to reflect this experience. At some point, given many repeats of the exchange process, the evaluation process may become relatively routine even though the subject of the exchanges is still highly involving. This distinction is indicated in Table 4-1.

There are also many exchanges, especially in the private sector, in which consumers are not personally involved to any great degree. However, it is very likely that a great many of the exchanges nonprofit marketing managers are attempting to influence are high, rather than low, involvement. The manager should be extremely careful, however, *not* to assume that the elaborate cognitive model outlined in the next section applies to all consumer decisions about behavior that many nonprofit marketers attempt to influence. It is possible that many other nonprofit exchanges, such as small donations, voting on trivial public issues, signing a simple petition, and so on, are really low-involvement actions. It is our experience that there is the real danger that a myopic company-oriented view of marketing will assume that the exchange is highly involving to consumers *since it is to the marketer.* The marketer then may seek to develop an elaborate level of understanding of an exchange that is basically relatively simple.

Having raised this important caution, we must repeat our position that a much larger number—perhaps the majority—of exchanges with which marketers in nonprofit organizations are involved are in fact considered high involvement and therefore involve what Hoyer and MacInnis call high processing, high elaboration.[7] Decisions about changing health habits, voting for major candidates, choosing a school or a career, giving a significant donation of time or money, attending the arts, changing religious institutions, supporting tax referenda, obeying the laws, and so forth all may be characterized as:

- involving very elemental aspects of one's self-image.
- involving major personal or economic sacrifices.

- risking major personal or social costs if a wrong choice is made.
- involving considerable peer pressure for or against.

HIGHLY COMPLEX DECISIONS

Stages of Change

The typical highly complex decision is one in which the consumer is considering undertaking a behavior for the first time. One of the key conceptual breakthroughs emerging from the nonprofit area called social marketing (see Chapter 13) is the recognition that high-involvement behaviors do not come about quickly, that they evolve over time. One does not go from being obese to being a conscientious dieter for a lifetime overnight—or even in a few months. People do not become opera-goers in a month. Villagers in the developing world do not adopt new sanitation practices as the result of a single lecture from a government health worker.

While one may admit that nonprofit marketers have challenges that take a long time to achieve, the breakthrough in the marketing literature (coming originally from social psychology) is that the process over time can be broken up into stages. Further, as research by James Prochaska and his colleagues have made clear,[8] campaigns can be more effective if they tailor interventions to the stage at which the consumer is found.[9] That is, the marketer's challenge ought to be seen, not as getting immediate action, but as moving the individual to the next stage. This, of course, is an approach long recognized by fundraisers seeking major donations. One does not go into an executive's office on day one and ask for a million dollars. The prospect requires a good deal of what the fundraisers call "cultivation." The advantage of the approach offered here is that the stages are given specific labels and their implications for strategy are clearly spelled out.

There are so-called stage models with anywhere from four to six stages. We adopt a four-stage model based on Prochaska and DiClemente's five-stage model, collapsing the Preparation and Action stages into one for simplicity and mental portability. The stages and their brief implications are these:

- *Precontemplation.* There are always a great many members in any given target audience who are not thinking about the behavior in which the nonprofit marketer is interested. This may be a case where they have never heard about the desirability of the behavior (e.g., they don't know there is a vaccine for a particular disease that is killing their neighbors). This would be very common when some new idea emerges, such as laying babies on their backs to reduce the risk of Sudden Infant Death Syndrome (SIDS). In other cases, it may be that the individual has heard about the behavior and concluded that he or she is not interested. This may be because social pressures strongly oppose it. It may be because the individual believes it is against his or her religion. He or she may think it is just not individually appropriate (e.g., it is a "Western idea" in an Eastern culture).

- *Contemplation.* This, of course, is where most marketing is done and it is where most marketers hope to encounter the market. It is where the target audience is thinking about the behavior. The audience is weighing the costs and benefits in the exchange, considering what others who are important do or do not want them to do, and forming a sense of whether they can actually carry the behavior out. Andreasen makes a distinction between early and late contemplation:

- *Early Contemplation.* This is where the target audience is just beginning to think about the behavior. Here, the benefits and costs will be a central focus. Benefits will be especially important because, if the target audience does not see significant benefits, they are unlikely to go further in the process (unless there are very strong social pressures to do so).

- *Late Contemplation.* This is where the target audience is actively considering the option. At this point, the audience is no longer dwelling on the benefits— they pretty much know they are there. They worry more about the costs. This is something we all do when something that once seemed like a really good idea gets closer to hand—the much-anticipated after-work party becomes less appealing as the time draws near, exhaustion sets in, and other obligations grow in importance. Consumers in Late Contemplation also worry more about what others think and about their own abilities to be successful.

- *Preparation and Action.* As a campaign gains momentum, a great many members of the target audience will be at the stage where they have thought through the behavior and are ready to act. They have just not taken that first step! Sometimes this is a question of a lingering sense of self-doubt. Sometimes, however, it is simply a matter of opportunity and some final push.

- *Maintenance.* Some campaigns are successful if people only act once, but many campaigns really need target audience members to continue the behavior. Many smokers quit, but 80 percent or more of them go back to smoking. The National High Blood Pressure Education Program focused much of its early efforts on getting target audience members aware of the problem of high blood pressure, getting them worried about its effects, and taking preventive action. Monitoring research well into the multi-year campaign showed managers that many sufferers were dropping out—in part because prevention offers no personally observable benefits (i.e., one does not feel any different). Subsequent focus in the campaign then had to turn to questions of how to keep people doing the desired behavior.

The Stages approach implies different marketing emphases at different stages:

- For Precontemplators, the marketer's principal challenge is creating awareness and knowledge and creating interest (i.e., a sense of personal relevance). Marketers often refer to this as "need arousal." Need arousal can occur spontaneously within the individual. Thus, as Bob Jones graduates from high school, he may recognize that he must pick a college and get further education. This *internal information* is one major source of need arousal. Arousing internal information could also come in the form of physiological drives (e.g., hunger, sex, and so on). Arousing *external information* can come from others (e.g., friends or family who insist that Bob Jones consider college) or from the media (e.g., college advertisements or brochures, posters, magazine articles). These types of information can often be very powerful in getting an individual to look into something that he or she might not otherwise consider.

- For Early Contemplators, the marketer must devise and communicate strong benefits. As noted below, these must be personal benefits, not benefits to others or "society."

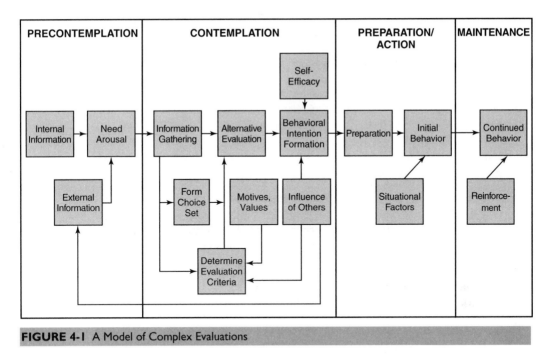

FIGURE 4-1 A Model of Complex Evaluations

• For Late Contemplators, emphasis must shift to reducing costs and bringing social pressure to bear. The marketer must avoid the natural tendency to "push benefits" on a slow-to-act target audience—they will know the benefits; it is the costs and the social issues that are looming large.

• For those in Preparation and Action, the key is to help bolster self-efficacy and maximize opportunities to act.

• For those in Maintenance, attention must shift to creating reward systems, making repeat behavior easy, and keeping social pressure bearing down on the good behavior.

The Contemplation Process

During the Contemplation Stage, the target audience member is seriously considering the campaign's recommended behavior—and, quite probably, other alternatives. The factors and processes that come into play at this stage are outlined in general terms in Figure 4-1, which also reflects factors important at the other three stages.

Information Gathering

Following need arousal, the involved target audience member typically will begin gathering information to help him or her decide what to do. It is important for marketers to understand what this process is because it represents a key *aperture* for marketer influence. As noted in Figure 4-1, one can imagine the consumer seeking information to form a *choice set* and then to evaluate it in terms of costs and benefits in order to decide what he or she is likely to do. "What they are likely to do" is usually conceptualized as their *behavioral intention,* a state that the BCOS model indicates is also influenced by

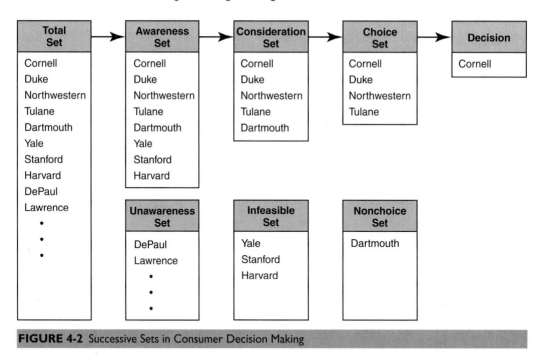

FIGURE 4-2 Successive Sets in Consumer Decision Making

others and self-efficacy. Evaluating the choice set in first-time decisions requires that the consumer figure out on what bases the choice will be made, the *evaluation criteria,* which in turn are influenced by the person's *motives and values* and by the opinions of others.

Forming the Choice Set

Through the process of gathering information, the consumer arrives at an increasingly clear picture of the major available choices. He or she eliminates certain alternatives and moves toward making a choice among the few remaining alternatives. This process of *choice narrowing* can be illustrated for Bob Jones. Jones considered a number of alternatives to college, including working, joining the army, traveling, and loafing. He decided that going to college made the most sense. Should it be a community college, a state university, or a private college? Examining his needs and values, he decided to attend a private college.

We can now examine how Bob narrowed his choice to a specific set of colleges. Figure 4-2 shows a succession of sets involved in this consumer's decision process. The *total set* represents all private colleges that exist, whether or not the consumer knows about them; this list runs into the thousands. The total set can be divided into the consumer's *awareness set* (the colleges he has heard of) and the *unawareness set.* Of those he is aware of, he will only want to consider a limited number; these constitute his *consideration set,* and the others are relegated to an *infeasible set.* As he gathers additional information, a few colleges remain strong candidates, and they constitute his *choice set,* the others being relegated to a *nonchoice set.* (Some research has suggested that choice sets seldom exceed seven alternatives, plus or minus two.) Let us assume that the student sends applications to the four colleges in his choice set and is accepted by all four.

In the final step, he carefully evaluates the colleges in the choice set (we shall examine this process shortly) and then makes a final choice, in this case Cornell University.

The implication of this choice-narrowing process is that a nonprofit marketer potentially competes with a large number of other choices for the consumer's interest. Therefore, before making plans to market to a particular segment, the nonprofit marketer must study consumers to learn (1) whether the recommended behavior is in the segment's awareness, consideration, and choice sets, and (2) if the behavior *is* in the various sets, who the competitors are. If the behavior is not in the choice set, for example, then the desired exchange will not be possible. The first marketing task, then, is to get the alternative into the choice set of the target buyers.

Forming Evaluation Criteria

To make an eventual judgment about which of the alternative behaviors he will select, Bob Jones must develop some basis for forming an overall evaluation of the alternatives in the final choice set. Presumably, developing these criteria is a step he could have taken before or—more likely—during the process of defining his choice set. Clearly, if a college marketer wants to influence Jones, he ought to understand what is important to Jones. And finding what is important to Jones is really finding out two things: (1) what factors Bob Jones considers in judging the various alternatives and (2) the relative value he assigns to each factor. We shall refer to the former as *choice criteria* and the latter as *criteria weights.*

One of the key factors determining Bob Jones's criteria in choosing his college is his own needs. While individuals have many basic needs, the marketer must discover which ones apply in this specific case.

One of the most useful typologies of basic needs is Maslow's *Hierarchy of Needs,* shown in Figure 4-3. Maslow held that people act to satisfy the lower needs before satisfying their higher needs.[10] A starving man, for example, first devotes his energy to finding food. If this basic need is satisfied, he can spend more time on his safety needs, such as eating the right foods and breathing good air. When he feels safe, he can take the time to deepen his social affiliations and friendships. Still later, he can develop pursuits that will meet his need for self-esteem and the esteem of others. Once this is satisfied, he is free to actualize his potential in other ways. As each lower-level need is satisfied, it ceases to be a motivator and a higher need starts defining the person's motivational orientation.

We can ask what basic needs are stimulated by the aroused interest in college. Some high school seniors become concerned about whether they can afford college and meet their basic needs for food and adequate housing. Others wonder about how safe they will be away from home. Still others are concerned with whether they can find people they like and who like them. And others are concerned with self-esteem or self-actualization. A college will not be able to give attention to all these needs. Thus, we find colleges that cater primarily to the need for belonging (small schools with small classes, a caring faculty, and a good social life), others to the students' need for esteem (many "name" colleges), and still others to the need for self-actualization (many "arty" schools).

Students often want to satisfy several needs, some of which are in conflict, by the same behavior. Thus, a student may have a high need for both achieving and belonging. This can create mental conflict, which can be resolved either by treating one need

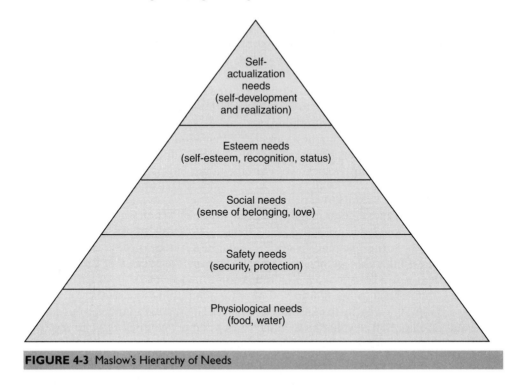

FIGURE 4-3 Maslow's Hierarchy of Needs

as more important or by fluctuating between the two needs at different times. Here is where the person's *values* come into play, namely, the principles the person employs to weight the various consequences that might follow a particular choice.

Four different methods for determining evaluation criteria are (1) direct questions, (2) indirect measurements, (3) perceptual mapping, or (4) conjoint analysis. These are outlined in Appendix I of this chapter.

Evaluating Alternatives

The bottom line in understanding highly complex decisions is determining how consumers ultimately come to a conclusion about each alternative in the choice set. Although the range of approaches to this very difficult issue would fill several volumes, we prefer to adapt a model developed by psychologists Martin Fishbein and Icek Ajzen in the late 1960s and early 1970s.[11] The central features of this approach have received wide acceptance in the private sector and play a central role in basic consumer behavior texts.

To understand Fishbein and Ajzen's approach, it is necessary to recall that our principal interest as a marketer is influencing behavior. Further, we proposed earlier that consumers choose whether or not to undertake a particular behavior by, in part, evaluating the benefits and costs they expect to result from taking that action. It logically follows that at any point in time, a consumer who has not yet decided whether to take a particular action, or which of several actions to take, will consider two things:

1. First, each consumer will possess a set of perceptions (which we shall call *beliefs*) about the likelihood of specific positive and negative consequences in undertaking each act in the choice set (that is, the benefits and costs). Thus, in a research study, assuming that we have already learned that Bob Jones has four criteria for choosing among colleges (class size, cost, friendship opportunities, and the quality of teachers), we could then ask the following questions.

a. How likely is it that classes will be small if you choose to attend each of the following?

	Very unlikely						*Very likely*
1. Cornell	−3	−2	−1	0	+1	+2	+3
2. Duke	−3	−2	−1	0	+1	+2	+3
3. Northwestern	−3	−2	−1	0	+1	+2	+3
4. Tulane	−3	−2	−1	0	+1	+2	+3

b. How likely is it that you and your family will *not* make a major financial sacrifice if you choose to attend?

	Very unlikely						*Very likely*
1. Cornell	−3	−2	−1	0	+1	+2	+3
2. Duke	−3	−2	−1	0	+1	+2	+3
3. Northwestern	−3	−2	−1	0	+1	+2	+3
4. Tulane	−3	−2	−1	0	+1	+2	+3

c. How likely is it that you will make many lifelong friends if you choose to attend?

	Very unlikely						*Very likely*
1. Cornell	−3	−2	−1	0	+1	+2	+3
2. Duke	−3	−2	−1	0	+1	+2	+3
3. Northwestern	−3	−2	−1	0	+1	+2	+3
4. Tulane	−3	−2	−1	0	+1	+2	+3

d. How likely is it that you will have excellent teachers if you choose to attend?

	Very unlikely						*Very likely*
1. Cornell	−3	−2	−1	0	+1	+2	+3
2. Duke	−3	−2	−1	0	+1	+2	+3
3. Northwestern	−3	−2	−1	0	+1	+2	+3
4. Tulane	−3	−2	−1	0	+1	+2	+3

2.   Second, we must determine the value the target audience member places on the various outcomes. These values we shall refer to as the *criteria weightings*. Thus, Bob Jones might be asked:

e. Please indicate how good or bad it would be for these outcomes to occur:

	Very bad						*Very good*
1. Small classes	−3	−2	−1	0	+1	+2	+3
2. Low cost	−3	−2	−1	0	+1	+2	+3
3. Lifelong friends	−3	−2	−1	0	+1	+2	+3
4. Excellent teachers	−3	−2	−1	0	+1	+2	+3

TABLE 4-2 A High School Student's Beliefs About Four Colleges

Alternative	Small Classes	No Large Financial Sacrifice	Many Lifelong Friends	Excellent Teachers
Cornell	+2	−3	+1	+1
Duke	+1	−3	+2	+1
Northwestern	−1	−1	0	+3
Tulane	−3	+1	0	−3
Weightings	**+3**	**+1**	**+2**	**+1**

Once we have these measurements, we can compute a summary evaluation which ought to contribute significantly to a prediction of his *behavioral intentions*. However, as we shall see, combining the information requires that we make some assumptions about how Bob Jones might carry out this step.

Combining Beliefs and Weightings

To understand the possibilities for combining the information, let us return to Bob Jones and assume that he has revealed his beliefs about the likelihood that his college alternatives will yield the consequences he considers important as indicated in Table 4-2. Table 4-2 also portrays Jones's judgments about the goodness and badness of the four basic criteria. How, then, might he "use" these beliefs and values to reach a decision about which school to attend?

Decision theory and consumer research suggest that Bob Jones is most likely to proceed in one of two ways. He may begin by attempting to simplify the decision using one of the following rules:[12]

1. *Elimination by Criteria.* Jones may eliminate any school that does not meet a minimum cutoff on *any* of the criteria (e.g., Duke is dropped because the probability of no financial sacrifice is too low).
2. *Elimination of Nondeterminative Criteria.* Jones could drop criteria where candidates vary little (e.g., "many lifelong friends").
3. *Evaluate Options One Attribute at a Time.* Jones could consider his most important attribute (small classes) and determine whether there is a clear winner (Cornell and Duke both score high). If not, he could proceed to his next most important attribute and see if there is a superior choice among those surviving at the first stage, and so on.

The three approaches may not yield a clear choice. In such a case (or instead of these approaches), Jones may attempt to mentally combine the information to yield a single overall "score" for each candidate and choose the one with the highest score. While there are a number of alternative formulas that consumer behavior theorists postulate are used, the most widely accepted is what is called formally *the linear additive expectancy–value model*.

Linear Additive Expectancy–Value Model Here the consumer combines and then adds the beliefs and weighting data for each alternative into a variable that is formally labeled the individual's Attitude toward the Act or $A_{(act)}$. In this approach, each *expectation* about a consequence from choosing an alternative is weighted by the *value* of the consequence. All weighted consequences for a given alternative are then added to yield an overall "score" for that alternative. The weighted sum is then considered to be a mathematical representation of an *attitude* toward an act. Algebraically, this is

$$A_{act_j} = \sum_{i=1}^{n} b_{ij}\, a_i \qquad (4\text{-}1)$$

A_{actj} = attitude toward act j
b_{ij} = belief about the likelihood of experiencing consequence i from taking act j
a_i = value of consequence i
n = number of salient consequences

In the case of Bob Jones, we would have

$$A_{\text{Cornell}} = +3(+2)+1\,(-3)+2(+1)+1\,(+1)=6$$
$$A_{\text{Duke}} = +3(+1)+1(-3)+2(+2)+1(+1)=5$$
$$A_{\text{Northwestern}} = +3(-1)+1(-1)+2(0)+1(+3)=-1$$
$$A_{\text{Tulane}} = +3(-3)+1(+1)+2(0)+1(-3)=-11$$

As a result of these (perhaps subconscious) computations, Bob Jones would be most likely to choose Cornell, followed by Duke, Northwestern, and Tulane, in that order.

Several comments need to be made about this model. First, it is the only model with which a choice is almost always determined. Thus, this processing approach typically comes into play in cases where one of the other models is not determinant. This is one reason that the linear additive model will be a major focus of our remaining discussions of highly complex consumer behavior. The second and more important reason is that the linear additive model has been shown empirically to be an excellent predictor of behavioral intentions,[13] and behavioral intentions are good predictors of behavior under certain conditions. All these conditions make the model potentially very useful for strategic marketing decisions.

There are, however, defects in the linear additive model. First, it does not take into account possible interactions among dimensions. Second, it is a *compensatory* model. That is, low scores with respect to one consequence can be compensated for by high scores with respect to another consequence. Thus, in Bob Jones's case, Cornell and Duke both compensate for their significantly poorer scores on financial sacrifice (that is, they cost more) by having good scores on the other three dimensions. By contrast, Tulane is perceived to be very good on the financial dimension, but this cannot make up for poor scores in Jones's mind on the other three dimensions.

Objects Versus Behaviors

It is important to realize that the approach we are using here is to model individual attitudes toward an *act*. This is consistent with the entire approach of this book, namely that it emphasizes *behavior*. The predicted consequences of behavior are a central determinant of action. Unfortunately, many marketers and researchers in both the profit and nonprofit sectors believe they ought to study individuals' perceptions of objects, especially the *attributes of objects* involved in an exchange, rather than the consequences of taking an act with respect to the object. In Bob Jones's case, these misguided researchers might try to study Jones's perceptions of Duke or Cornell as an object itself, not his perception of what it would be like to go there. This approach can very often yield predictions that are far off the mark. If one were to ask Bob Jones to evaluate *colleges,* for example, he might indicate as important *attributes* such features as the reputation of the faculty for research and scholarship, the attractiveness of the campus, the innovativeness of curricula, and so forth. All of these may be very important to Bob Jones's evaluation of *these colleges* but have little or nothing to do with his evaluation of the opportunity to *attend* them. Questions about college attributes might never reveal that Jones was very concerned about whom he might meet there and turn into lifelong friends. It might not occur to him that this is what an interviewer meant when asking about the attributes of a college (an object) rather than about going there (a behavior).

We are firmly of the opinion that in complex high-involvement decisions, it is behavioral intentions that determine behavior, and perceptions of consequences of the behavior are major determinants of those behavioral intentions (along with other interpersonal factors to be noted shortly). This approach will be central to our consideration of strategic planning throughout the rest of the book.

Influence of Others

The evaluation stage leads consumers like Bob Jones to form A_{act_j}. However, as the BCOS model points out, whether or not benefits and costs are sufficient to predict *behavioral intention* also depends on *the influence of others* and on the individual's sense of self-efficacy. As David Reisman pointed out many years ago, there are many individuals who go through life taking their cues about appropriate behavior largely from what are called by sociologists "significant others" or "referents."[14] These referent individuals or groups could be people they know or people they've only seen or read about (for example, movie or rock stars). Further, they can be people they identify with (membership referents), envy and want to be like someday (aspiration referents), or people they *don't* wish to be like (negative referents). The latter would be exemplified by teenagers who refuse to go to the college where their parents went or to dress or to cut their hair as parents want them to. These referents can provide input into the criteria individuals use to form their personal attitude toward an act. They can also have *direct* influence on behavioral intentions by exerting pressure on the individual to act in certain ways.[15]

Some individuals may be directly influenced by several referents at once. Others may not be affected by referents at all. To obtain the best possible estimator of Bob Jones's behavioral intentions—and thus to have a true understanding of how his present perceptions affect his behavior—we must "add in" a factor for the possible influence of significant others. In a research context, this would involve three steps.

First, we must identify all of the definable sets of referents to whom Bob Jones might pay attention. These could include parents, high school counselors, brothers and sisters, and friends.

Second, we must ask Jones what he *perceives* each of the significant others as wanting him to do. Fishbein and his disciples refer to this as *normative behavior* and define it algebraically as NB_{kj} where k is an index referring to each set of significant others and j refers to the action in question.[16] Normative behavior is measured by asking Jones whether he believes each significant other wants him to take a particular action on a scale from, say, "Does not want it at all" (-3) or "Wants it very much" ($+3$). It must be emphasized once again that we must measure here what he *perceives* to be the position of others. Whether he has an accurate perception of reality does not matter. *"Reality" is what the consumer thinks it is,* a point we shall continue to emphasize.

Third, we must ask Jones how motivated he is, in general, to comply with the wishes of each referent group. This factor, defined as MC_k (motivation to conform), is in effect a *weighting factor* for each NB_{kj}. We can measure the extent to which Bob Jones cares about the opinion of each significant other on a scale from "Don't care at all" (-3) to "Care deeply" $(+3)$. Thus, if one parent leans toward, say, Duke, and Bob cares about this person's opinion a great deal, this influence on the ultimate choice could prove to be quite significant.[17]

With this consideration of the often-important role of significant others on possible behaviors, we can now expand our model of the predictors of behavioral intention (*BI*) as follows:

$$BI_j = (\sum_{i=1}^{n} b_{ij} a_i) W_1 + \sum_{k=1}^{m} NB_{kj} \cdot MC_k) W_2 \qquad (4\text{-}2)$$

It should be noted that this model has one additional feature. There are two weighting coefficients, W_1 and W_2, which signify the relative importance of the individual and group influences on behavioral intention, respectively. In practice, these weighting coefficients are usually derived statistically, which requires that we first find out from Bob Jones his behavioral intentions by asking him directly how likely he is to attend each school as follows:

	Very unlikely						*Very likely*
1. Cornell	-3	-2	-1	0	$+1$	$+2$	$+3$
2. Duke	-3	-2	-1	0	$+1$	$+2$	$+3$
3. Northwestern	-3	-2	-1	0	$+1$	$+2$	$+3$
4. Tulane	-3	-2	-1	0	$+1$	$+2$	$+3$

We then carry out a multiple regression analysis using equation 4-2. If the best fit of the equation to Bob Jones's interview responses yields a value of W_1 greater than W_2, then we could conclude that Jones is what Reisman would call "inner directed," more driven by his own evaluation of the benefits and costs of the behavior. However, if we find that W_2 exceeds W_1, Jones could be characterized as relatively more "other directed," more driven by what he thinks and feels others expect of him.

There is, however, one last factor to take into account.

Efficacy

As the BCOS model emphasizes, behavioral intentions are also influenced by self-efficacy, which may account for much of the remaining "unexplained" variance left over from the previous equation. We could measure *self-efficacy* by asking Bob Jones to reveal his perception of the likelihood that he can successfully complete a course of study at each university. In each case, Jones might consider whether he would "fit in," whether he could handle the tough courses, whether he could earn enough money near campus to meet his incidental spending needs, and so on. A final equation including an efficacy measure should yield the best prediction of behavioral intentions and give marketers from each campus the best insight into how they might influence Bob to choose their option.

Strategy Implications

What then does a marketer *do* with research findings such as those hypothesized for Bob Jones? Suppose one is the marketing director for Tulane University—what can one do to improve the university's chances of attracting him (besides hope that the other three colleges turn Bob Jones down!)?

Tulane has five options with respect to Jones's personal attitudes (A_{act}):

1. *Change beliefs about alternatives.* Tulane could attempt to change Jones's beliefs about Tulane University (his b_{ij}'s) on key dimensions on which Tulane scores poorly. There are two alternatives here, depending on whether Bob Jones's perceptions are accurate or not.

   a. If Jones's perceptions *are* accurate and there are a great many otherwise highly attractive prospective students like him, Tulane might consider reducing its class sizes or improving the quality of its teachers (dimensions on which it scores poorly).

   b. If Jones's perceptions are *not* accurate and it is clear he and others have a misunderstanding of what Tulane is really like, then Tulane has a communication problem. By words, pictures, testimonials, informal research reports, and the like, Tulane must tell its story more effectively, being sure that it begins by responding to Bob Jones and his needs and perceptions rather than just telling him what *they* think he should know.

2. *Change beliefs about competitors.* Similarly, Tulane might attempt to change Bob Jones's beliefs about Tulane's competition (which the research has specifically identified as being in his choice set). This would be particularly appropriate if Tulane knew that Jones's perceptions were, in fact, wrong. That is, Tulane could offer comparative data (if such were available) showing that, for example, Tulane had below-average class sizes while major competitors had above-average class sizes.

3. *Change weightings.* A third strategy available to Tulane is to attempt to change the importance of weightings assigned to the dimensions. One way to look at Tulane's problem is not that it is perceived badly but that the dimension on which it is rated highly, its lack of financial sacrifice, is not valued highly enough by Bob Jones and his cohorts. Tulane would be the *most favored alternative* if it were to shift its target audience's weights for the four criteria as follows:

Consequence	Weight
Small classes	−2
No large financial sacrifice	+3
Many lifelong friends	+1
Excellent teachers	−2

4. *Call attention to neglected favorable consequences.* Attendance at Tulane may have consequences that Bob Jones didn't realize. These might include better weather or the chance to visit nearby recreational or cultural centers. The college would attempt to have its target audience add these consequences to their salient criteria, especially if they are features that are not offered by competitors.

5. *Add new favorable consequences.* Just as products add new ingredients or new packaging to revive flagging sales, so too could Tulane offer such new features as the chance to attend a new study-abroad program or participate in a local work-study option that would meet important basic needs of the target audience that they heretofore had not thought relevant to the college decision.

In addition to these actions, Tulane could seek to work through the reference groups found to be important influences on Bob Jones. Business alumni in Bob's hometown might be contacted to speak to Jones. Letters or phone calls could be directed to his parents. Possibly the applications of Jones and several of his friends could be treated as a "package."

Finally, if perceived self-efficacy seemed to be holding Jones back, Tulane might promote its career placement services, offer campus employment, or show how there are many campus programs to assist students having social or academic difficulties.

Tulane will need to carefully evaluate these alternative strategies according to their feasibility and cost. The difficulty of implementing each strategy, such as repositioning the college or shifting the importance of weights, should not be minimized. However, the marketer can take comfort that, at least for these kinds of first-time complex decisions, there are many points at which the decision can be influenced. As we shall see, however, the marketer's degrees of freedom decline as the consumer gains experience.

The reader should note that the beliefs and weightings data can also be used to segment markets, as can the Stages of Change. We shall return to these considerations in Chapter 6.

Simplified Behavior

The complex process undergone by Bob Jones in evaluating his college choices is typical of many behaviors that nonprofits wish to influence because these decisions are highly involving. It is also complex because Jones was making the decision for the first time. If this were a decision that the consumer would be making a second, third, or fourth time, however, we would expect to observe some simplifications of the elaborate process outlined in Figure 4-1 as a result of experience. In such cases, we would still expect considerable information seeking and information processing to take place because the decision is an important one. Consumer behavior theory postulates, however, that four kinds of simplification will probably take place when the target audience has experience.

First, little information seeking and thinking will be devoted to defining the evaluative criteria. The first time around, say in evaluating charities, a consumer might be expected not only to try to learn about the charities to which she might give but also how she should go about evaluating her potential behavior. The consumer will take stock of what she really wants as benefits from charitable giving and what the costs might be. Friends and co-workers might be asked about how they choose charities. In these circumstances, the marketer has considerable opportunity to influence the criteria since consumers are still in their formative stage. (This would certainly be the case for the colleges communicating with Bob Jones.) With repeated behavior occasions (additional charity drives), however, it may be expected that after the first time the consumer will have fixed the criteria on which alternatives are assessed. Marketers thus will have very limited opportunity to intervene to change these criteria.

Second, the weights of the criteria may also be largely set, although they will be somewhat more changeable than the criteria themselves. That is, a consumer considering charitable donations from year to year may change the total amount dispensed depending on the *weightings* of a financial sacrifice dimension, which in turn might depend on personal economic fortunes or the relative desirability of other types of expenditures.

Third, the choice set may also be relatively well defined in second and third decisions. At least, a core subset of alternatives is likely to be constant from exchange to exchange, with marginal alternatives coming and going at the periphery in response to new information or changing criteria or decision rules on the part of the individual consumer.

Fourth, because they have undertaken the behavior, they know *how* to do it and will have evaluated its outcomes. Thus, in subsequent decisions, self-efficacy should not be a major determinant of action.

Thus, in complex cognitive exchanges, the experienced consumer will be primarily evaluating *given* choices on *given* criteria with relatively *constant* weightings and little concern for efficacy. The marketer's first task in such circumstances, therefore, is to learn the contents of the choice set and the set of operative criteria, as well as the consumer's beliefs about the consequences of accepting the marketer's alternative or those of competitors. If the marketer is *not* in the choice set, a kind of Catch-22 sets in. As we shall see later, consumers selectively attend to incoming information (e.g., from marketers). Thus, in the case of behavioral choices, they tend to pay attention to the options they are considering. Therefore, the poor marketer is in the position of not being able to influence the choice set until his or her option is in the choice set.

However, assuming that the marketer is a part of the choice set, the main option available is to devise marketing strategies to modify *beliefs* to secure greater market penetration. This may be the only area in which the marketer can maneuver. Relatively little can be done at this point to influence criteria or their weighting. In general, it may be expected that the less involving the decision, the faster the consumer will simplify the evaluation process with experience and the less flexibility the marketer will have to improve a flagging market share.

Low-Involvement Behavior

After considerable experience on the consumer's part, one may observe the development of relatively habitual routine behavior. In such cases, relatively little cognitive evaluation will appear to be taking place. Future behavior will be better predicted by past behavior than by attitudes. Influences may operate much more often by what Petty, Cacioppo, and Schumann refer to as the peripheral route of influence.[18]

This is shown in a recent study by Richard Bagozzi of prospective blood donors. Bagozzi found that if one only knew expectancy-value attitudes, one could explain from 10 to 22 percent of the variance in behavior at a blood drive one week away. If one knew how often the respondents had given in the past *and* what they did on the first blood drive, however, one could explain *40 percent of the variance* in behavior in the second drive.[19] Since these study participants had given an average of 13.08 times in the past five years, they were clearly experienced givers. For many, the behavior may well be described as having become highly simplified, if not routine. This would explain the greater role of behavioral over attitudinal predictors in Bagozzi's study. In such cases of routinized decisions, it is likely that the best approach to understanding the market is to study past behavior. Studying attitudes may not be particularly useful either because consumers cannot really recall what evaluation they went through many years ago or because their attitudes today have been simplified and aligned to support their behavior. Left with behavior only, the marketer can take several approaches.

1. Use past behavior frequencies to segregate the market and concentrate on the "heavy users" (see Chapter 6).
2. Seek to discover behavior modification strategies that "bypass" cognition—for example, use special incentives, free trials, and so on to change behavior (see Chapter 17).
3. Seek to discover persuasion strategies to "shock" habituated consumers into once again undertaking extensive cognitive activity.

Another approach would be to use what Krugman and others have called *low-involvement* or *incidental learning*.[20] Krugman points out that consumers in developed countries are inundated with hundreds of advertising messages daily. When these messages are about exchanges in which the consumers are highly involved, they will become perceptually vigilant and process the information vigorously.

The question, then, is what happens to the remaining messages that aren't immediately relevant? Krugman suggests that, precisely because the exchange addressed in the message is one of trivial interest to the consumer, he or she will be neither perceptually vigilant nor perceptually defensive. The message, so the theory goes, bypasses the cognitive evaluation stage and goes directly into long-term memory to be stored in detail or as some vague overall impression. This is what Petty and Cacioppo mean by "the peripheral route." This trace then resides in memory until some cue at the time of purchase reactivates it (perhaps subconsciously). It *then* becomes a factor influencing the immediate choice. Since the more often a given message passes the consumer's sensory field (i.e., is repeated), the more likely it is to become lodged in long-term memory, Krugman's postulation of low-involvement learning has led many marketers in "trivial" categories to emphasize memorable visual images (e.g., cartoon characters, the Energizer Bunny, and so on), jingles or "haunting" melodies (e.g., Coke or McDonald's), or outright repetition (e.g., Sprint long-distance commercials) to increase the probability that a subconscious memory trace will be built. Since most nonprofits cannot afford the budgets necessary to adopt these tactics, it may be expected that where they (reluctantly) conclude that a particular target segment considers the decision to be trivial, imaginative attempts must be developed to build trace recognitions through visual imagery, clever dialogue, or music that someday can be activated when an exchange is contemplated.

Emotion and Mood

Under medium- to high-involvement situations, it is assumed that behavior follows what Ray has called the "think-feel-do" model of consumer behavior.[21] That is, consumers are assumed to take in information, form some emotional response, and then act when the appropriate resources are available. However, Ray suggests there may be sequences other than think-feel-do.

One of those that has recently attracted considerable interest in private sector marketing is "feel-do-think." This model suggests that many consumers may be influenced to take actions not by their thoughts but by their feelings.[22] This may happen in low-involvement situations and potentially in high-involvement situations in which the marketer is promoting such behaviors as drug rehabilitation or safe sex where very powerful feelings are relevant.

Attention to this alternative model has led to a growing interest in the private sector in manipulating emotions through television or magazine advertisements that communicate few "facts" but attempt to create feelings or moods and positive associations with an organization's offering. Thus, Pepsi commercials try to create an emotional response to "the Pepsi Generation" while Coke hopes we will feel "warm and fuzzy" when we hear its commercial refrain "I'd like to teach the world to sing in perfect harmony."

Many nonprofit marketers seek to influence behaviors where emotions could be used effectively as a key strategy component. Hospitals are a good example of where dramatic portrayals of caring nurses and attractive maternity rooms may have a major impact on market share. Drug programs may have more effect by showing the warm, supportive camaraderie of a treatment group rather than emphasizing the facts about the harsh consequences of continuing drug abuse.

It may be expected that the use of such appeals will be given much more attention in the future.

SUMMARY

The ultimate objective of all marketing strategy and tactics is to influence target audience behavior. While the short-term focus may be communicating facts or changing attitudes and values, what distinguishes these activities from education or propaganda is that they are not ends but means to other goals. And since the ultimate goal is behavior change and the proper philosophy is customer-centered, it is essential that all strategic planning start with understanding customer behavior.

In this book, we emphasize the fact that consumer behavior is driven by four factors: Benefits, Costs, Others, and Self-efficacy—the BCOS Factors.

The targets of nonprofit marketers' influence strategies can be as diverse as legislators, donors, journalists, or consumers. In all cases, the marketer's objective is to bring about exchanges wherein target audience members give up some costs in return for some expected positive consequences. Exchanges may involve two or multiple parties and be of fixed or continuing duration. The starting point for understanding customer behavior thus must be an understanding of the exchange relationship to be affected. Most importantly, that exchange must be seen from the target audience's perspective.

Exchanges in the nonprofit sector are usually high involvement and often concern target audience behaviors with which audience members have little or no experience. In such highly complex decision situations, once a need has been felt, customers move through four stages: Precontemplation, Contemplation, Preparation/Action, and Maintenance. They begin by gathering information to form a choice set of alternative behaviors and to determine the criteria that will eventually be used to choose among them. The criteria, in turn, will be affected by the customer's own needs and wants and by the influences of significant others.

The next step in the typical process is to evaluate the chosen alternatives on the relevant criteria and to form attitudes and behavioral intentions toward each. These behavioral intentions will again be influenced by others and by perceptions of self-efficacy.

Marketers have several options in seeking to influence complex exchanges that are not turning out as a marketer wishes: The marketer can attempt to change the target customer's perceptions of the probable outcomes of choosing the marketer's alternative and/or the alternatives of competitors; weightings on the criteria can be changed—

although this is more difficult; or the customer can be pointed toward new or neglected favorable consequences.

With experience, customers proceed to simplify and then routinize behavioral patterns. In such cases, criteria are relatively fixed and alternatives are narrowed considerably. Efficacy is no longer a concern. At the routine stage, behavior may appear to occur with little conscious thought or even may appear probabilistic. In cases of low-involvement decisions, relatively little cognition may be the norm even when the customer has little experience.

APPENDIX I METHODS FOR DETERMINING DECISION CRITERIA AND WEIGHTINGS

Direct Questioning

Most marketing researchers use direct questioning to assess consumer needs and wants. They may conduct an interview with a single individual or lead a focused group discussion. They may use open-ended questions, such as "What courses would you like to see added to the college curriculum?" or "What recreational facilities would you like to see added on the campus?" Closed-ended questions may also be included, such as "Rank the following activities in terms of your level of interest" or "Rate each of the following services on a scale from one to ten." Closed-ended questions are simple to administer and code. They ensure uniformity of responses across consumers (they are all responding to the same stimulus). But they have two major disadvantages in comparison to open-ended questions. First, they require that the nonprofit marketer know the "master list" of criteria in advance. The marketer, then, is really asking the consumer *which* of a set of criteria applies (and, perhaps, how heavily weighted each is or will be). Second, direct questions risk influencing how the consumer thinks about the behavior. By telling the interviewee in advance what the *marketer* thinks are the key dimensions, the questioner risks inducing the effect by which the thing being measured is changed by the process of measurement itself.

Indirect Methods

The direct questioning method assumes that consumers are aware of their own needs and wants and are willing to share the information with interviewers. But there are many issues on which they may not know or want to share their true feelings. College students, for example, may mention a desire for more study time when what they really want is less work. Or they may say they want younger teachers when they really believe that younger teachers will be less demanding, and less demanding teachers are what they really want.

Thus, the needs a person verbalizes may mask his or her real needs. Various projective techniques have been proposed to probe more deeply into the real needs of consumers. The four main projective techniques are these:

1. *Word association or sentence completion.* Here the person might be asked to name the word that first comes to mind when each of a set of words is mentioned. The interviewer might say "college" and the person might respond with "boring." By mentioning key words, the interviewer hopes to infer a pattern of needs and wants that people connect with a particular object or behavior.

2. *Projection.* Rather than being asked about himself or herself directly, the individual is asked about a vaguely defined "someone else." A questioner, for example, might ask an individual what he or she thinks is the basic reason "most people" go to college. Another approach is to present a picture or drawing of someone and ask the subject what that person is thinking about when considering college. Alternatively, the person might be presented with a set of incomplete sentences and asked to finish them. One sentence might read, "College is for people who ____." The basic assumption of these techniques is that, in the absence of specific information about the other individuals, consumers will project onto them their own true feelings.

3. *Picture completion.* The person is shown a vague picture and asked to make up a story about what he or she sees (called the Thematic Apperception Test or TAT). He or she may also be shown a cartoon involving two people talking to each other, with one of their remarks deleted. The person is asked to fill in the words, which are thought to reflect the respondent's own attitudes toward the subject.

4. *Role playing.* In this technique, one or more respondents are asked to act out a given role in a situation that is described in the briefest terms. One person, for example, may be asked to play the role of a successful business alumnus of a major university and the other the university president asking for a larger contribution. Through role playing, the respondents again project their needs and personalities into the amorphous situation, thereby providing useful clues for fundraising.

Perceptual Mapping

The direct and indirect approaches require that the respondents explicitly indicate both the nature and the relative weightings of alternative criteria. A different approach, called perceptual mapping, permits the researcher or manager to *deduce* either the weightings or both criteria and weightings from consumer judgments about the available alternatives. Two techniques are typically employed in perceptual mapping: direct and indirect. In direct perceptual mapping, consumers are asked to rate the various alternatives on a set of dimensions supplied by the researcher. A mathematical technique called factor analysis is then applied to these responses to yield one or more statistically independent underlying dimensions that best represent the original responses. These factors can then be used to produce a "map" on which the alternatives can be placed.

Factor analysis assumes that the original responses contain a great deal of redundancy and are really just surface outcroppings of more basic underlying criteria (factors). Thus, for example, Bob Jones may constantly give similar ratings to different colleges on scales labeled "student centeredness," "classroom size," and "teacher approachability" because they all reflect an underlying "intimacy" factor that he believes is *really* the important difference between big state colleges and smaller private institutions.

The disadvantages of the direct approach were pointed out earlier: It assumes that the researcher knows all the relevant dimensions in advance, and the questioning process may well influence the consumer's judgments.

The indirect approach does not place these burdens on the research designer. The indirect approach simply asks respondents to rate alternatives in terms of their similarity to each other, letting the individual apply to these "similarities judgments" whatever criteria he or she wants. Again, a computerized mathematical algorithm is used to reduce the similarities data to one or more underlying dimensions. While this technique does not bias the respondent by presenting dimensions in advance, it does require that the *researcher* label the dimension after the fact. Such labeling is often as much an art as a science.

Conjoint Analysis

An even newer technique that can be used in this context is called conjoint analysis. Conjoint analysis was developed, in part, to remedy the problem of more naïve direct rating approaches, namely that ratings of alternatives are developed with respect to one benefit or cost dimension at a time. The traditional approach ignores two important features of the real world. First, when target consumers are evaluating courses of action, they implicitly or explicitly realize that the actions will generate *bundles* of benefits and *bundles* of costs. Second, in judging these various bundles, people are often willing to make *trade-offs*. That is, Bob Jones, if asked directly, may say that he prefers small classes to large classes and tuition under $1,000 to tuition over $1,000. Suppose, however, that he were offered the two conjointly. How would he respond if given the choice of (1) classes averaging 12 students and a tuition of $2,500 versus (2) classes averaging 45 students and a tuition of $800? The answer is that it depends on how he makes trade-offs between the two criteria. This, in turn, depends on the weight he has in mind for the two dimensions. The mathematical algorithm underlying conjoint analysis is specifically designed to reveal these weights, which are known as "part-worths" in the conjoint lexicon.

QUESTIONS

1. A marketer for the Smithsonian Institute in Washington, D.C., identifies an association between attendance and family composition. Namely, families with up to three children are much more likely to patronize the Smithsonian than families with four or more children. List possible causations for this association. How might this marketer increase attendance by larger families?
2. Lisa is the president of her company, and is helping her daughter Ella sell Girl Scout cookies at her place of work. Explain how personal involvement will affect Lisa's ability to sell cookies to her subordinates.
3. Reference the situation in question 2. Explain how the decision-making process for "consumers" would be different when Lisa tries to sell Girl Scout cookies to her co-workers versus when she asks the company's board to make a $1,000 donation to the Girl Scouts.
4. When you selected the university you attend (or attended), what decision criteria did you use to compare it to other universities? For the universities you did not select, was there something that the admissions offices could have done to influence your decision that they did not do? Did your decision criteria change as you moved along the evaluation process? Why?
5. How might a gang member incorporate efficacy considerations into his decision to leave a gang? How might a social worker use this information to develop a behavior change strategy for youths that she counsels?

NOTES

1. Robert Bartels, "The Identity Crisis in Marketing," *Journal of Marketing,* October 1974, pp. 73–76; David J. Luck, "Broadening the Concept of Marketing—Too Far," *Journal of Marketing,* January 1969, pp. 53–54.

2. Alan R. Andreasen, *Marketing Social Change* (San Francisco: Jossey-Bass Publisher, 1995).

3. Albert Bandura, "Self-Efficacy: Toward a Unifying Theory of Behavior Change," *Psychological Review,* 1977, Vol. 84, pp. 191–215.

4. For additional discussion of the concept of exchange in marketing, see Richard P. Bagozzi, "Marketing as an Organized Behavioral System of Exchange," *Journal of Marketing,* October 1974, pp. 77–81; and "Marketing as Exchange," *American Behavioral Scientist,* March–April 1978, pp. 535–556.

5. Jagdish Sheth and Atul Parvatiyar (eds.), *Handbook of Relationship Marketing* (Thousand Oaks, Calif.: Sage Publications, 2000); Mary Jo Bitner, "Building Service Relationships: It's All about Promises," *Journal of the Academy of Marketing Science,* Fall 1995, pp. 246–251.

6. James F. Engel and Roger D. Blackwell, *Consumer Behavior,* 4th ed. (Chicago: Dryden Press, 1982), p. 24. See also Richard L. Celsi and Jerry C. Olson, "The Role of Involvement in Attention and Comprehension Processes," *Journal of Consumer Research,* 15 (September) 1988, pp. 210–224.

7. Wayne D. Hoyer and Deborah J. MacInnis, *Consumer Behavior* (Boston: Houghton-Mifflin Company, 2001).

8. James O. Prochaska and Carlo C. DiClemente, "Stages and Processes of Self-Change of Smoking: Toward an Integrative Model of Change," *Journal of Consulting and Clinical Psychology,* 1983, pp. 390–395; James O. Prochaska, and Carlo C. DiClemente, "Self-Change Processes, Self-Efficacy and Decisional Balance Across Five Stages of Smoking Cessation," in P. F. Anderson, I. E. Mortenson, and L. E. Epstein (eds.), *Advances in Cancer Control* (New York: Alan R. Liss, Inc., 1984); James

O. Prochaska and Carlo C. DiClemente, "Toward a Comprehensive Model of Change," in W. R. Miller and N. Heather (eds.), *Treating Addictive Behaviors: Processes of Change* (New York: Plenum Press, 1986); James O. Prochaska and Carlo C. DiClemente, *The Transtheoretical Approach: Crossing the Traditional Boundaries of Therapy* (Homewood, IL: Dow Jones-Irwin, 1984).

9. For examples, see their Web site at www.uri.edu/research/cprc/.

10. Abraham H. Maslow, *Motivation and Personality* (New York: Harper & Row, 1954), pp. 80–106.

11. See Martin Fishbein and Icek Ajzen, *Belief, Attitude, Intention and Behavior* (Reading, Mass.: Addison-Wesley, 1975). For more recent theories on attitude change and behavior, see Icek Ajzen, "The Theory of Planned Behavior: Some Unresolved Issues," in *Organizational Behavior and Human Decision Processes,* 1991, pp. 179–211; Richard P. Bagozzi and Paul Warshaw, "Trying To Consume," *Journal of Consumer Research,* 1990, Vol. 17, pp. 127–140; and Edward W. Maibach and David Cotton, "Moving People to Behavior Change: A Staged Social Cognitive Approach to Message Design," in E. W. Maibach and R. L. Parrott (eds.), *Designing Health Messages* (Newbury Park, Calif.: Sage Publications, 1995), pp. 41–64.

12. See Paul E. Green and Yoram Wind, *Multiattribute Decisions in Marketing: A Measurement Approach* (Hinsdale, Ill.: Dryden Press, 1973), Chapter 2.

13. Fishbein and Ajzen, *Belief, Attitude, Intention, and Behavior.*

14. David Reisman with Nathan Glazer and Revel Demney, *The Lonely Crowd: A Study of the Changing American Character* (New Haven: Yale University Press, 1961).

15. Robert Burnkrant and Alain Cousineau, "Informational and Normative Social Influence in Buyer Behavior," *Journal of Consumer Research,* 1975, pp. 206–215.

16. Michael J. Ryan and Edwin H. Bonfield, "The Extended Fishbein Model and

Consumer Behavior," *Journal of Consumer Research,* September 1975, pp. 118–136.

17. The reader will note that the relationship among the NB_{kj} and MC_k components is compensatory, as is the relationship among the a_i and b_{ij} factors.

18. Richard E. Petty, John T. Cacioppo, and David Schumann, "Central and Peripheral Routes to Advertising Effectiveness: The Moderating Role of Involvement," *Journal of Consumer Research,* Vol. 10 (September 1983), pp. 135–146.

19. Richard P. Bagozzi, "Attitudes, Intentions and Behavior: A Test of Some Key Hypotheses," *Journal of Personality and Social Psychology,* 1981, pp. 607–627.

20. Herbert E. Krugman, "Low-Involvement Theory in the Light of New Brain Research," in John C. Maloney and Bernard Silverman (eds.), *Attitude Research Plays for High Stakes* (Chicago: American Marketing Association, 1979), pp. 16–22; and "The Impact of Television Advertising: Learning Without Involvement," *Public Opinion Quarterly,* Fall 1965, pp. 349–356. See also F. Stewart DeBruiker, "An Appraisal of Low-Involvement Consumer Information Processing," in Maloney and Silverman, *Attitude Research Plays for High Stakes,* pp. 112–132.

21. Michael L. Ray, "Psychological Theories and Interpretations of Learning," in S. Ward and T. S. Robertson (eds.), *Consumer Behavior: Theoretical Sources* (Englewood Cliffs, N.J.: Prentice-Hall, 1973), pp. 45–117.

22. See, for example, Meryl P. Gardner, "Mood States and Consumer Behavior: A Critical Review," *Journal of Consumer Research,* Vol. 12, No. 3, 1985, pp. 281–300; and Gerald Gorn, "The Effects of Music in Advertising on Choice Behavior: A Classical Conditioning Approach," *Journal of Marketing,* Winter, 1982, pp. 94–101.

CHAPTER 5

Acquiring and Using Marketing Information

Attending cultural events is an involving experience. This is particularly so for the opera, which can be a musical event, a social occasion, a learning experience, and a chance to participate in something more grand than one's humdrum daily existence. However, when arts marketers think about promoting their offerings, they tend to emphasize the performances and worry about creating attractive pricing options and series packages. These tactics have had only limited success. While opera attendance is growing, this is, at least in part, a result of the popularizing influence of "The Three Tenors" Concerts. Industry observers believe that there is much more that could be done to build future audiences.

One imaginative approach recently initiated by Opera America is to study the total opera experience of opera attendees. To do this, they engaged the services of an innovative research organization, Envirosell, that specializes in applying anthropological techniques to understanding consumer behavior. The company's CEO, Paco Underhill, has become something of a media celebrity, and his book, *Why We Buy—The Science of Shopping,* is a business best-seller in significant part because of the rare insights it offers into customer behavior. To study opera, Envirosell sent observers out to eight opera performances around the country and simply watched and photographed people before, during, and after the performances. They did not speak with anyone, nor did they observe people in their seats actually watching the opera.

As a result of these observations, the team came up with a number of unexpected recommendations:

1. Improve the simplicity and friendliness of the curbside locations where drivers drop off people—primarily women—for each event.
2. Start the theater outside the theater—make the excitement start sooner, perhaps with a formally dressed doorman or with wandering musicians in the lobby.
3. Provide places to sit before the performance so that people—especially older people—can read about the event before going to their seats.
4. Help audiences get the most from the experience with a pre-performance lecture—but don't call it a lecture; call it a preview or warm-up.
5. Take the guesswork out of everything—provide adequate signage (especially at the box office), lots of volunteers, and staff to answer questions.

6. Tell people how long intermissions are so they can plan.
7. Use any intermission as another chance to communicate with the audience about upcoming events.
8. After the event, people are in the mood to talk and to get more information; provide them with take-home information about future operas.
9. Leave a good impression—thank the audience for coming.

Source: Drawn from: *Observing Opera Attendance* (Envirosell Consulting Report for Opera America, May 5, 2001).

We saw in the preceding chapters the critical role marketing research must play in understanding customer attitudes and behavior and planning marketing strategy both at the organization and campaign levels. We define marketing research as follows:

Marketing research is the planned acquisition and analysis of data measuring some aspect or aspects of the marketing system for the purpose of improving an organization's marketing decisions.

Marketing research can be very diverse. It can involve conducting one-time field research studies. It can comprise the analysis of data provided by internal record systems or by secondary sources of information. It can involve experiments or panel studies. It can be complex and expensive and it can be low-cost and straightforward. What distinguishes it from simple observation and systematic reflection is that it is (1) planned and (2) tied to specific decision-making situations.

MARKETING RESEARCH IN NONPROFIT ORGANIZATIONS

Nonprofit organizations carry out much less marketing research than they can *or ought to*.[1] This is a consequence of their limited budgets, their relative newness in the marketing field, and their limited research expertise. Increasing the amount of marketing research, therefore, calls for both education and motivation, showing nonprofit executives what marketing research can do and how to do it properly, as well as encouraging them to do it more often.

Six myths keep nonprofit managers from engaging in more marketing research:

- The "big decision" myth
- The "survey myopia" myth
- The "big bucks" myth
- The "we can't wait" myth
- The "sophisticated researcher" myth
- The "most-research-is-not-read" myth

If nonprofit managers are to even consider doing more research, these six myths must be directly challenged.

The "Big Decision" Myth

Too often marketing research is considered necessary only for decisions involving large financial stakes, and in such cases it should always be carried out. But research should be viewed from a benefit/cost perspective. Its costs are usually of two types—the expenses for research itself and the amount of behavior change and competitive advantage lost by delaying a decision until the results are in. The benefits are measured in improvements in the decision under consideration. The value of the improvements, in turn, is a function of the stakes involved and how certain the manager is about the rightness of the contemplated decision.

It surprises managers that sometimes the benefit/cost ratio comes out against research even when the stakes are high. Take the case of the hospital manager who is thinking of adding an outpatient plastic surgery clinic and investing in a series of advertisements to promote this new service. He calls in a research professional to design a study of consumer interest in plastic surgery that would show how likely acceptance of such a service would be. Although such a study could cost several thousand dollars, in extended discussions with the manager the researcher determines that, unless the survey found virtually *no* interest in outpatient plastic surgery, the manager would go ahead with the decision to add the clinic.

The manager was highly uncertain about the market, but he was certain that his decision to add the clinic was best. The researcher convinced the manager that the research expenditure was unnecessary and that the money could be used more productively to ensure that the new clinic got the advertising send-off needed in order to have the best chances of succeeding.

However, research can often be justified even when the amount at stake is not very great. This is the case whenever the research can be done inexpensively, will not take very long to complete, and will help clarify which actions to take.

These conditions often accompany advertising copy decisions. While total expenditures are small, managers usually have two or three candidate ads, each of which seems to have potential worth. Showing the ads to a small but representative set of prospective target customers—very modest research—usually reveals one superior candidate, or at least, by pointing out serious defects in one or two candidate ads, allows the choice to be narrowed. This process has the fringe benefit that once in a while it produces extremely good suggestions for entirely different ads.

The "Survey Myopia" Myth

Many managers, when they think of marketing research, think of field surveys. However, any reliable information that improves marketing decisions can be considered marketing research. If one takes this view, many alternatives to formal survey research come to mind. Consider a social marketing manager thinking of introducing a new low-cost, high-nutrition food product for young children who has no idea whether the target market will accept the product or, once it is accepted, how quickly it can be expected to break even. If successful, the new product would produce profits of only a few thousand dollars in the first few years. The manager could conduct a survey to reduce this uncertainty. However, to make the research 95 percent certain of being within 2 percentage points of the break-even market share figure of 10 percent, the manager must use a sample of 900 people.

An experienced survey researcher would estimate, assuming the questionnaire and sampling plan are already designed and ignoring analysis and report preparation costs, that simply completing the interviews would cost between $4,000 and $8,000 in the United States. (The amount would depend on the duration and type of interviews done.)[2]

Clearly, such research could easily eat up the manager's initial years' contribution profits from product sales. More important is the question of whether the research would yield valid data in any case. One should ask whether it is reasonable to expect respondents to be candid about or even to know their likely behavior with respect to this new food product, especially if many do not want to disappoint the interviewer or the research sponsor by showing little enthusiasm for it.

How else, then, might the survey research objectives be achieved at lower cost? The company could try test marketing in representative markets. This approach has the virtue of not only lowering costs but yielding useful data (that is, it shows what people will actually do, not what they say they will do). Testing in a number of markets also allows alternative marketing strategies to be systematically evaluated.

Another approach would be to commission focus group interviews of 8 to 12 members at a time of the target audience.[3] Although focus groups are not the cheapest design and the results are not strictly projectable to the larger market because the groups are not randomly selected, these results can cut the cost of interviewing by a quarter or a half. In addition, interviewers can sometimes develop richer data in the relaxed, chatty format of the focus group.

The "Big Bucks" Myth

We have already seen that there are often low-cost alternatives to the kinds of field surveys most nonprofit managers normally consider. To be knowledgeable users of marketing research, managers must know how and when to do traditional survey research and how and when to use a wide range of alternative low-cost research techniques. We shall consider these low-cost research techniques in later sections since nonprofits typically have seriously restricted budgets.

The "We Can't Wait" Myth

Many managers hold off doing research because they believe that it will take much too long and seriously delay getting ahead with the *real* work of the organization — saving lives, improving health, or overhauling communities. Again, this myth follows from the notion that market research involves surveys, sampling, and long periods preparing, implementing, and analyzing research. However, there are many methods that can be carried out in a few days or a couple of weeks that will yield all of the information a manager needs for a particular decision or set of decisions. Telephone interviews can be done overnight—this is done in modern political polling all the time. The Internet now provides vehicles for "instant surveys" that, with the proper software, not only collect data but analyze it and produce tables of results.

Careful consideration of the question "Just what do I need to know in order to make a good decision?" will often tell a manager that all that is needed is simple, quick, reasonably representative data that can sway a decision one way or another.

The "Sophisticated Researcher" Myth

Just as marketing research need not involve complex sampling and elaborate designs, a high level of sophistication in sampling techniques, statistics, and computer analysis is not essential. Of course, executives of nonprofits planning to undertake research programs should acquaint themselves with at least the rudimentary principles of probability sampling, questionnaire design, and graphic presentation of results. This knowledge will help them evaluate research proposals submitted by contractors and evaluate results.

Even when managers need high levels of sophistication—for example, if elaborate experiments or careful field study projects are being planned—they can get low-cost assistance on an ad hoc basis. Professors at local colleges are one resource. An alternative particularly appropriate to nonprofit organizations is the voluntary help of local professional researchers. Nonprofits contemplating extended research programs may want to ask marketing research professionals to sit on their boards of directors.

The "Most-Research-Is-Not-Read" Myth

Executives who would rather not bother with research or who subconsciously fear the results use this last rationale for their inaction. Poor research certainly is undertaken, but when it is, it is usually a testimonial to poor planning. In our experience, few pieces of *well-planned* research are rejected as unhelpful, although they may be ignored on other, often political, grounds.

How can one ensure that research will not be wasted effort? The responsibility rests with both the manager requesting the research and the researcher doing it. Research will be most valuable when the following are true:

1. It is undertaken after the manager has made clear to the researcher what the decision alternatives are and what it is about those decisions that necessitates additional information.
2. The relationship between the results and the decision is clearly understood.
3. The results are communicated well.

ORGANIZATIONAL AND CAMPAIGN MARKETING RESEARCH STRATEGY

Marketing research can be an extremely valuable management tool, especially in a customer-centered organization. It can help with both organization-level and campaign planning. At the campaign level, what is needed are specific studies at the formative "listening," pretesting, and monitoring stages designed around the campaign's particular audiences and focal behaviors. At the organization level, managers must think of research not as a series of studies undertaken as need arises but as a system of information steadily flowing into management decisions. The sophisticated nonprofit manager should plan to invest in a *marketing information system.*

MARKETING INFORMATION SYSTEMS

As we have seen, nonprofit managers need timely, accurate, and adequate market information as a basis for making sound marketing decisions. We shall use the term *marketing information system (MIS)* to describe the organization's system for routinely gathering, analyzing, storing, and disseminating relevant marketing information. More formally

A marketing information system is a continuing and interacting structure of people, equipment, and procedures designed to gather, sort, analyze, evaluate, and distribute

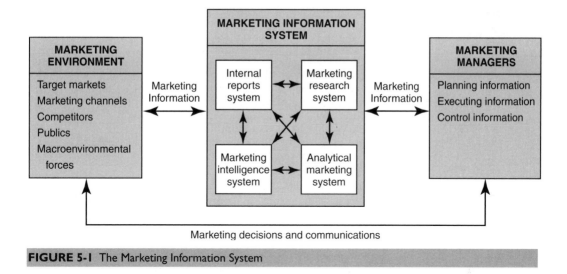

FIGURE 5-1 The Marketing Information System

pertinent, timely, and accurate information for use by marketing decision makers to improve their marketing planning, execution, and control.[4]

A sophisticated MIS has a number of subsystems as illustrated in Figure 5-1. At the left is shown the marketing environment that marketing managers must monitor—specifically, target markets, marketing channels, competitors, publics, and macroenvironmental forces. Developments and trends in the marketing environment are picked up in the company through one of four subsystems making up the marketing information system—the internal reports system, the marketing intelligence system, the marketing research system, and the analytical marketing system. The information then flows to the appropriate marketing managers to help them in their marketing planning, execution, and control. The resulting decisions and communications then flow back to the marketing environment.

Not all nonprofits will have the resources to include all four elements of the MIS and, even if they do, will wish to develop it slowly piece by piece. A good place to begin is with the internal reports system. As we shall note below, an organization's own archives can serve as one of the best low-cost research alternatives available.

Internal Reports System

Every organization accumulates information in the regular course of its operations. A hospital will keep records on its patients, including their names, addresses, ages, illnesses, lengths of stay, supplies and room charges, attending physicians, complaints, and so on. From these patient records the hospital can develop statistics on the number of daily admissions, average length of patients' stay, average patient charge, frequency distribution of different illnesses, and so on. The hospital will also have records on its physicians, nurses, costs, billings, assets, and liabilities, all of which are indispensable information for making management decisions.

TABLE 5-1 **Questionnaire for Determining Marketing Information Needs of Managers**

1. What types of decisions are you regularly called upon to make?
2. What types of information do you need to make these decisions?
3. What types of information do you regularly get?
4. What types of special studies do you periodically request?
5. What types of information would you like to get that you are not now getting?
6. What information would you want daily? weekly? monthly? yearly?
7. What magazines and reports would you like to see routed to you on a regular basis?
8. What specific topics would you like to be kept informed of?
9. What types of data analysis programs would you like to see made available?
10. What do you think would be the four most helpful improvements that could be made in the present marketing information system?

A museum will keep several record systems. Its contributor file will list the names, addresses, past contributions, and other data on its contributors. Its campaign progress file will show the amount raised to date from each major source, such as individuals, foundations, corporations, and government grants. Its cost file will show how much money has been spent on direct mail, newspaper advertising, brochures, salaries, consultant fees, and so on.

Every internal reports system can be improved in its speed, comprehensiveness, and accuracy. Periodically, an organization should survey its managers for possible improvements in the internal reports system. The goal is not to design the most elegant system, but one that is cost-effective in meeting the managers' (decision) needs. A cross-section of managers should be queried as to their information needs. Table 5-1 shows the major questions that can be put to them. Once their opinions are gathered, the information system designers can design an internal reports system that reconciles (1) what managers think they need, (2) what managers *really* need, and (3) what is economically feasible.

Market Intelligence System

As we noted in Chapter 3, marketers need information from both inside and outside the organization to do effective planning. The internal records system is a major source of insight into how the organization is performing. But these data are, by definition, about the past. What marketers also need is information about the future. In particular, they need information about the external environment around them that will have a major impact on what they can do and what they ought to do. This is the role of the market intelligence system.

Good marketing managers, of course, have always had an informal market intelligence system in place through their reading of newspapers and trade publications and talking to various people inside and outside the organization, often at national and international conferences. In this way, they are able to spot important developments. However, reliance on this casual approach to gathering marketing intelligence can also result in missing or learning too late of some other important developments, such as a fundraising opportunity with an important donor or a new law that might hurt the organization's nonprofit status. A good market intelligence system needs to be more systematic and more formal.

A simple first step is to improve the collection and transmission of insights gained by everyone in the organization. Often bits and pieces of important intelligence are located in nooks and crannies of the organization but never assembled in one place or transmitted to the people who can really use them. A person working on a commercial alliance might hear about a rival nonprofit's new venture but not tell the organization's strategic planning team, who may be considering something very similar and thinking they will be offering a unique service. To combat this, the organization must "sell" its managers and staff on the importance of gathering marketing intelligence and passing it on to others in the organization. Their intelligence responsibilities can be facilitated by designing information forms that are easy to fill out and circulate. Software can be created for this end and weekly e-mail "surveys" of internal staff can centralize a lot of market wisdom.

Second, the organization should encourage outside parties with whom it deals—advertising agencies, professional associations, lawyers, accountants, and its own board members—to pass on any useful bits of information. A museum's lawyer, for example, may hear about a wealthy donor who is revising his will, and this information can be useful to the development office of the museum.

Third, the organization can designate a person to be specifically responsible for gathering and disseminating marketing intelligence. This person would perform a number of services. He or she would scan major publications, abstract the relevant news, and disseminate the news to appropriate managers. Outside "clipping services" can be very useful in this regard.

Today, much of this information can be obtained from search engines on the Web, such as Lycos, Google, or Yahoo. In addition, there are a number of Web sites that are dedicated to aggregating market research information. These include the following:

www.AllNetResearch.Com

www.Bitpipe.com

www.MarketResearch.com ✓

www.Profound.com

www.USADATA.com

Marketing Research System

Although campaign managers may be carrying out market research studies all the time, central office managers may occasionally need to commission specific qualitative or quantitative marketing research studies in order to have adequate information to make pending organization-level decisions. For example, they may wish to learn how the organization is positioned in the minds of key publics. A college may want to determine what kind of image it has among high school counselors, or a political organization may want to find out what voters think of its candidates and other candidates. Many major non-profits and government agencies, such as the Centers for Disease Control and Prevention and the American Cancer Society, currently conduct formal branding studies. We will return to the problem of making these studies valuable below.

Analytical Marketing System

Data coming from internal records, marketing intelligence, and specific marketing research studies are only data until they are turned into information and insights that managers can use. This is the role of the analytical marketing system. The analytical marketing system consists of a set of techniques for analyzing marketing data and marketing problems. These systems are able to produce more findings and conclusions than can be gained by only commonsense manipulation of the data. Large organizations tend to make extensive use of analytical marketing systems. In smaller organizations, managers resist these approaches as too technical or expensive without realizing that inexpensive consulting help (e.g., from volunteers) can compensate for their own shortcomings.

A marketing research capability does not come about without careful planning. This requires that the nonprofit organization have (1) a marketing research mission, (2) a long-range strategy, (3) a budget, (4) an approach to carrying out individual projects, (5) an organization, and (6) a system of evaluation and control. We will comment in detail on (1) through (4) here and mention (5) and (6) briefly at the end of the chapter.

Marketing Research Mission

A marketing information system has as its basic mission *helping marketing managers make better decisions.* Thus, the first place to start when planning such a system is with managers' decisions. The research manager should think through the major kinds of decisions that managers will be making over the planning horizon for which marketing research might be useful. These include *routine decisions* to be made over and over, such as where to place advertising, which products or services to promote, what to do with prices and channels of distribution, and so forth. The planning period typically also includes *one-time decisions* such as whether to add a specific new product or service; reposition the enterprise; focus on a new target group; seek new funding sources; drop certain products, services, or customers; and so on. Some of these one-time decision needs can be anticipated, but some cannot.

For nonprofit organizations with very limited budgets, we would argue forcefully that *no* market research should ever be undertaken unless it can be *applied* directly to a decision. However, where one has a more generous budget, a nonprofit marketer might wish to establish capabilities to undertake one or both of two other kinds of research. One is *basic research.* Basic research has no immediate application to specific management decisions but is generally expected to lay the groundwork for better decisions somewhere down the road. Thus, the Association of College, University, and Community Arts Administrators has used part of its members' dues to explore the potential of lifestyle research—specifically, the original VALS approach—to understand consumers' reactions to the performing arts.[5]

The other type of research a nonprofit might undertake alone or jointly is *methodological research*—that is, research designed to improve the organization's ability to do more effective research in the future. Organizations involved in contraceptive marketing programs in developing countries, for example, have invested in two kinds of methodological research in recent years. One research stream has focused on figuring out how to measure the impacts of contraceptive marketing programs on a country's marketing system. The organizations need to know whether contraceptive program sales come at the expense of existing private sector firms or whether subsidized contraceptive marketing programs expand the entire market. In this connection, SOMARC, one of the key groups involved in international contraceptive social marketing, has sponsored research in Bangladesh to develop a standardized *retail audit* methodology for tracking condom and oral contraceptive sales for all brands in the markets they serve.[6]

Another more difficult methodological problem in family planning programs is how to get valid information on consumer attitudes and behavior concerning family planning. In this highly sensitive subject area, respondents very often distort the truth, withhold information, and make claims of use (or nonuse) that simply do not reconcile with, say, known sales data. In some cultures, research has discovered significant differences even within given households with respect to relatively simple matters, such as whether the family has ever actually used a particular method. Tackling this crucial methodological dilemma must be part of the marketing research mission of one or more of the key players in the social marketing arena over the next several years.

Most nonprofit marketing research should be designed to be *applied.* In such cases, it is likely to serve one of three purposes: description, explanation, or prediction.

Description

Marketing research can be designed to tell a nonprofit manager what his or her marketing environment is like. It can, for example, tell a hospital manager how many patients were served in each hospital facility each hour of each day of each year and indicate the sex and home address of each patient, his or her attending doctor, any previous admissions to the hospital, and the diagnosis.

While internal reports can often provide these data to hospital management, additional descriptive information could be acquired from a telephone survey to ascertain the patient's family status, occupation, education, media habits, satisfaction with various hospital services, and intentions as to word of mouth and future patronage. At the same time, the manager could acquire from published sources descriptive data on competitors' pricing and advertising expenditures as well as information on national trends in payment methods, wages of specific hospital departments, cost of equipment, and so on. All of these data have in common the fact that they are descriptions at one point in time or descriptions of trends or pattern changes over time. Descriptive data usually serve management decisions in three ways: (1) monitoring performance to indicate whether strategy changes are needed, (2) describing consumers for segmentation decisions, and (3) serving as the basis for more sophisticated analysis.

Explanation

Usually a manager is not satisfied with merely seeing what the market environment looks like. He or she would typically like to know what makes it "tick." In principle, there are really three possible levels of explanatory sophistication that a manager could attempt to build into the nonprofit organization's marketing research system. Each succeeding level has higher costs and greater resource requirements than the one preceding it, but it also has a higher potential payoff.

Association.   The simplest level of explanation is to discover what seems to be associated with what. Thus, the hospital manager might like to know which socioeconomic and demographic characteristics of patients characterize those who are repeat users of the hospital, or those who are satisfied or dissatisfied with past services, or those who are not favorably disposed toward competitors' offerings. Such data would be very useful in helping management decide which segment to address through what channels with which general strategy to use.

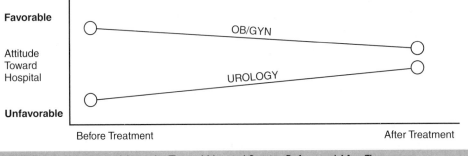

FIGURE 5-2 Hypothetical Attitudes Toward Hospital Service Before and After Treatment

Causation. A nasty feature of associations data that is learned by every freshman statistics student is that association is not the same as causation. Thus, the hospital manager may find that OB/GYN patients are more satisfied with their hospital care than those who were admitted for treatment of, say, urological problems. The manager may be tempted to think that the OB/GYN service is doing a better job than urology in terms of the technical quality and warmth of service offered. But suppose the manager had data like that displayed in Figure 5-2 showing patients' perceptions of the hospital before and after admission. The manager would quickly see that at admission, urology patients thought worse of the hospital than OB/GYN patients, but that the attitudes of OB/GYN patients *worsened* over the course of their treatment in the hospital, while the attitudes of urology patients improved. An "association" level of explanation would have given misleading indications about causation. For a manager to be sure of taking appropriate action, he or she must know what causes what. If the hospital manager subsequently took action to improve OB/GYN satisfaction scores, it would be critical to know whether these actions in fact led to the necessary changes. Only when the research strategy is specifically designed to trace antecedents and consequents, to measure effects under very controlled conditions, or to be subject to rather rigorous statistical procedures, does the strategy yield causative explanations.

Reasons Why. The ultimate level of explanation for marketing researchers is to know not only that A caused B, but *why* A caused B. Thus, the hospital manager looking at the data in Figure 5-2 may be willing to conclude that treatment by the urology service leaves patients satisfied, while treatment by the OB/GYN service does not. Before rushing to reward one service and castigate the other, the manager should have a better understanding of the nature of the causation, that is, of the "reasons why." To consider just one possibility, it may be that a significant number of patients in urology at the time of the study were there for the treatment of kidney stones and were simply relieved to have them removed. Any set of nurses or doctors who treated them in *any* way, from very competently and warmly to very incompetently and coldly, would have found them happier after treatment than before. If treatment per se, not staff, is the reason for the pattern of causation in Figure 5-2, then clearly rewards are not due to the urology staff. Indeed, there could even be serious problems on the urology floor that the warm afterglow of treatment is hiding. Management must often dig beneath simple causation if research is to lead to the right decision and action.

Prediction

Of course, descriptions or explanations of what exists or existed in the past are only useful to the manager if they tell about the future. As we noted in Chapter 3, marketing decisions play out in the future. Suppose the hospital manager in our hypothetical example finds that the reason for the post-treatment decline in OB/GYN patients' perceptions of the hospital is real and is due to the professional style of the staff, who emphasize doing the job right and efficiently rather than investing a lot of time in being solicitous and talkative with patients. But suppose it is also true that there are many patients who prefer this style—for example, those who have more education, those who are not having their first child, and those who are having birth complications. For the hospital manager to make a judgment about whether to try to change the style of the OB/GYN service to emphasize "warmth," it is essential to know what the future pool of potential parents will be and which strategic competitors will target them. This clearly requires a different set of information than is available from a typical descriptive or explanatory study.

MAKING RESEARCH USEFUL—THE BACKWARD RESEARCH PROCESS

At both the organizational and campaign levels, marketing managers will want to undertake specific studies to address specific problems or issues.[7] In unsophisticated organizations the standard approach to the research process is to start by defining the problem. The problem is then translated into a research methodology. This leads to the development of research instruments, a sampling plan, coding and interviewing instructions, and other details. The researcher takes to the field, examines the resulting data, and writes a report. The executive then steps in to translate the researcher's findings into action.

In the typical case, managers leave the problem vague and general. They say, in effect, "Here are some things I don't know. When the results come in, I'll know more. And when I know more, then I can figure out what to do." This approach makes it highly likely that the findings will be off target (i.e., not maximally useful).

We advocate instead a procedure that turns the traditional approach to research design on its head. The procedure stresses close collaboration between researchers and decision makers. It markedly raises the odds that the organization will come up with findings that are not only "interesting" but also actionable.

The "backward" approach advocated here rests on the premise that the best way to design usable research is to start where the process usually *ends* and then work backward. Each stage in the design is developed on the basis of what comes after it, not before. The steps in the procedure are outlined in Figure 5-3. They are as follows:

The backward research process may seem time-consuming at first. Indeed, it forces the participants from marketing research and management to spend a considerable number of hours together shaping and refining the goals and structure of the research project. This will be particularly frustrating the first time the approach is used and in the early steps each time thereafter. However, experience has shown that the long run effects in terms of reduced cost and increased effectiveness can be substantial.

At times, the early discussions will reveal that the research is not needed at all—that management will not act differently unless the results are very far from their

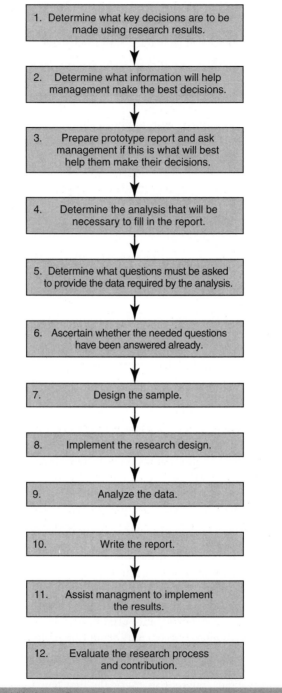

1. Determine what key decisions are to be made using research results.

2. Determine what information will help management make the best decisions.

3. Prepare prototype report and ask management if this is what will best help them make their decisions.

4. Determine the analysis that will be necessary to fill in the report.

5. Determine what questions must be asked to provide the data required by the analysis.

6. Ascertain whether the needed questions have been answered already.

7. Design the sample.

8. Implement the research design.

9. Analyze the data.

10. Write the report.

11. Assist management to implement the results.

12. Evaluate the research process and contribution.

FIGURE 5-3 Backward Marketing Research

Source: Alan R. Andreasen, *Marketing Research that Won't Break the Bank* (San Francisco: Jossey-Bass Publishers, 2003)

expectations. The discussions will also make sure that each element of the design ultimately chosen is necessary for decisions—there are no extraneous questions or "special subsamples" included. Lastly, close up-front collaboration will increase the likelihood that the final product will be one that management can understand, appreciate and implement with minimum delay. The ultimate test is: did the research make a real difference in organizational effectiveness? I takes hard work to achieve this goal.

Steps 1 and 2

To most managers, the research "problem" is seen as a lack of important information about their marketing environment. The manager of a social services program might say, "The problem is that I don't know who I am serving and who I am not serving" or "The problem is that I don't know whether my clients are more satisfied with my program than my major competitor's clients are satisfied with hers."

If the problem is defined this way, the "solution" is simply to reduce the manager's ignorance. Research is carried out that simply describes the patient population or that measures the level of satisfaction with alternative programs. These data may be very "interesting" and may give managers a great deal of satisfaction in revealing things they didn't know. But satisfaction can quickly turn to frustration and disappointment when the executive tries to use the results.

Take, for example, a lifestyle study done several years ago on over-the-counter drugs. Some respondents who claimed they were always getting colds and the flu frequently went to doctors, but the doctors were never of much help. The respondents thought that the over-the-counter drugs were often very beneficial, but they weren't sure why. This information, together with other details, caused the researchers to label this group "the hypochondriacs."

What can be done with these results? As is usually the case with segmentation strategies, there are quantity and quality decisions to make. The company has to decide whether to pump more marketing resources into the hypochondriac group than its proportion of the population would justify. The marketing vice-president might first say "yes" because the hypochondriacs are heavy drug users.

However, the picture is more complicated than that. Perhaps hypochondriacs are sophisticated buyers, set in their purchase patterns, and very loyal to their favorite brands. If so, money aimed at them would have little impact on the market shares. Light users, however, may have fragile loyalties, and throwing money at them could entice them to switch brands. Of course, just the opposite might be true: The hypochondriacs, being heavy users, might prove to be very impressionable and responsive to compelling ads.

On the qualitative side, lifestyle research could be much more helpful. Since it generates a rich profile describing each group's jobs, families, values, and preferences, this research could tell the company what to say. However, the frustrated manager is not likely to know *where* to say these things. There is no *Hypochondriac's Journal* in which to advertise, and there may be no viewing and reading patterns that apply to heavy users specifically—hypochondriacs or not.

A self-selection strategy could be tried in which the organization develops an ad speaking to hypochondriacs' fears and worries in the hope that they will see the message and say to themselves, "Ah, they're talking about me!" But non-hypochondriac heavy users who read the ad might say, "Well, if this product is really for those wimpy worry-warts, it certainly is not for sensible, rational me! I'll take my patronage elsewhere." In this case, the research will be very interesting (fine fodder for cocktail party banter) but not actionable.

But suppose that the company had first laid out all the action alternatives it might take after the study. If the marketing vice-president had made it clear that his problems were (1) whether to allocate marketing dollars differently and (2) whether to develop marketing campaigns aimed at particular, newly discovered segments, he would have launched the project in a more appropriate direction.

In the first case, discussions with the researcher would help the vice-president determine the criteria that would justify a different allocation. The manager needs research on the likely responses of different segments to advertising and promotional money. In the second case, the manager needs to know whether there are effective channels for reaching these segments. Only by first thinking through the decisions to be made with the research results will the project have a high likelihood of actionability.

Step 3

After step 1, management should ask, "What should the final report look like so that we'll know exactly what moves to make when the findings are in?" Now the collaboration between the researcher and the manager should intensify and prove both dynamic and exceedingly creative.

Scenarios are a good technique for developing ideas for the contents of the report. The initiative here lies with the researcher, who generates elements of a hypothetical report and then confronts management with tough questions, like "If I came up with this cross-tabulation with these numbers in it, what would you do?"

The first payoff from this exercise arises from improvements in the research itself. The exercise can move the project forward by sharpening the decision alternatives and backward by indicating the best design for the questionnaire or how the analysis of the findings should be carried out.

Suppose an arts manager is considering canceling a multiple-purchase discount offer because most of the people taking advantage of it may be loyal customers who are already heavy users, are upscale, and are largely price inelastic. The manager speculates that the discount mainly represents lost revenue. To decide whether to eliminate the discount, one must of course predict the responses of old and new customers to this step. The researcher should hypothesize tables showing various results.

Suppose the first iteration shows longtime customers to be price inelastic and new customers to be price elastic. This result suggests to the manager to only offer a discount to new customers. In considering this alternative, the manager will need to know whether potential new customers can be reached with the special offer in a way that will minimize or eliminate purchases at a discount by longtime customers.

This new formulation of the decision leads to a discussion of results set out in another set of dummy tables showing responsiveness to the proposed one-time discount by past patronage behavior. Other tables would then reveal what television shows various consumer segments watch and what they read or listen to, which will indicate whether they are differentially reachable. And so goes the process of recycling between the decision context and the research design.

The recycling will reveal what research is needed. Sometimes, the researcher will present contrasting tables of regression results only to discover that management would take the same course of action no matter what the results. This is actually a prima facie case for doing away with that part of the research design altogether.

Management participation in the design decision has other advantages. It serves to win managers' support of marketing research and deepens their understanding of research details. That understanding permits the researcher to simplify the report immeasurably. Working with contrasting, hypothetical tables can make the manager eager for the findings and unlikely to be startled by surprising results. Participation will also sensitize management to the study's limitations. Managers are often tempted to go far beyond research "truth" when implementing the results, especially if the reported truth supports the course of action they prefer to take anyway.

Step 4

The form of the report will clearly dictate the nature of the analysis. If management is leery of multivariate analysis, the researchers should design a series of step-by-step cross-tabulations. If management is comfortable with the higher reaches of statistics, the researcher can draw on more advanced analytic procedures. In general, the analysis phase should be straightforward. If the exercise of scenario writing has gone well, the analysis should amount to little more than filling in the blanks.

Step 5 through 7

The backward approach is very helpful in data gathering. In one study, management wanted to gauge young consumers' knowledge of the preferences for the organization's offering. Not until the researcher had prepared mock tables showing preference data by age and sex did the manager's wishes become clear. By "young," the manager meant children as young as 10. The manager also believed that preteens, being a very volatile group, undergo radical changes from year to year, especially as they approach puberty. Design plans to set a low age cutoff for the sample at 13 and to group respondents by age category—such as 13 to 17 and 17 to 20—went out the window. If the researcher had been following the usual design approach, the manager's expectations may not have surfaced until the study was well underway.

Backward design can also help determine the appropriateness of using strict probability techniques. If, for example, management wants to project certain findings to some universe, the research must employ precise probability methods. However, if the manager is chiefly interested in frequency counts (say, of words used by consumers to describe the organization's offerings or of complaints voiced about its staff), sampling restrictions need not be so tight. Researchers often build either too much or too little sampling quality for the uses the organization has in mind. Similarly, scenario writing will often also reveal that management wants more breakdowns of the results, requiring larger sample sizes or more precise stratification procedures than initially planned. Through simulating the application of the findings, the final research design is much more likely to meet management's needs with substantially lower field costs.

Steps 8 through 10

The first five steps encompass the major advantages of the backward technique. Steps 6 through 10 revert to a traditional forward approach that implements the research decisions and judgments made earlier. If all parties have collaborated well in the early stages, steps 6 through 10 should merely carry through what has already been decided.

Steps 11 and 12

The traditional research project concludes when the report is dropped on the manager's desk. This, however, is premature and shortsighted. The process began with the researcher and the manager thinking collaboratively about what the research would do to help management decision making. Now that the data are in hand, the researcher should continue to be involved because he or she (1) understands the database and its nuances and (2) has already thought hard about what the results should mean to the manager. Continued teamwork through the application stage will ensure not only good decisions, but that the data are mined as thoroughly as possible and that they are not subject to inadvertent misinterpretations (for example, when the manager *wishes* to believe that a finding is present when it really isn't).

The last step in the process is equally necessary if the research project is not to be a unique event but is to fit into an organization's long-run research strategy. Sometime after the application steps have been inaugurated, the researcher and manager should review the entire research process and ask whether there were any ways in which it could have been carried out better. Only through such careful reflection will the entire research enterprise be perfected and the nonprofit get the most out of the limited resources it allocates to this critical function.

Low-Cost Research Alternatives

The second requirement for effective implementation of research projects is to choose the right research methodology.[8] As we have noted earlier, when the nonprofit researcher thinks of carrying out research on key issues, the technique that usually comes to mind first is the one-time field survey, usually a mail or telephone study using conventionally designed questionnaires. However, this technique can be very expensive and time-consuming. There are many low-cost alternatives, especially at the formative and pretest phases of campaigns.

Qualitative Research

There are many situations in which management may wish to carry out research that does not require projections to broader populations or the use of sophisticated statistical techniques. In such situations, *qualitative research* techniques are appropriate. Among the uses of qualitative research by nonprofits are the following:

1. Identifying a problem.
2. Gathering initial customer insights around the BCOS model (introduced in Chapter 4)
3. Preparing for a subsequent quantitative study:
   a. Generating ideas and hypotheses.
   b. Learning appropriate language for questions.
   c. Pretesting questionnaires.
4. Helping interpret a prior quantitative study.
5. Pretesting alternative advertisements, product concepts, packaging, or brochures.
6. Generating ideas for new products or services.
7. Generating ideas for advertisements or product positioning.

Two approaches that are frequently used for qualitative research are *individual depth interviews* and *focus groups*. Individual depth interviews involve lengthy questioning of a small number of respondents (rather than brief questioning of large samples) one at a time, often using disguised questions and minimal interviewer prompting. Focus groups involve bringing together groups of 5 to 10 consumers, usually (but not always) a relatively homogeneous group, to discuss a specific set of issues under the guidance of a leader trained to stimulate and focus the discussion. Figure 5-4 indicates conditions under which each of these techniques might be used.

Issue to Consider	Use focus groups when . . .	Use individual depth interviews when . . .
Group interaction	interaction of respondents may stimulate a richer response or new and valuable thoughts.	group interaction is likely to be limited or nonproductive.
Group/peer pressure	group/peer pressure will be valuable in challenging the thinking of respondents and illuminating conflicting opinions	group/peer pressure would inhibit responses and cloud the meaning of results.
Subjectivity of subject matter	subject matter is not so sensitive that respondents will temper responses or withhold information.	subject matter is so sensitive that respondents would be unwilling to talk openly in a group.
Depth of individual responses	the topic is such that most respondents can say all that is relevant or all that they know in less than 10 minutes	the topic is such that a greater depth of response per individual is desirable, as with complex subject matter and very knowledgeable respondents.
Interviewer fatigue	it is desirable to have one interviewer conduct the research; several groups will not create interviewer fatigue or boredom.	it is desirable to have numerous interviewers on the project. One interviewer would become fatigued or bored conducting the interviews.
Stimulus materials	the volume of stimulus material is not extensive.	a large amount of stimulus material must be evaluated.
Continuity of information	a single subject area is being examined in depth and strings of behaviors are less relevant.	it is necessary to understand how attitudes and behaviors link together on an individual pattern basis.
Experimentation with interview guide	enough is known to establish a meaningful topic guide.	it may be necessary to develop the interview guide by altering it after each of the initial interviews.
Observation	it is possible and desirable for key decision makers to observe "firsthand" consumer information.	"firsthand" consumer information is not critical or observation is not logistically possible.
Logistics	an acceptable number of target respondents can be assembled in one location.	respondents are geographically dispersed or not easily assembled for other reasons.
Cost and timing	quick turnaround is critical, and funds are limited.	quick turnaround is not critical, and the budget will permit higher cost.

FIGURE 5-4 Which to Use: Focus Groups or Individual Depth Interviews?

Source: Mary Debus, *Handbook for Excellence in Focus Group Research* (Washington, D.C.: Academy for Educational Development, n.d.), p. 10. Reproduced with permission.

1. ***Build the relevant context information***—What are the experiences or issues that surround a product or a practice that influence how it/he/she is viewed?
2. ***Top-of-mind associations***—What's the first thing that comes to mind when I say "family planning"?
3. ***Constructing images***—Who are the people who buy Panther condoms? What do they look like? What are their lives about? (Or) Where are you when you buy condoms? Describe the place. What do you see? What do you feel? What do you do?
4. ***Querying the meaning of the obvious***—What does "soft" mean to you? What does the phrase "It's homemade" mean to you?
5. ***Establishing conceptual maps of a product category***—How would you group these different family planning methods? How do they go together for you? How are groups similar/different? What would you call these groups?
6. ***Metaphors***—If this birth control pill were a flower, what kind would it be and who would pick it? If this group of products were a family, who would the different members be and how do they relate to each other?
7. ***Image matching***—Here are pictures of ten different situations/people. Which go with this wine and, which do not? Why?
8. ***"Man from the moon" routine***—I'm from the moon; I've never heard of Fritos. Describe them to me. Why would I want to try one? Convince me.
9. ***Conditions that give permission and create barriers***—Tell me about two or three situations in which you would decide to buy this chocolate and two to three situations in which you would decide to buy something else.
10. ***Chain of questions***—Why do you buy "X"? Why is that important? Why does that make a difference to you? Would it ever not be important? (Ask until the respondent is ready to kill the interviewer!)

FIGURE 5–5 Suggestions for Soliciting Responses in Focus Groups

Source: Mary Debus, *Handbook for Excellence in Focus Group Research* (Washington, D.C.: Academy for Educational Development, n.d.), p. 10. Reproduced with permission.

The objective of both in-depth interviewing and focus groups is to get beneath the surface of some issue. These approaches are based on the presumption that individuals will reveal more either when they talk at length with a sympathetic and resourceful interviewer or when they are in a relaxed group setting and are stimulated by the camaraderie and comments of others (the "coffee klatsch" model). The trick in both circumstances is to bring out "hidden" or deeper aspects of a subject or issue. Mary Debus, formerly of Porter Novelli, has suggested several techniques that skilled interviewers and group moderators use to achieve this, which are listed in Figure 5-5.

Experimentation

A major problem with survey and much qualitative research is that it relies upon what people say. The quality of such data can be biased in all sorts of ways, including by the interviewees or interviewers themselves. An alternative approach is to observe what people do. Much archival data in fact provide such information. However, such data simply record what happened in the past. Marketers are often interested in "what-if scenarios," and this is the role of experimentation. Experimental opportunities abound. For example:

11. *Benefit chain*—This cake mix has more egg whites; what's the benefit of that? (Answer: "It's moister.") What is the benefit of a moister cake? (Answer: "It tastes homemade.") And why is homemade better? (Answer: "It's more effort.") And what's the benefit of that? (Answer: "My family will appreciate it.") And? (Answer: "They will know I love them.") And? (Answer: "I'll feel better; they'll love me back.")

12. *Laddering (chains of association)*—What do you think of when you think of Maxwell House coffee? (Answer: "Morning.") And when you think of morning, what comes to mind? (Answer: "A new day.") And when you think of a new day? (Answer: "I feel optimistic.")

13. *Pointing out contradictions*—Wait a minute, you just told me you would like it to be less greasy and now you're telling me it works because it's greasy and oily—how do you explain that?

14. *Sentence completions and extensions*—The ideal ORS product is one that. . . . The best thing about this new product is. . . .It makes me feel. . . .

15. *Role playing*—Okay, now you're the chairman of the board, or the mayor of this city. What would you do? (Or) I'm the mayor, talk to me, tell me what you want.

16. *Best-of-all-possible-worlds scenario*—Forget about reality for a minute. If you could design your own diaper that has everything you ever wanted in a diaper and more, what would it be like? Use your imagination. There are no limits. Don't worry about whether it's possible or not.

17. *Script writing*—If you were able to tell a story or write a movie about this company or city (or whatever), what would it be about? Who are the heroines and heroes? Does the movie have a message? Would you go see it? Who would?

FIGURE 5–5 *Continued*

- A fundraiser could divide a mailing list into three groups and send out solicitations with varying degrees of "personalization."
- A manager of an adolescent drug program could place a television set in the waiting rooms of half the centers and video games in the other half and observe the effects on the return rates of patients.
- A museum's cafeteria manager could systematically change prices on the assorted cheesecakes every day over a three-month period and estimate the price–volume relationship.
- Hospital rooms could be decorated in different colors or nurses' uniforms changed on different floors to assess their effects on patients' satisfaction with the quality of care.

These experimental manipulations often require little effort on the part of managers. Often they can be done as simple "variations" in marketing projects that would be undertaken anyway. In contrast to surveys and many qualitative techniques, they usually can be carried out *unobtrusively*—that is, without the target audience knowing they are part of a study. Researchers, however, should avoid thinking that "just trying something" makes for good experimentation. Careful attention must be paid to random assignment of experimental treatments across subjects, use of control groups

wherever possible, and monitoring the surrounding circumstances for possible con-
founding effects.[9]

Convenience Sampling

A nonprofit organization with a very limited budget often can get useful data
(although again not projectable) from respondents close at hand. Hospitals, for
example, could study patients, visitors, and service delivery people coming into the
hospital. These groups would obviously know more about the hospital and may be
more biased than strangers. Still, the hospital might argue that these people are
exactly their target market and that knowing more about them (and the differences
among them) could be very useful.

Snowball Sampling

Participants in the previous study could be asked to suggest the names of others
"like them" who could be contacted. This would add a group that (1) did not have the
familiarity biases of the first group, (2) would be likely to cooperate in the study (especially if the initial respondents allowed their names to be used as references), and
(3) would closely *match* the first sample in all other socioeconomic characteristics but
that which characterized the initial sample (for example, people already coming to the
hospital). Snowball sampling is a particularly good technique for finding rare populations. A hospital trying to broaden its appeal to hemophiliacs, for example, might ask
those hemophiliacs already attending the hospital to identify others. Conducting a full-
scale random sample to find rare populations, such as paraplegics or bus riders with
disabilities or the deaf, would be prohibitively expensive. Yet members of such rare
groups may well be known to many others like themselves.

Piggybacking

Nonprofit organizations may be able to add questions onto studies undertaken by
others. Several national research organizations regularly conduct omnibus surveys that
combine questions from a number of sponsors. Nonprofits could add questions for
close to the incremental cost of the question or questions. Corporations or other private firms with a public service inclination may be willing to add such questions to
planned studies at no charge or at reduced rates.

Volunteer Field Workers

Nonprofits such as hospitals or charities may enlist volunteers to conduct telephone, mail, or "convenience" interviews, or to tabulate questionnaires.

Student Projects

Students in business schools, and sometimes in psychology and sociology departments, are frequently looking for outside, real-world term projects. They can be an
excellent source of thought and legwork for nonprofit organizations. However, certain
caveats should be observed. First, student interviewers are not the same as trained professional interviewers. The nonprofit manager must give them guidance or be sure that
a professor is overseeing the research process. Second, plenty of lead time is necessary.
Student projects must fit within semester or quarter academic systems. Third, the nonprofit manager should set time aside to consult with the students—they are doing this
to learn. Finally, the nonprofit manager should be sensitive to the university's research
norms. The students cannot be ordered to do the research in a particular way, the pro-

fessor cannot be treated as a paid consultant or a field supervisor, and the professor may request that the results be made public (although possibly in disguised form).

Secondary Sources

Various published sources can provide comparative data or suggestions for question wording, sample design, and data analysis. Trade articles, marketing journals, and government reports can all prove very valuable, especially at the beginning stages of a project. Researchers, however, need to be careful to investigate the validity of other people's research. Oftentimes a careful reading of footnotes and appendices can reveal serious biases or deficiencies that require caution in the use of the findings.

Among the valuable sources of secondary marketing data are these:[10]

1. *American Demographics* magazine (www.marketingtools.com). Texts of publications.
2. Dow Jones and Company (www.dowjones.com). Web links to a wide range of financial and company data.
3. Mead Data Central. The LEXIS-NEXIS databases (www.lexis-nexis.com) provide full-text information on legal, business, and general news. Fee for subscription.
4. Find/SVP (www.findsvp.com). Provides fee-based information searches.
5. USA Data (www.usadata.com). Reports on industries, geographic locations, and brands available for a fee.
6. The Dialog Company (www.dialog.com). Over 450 databases with millions of documents.
7. Forrester (www.forrester.com). Information on the Web and other business issues.
8. Allnet (allnetresearch.internet.com). Wide range of data sources.

Board of Directors

Most nonprofit organizations select board members who will serve the nonprofit in some beneficial way. A typical board has lawyers, bankers, accountants, and individuals who have access to influential financial and political figures. There is every reason to add a marketing research professional (and advertising, public relations, and other marketing professionals) to the board. Such experts can provide useful advice, and possibly offer the services of their agencies gratis or at reduced rates.

SUMMARY

Most nonprofit organizations carry out much less marketing research than they should. This is because they have accepted certain myths. They assume that marketing research should only be used for major decisions, that it involves big surveys and takes a long time, that it is always expensive, that it requires sophisticated researchers, and, when it is finished, that it is usually not read or used. But research using a diversity of techniques, many at low cost, can be extremely valuable to a wide range of decisions.

Research, like any other management activity, must be planned strategically with a mission, strategy, budgets, implementation plan, organization, and control. Eventually, the nonprofit organization should develop a marketing information system. A marketing information system has four major subsystems: an internal records system, a market intelligence system, a marketing research system, and an analytical marketing system.

Research can help managers by describing, explaining, or predicting market characteristics. Most nonprofit research is applied, although some could be basic or methodological research. The applied nature of the research provides a good framework for decisions about budgets and for designing specific research projects.

An applied orientation also recommends a "backward" research design process. Here the research manager first looks to the decisions to be made using the research results and then works backward to design a study that would best inform such decisions. An important step would be determining what report format would provide the most managerially useful information. The report form would then suggest the type of analysis needed, which, in turn, would specify how the data are to be collected and processed.

Research can be quantitative or qualitative, high cost or low cost. Qualitative research, such as in-depth interviewing or focus groups, can be useful in identifying a problem, gathering background for later quantitative studies, interpreting past studies, pretesting advertisements, product concepts, packaging and brochures, and generating ideas for new products, services, and advertisements. Other techniques for keeping research costs low are experimentation, low-cost sampling designs, and the use of secondary data and volunteer assistance.

QUESTIONS

1. The director of a soup kitchen notices that donations of food increase significantly in April and December. She would like to understand why this happens. What type of research would be helpful in explaining this phenomenon? How could you design the research to obtain the causality of this consumer behavior?
2. Utilize the "backward" approach to research to design a questionnaire for a marketing manager who wants to curb teen smoking. Assume that the marketing manager is specifically interested in answering the following question: "How do social factors (e.g., peer pressure, fashion) influence teen smoking?"
3. You are appointed as the marketing director for a new AIDS awareness organization. Your boss has given you a limited budget for marketing research over the next year and wants to hear your plans for research by the end of the week. What types of research are you likely to undertake? What are the strengths and weaknesses of the research methods you identified?
4. You are an anti-violence counselor for teen youths. Prepare a guide for a focus group discussion that will include 10- to 15-year-old, underprivileged boys from inner cities. The objective of the study is to develop a strategy to keep young boys from joining street gangs and engaging in violence.
5. A trust has just provided your community organization with $1 million, and the direction to improve the well-being of local orphaned children. The board of the trust wants you to develop a budget proposal in one week before they release the funds. How much money will you spend on market research? How will you justify this decision?

NOTES

1. This section draws upon Alan R. Andreasen, "Cost-Conscious Marketing Research," *Harvard Business Review,* July-August 1983, pp. 74–77.
2. For further information on research costs, see Seymour Sudman, *Reducing the Costs of Surveys* (Chicago: Aldine, 1967).
3. See, for example, Thomas L. Greenbaum, *The Handbook of Focus Group Research,* 2nd ed. (Thousand Oaks, Calif.: Sage Publications, 1998).
4. The definition is adapted from Samuel V. Smith, Richard L. Brien, and James E. Stafford, "Marketing Information Systems: An Introductory Overview," in their *Readings in Marketing Information Systems* (Boston: Houghton Mifflin, 1968), p. 7. See also Lee G. Cooper and Daniel Jacobs, "Marketing Information Systems for the Profession and Science of Arts Management," *The Journal of Arts Management and the Law,* Vol. 14, No. 1, Spring 1984, pp. 77–89.
5. *The Professional Performing Arts: Attendance, Preferences and Motives* (Madison, Wisc.: Association of College, University and Community Arts Administrators, 1977).
6. Alan R. Andreasen, *Conducting an Effective Retail Audit,* Practical Guide #4 (Washington, D.C.: SOMARC/The Futures Group, 1988).
7. This section is drawn from Alan R. Andreasen, " 'Backward' Marketing Research," *Harvard Business Review,* May-June 1985, pp. 176–182.
8. For more information on low-cost methods, see Alan R. Andreasen, *Marketing Research That Won't Break the Bank* (San Francisco: Jossey-Bass Publishers, 2002).
9. A good introduction to alternative field experimental designs is found in Donald T. Campbell and Julian C. Stanley, *Experimental and Quasi-Experimental Designs for Research* (Chicago: Rand McNally, 1966). For a good example of a nonprofit experiment, see Richard A. Winett, Ingrid N. Lecklite, Donna E. Chinn, and Brian Stahl, "Reducing Energy Consumption: The Long-Term Effects of a Single TV Program," *Journal of Communications,* Summer 1984, pp. 37–51.
10. Alan R. Andreasen, *Marketing Research That Won't Break the Bank.*

CHAPTER 6

Segmentation, Positioning, and Branding

Every 10 years, the U.S. Bureau of the Census has a monumental marketing challenge. Its mandate is to collect information on every resident in the country; unfortunately, its performance over the last half-century has slowly been deteriorating. Part of the problem is that more of the country is mobile and hard to pin down. In addition, people are increasingly suspicious of anything (e.g., census forms) that looks like junk mail. The biggest problem is not finding people but getting them to fill out the forms, especially the mail version. If individuals do not respond by mail, the Census Bureau incurs significant costs in sending one of its enumerators into the field to collect the information in person. In 1990, only 65 percent of Americans responded by mail, down 10 percent from 1980. Bureau predictions forecasted a response rate for Census 2000 below 60 percent.

The bureau believed that its major challenges were in the diverse racial and ethnic communities of the United States where there is broad suspicion of government inquiries of any kind. Previous research found immigrant groups who are not yet citizens to be especially wary. One-half of those not counted in 1990 were minorities. As a consequence, the bureau spent four years planning an extensive multiethnic campaign involving a team of agencies specializing in these markets to change this pattern. For the 2000 census, it also decided to rely on $167 million in paid advertising to achieve results instead of relying on mostly pro bono PSA contributions as they did in 1990. This allowed messages to be targeted more precisely at these special audiences. The campaign also emphasized integration and consistency across audiences and a significant reliance on grassroots help and local partnerships.

Some messages were blunt: Telling various minority groups that the INS, IRS, FBI, and CIA have no access to census data thus significantly reducing what many minorities saw as the major cost of participating. However, the bureau's multicultural marketing team also emphasized benefits—what the minority groups would get in terms of government benefits if they were only fully counted. The bureau also hired 700 community spokespeople and business leaders, and recruited another 140,000 partners from each market to help show that "others" supported the effort. Events were held around census issues, and census partners reached Central and South American Hispanic groups by going into the communities and talking up the census at events like the soccer games these special audiences were known to attend. School kits were also developed so that minority kids would bring the message—and some pressure—home to their parents. It was estimated that the census message reached 93 percent of the Spanish-speaking population.

The payoff was significant. Undercounting in the Hispanic market was reduced 50 percent despite the fact that this market had become much more complex in the last 10 years. Best of all, the overall mail-back response rate for the entire population rose to 67 percent, well above the predicted 61 percent. It was estimated that this alone saved the government $300 million.

Source: Adapted from Dana James, "Census Says: Multiculti Works," Marketing News, July 30, 2001, pp. 1, 9–10.

A central theme of this text is that, whether a nonprofit marketer is undertaking organization-level or campaign planning, the central issue is—or ought to be—how to induce desired behavior from target audiences. Thus, we argue that the two most fundamental challenges of nonprofit marketers is deciding (1) who should be their target audiences and (2) what sort of behavior or behaviors do they want them to take? With respect to audiences and behaviors, nonprofit organizations with huge challenges and limited budgets cannot be all things to all people (even though their mission statement may grandly imply such ambitions). They must choose audiences and they must choose behaviors. We refer to the former as the Segmentation Problem and the latter as the Positioning Problem. A central feature of the latter for many nonprofits is the development of a conscious Branding Strategy.

We treat each of these planning challenges in turn.

SEGMENTATION

Good marketing starts with the target audience that determines success. Thus, the first element to be set out in any marketing strategy is the organization's approach toward market targets. However, target audiences come in many different shapes and sizes and a fundamental problem for marketing managers is how to deal with this complexity. Treating all customers the same may achieve economies of scale, but it ignores the diversity that is typically present in most markets, and it probably means that what is offered never really meets any one target audience member's needs very well. However, treating everyone as a unique individual deserving customized attention has been historically too expensive and impractical for most nonprofit situations (except in fundraising, where individualized approaches to foundations, corporations, and major donors are certainly merited).

Today, however, treating audience members individually—as markets of one—is becoming ever more practical. Computers and information technology have made individualized approaches through direct mail and the Internet much more cost-effective. For example, direct mail technology allows a political fundraiser to send letters to Lexus and Hyundai owners living next to each other and to ask for $500 from the Lexus owner and $100 from the Hyundai owner.[1] Even more promising are developments on the Internet where sophisticated software allows marketers to address individuals by name and respond to inquiries with custom-tailored responses. As the work of Williams and Flora and others has demonstrated, tailored approaches can be especially valuable in health care.[2]

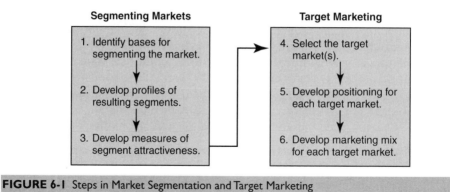

FIGURE 6-1 Steps in Market Segmentation and Target Marketing

For the marketer seeking to develop a sophisticated segmentation approach, a process is needed to cope with the sheer enormity of the task. There are really *two* stages to this process. First is a conceptualization and research stage to identify and describe the groups the marketer *may* wish to target. This stage we shall refer to as *developing market segments.* As can be seen in the left side of Figure 6-1, market segmentation requires (1) identifying the different bases for segmenting the market, (2) developing profiles of the resulting market segments, and (3) developing measures of each segment's attractiveness. The second stage is *target marketing,* the act of selecting one or more of the market segments, deciding how many resources and of what kind to apply to each, and developing a positioning and marketing mix strategy for each.

Segmenting Markets

There are a great many ways in which a given market can be divided for purposes of marketing strategy. In determining which way one ought to proceed, the manager should first consider *why* segmentation is to be carried out. That is, segmenting the market is a research task and, as we noted in Chapter 5, good "backward" research starts with an understanding of how the data will be used to help managers make decisions. There are three types of decisions for which segmentation information is valuable:

1. *Quantity decisions.* How much of the organization's financial, human, and mental resources are to be devoted to various groups in the target population? Which groups merit zero attention, if any?
2. *Quality decisions.* Among the chosen segments, how should each segment be approached in terms of specific offerings, communications, place of offering, prices, and the like?
3. *Timing decisions.* Should some segments be targeted earlier and some later with a specific marketing effort?

How, then, to divide up the market? In theory, the criteria are well-defined. A segmentation base is optimal if it yields segments possessing the following characteristics:

1. *Mutual exclusivity.* Is each segment conceptually separable from all other segments? Breaking donors into present givers and past givers, for example, would be confusing for a respondent who could be both a past and a present giver.

2. *Exhaustiveness.* Is every potential target member included in some segment? Thus, if there is to be segmentation according to household status, one should have categories to cover relationships like unmarried couples and religious communes where the notion of "household head" really does not apply.
3. *Measurability.* Can you measure the size, motivation, ability to act, and so on of the resulting segments? Certain segments are hard to measure, such as the segment of white upper-income teenage female drug addicts engaged in secretive behavior.
4. *Reachability.* Can the resulting segments be effectively reached and served? Thus, it would be hard for a drug treatment center to develop efficient media to locate and communicate with white female drug addicts.
5. *Substantiality.* Are the resulting segments large enough to be worth pursuing? The drug treatment center is likely to decide that white affluent female drug addicts are too few in number to be worth the development of a special marketing program. Size is a combination of both number of consumer units and the amount of consumption.
6. *Differential responsiveness.* This is perhaps the most crucial criterion. A segmentation scheme may meet all of the previous criteria but several or all segments may respond exactly alike to different amounts, types, and timings of strategy. In such cases, although it may be *conceptually* useful to develop separate segments in this way, *managerially* it is not useful.

It is typically difficult to answer all of the previous questions when considering a particular segmentation scheme. Responsiveness and reachability are very often impossible to measure and, as a result, managers typically use *surrogates* for what they *ideally* would like to measure. Segmentation is often based on demographics, for example, because managers assume that such characteristics will be related to likely responsiveness and reachability. Thus, one might choose to segment potential symphony customers on the basis of gender because it is believed (or past research has shown) that women respond more to communications focusing on the performance itself, whereas men respond more to communications about the social aspects of attending the symphony *event*. At the same time, it may be found (or assumed) that ads placed in the sports section of a newspaper would reach a predominantly male audience and ads in the metropolitan news section would be an excellent way to reach females. Symphony marketers may initially conclude—with or without past research evidence—that the added costs of placing two such ads in a given paper may be justified by the better *total* responses achieved over a less costly, single ad that tried a middle approach or tried to combine the two approaches in one (possibly confusing) message.

At the outset of a segmentation process, reachability and responsiveness often must be estimated. However, as a strategy or campaign unfolds, a careful program of *experimentation* could directly test which segmentation approach (for example, separate or single ads) generated more mail orders or more box office sales. By carrying out a systematic program of experiments over a long time, savvy marketing managers can accumulate considerable experience on the responsiveness and reachability of key market segments.

Alternative Segmentation Bases

Variables that have been used to segment markets in particular cases vary according to whether they were *primarily* chosen to reflect expected differences in responsiveness

	General	**Behavior-Specific**
Objective Measures	Age, income, sex Place of residence Status change Family life cycle Social class	Past behavior • Purchase quantity • Outlet/brand preference • Loyalty Decision role
Inferred Measures	Personality Psychographics/lifestyles (e.g., PRIZM) Values (e.g., VALS 2)	Beliefs, perceptions BCOS drivers Stage in decision

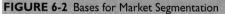

FIGURE 6-2 Bases for Market Segmentation

or differences in reachability. Frank, Massy, and Wind have developed a two-by-two matrix that serves as a useful vehicle for categorizing segmentation approaches that may be used to achieve these ends.[3] These authors note that two important ways in which segmentation variables differ are in the extent to which they are (1) objective or inferred and (2) general or behavior-specific (Figure 6-2). *Objective measures* are those that can be verified by an independent observer—for example, status indicators such as age, income, sex, and the like. *Inferred measures* are mental states peculiar to each respondent that have to be deduced from what people tell us; included are such cognitive factors as perceptions, beliefs, benefits sought, and so forth. Inferred variables depend on the candor and cooperation of a target consumer through answers to a questionnaire, a paper-and-pencil test, or a similar assessment device.

General variables are those that might apply to any exchange, whereas *behavior-specific* variables are those that are unique to one type or class of behaviors (for example, the purchase of a particular brand or patronage of a particular hospital or museum). Thus, the extent to which an individual consumer possesses an "aggressive" or "risk-averse" personality would be a general inferred variable, whereas beliefs about the likelihood of getting friendly nursing service or the latest diagnostic procedures at Good Samaritan Hospital would be a behavior-specific inferred variable.

In some respects, marketers would prefer to use objective rather than inferred measures as the basis for segmentation. There are several reasons for this. First, there is the *ease* of identifying target consumers. Most objective general measures such as sex and geographic location are instantly observable. Others, such as education level, occupation, household size, and family composition are relatively easily determined and verifiable. Unlike inferred measures, objective indicators do not always require consumer cooperation, nor is there a strong likelihood that an error in measurement would be made either because the wrong wording was used for a question or because respondents did not know the answer or consciously or unconsciously distorted their responses. Second, target consumers can be fairly easily allocated to specific, nonarbitrary categories. Third, the measures can be adapted easily by different researchers to different contexts, permitting extensive comparison of segmentation findings across

EXHIBIT 6-1   A Taxonomy of Beneficiaries of Nonprofit Organization Programs

I. *General*
1. All, general public, no specific beneficiary
II. *Age related*
1. Infants, babies
2. Children and youth
3. Aging, elderly, senior citizens, and retired
III. *Sex*
1. Boys 5 to 19
2. Boys and men (i.e., males 5 and older)
3. Girls 5 to 19
4. Girls and women (i.e., females 5 and older)
5. Men 19 and older
6. Women 19 and older
IV. *Race*
1. Asian, Pacific Islander
2. Blacks
3. Hispanics
4. Native Americans, American Indians
5. Other Minorities
6. Minorities, general, unspecified
V. *Other beneficiaries*
1. Disabled, general, unspecified
2. Disabled, physically
3. Disabled, mentally, emotionally
4. Immigrants, newcomers, refugees, stateless
5. Member or affiliates (organizations)
6. Member (individual)
7. Military, veterans
8. Offenders, ex-offenders
9. Poor, economically disadvantaged

Source: National Center for Charitable Statistics, *National Taxonomy of Exempt Entities* (Washington, D.C.: The Independent Sector, 1987).

studies. This is typically not possible with inferred characteristics, where subtle changes in wording can yield major differences in results.

Finally, objective measures are often preferred because they are available in a wide range of secondary sources including Census Bureau data, Simmons reports, Nielsen audience measures, and so on. Thus, if one believes that households with young children are the best prospects for a charity drive, then publicly available census data can be used to discover cities or census tracts within cities that have above-average frequencies of households with that characteristic. Thus, socioeconomic characteristics were the principal criteria used by the National Center for Charitable Statistics to segment the target markets for exempt nonprofit agencies in the 1980s. Their taxonomy of beneficiaries reproduced in Exhibit 6-1.

Objective General Measures
Among the most commonly used objective general measures are the following:

Demographic Segmentation   In demographic segmentation, the market is divided into different groups on the basis of demographic variables such as age, sex, family size,

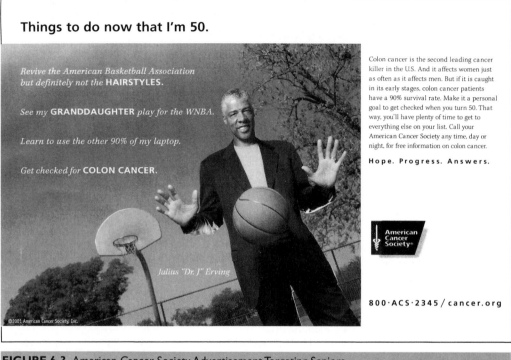

FIGURE 6-3 American Cancer Society Advertisement Targeting Seniors

Source: American Cancer Society. Reproduced with permission.

family life cycle, income, occupation, education, religion, race, and nationality. Demographic variables have long been among the most popular bases for distinguishing consumer groups. One reason is that consumer wants, preferences, and usage rates are often highly associated with demographic variables. Another is that demographic variables are easier to measure than most other types of variables. Even when the target market is described in nondemographic terms (say, a personality type), the link back to demographic characteristics is necessary in order to know the size of the target market and how to reach it efficiently.

Here we will illustrate how certain demographic variables have been applied creatively to market segmentation.

Age Consumer wants and capacities change with age. Thus, churches have developed different programs for children, youths, singles, married adults, and senior citizens. The churches try to "customize" the religious and social experiences to the interests of these different groups. Some churches are even subsegmenting the senior citizens into those between 55 and 70 ("the young old") and 70 and up ("the old old"). The "young old" still feel vigorous and want challenge and variety in their lives, and the "old old" want to settle into a comfortable and routine existence.[4] The American Cancer Society makes extensive use of age to target audiences (Figure 6-3).

Generation   Many scholars believe that age should not be looked at as simply an issue of maturation but as an indicator of the distinctive norms, values, and goals that one has acquired growing up in a particular generation. Neil Howe and William Strauss have produced a series of extremely complex and thoughtful studies of generational patterns in the U.S. and British populations since 1433.[5] They conclude that there are four basic patterns that always follow each other (what they call "turnings") that have repeated over 24 generations of Anglo-American history. They call these the Awakening, Unraveling, Crisis, and High periods that, depending on the period into which one is born, produce archetypal individuals they call Prophets, Nomads, Heroes, and Artists. It is prescient that these authors predicted that the early twenty-first century would be a Crisis turning—a prophesy borne out in the significant impact that the world has felt in the wake of the September 11, 2001, terrorist attacks. Howe and Strauss state that in the early twenty-first century the four archetypes are distributed across age groups as follows:

Age Group	Archetypes
Elderhood	Prophet
Midlife (boomers)	Nomad
Young Adulthood	Hero
Childhood	Artist

Sex   Sex segmentation appears in many nonprofit sectors, such as male and female colleges, service and social clubs, prisons, and military services. Within a single sex, further segmentation can be applied. The continuing education department of a large university segments the female adult learners into "at homes" and "working outside the homes." The "at homes" are subdivided into homemakers and displaced homemakers. Homemakers are attracted to courses for self-enrichment and improved homemaking skills, whereas displaced homemakers are more interested in career preparation. The "working outside the home" segment breaks into two subsegments, clerical–technical businesswomen and management businesswomen. Each segment has a different set of motivations for attending college, and different programs are appropriate for each. Furthermore, each segment faces certain efficacy problems in attending college. By addressing the specific problems of each segment, the college is in a better position to attract more women to its campus.

Income   Income segmentation is another long-standing practice in the nonprofit sector. In the medical field, the standard health insurance policy pays for semi-private rooms. Most hospitals, however, offer patients the option of a private room at an additional cost in order to cater to the preferences of higher income groups. Some hospitals have designed entire wings and even whole buildings to serve more affluent patients. Hospitals that establish outreach ambulatory centers vary the decor and service to match different income groups.

Race and Ethnicity   Two variables that are often used to segment nonprofit marketing programs are race and ethnicity. There are many reasons for this. One is that different issues impact different racial and ethnic groups. Hispanics and Southeast Asians are particularly concerned with immigration issues, and African-Americans are especially concerned with sickle-cell anemia. However, problems of drugs, poverty, education, and homelessness affect all groups.

Second, racial and ethnic groups differ in their media habits and organizational ties. In the United States, most major minority groups have their own newspapers, magazines, and, in some cases, radio and television programming. These permit very precise targeting of marketing messages.

Finally, the way one appeals to different races and ethnic groups is different. As shown in Figures 6-4 and 6-5, it is often essential to use different models and settings in ads for different audiences. Language and colloquialisms often should differ in communications to each segment as well as the basic appeals. Spokespeople will differ. For example, religious leaders can often be extremely effective in transmitting important social messages in Hispanic and African-American markets where preachers and priests are highly respected leaders.

The vignette at the beginning of this chapter shows how the U.S. Bureau of the Census developed a multiethnic, multicultural strategy to maximize participation in the 2000 census.

Geographical Segmentation   In geographical segmentation, the market is divided into different geographical entities, such as nations, states, regions, counties, cities, zip code areas, or neighborhoods, based on the notion that consumer needs or responses vary geographically. The organization either decides to operate in one or a few parts of the country as a specialist in meeting the needs of those areas or to operate broadly but paying attention to regional variations in needs and preferences. Geographical segmentation is often used as the basis for direct mail or billboard campaigns. More recently, information on geographical location has been combined imaginatively with lifestyle information (discussed below) to yield descriptions of neighborhoods richer than traditional demographics. This lifestyle approach is called *geoclustering*. It is typified by the PRIZM system and is based on the notion that people who live near each other are likely to have similar interests and behaviors.[6] As noted in *Business Week*, PRIZM is founded on the notion that "Birds of a feather flock together."

PRIZM was developed by the Claritas Corporation. Claritas collects a vast amount of information on geographic areas in the United States, including standard demographic data, product and service purchases, and media use. In the latest PRIZM approach, released in 1994, clustering procedures are used to group the census block areas into 62 categories in 15 social groups, which are given colorful names, such as "Shotguns and Pickups" and "Norma Rae-Ville." The 62 categories and the major demographic characteristics associated with them are shown in Exhibit 6-2. A nonprofit marketer can use the information in the PRIZM system to locate new markets or learn what would be appealing to existing markets. For a predetermined fee, the organization can acquire a list of all the zip codes in a selected area with lifestyles that would suggest they are good targets for fundraising or for products or services the organization offers. PRIZM can also help define markets, telling the organization which zip codes are the best prospects for the organization's offering. PRIZM can "tell you more than you probably ever wanted to know about [an] area's typical residents: what they like to eat, which cars they like to drive, whether they prefer scotch or sangria, tuna extender or yogurt, hunting or tennis . . . which magazines they read, which TV shows they watch, whether they are more likely to buy calculators or laxatives, and whether they're single or potential customers for a diaper service."[7]

A version of the PRIZM system has been used by the American Cancer Society for various purposes. Donors to the American Cancer Society are now being coded as to their PRIZM cluster, and these data are used to plot future allocations and strategic emphasis.

FIGURE 6-4 Family of the Future Contraceptive Point-of-Sale Placard for Non-Cairo Markets

Source: Porter Novelli. Reprinted with permission.

FIGURE 6-5 Family of the Future Contraceptive Point-of-Sale Placard
for the Cairo Markets.

Source: Porter Novelli. Reprinted with permission.

	Label	Description	% of Pop.
	EXHIBIT 6-2 PRIZM Cluster Categories (and % of 2000 Population)		
01	Blue Blood Estates	Elite Super-Rich Families	1.35
02	Winner's Circle	Executive Urban Families	2.45
03	Executive Suites	Upscale White-Collar Couples	1.15
04	Pools & Patios	Established Empty Nesters	1.89
05	Kids & Cul-de-Sacs	Upscale Suburban Families	3.48
06	Urban Gold Coast	Elite Urban Singles & Couples	0.37
07	Money & Brains	Sophisticated Townhouse Couples	1.10
08	Young Literati	Upscale Urban Singles & Couples	0.76
09	American Dreams	Established Urban Immigrant Families	1.74
10	Bohemian Mix	Bohemian Singles & Couples	1.02
11	Second City Elite	Upscale Executive Families	1.96
12	Upward Bound	Young Upscale White-Collar Families	1.94
13	Gray Power	Affluent Retirees in Sunbelt Cities	1.67
14	Country Squires	Elite Exurban Families	1.53
15	God's Country	Executive Exurban Families	2.96
16	Big Fish, Small Pond	Small Town Executive Families	1.41
17	Greenbelt Families	Young, Middle-Class Town Families	1.59
18	Young Influentials	Upwardly Mobile Singles & Couples	1.08
19	New Empty Nests	Upscale Suburban Fringe Couple	2.12
20	Boomers & Babies	Young White-Collar Suburban Families	1.13
21	Suburban Sprawl	Young Suburban Townhouse Couples	1.34
22	Blue-Chip Blues	Upscale Blue-Collar Families	2.21
23	Upstarts & Seniors	Middle-Income Empty Nesters	1.12
24	New Beginnings	Young Mobile City Singles	0.92
25	Mobility Blues	Young Blue Collar/Service Families	1.54
26	Gray Collars	Aging Couples in Inner Suburbs	1.95
27	Urban Achievers	Mid-level, White-Collar Urban Couples	1.40
28	Big City Blend	Middle-Income Immigrant Families	1.16
29	Old Yankee Rows	Empty-Nest, Middle-Class Families	1.26
30	Mid-City Mix	African-American Singles & Families	1.21
31	Latino America	Hispanic Middle-Class Families	1.58
32	Middleburg Managers	Mid-Level White-Collar Couples	1.65
33	Boomtown Singles	Middle-Income Young Singles	0.73
34	Starter Families	Young Middle-Class Families	1.59
35	Sunset City Blues	Empty Nests in Aging Industrial Cities	1.65
36	Towns & Gowns	College Town Singles	1.34
37	New Homesteaders	Young Middle-Class Families	1.64
38	Middle America	Midscale Families in Midsize Towns	2.34
39	Red, White, and Blues	Small Town Blue-Collar Families	1.85
40	Military Quarters	GIs & Surrounding Off-Base Families	0.67
41	Big Sky Families	Midscale Couples, Kids & Farmland	1.63
42	New Eco-Topia	Rural White/Blue-Collar/Farm Families	0.87
43	River City, USA	Middle-Class, Rural Families	1.90
44	Shotguns & Pickups	Rural Blue-Collar Workers & Families	2.03
45	Single City Blues	Ethnically Mixed Urban Singles	1.40
46	Hispanic Mix	Urban Hispanic Singles & Families	1.74
47	Inner Cities	Inner City, Solo-Parent Families	1.99
48	Smalltown Downtown	Older Renters & Young Families	1.51
49	Hometown Retired	Low-Income, Older Singles & Families	0.93
50	Family Scramble	Low-Income Hispanic Families	2.28

(continued)

	Label	Description	% of Pop.
EXHIBIT 6-2	**PRIZM Cluster Categories (and % of 2000 Population)** *continued*		
51	Southside City	African-American Service Workers	1.94
52	Golden Ponds	Retirement Town Seniors	1.47
53	Rural Industria	Low-Income, Blue-Collar Families	1.75
54	Norma Rae-Ville	Young Families, Bi-Racial Mill Towns	1.37
55	Mines & Mills	Older Families, Mine & Mill Towns	1.96
56	Agri-Business	Rural Farm-Town & Ranch Families	1.56
57	Grain Belt	Farm Owners & Tenants	2.36
58	Blue Highways	Moderate Blue-Collar/Farm Families	2.02
59	Rustic Elders	Low-Income, Older, Rural Couples	1.77
60	Back Country Folks	Remote Rural/Town Families	2.18
61	Scrub Pine Flats	Older African-American Farm Families	1.58
62	Hard Scrabble	Older Families in Poor Isolated Areas	1.92

Source: Copyright 2001, Claritas Inc.

In addition to PRIZM, there are other syndicated geoclustering approaches available nationally. These include ACORN (A Classification of Residential Neighborhoods) from C.A.C.I. in Arlington, Virginia; ClusterPlus 2000 from Strategic Mapping, Inc.; and MicroVision 50 from Equifax.

Complex General Objective Measures

As nonprofit marketers grow more sophisticated in their use of objective segmentation variables, two steps can be taken. First, marketers can be more precise in operationalizing the measures they use. Income, for example, is a frequently used variable in attempts to segment the charity market—for obvious reasons. Miller, however, found that donation behavior in various zip codes in Oklahoma is often more closely associated with the *source* of income than the amount of income.[8] He found, for example, that the number of households in a zip code area receiving some form of interest income was a better predictor of total donations than was total adjusted gross income. Predictions of the *percentage* who would donate were better with measures of the percentage of households receiving dividends, or of the percentage receiving interest, than with average household income. Clearly, routinely using total income in studies may miss insights that more careful measures might yield.

Complex measures can also be developed by combining objective measures in a single index. Two such combined measures, social class and family life cycle, have been used extensively in marketing.

Social Class   Social classes are relatively homogeneous and enduring divisions in a society that is hierarchically ordered and whose members share similar values, interests, and behavior. Social scientists have distinguished six social classes: (1) upper uppers, (2) lower uppers, (3) upper middles, (4) lower middles, (5) upper lowers, and (6) lower lowers, using objective variables such as income, occupation, education, and type of residence. Social classes show distinct consumption preferences in the nonprofit area. Operas, plays, the ballet, symphonies, and lectures attract the upper classes most heavily. Cultural institutions that wish to overcome their elitist image and attract lower-class audiences to appreciate their art forms will have to develop separate marketing programs and strategies for them.

Family Life Cycle   The family life cycle concept is based on the notion that over one's lifetime there are critical transition points when major changes in consumer behavior (and other behaviors) take place. These transition points are generally defined in terms of objective variables such as marital status, workforce status, and the presence and age of children. Eight stages are typically specified as the model family life cycle pattern:

1. Young single (under 40, not married, no children at home)
2. Newly married (young, married, no children)
3. Full nest I (young, married, youngest child less than 6)
4. Full nest II (young, married, youngest child 6 to 13)
5. Full nest III (older married, dependent children 14 or older)
6. Empty nest I (older married, no children at home, head working)
7. Empty nest II (older married, no children at home, head retired)
8. Solitary survivor (older single, working or retired)

In an analysis of performing arts attendance data, Andreasen found that family life cycle appeared to have an important effect on attendance at six different types of performing arts. The proportions of households attending multiple events were as follows:

Young, single	17.9%
Young, married, no children	10.7%
Infants at home	8.7%
Children 6 or older	12.4%
Older, no children	15.4%
Elderly	8.8%

Obviously, the elderly represent a poor market. Among the remaining lifestyle categories, the relationship is clearly curvilinear: Multiple attendance is high at each end of these life cycle categories but low in the middle. It would appear that the presence of children has a dampening effect on arts involvement. Undoubtedly, this is due to several factors, including reductions in leisure time and discretionary income, changes in household priorities, and increased costs for "going out."[9]

It should be noted that while the family life cycle concept can prove to be a useful segmentation variable, it is not *exhaustive* in that it omits important groups of households. For example, older never-marrieds, and divorced or single parents with spouses absent, are often not included. For some nonprofit social service marketing programs, such households may be very important.

Multivariate Segments   Skilled market analysts can use multivariate statistical procedures to develop customized sets of objective predictors that, when considered together, best segment target markets. These procedures consider all possible segmentation variables together and develop (1) a parsimonious subset that jointly does the best job of predicting the behavior in question, and (2) a measure of the relative contribution of each variable to the final predictions. Beik and Smith, for example, collected survey data on 2,291 households in Allegheny County, Pennsylvania, describing their charitable giving of all kinds. They also assembled objective data on the tracts in which the respondents resided.[10] By analyzing these results with a technique called multiple discriminant analysis, the researchers found they could best discriminate between households making donations of $50 or more to medical charities and all other households with the following equation:

$$Y_1 = .5832\, X_1 + .53414\, X_3 + .31493\, X_4 \qquad (6\text{-}1)$$

where

Y_1 = donate \$50+ to medical charities (1 = yes, 0 = no)
X_1 = proportion of households with income $\geq$ \$15,000
X_3 = proportion of household heads $\geq$ 55 years of age
X_4 = proportion of household heads in managerial, professional, or entrepreneurial positions.[11]

Note three features of this analysis. First, to discriminate donation behavior, the researchers attempted to use objective variables other than age, income, and occupation, such as the proportion of owned homes and the proportion of household heads who were college graduates. These variables, however, turned out not to be useful for segmentation in the multivariate analysis framework. Second, the coefficients in the final equation indicate that income contributed somewhat more as a predictor of medical donations than did age, while both were substantially more important than occupation. Finally, because the predictors are all available in government census data, if one assumed that the Oklahoma results applied elsewhere, one could, in theory, segment every area in the United States as to whether they are likely to be better or poorer prospects for solicitations by medical charities using the three variables and weightings reported in the equation.

Objective Behavior-Specific Measures

For target audience decisions involving little or no cognitive activity, the best predictor of future responsiveness often is past behavior in the exchange category or closely related exchanges. Among the objective specific variables relating to behavior often used in marketing are the following:

Occasion Buyers can be distinguished by the occasions when they engage in the behavior. Commuters using public transportation, for example, include those who are traveling to work, those who are shopping, those who are going to entertainment, and those who are visiting friends. Some public transit companies have launched campaigns to encourage the shopping segment to travel in off-peak hours and have even charged lower fares as an incentive.[12]

User Status Many markets can be segmented into nonusers, ex-users, potential users, first-time users, and regular users of a product or service. This segmentation variable is helpful to antidrug agencies in planning their education programs and campaigns. Much of their effort is directed at identifying potential users of hard drugs and discouraging them through information and persuasion campaigns. They also sponsor rehabilitation programs to help regular users who want to quit their habits. They utilize ex-users in various programs to add credibility to their efforts.

Usage Rate Many markets can be segmented into light-, medium-, and heavy-user groups for the offer (called volume segmentation). Heavy users may constitute only a small percentage of the numerical size of the market but a major percentage of the unit activity. Marketers make a great effort to determine the demographic characteristics and media habits of the heavy users and aim their marketing programs at them. An anti-smoking campaign, for example, might be aimed at the heaviest smokers, a safe driving campaign at those having the most accidents, and a family planning campaign at those likely to have the most children. Unfortunately, the heaviest users are often the most resistant to change. Fertile families are the most resistant to birth control messages, and unsafe drivers are the most resistant to safe driving messages. The agencies must consider whether to use their limited budget to go after a few heavy users who are highly resistant or many light users who are less resistant.

Semenik and Young segmented the audience attending opera into three attendance-level segments—subscribers, frequent attenders, and infrequent attenders—and found significant differences.[13] Subscribers tended to be longtime patrons, attended as a married couple, and considered themselves to be opera fans. Frequent attenders had similar characteristics but were younger and lower in income and often attended with a friend rather than a spouse. Infrequent attenders did not consider themselves opera fans but attended because of a featured star or well-known opera. The identification of segment characteristics enables the development of separate market strategies designed to maximize attendance and loyalty.

Loyalty Status   Loyalty status describes the strength of a consumer's preference for a particular entity. The amount of loyalty can range from zero to absolute. We find consumers who are deeply loyal to a brand (Budweiser beer, Crest toothpaste, Cadillac automobiles), an organization (Harvard University, the Republican Party), a place (New England, Southern California), a person (Dan Rather), and so on. Being loyal means preferring the particular object in spite of increased incentives to switch to something else.

Inferred General Measures

Most of the measures in this category seek to identify consumers in terms of relatively enduring general intrapsychic predispositions that presumably would affect a range of behavior categories. The most widely used approaches are those that segment consumers by personality, by values, and by lifestyle.

Personality   It has long been believed that variations in consumer personality would be reflected in their marketplace behavior. However, in the main, general personality traits have not been useful in past studies, in part because they are very difficult to measure (i.e., they are highly subjective and unreliable across studies) and therefore very hard to link to specific marketplace actions. In contrast, past studies have focused on relatively trivial behavior, such as beer preferences and car choices. It may be that in the future personality measures may finally prove to be helpful in segmenting markets for the more highly involving exchanges that are of interest to nonprofit marketers.

Values   A number of disciplines argue that individuals organize and evaluate their behavioral choices in terms of the values they hold. The best-known scholar in this area, Milton Rokeach, distinguishes between *instrumental values* and *terminal values*.[14] Instrumental values guide our ongoing behavior to achieve certain end states. Terminal values guide our choices among those end states. Research has shown that values of both types are closely related to other segmentation variables such as age, family structure and life cycle, race and ethnicity, and geographical location. They are also closely related to attitudes and predispositions, product choices (e.g., automobiles), allocations of time between work and leisure, and the use of various media.

Values are much less permanent than personality traits. Individuals slowly change some of the values they use to guide their lives as they age. Values can also be influenced by life status changes. For example, rural people moving to a competitive big city may come to value prudence over openness in their interpersonal relations. Values also change as societies change. Americans in the twenty-first century approve of many conservative programs (e.g., privatization of prisons) that would have been considered highly reactionary 25 years earlier.

How does a manager develop information on a target segment's values? One approach is to use Rokeach's value survey and then link it to specific attitudes, preferences, or behaviors of the target market. An alternative approach works backward from specific choices and preferences (e.g., the focal issues in a campaign) to discern fundamental values that drive these choices and preferences. The technique, called *laddering,* begins with choices and preferences and then asks consumers to reveal reasons for those preferences (e.g., to secure specific benefits or avoid certain costs). The interviewer then proceeds further backward to learn why these benefits and costs are important, and then why those reasons are important, and so on. One finally "moves up the ladder" to the basic values that characterize the particular customer and that presumably guide a great many choices and behaviors. These fundamental values can then be used to form segments holding similar values.[15]

Lifestyles Dissatisfaction with personality and value-based approaches has led to the very rapid growth of lifestyle research in the last 25 years. If segmentation by personality is based on the notion that "We do what we do because of the kind of people we are," then lifestyle segmentation is based on the notion that "We do what we do because it fits into the kind of life we are living or want to live." A further distinction is that whereas personality is seen to be a very enduring, perhaps lifelong characteristic, lifestyle is seen as more transient, something that can change even from one year to the next.

There are several different approaches to identifying lifestyle groups in the population. Most, however, are based on measures of consumers' *activities, interests, and opinions* (AIOs). When lifestyle measures are combined with demographic measurements, they are often called *psychographics.*

Many lifestyle approaches are customized for specific research needs. For example, Andreasen and Belk used information on the leisure-time activities of respondents in four Southern cities to group potential attenders at symphonies and the theater in six broad categories.[16] The six groups were labeled Passive Homebodies, Active Sports Enthusiasts, Inner-Directed Self-Sufficients, Active Homebodies, Culture Patrons, and Social Actives. The researchers found that membership in the Culture Patron lifestyle group was a very good predictor of attendance at the theater or symphony, presumably because the aesthetic benefits of these performances fit their lifestyles. In contrast, membership in the Socially Active group predicted symphony attendance only, suggesting that it is the symphony performance *event* that meets the lifestyle needs of this group. Lifestyle was found to be a better explanatory variable than any of the traditional socioeconomic characteristics, such as income and education, that are usually used to explain performing arts attendance. Andreasen and Belk suggest that these socioeconomic indicators may simply be masking what are really the more profound explanations—lifestyle compatibility.

Lifestyle information is valuable in many ways. One advantage is that it can give communications specialists rich portraits of their various target market segments.

Inferred Behavior-Specific Measures

Segmenting consumers subjectively around specific behaviors, of course, usually requires original field data. Rarely are such data available from secondary sources. Thus, nonprofit managers are often reluctant to use them. In cases where the behavior at issue is highly involving, a very useful framework for such research is the Extended Fishbein Attitude Model described in detail in Chapter 4. Algebraically, this model was as follows:

$$\text{Behavior} = BI_j = (\sum_{i=1}^{n} b_{ij} a_i) W_1 + \sum_{k=1}^{m} NB_{kj} \cdot MC_k) W_2 \qquad (6\text{-}2)$$

The model contains a wide array of specific subjective measures that can be used to segment markets. Referring to the algebraic notations, these measures and their segmentation possibilities include:

1. j: the exchange alternatives in the consideration set (e.g., segmenting those consumers that include your alternative in their set separately from those who do not).
2. i: the criteria used to evaluate the alternatives (e.g., segmenting those who *consider* consequences you offer from those who don't).
3. a_i: the pattern of weightings applied to the criteria (e.g., segmenting those who give high weight to the set of consequences at which you excel from those who give them low weight).
4. b_{ij}: beliefs about consequences of taking particular action alternatives (e.g., segmenting those who accurately see the consequences of choosing your alternative from those who have inaccurate perceptions or segmenting those who have more favorable beliefs about a competitive alternative than about yours from those for whom the reverse is true).
5. k: the significant others whose views about the behavior might influence behavioral intentions (e.g., segmenting those who consider family only from those who consider peers only).
6. MC_k: the pattern of motivations to conform to the views of these significant others (e.g., segmenting those who say they are heavily influenced by parents from those who are only "somewhat" influenced).
7. NB_{kj}: perceptions of the behavioral expectations of specific significant others (e.g., segmenting those whose significant others are generally favorably disposed toward your alternative from those whose significant others are negative).
8. W_1/W_2: the relative weight of the person's own attitude versus the perceived views of significant others in affecting behavioral intentions (e.g., segmenting those who are inner directed from those who are other directed).

Stages of Change As noted in Chapter 4, an extremely powerful approach to segmenting markets in high-involvement situations is where they are in the change process. As described there, the marketer's challenge is significantly different if an audience member is in Precontemplation, Early or Late Contemplation, Preparation/Action, or Maintenance. Prochaska and his colleagues have used this form of segmentation to successfully influence target audiences to quit smoking, use condoms, lose weight, and exercise.[17]

Benefit Segmentation Research suggests that some consumers look for one dominant benefit from the offering, and others seek a particular *benefit bundle*.[18] In one application, Bonaguro and Miaoulis developed eight benefit segments for a multiservice family planning agency. These segments are outlined in Table 6-1.

TABLE 6-1 Benefit Segments for a Family Planning Agency	
Immediate solutions to a problem (pregnancy, breast lump, etc.), shoulder to lean on	1. Firefighters
Relief from feeling of desperation, financial stability, marital harmony	2. Desperates
Security about good health, relief from worry	3. Worriers
Conception, birth, children	4. Infertiles
Freedom of choice, control, financial stability, marital harmony	5. Married Rationals
Freedom of choice, financial stability	6. Married—No Children
Pregnancy prevention, financial stability, avoid social stigma	7. Married—With Children
Pregnancy prevention to avoid social stigma, retain independence, financial stability	8. Singles—Without Children

Source: John A. Bonaguro and George Miaoulis, "Marketing: A Tool for Health Education Planning," *Health Education,* January–February 1983, p. 9.

The eight segments were then combined into more manageable subsets. The Firefighters and Desperates were joined into a group that had in common a sense of urgency about health needs. They only seek information and take action in an emergency, at which point they are likely to be agitated, confused, and perhaps irrational. It was decided to ignore the Worriers and Infertile benefit segments because of the agency's limited budget and to group the four remaining original segments as Rationals. This combined group was likely to seek information on their own as a means of improving their families' health and future prospects. Print media, lectures, pamphlets, and posters, all with longer messages, were emphasized within the strategy destined for this group under the theme: "A brighter future—plan it now." Note that in this example, the marketer segmented the market by benefits and then decided to concentrate on only those segments where the organization could have the best impact for its limited resources.

Sacrifice Segmentation In Chapter 4, we noted that consumers are likely to undertake exchanges if the benefits outweigh the costs. We further noted that in many cases there is wide appreciation of the *benefits* of a particular action, while it is the *costs* that are the major inhibitors to action. In Chapter 4, we noted that Bagozzi, in his study of blood donors, found little difference among consumers in the perceived positive consequences that would follow from their behavior. However, Bagozzi found considerable variation in the perceptions of *negative* consequences and learned that they were good predictors of behavioral intentions. These results give rise to the speculation that some markets could be usefully segmented in terms of the relative weight individuals attach to the various *barriers* to action rather than to the benefits. Thus, in the blood donation case, consumers could be subdivided into those who are highly sensitive to physiological risks (infections, AIDS, physical pain); social risks (not being "brave" in the eyes of others); and psychological fears (fears of needles, blood, and "hospitals").[19]

TARGET MARKETING

Market segmentation reveals the market segmentation opportunities facing the organization. The organization must next decide how to target these segments. There are four broad strategic choices:

1. *Undifferentiated (mass) marketing.* The organization can decide to go after the whole market with one offer and marketing mix, trying to attract as many consumers as possible (this is another name for mass marketing).
2. *Differentiated marketing.* The organization can decide to go after several market segments, developing an effective offer and marketing mix for each.
3. *Concentrated marketing.* The organization can decide to go after one market segment and develop the ideal offer and marketing mix.
4. *Mass Customization.* This the case where a marketer seeks to reach almost everyone in the market but through some form of information exchange is able to customize the offering to the individual. Dell Computers and Levi Jeans both practice this approach.

The logic and merits of each of these strategies follows.

Undifferentiated Marketing

In undifferentiated—or mass—marketing,[20] the organization chooses not to recognize the different market segments making up the market. It treats the audience as an aggregate, focusing on what is common in the needs of consumers rather than on what is different. It tries to design an offer and a marketing program that appeals to the broadest number of buyers. It would be exemplified by a church that runs only one religious service for everyone, a politician who gives the same speech to everyone, and a museum that highlights the same exhibits to everyone.

Undifferentiated marketing is typically defended on the grounds of cost economies. It is "the marketing counterpart to standardization and mass production in manufacturing."[21] Production costs, research costs, media costs, and training costs are all kept low through promoting only one offering. The lower cost, however, is often accompanied by reduced target audience responsiveness through failure of the organization to meet individually varying needs. In many health care and environmental areas, this can border on the tragic.

Differentiated Marketing

Under differentiated marketing, an organization decides to operate in multiple segments of the market but designs separate offerings or marketing programs for each. There are two basic options here. One involves creating fundamentally different offerings for each chosen segment. For example, an art museum could develop a children's wing as a differentiated addition to its regular collection or put on "singles nights" for unattached urban workers who want to avoid the "bar scene." The alternative option, as we shall suggest below, is to take an existing offering and position it differently to different segments. For example, the art museum could show how its basic art collection meets the needs of educators eager to teach their students about the history of various cultures. At the same time, it could position the collection to seniors in the general public who might be interested in a self-taught art-appreciation experience. Similarly, a hospital could take its basic set of services and emphasize (1) the "tender loving care" of its nurses to an elderly market, (2) the national reputations of its leading physicians to a young professional market, and (3) the cost efficiency of its entire operation to business HR officers.

While the net effect of differentiated marketing is to create greater responsiveness, it can lead to higher costs of doing business since the organization has to spend more in offer management, marketing research, communication materials, advertising, and staff training

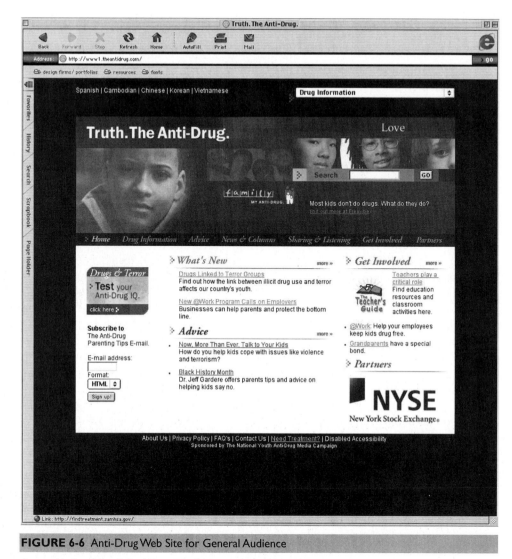

FIGURE 6-6 Anti-Drug Web Site for General Audience

Source: National Youth Anti-Drug Media Campaign, White House Office of National Drug Control Policy. Reproduced by permission.

for the given segments. However, the other principal advantage of a differentiated strategy is that it allows the marketing manager to vary the amount of resources applied to each of the segments—*including zero!* Thus, the manager can trade off the higher costs of differentiation by reducing the number of segments treated. The net effect can often be achieving significantly higher returns for a given budget or a lower budget for given returns.

A good example of a differentiated strategy is found in the Office of the National Drug Control Policy campaign for "the Anti-Drug." They and one of the agencies, Fleishman Hillard, recognized that the Web is an important vehicle for reaching various market segments but that the "look and feel" of each Web site should be appropriate to each segment. Thus, Figure 6-6 shows the main home page, primarily for

FIGURE 6-7 Summit High Episode 3

Source: National Youth Anti-Drug Media Campaign, White House Office of National Drug Control Policy. Reproduced by permission.

parents, which is available in English, Spanish, Chinese, Cambodian, Korean, and Vietnamese. The page features a good deal of text and warm photos of kids. In contrast, the Web site aimed at their children (Figure 6-7) not only has an entirely different address (Freevibe.com), but also a much busier, cooler look and much more

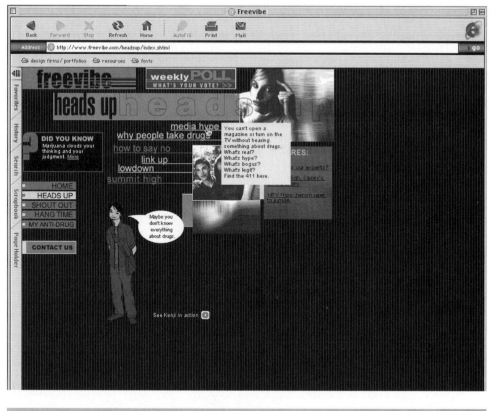

FIGURE 6-8 Freevibe Heads Up

Source: National Youth Anti-Drug Media Campaign, White House Office of National Drug Control Policy. Reproduced by permission.

potential for interaction on the part of visitors (see Figure 6-8). Finally, the page aimed at teachers (Figure 6-9) is much more prosaic and matter-of-fact with no emotional photos and more text.

Concentrated Marketing

Concentrated marketing occurs when an organization decides to divide the market into meaningful segments and devote its major marketing effort only to one or two segments. This is often referred to as "*niche marketing.*" Instead of spreading itself thin in many parts of the market, it concentrates on serving a particular market segment very well. Through concentrated marketing, the organization usually achieves a strong following and standing in a particular market segment. It can afford to develop greater knowledge of the market segment's needs and behavior and it can achieve operating economies through specialization in production, distribution, and promotion. This type of marketing is done, for example, by a private museum that decides to concentrate only on African art; an environmental group that concentrates only on the problem of noise pollution; or a private foundation that awards grants only to transportation researchers.

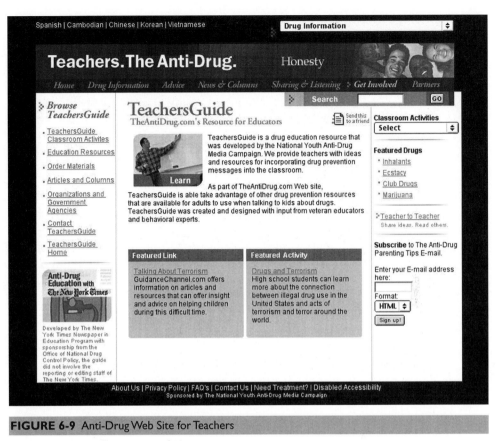

FIGURE 6-9 Anti-Drug Web Site for Teachers

Source: National Youth Anti-Drug Media Campaign, White House Office of National Drug Control Policy. Reproduced by permission.

Concentrated marketing does involve higher-than-normal risk, in that the market may suddenly decline or disappear. The National Foundation for Infantile Paralysis almost folded when the Salk vaccine was developed. Fortunately, the National Foundation was able to turn its huge fundraising apparatus over to another medical cause.

Mass Customization

Technology—in particular the Internet—has allowed many marketers to adopt their strategies to individuals who seek out their offerings. Thus, behavior change programs, such as smoking clinics, can promise to "tailor a program to your individual needs and lifestyles," whereas a marketer of a nicotine patch must use either a mass or differentiated approach. A significant benefit of this approach—besides its unique ability to respond to customers' data about themselves—is that it allows the "production" of the offering only "on demand." The latter obviously can produce significant scheduling and cost savings.[22]

Choosing Among Market Segmentation Strategies

The actual choice of a marketing strategy depends on specific factors facing the organization. If the organization has *limited resources,* it will probably choose concentrated marketing because it does not have enough resources to relate to the whole market and/or to tailor special services for each segment. If the market is fairly *homogeneous* in its needs and desires, the organization will probably choose undifferentiated marketing because little would be gained by differentiated offerings. If the organization aspires to be a leader in several segments of the market, it will choose differentiated marketing. If *competitors* have already established dominance in all but a few segments of the market, the organization might try to concentrate its marketing in one of the remaining segments. Many organizations start out with a strategy of undifferentiated or concentrated marketing and, if they are successful, evolve into a strategy of differentiated marketing. Some are able to evolve to mass customization.

If the organization elects to use a concentrated or differentiated strategy, it has to evaluate the best segment(s) to serve. Each should be evaluated in terms of the following:

- Its relative attractiveness
- The requirements for success within it
- The organization's strengths and weaknesses in competing effectively

The organization should focus on market segments that have intrinsic attractiveness and that it has a differential advantage in serving. A detailed example of a step-by-step approach for allocating resources across a hypothetical AIDS program is outlined in Andreasen's 1995 book, *Marketing Social Change.*

POSITIONING

Nonprofit organizations are in competition. Many nonprofit managers would like to believe otherwise or think it is "not nice to compete," but it is a reality. Nonprofit marketing objectives *always* involve influencing the behavior of target consumers, and consumers *always* have something else they can do. Potential donors can give money to a different charity, give their *time* to the charity instead of money, or not give at all. High schoolers can attend a different university or not go to college at all. Mothers in Zimbabwe can feed oral rehydration solution to their children when they have diarrhea or they can apply herbal potions or they can do nothing at all.

In each case, there are alternatives *in the mind* of the target consumer, and therefore it is in the mind where the marketer must compete.[23] Thus, at the beginning of any strategic planning cycle, it is important to understand how target audience members view the offering. In an important sense, the marketer needs to know where the marketer's offering "resides" in the target audience's mind and what associations the audience has with it. This set of perceptions is collectively referred to as the offering's *position.* For customers at the Precontemplation Stage, the marketer's challenge is to have *any* position at all—the audience here is simply not thinking about the option.

For audiences at the Contemplation Stage and beyond, marketers must position their offerings as a superior value to those of their competition—which may simply be inaction or the status quo.

Frequently research will tell marketers that they need to *reposition* themselves and/or their offerings.[24] In many cases, repositioning first requires that the organization itself *become* different. In other cases, the reality is fine—it is the market's perception that is the problem. Many nonprofit service organizations fail to succeed at fundraising because they are not seen as different from their competitors. How do the following differ?

- The Reilly Smith Women's Center
- The Caring Woman
- Abused Wives Recovery Program
- Alice Torrance Women's Refuge
- Western Memorial Hospital's Women-Together Program

They all seem to have something vaguely to do with women. But why should someone become involved with—or give money to—one over another? What services do they offer? How are they staffed (do they need volunteers)? How are they funded (do they need contributions)? Whom do they serve? Who works there? Who supports them? Are they licensed? And so on. If any one of these organizations is to be successful in getting clients and getting volunteer and financial support, it must differentiate itself in the eyes of the target audience. Similarly, in the developing world, an organization seeking to get mothers to use oral rehydration therapy must distinguish this approach to child survival from other means of achieving the target audience's ends and show that it provides superior value in terms of the target audience's own needs and wants.

It is also frequently the case that, as noted in earlier sections, the marketer must position itself differently for different segments. Oral rehydration therapy may be *positioned* as a "modern" approach to urban women, as a way to please mothers-in-law to new wives, and as a means of quick recovery for village mothers with many other children and multiple household duties.

Measuring the Present Position

The starting point for any positioning strategy is to understand how the organization or the proposed behavior is perceived at the present time in comparison with its major competitors. This involves measurement of what is often called "perception." Perception is a term that became popular in the 1950s and has been used to describe products (Ford, Mustang, Macintosh Computer), institutions (Harvard, McDonald's, the United Way, IBM), individuals (Madonna, Newt Gingrich), and places (San Francisco, Thailand, Brooklyn).[25] However, in all of these cases, the term is used to apply to an *object.*

Certainly, target audiences have perceptions of objects, and very often those perceptions can influence their behavior. The perception they hold of "The Caring Woman," an organization that helps abused women, will affect whether they volunteer, donate, or even go there if they are a victim. But remember, as we emphasize throughout the chapters in this book, the *perception of objects* should not be our ultimate concern. Our real interest is not what people think about objects but what they think about the behaviors we are seeking to induce (e.g., donating, volunteering, or using an organization's services).

As we noted in Chapter 4, what we really need to know is information about the BCOS factors—what the target audience believes about the Benefits and Costs of the action or actions we are promoting, beliefs about what Others who are important to them think about the behavior(s), and beliefs about whether they think they can do the behavior(s)—their sense of Self-efficacy.

It is not unusual for target audiences to have serious misperceptions of the proposed behaviors. These misperceptions may be based on erroneous information or from stereotypes. A stereotype suggests a widely held perception that is highly distorted and simplistic and that implies a favorable or unfavorable attitude toward the object or behavior (e.g., what will happen if you join a Boys & Girls Club that is heavily populated with African Americans). If a positioning is based on a stereotype, the marketer's challenge will be especially difficult (because logic or information usually does not help much). Such stereotypes are likely to keep target audience members in the Precontemplation Stage for a very long time.

Finally, we should note that a person's perception of an object or behavior does not incorporate his or her feelings toward it. Feelings may be driven by perceptions but they are different. One can believe that joining a YMCA will help one lose weight, but one may feel negatively about the atmosphere when one drops by, or "uncomfortable" about the kind of participants one finds there. Often feelings are more determinative than perceptions, especially when the behavior involves other human beings.[26]

Measuring the Positioning of Behaviors

Many methods have been proposed for measuring the perceptions of organizations and behaviors. Many of these were developed in the private sector and focus on objects. They ask for our perception of Ford cars, Microsoft software, or Marriott hotels. In many cases, they are found in the political realm where we regularly read polling data on how the president or Congress is doing. Fortunately, most of the approaches can be adapted to studying the perception of behaviors.

We have already described in Chapter 4 how one can measure beliefs about the likelihood of experiencing certain benefits and costs surrounding behaviors and what significant reference groups think of those behaviors. These data can be inputs into one of many software packages that can yield sophisticated portraits of an organization's behavioral offering and those of its prime competitors.

One approach to measuring these perceptions is called the *semantic differential.*

Semantic Differential   The semantic differential[27] is based on bipolar adjectives and involves the following steps:

1.   *Develop a set of relevant dimensions.* The researcher first asks people to identify the dimensions they would use in thinking about the behavior. People could be asked: "What things do you think of when you consider checking into a hospital for surgery?" If someone suggests "quality of medical care," this would be turned into a bipolar adjective scale—say, "inferior medical care" at one end and "superior medical care" at the other. The scale could be rendered as a five- or seven-point scale. A set of relevant dimensions for checking into one of three hospitals is shown in Figure 6-10.

2.   *Reduce the set of relevant dimensions.* The number of dimensions should be kept small to avoid respondent fatigue in having to rate n behaviors on m scales. The typical

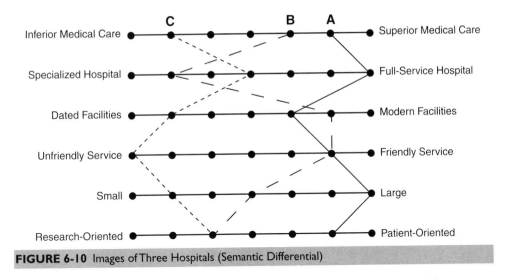

FIGURE 6-10 Images of Three Hospitals (Semantic Differential)

procedure is for the researcher to conduct a pilot study and then employ a technique called *factor analysis* to remove redundant scales that fail to add much information.

3. *Administer the instrument to a sample of respondents in the Contemplation Stage.* The respondents are asked to rate one behavior at a time. The bipolar adjectives should be arranged so as not to load all of the poor adjectives on one side.

4. *Average the results.* Figure 6-10 shows the results of averaging the respondents' pictures of going to Hospitals A, B, and C. Each hospital's perception with respect to the behavior is represented by a vertical "line of means" that summarizes how the average respondent sees going to that institution. Thus, Hospital A is seen as a large, modern, friendly, and superior hospital. Hospital C, however, is seen as a small, dated, impersonal, and inferior hospital.

5. *Check on the perception variance.* The variance of an perception can yield very valuable information. Since each perception profile portrays a series of mean values, it does not reveal how variable the perception actually is. If there were 100 respondents, did they all see going to Hospital B, for example, exactly as shown, or was there considerable variation? In the first case, we would say that the perception is highly *specific* and well-defined, and in the second case that the perception is highly *diffused* or *fuzzy*. The organization will want to analyze whether a highly variable perception is really the result of different subgroups rating the organization's offering differently but each with a highly specific perception or whether the offering is very ill-defined.

Positioning Alternatives

Once the organization analyzes the perceptions that target audiences hold about a specific behavior or perhaps about the organization itself as well as perceptions of its major alternatives, the next step is developing a positioning strategy. To repeat: effective positioning involves (1) understanding your present position; (2) understanding the position of your principal competitors; (3) deciding on whether and how to differentiate your offerings from those of competitors; and (4) making this positioning known to others. Al Reis and Jack Trout, in their book *Positioning: The Battle for Your Mind,*[28] argue that differentiation is largely a creative exercise carried out to achieve one of three strategies:

1. *Building upon your present strengths.* Avis capitalized creatively on what would appear to be a weak second-place status with its "We Try Harder" positioning. In a similar manner, a hospital with only limited facilities could emphasize its concern with delivering great care in a concentrated number of very important practice areas.

2. *Searching for a niche.* If every hospital in an area understaffs its emergency room and uses interns and residents to treat most patients there, an innovative hospital could position itself as having an emergency room that treats everyone quickly and personally, and with the highest-quality medical staff.

3. *Repositioning the competition.* Wendy's hamburger chain challenged the opposition by asking "Where's the beef?" A hospital that emphasizes high-touch personal treatment could develop a positioning strategy that portrays competitors as high-tech sterile environments treating patients as serial numbers.

If the organization decides that it does not like its present position, it needs to decide whether the problem is a matter of reality or of the perception of reality. If it is the former, then it must make fundamental changes before broadcasting to the world its new position. If it is a perception problem, then much more can be done with creative communications. Indeed, the entire nonprofit sector has something of a perception problem. As our example previously noted, there are many look-alike organizations and campaigns. In addition, there is increased blurring between the sectors. For example, many people believe that Newman's Own is a charitable organization; it is not, although the company gives all of its profits to charity (see Figure 6-11). Similarly, many "social responsibility" mutual funds are not charitable operations but potential moneymaking ventures in the private sector. The former director of the Internal Revenue Service's Exempt Organizations Division, Mark Owens, recently noted, "There is a danger of the charities starting to lose their special place and sense of purpose and becoming just part of the way business is done." He feels that the shift of many nonprofits toward generating more revenue from the marketing of products and services has contributed to this blurring of sector positions.[29]

BRANDING

Many organizations see their positioning challenge to be one of building or differentiating their brand or brands. A brand like the American Cancer Society or the "Truth" teen anti-smoking campaign can become valuable shorthand for a wide range of characteristics and outcomes. A brand can imply certain information (the American Red Cross is there in disasters). It can convey certain emotions (the YMCA). It can even have its own personality (the Salvation Army).

However, developing, nourishing, and maintaining a brand is a challenging task. For many organizations that place great emphasis on their brand, it must be a continu-

FIGURE 6-11 Newman's Own

Source: Newman's Own. Reproduced with permission.

ing focus. For example, the Make-a-Wish Foundation is well-known and has a name that "says it all." Yet, in 1998–1999 it reconsidered its identity and brand positioning and launched a new brand strategy with PSAs, a new logo, and a revised Web site. Similar efforts were recently undertaken by Goodwill Industries.[30] Another example is Volunteers of America (VOA). The VOA is a very large organization with over 10,000 full-time professional staff and 40,000 volunteers reporting total income of just under half a billion dollars in 1999. Yet, although it offers 300 different services and is one of the largest providers of affordable housing to the poor, few people know about it and what it stands for. As a consequence, VOA also undertook a branding campaign in 2000.

This is not to say that everyone in the nonprofit sector thinks that an emphasis on organizational branding and positioning is a good idea. In an editorial commentary in the June 14, 2001, edition of *The Chronicle of Philanthropy,* Vikki Spruill, Executive Director of SeaWeb, said the approach is misdirected:

> [T]he nonprofit world—especially advocacy groups working in fields such as health, education, and the environment—can ill afford to wage corporate-style branding battles. Instead of helping charitable groups work together to build a broad base of support from donors, volunteers and activists, branding becomes a barrier. It fosters unhealthy competition among nonprofit groups for visibility, promotes the hoarding of proprietary information, and leaves donors confused about how their support is making a difference.[31]

Spruill goes on to argue that branding, per se, is acceptable but it ought to be applied to causes, not individual organizations. Her position was countered by Kurt Aschermann, Senior Vice-President at the Boys & Girls Clubs of America. Aschermann's response is reported in Exhibit 6-3.

There is now very strong pressure to use branding and positioning concepts in a wide range of settings. Government agencies have developed branding programs, including the Bureau of the Census and the Centers for Disease Control and Prevention.[32] Universities are adopting the approach. Rensselaer Polytechnic Institute in Troy, New York, hired Media Logic, Inc. and launched a branding campaign in 1999 to raise the university's stature around a tagline—"Why not change the world?"[33] The American Legacy Foundation decided to brand its teen anti-smoking campaign as "Truth" (www.thetruth.com).

Perhaps the most unusual branding initiative emerged when U.S. Secretary of State Colin Powell said that he wanted to "brand the State Department."

> I am going to bring people into the public diplomacy function of the department who are going to change from just selling us in an old [U.S. Information Agency] way to really branding foreign policy. [His goal is] branding the department, marketing the department, marketing American values to the world, and not just putting out pamphlets."[34]

To further this agenda, Secretary Powell appointed Charlotte Beers, former chair of the J. Walter Thompson advertising agency, to the position of Assistant Secretary for Public Diplomacy. Ms. Beers has the credentials to bring first-rate private sector marketing concepts to her new "client." Her job has been made much more difficult since September 11, 2001.

Developing a Branding Strategy

Susan Kirby, formerly at the Centers for Disease Control and Prevention, offers her thoughts on how to undertake a branding strategy in Exhibit 6-4. As Susan Kirby suggests, there are a number of stages in building a brand or repositioning it. In many ways, the early steps and the general thinking parallel those previously suggested for positioning.[35]

EXHIBIT 6-3

KURT ASCHERMANN, SENIOR VICE-PRESIDENT FOR MARKETING AND COMMUNICATIONS OF THE BOYS & GIRLS CLUBS OF AMERICA, ON THE VALUE OF NONPROFIT BRANDING

Vikki Spruill's column . . . did a wonderful job explaining exactly why her premise is flawed. Ms. Spruill's comments, surprising as they may be coming from a former public-relations executive, nevertheless are prominent in nonprofit circles.

The idea that a nonprofit would perform like a for-profit in order to differentiate itself (create its own unique selling or service proposition, if you will) seems dangerous to Ms. Spruill because, she says, it will cause competition and perhaps result in questionable practices by nonprofit leaders. Yet in the end she asks nonprofits to consider three important questions that are at the heart of branding: Where does the soul of the organization lie? What was the impetus behind its formation? What need did it fill then, and does that need still exist?

Sorry, Ms. Spruill, you just asked the three fundamental questions of branding. You are asking the nonprofit to simply determine what makes it unique, why it exists, and why someone should support it—all questions that need to be asked in order to create a brand, protect a brand, and enhance a brand's position in the marketplace.

In the for-profit world the questions might be, Why should this company exist? Why was the company formed? And why would the consumer buy the product the company makes or service it offers?

The nonprofit-branding naysayers, in my experience, don't understand marketing or branding and see it as some kind of violation of charitable purity. In reality it is an exercise designed to help the nonprofit serve its constituents better by establishing its uniqueness in a very cluttered nonprofit world.

A decade ago Boys & Girls Clubs of America was a $180-million organization, with about 1,000 Clubs nationwide. In the early 90's, with the help of some very savvy board members who were CEO's of Fortune 500 companies, we created and implemented a very aggressive brand strategy.

The strategy required us first to determine who and what we were, second to focus messaging on a limited number of issues that describe what we do for kids, and third to seek corporate, government, and private partners to support our strategy and support our public-relations and information campaign on that strategy.

Result: In 2001 our combined budgets are more than $1 billion, and we are going to open our 3,000th Club this year. In a little more than 10 years we have increased our budgets by more than $800 million and we have opened over 2,000 new Clubs. In the past few years we have opened a new Boys & Girls Club every other day. Two years ago we opened 337 Clubs in one calendar year.

Now, there is no way I will say the brand strategy was single-handedly responsible for this unbelievable growth. But I sure can tell you the American donor knows who we are, what we stand for, and what we do to serve American children well. In short, they know what this brand stands for, and they're "buying."

Source: The Chronicle of Philanthropy, July 26, 2001. Reproduced with permission.

EXHIBIT 6-4

SUSAN D. KIRBY, FORMERLY OF THE CENTERS FOR DISEASE CONTROL AND PREVENTION AND NOW A PRIVATE CONSULTANT ON HOW STRATEGIC IDENTITY AND BRANDING CAN IMPACT SOCIAL ORGANIZATIONS AND PROGRAMS

If your social/public organization or program has competitors and a limited funding stream, strategic identity and branding can help ensure your programs/products are created to provide relevant value to your target audiences and that target audiences view those programs or your organization as valuable and different from competitors. Identity and branding focus on perceived differentiation and value, which can contribute to long term success for social programs and the organizations that offer them in many ways. Three of these expected outcomes are discussed below.

In a competitive arena, strategic identity and branding can significantly help organizations achieve increased program awareness, utilization and satisfaction (e.g., market share), improve funding and donations, and ultimately improved social welfare through the following outcomes, which Aaker (1991)35 describes more fully for the private sector:

1) Brand Awareness
2) Brand Mindshare and
3) Brand Loyalty

Brand Awareness and Mindshare

In today's crowded communications environment, it is critical for social organizations and programs to be visible and to stand out from others. If your program is not recognized or recalled as part of your organization's portfolio of programs, organizations can lose valuable stakeholder and public support for these programs, users may be less likely to use the programs if they are unaware of the program or its link to credible organizations, and partners may not initiate or consider partnerships if they are unaware of the programs and services you offer. Brand awareness is most often measured by asking respondents which brands they recall from a list of names (Aaker, 1991). Mindshare is measured by asking respondents to name brands in a specific category (e.g., name computer chip brands), which usually signifies a rank ordering of the brands in the market category. Mindshare is important because it usually means the "top-of-mind" brands are the ones in the users' consideration set when they are contemplating a purchase, stock purchase, or co-branding opportunity. For social brands it can mean that your organization (American Red Cross) or one of your programs (Blood Donations) is at least recognized from a list of possible competitors or at best is the "top-of-mind" choice when a donor is contemplating donations, a volunteer is thinking about volunteering, or when your programs' audiences' need services, programs, or products.

Brand Loyalty

Brand loyalty basically means repeat customers, even in the face of new competition, price increases, product scandals (e.g., the Tylenol scare), or even product changes. Brand loyalty is most often created by tapping into either self-expressive or relational aspects of an identity. Imagine Harley-Davidson without its self-expressive traits. Harley owners are diehard owners, not so much because of functional features of the

Harley motorcycles, but because owning a Harley says something about them as people. Just as owning a Harley says something about the motorcycle enthusiast, contributing to the American Cancer Society or participating in breast cancer programs can say something personal about the participants, something they want to express about themselves. Think of how many people are proud to wear pink ribbons, if only to signify to others that they support breast cancer research and prevention. When the identity or branding of a program or organization taps into our self-expressive desires, it creates a stronger link to us and begins to create a relationship. This level of brand loyalty should also be highly desired in the social sector because, just like the private sector, we have enormous start-up costs to convert newcomers to long time users of a program or organizational brand. When we develop self-expressive and relationship-based benefits, we reduce those start-up costs by building brand loyalty.

1. Know your brand's present position and that of your competitors' brands. This often involves first figuring out who your competitors actually are. With what does a teen anti-smoking campaign compete? With whom does the Centers for Disease Control and Prevention compete? In each case, a key element is determining the principal behavior or set of behaviors around which the competition will take place. This also involves determining your target audience or audiences because it is these individuals you must contact in order to understand how your brand is perceived with those who count.

2. Analyze what you have learned and decide where you want to go. This requires understanding the dimensions on which brands are evaluated, which ones are most important to the target audiences, and what their ideal positioning for any alternative would be. There will be several clusters of audience preferences, and the marketer needs to decide which group or groups are most important, then how to reposition to be most appealing to them. (Sometimes the decision will be to develop a family of brands, each aimed at a different segment.) This is the kind of problem that has been faced by older nonprofits where perceptions about it are out of date. Recently, the Boy Scouts has been undertaking a significant repositioning as shown in Figure 6-12.

3. Determine how to get to the new branding position. As noted above, this means determining if you have a reality problem, a perception problem, or some combination. Usually it is the latter.

4. Put your house in order and craft the necessary creative communications. Getting consensus in a nonprofit organization around branding and positioning may take a very long time because it will raise issues about the organization's mission and basic strategies. This task should never be neglected because staff or various centers or divisions can easily undermine the best branding initiative. Staff must also be the ones to carry out the repositioning. For example, if a hospital or hotline is seen as uninformed and vaguely unfriendly, it may take significant changes in personnel and extensive training before a marketer can tout a brand as offering "the most friendly and knowledgeable health care for [the target audience]." Beware thinking that a "communications fix" will solve the branding problem!

5. Make sure there is an integrated strategy. A brand is something that conveys meaning and emotion about your organization and its offerings in a great many manifestations.

FIGURE 6-12 Life's an Adventure

Source: Boy Scouts of America. Reproduced with permission.

Everyone who works on anything related to the brand and every physical or electronic element involved with it must be supportive of—and integrated with—the branding effort. Thus, if the new positioning is "state-of-the-art," then the letterhead should look very "cool," switchboard people (or the answering system) should be super-competent and glitch-free, and the Web site should use cutting-edge Flash technology.

6. Make sure everyone buys in. Brands need to be created and then maintained. It is often valuable to have a "brand steward" whose challenge it is to keep everyone and everything protecting the brand and its perception in line. This is especially a challenge in multi-site or multi-division nonprofits. One of the major challenges faced by the Centers for Disease Control and Prevention when it sought to implement a branding effort was getting all the various divisions (in fact, mini-fiefdoms) to agree on one strategy, implement it fully in their own domains, and then stick to a process of enhancing and protecting that positioning.

7. Pretest as much as possible. The objective is to move somewhere in the minds of key target audience members. They are the ones who can tell you if you are likely to succeed.

8. Routinely monitor. This means both tracking what is being done internally to protect and enhance the equity in this critical asset—the brand—and monitoring how it is being perceived over time by the target audience. The reality of the competitive world is that it changes. In many fields, it changes dramatically and quickly. Regular monitoring is crucial. Monitoring should also be supplemented from time to time by deeper special studies, especially after major environmental shocks. Many charitable organizations undertook studies of their brand positions after the September 11, 2001, terrorist crisis and the subsequent negative publicity surrounding the efforts of the American Red Cross in its handling of donated funds.[36]

SUMMARY

The first steps in developing a marketing strategy designed to influence target audiences are segmenting the audience and then developing a positioning strategy for the offering. The latter often involves branding the organization and/or its offerings. Segmentation can help make quality, quantity, and timing decisions with regard to marketing strategies.

Segmenting the market requires partitioning the market into subgroups that are mutually exclusive, exhaustive, measurable, accessible, substantial, and possessing differential responsiveness. Bases for segmentation are general or behavior-specific, objective or inferred. Many marketers think first of simple objective general measures such as age, income, geographical location, and marital status. Over the years, more complex general objective measures (such as social class and family life cycle) and inferred general measures (such as values and lifestyles) have become more popular. Behavior-specific bases for segmentation apply to a specific behavior. They include objective measures such as user status, usage rate, and loyalty. Inferred specific measures include beliefs, benefits, and perceived sacrifices. Once markets are divided up, one of four approaches to market segmentation can be chosen: mass marketing, differentiated marketing, niche marketing, and mass customization.

The next step is positioning the organization and/or its offering. This requires research on target audience perceptions and the key dimensions on which the perceptions are based. The semantic differential is a useful research tool here. Marketers then need to look for potential positions that will achieve the maximum impact. Reis and Trout suggest three possibilities: Building upon your present strengths, searching for a niche, and repositioning the competition.

More and more nonprofits are employing branding strategies as a way of managing their positioning. Brands can convey a lot about an organization and specific behaviors. It can have cognitive and emotional content. It can have its own personality. Building or rebuilding a brand is a challenging task and requires careful steps including background research, developing an integrated strategy, getting "total buy-in," and careful pretesting and monitoring.

QUESTIONS

1. Assume that you are the marketing director of your local YMCA. You have been charged with increasing membership in various "Y" activities. Identify five PRIZM clusters and suggest how you would develop different approaches for each cluster.

2. Compare and contrast (a) objective general and (b) inferred behavior-specific segmentation bases. What are the advantages and disadvantages of each? Under what circumstances would you recommend the use of each? Why?

3. You have just been assigned to be the head of a research group whose objective is to issue recommendations on how to stomp out drug use in America. Prescribe a market segmentation framework, and explain why you choose specific segmentation variables.

4. Identify the four long-term market positions that an organization might strive for. If you were establishing a new graduate business school at a public university known for its public policy curriculum, which of these market positions might you pursue? Why?

5. How often should an organization consider its market positioning? What are some key events that might trigger an evaluation of one's market positioning? Explain the relationship between an organization's strengths and weaknesses and its market positioning.

NOTES

1. "Devising Mailing Lists for Every Market," *Wall Street Journal,* May 7, 1991, p. B1; Stephen W. Colford, "Direct Mail Sophistication Aids Political Campaigns," *Advertising Age,* October 10, 1994, S-10, p. 15.

2. J. E. Williams and J. A. Flora, "Health Behavior Segmentation and Campaign Planning to Reduce Cardiovascular Disease Risk Among Hispanics," *Health Education Quarterly,* 22 (1995), pp. 36–48.

3. A basic review of the segmentation literature is found in Ronald E. Frank, William F. Massy, and Yoram Wind, *Market Segmentation* (Upper Saddle River, N.J.: Prentice-Hall, 1972). See also Yoram Wind, "Issues and Advances in Segmentation Research," *Journal of Marketing Research,* August 1978, pp. 317–337.

4. Pam Weisz, "The New Boom Is Colored Gray," *Brandweek,* January 22, 1996, p. 28; Paula Fitzgerald Bone, "Identifying Mature Segments," *Journal of Services Marketing,* Vol. 5, No. 1 (Winter 1991), pp. 47–60.

5. William Strauss and Neil Howe, *Generations: The History of America's Future* (New York: William Morrow/Quill,

1991). See also William Strauss and Neil Howe, *The Fourth Turning: An American Prophesy* (New York: Broadway Books, 1997) and Neil Howe and William Strauss, *Millennials Rising: The Next Generation* (New York: Vintage Books, 2000).

6. Bob Minzesheimer, "You Are What You ZIP!" *Los Angeles,* November 1984, pp. 175–192.

7. Christina Del Valle, "They Know Where You Live—and How You Buy," *Business Week,* February 7, 1994, p. 89.

8. Stephen J. Miller, "Source of Income as a Market Descriptor," *Journal of Marketing Research,* February 1978, pp. 129–131.

9. Alan R. Andreasen, "Acquiring a Lifestyle: An Innovation Adoption Approach," Working Paper, Department of Marketing, California State University, Long Beach, 1988.

10. Leland L. Beik and Scott M. Smith, "Practical Segmentation: A Fund Raising Example," Working Paper No. 68, College of Business Administration, Pennsylvania State University, February 1978.

11. Their analysis also included a second function using five variables to separate those

who were not large medical givers into those who were large and small donors to all charities.

12. Christopher H. Lovelock, "A Market Segmentation Approach to Transit Planning, Modeling, and Management," *Proceedings, Sixteenth Annual Meeting Transportation Research Forum* (1975), pp. 247–258.

13. Richard J. Semenik and Clifford E. Young, "Market Segmentation in Arts Organizations," in N. Beckwith, M. Houston, R. Mittelstaedt, K. Monroe, and S. Ward, (eds.), *1979 American Marketing Association Educators' Conference,* pp. 474–478.

14. Milton J. Rokeach, *The Nature of Human Values* (New York: The Free Press, 1973). See also Donald E. Vinson, J. Michael Munson, and Masao Nakanishi, "An Investigation of the Rokeach Value Survey for Consumer Research Applications," in W. D. Perrault, (ed.), *Advances in Consumer Research,* Vol. 4 (Atlanta, Ga.: Association for Consumer Research, 1977), pp. 247–252; and Robert E. Pitts Jr. and Arch G. Woodside (eds.), *Personal Values and Consumer Psychology* (Lexington, Mass.: Lexington Books, 1984).

15. Thomas J. Reynolds and Jonathan Gutman, "Laddering: Extending the Repertory Grid Methodology to Construct Attribute-Consequence-Value Hierarchies," in R. Pitts and A. Woodside (eds.), *Personal Values and Consumer Psychology,* pp. 155–168.

16. Alan R. Andreasen and Russell W. Belk, "Predictors of Attendance at the Performing Arts," *Journal of Consumer Research,* 7, 2 (September 1980), pp. 112–120.

17. James O. Prochaska and Carlo C. DiClemente, "Stages and Processes of Self-Change of Smoking: Toward an Integrative Model of Change," *Journal of Consulting and Clinical Psychology,* 1983, pp. 51, 390–395.

18. Martha Farnsworth Riche, "Psychographics for the 1990s," *American Demographics,* July 1989, pp. 24–31, 53–54.

19. Richard P. Bagozzi, "Marketing as an Organized Behavioral System of Exchange," *Journal of Marketing,* October 1974, pp. 77–81; and "Marketing as Exchange," *American Behavioral Scientist,* March–April 1978, pp. 535–556.

20. Wendell R. Smith, "Product Differentiation and Market Segmentation," *Business Horizons,* Fall 1961, pp. 65–72; Theodore Levitt, "Marketing Success Through Differentiation—Of Anything," *Harvard Business Review,* May/June 1980, pp. 83–91.

21. Wendell R. Smith, "Product Differentiation."

22. B. Joseph Pine III, Bart Victor, and Andrew C. Boynton, "Making Mass Customization Work," *Harvard Business Review,* September/October 1993, pp. 108–119.

23. Al Reis and Jack Trout, *Positioning: The Battle for Your Mind* (New York: Warner Books, 1982); Jack Trout and Steve Rivkin, *The New Positioning: The Latest on the World's #1 Business Strategy.* (New York: McGraw-Hill Professional Publishing, 1997).

24. Glen L. Urban and Steven H. Star, *Advanced Marketing Strategy: Phenomena, Analysis, Decisions* (Upper Saddle River, N.J.: Prentice Hall, 1991).

25. Philip Kotler, Donald H. Haider, and Irving Rein, *Marketing Places* (New York: The Free Press, 1993).

26. Julie Edell and Marian Burke, "The Power of Feelings in Understanding Advertising Effects," *Journal of Consumer Research,* Vol. 14 (December 1987), pp. 421–433; Meryl Gardner, "Effects of Mood States on Consumer Information Processing," *Research in Consumer Behavior,* Vol. 2 (1987), pp. 113–135.

27. C. E. Osgood, G. J. Suci, and P. H. Tannenbaum, *The Measurement of Meaning* (Urbana: University of Illinois Press, 1957). Other image-measuring tools exist, such as *object sorting* [see W. A. Scott, "A Structure of Natural Cognitions," *Journal of Personality and Social Psychology,* Vol. 12, No. 4, 1969, pp. 261–278], *multidimensional scaling* [see Paul E. Green and Vithala R. Rao, *Applied Multidimensional Scaling* (New York: Holt, Rinehart and Winston, 1972)], and *item lists* [see John W. Riley, Jr. (ed.), *The Corporation and Its Public* (New York: John Wiley, 1963), pp. 51–62].

28. Al Reis and Jack Trout, *Positioning.*

29. "Reflections of a Top Regulator," *The Chronicle of Philanthropy,* February 24, 2000, pp. 35–37.

30. Tom Pope, "Make-A-Wish Redesign," *The NonProfit Times,* July 15, 2000, pp. 4–6; Tom Pope, "Repositioning Goodwill through TV Ads," *The NonProfit Times,* March 15, 1999, pp. 1, 4.

31. Vikki Spruill, "Build Brand Identity for Causes, Not Groups," *The Chronicle of Philanthropy,* June 14, 2001, pp. 45–46.

32. Susan Kirby, Melissa Kraus Taylor, Vicki S. Friemuth, and Claudia Fishman Parvanta, "Identity Building and Branding at CDC: A Case Study," *Social Marketing Quarterly,* VII, 2 (June 2001), pp. 16–35.

33. Jamie Smith, "Put Out the Word: University Sets Branding Example," *Marketing News,* May 7, 2001, pp. 6–8.

34. Ira Teinowitz, "Affairs of State: Looking for Love through Branding," *Advertising Age,* April 9, 2001, p. 8.

35. David A. Aaker, *Managing Brand Equity: Capitalizing on the Value of a Brand Name* (New York: The Free Press, 1991); David A. Aaker and Erich Joachimsthaler, *Brand Leadership* (New York: The Free Press, 2000); Kevin L. Keller, *Strategic Brand Management: Building, Measuring and Managing Brand Equity* (Upper Saddle River, N.J.: Prentice Hall, 1998); Marc Gobé, *Emotional Branding: The New Paradigm for Connecting Brands to People* (New York: Allworth Press, 2001); Gil Bashe, Nancy J. Hicks, and Amy Zeigenfuss (eds.), *Branding Health Services: Defining Yourself in the Marketplace* (Gaithersburg, Md.: Aspen Publishers, 2000).

36. "Recovering from Controversy: Experts Offer Advice to the Red Cross," *The Chronicle of Philanthropy,* November 15, 2001.

SECTION III

Developing and Organizing Resources

CHAPTER 7

Generating Funds

CHAPTER 8

Attracting Human Resources: Staff, Volunteers, and Boards

CHAPTER 9

Working with the Private Sector

CHAPTER 10

Organizing for Implementation

CHAPTER 11

Planning and Budgeting the Marketing Mix

CHAPTER 7

Generating Funds

In the 1980s in Budapest, a man in his 50s once known in that country as Dzjcgdzhe Shorash bought 400 photocopying machines and gave them to libraries and universities around the country. He believed that a good future for his former countrymen would come from free expression—and photocopiers would help promote that. He also invested in dissident and grass roots organizations there and in other Eastern European countries because he thought they were the ones to bring about change in repressive regimes.

The idea of investing as a way to make progress was something with which the man, now known as George Soros, was quite familiar. Starting with only a few thousand dollars in London in 1954, Soros used analysis and a sensitive "gut instinct" for the way markets and currencies would move to amass a fortune of over $8 billion over the next three decades. He also became one of the world's most famous money managers when in September 1992 he bet $10 billion through his Quantum funds that the British pound would fall. He was right, earning over $1 billion on the transaction and becoming so well-known—and feared—that heads of state treated him very well lest he turn against their currencies.

Soros has had some important setbacks since those heady years but is still very rich and still able to converse with powerful movers and shakers around the world. Today, he spends much of his energy on the network of Open Society funds he has set up using the $2.8 billion endowment he has given to the Soros Foundation. Initially, he sought to promote free expression and liberal democracy in Central Europe and the former Soviet Union through many kinds of investments, including creating radio stations for nomadic Mongol tribesmen and starting the Central European University in Budapest in 1989 (www.soros.org/ceu). Soros's Open Society Institute today also operates in Central Eurasia, South Africa, Haiti, Guatemala, and the United States.

George Soros continues to be very outspoken in his efforts to promote individual freedom as he sees it. He draws headlines for his stance against the criminalization of drug use and his support for medical uses of marijuana. Having retired from his Quantum money management firm, Soros is now a source of grants and other support for democratic causes in which he believes.

A small measure of his impact is that, in the Russian language today, the word that means "to apply for a grant" is *sorosovayt*.

Source: Drawn from several sources including Alan Deutschman, "George Soros," *Salon,* March 27, 2001.

BALANCING MISSION AND FUNDRAISING

Nonprofit organizations are constantly in search of financial support. Sometimes this activity overwhelms everything else the organization tries to do, distorts its operations, and drives it away from its core mission. Some have accused organizations in the social services sector for behaving like budget maximizers. Such an orientation can lead to excessive pursuit of donors and foundation grants that can lead a nonprofit far afield from its motivating ideals and objectives. In more recent years, "mission creep" has also resulted from many nonprofits venturing into product and service marketing, much like commercial firms. This tactic is pursued to generate revenues that the nonprofit organization can control itself and that, ideally, can free it from reliance on the whims of grant makers and politicians. Such a pursuit can also lead to organizational distortion.

Thus, a primary challenge in generating funds is to achieve an appropriate balance. We argue that this criterion is a more important measure of successful fundraising than is revenue growth or the financial success of individual campaigns and events.

An Important Balancing Act

Broadly speaking, there are three major sources of funds for a nonprofit organization:

1. Donations and grants
   a. Major individual gifts (e.g., grants, bequests, planned giving)
   b. Corporate and corporate foundation donations (e.g., an AOL–Time Warner Foundation grant)
   c. Non-corporate foundation grants (e.g., a Gates Foundation grant)
   d. Cause-marketing proceeds (e.g., proceeds from the annual Race for the Cure)

2. Revenues
   a. Sales of principal products and services (e.g., hospital charges, university tuitions, sales of oral rehydration solutions)
   b. Revenues from unrelated enterprises (e.g., catalogue sales, Girl Scout cookies)
   c. Membership dues (e.g., payments to American Marketing Association, American Medical Association)

3. Miscellaneous (e.g., investment income)

In a 1993 study, Segal and Weisbrod found that nonprofit organizations generated about 18 percent of their total revenues from various kinds of donations and 71 percent from program service revenue.[1] Furthermore, the proportion generated from program services had grown significantly since the early 1980s. The researchers also found that the proportion of total revenue that comes from self-generated program service revenues varied across nonprofit classifications from 89 percent for health care organizations (such as hospitals, nursing homes, and the like) and 69 percent for youth development organizations to 11 percent for community improvement organizations and 27 percent for arts, culture, and the humanities.

Even within categories, different organizations have different revenue streams. As shown in Table 7-1, the largest fundraiser, the Salvation Army, raises about 50 percent of its income from private support whereas, for the third-largest private fundraiser (the YMCA), fundraising provides only about one-fifth of its income. (It should be noted that the largest fundraising organization is not listed in Table 7-1. The United Way system is a collection of individual local United Ways. If their fundraising for 1999–2000 were added together, it would amount to $3.77 billion, 2.6 times the donations to the Salvation Army.)

A principal challenge for each organization is how to generate optimal revenue streams in the future. As we previously noted, the challenge is to maximize revenues while maintaining the proper balance. Balance implies that not all revenues are equally desirable. Revenues can be undesirable for one of two reasons: They may distort the mission and they may not be cost-effective.

TABLE 7-1   Income Sources for Top Twenty Fundraisers, 2001

Rank	Organization	Private Support	Total Income	Private Support %	Total Expenses
1.	Salvation Army (Alexandria, Va.)	$1,440,442,000	$2,792,816,000	51.6%	$2,124,966,000
2.	Fidelity Investments Charitable Gift Fund (Boston)	$1,087,748,356	$1,260,524,937	86.3%	$588,649,874
3.	YMCA of the USA (Chicago)	$812,098,000	$3,987,476,000	20.4%	$3,555,563,000
4.	American Cancer Society (Atlanta)	$746,391,000	$812,297,000	91.9%	$648,619,000
5.	Lutheran Services in America (St. Paul)	$710,263,416	$6,909,130,967	10.3%	$6,505,034,591
6.	American Red Cross (Washington, D.C.)	$637,664,249	$2,492,418,155	25.6%	$2,456,102,744
7.	Gifts In Kind International (Alexandria, Va.)	$601,926,952	$605,112,093	99.5%	$631,560,761
8.	Stanford University (Palo Alto, Calif.)	$580,473,838	$3,780,956,626	15.4%	$2,052,942,117
9.	Harvard University (Cambridge, Mass.)	$485,238,498	$5,967,156,304	8.1%	$1,950,134,900
10.	The Nature Conservancy (Arlington, Va.)	$445,326,081	$784,263,611	56.8%	$392,799,844
11.	Boys & Girls Clubs of America (Atlanta)	$425,125,115	$894,915,513	47.5%	$798,016,647
12.	America's Second Harvest (Chicago)	$421,665,967	$424,178,750	99.4%	$416,475,383
13.	Catholic Charities USA (Alexandria, Va.)	$414,440,601	$2,342,188,556	17.7%	$2,261,594,311
14.	Duke University (Durham, N.C.)	$407,952,525	$2,742,466,603	14.9%	$2,105,275,052
15.	American Heart Association (Dallas)	$396,388,909	$471,623,812	84.0%	$448,154,348
16.	Feed the Children (Oklahoma City)	$395,581,981	$398,455,754	99.3%	$360,002,085
17.	World Vision (Federal Way, Wash.)	$372,045,000	$468,045,000	79.5%	$466,903,000
18.	Habitat for Humanity International (Americus, Ga.)	$371,086,000	$548,881,000	67.6%	$421,062,000
19.	Yale University (New Haven, Conn.)	$358,102,600	$3,081,904,467	11.6%	$1,330,494,071
20.	AmeriCares Foundation (New Canaan, Conn.)	$326,373,880	$328,117,182	99.5%	$313,390,214

Source: The Chronicle of Philanthropy, The Philanthropy 400, November 2001.

Mission Distortion

This can happen due to external factors and internal factors.

1. *External causes.* An example of a problematic external influence is when a donor dangles large amounts of money with strings attached. The donor will give funding to a museum, but it must "improve the 'good taste' of its exhibits." A donor will endow a chair at a university but insists on having final say on who holds the chair. A drug company will fund university research but states that research results may not be published for five years. In each case, the nonprofit is tempted to move in a direction it did not want or, perhaps more critically, forced to compromise its standards and ethics.

2. *Internal causes.* Many nonprofits that rely extensively on foundation grants live a fluctuating and anxiety-prone existence. Staff are attached to projects funded by grants and risk losing their jobs if the grant is not renewed. Such funding is often short-run (one to three years) and may or may not be renewable (and, even if it is renewable, it must be "competed"—i.e., it might go to someone else). The organization then has both the pressure to grow and the pressure not to shrink and to have to lay off valued friends and co-workers. There is great pressure to "chase grants" where the organization may have some competency, some personal connection, or some small reason to believe a proposal might succeed. Like rich desserts, grants off-mission may be immensely satisfying in the short run but very damaging in the long run if relied on for continual nourishment.

Lack of Profitability

Some revenue sources may be undesirable because they cost more than they bring in. Again, the causes may be internal and external.

1. *External causes.* Many promoters come to nonprofits with good ideas for fundraising. These can include both fast-talking con artists and legitimate corporations. Many rock concerts promising to be high-profile moneymakers turn out to have unexpectedly high costs—including fees to the promoter that, when accompanied by negative publicity about fans being ripped off, are not worth the undertaking. Many corporate partnerships (discussed in Chapter 9) turn out to be extremely time-consuming such that if the opportunity cost of the nonprofit's staff time is included, the venture would be clearly unprofitable. (Still, it is not uncommon for nonprofits to put up with such off-book costs in the hopes that the investment in personal connections will yield future, more profitable alliances.)

2. *Internal causes.* A great many nonprofits are tempted to think they can generate great amounts of revenue by selling products largely unrelated to their core businesses.[2] These can range from T-shirts and mugs to extensive lines of clothing, gift items, or products closely related to their main business. They can prove to be good revenue sources but also can be distractions or, at worst, disasters. For example, in the 1980s one of the authors investigated attempts by several nonprofit family planning organizations worldwide to add over-the-counter health products like facial tissues and medications to the distribution systems they had built for their condoms, pills, and other contraceptive products. What they found was that they simply could not compete with the private sector and lost considerable time and money.

With this caveat in mind, we now turn to the marketing challenges involved in generating the two major revenue streams for most nonprofits: fundraising and revenue generation.

FUNDRAISING

Although many nonprofit organizations are increasing the range of products and services that they offer for a fee, the major source of their support continues to be fundraising. Government organizations raise funds through taxation. Private nonprofits, however, must rely on three major sources: foundations, corporations, and individuals. Fundraising is, therefore, one of the most important applications of marketing principles in the nonprofit world, and, because of increasing competition, one of the most difficult.

The total amount of charitable money raised by all organizations in the United States in 2000 was $203.45 billion. Seventy-five percent of these contributions came from *individuals* ($152.07 billion), with the remainder coming from *bequests* ($16.02 billion), *foundations* ($24.50 billion), and *corporations* ($10.86 billion). By far, the largest proportion of the money ($74.31 billion or 36.5 percent) was raised by religious organizations; the rest was raised by educational institutions ($28.18 billion), health-related groups ($18.82 billion), human services organizations ($17.99 billion), groups concerned with arts, culture, and the humanities ($11.50 billion), public and societal benefit organizations ($11.59 billion), environment and wildlife organizations ($6.16 billion), international affairs organizations ($2.71 billion), and other groups ($32.15 billion).[3]

Customer-Centered Fundraising

Organizations that raise money typically pass through three stages of marketing orientation in their thinking about how to raise funds effectively—similar to the stages described in Chapter 1.

• *Product orientation stage.* Here the prevailing attitude is "We have a good cause; people ought to support us." Many churches and colleges operate on this concept. Money is raised primarily by the top officers through an "old boy network." The organization relies on volunteers to help raise additional funds. A few loyal donors supply most of the funds.

• *Sales orientation stage.* Here the prevailing attitude is "There are a lot of people out there who might give money, and we must go out and find them and convince them to give." The institution appoints a development director who eventually hires a staff. This staff raises money from all possible sources, typically using a "hard sell" approach or dramatic emotional appeals featuring emaciated children in Ethiopia, AIDS patient on their deathbeds, and so on. The fundraisers have little influence on the institution's policies or personality because their job is to raise money, not improve the organization. A majority of large nonprofit organizations are in this stage. In the 1970s this mentality very much described the United Way of America, the nation's largest charitable giving intermediary.

• *Customer orientation stage.* Here the prevailing attitude is "Like all marketers, our challenge is to start with the needs and wants of our target market and then figure out how to meet them."

A signal that an organization has shifted from a sales to a customer orientation in its fundraising is when it sees fundraising as first meeting donors' needs and not the organization's needs—which, of course, will be met if the donor is satisfied.

One of the authors sought to redirect the United Way of America from being organization-centered to being customer-centered in the 1980s. At that point, the United Way marketing approach might be described as "You ought to give to us because we are supporting all these very good charities like the Girl Scouts and your local homeless shelter!" However, they were experiencing difficulties reaching and influencing the rapidly growing class of young professionals who were not part of the old system where one gave at the office through payroll deduction. Interviews with members of this target market revealed clearly that the United Way did not really understand its needs and wants and was certainly not positioning itself to meet those needs.

What the interviews showed was that these young professionals looked upon charitable giving much like their other investments. In the main, they wanted to give back to their communities and support some of the organizations that they thought were doing meritorious work. However, they were unsure how much they should give and how to distribute it across the various charities they were considering. These individuals were accustomed to investing in the stock market where they could get a lot of data and much advice. They could choose individual stocks that met their portfolio needs or they could choose one or more of hundreds of mutual funds that would spread their risk. To them, charitable "investing" was nothing similar—and so many just made token gifts and tended to repeat patterns established years earlier.

As a result of this investigation and an analysis of the United Way's strengths and weaknesses in influencing this market, the following recommendations were made:

1. The United Way should reposition itself from being a collection agency for its charity partners to being a "Charity Investment Counselor." As part of its fund allocation process, the United Way accumulated a great deal of information about all of the major charities in its communities (i.e., the ones that had asked for funding). It was just the kind of data—and expertise—that the young professionals said they were seeking.

2. It needed to abandon its tradition (at the time) of not giving donors any choice. Consistent with its self-image, the United Way of America believed that it knew best what was needed in its community and therefore donors should just trust it to use donations wisely.

3. Rather than one take-it-or-leave-it portfolio of charities, it should offer distinctive "Charitable Mutual Funds" around themes significant to blocks of donors. Thus, it could have a "mutual fund" comprised of charities concerned with the elderly or with children. There could be "mutual funds" built around the poor or minorities or around education. The funds could be tested, the ones that were desired retained, and the "losers" disbanded and their charities absorbed elsewhere or into a "general fund."

4. Extensive resources should be put into reporting back to donors. Young professionals were accustomed to tracking their portfolios without delay, but their experience with most charities was that they would hear from them every once in a while and then often with information that did not speak to their interests. Among other advantages, the mutual fund approach would allow the United Way to identify the interests of donors and provide them with personally relevant feedback much more likely to build long-term mutually satisfying relationships.

Of course, change took a very long time to happen. The United Way of America is a very large organization with an elaborate chapter structure that is promised significant local autonomy. The fact that both national and local United Ways were driven in major part by volunteers who rapidly turned over added to the inertia. However, some local chapters, such as Southern Pennsylvania, did experiment with the "Mutual Fund" concept. Over time, in part because of new competitive pressures and internal scandals, the United Way began to offer donor choice in most chapters around the country.

FUNDRAISING IN THE TWENTY-FIRST CENTURY

When nonprofit organizations start up, they tend to seek support from one or two sources, often wealthy individuals or friendly foundations. As organizations grow, they (1) diversify their donor bases; (2) shift from periodic fundraising efforts to year-round programs; (3) hire specialists in fundraising; (4) develop extensive databases for tracking donors and donor prospects; and (5) seek increasingly imaginative means to help people and organizations give—including elaborate, tax-friendly estate-planning options.

The fundraising environment has seen a number of significant innovations develop in the twenty-first century. Principal among these are Internet options for individual donors, the emergence of charitable mutual funds from organizations like Fidelity and Charles Schwab, and the rise of so-called "venture philanthropists." The Fidelity Investments Charitable Gift Fund is now the second-largest private fundraiser. Venture philanthropists are individuals such as Mario Morino or George Roberts who are millionaires from the high-tech or investment communities. They have established foundations like the Roberts Foundation that "invest" in nonprofits, treating them like entrepreneurial ventures. The venture philanthropists seek to build portfolios of promising organizations and then, rather than stand aside and hope for good outcomes, directly intervene with management assistance and insist on tough reporting standards to monitor performance.[4]

In the United States, charitable organizations are concerned that future fundraising, especially among major individual donors, may be seriously reduced because of the provisions of the 2001 tax bill that established a course of action for eliminating the estate tax.[5]

We elaborate on these developments in the following pages.

ANALYZING DONOR MARKETS

An organization can tap into a variety of sources for donations. The four major donor markets are *foundations, corporations, government,* and *individuals.* Here we will examine the institutional and behavioral characteristics of each donor market.

Foundations

According to *The Chronicle of Philanthropy,* in 1999 there were 50,201 foundations in the United States, a 7 percent increase over 1998. These foundations held almost a half-trillion dollars in assets and made grants totaling over $23 billion.[6] They fall into the following groups:

1. *Independent foundations,* set up to support a wide range of activities and usually run by a professional staff. There were 44,824 of these foundations in 1999 holding $381 billion in assets and giving out $18 billion in grants. Independent foundations include large well-known organizations such as the John D. and Catherine T. MacArthur Foundation and the Ford and Rockefeller Foundations, which support a wide range of causes, to more specialized general foundations that give money in a particular area, such as health (Robert Wood Johnson Foundation) or education (Carnegie Foundation).

 • *Family foundations,* set up by wealthy individuals to support a limited number of activities of interest to the founders. Family foundations sometimes do not have permanent offices or full-time staff members. Decisions tend to be made by family

TABLE 7-2   Twenty Largest Foundations in Terms of Awards Approved, 2000

Foundation	2000 (thousands)
Bill & Melinda Gates Foundation	$1,498,728
Ford Foundation	$669,705
David and Lucille Packard Foundation	$645,261
Robert Wood Johnson Foundation	$645,261
Pew Charitable Trusts	$235,605
Andrew W. Mellon Foundation	$220,328
California Endowment	$195,000
John D. and Catherine T. MacArthur Foundation	$174,700
Charles Stewart Mott Foundation	$153,696
Rockefeller Foundation	$141,000
Annenberg Foundation	$139,880
William & Flora Hewitt Foundation	$134,911
Kresge Foundation	$133,525
W. K. Kellogg Foundation	$128,435
Ann E. Casey Foundation	$127,537
Doris Duke Charitable Foundation	$116,466
Robert R. McCormick Tribune Foundation	$101,000
Donald W. Reynolds Foundation	$99,650
Duke Endowment	$98,400
McKnight Foundation	$94,125

Source: The Chronicle of Philanthropy, April 4, 2001.

members, counsel, or both. There were 18,276 family foundations in 1998 holding $154 billion in assets and giving out just over $7 billion in grants. The largest, fastest-growing, and best-known family foundation is the Gates Foundation, which in 1998 held over $5 billion in assets and gave out almost $1.5 billion in 2000 (see Table 7-2).

2. *Corporate foundations,* set up by corporations and allowed to give away up to 5 percent of the corporation's adjusted gross income. There were 2,019 corporate foundations in 1999, holding over $15 billion in assets and giving out $2.8 billion in grants.

3. *Community foundations,* set up as vehicles for pooling bequests from many private sources, including individuals, corporations, foundations, and nonprofit organizations. There were 519 community foundations in 1999 holding over $27.6 billion in assets and giving out $1.8 billion.

The 20 foundations that gave away the most money in 2000 are listed in Table 7-2. With 50,000+ foundations, it is important for the fundraiser to know how to locate the few that would be the most likely to support a given project or cause. Fortunately, there are many resources available for researching foundations. Most of these can be searched on the Internet. An important resource is the Foundation Center, a nonprofit organization with research centers in New York, Washington, D.C., and Chicago, which collects and distributes information on foundations. Similar databases are maintained by *The Chronicle of Philanthropy.*

Even these guides do not reflect subtle changes in the direction of a particular foundation. Many foundations, especially those organized by the new venture-philanthropists are becoming directly involved in seeing that their grants have impact. In Exhibit 7-1, Tom Reis describes the new approach of the Kellogg Foundation.

EXHIBIT 7-1

TOM REIS, DIRECTOR OF MARKETING AND DISSEMINATION FOR THE W. K. KELLOGG FOUNDATION, ON THE FOUNDATION'S NEW DIRECTIONS

The intent and purpose of the W. K. Kellogg Foundation grantmaking is to promote social development and achieve sustainable systemic change. Through the wise investment of its resources, the Foundation pursues its mission of "helping people help themselves through the practical application of knowledge and resources to improve the quality of life and that of future generations."

An underlying Kellogg philosophy is to collect, disseminate and extend the lessons learned resulting from its grantmaking. As such, the Foundation takes a utilization-focused approach to its evaluation work and is committed to creative marketing and outreach methodologies.

Over the past few years, the W. K. Kellogg Foundation has established a communications and strategic planning group which provides integrated management services for its grantmaking efforts. Those services include: media resources, marketing/dissemination, technology, evaluation, and public policy education.

The marketing/dissemination function provides a menu of services related to strategic grantmaking support. These include planning, message development, program and product design, audience identification and segmentation, documenting and archiving grantmaking activities and lessons learned. The Foundation refers to the systematic, creative sharing of results as "strategic dissemination."

Through this approach, the Foundation views dissemination as both the alpha and the omega. Dissemination becomes a major ingredient throughout the grantmaking process, from planning and design, through implementation and monitoring, and finally by using lessons learned from grantees to help shape future Foundation grantmaking.

By conducting a "stakeholder analysis," marketing support employs the basic marketing tools and methods to build support strategies for social change initiatives in grantmaking. This consists of identifying the key stakeholders around a specific grant initiative, prioritizing and profiling those stakeholders, and establishing their current attitudes and practices related to the initiative's objectives. Finally, the task shifts to determining what types of specific communication strategies will work best with each stakeholder group. This planning helps move stakeholders along a continuum toward the change objectives for that grantmaking initiative.

The Foundation often explains its approach to program development and grantmaking with what it calls the "strategic programming wheel." At each step, the program support services of marketing/dissemination, evaluation, and public policy education work closely on the planning and design activities being conducted in team multidisciplinary settings (with the program director taking a leadership role). The

(continued)

"stages" on the program development wheel are as follows:

1. *Situation Analysis.* Program directors look at current situations—external and internal—related to a specific grantmaking area. They conduct needs assessments and engage in "environmental scanning" through literature reviews, etc., to determine the need and social climate for grantmaking in the proposed area.

2. *Strategic Discussion.* Here, the information derived from the situation analysis is reviewed by multidisciplinary teams made up of program directors and integrated program support staff. The teams determine whether this potential area of grantmaking will fit within the Foundation's programming priorities. If so, the initial conceptual work of exploring that emerging programming area is completed and presented to the Board of Trustees for discussion.

3. *Strategic Plans.* If the Trustees decide to pursue the emerging grantmaking area, the multidisciplinary teams come together again. They create a strategic plan consisting of goals and strategies and clustered grantmaking approaches.

4. *Integrated Action Plans.* This is the implementation planning stage. Explicit individual plans for marketing/dissemination, evaluation, and public policy education are established and designed to interact together and create integrated synergistic support activities. Consensus is reached, roles and responsibilities are established,

and activities rally around critical action points in the implementation plan.

5. *Implementation Monitoring.* Grants are made and monitored against the major intended outcomes agreed upon in the implementation plan.

6. *Recording and Reporting.* This phase involves documentation and analysis of evaluation results and project report summaries. Data and information assessments are also codified and input into a database for ongoing planning purposes.

7. *Use Analysis and Dissemination.* An analysis of lessons learned is conducted and those lessons are disseminated using creative marketing methods to develop activities and products.

8. *Long-range Planning.* This stage involves using the information and best practices gleaned from our previous grantmaking to guide Kellogg planning efforts in new areas of opportunity.

This methodical, systematic approach to strategic grantmaking has been instrumental in helping the W. K. Kellogg Foundation achieve sustainable, system-wide social change in its priority grantmaking areas. Determining how to integrate programming support services, such as marketing/dissemination, evaluation, and public policy education, has been a learning experience for the Foundation's programming staff. These approaches are already beginning to show evidence of significant impact in Foundation grantmaking.

The first step in seeking foundation grants is finding a match between the foundation's interests and scale of operation and that of the nonprofit. Too often a small nonprofit organization will send a proposal to the Ford Foundation because it would like to get the support of this well-known foundation. However, the Ford Foundation only accepts about 1 out of every 100 proposals and may be less disposed toward helping small nonprofit organizations than more regional or specialized foundations would be.

After identifying a few foundations that might have strong interest in its project, the organization should try to estimate more accurately its level of interest before investing a lot of time in grant preparation. Most foundations are willing to respond to a simple, straightforward letter of inquiry, telephone call, or personal visit and indicate how interested they would be in a project. The foundation officer may be very encouraging or discouraging and may suggest ways in which the nonprofit's interests may match those of the foundation. If the foundation appears receptive, the fund-seeking organization can then make an investment in preparing an elaborate proposal for this foundation. However, it is extremely important that the nonprofit make sure that, in the course of adapting a proposal to a foundation's interests, the organization not distort its mission.

Writing successful grant proposals is becoming a fine art, with many guides currently available to help the grant seeker, including sources on the worldwide Web.[7] The larger foundations will have clear guidelines and will usually make these available on their Web site. Each proposal should contain at least the following elements:

1. *A cover letter* describing the history of the proposal; its title; a one-sentence overview; who has been contacted, if anyone, in the foundation; and the kinds and levels of support being sought.
2. *The proposal,* describing the project, its uniqueness, and its importance.
3. *The budget* for the project.
4. *The personnel* working on the project, along with their resumes.

This is, of course, simply another occasion for effective marketing. Each solicitation is a "campaign" as discussed in Chapter 3. Thus, it ought to begin with the right mindset and then a thorough "listening" to the target audience (i.e., careful formative research). As always, the right mindset is to be customer-driven. Target audiences in this case (i.e., foundations) make grants because it is in *their* interest. A fundamental mistake many grant seekers make is to ask for the grant because the grant seeker needs and wants it. But the foundation knows this—what it will be asking is this: Compared to the many other solicitations we receive, is this a good way for us to invest our limited funds?

The challenge, therefore, is to conduct formative research in order to understand as thoroughly as possible a foundation's interests and "needs." Many foundations describe their broad funding priorities on their Web site, and in their annual reports or press releases. A review of recent grants given (available from the Foundation Center or *The Chronicle of Philanthropy*) will indicate preferences and priorities. Conversations with recent grantees can also be instructive.

An important piece of information to learn in this process is the relative importance of typical criteria for projects that are clearly within the foundation's areas of interest. These data have clear implications for the "campaign." Typical criteria include the following:

1. *Track record.* Most foundations prefer to bet on likely winners and, in such cases, the proposal marketer should stress, if possible, his or her organization's longevity and previous successes.
2. *Quality of staff.* In the absence of a track record—and/or in addition to one—Foundations may look at the credentials and character of key personnel. This can be a matter of providing impressive resumes (or taking on board consultants with impressive resumes) or promoting a charismatic leader. It is said that many foundations like to give to *people* as much as to good ideas. If this is the case, the organization should send its highest-ranking, most impressive officials to the foundation.

3. *Ability to measure results.* In the twenty-first century, more and more foundations want to see potential grantees indicate clearly how they are going to track performance. Monitoring systems of the type described in Chapter 20 are crucial.
4. *Generalizability.* Many foundations now have significant communications staffs whose task it is to disseminate to others findings from the work of their grantees. These can be research findings or data on best practices. The grantee's campaign can anticipate this step by making clear how the results are likely to have relevance far beyond the relatively narrow focus of the specific undertaking.

Marketing to foundations should not be solely a matter of campaigns. Nonprofit organizations that plan to have foundation grants as a continuing source of revenue need to develop an overall organization strategy based on long-term relationships with key foundations. They should not contact foundations only on the occasion of a specific proposal. Each organization should cultivate a handful of appropriate foundations in advance of specific proposals. In the private sector, this is called "relationship marketing." One major university sees the Ford Foundation as a "key customer account." The development officer arranges for various people within the university to get to know people at corresponding levels within the foundation. One or more members of the university's board arrange to see corresponding board members of the foundation each year. The university president visits the foundation's president each year for a luncheon or dinner. One or more members of the university's development staff cultivate relations with foundation staff members at their levels. When the university has a proposal, it knows exactly who should present it to the foundation and who to see in the foundation. Furthermore, the foundation is more favorably disposed toward the organization because of the long relationship and special understanding they enjoy. Finally, the organization is able to do a better job of tracking the proposal as it is being reviewed by the foundation.

Corporations

Business organizations represent another distinct source of funds for nonprofit organizations. Corporations may hold particular interest for nonprofits seeking support for projects with a marketing orientation. The corporations with the largest cash giving in 2000 according to *The Chronicle of Philanthropy* were the following:[8]

Wal-Mart Stores	$150.4 million
Ford Motor Company	$110.5 million
Philip Morris Companies	$107.0 million
SBC Communications	$101.7 million
ExxonMobil Corporation	$ 91.7 million
Bank of America	$ 87.3 million
J. P. Morgan Chase & Company	$ 84.0 million
Target Corporation	$ 80.8 million
Verizon Communications	$ 70.0 million

There are also a significant number of corporations that have much larger giving levels when one includes product donations. This applies particularly to corporations marketing pharmaceuticals and computers. Total giving in 2000 for the largest of these was as follows:

Pfizer	$340.5 million
Merck & Company	$249.0 million
Microsoft	$231.8 million
Johnson & Johnson	$217.6 million
Bristol-Meyers Squibb	$172.2 million
IBM	$126.1 million
Intel	$111.5 million

Some corporations give a significant portion of their donations outside the United States. For example, in 2000 Merck allocated 81.8 percent of its giving overseas, Hewlett-Packard gave 45.5 percent abroad, and Chevron gave 34.2 percent.

Corporate giving has changed dramatically in recent years. As Craig Smith points out,[9] at the turn of the century corporate philanthropy was the special province of corporate barons like Morgan and Rockefeller, who decided on their own which favorite charities would benefit from business-generated profits. The corporations themselves did not have giving programs, believing that society did not want them to be involved in social issues. In the 1950s, barriers to such involvement were removed, and corporations began to establish major giving programs. Most corporations created in-house foundations, and companies like Dayton Hudson, Levi Strauss, and Cummins gave up to 5 percent of pretax earnings. In most cases, the foundations were intentionally divorced from mainstream corporation activities.

But in the 1990s, strong pressures from stockholders and the competitive marketplace forced corporations to become leaner and more efficient. This caused firms to rethink their approach to philanthropy. Smith identified a new paradigm, now labeled "strategic philanthropy," in which companies have come to think of philanthropy as a *competitive weapon.* As Weeden and others have pointed out, corporations have learned that they can "do well by doing good." Strategic philanthropy can meet a number of corporate goals:

- Changing the image of an organization, as when AT&T's sponsorship of the arts changed it from dull and boring to sophisticated and upscale.
- Building alliances that give the corporation public support in times of crises such as ecological disasters or product problems.
- Creating awareness and interest in the organization for future customers and future employees.
- Providing a means of binding together employees and distributors in projects that elevate their job time to working on something "bigger" than merely making money.
- Producing increased sales, as when American Express or Coca-Cola engage in cause-related marketing (discussed in Chapter 9).

In the twenty-first century, corporations have also become more active in involving their own workers in community and social projects. Corporations now have significant volunteer programs (as described in Chapter 8). And many also have active "matching gift programs." A study of 1,007 companies by the Council for Advancement and Support of Education in 2000 found that 51 percent matched employee gifts to at least one non-educational organization the previous year.

(Corporations often have tuition-matching programs as well.) There are usually minimum and maximum levels set. Exxon contributes funds in proportion to the time volunteered by staff ($600 for each 20 hours worked). It will also contribute $500 to events that its employees coordinate.[10]

Philanthropy has also become a tool of international competition. Foreign companies such as Hitachi are establishing foundations in the United States, and many U.S. companies with international operations are beginning giving programs abroad. Smith argues that in markets such as Brazil and Hungary where philanthropy is weak at present, real opportunities exist for U.S. corporations to obtain differential advantages.

Seeking funds from corporations and their foundations is, conceptually, no different from the approach recommended for independent and family foundations. Both specific campaigns should be mounted while at the same time carrying out long-term relationship marketing. Of the millions of business enterprises that might be approached, relatively few are appropriate to any specific nonprofit organization. The best prospects for corporate fundraising will be those where the nonprofit can easily demonstrate that it provides the corporation with strategic payoffs. Such corporations are likely to have one or more of the following characteristics:

1. *Local corporations.* Corporations located in the same area as the nonprofit organization are likely to see direct benefits to it and its staff from grantmaking. A hospital, for example, can base its appeal on the health care it offers to the corporation's employees, and a performing arts group can argue that its cultural offerings improve the local climate and thus help corporations attract and keep top-flight talent. Further, it is logistically easier to build long-term corporate relationships where corporate and nonprofit executives can find time for cultivation off the job.

2. *Kindred activities.* Corporations located in a field kindred to the nonprofit organization's are excellent prospects. Hospitals can effectively solicit funds from pharmaceutical companies, and colleges can attract funds from companies that hire many of their graduates.

3. *Personal relationships or contacts.* Nonprofit organizations should review their personal contacts to obtain clues to which corporations they might solicit. A university's board of trustees consists of influential individuals who can open many doors for corporate solicitations. Corporations tend to respond to peer influence in their giving. It is a maxim of fundraising that people do not give to institutions or causes: *People give to people.* This is especially true in corporate fundraising. As Austin points out, many valuable long-term relationships between corporations like Starbucks and Timberland first began through personal acquaintance.[11]

4. *Structural similarity.* Nonprofits with a national or international scope should seek out corporations that match them structurally. Thus, Coca-Cola developed a partnership with Boys & Girls Clubs of America, in part because they both catered to the teen market and in part because they both have an organizational structure comprised of a headquarters and multiple local independent operators (club branches and franchised bottlers).

The preceding criteria will help the nonprofit organization identify a number of corporations that are worth approaching for contributions. Corporations in the organization's geographical area or field are worth cultivating on a continuous basis ("relationship marketing") aside from specific grant requests. When the organization is seeking to fund a specific project, however, it needs to identify the best prospects and develop a marketing plan from scratch.

Nonprofits that rely heavily on corporate support must constantly keep up on changes in corporate philosophy toward philanthropy. For example, in the 1990s, a great many corporations were downsizing and feeling very strong pressures on their bottom line. This means that they will give out fewer, more focused cash grants and will more often look for ways to give in-kind support, such as loaning their workers for charitable activities. Also, as Paul Ostergard, Citibank's Director of Corporate Contributions and Civic Responsibility, argues, many corporate philanthropy directors are turning their attention toward subject areas that are more closely attuned to the corporation's own long-run interest.[12] Thus, in the next decade, they are likely to spend more on the following:

- Education that will produce better workers.
- Human services and job-creation programs that will get more people off the welfare system and into productive careers.
- Environmental causes that reinforce the corporation's growing internal efforts at environmentally friendly behavior.
- Wiring the world to have Internet access.

The latter is a particular priority of many of the so-called dot-coms that have proliferated in recent years. Their leaders are eager to give back to the society that helped them be successful. They have particularly focused on eliminating what has come to be called the "digital divide." Among corporations taking leadership here are Intel, Cisco, and Microsoft.

Government

Another major source of funds is government agencies at the federal, state, and local levels that are able to make grants to worthwhile causes. As an example, the federal government set up the National Endowment for the Arts (NEA) to make grants to support museums, ballet companies, art groups, and other arts organizations, large and small. Other government agencies make grants to support health care, university teaching and research, social services, and other worthwhile causes. Web sites announcing government Requests for Proposals (RFPs) are routinely watched by organizations that have projects of likely interest to government agencies.

Government agencies normally require the most detailed paperwork in preparing proposals. They tend to place the main weight on the proposal's probable contribution to the public interest as well as the agency's own agenda. Reputation of the proposing agency is important while personal relations between the agency and grantee are less determinative. Nonprofits with good performance records can often successfully "re-compete" for extensions of current grants.

Individual Givers

Individuals are the major source of all charitable giving, accounting for some 81 percent of the total. According to *The Independent Sector,* 70.1 percent of all households gave to charities in 1998, averaging $1,075 in cash contributions. Cash giving represented 2.1 percent of the giving household's total income, a decline from 2.5 percent in

1989 that undoubtedly reflected the national economic recession that was occurring during that period. Among the households in the 1999 study, 84 percent made in-kind donations of food or clothing, 79 percent contributed cash, and 80 percent said they gave indirectly through cause-related marketing programs.[13]

Characteristics

Robert Sharpe suggests that individual givers can be divided into three groups based on their life cycle stage and giving patterns:[14]

- *The early years.* Up to age 50, potential donors are absorbed in establishing their families and their careers. They have limited discretionary income; when they do give, it is in relatively small amounts. They are regular givers, often to their churches or synagogues. They give cash and sometimes property.

- *The middle years.* Between 50 and 70 years of age, donors are at a stage where they are relatively settled. The children have been through college and most major assets are paid off. Regular giving continues during this period, but middle-year households are beginning to be candidates for making large gifts for the special needs of a non-profit organization. These households could buy a new van for the YMCA, endow a scholarship at a local college, or underwrite a major fundraising event.

- *The later years.* Households with members over the age of 70 are prime candidates for giving what Sharpe calls "the Ultimate Gift." They are less likely to be regular givers because their incomes are shrinking. They can, however, be approached for bequests and other forms of planned giving.

The distribution of the population across these three categories in the early twenty-first century is affected by the baby boom, which has resulted in relatively fewer households in the Middle Years category than in earlier periods. This pattern will soon change, however, and fundraising prospects should improve. Other interesting correlations from the Independent Sector data are these:

- Whites give more than African Americans, who give more than Hispanics. Religious donations per household are lowest for Catholics, next are Protestants, highest are "other religions."
- Most giving came from 35- to 44-year-olds (67 percent) followed by 45- to 54-year-olds.
- As expected, there is a strong positive correlation between income and giving to charities. Over 80 percent of those earning above $50,000 in annual income gave. However, those with incomes under $10,000 gave at a higher rate—5.2 percent—than other groups. The latter is partly a matter of age as 26 percent of those in this income group are retired.
- Those who are married and have more than a high school education gave more often.
- Being asked was an important precipitant of giving; of those asked, 81 percent gave.[15]

People say that the major reason they give is that they "feel strongly about the cause." Over half say this. However, this reason is even more important for wealthy individuals. Recent online studies by Harris Interactive also established important differences between men and women in motivations. In the study, women were more likely to give because of a health problem of a family member or friend while men (and

TABLE 7-3 Reasons for Giving by Gender and Wealth Status

	Women (%)	Men (%)	Wealthy (%)	All (%)
Why People Give				
Feel strongly about the cause	59	59	74	59
Personal experience with the organization	38	41	55	40
Tax benefit	18	36	54	28
Response to specific request	22	28	46	25
Moral imperative—the right thing to do	43	50	42	47
Involvement of family member, friend, co-worker	32	35	38	33
Religion, spirituality	36	37	37	36
Charity event	25	27	35	26
Illness of family member, friend, co-worker	39	22	30	30
Family tradition	17	14	21	16
Tithing	18	23	17	21
News or media story	20	11	16	15
New wealth	8	3	14	5
Business connection	5	4	13	4
Where People Give				
Educational institutions	28	33	53	30
Children and youth services	41	47	52	44
Health and medical charities	45	35	51	40
Religious and faith-based organizations	47	50	45	49
Homeless or low-income services	37	32	36	35
Disaster relief organizations	21	26	35	24
Arts or cultural organizations	11	16	35	14
Political or advocacy organizations	11	17	32	14
Disability organizations	31	30	31	30
Elderly or aging services	25	17	25	21
Animal-rights groups	28	21	24	24
Environmental groups	12	14	22	13
Sports or recreational groups	13	20	21	16
Women's organizations	20	7	21	14
Civil-rights groups	9	10	16	9
Family planning or child-rearing organizations	12	5	10	8

Source: Elizabeth Greene, "Study Finds Differences in Giving Patterns between Wealthy Men and Women," *The Chronicle of Philanthropy,* May 3, 2001, pp. 12–15.

wealthy Americans of both sexes) emphasized tax benefits. Women are more likely to give to health charities and women's organizations and men to sports and recreation. The wealthy give more than the general population to educational institutions, health organizations, arts or cultural organizations, and organizations involved in political advocacy. Selected results are reported in Table 7-3.

In health care, a larger part of the difference in giving levels is attributable to interest in specific health problems, particularly about the disease's *severity, prevalence,* and *remediability.* Thus, heart disease and cancer are severe diseases—they kill—whereas arthritis and most birth defects are considered less serious since they do not kill. Cancer has a higher prevalence than muscular dystrophy and therefore attracts more support. Finally, people believe that cures or preventions are possible for

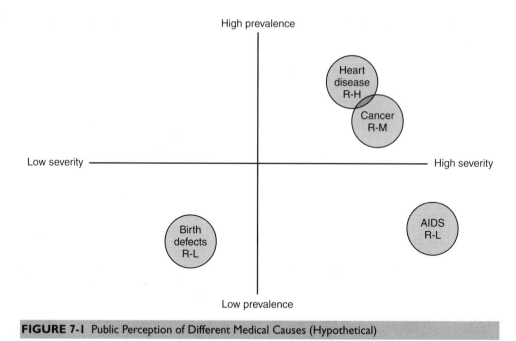

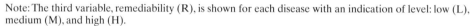

FIGURE 7-1 Public Perception of Different Medical Causes (Hypothetical)

Note: The third variable, remediability (R), is shown for each disease with an indication of level: low (L), medium (M), and high (H).

heart disease and less so for birth defects, which leads to more giving to heart disease. Figure 7-1 shows the hypothetical positions of four diseases on the three variables. If the March of Dimes wanted to attract more funds for birth defects, it must try to increase the perceived severity, prevalence, and remediability of birth defects.

Motives

When a nonprofit organization plans a fundraising campaign aimed at individuals, it needs to begin with a clear sense of why people give in general and then why they do—or might—give to them. We argue that most often individuals give in order to get something back. In other words, donations should not be viewed as a *gift* but as a *transaction* where the nonprofit offers significant benefits that the donor wants and the donor "pays" with his or her donation. The question is, what does—or could—the donor *get?* Table 7-4 lists several motives underlying giving behavior. Figure 7-2 shows some of the benefits the American Cancer Society offers to those who support its fight on breast cancer.

Is there such a thing as giving without "getting" (i.e., pure altruism)? Some people give and say that they expect nothing back. But, in our view, actually they most likely privately enjoy the self-esteem of being "big enough" to give money without requiring recognition.

A problem for a great many nonprofit organizations that do *not* have a customer orientation is that they attempt to solicit funds by telling potential donors that *the organization* needs the money. They describe at great length and with enthusiasm all

---

TABLE 7-4   Individual Giving Motives

1. *Need for self-esteem.* These people attempt to build their self-esteem and self-image by playing "God," by feeling good from giving. The opposite of this would be shame or guilt.
2. *Need for recognition from others.* These people attempt to build their social status or enhance their prestige in the eyes of others. They have a strong need to belong.
3. *Fear of contracting the problem.* This need centers on people's fear that they or members of their families will contract a particular disease or fall into poverty or neglect in their old age. They hope in some sense to buy "protection."
4. *The habit giver.* These people give out of habit for no real reason other than a desire not to be embarrassed by not contributing to the cause. They are indifferent to contributions, but feel that they must give to someone because everyone else does. A benefit may be not having to agonize over choosing charities (for example, *not* giving to a needy cause).
5. *Nuisance giver.* These people only give to get rid of the caller. They feel that contributing to a cause is of no real significance, but would rather donate a few dollars than be troubled by others.
6. *Required to give.* These people are required to give at work; they feel they are under pressure from superiors to donate part of their checks to a fund. They therefore demand efficiency and credibility from the organization that they contribute to.
7. *Captive givers.* These people feel real sorrow for someone they know who has a particular problem. They are other-centered in that they earnestly would like to aid the victim in some way. Givers in this category may contribute at the death of a friend rather than sending flowers, and so on.
8. *People-to-people givers.* These people have a real feeling of the "commonness of human beings," a solidarity with other people. This group of people has internalized the idea of helping others because they want to.
9. *Concern for humanity.* This segment of givers is concerned about others for religious reasons and because they are "God's children." They feel a moral obligation to contribute to a charity. They have accepted the love-for-humanity idea because it is a requirement of their faith.

---

the good work the organization does and then point out how much more could be done if only they had more funds. They have the fundraising transaction exactly backward. They try to motivate giving to meet the organization's needs. But, as the BCOS model introduced in Chapter 4 makes clear, people (i.e., donors) take actions to meet their own needs. Fundraisers need to find out what each target audience wants and then show them how the proposed action (i.e., donating) meets *their* needs.

These motivations reflect the benefits and influence-of-others specified in the BCOS model. However, that model also points out the importance of the perceived costs of the donation. It is important to also understand what potential donors think might be the negatives of giving—is it giving up some other expenditure, being identified as "an easy mark" for other solicitors, or perhaps feeling that they have given to an organization that will waste their money. If such costs are identified, the fundraiser must address them, not just (as is typical) try to overpower them by emphasizing benefits.

The BCOS model also emphasizes the importance of self-efficacy. Many donors may feel that, despite the worthiness of a cause, they cannot give because they just don't know how to manage the expenditure financially. Fundraisers who solicit major gifts have many devices to cope with these concerns. However, financing help may also be important for the low-income person solicited in an annual drive.

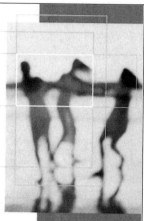

Five Things to Tell Your Friends About Breast Cancer

1. All women are at risk for breast cancer — even those who have no family history of the disease.

2. The two greatest risk factors for breast cancer are being a woman and growing older.

3. Survival rates are high for women diagnosed with early stage breast cancer, when the cancer is small and has not spread. Get annual mammograms beginning at age 40, and start regular breast exams by your doctor and monthly breast self-exams at age 20.

4. Smart strategies to reduce your risk of cancer include regular physical activity, maintaining a healthy weight, and limiting alcohol intake.

5. Through early detection and improved treatment, more women than ever are beating breast cancer.

Tell your friends, your family — any women you care about. You could save a life.

American Cancer Society®

FIGURE 7-2 American Cancer Society

Source: American Cancer Society. Reproduced with permission.

TYPES OF INDIVIDUAL FUNDRAISING

Fundraising at the individual level for larger nonprofit organizations is typically divided into annual giving, major giving, and planned giving. We will discuss each of these in turn.

Annual Giving

Although some new nonprofit organizations rely heavily on a few principal donors to keep them going in the early years, eventually most charitable organizations come to rely on annual giving campaigns as the bedrock of their fundraising activities. As pointed out by several authors,[16] there are a number of basic components that must be present for an effective annual giving campaign: (1) strong volunteer leadership and staff support, (2) clear organization structure, (3) ambitious but realistic goals, (4) careful segmentation of donors and prospects, (5) extensive prior research, (6) thorough training of volunteer solicitors, (7) a detailed timetable of activities and mileposts, (8) extensive reports and accountability, (9) donor and volunteer recognition, (10) online giving options, and (11) building of lifetime donors. We address several of these challenges below.

Leadership

Most nonprofits rely on volunteers to lead and staff their annual fund drives. This approach not only provides large numbers of solicitors, but it also is a way of binding those solicitors more closely to the organization. For the campaign to be effective, strong, dedicated leadership among these volunteers is necessary. Annual fund drive leaders typically emerge from the ranks of past volunteers. They are often community leaders or nationally known figures. In many cases, they are senior members of the organization's board of directors. Although the leadership task is very demanding, it is one often sought after by up-and-coming business and professional people for the prestige and networking it affords.

This volunteer leadership must be fully backed by a cadre of professional staffers who will (1) ensure that the volunteers have the information they need to take effective action, (2) maintain continuity between each program stage, and (3) prepare the reports and other materials used to track performance. Senior management must be cautious so that rivalries among professional staff and volunteers do not emerge in the heat of a high-pressure campaign.

Organization

Today, most major annual campaigns use multiple approaches to raising money. There may be direct mail, telephone solicitations, personal contact, fundraising events, telethons, and imaginative use of the Internet and the organization's own Web site, as well as Web sites of cooperating partners or intermediaries. Under the general guidance of a campaign committee, specific individuals are made responsible for each of these tactical areas. In many sophisticated campaigns, workers within telephone and person-to-person solicitation divisions may be further organized into groups responsible for specific geographic areas or particular professions. Thus, one group may be responsible for telephoning every household on the upper east side while another group might be responsible for personal solicitation among lawyers. Obviously, there is a careful attempt to match the skills and personalities of volunteer fundraisers to the tasks they are likely to do best. Team captains and subcaptains are often employed to ensure continuity and increase motivation and enthusiasm among the field workers. Captains often rise upward to become campaign CEOs of the future.

Goals

Setting the annual campaign goals, overall and for each segment and tactic, is one of the most important tasks of any annual campaign committee. Goal setting is usually preceded by a careful environmental scan. The committee begins with the previous year's performance: Were goals met? Why or why not? What changes have taken place in the social and economic environment? Have there been plant layoffs, an economic downturn, or wage freezes? What is the competitive situation? Are new charities coming on the horizon? Does the local university or art museum have a special campaign planned this year that will drain funds from major corporate and individual donors? All of these considerations are investigated so that the campaign committee can set goals that have the following characteristics:

- *Realistic.* They must be *attainable* by campaign workers or else the workers will be discouraged at the outset.
- *Motivating.* They should be just beyond the current reach of the workers so that the workers will try especially hard to reach them.
- *Clear.* Specific numeric target amounts should be set for each specific component.
- *Benchmarked.* Goals should be set for various stages of the campaign so that workers will know if they are on target for achieving overall goals or whether extra effort is necessary.
- *Assigned.* Each goal should be assigned to a specific individual so that someone can be held accountable for ultimate success or failure. There should be no room for finger-pointing.

Segmenting Markets

Successful campaigns make extensive use of the segmentation concepts discussed in Chapter 6. The overall target market is subdivided in ways that will help campaign managers decide (1) how much effort to assign to each target member and (2) how specifically to approach him or her. Effort level is typically based on donation potential: The more one is likely to give, the more effort should be devoted. Prospects with small donation potential typically are approached by direct mail, the least cost-per-contact method. Those with larger potential then may be approached by telephone, and the most significant donors may be reached with person-to-person solicitation. Within all three groups, there may be further opportunity for segmentation.

Direct mail and Internet solicitations may differ according to what is known about the likely recipients. For example, the American Cancer Society bases much of its direct-mail fundraising on the PRIZM geodemographic system described in Chapter 6. The American Cancer Society's marketing director obtains detailed lifestyle information about each of the zip code areas to which the society might direct solicitations. He or she can then tailor the type of appeal to the destination zip code. Thus, different messages would go to areas best characterized as "Money and Brains" than to areas categorized as "Shotguns and Pickups." Other organizations that do not subscribe to the PRIZM system can make adjustments based on the type of database they use. Most direct solicitations are aimed at members on a list. The best list is the organization's past contributors. However, many organizations seeking *new* donors move beyond present members to new databases that they purchase from other organizations that they know (e.g., the local museum or public television station) or they may buy them from independent suppliers that can supply highly specialized lists of specific types of potential donors. Thus, one can buy lists of heating contractors or school superintendents or physicians. Obviously, one can tailor different messages to each audience based on reasonable assumptions about their interests and lifestyles.

The availability of computers enhances careful record keeping and allows the charity's direct solicitation specialists to evaluate the productivity of the various lists they acquire and, over time, to fine tune the database to include only the very best prospects. These databases can contain detailed information on each prospective donor (interests, children's names, employer, and so on) that are particularly valuable for telephone and personal solicitations. These can also be segmented. In the last year, the American Cancer Society has gone to the costly trouble of attaching geographic coordinates to every donor record in its possession. It can now look to see how successful it has been in reaching people in "Shotguns and Pickups" neighborhoods and how this level of success differs in different parts of the country. Such data allow the organization to evaluate present programs and also to identify undertapped markets and to set dollar targets for such neighborhoods in future campaigns.

Distinguishing between repeat donors and new donors is always a sound strategy. It is an old marketing maxim from the private sector that it is always easier to sell to existing customers than it is to find new ones. Yet, the drop-out rate for many annual fund drives, especially those that rely on direct mail, can be as high as 40 percent to 60 percent, often because this key group is neglected. Of course, there are always substantive reasons people drop out of annual drives or give up their memberships, including changes in economic circumstances or social interests or disappointment with the organization itself; however, the most common reason for not renewing is simply forgetting. Mal Warwick suggests that a planned sequence of messages directed to past donors can effectively reduce the drop-out rate. For annual memberships, he proposed that "renew early" messages be sent out 90 days in advance of the expiration date, followed by "time to renew" mailings and substantive appeals. Once the membership has expired, he suggests messages such as "Have you forgotten?" followed by later messages talking about "the last newsletter" or asking "Why forsake us?" He suggests telephone calls to stragglers 120 days after expiration.[17]

In tackling new members, there are many techniques that can be used in annual campaigns to appeal to particular interests. These include walkathons, bike-athons, dance-athons, and so on; bingo nights; fairs; TV or radio marathons; book or craft sales; parties in usual places; cause-related marketing (discussed in Chapter 9); on-street solicitation (i.e., the Salvation Army); lotteries and sweepstakes; and commemorative gifts.

Training

The most critical aspect of training campaign workers from a marketing standpoint is one that frequently gets ignored. Workers are typically given extensive details about campaign objectives, facts about the charity, donor information, forms on which to report activities and accomplishments, handouts for in-person solicitations, and tips on how to actually ask for money and get a commitment. However, they are rarely shown how to apply a *customer mindset* to the donation opportunity; in other words, how to state the opportunity for giving in terms of the target audience's needs and wants. Campaign trainers typically put so much emphasis on telling the *charity's* story and making clear the *charity's* needs that target audience members often feel that giving is something one does only because it benefits the charity. Solicitors need to be trained to show the target audience how giving will meet *the audience's* needs and wants, not just the charity's. We have outlined some of the possible needs that can be addressed earlier in this chapter. Solicitors who will be talking to potential donors either face-to-face or over the telephone must learn how to find out what the donor is looking for in the giving situation and show him or her how the charity provides an opportunity to meet those needs.

Recognition

Both donors and volunteers should be recognized for their contributions after the campaign is completed. In many campaigns, donors are directly rewarded with some type of premium. This is particularly popular in fundraising for public television. Donors giving at different levels can get T-shirts or dinners or membership in some inner circle. But concrete tokens can only go so far. One of the frequent complaints of donors to charities is that they never hear from the organization once they have donated their money. Yet, individuals like to know how their money is being used, especially if it is a significant amount. Remember that 60 percent of all donors give to only *one* organization. Typically, they feel close ties to that organization, and careful feedback after the campaign can do much to cement the all-important relationship between donor and charity that can last a lifetime.

Warwick suggests a number of ways to make sure donors are "yours" for a lifetime:[18]

- Thank donors quickly.
- Send new donors a welcome package.
- Telephone every new donor who gives over a given threshold (e.g., $500.00).
- Set up a donor information hotline.
- Offer donors choices as to how gifts will be used.
- Host special events especially for donors.
- Send unsolicited pins, autographed books, or certificates to top donors.
- Send personal notes and annotated news clippings to the very best donors.

Online Giving

A phenomenon appearing at the turn of this century was the availability of giving opportunities on the Web. In the dot-com boom years in 2000 and 2001, a number of central "collection" sites sprang up, but many quickly disappeared when the boom deflated and when donors did not rush to the sites. However, most major charities now provide donation opportunities on their Web sites. This has proved particularly valuable for organizations that are featured in the evening news, such as those involved with disasters or the homeless. However, as yet, online donations are still a minor part of organizational fundraising. In a June 2001 survey, only two organizations, Campus Crusade for Christ and the American Red Cross, reported receiving more than a million dollars over the Web.[19] However, this method is expected to grow significantly in importance in the next decade. The success of Campus Crusade for Christ would suggest that today's college graduates are much more accustomed to using the Web for various financial transactions.

Disaster and relief organizations should also benefit from being able to portray recent traumatic events on their Web sites (Figure 7-3). CARE has already invested in this possibility by using a grant from the Kresge Foundation. CARE developed a capability to "whisk potential donors away on field trips over several days where they feel

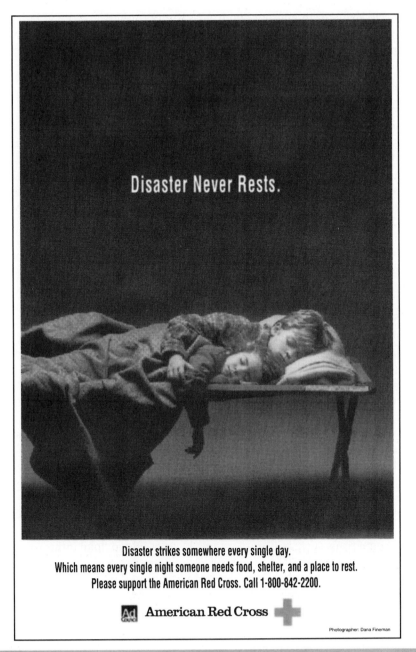

FIGURE 7-3 American Red Cross

Source: The Advertising Council. Reproduced with permission.

and see sights from another country." Visitors to the site were able to follow CARE workers as they went about their efforts to help those impacted by Hurricane Mitch in Honduras and Nicaragua.[20]

Building Lifetime Donors

Of course, nonprofits are interested not just in individual gifts but in attracting a donor for his or her lifetime. Much thought is put into those donors we would describe as in the Maintenance Stage to build high loyalty.[21] The change in focus of many fundraisers has been to be willing to invest more heavily in donor acquisition with the expectation that each donor recruited would yield significant returns over many years, not just the year of the recruitment. It is proposed that fundraisers calculate not just the benefit/cost ratio of a specific donation but the *lifetime value* of a donor against the cost of acquiring him or her. In a recent study in the United Kingdom, Adrian Sargeant and Jane McKenzie analyzed databases of four charities to develop statistical models of "life time value" (LTV). The procedure uses retention rates to calculate the present value of future donations of all of those recruited through each medium. The LTV of donors is then compared to the cost of the medium to provide recommendations as to the amount that should be invested in each method of donor recruitiment.[22]

Major Giving

Both individuals and corporations are sought out for major gifts, which often generate 80 percent of fundraising dollars with 20 percent of the effort. Major gifts are those designed for a specific purpose, and the tactics used to raise them are much different from those used for annual campaigns. There is a much more intense effort made to identify prospects who might be able to make the major gift to the museum's acquisition fund or the university's scholarship pool or to the YMCA's capital campaign. This is now made easier by the availability of search engines and other services on the Internet such as those from Yahoo!, Northern Light, Scoop, and Forbes that can track high-potential donors on a regular basis.[23]

The number of high-potential givers has risen significantly in the last 10 years with the so-called dot-com boom. While the subsequent downturn in this area deflated many portfolios, firms like Microsoft and AOL have created dozens of new millionaires. These newly rich often need help in using their wealth for social contributions, and some firms such as Cisco Systems have provided "philanthropy counseling" services for this purpose.[24]

There are typically several steps involved in developing a major gift program: (1) identifying prospects; (2) "qualifying them" (i.e., looking into secondary records or past giving history to see if they would have the *capacity* to donate the required amount); (3) determining appeals that might be used; (4) assigning one or more volunteers or professional staff members to make the personal solicitation (usually over several calls and visits); (5) preparing the presentation and making the solicitation; and (6) following up the gift with full recognition (in public, if the donor is willing; many are not) and involvement of the donor in the organization and activities that relate to the gift area.

As with many kinds of marketing activities, it is extremely important to understand the *benefits* and *costs* that each prospect might see in the giving opportunity. As we noted in Chapter 4, it is these costs and benefits along with social pressure that will be the major determinants of their actions. However, as we have repeatedly said, volunteer solicitors and fund managers, in their enthusiasm about their own organizations and the fundraising activity itself, tend to emphasize the *benefits* when talking to donors. Benefits, of course, are important. However, when outlining benefits, volunteers must be careful to do two things:

1. Emphasize benefits *to the donor,* not benefits to the organization. Thus, the volunteer solicitor should learn *not* to say "If you give us this money for a minority scholarship, we can attract more high-quality African American and Hispanic applicants." Rather, the benefit should be stated in the *donor's* terms, saying "If you give us money for a minority scholarship, you can feel that you are helping your alma mater increase the richness of the educational experience it can give future students like you."

2. Tailor the benefits to the individual's own needs, wants, and lifestyle situation. Thus, the minority scholarship presentation might be different for a potential donor who is seeking more high-quality minority workers for his or her organization; for a donor who has a son, daughter, niece, or nephew thinking of going to the alma mater; or for a donor who wants to have some influence on the direction that the university will take in the future.

However, benefits are only part of the story. As we noted in Chapter 4, individuals undertake difficult behaviors in stages.[25] In the early Contemplation Stage of thinking about the action (i.e., giving a major gift), potential donors will be weighing benefits and costs but will be paying most attention to the benefits. Certainly, if they do not see major benefits, they are not likely to act. However, as they get closer to action (Late Contemplation), the potential negative factors will become much more dominant in their minds. As noted earlier, the kinds of costs a major giver might consider would include the following:

- Opportunity costs (other expenditures that would have to be foregone, including donations to other charities).
- Publicity that might lead them to be inundated with solicitations from other organizations.
- Worries that the money might be misused or wasted (this was the major barrier mentioned by wealthy donors in the study reported in Table 7-3).
- Worries that a large payment might temporarily put the family at risk in case an emergency arises.

Solicitors should seek to minimize all of these potential costs, especially if they seem significant to the donor. For example, the organization could propose a phased payment plan for the donor who is concerned about having to make a very large single payment.

Tactics

There are a great many techniques that nonprofit organizations use to solicit major gifts. These include auctions, benefit events (theater, sports), invitational dinners (e.g., the $1,000 a plate political "roast"), dances (especially in exotic locales such as a museum or zoo), fairs, fashion shows, small gatherings in a sponsor's home, celebrity meetings, and challenge grants.

An issue in designing solicitation for major gifts is to decide whether potential donors should be "coached" in how much to give or whether this should be left to their judgment. In fact, there are three possibilities:

1. Don't specify any amount.
2. Suggest a specific dollar amount on the low side.
3. Suggest a specific dollar amount on the high side.

The first approach is the most common. People differ in what they can give, and it is felt that this is best left to their individual judgments.

Suggesting a specific amount on the low side is seen as accomplishing two things. It helps prospects know what is considered a minimum proper amount to give. And the "low-amount feature" allows people to get into the habit of giving (the "foot-in-the-door" theory).[26] While there is the problem that many people might have given more, research suggests that the technique can be quite effective. Brockner and others found that in a campaign for a relatively obscure charity, the National Reye's Syndrome Foundation, concluding the sales presentation with the phrase "even a dollar will help" resulted in *twenty times* as much money being raised as when this suggestion was not made.[27] Further, this was more effective than saying "even five dollars will help." The researchers found that the latter yielded more total dollars than the control condition (no request), but *less* than the "even a dollar" condition. This was due to increased frequency of donating under the "dollar" condition, rather than larger amounts being donated. Finally, the research found that the technique applies to both telephone and face-to-face solicitation. Citing earlier research, they also claim that the technique has been shown to work for at least three different charities: Reye's Syndrome, the American Cancer Society, and the Heart Association.[28]

Suggesting a high amount to give works on the theory of the "door-in-the-face." It stretches people's idea of what they should give, and it is hoped that they will give this much or something close to it. Thus, the Give Five Program suggests that citizens give 5 percent of their income and/or 5 percent of their time each week to help others. Most people regard these amounts as too high, but end up giving more than they normally would, that is not shutting the door on the solicitor.

Planned Giving

Of growing importance to many nonprofit organizations is planned giving. Planned giving is a euphemism for charitable gifts that are made at the time of the donor's death. These gifts are often very substantial amounts and, therefore, are of considerable interest for nonprofits with major capital needs (e.g., arts organizations, universities, research-based charities, and hospitals). The approach to securing planned gifts is similar to that for major gifts but often the time period is much longer. It is only after considerable cultivation that many major planned gifts are awarded.[29]

Planned giving can take a wide range of forms, and each vehicle has its own requirements for when and if cash must be turned over and its own tax implications. The two simplest forms of planned giving are through ordinary wills in which the donor pledges a fixed amount or percentage of the estate, and life insurance in which the charity is named as the beneficiary. More complicated forms are also possible.

Charitable Remainder Trusts

Cash and/or property is donated during the donor's lifetime, and the donor and the charity receive income and/or other distributions based on the trust's assets. In a *unitrust,* the income interest is variable, based on each year's appraisal of the assets. In an *annuity trust,* the income interest is a fixed amount based on the assets' fair market value. In both cases, the nonprofit receives the assets upon the death of the donor.

Pooled Income Fund

Donated cash and/or property is pooled by the nonprofit with assets of other donors, and each donor receives income as a proportional share of the earnings of the pool.

Charitable Gift Annuity

Cash or property is donated during the donor's lifetime in return for an annuity to the donor. The nonprofit receives the assets upon the donor's death.

Charitable Lead Trust

Cash or property is donated for a fixed period of at least 10 years, during which time the charity receives all the earnings. Assets revert to the donor at the end of the period.

Life Estate Agreement

A residence is donated to the nonprofit although the donor reserves the right to live in the property for life.

The major benefit of a planned gift to the donor is that he or she can make a major contribution to a favored nonprofit while at the same time reaping significant tax advantages, particularly the avoidance of estate taxes. Because planned gifts represent major investments for donors and because they are subject to tax regulations that change regularly, most nonprofits retain specialists to market and manage these giving opportunities. These specialists can then tailor the planned gift to meet the financial circumstances, age, and number of heirs and dependents of each potential donor.

Nonprofits that do receive assets as part of planned giving programs must be especially careful to manage them with the greatest degree of fiduciary responsibility. Nothing can tarnish the credibility of a nonprofit as fast as poor trust management or inappropriate investments. For example, nonprofit CEOs or boards that have authorized loans to officers out of trust funds have quickly found themselves the subject of public scrutiny and early dismissal.

REVENUE FROM SALES AND SERVICES

As we noted at the outset of this chapter, an important growth area for many nonprofit organizations is in the generation of their own revenue. This growth has resulted from two forces. On the one hand, competition for traditional sources of funding has intensified. There has not been strong growth in corporate or individual donations that can sustain the even faster growth in the number of nonprofits competing for such funds. On the other hand, it has long been the dream of many nonprofit managers, especially those involved in international assistance, to make their programs self-sufficient. The data make clear that they have improved their chances for independence, since the proportion of internally generated nonprofit revenues has risen from 63.4 percent in 1982 to 71.3 percent in 1993.[30]

The growth has come through expanding three kinds of activities. First, nonprofits that market products and services as their principal mission—universities, hospitals, clinics, museums, the performing arts—have all improved their marketing skills, and many have significantly increased their market share vis-à-vis the private sector.[31] These marketers have also been more effective in their pricing strategies so as to increase returns per customer.

Second, many organizations have added retail operations to their main mission. This has been in two principal forms. Where feasible and appropriate, organizations like the Smithsonian, the Kennedy Center, and many, many local museums have gift shops that market both goods related to their prime mission (e.g., health products at the Mayo Clinic) and goods that might appeal to their typical clientele (i.e., "artistic" products in museum shops). A few organizations, such as the Metropolitan Museum of Art and some PBS stations, have opened retail outlets in malls. Many have sought a second line of growth by extending these activities through catalogue and Web site operations. For example, a visit to the Smithsonian Web site (www.smithsonianstore.com) allows anyone anywhere in the world to acquire such exotic items as a "Captivating Cat Lamp" or a "Leonardo DaVinci leather journal."

Third, the more imaginative nonprofits have sought to capitalize on their unique skills, marketing them to private sector, government, and other nonprofit organizations. A major promoter of this perspective is Billy Shore, the charismatic co-founder of Share Our Strength, one of the earliest participants in cause-related marketing. Shore has written extensively about his views in *Revolution of the Heart* and *The Cathedral Within*. His central thesis is that nonprofits can "make money—lots of money potentially—by selling things none of them understood they had: their good names, their expertise at solving difficult social problems, their ability to organize and train untapped labor pools, their artistic talents, even their access to inner-city youth markets."[32] Nonprofits like JumpStart can market their know-how about teaching at-risk preschoolers through profitable educational books and software. Other organizations can help corporations by training special populations, such as training former prison inmates to work in the sheet metal industry. Shore says that, today, 80 percent of Share Our Strength's operations budget is generated from corporate partnerships and licensing arrangements.

This effort is not without its critics. There are those who decry the competitive advantages that tax-free nonprofit product marketers have that allegedly hurt small businesses. Others feel that commercializing nonprofits takes them away from their core missions. The expectation was that they were supposed to be filling in where the private sector and governments have failed instead of becoming just like the private sector in too many ways. Shore and other "social entrepreneurs" have responded that what they recommend is, at bottom, really mission-driven. What they are doing is helping nonprofits to move away from handouts toward responsibility and independence.

There are a number of scholars who think that the move toward increasing revenue from these sources in not a good thing for the nonprofit sector. Burton Weisbrod, a senior Northwestern professor who has studied this phenomenon extensively, argues "forcing nonprofits into either alliances or competition with profit-oriented firms is the root to breaking down the lifeblood of many nonprofits—robbing them of the public trust in their integrity."[33]

SUMMARY

Although nonprofits obtain funds from other sources, fundraising remains essential to their survival and growth. Organizations are gradually shifting from a product or sales orientation to a customer orientation in their approach to fundraising. Greater attention is being paid to establishing relationships with donors rather than merely to raising funds.

Donor markets are of four basic types: foundations, corporations, government, and individual donors. The first three groups are no different from individuals in that fundraisers must understand the potential donor's needs and wants and then show how giving to the nonprofit organization is a way of meeting those needs and wants. Often careful paperwork will be necessary. In particular, foundations, corporations, and governments will look for indications that the nonprofit has a clear mission, careful controls, experienced staff, and a track record of achievement. Secondary sources can help identify grantmakers, but nonprofits are urged to look at various programs more carefully, especially those of foundations, because their views of their roles are changing.

Individual donors go through three stages over their donation history. The early years involve regular small gifts. The middle years provide opportunities for nonprofits to secure major gifts, and the later years provide opportunities for planned giving. In each case, it is crucial that fundraisers be aware of the demographic characteristics of potential donors and their likely motives for giving.

Every fundraising activity starts with clear goals and a well-thought-out strategy. The approach differs depending on the type of campaign. For annual giving campaigns, strong volunteer leadership must first be established and backed up with thorough staff support. Organizational design should match the types of solicitation to be used, and specific goals and accountability should be established to ensure that someone is responsible for every key outcome.

Major gift campaigns involve the use of tools similar to annual drives. However, major gift solicitations are always in person and they often require very long investments of time. Planned gifts also often require long cultivation and, because of their complexity, usually are turned over to highly trained specialists.

Raising funds from the nonprofits' own activities has become an increasing source of revenue for the sector. However, these initiatives are not without their critics who believe they are taking organizations away from their core missions.

QUESTIONS

1. Why is it important to diversify funding sources? Does this complicate the development of a marketing program aimed at resource attraction? Why?
2. Describe the fundraising transition that an organization undergoes as it grows from a new organization to a mature, established organization. Relate the transition stages to the changes that the United Way has undergone.
3. Describe how you would go about seeking corporate donors for a specific nonprofit organization. How would your process and tactics differ if you were targeting a foundation for donations?

4. Identify the key elements of a grant proposal written to secure funds. Imagine you must write a proposal for a grant to fund scientific research on the effects of smoking. Outline the grant proposal and identify key information needs that you must satisfy in order to write a compelling proposal.
5. Some nonprofits have secured funding through product and service sales. What criticisms has this strategy drawn? Do you think that nonprofits should retain tax-exempt status when engaging in commercial activities? Support your position.

NOTES

1. Lewis M. Segal and Burton A. Weisbrod, "Interdependence of Commercial and Donative Resources," in Burton A. Weisbrod (ed.), *To Profit or Not to Profit: The Commercialization of the Nonprofit Sector* (Cambridge: Harvard University Press, 1998), pp. 105–128.
2. Burton A. Weisbrod, "The Nonprofit Mission and Its Financing," *Journal of Policy Analysis and Management,* Vol. 17, No. 2 (Spring 1998), pp. 165–174.
3. *Giving USA* (Sewickley, Pa.: Fundraising Council Trust for Philanthropy, 2001).
4. Thomas J. Billitteri, "Venturing a Bet on Giving," *The Chronicle of Philanthropy,* June 1, 2000, pp. 1, 7–10.
5. Elizabeth Schwinn, "Phaseout of Estate Tax Will Make It Tougher to Raise Funds Over Long Term, Experts Say," *The Chronicle of Philanthropy,* June 14, 2001, p. 27. See also Paul G. Shervish, "Philanthropy Can Thrive without Estate Tax," *The Chronicle of Philanthropy,* January 11, 2001, p. 47.
6. *The Chronicle of Philanthropy* Web site at http://philanthropy.com/stats.
7. *The Foundation Directory Online* at http://www.fconline.fdncenter.org. See also Sandra A. Glass, *Approaching Foundations: Suggestions and Insights for Fundraisers: New Directions for Philanthropic Fundraising #28* (San Francisco: Jossey-Bass Publisher, 2001).
8. *The Chronicle of Philanthropy* Web site at http://philanthropy.com/stats. See also Mark Dowie, *American Foundations: An Investigative History* (Cambridge, Ma.: The MIT Press, 2001).
9. Craig Smith, "The New Corporate Philanthropy," *Harvard Business Review,* May–June 1994, pp. 105–116. See also

Michael Skapinker, "Philanthropy during a Downturn," *Financial Times,* April 27, 2001, p. 12.
10. Elizabeth Greene, "Making the Most of Matches," *The Chronicle of Philanthropy,* April 19, 2001, pp. 27–28.
11. James E. Austin, The Collaboration Challenge (San Francisco: Jossey-Bass Publisher 2000).
12. Paul M. Ostergard, "Fasten Your Seatbelts! Corporate Philanthropy in the 21st Century," *Fund Raising Management,* Vol. 25, No. 1 (March 1994), p. 36.
13. *Giving and Volunteering in the United States 1999,* Washington, D.C.: The Independent Sector, 2001, pp. 4–5.
14. Robert F. Sharpe, Jr., "Successful Fundraising in Challenging Times," presentation to American Cancer Society National Fundraising Leadership Conference, Orlando, Fl., September 23, 1994.
15. *Giving and Volunteering in the United States 1999,* pp. 6–8.
16. Stanley Weinstein, *The Complete Guide to Fund-Raising Management* (San Francisco: Jossey-Bass Publisher, 1998); Kent E. Dove, Jeffrey A. Lindauer, and Carolyn P. Madvig, *Conducting a Successful Annual Giving Program* (San Francisco: Jossey-Bass Publisher, 2001).
17. Mal Warwick, "How to Boost Your Renewal Rate," *The NonProfit Times,* December 1993, p. 40.
18. Mal Warwick, "Increase Donors' Lifetime Value," *The NonProfit Times,* November, 1993, pp. 58–59.
19. *The Chronicle of Philanthropy,* June 14, 2001, p. 10.
20. Tom Pope, "Virtual Events: Field Trips for Your Donors," *The Chronicle of Philanthropy,*

March 15, 2001, p. 4. See also Janet L. Fix, "Nonvirtual Reality Hits Giving Sites," *The Chronicle of Philanthropy,* June 14, 2001, pp. 9, 12; Thomas K. Reis and Stephanie J. Clohesy, *e-Philanthropy, Volunteerism and Social Changemaking* (Battle Creek, Mi.: W. K. Kellogg Foundation, 2000).

21. Kenneth Burnet, *Relationship Fundraising* (London: White Lion Press Limited, 1992). See also Alan R. Andreasen, *Marketing Social Change* (San Francisco: Jossey-Bass Publisher, 1995).

22. Adrian Sargeant and Jane McKenzie, "A Lifetime of Giving: An Analysis of Donor Lifetime Value," London: Charities Aid Foundation, Research Report 4, 1998.

23. Meg Sommerfeld, "Prospecting the Web for Donors," *The Chronicle of Philanthropy,* August 9, 2001, p. 27.

24. Nicole Lewis, "Philanthropy Counseling: The Latest Benefit for High-Tech Workers," *The Chronicle of Philanthropy,* December 14, 2000, p. 10.

25. James O. Prochaska and Carlo C. DiClemente, "Toward a Comprehensive Model of Change," in W. R. Miller and N. Heather (eds.), *Treating Addictive Behaviors: Processes of Change* (New York: Plenum Press, 1986).

26. In a study by Freedman and Fraser, the experimenters asked subjects to comply with a small initial request. Two weeks later, they were contacted and asked to comply with a large request. It was found that 76 percent of the experimental participants *agreed* to comply with the large request, compared to a 17 percent compliance rate by those subjects approached with *only* the large request. See J. L. Freedman and S. Fraser, "Compliance Without Pressure: The Foot-in-the-Door Technique," *Journal of Personality and Social Psychology,* Vol. 4, 1996, pp. 195–202. See also Chapter 17 of this text.

27. Joel Brockner, Beth Guzzi, Julie Kane, Ellen Levine, and Kate Shaplen, "Organizational Fundraising: Further Evidence of the Effects of Legitimizing Small Donations," *Journal of Consumer Research,* June 1984, pp. 611–613.

28. Peter H. Reingen, "On Inducing Compliance with Requests," *Journal of Consumer Research,* September 1978, pp. 96–102; Robert B. Cialdini and David A. Schroeder, "Increasing Compliance by Legitimizing Paltry Contributions: When Even a Penny Helps," *Journal of Personality and Social Psychology,* October 1976, pp. 599–604.

29. Douglas E. White, *The Art of Planned Giving: Understanding Donors and the Culture of Giving* (San Francisco: Jossey-Bass Publisher, 1998).

30. Lewis M. Segal and Burton A. Weisbrod, "Interdependence of Commercial and Donative Resources," in Burton A. Weisbrod (ed.), *To Profit or Not to Profit: The Commercialization of the Nonprofit Sector* (Cambridge: Harvard University Press, 1998), pp. 105–127.

31. Howard P. Tuckman, "Competition, Commercialization, and the Evolution of Nonprofit Organizational Structures," in Burton A. Weisbrod (ed.), *To Profit or Not to Profit: The Commercialization of the Nonprofit Sector* (Cambridge: Harvard University Press, 1998), pp. 25–45.

32. Tracy Thompson, "Profit with Honor," *Washington Post Magazine,* December 19, 1999, pp. 7–10.

33. Burton A. Weisbrod, "Some Unhealthy Alliances," *Atlanta Constitution,* June 27, 1999.

CHAPTER 8

Attracting Human Resources: Staff, Volunteers, and Boards

Volunteers of America in 1997 merged the organization's housing and health services divisions. According to national president Charles Gould, combining these operations has produced synergies in home management and services for the poor, fostering an entrepreneurial culture while preserving and sharpening the focus on people, not properties. The merger also has set the stage for growth, building on a nationwide portfolio of more than 200 housing facilities, home to more than 18,000 low-income people. To meet growing demands for affordable housing, the organization is actively courting as development partners the private sector, other nonprofits, state and local agencies, and nongovernmental organizations.

The $2.8 million Pavilion Apartments in Montrose, Colorado, are a prime example of its approach. Like most new Volunteers of America developments, building Pavilion involved a long list of players and complicated financing. Partial financing came through private placement of $1.8 million in federal tax credits with a for-profit corporation. The placement was arranged by the National Affordable Housing Foundation, a consortium of the nation's three largest nonprofit developers of affordable housing—Volunteers of America; National Church Residences, Columbus, Ohio; and the Retirement Housing Foundation, Long Beach, California. With permanent financing from the Colorado Housing Finance Authority through the SMART loan program, Volunteers of America paid off construction financing from Wells Fargo Bank.

Opened in October, 2000, the Pavilion Apartments were 100 percent occupied within 90 days. Last year, the U.S. Congress increased the affordable housing tax credit allowance to each state from $1.25 per capita, where it had been since the program began in 1986, to $1.50 in 2001 and $1.75 in 2002. The move created powerful new incentives for for-profit corporations to invest with Volunteers of America and other nonprofits in affordable housing. Congress also raised the ceiling on the amount of tax-free bonds that states can issue to finance affordable housing. The debt limits will increase by 50 percent in the next year. "These are very positive developments that will impact millions of low-income families," said Gould.

Source: Reproduced from *Spirit: The Magazine of Volunteers of America,* Spring 2001, p. 9. Reproduced with permission.

To be effective, all organizations need effective planning, management, and operations. In the private sector, more and more of this work is done by systems and not people. However, the nonprofit world is very much dependent on individuals and their contributions—it is very much a "people sector." The human resource challenges for marketers lie in three areas, each with unique features. First, permanent staff in nonprofits must be recruited at wages that are typically below market. Second, in a great many sectors, this staff must be supplemented by volunteers. And, finally, board members must be attracted. Board members are especially important because of their unique role in the nonprofit sector. In contrast to the private sector, nonprofit boards set the strategy for the organization and approve major initiatives. They have special fiduciary responsibilities and are typically careful critics of the performance of the nonprofit CEO.

There are two major advantages that the nonprofit world has in meeting these challenges. First, as Peter Frumkin has noted, nonprofit organizations have an expressive character. They "allow people to demonstrate commitment to social ends and values."[1] In effect, this means that a significant proportion of the population—particularly in developing countries—is willing to accept "psychic rewards" to augment meager (or zero) salaries and modest perks. Second, the corporate sector increasingly sees value in worker volunteer programs and executive participation on nonprofit boards.

However, marketing to attract human resources is still critical. It is our position that, while the special elevated status of nonprofit and public service organizations offers a highly positive platform for seeking help, the organization must also explicitly or implicitly have other benefits to offer as well. This is in part due to the fact that all nonprofits have real competition. Doctors who could help with an anti-smoking campaign or contribute to a charitable activity may agree that what you're doing is admirable and ought to be supported. Nonetheless, they may have many demands placed on their time by other organizations and, indeed, make their social contribution by providing free services to impoverished patients. To get their help, the nonprofit marketer must make them see that the benefits exceed the costs of the help and the benefit/cost ratio for this contribution is better than anyone else's.

RECRUITING AND MANAGING VOLUNTEERS

Volunteers are critical to the success of most nonprofit organizations. Volunteers staff the fund drives, serve as candy-stripers in hospitals, coach the sports teams, take the meals into the homes of the house bound elderly, and are assistants in elementary school classrooms. Their ranks include a majority of the adult population in the United States and a growing number of individuals in both the developed and developing parts of the rest of the world. Volunteerism helps to keep down expenses while providing a channel for socially conscious people to contribute time to a cause they believe in. Among the organizations that make heavy use of volunteers are hospitals, political parties, trade associations, arts organizations, charitable institutions, churches, and social reform organizations. Also, smaller volunteer units are found in schools and social service organizations.

The core concept of volunteerism is that individuals participate in spontaneous, private, and freely chosen activities that promote or advance some aspect of the common good, as it is perceived by the persons participating in it. These activities are not coerced by any institution in society, and the behavior is not engaged in primarily for financial gain. Volunteerism is a significant activity in the United States. Recent data collected by the Gallup Organization for the Independent Sector report the following statistics for 1998:[2]

- 109.4 million Americans (55.5 percent of adults 18 years or older) volunteered an average of 3.5 hours per week in 1998.
- Total volunteered time amounted to 19.9 billion hours. Of this, about 15.8 billion (79.4 percent) was formal volunteering to specific nonprofit organizations.
- Formal volunteering to nonprofits amounted to the equivalent of 9.3 million full-time employees with an estimated value of $225.9 billion.

A distribution of the jobs performed by volunteers in 1998 is as follows:

23.6 percent direct service (e.g., serving food, doing repairs, providing transportation)
16.0 percent fundraising
10.5 percent giving advice, information, or counseling
9.8 percent organizing an event
8.6 percent visiting people, companionship
7.4 percent administrative or clerical work
4.5 percent board member, trustee
4.0 percent advocacy
3.4 percent other
12.2 percent no answer

The kinds of organizations they joined (many of them multiple organizations) are the following:

24.4 percent religious organizations
17.6 percent youth development
17.3 percent education
15.9 percent human service
11.4 percent health
10.3 percent work-related organizations
9.2 percent environment
8.6 percent arts, culture, & humanities
7.9 percent public and societal benefit
4.6 percent political organizations
3.4 percent private and community foundations
2.5 percent international organizations
2.2 percent other
24.4 percent informal volunteering

Cross-National Comparisons

The concept of volunteering is well-ingrained in the modern American experience. Early colonists actively supported each other through barn raisings, community socials, and clothing collections for the needy. The rigors of frontier living made community reciprocity essential for survival. Further, the notion that a person ought to be his or her "brother's keeper" is explicit or implicit in many Christian theologies. Indeed, in his analysis of the American "experiment" in democracy, Alexis de Toqueville[3] argued that the willingness of Americans to establish voluntary associations to meet community needs was one of the key sources of democracy itself.

However, the concept of volunteerism is less well-accepted in other parts of the world. In some countries, especially in Scandinavia, the society is governed by a "social democratic" model that tends to let the state carry out many of the charitable activities one finds handled privately in countries such as the United States, the United Kingdom, and Australia, where "welfare capitalism" is the governing norm. In Sweden and Denmark, there is simply less need for volunteerism.[4] There also used to be little need for volunteerism in the Socialist states of the former Soviet Union and the Iron Curtain countries. Today, however, as newly democratic states are less willing, and even less *able,* to provide social services, countries like Russia and Hungary are turning to private volunteerism and the nonprofit sector to provide needed services and safety nets.[5]

Private voluntary organizations (PVOs) are also becoming more important in Africa, where private sector and state-run efforts at economic and social development have had limited success. Hyden and others[6] have argued that PVOs are to be preferred because they (1) have lower overhead costs; (2) are less bureaucratic; (3) are less subject to political influence; (4) are more sensitive to grass-roots needs and wants; and (5) are better able to mobilize the poor while at the same time providing services when the public sector fails.

In Asia, the pattern of volunteerism is also ingrained as it is in the United States; however, in countries such as Japan, it is rooted in a different religious culture. Thornhardt notes that the Japanese have an extremely effective voluntary self-help system organized through neighborhood associations, called *jichikai.*[7] She quotes Vogel: "The Japanese have been able to provide for the well-being of their population without requiring many except the very old and infirm to become economically dependent on the state, and they have done it in such a way as to reinforce their communitarian ideals."[8] These ideals are rooted in Confucianism, which promotes the community over the individual. Under Confucianism, the individual is expected to help others and to seek harmony and cooperation in interpersonal relations. Today's *jichikai* not only promote social services but also have adapted to the times by becoming active lobbyists and environmentalists.

Voluntary participation in 24 countries worldwide is reported in a recent paper by Salamon and Sokolowski.[9] The level of volunteering was found to be equivalent to 11 million FTE jobs. However, as suggested in the preceding paragraphs and indicated in Table 8-1, the rate of volunteering varies significantly across the 24 countries from a high of 8 percent for Sweden and 7.55 for the Netherlands to a low under a half percent for Slovakia, Brazil, Hungary, and Mexico. The structure of volunteering also varies across the 24 countries.

Salamon and Sokolowski group the activities in which nonprofits participate into two broad categories based on the role the nonprofit plays in the society. The *service role* is the provision of specific valuable services such as emergency relief, social assistance, and health care. The *expressive role* is "the actualization of values and preferences" such as in the arts, protecting the environment, and heritage preservation. The

TABLE 8-1	Volunteering in 24 Countries		
Country	Labor Force[*] (%)	Expressive Role (%)	Service Role (%)
Sweden	8.0	82	14
Netherlands	7.5	52	46
France	5.2	64	32
United Kingdom	4.9	38	56
United States	4.6	30	64
Finland	3.5	78	21
Germany	3.3	57	22
Australia	3.2	44	53
Ireland	3.1	29	66
Belgium	2.9	39	60
Argentina	2.5	29	70
Spain	2.4	42	54
Israel	2.0	31	69
Italy	1.3	36	62
Austria	1.3	NA	NA
Japan	1.1	21	39
Czech Republic	1.0	61	34
Colombia	0.8	19	77
Romania	0.7	32	60
Peru	0.5	1	99
Slovakia	0.4	64	26
Brazil	0.3	3	94
Hungary	0.3	46.5	45.8
Mexico	0.2	49	49
Average	2.5		

[*]*Non-agricultural labor force.*
Source: Lester M. Salamon and Wojciech Sokolowski, "Volunteering in Cross-National Perspective: Evidence from 24 Countries," Working Paper, The Johns Hopkins Comparative Nonprofit Sector Project, 2001.

extent to which each country's voluntary activity is engaged in each role is also shown in Table 8-1.

Salamon and Sokolowski propose that the patterns reflected in Table 8-1 could possibly be explained by the factors outlined in Chapter 1. One possibility is subsumed under what they call "macro-structural" arguments, namely that the extent of volunteerism in the nonprofit sector can be explained by the attitude of a country's government toward social services and the voluntary sector. Thus, one might expect to find less volunteering when governments carry out many services themselves (the "crowding out" hypothesis) and/or if they are hostile to the sector and impose restrictions on it. Their analysis of the data in 24 countries reveals that the first explanation is not supported by their data; indeed, high levels of government spending are associated with high levels of voluntary activity (e.g., Sweden, Finland, France). The "restrictiveness hypothesis" is not supported.

A second set of "micro-structural" arguments proposes that volunteering is associated with a social climate that supports and encourages social connections. They test this notion by treating the size of the nonprofit sector in each country (as measured by FTE) as a proxy for societal support for the nonprofit concept. They find a good correlation between these measures of FTE and volunteerism.

TABLE 8-2 Political Regime and the Amount and Roles of Volunteering		
Political Regime	*Amount of Volunteering*	*Dominant Volunteering Type*
Social-democratic	High	Expressive
Liberal	High	Service
Corporatist	Moderate	Service
Statist	Low	Service

Source: Lester M. Salamon and Wojciech Sokolowski, "Volunteering in Cross-National Perspective: Evidence from 24 Countries," Working Paper, The Johns Hopkins Comparative Nonprofit Sector Project, 2001. Reproduced with permission.

TABLE 8-3 Volunteering in the United States, 1989 to 1998					
	1989	*1991*	*1993*	*1995*	*1998*
Number (in millions)	109.4	93.0	89.2	94.2	98.4
Percent of adults	55.5%	48.8%	47.7%	51.1%	54.4%
Average weekly hours	3.5	4.2	4.2	4.2	4.0
FTE employees (in millions)	9.3	9.2	8.8	9.0	9.2

Source: The New Nonprofit Almanac, Washington, D.C.: The Independent Sector, 2002.

Salamon and his colleagues further explore the relationship between their categorization of the nature of a country's political regime—social-democratic, liberal, corporatist, or statist—as a major predictor of the size of the voluntary sector. In their recent paper, Salamon and Sokolowski demonstrate that this distinction generally does a good job predicting both the extent of volunteering and the dominant type of volunteering as indicated in Table 8-2.

Trends

Trends in volunteering over time in the United States indicate a curvilinear pattern between 1989 and 1998. Nonprofit executives have been worried that volunteering would suffer as more women entered the labor force and work weeks became longer. This may have been the case in the mid-1990s. In 1998, there appeared to be a rebounding in the number of Americans volunteering, although the average hours that each contributed had fallen off. Table 8-3 reports the numbers on adult formal and informal volunteering.

There have also been changes in the *kinds* of nonprofit organizations in which individuals volunteered. Between 1989 and 1998, there were the following changes:

Increasing: Arts and culture, environment, human services, international, work-related, and youth development

Decreasing: Religion[10]

Taking a longer perspective, data from the DDB Needham lifestyle survey collected since the mid-1970s paints a somewhat different picture. These data suggest that there has not been a major change in the proportion of households volunteering. However, an analysis of these data by Kristin Goss indicates that the amount of volunteer *effort* as measured by the number of episodes of volunteering per year has increased 20 percent over this period, from 6.3 to 7.6 times per year.[11]

This growth in volunteering is unexpected. First, Robert Putnam, in his provocative book *Bowling Alone* has hypothesized that, Americans are becoming less and less engaged in a number of ways—voting, joining unions, attending public meetings, and joining churches and community groups.[12] Our social capital appears to be diminishing—but not with respect to volunteering for nonprofit organizations. Traditional predictors of volunteer participation would seem to work for and against growth in this sector. Since the 1970s, socioeconomic status indicators like education, income, and occupation have all increased; historically, they have predicted increased volunteering. However, growing female participation in the labor force would work against volunteering. To sort out these factors, Goss conducted a cohort analysis and found that "Seniors—those who are at least 60 years old—are responsible for virtually all of the increase in voluntary effort." She found that between 1975 and 1997, the number of occasions of volunteerism for those between 30 and 59 remained essentially constant at seven times a year and for those under 30 constant at around four times. However, the yearly rate of volunteering for those over 60 jumped from 6 to 11![13]

One intriguing possibility is the generational effect highlighted by Putnam. Putnam finds that one of the most powerful predictors of overall social involvement is the generation into which one is born. Consistent with the recent work by Strauss and Howe,[14] he believes that different generations are driven by different values that were determined by the year of their birth and the circumstances of their formative years. Goss and Putnam describe a segment of the 60-plus group (born between 1910 and 1930) as the "long civic generation."

Goss, however, remains puzzled by her analysis. She sees what she calls a "wind" driving an increase in volunteering among seniors (especially women) that is not explained by conventional socioeconomic and sociological measures and, in many cases, seems to counteract the potential negative effects of other trends. This same wind has had a much smaller effect on the middle age group and no effect on the youngest cohorts.

What is very troubling to nonprofit marketers is the finding that the largest group, the middle-aged Baby Boomers, may be declining in volunteering and, as Skocpol suggests, trading financial involvement in civic issues for face-to-face involvement.[15] Goss attributes this to four factors:

- Decreased club participation (i.e., overall civic engagement)
- Fewer children at home (prompting PTA membership, coaching, and so on)
- More reliance on television for entertainment
- More full-time work for all adults

Altogether these data suggest that the pool available to nonprofit marketers who seek to increase volunteering is shrinking. However, a bright note is Goss's finding that being asked is a major predictor of being involved.

Recruiting Volunteers

Recruiting volunteers is simply another marketing task and should proceed in a planned strategic way. Consistent with our discussions in earlier chapters, the challenge for each nonprofit marketer is to do the following:

- Determine the target *market segments* he or she is going to pursue.

- Determine the organization's own *positioning* vis-à-vis its competitors—which includes not volunteering.
- Craft a powerful marketing mix to implement the positioning against the target markets.

Positioning and Targeting

In seeking market segments that might be responsive to recruiting efforts, one place to begin is with data on characteristics associated with volunteering. Data from Goss's analysis of the DDB Needham data on volunteering between 1975 and 1998 reveal a number of factors—demographic, lifestyle, and attitudinal—that were positively (+) and negatively (−) associated with volunteering—or not associated at all (blank). These data are reported in Table 8-4.

Data from the Independent Sector add other characteristics not covered in Goss's study. These suggest that volunteering was higher for certain groups:

- 35- to 44-year-olds, followed by those 45 to 54 years old.
- Whites (although rates for African Americans and Hispanics are rising).
- Those living in the Midwest and West.
- Home owners.
- Those born in the United States.[16]

Clearly the choice of targets for each specific organization will depend on its own mission and what it knows about its geographic and social environment. Analysis of the

TABLE 8-4   Correlates of Reported Volunteering by Age Group

Factor	Young adults (<30 yrs.)	Middle-aged (30–59 yrs.)	Seniors (60+ yrs.)
Year (1975–1998)	+ +	+ +	+ +
Employment status	+ +	+ +	+ +
Married			− −
Education		+ +	+ +
Children at home		+ +	
Female	−		+
Good health			
Live in county with high volunteering	+ +	+ +	+ +
Gave/attended dinner parties	+ +	+ +	+ +
Attended club meetings	+ +	+ +	+ +
Attended church	+ +	+ +	+ +
TV is primary entertainment	− −	− −	− −
Feel "hassled"	+		+ +
Financial worries			− −
See most people as honest		+	
Wish for the good old days		−	− −
Like to be thought of as a leader	+	+ +	+ +
Overall R^2	.141	.187	.175

+ + or − − Significant at .01 level.
+ or − Significant at .05 level.
Source: Kristin A. Goss, "Volunteering and the Long Civic Generation," *Nonprofit and Voluntary Sector Quarterly,* 28, 4 (December 1999), p. 409.

characteristics of existing volunteers is also an excellent way to assess market potential. The next step, positioning, is a matter of positioning both the organization and the volunteering opportunity. Positioning the volunteer opportunity requires more extensive analysis of the factors that are likely to cause someone to volunteer.

Developing a Recruitment Strategy

As we indicated in Chapter 3, the conduct of any campaign must begin with an in-depth understanding of the potential target audience. This means understanding what is likely to make them act as the organization wishes and determining what is the organization's major competition. In most instances, competition is at one of four levels.

First, the organization may be competing against inertia. Certainly, Robert Putnam would argue that this is an increasing problem in the American culture. A second level of competition is for the type of contribution the individual might make. Given that the person wishes to give something back to his or her society, this can take many forms. The person can donate, can perform free services (as lawyers and doctors typically do), or can volunteer for some organization. Third, given that the person wishes to give time for volunteering outside of work, he or she may decide among broad categories, such as fundraising for some charity, coaching a soccer team, or helping political candidates. The final level of competition is among various enterprises in the same category—different charities, different soccer teams, and so forth.

A recruiting campaign needs to make decisions early on as to where it plans to focus its competitive energies. This may well come from formative research that looks at the most likely target audiences and what these audiences say is the real competitor or competitors for volunteer time. The next step is to then understand how to bring about the desired action—namely, volunteering for the marketer's organization. The approach we recommend is to use the consumer behavior model introduced in Chapter 4. There, we pointed out that there are two concepts that should drive market analysis at this stage. First, it should be recognized that people will become volunteers in stages and it is, therefore, important to (1) figure out what stage they are in at present and then (2) tailor a strategy to that stage. There are four such stages:

- *Precontemplation*—where the challenge is to get the target audience considering volunteering—possibly instead of doing nothing or just giving money.
- *Contemplation*—where the challenge is to get the target audience to conclude that this is a sensible and desirable thing to do.
- *Preparation/Action*—where the challenge is to get those predisposed to volunteer to actually step forward and take action.
- *Maintenance*—where the challenge is to get the beginning volunteer to continue with this effort and possibly extend his or her service.

Efforts to move audiences from Precontemplation to Contemplation might well be a challenge left to broad-based organizations and associations like Volunteers of America (www.voa.org), the Independent Sector (www.independentsector.org), or the Points of Light Foundation (www.pointsoflight.org), which are concerned with creating a more civil, involved society. The challenge for most specific organizations is with the Contemplators. There, our second consumer framework, the BCOS model, becomes a useful organizing framework.

From Contemplation to Action

As suggested in Chapter 4, when individuals are considering a high-involvement action, there are typically four factors that will have a major impact on their decisions to move forward. These are, first of all, the benefits and costs the target perceives to be involved in taking the action to volunteer—the *exchange* the individual thinks he or she will have to make. But also weighing on the decision will be the influence of others—both for and against—and the individual's sense of self-efficacy, whether he or she thinks that one can actually make the volunteering experience happen. Let's consider each of these BCOS factors in turn.

Benefits

There are a great many benefits that have been found to cross the minds of individuals considering volunteering. A comprehensive list recently compiled by the Tallaght Volunteer Center at Coleraine House in Dublin, Ireland, included the following as possible motivations for people to volunteer:[17]

To feel needed	To become an "insider"	To experiment
To make a difference	To be an agent of change	To have something to get up for
To get to know a new neighborhood	To do something with a family member	For fun
To help someone	To learn the truth	For religious reasons
Because a friend pressured them	To do one's share	To repay a debt
To gain or improve skills	For recognition	To learn about Irish culture
Because they have time on their hands	To get a better balance in life	For work experience
To do their civic duty	To make new friends	To give something back
To be with people who are different	To explore a new career	As an excuse to do something they love
To keep busy	Because they are bored	To donate their professional skills
Because the agency is close by	To demonstrate commitment to a cause	Because there is no one else to do it
To have an impact	As therapy	To feel good
Because they can't do paid work	To do something different from their job	As an alternative to giving money
To be part of a team	Personal experience with a problem	To be a watchdog
To be an advocate	Guilt	To feel proud
To gain status	Because of concern for the client group	Because they were asked
To get out of the house	To gain access to services themselves	To stand up and be counted
To test themselves	To be challenged	
To escape		

Surveys are also a useful way to learn about what motivates volunteers. The Gallup study for the Independent Sector produced a great deal of information on motivations of volunteers and how they became connected to their nonprofit organizations. The reasons for volunteering that were most often considered "very important" in 1999 were the following:[18]

Having an interest in the activity or work	72%
Feeling compassion toward people in need	86%
Gaining a new perspective on things	70%
The importance of the activity to people the volunteer respects	63%

A recent review of past studies of the benefits and costs of volunteering by Chinman and Wandersman drew the following conclusions:

1. Benefits seem to be grouped into three categories first identified by Clark and Wilson in 1961.

   a. *Material*—tangible rewards associated with monetary value

   b. *Solidarity*—intangible social rewards

   c. *Purposive*—intangible rewards from identification with the organization and its mission

2. The relevance and importance of particular benefits vary by the type of organization—those involved in community activities seek different benefits from those involved in, say, international peace or national conservation or child violence efforts.

3. Normative and social benefits appear to be relatively more important.[19]

Costs

The Chinman and Wandersman study found that there has been less research on costs in the literature—perhaps a reflection of the absence of a marketing (or exchange) perspective. A surprising result of their review is that it was often the case that higher participation rates were associated with higher costs as perceived by the participant. This is undoubtedly due to the deeper involvement and perhaps greater participation in volunteering. However, the studies also showed that these higher costs were well exceeded by higher levels of perceived benefits—as expected from their continuing participation. These authors argue for careful attention to benefit cost *ratios,* an approach consistent with exchange theory.

Others

A number of studies have shown that having a personal motivation to volunteer (i.e., a high benefit/cost ratio) is not enough to promote action; others can be a very important influence. First of all, a great many studies show that a prime prompter of action is being asked to volunteer by someone else. The Independent Sector[20] found that only 22.3 percent of people volunteer when not asked, whereas 89.5 percent volunteer when asked. In a number of studies, a great many individuals indicate that they learned about volunteer opportunities from others or they simply joined with others in volunteering. The 1999 Independent Sector study found that friends were the most commonly mentioned person who recruited a volunteer (50 percent), followed by someone at a church or synagogue (32 percent), a family member or relative (19 percent), or someone at work (12 percent).

It is important to recognize that "others" can often act as a deterrent to volunteering. A wide range of anthropological studies have established the importance of group norms in guiding action. Certainly, the positive norms of group solidarity and mutual help found among some religious groups like the Quakers is a strong determinant of volunteering. At the same time, although the evidence is only anecdotal, it is very likely that volunteering is not "cool" among many specific subgroups of the population. This undoubtedly is the case among some teenage groups, and perhaps those not born into the local culture.

Self-Efficacy

Motivating individuals and getting their friends or co-workers to support this behavior is not enough to ensure action. Everyone can recount volunteering opportunities that seemed promising and that others supported but were never acted on. Organizations seeking volunteers must pay careful attention to removing all barriers that may cause people to feel that they just cannot make the volunteer experience happen and be successful. Barriers to action must be removed. A recent study of teenagers who did not volunteer made clear that many of them just did not know how to "make it happen."[21] Among the reasons mentioned were these:

Personal schedule too full	33.1 percent
I'm too young	19.6 percent
No transportation	14.8 percent
Didn't know how to become involved	13.2 percent
May not be able to honor the volunteer commitment	7.1 percent
Don't have the necessary skills	4.6 percent

Clearly, significant increases in volunteering among this population could be achieved by simply showing them how to fit it into busy schedules (e.g., as other role models have done), describing activities for all age groups, providing transportation or carpooling, being clear on the steps involved, showing that the organization will be flexible in case the volunteer's future circumstances change, and making clear that all volunteers will be carefully trained.

In this regard, one development that has significantly increased the ease of volunteering is the Worldwide Web. The Web is important in three ways. First, it provides access to sites like Give.com, the Better Business Bureau's site that rates various charities. Second, it allows individuals to go to a potential organization's own Web site and learn something about it and its volunteering opportunities. This is particularly valuable because many would-be volunteers may be more willing to explore an opportunity anonymously rather than risk the embarrassment or the potential "sales pressure" should they make a personal appearance. The Independent Sector reported that 1 percent of its respondents said that they learned about volunteering possibilities through the Web.

The final contribution is using the Web to match organizations with individual interests. The following are some sites available in the summer of 2001:

United Kingdom: National Centre for Volunteering (www.volunteering.org.uk)

Africa relief organizations: NetAid (app.netaid.org/OV)

United States: VolunteerMatch (www.volunteermatch.org)

Federal volunteering: U.S. Department for Housing and Urban Development (www.hud.gov/volunteering/index.cfm)

Opportunities abroad (many educational): University of California, Irvine (www.cie.uci.edu/iop/voluntee.html)

Western Australia: Volunteer Western Australia (www.volunteer.org.au)

Canada: Volunteer Canada (www.volunteer)

Teens in United States: About (www.teennewsgossip.about.com/cs/volunteering)

Preparation/Action

Besides removing all of the barriers to possible action, organizations should design opportunities for potential volunteers to experiment with a new behavior. Many potential volunteers will have hesitancies about their own competence, will be unsure about the possible benefits and costs, and may even feel that they won't know anyone at the volunteer site. Thus, giving them a trial experience may do much to get over remaining hurdles and prompt permanent action. Certainly, this is a clear, consistent finding in the literature on the adoption of innovations: New products and practices that permit trial are adopted faster than those that do not have this option.[22]

Maintenance—Retaining Volunteers

As we have said earlier in this text, marketing is not simply an external activity. It applies wherever the organization has a target audience and a behavior it needs to influence to be successful. Present volunteers represent just such an important target and clearly merit a specific effort of internal marketing. This is necessary for three reasons. First, internal marketing will help make volunteers better, harder-working, more loyal, and more involved thus making the organization more effective. Second, internal marketing will make it less likely that they will leave. Private sector marketers know very well it is much less costly to market to "present customers" than always going out to find new customers. Finally, satisfied volunteers are likely to be an organization's best source for future volunteers as well as positive word of mouth to the general community.

In considering how to approach target audiences in the Maintenance stage, a useful starting point is with some kind of formative research. This can involve simple conversations and regular tracking of satisfaction levels. From time to time, it will be desirable to conduct formal surveys of volunteers. Another important source of data would be to survey "dropouts" to ascertain what it is that made them quit. A final approach is to conduct periodic assessments of present volunteers' satisfactions and dissatisfactions. Among the sources of dissatisfaction that frequently surface are the following:

1. Unreal expectations when volunteering. This is sometimes the recruit's own fault in that he or she has unrealistic fantasies about how exciting it would be to join the Peace Corps, participate in a political campaign, or become part of the "United Way team," or about how much time would be involved. But just as often the culprit is the nonprofit organization, which, in its zeal to get recruits, paints an excessively optimistic picture of the volunteer's time commitment, type of work, and probable influence.
2. Lack of appreciative feedback from clients and co-workers.
3. Lack of appropriate training and supervision.
4. Feelings of second-class status vis-à-vis full-time staff.

5. Excessive demands on time.
6. Lack of a sense of personal accomplishment.

Another approach is to ask both present and past volunteers what their expectations were for volunteering and how the experience matched—or did not match—these expectations. This is consistent with recent research by Farmer and Fedor that introduces a concept they call *the psychological contract,* first developed by Rousseau in a private sector context in 1989.[23] In a sense, the psychological contract is related to the marketing concept of exchange in that the volunteer comes to have expectations about what the benefits will be from volunteering and of the costs he or she is likely to endure—or will be expected to endure. As we know from the private sector, nothing will yield dissatisfaction and complaining as much as expectations not met. In consumer markets as well as nonprofit volunteering, the marketer has a dual challenge—managing expectations so that they are realistic and deliverable and making sure that the benefits are, in fact, delivered. In the area of volunteering the former are realistically marketing responsibilities, while the latter are more typically the purview of human resource professionals.

The important difference between consumer and volunteer contracts is that the former are transactions for the most part whereas the latter are relationships. Relationships are more likely to have higher emotional content, involve interpersonal trust, and are more likely to be subject to ambiguity and nuance. Nonprofit environments may be much riper places for unmet psychological contracts in part because the job expectations are often ill-defined, formal contracts are rare, screening is limited, formal evaluation and reward systems are rare, and job tasks often vary significantly over time, especially in smaller nonprofits. This is an environment rife with the dangers of broken promises, losses of trust, and hurt feelings.

In their study of a national nonprofit fundraising organization, Farmer and Fedor found good support for the psychological contract model as a predictor of both levels of active participation in the nonprofit's activities and intentions to withdraw. The effect on the latter was somewhat weaker. Indeed, they found that intentions to leave were more closely related to the amount of organizational support the person received. This is consistent with our notion that volunteers seek benefits from volunteering and weigh these against the costs of securing them. The organizational support items that individuals reported in this study can all be seen as benefits "given" by the organization to the volunteer. They see that the organization:

1. values their contribution.
2. appreciates any extra effort from them.
3. does not ignore their complaints.
4. cares about their well-being.
5. cares about their opinions.
6. tries to make their jobs as interesting as possible.

Managing Volunteers

The use of volunteers is not an unmixed blessing for a nonprofit organization. The mix of volunteers and full-time staff can be a volatile one. There can be problems on both sides. On the side of the volunteer, because they are donating their services to the nonprofit and are not paid by the organization, many have the attitude that (1) they don't really *work* for the organization and so shouldn't be *told* what to do, rather, they should be *asked* if they would be willing to do something; (2) they should have a great deal to say about the content and timetable for their assignments; and (3) they deserve continual appreciation for their generosity and commitment. Further, some individuals volunteer, not because they really want to work, but because they have been coerced into volunteering by an employer or peers or because they wish to add an item to their resume. One manager of a large volunteer force has developed what he calls his "rule of thirds." One-third of his volunteer force works avidly with very little direction and encouragement. One-third will work only with considerable motivation and are only effective with careful supervision. And one-third will not work at all under any circumstances and are best ignored (unless they are causing morale problems among those who do work).

On the organization side, there is considerable opportunity for friction to develop if the professional full-time staff views on the volunteers as second-class workers. Among the opinions professionals have been known to offer these:

1. Volunteers are dilettantes. They are not there for the long haul and so don't have to live with the consequences of their impulsive or lethargic performance.
2. Volunteers never really pay attention to their training and instruction because they are only part time and so commit tactical and ethical missteps that hurt the organization.
3. Volunteers often come from occupations in which they boss others and so cannot or will not take direction.
4. Volunteers are often well-to-do members of the leisure classes who (a) consider themselves better than the professional staff (the "Junior Leaguers") and (b) are unwilling to perform grubby tasks like licking envelopes or cleaning bedpans.

In a recent article, Susan J. Ellis, president of Energize, a Philadelphia nonprofit, takes issue with society's "unquestioning acceptance of any work performed by volunteers as self-evidently good. . . . True service—to be of service—is an attitude, not an employment status." Ms. Ellis is concerned that great reliance on volunteers and with providing them with "helping" opportunities can affect the nonprofit's mission. For example, it may be inclined to continue providing help to the poor, the hungry, and the unemployed in order to give volunteers meaningful work. This, she worries, diverts attention from correcting underlying problems that may be causing the need for help.[24]

The potential for conflict between volunteers and professional full-time employees is therefore considerable. The situation can be exacerbated if management does not take firm control of the situation. Again, it is a matter of *attitude.* If management's attitude is dominated by feelings of gratitude that these individuals have so kindly volunteered, all is virtually lost. Management will be unwilling to ruffle the feathers of volunteers. This will only encourage the volunteers' tendencies toward undisciplined performance. At the same time, management will be likely to squelch grumblings of the paid staff for fear that they will upset these needed volunteers. This will only cause further unrest and surreptitious insubordination among the staff. The result will be that management loses control of *both* full-time and volunteer staff.

The solution that the more experienced programs have developed is simply to treat volunteers as much as possible as professional, full-time workers indistinguishable from paid staff. Among other things, authors such as Ken Nations[25] suggest using the following standards and managerial practices:

1. Assessing the volunteers' skills and, as nearly as possible, matching these skills to the tasks to be performed in the organization.
2. Setting out job responsibilities clearly and in detail in advance.

EXHIBIT 8-1   Eleven Characteristics of Effective Volunteer Management

1. The mission and priorities are framed in terms of the problem or issue the organization is addressing, not its short-range institutional concerns.
2. There is a positive vision—clearly articulated, widely shared, and openly discussed throughout the organization—of the role of volunteers.
3. Volunteers are seen as valuable human resources that can directly contribute to achievement of the organization's mission, not primarily as a means to obtaining financial or other material resources.
4. Leaders at all levels—policy making, executive, and middle management—work in concert to encourage and facilitate high-impact volunteer involvement.
5. There is a clear local point of leadership for volunteering but the volunteer management function is well-integrated at all levels and in all parts of the organization.
6. Paid staff are respected and empowered to fully participate in planning, decision making, and management related to volunteer involvement.
7. There is a conscious, active effort to reduce the boundaries and increase the teamwork between paid and volunteer staff.
8. Potential barriers to volunteer involvement—liability, confidentiality, location of the organization, hours of operation, and so on—are identified and dealt with forthrightly.
9. Success breeds success as stories of the contributions of volunteers—both historically and currently—are shared among both paid and volunteer staff.
10. There is an openness to the possibility for change, an eagerness to improve performance, and a conscious, organized effort to learn from and about volunteers' experiences in the organization.
11. There is a recognition of the value of involving, as volunteers, people from all segments of the community, including those the organization seeks to serve.

Source: The Points of Light Foundation, *Changing the Paradigm: The First Report,* 1992. Reproduced with permission.

3. Setting specific performance goals and benchmarks.

4. Clearly informing the volunteers of these goals and of the fact that they are expected to achieve them.

5. Informing the volunteers that if they do not perform satisfactorily in their jobs, they will be let go or assigned elsewhere (the most difficult task).

6. Following through on the standards of accountability, knocking heads, and dismissing volunteers until the word gets around that management is serious in its commitments (the most crucial task).

This straightforward, professional style of volunteer management may seem risky to the inexperienced manager. But both volunteer and professional staff respond very favorably to it. Most volunteers like to be taken seriously and challenged. They appreciate the opportunity to be well trained and well supervised. Those who do not are the one-third you do not want anyway. Full-time paid staff appreciate management's firmness and the fact that they, too, can treat the volunteer seriously, giving orders as necessary and reprimands as required. Performance standards for both groups improve enormously and the nonprofit's effectiveness, efficiency, and morale rise noticeably. Indeed, the organization's volunteer positions can be highly coveted.

Some organizations find principles for managing volunteers are very valuable. The Points of Light Foundation, a national organization dedicated to engaging more people effectively in volunteer community service, has developed eleven principles of effective volunteer management. These are outlined in Exhibit 8-1.

BOARDS OF DIRECTORS AND THE MARKETING FUNCTION

Boards of directors are extremely important groups for nonprofit organizations. Their members serve a number of important functions, many of which have direct impact on the marketing activities of the nonprofit. Marketing principles can be used to recruit future board members.

The Influence of Boards on Marketing

Boards of directors can serve a great many functions for the nonprofit organization. Of course, the most important function is *oversight.* By statute in most states, nonprofit boards have a fiduciary responsibility for ensuring that the organization and its staff members serve the purpose for which the nonprofit organization was founded and do so in an ethical fashion. Thus, boards are important to marketers whenever the marketers consider new ventures: Boards ultimately must decide whether new directions are legitimate undertakings. Suppose that a museum marketer is considering entering a joint venture with a private sector computer equipment maker to sell CD-ROMs containing the museum's collection, and the agreement calls for the museum to promote the CD-ROM at museum events even though the equipment maker keeps 80 percent of the profits on every sale. The board would be the one that decides whether such a venture was within the charter of the organization. The answers are seldom clear, and marketers must spend some of their time cultivating board members (i.e., marketing to them) so that the board sees the venture as being in the nonprofit's long-term interest.[26]

The board will also keep a close eye on the tactics used by the marketing department, asking whether they meet the board's concept of ethical behavior. Many boards will veto, for example, lotteries as fundraising devices if these lotteries are likely to appeal excessively to low-income people. Others will look askance at excessive hyperbole used to promote the product. Hospital boards are particularly sensitive in the latter regard.

A second function that some, but not all, boards serve is direct *decision making.* This is most often the case in small organizations and organizations in their earliest stages of growth. The board serves as a "joint CEO" until the enterprise is firmly established and it can afford a well-qualified independent CEO. In such situations, of course, the marketing manager may find that he or she is constantly going to the board to get approval for specific actions, ad budgets, prices, donation levels, and so on.

A third function of many boards is to *provide specific expertise.* Very often, board members are chosen because they are lawyers, politicians, accountants, physicians, or bankers with the express intention that such experts would be called upon to provide direct help to the nonprofit in their areas of special knowledge. Other board members who do not have direct expertise (e.g., general managers and CEOs) will be recruited because they will "volunteer" experts within their own organizations to be helpful. Thus, in 1995, Philip Marineau, then President of the Quaker Oats Company, agreed to assign staff from his marketing group to help Georgetown University's School of Business develop a position statement for itself and a plan to implement that positioning. Marineau serves on the Georgetown School of Business Board of Visitors.

Although marketing help can come indirectly as in the Quaker Oats–Georgetown case, surprisingly few nonprofits make an effort to have marketing people serve directly on their boards. A study of 1,190 board members in 66 agencies in Rochester, New York,[27] found the following representation of skills:

Function	Percentage	Function	Percentage
Legal, financial	27	General management	5
Medical	13	Marketing and sales	4
Human service	13	Manufacturing	4
Homemakers, retirees	11	Human resources	3
Educators	10	Public relations	3
Government personnel	6	Other	6

Only 7 percent were either marketing or public relations professionals. Yet, as we have indicated throughout this book, nonprofits could make great use of marketing managers, marketing researchers, advertisers, retailers, and other promotional specialists in designing and implementing their strategies.[28]

Of course, a very important function of board members is to help out in *fundraising*. Board members are not only expected to be major donors themselves but also to serve as fundraisers reaching out to their peers and members of their own businesses. Thus, board members many times serve as marketers themselves. Yet, it is typically the case that few of them have any marketing training. Moreover, because the board members are often very powerful in their own organizations or in the community, they are often very reluctant to take advice as to how they ought to approach their fundraising tasks. The approach to "training" such powerful fundraisers that seems to work best is to involve them in the fundraising planning process rather than just asking them to solicit at the end of the planning process. Such involvement very often gets them to understand what is needed to make the campaign be fully customer-centered. This exercise typically causes them to change their own views about how to approach potential donors.

Finally, boards of directors provide a very important function as a *link to the environment*. As we pointed out in Chapters 2 and 3, nonprofits must serve a wide range of publics and respond to a wide variety of environmental influences and changes. Board members who are bankers, politicians, community activists, and educators can serve marketers very well by helping them keep in touch with and, where necessary, influence key components of the nonprofit's marketing environment. Politicians are good at sensing changes in societal attitudes and preferences. Community activists can tell what energizes people the most. Bankers can be sources of demographic and economic trends. Educators can often conceptualize broad themes that can help guide the organization and its marketers.

Recruiting Board Members

For many organizations, securing board members is no problem at all. Inducing someone to be on the board of a church, a public television station, the YMCA, or the local museum of art is relatively simple because of the prestige that an invitation to join the board implies. The only holdout might be the prospect who suspects that the invitation to the board will soon be followed by a large donation request that the prospective member is not prepared to meet.

However, nonprofits would like to have effective board members and not have to spend time recruiting and retaining board members. This is one reason that the late 1990s and early twenty-first century has seen increasing attention paid to institutional branding (discussed in Chapter 6). Nonprofits have recognized that they face real direct competition for high-quality board members. Defining and maintaining an organization's brand has been found to be a powerful strategic and competitive tool. Shocks to well-established brands such as the United Way in the late 1980s and the Boy Scouts in the late 1990s have shown the need for careful cultivation and management of strong brands.

Some board members are easy to attract because they have a commitment to the "cause" of the nonprofit. They may have helped get it started. Or they may be seduced by a charismatic founder. They leap on board because they are believers.

For a large number of nonprofits, however, getting board members and the right *kind* of board members is a difficult task, especially if they wish members to serve many of the five functions outlined previously. It is here that the marketing principles enunciated in this book can be helpful. Probably the most important of these principles is that the best recruitment campaign is one that *starts with an understanding of the target audience's needs and wants.* Just what is it that motivates people to want to join boards of directors?

Candace Widmer proposes an Incentive-Barrier model of board member involvement[29] that parallels the benefit-cost exchange model in Chapter 4. She suggests that there are four kinds of incentives for participation in nonprofit boards:

- *Material incentives:* tangible rewards in goods, services, or money for oneself or one's group.
- *Social incentives:* intangible rewards following from associating with others, including friendship, status, and honors.
- *Development incentives:* intangible rewards that result from learning new skills or assuming civic responsibilities.
- *Ideological incentives:* intangible rewards that come from helping achieve something greater than oneself.

In her study of 98 members of boards of 10 human service agencies in Central New York State, Widmer found strong confirmation of this model as well as a number of implications for recruitment strategies. First of all, consistent with the BCOS model, she found that the *precipitant* for joining a nonprofit board was having a friend ask the person to join. Forty-three percent of the respondents first talked about volunteering with a present member of the board. A further 17 percent were asked by a staff member or the nonprofit's CEO. It is clear that most board members join *people,* not causes.

Among the reasons these 98 board members gave for joining were:

- wanting to help the community. Almost one-half gave altruistic reasons (involving social and ideological incentives).
- believing in the agency's mission (ideological incentives).
- wanting to accomplish something (developmental incentives).
- being obligated by their employer. Many were required to be involved by their job descriptions (material incentives).

- wanting personal development. Many wanted to learn, to grow, and to use skills (developmental incentives).
- repaying the agencies. Six board members came aboard because family members had benefited from the agency.

When asked about benefits directly, 15 percent mentioned employment benefits, 6 percent mentioned at least one social benefit, 50 percent mentioned learning, and 10 percent mentioned ideological considerations.

These findings offer a number of examples of incentives that might be used to recruit new board members. Marketers in a specific nonprofit organization might begin their own efforts by asking their own current board members to reveal the benefits that they get from participating. Such benefits can then be used as a solicitation platform for a new campaign. The real targets of such a campaign will not be current members but prospective members. This makes it obvious that the marketer must also understand how nonmembers perceive the costs or barriers to joining the board. One way to do this would be to have each current board member identify one or two people like themselves who might have been board members (an example of "snowball sampling" as described in Chapter 5). These prospects could then be asked to report on the positive and negative outcomes that they think might be associated with joining the board. These results, coupled with the real experience of current members, can then be used as the basis for a message strategy designed to recruit new members. Data on prospective new members and their perceptions can also be used to develop a clear segmentation strategy. The next step is to use current board members, staff, and the CEO to deliver the message about the benefits to those picked among the target audience. As we noted earlier, people join *people,* not causes.

SUMMARY

Nonprofits have limited resources. As a consequence, they must become experts at securing additional volunteer staffing, skills, and financial resources. This, too, is a marketing task. Others must be convinced that the benefits of helping exceed the costs, that others important to them support the effort, and that volunteering is easy to do.

Nonprofits are unique in needing volunteers to help them accomplish their basic goals. Strategies for recruiting and managing volunteers must take into account changes in the environment. Today's volunteers cover a wider spectrum of people. They are more demanding and have different motivations than volunteers in the past. More importantly, some groups are challenging the basic value of volunteer service.

Recruiting volunteers involves knowing the target audiences. The nonprofit should also know how to retain volunteers. Studies of former volunteers and the satisfaction and dissatisfaction of present volunteers can be helpful in this regard. Problems that emerge may involve volunteers' expectations, training, supervision, and feedback.

Managing volunteers can also be a problem if the organization is not truly professional in its approach. Many volunteers work hard and effectively with little incentive or guidance. Some hardly work at all under any circumstances. Most, however, respond best to being treated as professionals. This means matching responsibilities to skills; setting clear, achievable goals; and then holding volunteers to achieving them.

Boards of directors serve a number of functions that can have an effect on marketers. They carry out oversight, make decisions in some organizations, provide specific expertise, raise funds, and serve as a link to the external environment. Marketing skills can be used to recruit members of boards. Research carried out to determine the incentives and barriers to their participation can be used to develop effective recruitment strategies.

QUESTIONS

1. Is it reasonable to implement a standardized human resource attraction strategy for a global organization? Why? How might the strategy differ among the United States, Africa, and Russia?
2. Develop a research instrument that could be used for interviews with former volunteers of a nonprofit organization with which you are familiar. Describe how you would analyze the findings in ways that would lead to improved retention strategies in the future.
3. Write a recruitment ad that will be posted in local newspapers. Assume that you are recruiting unpaid volunteers to provide administrative assistance in local community centers. What other media might you use on a local level to recruit volunteers?
4. How can you as a manager suppress the natural tensions that exist between professional full-time employees and volunteers?
5. Assume that you are appointed the managing director for a new YMCA in your community, and that you must nominate 15 members to the board of directors. What kind of people would you nominate for the board? What functions would they serve that would benefit marketing? Would you have more than one person of a particular type? Why?

NOTES

1. Peter Frumkin, "Going Beyond Efficiency," *The Nonprofit Quarterly*, 8, 2 (July 2001), p. 22.
2. *Giving and Volunteering 1999*. Washington, D.C.: The Independent Sector, 2001.
3. Alexis de Toqueville, *Democracy in America* (New York: Vintage, 1954).
4. John Boli, "The Ties that Bind: The Nonprofit Sector and the State in Sweden," in Kathleen D. McCarthy, Virginia A. Hodgkinson, Russy D. Sumariwalla, and Associates (eds.), *The Nonprofit Sector in the Global Community* (San Francisco: Jossey-Bass Publisher, 1992), pp. 240–253.
5. Miklós Marschall, "The Nonprofit Sector in a Centrally Planned Economy," in Helmut K. Anheier and Wolfgang Seibel (eds.), *The Third Sector: Comparative Studies of Nonprofit Organizations* (Berlin: Walter de Gruyter, 1990), pp. 277–291.
6. G. Hyden, *No Shortcuts to Progress: African Development Management in Perspective* (Berkeley, Ca.: University of California Press, 1983), and Helmut K. Anheier, "Indigenous Voluntary Associations, Nonprofits, and Development in Africa," in W. Powell (ed.), *The Nonprofit Sector: A Research Handbook* (New Haven: Yale University Press, 1987), pp. 416–433.
7. Helmut K. Anheier, "Private Voluntary Organizations and the Third World: The Case of Africa," in Helmut K. Anheier and Wolfgang Seibel (eds.), *The Third Sector: Comparative Studies of Nonprofit Organizations* (Berlin: Walter de Gruyter, 1990), pp. 361–376.

8. Anna Maria Thränhardt, "Changing Concepts of Voluntarism in Japan," in Kathleen D. McCarthy, Virginia A. Hodgkinson, Russy D. Sumariwalla, and Associates (eds.), *The Nonprofit Sector in the Global Community* (San Francisco: Jossey-Bass Publisher, 1992), pp. 278–289. Also Anna Maria Thränhardt, "Traditional Neighborhood Associations in Industrial Society: The Case of Japan," in Helmut K. Anheier and Wolfgang Seibel (eds.), *The Third Sector: Comparative Studies of Nonprofit Organizations* (Berlin: Walter de Gruyter, 1990), pp. 347–360. Ezra F. Vogel, *Japan is Number One—Lessons for America.* (Cambridge, MA: Harvard University Press, 1980), p. 203.

9. *The New Nonprofit Almanac in Brief,* Washington, D.C.: The Independent Sector, 2001.

10. Lester A. Salamon and Wojciech Sokolowski, "Volunteering in Cross-National Perspective: Evidence from 24 Countries," Working Paper, The Johns Hopkin's Comparative Nonprofit Sector Project, 2001.

11. Kristin A. Goss, "Volunteering and the Long Civic Generation," *Nonprofit and Voluntary Sector Quarterly,* 28, 4 (December 1999), pp. 378–415.

12. Robert Putnam, *Bowling Alone: Civic Disengagement in America and What to Do About It* (New York: Simon & Schuster, 2000).

13. Kristin A. Goss, "Volunteering and the Long Civic Generation."

14. William Strauss and Neil Howe, *Generations: The History of America's Future* (New York: William Morrow/Quill, 1991). See also William Strauss and Neil Howe, *The Fourth Turning: An American Prophesy* (New York: Broadway Books, 1997) and Neil Howe and William Strauss, *Millennials Rising: The Next Generation* (New York: Vintage Books, 2000).

15. T. Skocpol, "Advocates without Members: Recent Transformation of American Civic Life," in T. Skocpol and M. P. Fiorina (eds.), *Civic Engagement in American Democracy* (Washington, D.C.: The Brookings Institution, 1999) (quoted in Goss, "Volunteering and the Long Civic Generation").

16. *The New Nonprofit Almanac in Brief*

17. http://www.volunteertallaght.ie/Resources/Motivations.html.

18. *The New Nonprofit Almanac in Brief.*

19. Matthew J. Chinman and Abraham Wandersman, "The Benefits and Costs of Volunteering in Community Organizations: Review and Practical Implications," *Nonprofit and Voluntary Sector Quarterly,* 28, 1 (March 1999), pp. 46–64.

20. *Giving and Volunteering 1999.*

21. Meg Sommerfeld, "More Than Half of Youths Plan to Volunteer," *The Chronicle of Philanthropy,* September 20, 2001, p. 46.

22. Everett M. Rogers, *Diffusion of Innovations,* 4th ed. (New York: The Free Press, 1995).

23. Steven M. Farmer and Donald B. Fedor, "Changing the Focus on Volunteering: An Investigation of Volunteers' Multiple Contributions for a Charitable Organization," *Journal of Management,* March 2001.

24. Susan J. Ellis, "Reverse Discrimination: Volunteers vs. Employers," *The NonProfit Times,* October 1999, pp. 16, 18.

25. Ken Nations, "Managing Difficult Volunteers Requires Structure and Limits," *The NonProfit Times,* February 1993, p. 36.

26. William G. Bowen, "When a Business Leader Joins a Nonprofit Board," *Harvard Business Review,* September–October 1994, pp. 38–43; F. Warren McFarlan, "Working on Nonprofit Boards: Don't Assume the Shoe Fits," *Harvard Business Review,* November–December 1999, pp. 64–80; Nancy Axelrod, "Who's in Charge?", *The NonProfit Times,* December 1994, p. 32.

27. Robert D. Herman, "Board Functions and Board–Staff Relations in Nonprofit Organizations: An Introduction," in Robert D. Herman and Jon Van Til (eds.), *Nonprofit Boards of Directors* (New Brunswick, N.J.: Transaction Publishers, 1989), pp. 1–7.

28. Eugene H. Fram, "Nonprofit Boards Would Profit with Marketers Aboard," *Marketing News,* April 29, 1991, p. 6.

29. Candace Widmer, "Why Board Members Participate," in Robert D. Herman and Jon Van Til (eds.), *Nonprofit Boards of Directors* (New Brunswick, N.J.: Transaction Publishers, 1989), pp. 8–23.

CHAPTER 9

Working with the Private Sector

The National Geographic Society is one of the world's best-known non-profit organizations. Rows and rows of its magazines are found on Baby Boomers' bookshelves. It is synonymous with exploration into the natural world. It funds major research studies and adventures into remote areas. Its television channel is widely viewed and admired. And its tradition of world-class photography has won it and its staff many awards.

Beginning in 1997, the National Geographic Society decided to embark on a major effort to build its brand and to use that brand to further its mission through licensing arrangements with the private sector. Two new executives were brought in from the Walt Disney Company and Universal Studios. They decided to move beyond the traditional society product portfolio of maps, books, and calendars and an affinity credit card with First USA Bank. Today the society has partnerships with 23 organizations and sells $200 million in merchandise. In 2002, it plans to introduce a wide array of hiking and camping products, including 110 styles of boots—all carrying the National Geographic brand.

The society has been very careful in its selection of products to make sure that each offering advances the organization's mission of expanding people's knowledge about geography. To generate ideas for such products, it sought the advice of its own photographers and explorers in extended brainstorming sessions. As one result, it was decided that every product should be delivered with educational materials and information about the society.

Products are now sold in 150 outlets including national parks and J.C. Penney. At the same time, catalogue marketing has been expanded from a holiday activity to a year-round monthly mailing that reaches 15 million consumers—double that reached in 1997.

The society is also taking its brand into other areas where it can generate support and further its mission. It is starting a magazine for children to be distributed through schools and has embarked on an aggressive venture travel program. Its TV channel provides great synergy in promoting the travel division including production of the 2002 Harrison Ford movie, K-19: The Widowmaker.

Source: Adopted from Martha McNeil Hamilton, "Mapping New Territory," *Washington Post,* June 25, 2001, pp. E1, E13.

One of the most important features of the nonprofit environment at the beginning of the twenty-first century is the growing number of interconnections between the interests of nonprofit organizations and the business world. On the one hand, nonprofits are increasingly finding themselves strapped for support from traditional sources such as private donations and government subsidies. They are increasingly interested in finding ways to leverage these limited resources.

At the same time, corporations are recognizing that there are many direct benefits to the bottom lines from working with nonprofits. Historically, most corporations have made direct contributions to nonprofit organizations and their operations. They have contributed money, loaned their executives and their facilities, and sought to build coalitions to achieve local, national, and international social objectives. Many corporate CEOs have taken direct part in nonprofit operations, serving on boards or heading up fund drives. Industry-funded agencies such as the Advertising Council have long offered specific services to help nonprofit organizations and campaigns achieve maximum impact.

But what is unusual about the twenty-first century is the increasing number of corporations and private-sector marketing executives who are looking for ways to become more closely involved in joint ventures that have a *direct* benefit to the corporation. For example, Chrysler Corporation found that it was having difficulty getting upscale consumers into its showrooms to look at the latest models. Therefore, the company worked out an arrangement with Boston Symphony Hall to place three brand-new luxury Chryslers in the lobby of the concert hall for a Handel and Hayden concert. Upon entering, patrons received marketing brochures and upon leaving got videotapes. In return for this opportunity, Chrysler donated generously to the orchestra's annual campaign.[1]

A sense of this increasing mutual support is found just in the August 27, 2001, issue of *People* magazine. Among the ads for automobiles, shampoos, and cosmetics are the following full-page color ads:

- An ad for *Lee National Denim Day*. The ad features actress Lucy Liu in Lee Jeans saying, "Breast cancer does not discriminate against age, race, or even gender. Please join me on Lee National Denim Day to work toward a cure while spreading the word about breast cancer education and options for treatment." The ad also says, "Participate by donating $5 and wearing jeans to work Friday, October 5. The Susan G. Koman Foundation will receive 100% of the donations. . . . For information and to register your company . . . visit www.denimday.com."

- An ad for *Partnership for a Drug Free America*. Two kids are shown together and the ad tells parents that if they don't know with whom their kid hangs out after school, "You need to start asking. It's a proven way to steer kids clear of drugs. It's not pestering. It's parenting. Contact www.drugfreeamerica.com."

- An ad for *Budweiser*. Headline is "Teenage drinking is down because parents are doing their homework." The copy then mentions the free Anheuser-Busch booklet "Family Talk About Drinking" and points to the company's Web site at www.beeresponsible.com. The ad concludes, "It's people like Susan [the parent in the ad] and programs like this that have helped reduce teenage drinking by 47% since 1982."

- *Reading Is Fundamental*. Special advertising section with people serving as a "Celebrity Storytellers." The copy under a photo of actor John Lithgow reads, in part, "Teach your kids that reading is FUN with these back-to-school reading tips from PEOPLE's 'Celebrity Storyteller' partner Reading Is Fundamental." The ads direct readers to RIF's at www.rif.org.

- A joint ad between the Merisant corporation (the maker of Equal sweetener) and the American Diabetes Association featuring the company president and promoting "America's Walk for Diabetes." The headline is "Nothing could be sweeter than a cure." The Web site is www.diabetes.org/walk/equal.
- An ad for *Staples* headlined "Put $5,000 of FREE school supplies into the right hands. And win a visit from your local NFL head coach." The partnership with the NFL and local schools is described at www.NFL.com/staples.
- An ad for *Target* featuring actress Camryn Mannheim and her high school history teacher, Mrs. O'Byrne. The headline is "Who's Your Mrs. O'Byrne?" and the copy says, "With the Target Take Charge of Education School Fundraising program, you can support your school and your Mrs. O'Byrne. When you shop at Target with your Target Guest Card, Target will donate an amount equal to 1% of your purchases to the K–12 school of your choice. We are who we are because of our schools."

This new set of relationships in which private marketers participate in nonprofit marketing activities for some private sector gain is referred to as *cause-related marketing*. Although cause-related marketing may have many benefits for the corporation and add important resources and expertise to nonprofit causes, the relationships are not without their risks for both sides. Working with corporations is a risky undertaking for nonprofit organizations because such partnerships may end up not serving the nonprofit's long-term interests. Nonprofits need to think very carefully before they risk hard-won reputations by temporarily teaming up with the wrong kind of partner. They also need to worry whether traditional sources of support will disappear as they seek more corporate assistance and partnerships. And they need to worry about how traditional internal constituencies, such as staff and board members, feel about these developments.

For example, many social commentators decry the extent to which corporate brands are appearing on all sorts of public and nonprofit sites. As a recent *New York Times* article noted, "Children visiting the expanded St. Louis Zoo can pet animals in the Emerson Electric Children's Zoo, watch a show at the Bank of America Amphitheater, study bugs at the Monsanto Insectarium and, starting this summer, view the underwater antics of hippopotamuses at the Anheuser-Busch Hippo Harbor."[2] Naming rights have become big business for nonprofits. Hospitals that once had buildings and clinics named in memory of loved ones now find Children's Hospitals in Los Angeles and Providence, Rhode Island, named for Mattel and Hasbro. City-owned sports arenas everywhere now have corporate names like FedEx Field, Target Center, and 3Com Park.

This influx of corporate sponsorships has led many to worry about the impact on a nonprofit's management discretion. Lawrence M. Small, appointed Secretary of the Smithsonian Institution in 2000, has found his appointment becoming controversial in part because of the management rigor he has introduced but also for his efforts to bring in new corporate sponsors that many staff feared would dictate exhibition designs and operation.[3]

In this chapter we consider a number of the ways in which corporations and nonprofits can work together and we point out some of the pitfalls along the way. We begin by looking at one of the best-known types of partnership between the private sector and nonprofit marketing efforts: the work of the advertising community on nonprofit campaigns, most notably the efforts of the Advertising Council.

ADVERTISING AGENCY PARTNERSHIPS

Almost every major community has advertising agencies that are willing to make contributions of their skills and services in the public interest. There are a number of reasons they contribute their services:

- They believe that the nonprofit organization will have important community executives among its other volunteers and so a volunteer campaign will be a major opportunity to make business contacts.
- Goodwill can be obtained by such public-spiritedness.
- Agency executives and staff can achieve personal psychic benefits from working on important social issues rather than just "selling soap."
- Opportunities in the campaign for individual creativity, agency creativity, or both may be considerably greater than when a paying client is "calling the tune." The agency may see a chance to make a major public impression with a highly innovative campaign.
- The campaign presents an opportunity to give experience to junior staff people where a major client is not at risk.

Like volunteers, contributed advertising services can be a mixed blessing for a nonprofit. First, if the donated campaign is costly, the agency may skimp on production values. If it assigns junior people, the execution may not be of the highest quality. Also, if the agency focuses too narrowly on the campaign as merely a chance to make a major creative impact, it may lose sight of the nonprofit organization's basic advertising goals. If the nonprofit managers are alert to these potential dangers, however, they can typically be avoided with timely interventions. Again, as with volunteers, it is up to the nonprofit to treat the donated relationship *as if* it were a professional, fully paid-for relationship rather than a "charity case" for which the nonprofit organization should be grateful (and thus non-interfering).

The Advertising Council

Perhaps the best-known example of donated advertising is the work of the Advertising Council. The council was founded in 1942 just four weeks after the Japanese bombing of Pearl Harbor. Its initial challenge was to promote war-related programs such as buying war bonds, planting victory gardens, and home canning of vegetables. Observers believe that the lives of thousands of American servicemen and servicewomen were saved by the campaign telling citizens that "Loose lips sink ships."

Over the years, the Advertising Council has been deeply involved in American life, creating over 1,000 campaigns (about 40 per year). It has developed advertising slogans that are now widely familiar:

- "Only you can prevent forest fires."
- "A mind is a terrible thing to waste."
- "Help take a bite out of crime."
- "Pollution: It's a crying shame."

Ad Council agencies have brought us such memorable characters as Rosie the Riveter, Smokey the Bear, McGruff the Crime Prevention Dog, and Vince and Larry the crash dummies (see Figures 9-1 to 9-4).

HOW CAN WE ENCOURAGE OUR KIDS TO HAVE DREAMS
THEN DENY THEM THE MEANS TO ACHIEVE THEM?

For nine-year-old Carolyn Michel, the dream is to become a doctor. For the
United Negro College Fund, that's a dream too precious to let die.

For more than 50 years, we've been helping bright, deserving students get the
education they need to turn their hopes into realities.

Please give generously. Your contribution could help someone like Carolyn
make a contribution that benefits everyone. Call 1 800 332-UNCF.

UNITED NEGRO COLLEGE FUND.
A mind is a terrible thing to waste.

FIGURE 9-1 United Negro College Fund

Source: The Advertising Council. Reproducd with permission.

FIGURE 9-2 Seatbelts and Airbags

Source: The Advertising Council. Reproduced with permission.

FIGURE 9-3 AIDS—Facing Reality

Source: The Advertising Council. Reproduced with permission.

FORTY-TWO PERCENT OF ALL MURDERED WOMEN ARE KILLED BY THE SAME MAN.

Each day women are beaten to death by their husbands or boyfriends. Just as frightening, each day neighbors just like us make excuses for not getting involved. For information about how you can help stop domestic violence, call 1-800-777-1960.

THERE'S **NO** EXCUSE
for **Domestic Violence.**

Family Violence
Prevention Fund

FIGURE 9-4 Domestic Violence

Source: The Advertising Council. Reproduced with permission.

The Ad Council operates through donations from industry and assessments from sponsors of its causes. Sponsors pay for material costs but receive creative and media support free. In 2000, the market value of donated media was approximately $1.5 billion and would place the council among the top 10 advertising spenders in the country. One-third of all public service announcements are from the Ad Council. A typical campaign receives the equivalent of $25 million in donated media support. The following is a list of campaigns that the Ad Council created in 2001:

ACT Against Violence	Child Hunger
Afterschool Programs	Community Drug Prevention Campaign
Child Abuse Prevention	Community Schools
Childhood Asthma	Connect for Kids
Crime Prevention	Learning Disabilities
Do Good. Be A Mentor.	Library of Congress
Domestic Violence Prevention	Math Is Power
Drunk Driving Prevention	Operation Graduation
Earth Share	Organ Donation
Employer Support of the Guard and Reserve	Parents as First Teachers
Fair Housing	Reduce, Reuse, Recycle
Fatherhood Initiative	Safe Gun Storage
Fire Safety	Safety Belt Education
Give Kids the World	United Negro College Fund
Healthy Start	Wildfire Prevention

Audio, video, and print materials can be seen on the Ad Council's Web site at www. adcouncil.org/fr_camp_current.html.

The Ad Council has changed many aspects of the way it operates over the years. It practices careful segmentation. Increasingly, it has focused on poor and African American issues. It has introduced campaigns aimed at new media such as the Web and interactive television. In the mid-1990s, it developed a strategic plan that increases its focus on issues relating to children. It has also paid much more attention to its impact. Critics have charged that public service announcements (PSAs, the Ad Council's primary tool) are not effective because they rely on volunteered time and space and often are shunted to remote time slots and unattractive billboard and magazine placements. Most critically, such voluntary placement significantly reduces the chance that the PSAs will be targeted to specific segments. To address this issue, the Ad Council has shifted from reliance on measures of placements and calls to 800 numbers to carefully designed research studies.

In addition to the Ad Council's work, a great many individual agencies in advertising, public relations, Web management, and the like have also volunteered their help in creating promotions for nonprofits, especially in local towns and cities. Because of their restricted budgets, these organizations are grateful for this help. However, a small but increasing trend in the nonprofit sector is for larger organizations and major federal programs to conduct paid advertising and promotion campaigns. One example of this is the national drug abuse campaign sponsored by the Office of National Drug Control Policy (www.mediacampaign.org/index.html) that supplements a program of many years from the nonprofit sector led by the Partnership for a Drug Free America (www.drugfreeamerica.org). A second important example is the national anti-tobacco campaign of the American Legacy Foundation, the prime beneficiary of hundreds of millions of dollars in the national U.S. tobacco litigation settlement (www.americanlegacy.org).

SOCIAL ALLIANCES AND CAUSE-RELATED MARKETING

Social Alliances

One of the most significant growth areas in nonprofit marketing in the last 10 years is cause-related marketing. Cause-related marketing started in 1982 when Jerry C. Welsh, then chief of worldwide marketing for the American Express Company, agreed to make a five cent donation to the arts in San Francisco every time someone used an American Express card and two dollars every time American Express got a new member. In three months, the campaign raised $108,000. The approach gained national attention when American Express (AmEx) tried it out on a country-wide basis. In 1983, AmEx agreed to set aside one cent for every card transaction and one dollar for each new card issued during the last quarter of 1983 to support the renovation of Ellis Island and the Statue of Liberty. The program was a great success. American Express reported sales increases of 28 percent over the same period a year earlier with a total of $1.7 million eventually donated to the renovation project.[4]

Since that first national event, cause-related marketing has grown dramatically. Cone Communications estimated that by 2000, cause marketing had grown into a $2 billion set of activities.[5] Cause-marketing has grown in two other ways. First, we have learned how to initiate and grow individual partnerships. Second, larger nonprofits have learned more about how to manage not just one partnership but a whole portfolio of relationships.

However, it is important to see that cause-related marketing is but one component of a larger trend that Minette Drumwright and her colleagues have defined as "social alliances." For present purposes, we define social alliances[6] as any formal or informal agreement between a nonprofit organization and one or more for-profit organizations to carry out a marketing program or activity over a significant period of time where:

1. both parties expect the outcome to advance their organizations' missions.
2. the corporation is not fully compensated for its participation.
3. there is a general social benefit expected.

These alliances may be either contractual or relational (i.e., having or not having a fixed termination point). If one considers the first cause-related marketing venture by American Express in 1982 as the starting point of the recent intense interest in social marketing partnerships, it seems fair to conclude that most reported social alliances to date have been contractual alliances. The early American Express project to contribute to the restoration of the Statue of Liberty was a contractual arrangement with a fixed closing date. The dominance of the contractual form may be changing as commercial organizations see the strategic potential of social alliances and so develop longer-term, more open-ended relationships. One example of a longer-term alliance is the agreement recently signed between Coca-Cola and the Boys & Girls Clubs of America (BGCA) through which Coca-Cola will invest $60 million and significant staff time over 10 years to help BCGA increase the number of young people participating in its programs (www.bcga.org). Such a relationship meets our criteria in that:

1. Coca-Cola will significantly increase its exposure to a prime market target (young people), improve staff morale in local community activities, and improve its corporate image.

2. BGCA will receive significant investment capital, volunteer assistance, and new promotional opportunities.
3. BGCA does not pay Coca-Cola for the services it renders to BCGA.
4. The result should be a significant increase in the number of at-risk young people involved in positive after-school activities.

It should be noted that our definition of social alliances *excludes* contractual agreements between nonprofit and commercial organizations where the former merely hires the latter (sometimes at below-market rates) to perform specific services. Such arrangements are increasingly common for such service areas as advertising, public relations, research, and distribution.

Contractual and strategic alliances are becoming more and more common and have proved to be very successful. For example, consider the ongoing Avon Breast Cancer Awareness Crusade, which was initiated in 1993 and is based on a partnership between Avon Products, Inc., and the National Alliance of Breast Cancer Organizations (NABCO). Through the crusade, Avon has raised $150 million for breast cancer education and research by carrying out walks and runs and by selling special merchandise (e.g., pins with the insignia of the pink breast cancer ribbon). NABCO distributes the funds to community programs throughout the United States that promote education and access to screening services for underserved women. In addition, Avon's 550,000 salespeople have been trained to talk about breast cancer–and the importance of early detection. They have distributed more than 80 million flyers on breast cancer detection. Some of them volunteer through local breast cancer-related organizations or through special events such as one of the Avon Breast Cancer Walks. The crusade has generated more than one billion media impressions.[7]

In the summer of 2001, Avon announced its most ambitious program to date, called "Kiss Goodbye to Breast Cancer." Two of six new lipstick shades, called "Strength" and "Courageous Spirit" in keeping with the program, are being introduced, and $1 of every $4 in lipstick sales will be turned over for breast cancer research. Promotions will target a number of ethnic groups with spokespeople like Cuba Gooding Jr., Serena and Venus Williams, and Lisa Ling.[8]

Since the Avon crusade began, NABCO has been transformed. Prior to its involvement with Avon, NABCO was an information and education resource with an annual budget of less than $2 million. In addition to augmenting NABCO's education and information efforts, the crusade has enabled NABCO to expand its mission, its clientele, and its annual budget. According to Amy Langer, NABCO's executive director:

> Before the crusade, we were busy empowering those patients who are information seekers, which meant that we were serving educated, white women— "the haves." I had begun to feel an ethical imperative about who we weren't serving—the "have nots"—the medically underserved women. Through Avon, NABCO was allowed to direct money and focus on an unsexy area—underserved women.

Avon is also very pleased with the arrangement. CEO Andrea Jung is quoted as saying: "It's incredibly beneficial to the overall business. When associates, reps, and consumers have an enhanced experience as a result, the shareholder obviously wins as well."[9]

Cause-Related Marketing

Cause-related marketing has a somewhat narrower definition. Adapting the approach of Varadarajan and Menon,[10] we define cause-related marketing as follows:

Cause-related marketing is any effort by a corporation to increase its own sales in both the short and long run by contributing to the objectives of one or more nonprofit organizations.

We employ a broad time horizon for "sales" because a great many activities that do not yield immediate sales can have long-term effects on sales and profitability through improved corporate or brand image, better employee morale, and so forth, brought about by the cause-related activity.

Cause-related marketing can be distinguished from traditional corporate philanthropy which involves simple donations of cash, goods, or services to deserving nonprofits without the expectation that the donations would be publicized or otherwise rebound to benefit the corporation. Thus, when Digital Equipment Corporation, IBM, and Sony agree to contribute equipment to the National Center for Missing and Exploited Children to help it create and distribute posters depicting missing children, these actions can be considered corporate philanthropy because reports indicate that none of the companies used its support for promotional purposes. The same is said to be true of ARCO's support of an educational program called ALIVE (Alternatives to Living in a Violent Environment). Although some might dispute it, ARCO claims the program is not designed to impress final consumers.[11] Many authors suggest the most important criterion is whether charitable donations from a cause-related marketing program come out of the firm's marketing budget or out of its regular charitable donations.[12]

The growth of cause-marketing has been propelled by a shift in corporate attitudes toward social involvement, an issue we discuss more fully below. It has put nonprofits in the current position of partnering with corporations and not, as Weeden notes, begging for help.[13] However, cause-related marketing can be troublesome for some nonprofits. It is clear that cigarette company sponsorships of sporting events or fairs are ways for tobacco companies to get product logos in front of television cameras where their advertising is banned. But Philip Morris's efforts to sponsor the Bill of Rights as a way of keeping its corporate brand name before the public is just a ploy for making people feel that maybe tobacco companies—and tobacco products—are not so bad after all, especially in light of the recent tobacco settlement. Each situation must be judged on its merits. In many cases, the corporation's ulterior motives are transparent and a backlash is created.[14] Philip Morris again presents a case in point. Although the company has, for years, given money to charitable organizations, especially in the arts, much of the goodwill generated by this activity was dissipated in New York City in October 1994 when the company called a number of arts organizations asking them to try to influence pending City Council anti-smoking legislation. Many New Yorkers were greatly offended by this tactic, as were a number of Philip Morris's grantees.[15]

There are several types of cause-related marketing.

Corporate Issue Promotion

This is the case where a corporation promotes some socially desirable behavior on its own without the involvement of any nonprofit. A prime example is the Anheuser-Busch campaign promoting responsible drinking and, over holiday periods, the use of designated drivers. While the ads promote socially desirable behavior, they also remind consumers of the product brand name and cast the corporate product line in the image of one that is purchased by sensible, mature drinkers.

Liz Claiborne has ads calling attention to domestic violence and the need for mammograms. The company also produces a book, *A Million Moms and Mine,* designed to explore what it means to a child to have a working mother. The latter is part of Claiborne's Women's Work Program designed to promote positive change on issues of interest to women. Profits from the book go to the Reading Is Fundamental (RIF) program.[16] Timberland attempts to combat racism on billboards in New York and Germany. Benetton produces shocking ads designed to energize consumers to care about AIDS[17] and a 96-page insert in major newspapers in late 1999 designed to protest the death sentence.[18]

Joint Issue Promotion

This is where a corporation, in cooperation with a nonprofit or government organization, pays for and/or designs a campaign to urge certain behaviors without expecting any direct payback.

For example, in 1992, *Glamour* magazine and Hanes Hosiery joined with the National Cancer Institute, the American College of Obstetricians and Gynecologists, and the American Health Foundation to promote breast-health education among young women 18 to 39 years old. The Hand-in-Hand program stressed lifestyle changes and regular breast cancer screening and involved articles in *Glamour,* promotions in stores sponsored by Hanes, and the production of a wide range of free educational materials. The program was designed to influence young women and to achieve a "trickle up" effect where women under 39 influence their mothers, aunts, and grandmothers to undertake regular exams. The latter group, of course, is at much higher risk for breast cancer. A study on four college campuses found that the Hand-in-Hand materials increased both knowledge of and desire to be proactive about breast health among the target population.

Sales-Related Fundraising

This is where a corporation agrees to donate funds or equipment to a nonprofit or charitable organization in proportion to the number of sales or other customer transactions that are made. This type of cause-related marketing was the very first to get the name. Examples include these:

*   One of the oldest and best-known examples of cause-related marketing is the line of Newman's Own products that boasts the slogan "All profits for charity" (see www.newmansown.com). Started by actor Paul Newman and writer A. E. Hotchner in 1982 with an investment of $20,000, the Newman's Own product line is now available all over the world. Its Web site describes its approach to marketing as "Shameless exploitation in pursuit of the common good." Since its beginnings, Newman's Own has donated $125 million in after-tax profits to thousands of charities in the United States and elsewhere.[19]

*   Safeway supermarkets is typical of many organizations with multitudes of programs tailored to specific communities. Among the programs supported by Safeway in the summer of 2001 in various regional divisions are the following (www.safeway.com/community_ caring.asp):

1. *East Coast*   Voter Registration

   Race for the Cure   Tied Up in Ribbons

   Club Card for Education   Because Vons Cares

2. *Midwest*   Holiday Food Convoy

   A Holiday Tradition   Hunger Free America

   Food Bank of the Rockies   4. *Northwest*

   Neighborhood Block Party   Charity of Choice

   Red Ribbon for Safety   Make a Wish

   Chicago Foundation for Women   Lupus

3. *West Coast*   Waterfront Blues Festival

   Race for the Cure   Taste of Portland

   Operation Blessing   5. *Southwest*

   Escrip   Safeway Charity Fundraisers

   Special Olympics   Thanksgiving Food Drive

- American Express until very recently had a campaign in which it donated two cents of every cardholder purchase to its campaign, "Charge against Hunger." It has donated millions of dollars to Share Our Strength, a Washington, D.C. hunger organization under this program.[20]

- Campbell's Soup Company and a number of other corporations have long had programs involving donations to schools. For example, in 1999, Campbell collected 250 million labels which it converted into purchases of school equipment. General Mills has a similar program involving boxtops.[21]

Licensing and Co-branding

Historically, a great many nonprofit organizations have licensed their logos to private sector marketers and reaped some sort of financial benefit, either a flat fee or a percentage of profits. Universities are prime examples of this approach—for example, Georgetown sweatshirts are found in all corners of the planet. In 1998, companies paid nonprofits more than a half billion dollars for the use of their names. Where the licensing arrangement involves another well-known brand, these programs are sometimes referred to as co-branding. The American Cancer Society (ACS) developed a co-branding relationship with SmithKlineBeecham, the makers of NicoDerm, and the Florida Citrus Commission whereby both businesses could use the ACS logo on their products. The American Cancer Society justified these arrangements not so much for the licensing fees they would produce but because consumption of these products could help prevent cancer. The ACS's view was that if its logo would increase consumption, then the society's own mission would be advanced. For example, the slogan in the television ads for NicoDerm in 2002 was "Partners in helping you quit."

In other examples, Bristol-Myers Squibb has run full-page advertisements for Pravachol, a cholesterol-lowering drug, that featured the name and logo of the American Heart Association. Similarly, Electrolux LLC negotiated an exclusive arrangement with the Asthma and Allergy Foundation to use its name and logo on the cartons in which its vacuum cleaners are packaged and in product literature.

Licensing can also work in the other direction. It is now common for nonprofit organizations like universities and some cultural institutions to have franchised restaurants and coffee shops on their premises. Perhaps the most unusual of these ventures was the decision of the Family Christian Center in Munster, Indiana, to put a Starbucks in its church lobby. Church officials say that the site does not generate a lot of revenue but "It tears down walls and the perception that church is stuffy and cold."[22]

Driving Forces

Social alliances came into being as the result of a number of factors both pushing and pulling private sector marketers to rethink their relationships to their communities. On the consumer side, a number of trends in the 1970s and 1980s significantly increased the demand for greater social responsibility on the part of businesses. The primary driver was undoubtedly the growing level of education of consumers. This education comprised not only formal education but also informal education through media about the environmental damage that corporations were doing.[23] Business scandals, including those involving the savings and loan and junk bond industries during the 1980s, caused many people to question the motives and behaviors of the private sector and made them potentially more responsive to companies that seemed to go against the self-interested corporate norm.

On the business side, a number of trends laid the groundwork for greater social involvement by marketers. Graham suggests the following:[24]

1. Marketers were seeking narrower and narrower target niches. As markets became increasingly competitive, organizations sought ways to differentiate themselves from other me-too organizations. Helping a charitable cause could appeal to those interested in a particular problem or cause or to those who simply responded to "good-hearted" firms.
2. Marketers sought to lower promotional expenses as part of their new approach to philanthropy.[25] As advertising became more and more expensive and promotional wars ate up profits, firms looked for ways to extend their marketing dollars. Cause-related marketing allowed them to leverage their budgets by getting considerable free publicity about their firms and their products. (Indeed, cause-related marketing program expenses typically compete with advertising and sales promotion as part of corporate marketing budgets.)
3. Marketers recognized that an "image lift" would help them in a time when the business world was looked upon with suspicion.

Other factors that encouraged the development and growth of cause-related marketing are the following:

1. Marketers were learning the advantages of building *relationships* with customers rather than just making sales. Having the customer and the marketer cooperate in helping a deserving charity could be seen as a way to build relationships and loyalty.

Indeed, many cause-related programs that give money to charities as a percentage of sales are, in part, designed to make customers loyal to a firm. It has been said that if a marketer can get someone to buy his or her product or service 10 times, that marketer has won them for life. Many cause-related programs are expressly designed to achieve such purchase repetitions. As John Mohrbacher, of Cone Communications, notes, cause-related marketing is a "relationship enhancer."[26]

2. Teamwork was one of the major watchwords of new management practice in the 1980s and 1990s. Firms have learned that staff members will develop better camaraderie and favorable feelings about a firm and will work better and harder when the corporation allows and encourages them to participate in a cause-related project.

3. Finally, many organizations undoubtedly shifted their charitable donations from outright gifts to cause-related marketing because the latter is much easier to justify to increasingly critical boards and stockholders.

Nonprofits have a good reason to seek out partnerships with corporations: It appears to pay off. The responses of consumers are clearly favorable. In two studies in 1993 and again in the 1999, Cone/Roper Cause Related Trends Report:

- Eight in ten Americans have a more positive image of companies who support a cause they care about (84 percent in 1993, 83 percent in 1998).

- As in 1993, nearly two-thirds of Americans, approximately 130 million consumers, report they would be likely to switch brands (66 percent, 65 percent) or retailers (62 percent, 61 percent) to one associated with a good cause.

- In 1993, 31 percent of respondents said when price and quality are equal that responsible business practices will make a difference in their brand choices; one in five, in fact, had made such a choice in the previous 12 months.

- In 1993, 54 percent would pay more for a product that supports a cause they care about.

Cone/Roper found that cause-related marketing was particularly appealing to social activists, opinion leaders, and people with incomes over $50,000. They also found that local issues were more important to respondents than national or global issues.[27] The latter may be one reason that American Express has recently shifted its cause-related programs from national to local issues.

Risks

It might seem that cause-related marketing is a classical win–win situation. The nonprofit marketer gets needed funds, assistance, and attention to an issue; the private sector marketer gets more sales, a better public image, improved employee morale, and, in many cases, better relations with distributors who participate in programs. There are, however, a number of potential pitfalls for both sides of the relationship.

For Marketers

For many private sector marketers, there is a potential for significant negative publicity if the relationship is not the proper one and is not handled in an ethical manner.

Consumers may be very cynical of actions that seem to be transparent attempts to win tolerance of unhealthy business practices. Despite its considerable investment in nonprofit causes such as the Bill of Rights commemorative promotion, Philip Morris has faced a great many critics of its action as cynical. Many thought that, through the Bill of Rights program, Phillip Morris was simply trying to curry favor with people for its efforts to stop increased restrictions on smoking. Similarly, Greenpeace criticized General Motors for its tree-planting program as "greenwashing" because the program tries to cover over the fact that GM has been "a leader in the lobby against fuel efficiency in cars, and that lack of fuel efficiency is one of the primary causes of the greenhouse effect."[28]

If the marketer is not fully candid with the public, its image may suffer. American Express is always very clear to say that it is involved in cause-related marketing at least in part because it hopes to increase sales, employee morale, and so forth. By contrast, Barnes & Noble initially ran into considerable public criticism for not being open with the public in a cause-related marketing project. In Minneapolis, the chain promoted "Operation Bookshelf" in which the public was invited to buy books for donation to children's programs. Two ads were run asking people to come to Barnes & Noble to donate books. What the chain did not tell the public was that the company donated *nothing* to the children's program. In fact, it kept the profits on the book sales: Customers made the donations. Further, the books were not delivered by Barnes & Noble but picked up by the charities, and the ads promoting the project were not run by the company but by a co-sponsor, *Minnesota Parent* magazine. The chain came under fire from the local newspaper, a retired director of the General Mills Foundation, and the executive director of the Minnesota Council for Nonprofits. One member of the public said, "They weren't doing what I thought they were doing, which was making a donation to charity. It seemed like they were lining their own pockets while trying to convince me they were doing something for charity."[29]

If the marketer is not candid with its partner nonprofit, similar bad feelings and bad press can emerge. A good example is the experience of the Women in Community Service (WICS) program. According to WICS, a public relations firm, Fleishman–Hillard, contacted the agency and said that the retailer Limited Express had designated WICS as the recipient of a program it had devised. Under the program, people would bring in used jeans to Express, get a 25 percent discount on new jeans, and WICS would get the used jeans. Limited Express put flyers announcing the program in billing statements to 200,000 of its customers. What it neglected to do was ask WICS if they wanted to participate, which they did not, in part because they had no way to make use of the used jeans they were to be given. Subsequently, no jeans were given to WICS, and WICS claimed that Limited Express owed it $110,200 for the use of its name in a promotion that sold 3,800 pairs of jeans at $29. Lawyers then became the beneficiary of the fiasco. As Carole Cone of Cone Communications noted, "This was just a case of bad business. A good cause-related marketing project is . . . not something shoved down the throat of one party."[30]

Excessive righteousness on the part of a corporation that is deeply committed to social problems can cause critics to lie in wait until the corporation shows its first flaw. In a 1994 editorial in *Advertising Age,* editor Rance Crain criticizes corporations like the Body Shop, saying "the common denominator of these kinds of companies is that they maintain a holier than thou attitude. But if they should stumble and show any evidence of not living up to their lofty preachings, their customers will hold them strictly accountable, more so than if they operated a more mundane—if less contentious—institution."[31]

The corporation runs the danger of being charged with exploitation. A good example was the effort by the maker of Stain Stick and Spray 'n Wash to include a Down syndrome child in a commercial. Presumably, the company thought that such an ad would make children affected with Down syndrome more acceptable in the general society. But, at least to *Advertising Age* columnist Bob Garfield, the effort backfired. Garfield describes the impact of having the child in the commercial: "Merely to say 'appalling' doesn't serve, because it doesn't capture the sense of utter betrayal we feel at having been suckered into what must be the most crassly contrived slice-of-life in advertising history. Can they possibly be using the notion of 'mentally challenged' as a segue to getting out those really tough stains? The spot isn't about raising awareness. It isn't about inclusiveness. It is about exploitation. It is 'My daughter is retarded. Buy Stain Stick.' The result is a stain on advertising that no laundry product can ever remove."[32]

For Nonprofits

There are also a number of important risks to nonprofits' revenues and prestige from becoming involved in cause-related marketing. For example, total nonprofit donations may decline if donors assume that, since they are giving to a charity through a cause-related marketing program, they need not give directly to the charity. The cause-related marketing program may generate much less revenue for the nonprofit than direct customer donations.

The private sector marketer may unduly restrict the nonprofit's operations because he or she may wish to "own" the charity. Many marketers feel they can benefit the most if they come to be very closely identified with a specific cause, as the Body Shop is with the environment or 7-Eleven is with the Muscular Dystrophy Society. Marketers may seek an exclusive arrangement with the nonprofit that is not in the latter's interests. They may also simply put pressure on the nonprofit not to engage in other cause-related marketing ventures or even certain kinds of fundraising that the marketer considers competitive.

The private sector marketer may attract unwanted negative publicity to the nonprofit from its actions in other domains. For example, in October 1993, Jenny Craig Inc. announced that it would give $10 for every new enrollment in its weight-loss programs to the Dallas-based Susan G. Komen Breast Cancer Foundation and would spend $7 million on advertising promoting breast cancer awareness. However, just before the program was announced, Jenny Craig was cited by the Federal Trade Commission for engaging in deceptive advertising practices by making unsubstantiated weight-loss claims. Although the Komen Foundation was aware of the pending charges when it entered the arrangement with Jenny Craig, it was hoping that the matter would be settled before the program was announced.[33]

Close identification with a major corporation may cause individual potential donors to believe that the nonprofit has less need for direct funding because they are "being taken care of" by the company. Donors and other supporters may also be put off by what they see as the nonprofit's excessive commercialism. The introduction of corporate partnerships in public schools has led many parents and social critics to say that schools are feeding their kids to the corporate world and mainly teaching them to be good consumers. Many think this should not be a major (or any) undertaking of school systems even when they are significantly strapped for cash.

Finally, there is a danger that the nonprofit will lose credibility or integrity through its corporate joint venture. The Arthritis Foundation once entered into an agreement with McNeil Consumer Products to market a product to be called "Arthritis

Foundation Pain Reliever." Although the product eventually was taken off the market because of a lack of sales, at the time many people wondered whether the Arthritis Foundation could be truly objective when investigating possible cures or treatments for arthritis since it was in a joint venture with a leading over-the-counter drug marketer. Similar criticisms were made of the American Heart Association. When new food labels were introduced in the United States in 1994, the makers of Quaker Oats Squares, Healthy Choice pasta sauce, Progresso Healthy Classic soups, and a home cholesterol test kit helped the association distribute brochures explaining the labels. Two-thirds of the brochures comprised cents-off coupons for the sponsoring products.[34] Many felt that this venture compromised the Heart Association's independence as a voice advocating the best heart-healthy eating and exercising.

Perhaps the most publicized recent example of co-branding gone wrong was the 1997 agreement between the American Medical Association (AMA) and Sunbeam, which permitted Sunbeam to put AMA's name on products ranging from blood pressure monitors to heating pads. This was an exclusive agreement whereby the American Medical Association name could not be used with rival products. AMA members raised a storm of protest over this agreement, fearing that the AMA name on these Sunbeam products would imply an endorsement and/or would signify that the products were superior to competitive products. The AMA abandoned the arrangement but paid Sunbeam $10 million to settle a breach-of-contract lawsuit.[35]

Developing a Sound Cause-Related Marketing Strategy

From the nonprofit marketer's standpoint, there are a number of steps to be followed if a cause-related marketing partnership is to be successful:

1. Use board members and community supporters to identify potential partners. They also can often detect possible problems.
2. Select a partner with whom there is a mutuality of interest. Thus, the Special Olympics should look to sporting goods companies as sponsors, hunger programs to supermarket chains, and alcohol abuse programs to the beer or liquor industries. It was natural for the National Center for Missing and Exploited Children to turn to Kodak to develop a photo identification system called KidCare ID that would assist police in cases of missing or abducted children.[36] Mutuality of interest has a number of advantages:

   - Both parties are likely to understand the nature of the social problem and the major solutions.
   - The public is likely to be less suspicious of the marketer's involvement. That is, they will not see it as the marketer doing a "cause-of-the-month."
   - Corporations with mutual interest will be much more receptive to solicitations for joint ventures.

3. Screen out partners who may present a conflict of interest. Wallace and Mintz list four potential disqualifiers. A nonprofit should exclude partners:

   - Whose product/service conflicts with the nonprofit's mandate (e.g., Frito-Lay should not sponsor a fat reduction program).
   - Whose product is hazardous to health or the environment.

- Who is under investigation for health, environment, or other violations.
- Whose product and service claims, especially in the area of health, are unsubstantiated.[37]

4. Ensure that the proposed relationship meets the corporation's needs and wants (remember that this is a *marketing* task). A typical set of objectives of a corporation's social responsibility program is the four principles set out by Sir Geoffrey Mulcahy of Kingfisher Ltd several years ago:

- Any supported issue must be relevant to the organization's mainstream commercial objectives. For example, they support crime prevention because safer streets means more shoppers.[38]
- The target audience must be very clear and related in some way to the organization's interests. Thus, Kingfisher supports women's issues because two-thirds of their workers are women.
- Kingfisher limits its involvement to a small number of causes.
- The company tries to build a leadership position to gain a competitive advantage. Thus, they often tackle leading-edge issues such as attitudes toward gay men and lesbians in the workplace.

The nonprofit marketer seeking a corporate partner should be imaginative in portraying how a cause-related marketing venture could meet corporate interests. For example, Second Harvest, a Chicago-based network of community food banks that feed the hungry, seeks out food company help noting how participation in Second Harvest food donations can meet some important bottom-line needs:

- Solving excess inventory problems
- Providing an opportunity for tax benefits
- Distributing products in a visible manner that can substitute for media promotion
- Deflecting charitable requests that would have gone to the retailers with which they are trying to build goodwill[39]

5. Develop a carefully designed, well-thought-through proposal before contacting the corporation. Sir Geoffrey Mulcahy of Kingfisher asks of each project proposed to him:

- Is the charitable organization well run and does it "have an acceptable brand?"
- How innovative is the project?
- Can Kingfisher add value to it?
- What is the resource level required?
- What is the quality of the nonprofit's organizational plan for the project? How will they evaluate their success and report back?[40]

The nonprofit should be prepared to answer each of these questions. Note that it is not necessary to have a proposal in writing to present. Kurt Aschermann of the Boys & Girls Clubs of America believes strongly in "proposal-less" partnership building. He believes that it is critical to have a dialogue with the potential partner and mutually build a personal relationship as well as an organizational one.

6. Make sure that there is a clear specification of the roles that each partner is to play. Make sure that there is full communication so that no one is surprised, especially with unpleasant publicity. Again. Kurt Aschermann is very careful to discuss with potential partners what he calls his "will do/won't do" list at the very outset of negotiations. Most importantly, this sets out what the Boys & Girls Clubs will not do for a partner. This has saved the organization from some awkward demands by partners with whom it really wants to work.

7. Insist on complete candor with the public. Nothing will sabotage a good cause-related marketing program faster than the public learning that while corporation X is donating 1 percent of sales to charity Y, there is a limit on total giving—and the limit is rather low! The Better Business Bureau keeps a close watch on such practices and points to dubious examples such as the pharmaceutical company that advertised that up to $400,000 would be donated to a health and education charity "based on the amount of donations paid to you." In fact, the company guaranteed the $400,000 in advance (which was good in itself) but the amount was totally unrelated to what any consumers did.[41] The corporate partners must agree to be totally candid about what they are putting into and what they are getting out of the arrangement. The public will respect organizations that acknowledge that a program helps their bottom line while benefiting a major social cause.

8. Make the relationship a long-term one. The nonprofit should beware of the corporation which jumps on an issue quickly, perhaps for a quick "image fix." The nonprofit may be hurt if it relies on a corporation with a short-term objective that bails out after a brief period—and plenty of publicity. (This is not good for the corporation either. For example, Burger King was criticized for its sudden involvement in the San Francisco earthquake in the late 1980s because, unlike McDonald's, it did not have a track record of social involvement.[42]) A long-term orientation to the partnership will also allow the partners to evolve into other projects as initial ventures serve their purpose.

9. Agreements with corporate partners should not be excessively restrictive so that the nonprofit's operating flexibility is unduly hampered. The nonprofit should, at minimum, agree not to involve competing organizations in the venture. Corporations like to dominate a charitable project or at least be dominant over direct competitors.

10. Evaluate the results honestly. It is very important to learn from each venture so as to improve future efforts. Careful research can often be the basis for attracting new partners in the future who, like Sir Geoffrey Mulcahy, want hard numbers about likely payouts. The appropriate evaluation depends on the project. After Texaco of Great Britain became involved in promoting child road safety, it looked at a number of measures that showed it was being successful:

- Pedestrian and cycling casualties were down 22 percent by the second quarter of Texaco's participation.
- Interviews with government officials, teachers, and police officers indicated an improvement in Texaco's reputation.
- Interviews showed that Texaco owned the tag line "Children should be seen and not hurt."
- Eight hundred sixty-two company employees volunteered to participate.
- Texaco was given an award by the Royal Automobile Club for its efforts. The award could be used in future advertising.

The Collaboration Continuum

In a 2000 book published by the Drucker Foundation,[43] James Austin of Harvard University summarized the experiences of a number of major social alliances including those between Timberland and City Year, Starbucks and CARE, and The Nature Conservancy and Georgia-Pacific. Austin discovered that these relationships tended to evolve through three stages:

- The *Philanthropic Stage* where organizations get to know each other through the traditional process of seeking and gaining corporate donations. This stage often leads to strong personal connections.
- The *Transactional Stage* where organizations move on to a specific partnership to exchange resources around a specific delineated activity. Much cause-related marketing is of this type.
- The *Integrative Stage* where "the partners' missions, people, and activities begin to experience more collective action and organizational integration."

Achieving the Integrative Stage is where the two partners really appreciate that various kinds of continuing collaborations produce important values for both sides. Based on his extensive experience, Austin has developed the "Seven C's of Strategic Collaboration" to guide potential partners. These are outlined in Exhibit 9-1.

EXHIBIT 9-1

JAMES AUSTIN'S SEVEN C'S OF STRATEGIC COLLABORATION

CONNECTION with Purpose and People. Alliances are successful when key individuals connect personally and emotionally with the alliance's social purpose and with each other.

CLARITY of Purpose. Collaborators need to be clear—preferably in writing—about the purpose of joint undertakings.

CONGRUENCY of Mission, Strategy, and Values. The closer the alignment between the two organizations' missions, strategies, and values, the greater the potential gains from collaboration.

CREATION of Value. High-performance collaborations are about mobilizing and combining multiple resources and capabilities to generate benefits for both parties and social value for society.

COMMUNICATION between Partners. Even in the presence of good personal relations and emotional connections, strategic fit, and successful value creation, a partnership is without a solid foundation if it lacks an effective ongoing communication process.

CONTINUAL Learning. A partnership's evolution cannot be completely planned or entirely predicted and so partners should view alliances as learning laboratories and cultivate a discovery ethic that supports continual learning.

COMMITMENT to the Partnership. Sustainable alliances institutionalize their collaboration process. They weave incentives to collaborate into their individual systems and imbed them in organizational culture. As insurance against the exit of key individuals, they ensure continuity by empowering all levels of the organization.

Source: James Austin, *The Collaboration Challenge* (San Francisco: Jossey-Bass Publisher, 2000). Reproduced with permission.

Portfolio Management

A very important development at the turn of the century with respect to corporate alliances is the growing number of nonprofits that are currently engaged in multiple simultaneous partnerships. For example, in the summer of 2001, the Boys & Girls Clubs of America had relationships with the following partners:

The Allstate Foundation	Fender Musical Instruments
America's Promise	Finish Line
Blimpie	The Gap Foundation
Church's Chicken	IHRSA
Circuit City Stores	J. C. Penney
The Coca-Cola Company	L'Oréal
Compaq Computer Corporation	Major League Baseball
Crest	Metropolitan Life Foundation
CSK Auto	Microsoft
Enesco	New York Life Foundation
Nike	Reader's Digest
Phillips	Taco Bell Foundation
Post Cereals	The Sports Authority
PowerUP	

A challenge for nonprofits is both how to manage all of these relationships at once and how to manage them over time. The latter can well be handled by the portfolio models as discussed in Chapter 3. Partnerships can be arrayed on three dimensions. First, following Austin, they can be considered philanthropic, transactional, or integrative. Second, they can be arrayed in terms of the particular resources they bring in: money, volunteers, and expertise (e.g., marketing skills). Third, they can be partitioned into those with high and low long-term potential. This yields the following matrix:

	Philanthropic Low potential	Philanthropic High potential	Transactional Low potential	Transactional High potential	Integrative Low potential	Integrative High potential
Brings money						
Brings people						
Brings expertise						

Finally, each potential venture could then be described (inside its cell) as to its present or potential scope, say large, medium, and small. Clearly, the nonprofit would want to:

1. Have ventures at all three stages of development. Ideally, one would like a large number of high-potential integrative partnerships of large size yielding resources

in all three areas. However, these will be rare and will not necessarily last forever—for example, as corporate (and nonprofit) goals change. Thus, the nonprofit needs to have other ventures in the transactional and philanthropic stages with high potential. These can be large or medium in scope and perhaps, on occasion, small if the potential seems huge (e.g., with a very close and obvious mission fit).

2. Have ventures yield resources of all three kinds. It is especially important to generate "expertise" resources. As we have said throughout this volume, the private sector has much to teach nonprofit managers, and partnerships are great vehicles for achieving this.[44]

3. Minimize the number of low-potential partnerships at all stages and involving all resources. In the private sector, it is well-known that weak products and brands will have huge hidden costs because managers will be spending too much time on them, wasting funds and staff time that could be productively used elsewhere. The same is true with weak partnerships.

4. Consider organizing the partnership staff around these divisions. It takes a different kind of person and different systems and management styles to run philanthropic ventures than those that are transactional or integrative. Similarly, managing partnerships where the "currency" is people will be very different from those that are organized around money.

Nonprofits are grappling with these options. Kurt Aschermann of the Boys & Girls Clubs of America describes his approach in Exhibit 9-2. This is an area in which we may expect considerable growth in the development of more sophisticated planning models over the next decade.

EXHIBIT 9-2

KURT ASCHERMANN OF BOYS & GIRLS CLUB OF AMERICA ON CAUSE PARTNERING

In the early '90's as Senior Vice President for Resource Development I realized, after approaching Reader's Digest for their annual 30K gift, that the corporate funding world was changing. Our usual contact, within the Chairman's office, referred us to the marketing and sales department in order to get our gift. After procrastinating, I did contact them and concluded they were looking for us to become more a partner with them in using the money to foster the understanding of Reader's Digest as a good corporate citizen. They were also asking us to be creative on reaching potential new customers. We stumbled around to provide what they were looking for and eventually presented an "awareness based" enhanced program.

Our new approach lead to the $30K annual gift growing to a five year, $1 million commitment. It seemed this new approach worked.

After discussions with a member of our board, Rick Goings, then CEO of Avon, we concluded we needed to formulate new strategies for reaching corporate donors with more than just a hand out. Our cause-related marketing strategy was the result, and we created new systems for doing business called Proposal-less fundraising.

(continued)

In the mid-1990s we realized we were on to something and began to fine-tune the system. We asked our board for staff, which we recruited from the for-profit sector, and created a relationship marketing team. This team changed our language, and our way of operating again, and began to formulate a Strategic Philanthropy strategy (Roberto Goizueta, the late CEO of Coca-Cola, was the first to use that term to describe how Coke was approaching its charitable work). This strategy called for the implementation of systems for exploring the corporation's marketing and sales strategy as well as its consumer targeting methods, and was centered on convincing potential partners we cared about their business, as well as what they could do for us. A $60 million commitment from Coca-Cola as well as several $7 million commitments from the likes of J. C. Penney, GAP, and others resulted.

Finally, though we quickly gained a reputation as a charity that "got it," as we approached the twenty-first century, we realized the new business climate, including the explosion of the dot.com world, mandated us to be even more sophisticated in our relationships with corporate partners.

Much of our success, we believed, resulted from our using business practices in our dealings with corporations. We understood that CRM, the acronym for cause-related marketing in the nonprofit world, meant customer relationship (or relations) marketing in the for-profit world, and we understood our customers were the corporations. We took specific steps to re-invent ourselves to behave in new ways:

- We began to treat our corporate partners as their ad agency and promotions agency would, with teams of people working on the account.

- We responded at all costs and encouraged our partners to think creatively about their business and how their charity could enhance it, then moved quickly to implement their ideas.

- The Corporate Opportunities Group was born, the first (we believe) formal nonprofit, cross-functional team ever constructed exclusively to target and "land" big corporate accounts for a charity. The strength of the COG was coming from an agency-wide commitment by senior management to "loan" employees to the team where their performance on the team entered into their compensation package. The COG works and has already seen great success with Crest/P&G, the Sports Authority, Post Cereals, and Circuit City, who have all signed multi-year, multi-million dollar cross-promotion deals with the Boys and Girls Clubs of America.

SUMMARY

In addition to cash donations and volunteer support, there are a great many other kinds of help that nonprofits need in order to carry out their objectives. More and more nonprofits are turning to business for help to leverage their own limited resources.

Advertising agency partnerships have been one of the longest-running sources of business support for nonprofits. Agencies often wish to help nonprofits because of the business contacts the relationship brings and for the goodwill, the chance to be highly creative, and the chance to give experience to junior staff where a major client is not at risk. However, there are risks for the nonprofit if the ad agency skimps on production values or loses sight of the nonprofit's goals.

A good example of the kind of good agency relationship that can be fostered is the work of the Advertising Council. Since 1942, the Ad Council has created over 1,000 campaigns, developing such familiar advertising slogans as "Only you can prevent forest fires" and "Help take a bite out of crime." One-third of all public service announcements on television today are from the Ad Council. Each campaign receives the equivalent of $25 million in donated media support. Recently, Ad Council campaigns have become increasingly focused on ethnic and racial minorities.

A rapidly growing form of business–nonprofit partnership is cause-related marketing. Cause-related marketing is an arrangement by which a corporation seeks to increase its own sales by contributing to the objectives of one or more nonprofit organizations. Started in 1982 by American Express, cause-related marketing is now estimated by some to be a $2 billion business. There are four main types of cause-related marketing: corporate issue promotion, joint issue promotion, sales-related fundraising, and licensing.

There are potential risks for both marketers and nonprofits in joint cause-related marketing ventures. Marketers can be accused of cynical attempts to cover up unhealthy business practices. A lack of candor can affect their corporate image or poison their relationship with the nonprofit. They can also be charged with excessive righteousness and/or exploitation. For the nonprofit, there are risks that total donations may be reduced. Corporate partners may overly restrict the nonprofit's actions. They may bring unwelcome "baggage," and the nonprofit may lose its own integrity in the wrong kind of partnership.

Steps involved in developing a sound cause-related marketing strategy involve careful selection of corporate partners with mutual interests, possibly using board members' advice. Partners with conflicts of interest should be screened out. Solicitation of partnerships should follow the sound marketing principle of showing them how the partnership will meet corporate needs and wants. The partnership proposal should be set out in careful, precise terms. Ideally, the relationship should be long-term and one of complete candor both with the public and between partners. Results should be evaluated honestly.

QUESTIONS

1. Explain why an advertising firm might enter into a "social alliance" with a nonprofit. How would such a relationship benefit the advertising firm? How would you attract a leading advertising firm to partner with your nonprofit organization?
2. A number of firms are increasingly engaged in Corporate Issue Promotion. Is this a desirable trend? What are some of the risks? Why have firms become more involved in cause-related marketing?
3. Imagine ExxonMobil decided to support Greenpeace by offering to donate a percentage of its sales (up to $20 million) to environmental restoration. What are some of the risks of this proposal from the perspective of Greenpeace? Should Greenpeace accept this offer? Why or why not?
4. Using the Seven C's of Strategic Collaboration framework (illustrated in Exhibit 9-1), identify key partnership linkages that would produce an effective alliance between a nonprofit group that you know and a public corporation.
5. The Arthritis Foundation loaned its name to an over-the-counter drug product. What other nonprofit organizations should consider this use of their "brand name"? What are the risks in doing this?

NOTES

1. Stephen H. Judson, "Maestro, Hand Me the Sales Brochure," *New York Times,* April 3, 1994.

2. Julie Edelson Halpert, "Dr. Pepper Hospital? Perhaps, For a Price, Company Names Are Busting Out All Over," *New York Times,* February 18, 2001, section 3, pp. 1, 21.

3. Jaqueline Trescott, "Smithsonian Benefactor Cancels $38 Million Gift," *Washington Post,* February 5, 2002, p. A1; Milo Beach, "Why I Think the Smithsonian Is Misguided," *Washington Post,* January 27, 2002, p. G1; Philip Kennicott, "Open Letter Berates Smithsonian's Small," *Washington Post,* Jan. 7, 2002, p. C4.

4. "Charity Fund-Raising Is a Popular Marketing Tool," *Washington Post,* September 3, 1991, p. D2.

5. Cone, Inc. at www.cause-branding.com/Pages/research.

6. Minette E. Drumwright, Peggy H. Cunningham, and Ida E. Berger, "Social Alliances: Company/Nonprofit Collaboration," Report # 00-101 (Cambridge, Ma.: Marketing Science Institute, 2000).

7. Alan R. Andreasen and Minette E. Drumwright, "Alliances and Ethics in Social Marketing" in Alan R. Andreasen (ed.), *Ethics in Social Marketing* (Washington, D.C.: Georgetown University Press, 2001), pp. 95–124.

8. Allison Fass, "A Campaign by Avon on Breast Cancer," *New York Times,* August 17, 2001, p. C3.

9. Ibid.

10. P. Rajan Varadarajan and Anil Menon, "Cause-Related Marketing," *Journal of Marketing,* 2 (1986), pp. 58–74.

11. Shari Caudron, "Fight Crime, Sell Products," *Industry Week,* November 7, 1994, p. 49.

12. P. Rajan Varadarajan and Anil Menon, p. 59.

13. Curt Weeden, *Corporate Social Investing* (San Francisco: Berrett–Koehler Publishers, Inc., 1998).

14. Richard Steckel and Jennifer Lehman, "Think It Through — *Again,*" *The NonProfit Times,* February 1994, p. 37.

15. Paul Goldberger, "Philip Morris Calls in I.O.U.s in the Arts," *New York Times,* October 5, 1994.

16. Don Oldenburg, "The Messages," *Washington Post,* June 23, 1992, p. C5.

17. Ibid.

18. Bob Garfield, "The Colors of Exploitation: Benetton on Death Row," *Advertising Age,* January 17, 2000.

19. Charles Champlin, "Hot, Sexy and (Almost) 70," *Los Angeles Times,* December 18, 1994.

20. Anthony Giorgianni, "Big Businesses Are Finding that Good Causes Are Good for Business," *The Hartford Courant,* November 25, 1994.

21. Stephanie Thompson, "Pepsi Hits High Note with Schools," *Advertising Age,* October 9, 2000, p. 30.

22. Michelle McCalope, "Church Retailing," *Time,* 2001, p. 11.

23. L. Lawrence Embley, *Doing Well While Doing Good* (Upper Saddle River, N.J.: Prentice Hall, Inc., 1993).

24. John R. Graham, "'Doing Good' Is Good and Bad for Business," *Supervision,* July 1994, pp. 11–13.

25. Craig Smith, "The New Corporate Philanthropy," *Harvard Business Review,* 72 (May–June 1994), pp. 105–116.

26. Mickey Meece, "Consumers Like 'Cause Marketing' Survey Finds," *The American Banker,* June 8, 1994, p. 13.

27. Ibid.

28. Jeffrey D. Zbar, "Wildlife Takes Center Stage as Cause-Related Marketing Becomes a $250 Million Show for Companies." *Advertising Age,* June 28, 1993, p. S-1.

29. Robert Franklin, "Help the Needy—and Maybe Merchants, Too," *Minneapolis Star Tribune,* December 24, 1993.

30. Stephen W. Colford, "Jeans Giveaway Labeled a Poor Fit." *The Hartford Courant,* November 25, 1994.

31. Rance Crain, "Social Marketing Misses the Mark," *Advertising Age,* September 26, 1994, p. 22.

32. Bob Garfield, "This Heavy-Handed Ad Exploits Someone New," *Advertising Age,* p. 50.

33. Anthony Giogianni, "Big Businesses Are Finding that Good Causes are Good for Business." *The Hartford Courant,* November 25, 1994.

34. Ibid.

35. Glenn Collins, "A.M.A. to Endorse Line of Products," *New York Times,* August 13, 1997, Section A, p. 1; and Greg Johnson, "Officials Urge Limits on Use of Nonprofit Logos," *Los Angeles Times,* April 7, 1999, Part C, p. 1.

36. Shari Caudron, "Fight Crime, Sell Products."

37. Gwynneth Wallace and James Mintz, "One Step at a Time," *Health Promotion in Canada,* Summer 1994, pp. 1–3.

38. Howard Schlossberg, "Surviving in a Cause-Related World: Social Agencies Grow into Sophisticated Marketers," *Marketing News,* December 18, 1989, p. 1.

39. Sir Geoffrey Mulcahy, "The Four Principles of Corporate Giving," *The Financial Times,* October 25, 1993, p. 15.

40. Albert B. Crenshaw, "Looking a Gift Horse in the Mouth: Consumers Should Be Cautious About Business/Charity Fund-Raisers," *Washington Post,* September 1, 1991, p. H3.

41. Howard Schlossberg, "Common Sense, Research Should Guide Cause-Related Marketing Campaigns," *Marketing News,* December 18, 1989, p. 12.

42. James Austin, *The Collaboration Challenge* (San Francisco: Jossey-Bass Publisher, 2000), pp. 21–29.

43. Kevin P. Kearns, *Private Sector Strategies for Social Sector Success* (San Francisco: Jossey-Bass Publisher, 2000).

CHAPTER 10

Organizing for Implementation

America's Promise is an ambitious organization. It was founded as a follow-up to the President's Summit in April of 1997. At that summit, Presidents Ford, Carter, Bush (Senior), and Clinton, along with Nancy Reagan, challenged the country to make youth a national priority. America's Promise's first executive director was General Colin Powell. The organization's mission is to build and strengthen the character and competence of our youth by fulfilling the Five Promises:

1. Caring adults
2. Safe places
3. Healthy start and future
4. Marketable skills
5. Opportunities to serve

Its principal method of operation is to work with—and energize—a great many kinds of partners. Over 500 organizations are now members of the Partners Alliance, who commit to significantly expanding their own efforts to have impact on at least one of the Five Promises. The partners include corporations, nonprofits, colleges and universities, faith-based groups, associations and federal agencies, and arts and culture organizations. (See the organization's Web site at www.americaspromise.org.)

The organization also focuses on over 550 "Communities of Promise" that have agreed to make a special effort to implement the Five Promises. In San Diego, one of the principal vehicles for organizing local participants is through the Internet using America's Promise's web platform called Promise Stations. This Web site provides a variety of tools that allow interested individuals, businesses, and organizations to find ways they can "buy into" the program, locate partners, and begin to take action. Each community can tailor the site to its own needs while making available the underlying support available from national headquarters. The San Diego leaders developed a partnership with a local college, California State San Marcos, to provide technical expertise for their efforts, and the college hopes to eventually serve as the site's webmaster.

Source: Drawn in part from Craig Causer, "Promise Stations Target Big Features, Low Cost," *Nonprofit Times,* September 1, 2001, pp. 23–26.

As we indicated in several places in the preceding chapters, nonprofits are increasingly becoming large-scale organizations involved in a range of complex undertakings. In the last chapter, we discussed the problem many organizations are now facing in managing significant numbers of partnerships with the private sector. We have also talked about the extent to which the nonprofit sector is becoming an international force. Certainly, many of the larger nonprofits, such as Habitat for Humanity, are undertaking significant offshore ventures. The other major organizational issue that many large nonprofits are facing is how to manage a multi-site organization (i.e., one with hundreds or thousands of chapters or local clubs).

In this chapter, we consider the organizational issues facing today's large, complex nonprofit marketers. However, we shall first consider the challenges of organizations that are only beginning to think that marketing might be a useful set of concepts and tools that may help them achieve their missions more effectively.

INTRODUCING MARKETING—PUSHING OR PULLING?

When marketing is first proposed as a philosophy and set of techniques for improving an organization's performance, this introduction typically comes about in one of two ways. One pattern is for marketing to be *pushed* into the organization by one or more key individuals who have been exposed to its potential in outside seminars or in formal academic training or who come to the nonprofit from a commercial enterprise where marketing is a very powerful force. These potential change agents shuttle about the organization trying to convince others, most importantly CEOs, of the wisdom of their views. They frequently encounter considerable intraorganization resistance, which is often reflected in disparagement of the marketing function and frequent allusions to its nastier manifestations. Unless the change agents are very highly placed in the organization or are extremely convincing in their personal promotion campaigns, the introduction period is likely to be quite prolonged under a "push" scenario.

The other common pattern for the introductory period is for marketing to be *pulled* into the organization by environmental forces. This condition occurred in health care in the 1980s as market conditions increased the pressures on nonprofit hospitals to improve performance. Marketing came to be viewed as a potentially highly useful approach to such improvement. Pressures to introduce marketing are further heightened if one or more direct competitors begin to use marketing or are rumored to be beginning soon. Marketing is likely to be introduced much faster under a "pull" scenario than if it is "pushed" into a sometimes reluctant institution.

In the growth phase following marketing's introduction, attempts are made to expand marketing's role and formalize its position in the organization. Typically, marketing is first formalized as a staff function *coordinating* programs and providing advice to others. Only later, as marketing proves its value and/or environmental pressures become more intense, is it often changed into a specific line function with its own staff and responsibilities for programs and specific volume results.

Even when marketing becomes a formal department during the growth phase, its role may be inconsequential. The mature phase can therefore be identified by the transition of marketing from being just another division or function to being a top-level management concern. In this phase, marketing philosophy has permeated much of the organization's planning. Marketing has relatively few detractors and virtually no effort is needed to market marketing itself. Concern has shifted to this issue: how to market *well.*

In this chapter, we initially discuss where marketing should be positioned within the organization. We then turn to a discussion of how marketing activities should be structured and how a marketing orientation can be implemented before turning to the important challenges now facing the very largest nonprofits.

MARKETING'S POSITION IN THE ORGANIZATION

The positioning of marketing in an organization, and even what to call it, is not a trivial decision. In the 1970s and 1980s, when marketing was first being introduced in a serious way in the nonprofit field, marketing was often positioned either far down in the organization or in some advisory staff position. When a marketing person was first introduced at the American Cancer Society, the candidate was responsible for "market intelligence" and was positioned far down the organizational chart, reporting to the vice-president of communications, who had a vice-president for public relations and advertising and a vice-president for product production. This reflected both a lack of understanding and acceptance of marketing across the organization and a lack of appreciation for the contributions that it might make to the organization's mission. After a number of years and considerable attention to demonstrating how strategic marketing works and promoting marketing successes, the chief marketing person became the vice-president of strategic marketing and branding, reporting directly to the CEO.

Even today, in many nonprofits there is much disagreement about where marketing ought to fit. In our view, marketing should be at the very top of the organization. Depending on the organization's mission, it may be quite appropriate for the CEO to have strong marketing skills and a "marketing mindset." This follows our argument at the very start of this book that marketing is vital because its role is to influence behavior and its armamentarium of concepts and tools is—in the best organizations—focused in a laser-like fashion on this behavioral bottom line. As we noted in Chapter 3, nonprofits have a large number of constituencies that they need to address, including clients, funders, regulators, commercial partners, and the media. Because influencing behaviors is critical to success, marketing must be central to the mission.

To be most effective, marketing therefore needs to have the resources and the control necessary to be successful—that is, to bring about the organizational impacts the nonprofit needs to prosper. This means that marketing must ultimately be a *line position* with significant budgets and direct authority to make designated behaviors happen. In early years, it may be prudent for marketers to adopt a staff role until such time as they prove their merit and ingratiate themselves with suspicious traditional staff.

The next question, then, is this: What should marketing control? This issue is still not resolved in 2003, as is reflected in the titles of the senior marketing people at some of America's top nonprofits attending one of the earliest "summits" of these managers organized by one of the authors. Here is a selection of those titles:

- Vice President of Strategic Marketing and Branding, American Cancer Society
- Senior Director of Line of Service Marketing, American Red Cross
- Vice President of University Relations, Baylor University
- Director, Sales and Marketing, Planned Parenthood Federation of America, Inc.

- Senior Vice President, Marketing and Communications, Boys & Girls Clubs of America
- Director, Relationships/Marketing Group, Boy Scouts of America
- National Director of Advancement, Girl Scouts of the USA
- Director, Association Advancement, YMCA of the USA
- Director, Marketing Services, John F. Kennedy Center for the Performing Arts
- Director of Development, Feed the Children
- Vice President of Communications, Volunteers of America
- National Director of Marketing, National Multiple Sclerosis Society
- Manager, Brand Stewardship, United Way of America
- Vice President, Development and Communications, Project Hope
- Executive Vice President & Director of Pubic Affairs, Partnership for a Drug-Free America

It is clear from these titles that, in the very best organizations, the word "marketing" is sometimes not even in the job title. Further, it is very often formally described as comprising one or more of the following functions:

- Communications
- Development (which usually means fundraising)
- Membership (which can also include fundraising)
- Public Affairs (which can mean Public Relations)
- Brand management
- Sales (which can include catalogue and retail operations)

What is interesting here is the frequency with which "communications" is in the title. This undoubtedly reflects higher management's view of marketing as the "message people." It also may be a tactical decision to "hide" marketing behind nonthreatening nomenclature. In either case, potentially the choice can cause one of several kinds of problems:

1. It may reflect an "image problem" where marketing is seen only as communications and so the organization misses its full potential.
2. Marketing will only be given control over communications and not have responsibility over other departments and functions that have major impacts on target audience behavior.
3. It reflects "turf wars" within the organization where other areas do not want to be subsumed under "marketing."

In contrast, one might ask this: What *should* marketing control (i.e., have responsibility for)? We would argue that, in the ideal organization, marketing would:

- Be directly responsible for functions and staff whose primary responsibility is to influence key target publics of the organization. This could mean responsibility for:
  a. Communications—directed at many publics
  b. Public relations—directed at influencing the media

    c. Direct sales (catalogues, sales)
    d. Volunteer recruitment
    e. Membership recruitment
    f. Fundraising

- Have an advisory role for functions that can *indirectly* impact target audiences (positively or negatively) or that have as their principal roles tasks more important than the marketing components of their portfolio. This could include:
  a. Volunteer management
  b. Human resources (negative staff interaction with a target audience can sabotage the best marketing campaigns)
  c. Membership management
  d. Information technology and Web site management

These are not ironclad distinctions. It may well be that some functions in the second category belong in the first. For example, as we shall discuss in a later chapter, a major component of the anti-drug campaign of the Office of National Drug Control Policy is an elaborate Web site marketing campaign. Where the target audience is teenagers, the Web is one of the single most important tools for reaching and having an impact on this group.

Recruiting Great Marketers

Once a marketing staff position is defined, the next critical step is recruiting a first-rate marketer to fill it. Here, an important change that has occurred in the 1990s is that the pool of talent now encompasses a significant number of mainstream commercial marketing people. A significant proportion of the nonprofit marketing managers who attended the "summit" conference noted above (and those who came to Summit II and Summit III) had commercial marketing experience. No longer are nonprofit marketers drawn from within the nonprofit world (e.g., former managers of fundraising, advertising, public relations, or direct mail divisions).

    Part of this shift in the human resource pool is attributable to the growing sophistication of nonprofit marketing and to its significant size and scope of operations. Commercial marketers know they are much more likely today to have the resources and supportive management that was not present even 10 years ago. However, there remain a number of barriers to attracting the best talent. An initial problem is salary.

The Salary Problem

One of the distinct problems managers have in attracting talented marketing people into the nonprofit world is the low salaries that are routinely paid to managers and staff. There are a number of reasons for this situation. First, decades ago, work in nonprofit organizations was "women's work," and job categories in all sectors in which women dominate have historically been underpaid.[1] Second, the culture of many nonprofit organizations is one of sacrifice in the face of daunting challenges. Members of an organization trying to do something about a dreadful social problem are not expected to reap private gain for doing so. Such a culture is common in organizations still in the "founder stage," during which they are dominated by dedicated leaders who will sacrifice for their cause and expect others to do so also.

    Third, most donors to nonprofit organizations (and many staff people and members of boards of directors) expect that most of the organization's revenues will go to services for their target audiences. Staff members should not take money that should be going elsewhere. Fourth, as we have noted throughout this book, nonprofits often have very limited budgets and feel they cannot afford higher salaries. Finally, a great many of those men and women who choose nonprofit careers are *willing* to take lower salaries because they gain significant psychic income from what they do.

There are also external pressures to keep salaries low. Concerns about "extravagant" salaries have led to scandals in organizations such as the United Way of America. These scandals have prompted a subcommittee of the United States House of Representatives to consider a federal law to place a cap on salaries paid to nonprofit executives.

The consequence of all of these forces is that low salaries are often set for marketing positions and nonprofit organizations often cannot attract the kind of talent they need if they are to become truly effective. As Marianne Briscoe said recently, "It can be difficult for . . . founders to understand that to move to higher levels of effectiveness people with experience and special skills must be brought into the organizations— people who know about computer systems, financial management and fund-raising for example." She could easily have added marketing researchers, product managers, advertising copywriters, and so on to her list. To attract the first-rate MBA majoring in marketing who could easily earn $75,000 at Procter & Gamble or IBM, the ambitious nonprofit has to offer a lot more than what Briscoe calls "Peace Corps wages."[2] Indeed, some nonprofit marketers have become so frustrated with the salary and perks in the nonprofit world that they have migrated back to the private sector. Jay Steenhuysen, director of philanthropic planning at Brown University, sees a "brain drain" among fundraisers as being a potentially very serious threat for nonprofits.[3]

The problem is even more serious overseas. Americans seeking to work in other countries find the wages there are even lower, unless they are able to work for a multinational nonprofit such as CARE or Childreach that provides cost-of-living adjustments to their expatriate workers.[4]

Two Cultures

In a recent series of in-depth interviews of marketers who have moved from the commercial to the nonprofit sectors organized by one of the authors,[5] a number of interviewees expressed frustration with their new environment. In part this reflects contrasts in the two cultures, as described in Chapter 3, where commercial marketers are accustomed to such tactics as segmenting markets and ignoring difficult-to-influence targets, to worrying about issues of efficiency, and the acceptance of risks. This often runs counter to the norms and values of those brought up in social service cultures, and heated battles often ensue.

Interviewees also found differences in the "decision styles" across the sectors. In the private sector, they were accustomed to decisions being made relatively quickly by some designated executive based on analysis and arguments raised by his or her staff and/or consultants. Once the decision was made, responsibility for performance was assigned and goals set, and the participants moved on to other issues and challenges. Marketers who did not perform well could reasonably be expected to lose their jobs!

In nonprofit organizations, marketers report important, frustrating differences. First, the process takes much longer. Two reasons for this appear to be that decisions are often considered the responsibility of a group rather than an individual and there is a felt need to consult with every possible stakeholder who might be affected by the decision. A second problem is that there is a reluctance to take risks. If analysis shows some downside potential, nonprofit managers are often reluctant to move forward or, at best, will postpone the decision, hoping some new, conclusive insight will emerge. Finally, there is a frequent tendency not to assign blame for inadequate performance.

A possible explanation for these differences in style goes something like this:

1. Individuals in nonprofit organizations join up because they wish to avoid the judgmental rat race of the commercial world.
2. They accept reduced salaries in return for not only working on socially important problems but also having a "workstyle" that is much less stressful.
3. They do not want to be responsible for making co-workers' work life unpleasant.
4. They attempt to make decisions that leave everyone happy or at least not feeling neglected.
5. They consider it harsh and unpleasant to be too judgmental about poor performance.

It may be expected that, over time, this environment will shift more in the direction of the commercial model as more and more nonprofits pay attention to achieving high performance as recommended by students of the field like Letts, Ryan, and Grossman[6] and increasingly demanded by foundations, philanthropists, and nonprofit watchdogs.

DEVELOPING INITIAL MARKETING PROJECTS

To maximize marketing's acceptance in the organization, marketing directors will want to demonstrate that marketing thinking can have major impacts on objectives that are important to the organization. Many members of the organization will be critical of marketing, arguing that it is inappropriate or a waste of money, or that the money could be spent better elsewhere. Others will be puzzled about what marketing is or does. Only a few will see it as a strong opportunity for the organization.

In the face of this skepticism, marketing managers must carefully choose high-visibility projects that, if successfully executed, demonstrate the value of marketing. The marketing director can devise these projects alone, but it would be better if he or she meets key groups and conducts a needs assessment to get ideas on important marketing needs. This is especially important when the marketing function is very new to the organization. For example, it would be good strategic planning for a new marketing director at a hospital to meet with department heads (individually or in groups), describe the work that can be done (marketing analyses, new program assessment, communication planning, and so on), and ask about any projects he or she might be interested in seeing done. This approach will build goodwill and understanding with various people in the organization and lead to many project ideas, often more than can be handled by a single marketing director operating with a small budget. The director should not promise to do work on any project until he or she reviews the possible projects and chooses the best ones. The best early projects to undertake would have four characteristics:

1. A high impact on making money or saving money for the institution.
2. A relatively small cost to carry out.
3. A short period of time for completion.
4. A high visibility potential if successful.

Presumably, some projects will stand up better than others under these criteria. The main thing is to avoid major projects that will take a long time, cost a lot of money, and not yield definitive results. The organization will not have the patience to support costly, drawn-out marketing projects, and this will significantly delay marketing's progress.

MANAGING MULTINATIONAL NONPROFITS

A growing phenomenon in the 1990s and early twenty-first century is for nonprofit organizations to locate in more than one country. Organizations such as CARE, the Red Cross, and the Salvation Army have had operations worldwide for many years. Many others, like the United Way and Habitat for Humanity, are becoming similarly international. This raises a number of important organizational questions with respect to marketing operations. When a nonprofit decides to move internationally, there are a number of options:[7]

- *The Export Department.* In this form, the marketing operation is headquartered in a single country such as the United States and marketing experts go from country to country carrying out their programs as need dictates. The Academy for Educational Development, a major nonprofit consulting firm, adopts this approach.

- *The Multinational (or Multi-Local) Organization.* The organization has operations in a number of countries. Each country has its own local management and a considerable amount of autonomy. Coordination is managed at headquarters. CARE operates as a multinational.

- *The Global Organization.* This organization treats the world as one single market and develops universal strategies that apply everywhere. Local managers may adapt programs slightly to meet local needs. Habitat for Humanity's programs reflect this thinking.

The strongest debate is between multinational and global organizations.[8] Managers with a global point of view argue that barriers between countries have broken down greatly, that nonprofit problems are surprisingly similar in various countries, and that there can be great savings by developing a single basic strategy. They also argue that global programs offer consistency around the world that can increase awareness and effectiveness. Global strategies also mean that the nonprofit marketing organization can, over time, become extremely good at the few things that are its central global strategy.

Managers with a multinational orientation argue the opposite. They say that, although barriers have broken down between countries, this applies mainly to middle- and upper-class markets. Thus, one might have a global strategy for certain kinds of direct mail fundraising directed at the middle classes. However, for programs targeting the lower classes, differences across countries are significant, especially when one considers differences in language and culture. Separate programs are needed for each country. Indeed, many argue that differences *within* countries merit treating local ethnic market segments as "mini-nations." Even for programs where cultural differences are of minimal importance, multinationalists argue that differences in rules and regulations across countries make local programs essential. They do not deny that much can be gained from standardizing across countries; however, they argue that too much is unique to each nation or to each subregion to have a single strategy that will fit every situation.[9]

The multinational form appears to dominate in the early twenty-first century. Tom Harris, chairman of the World Fund Raising Council, is quoted as saying, "Very few nonprofits operate effectively transnationally. Organizations like Save the Children have national organizations with perhaps an international secretariat: rarely will you find a Frenchman working permanently in the offices in another country." Harris attributes this pattern to the fact that "all nonprofit organizations throughout the world tend to be chauvinistic."[10] This observation suggests that, over time, as the nonprofit world itself becomes more global and chauvinism fades, we may see more globally centered organizations emerge as they have in the private sector.[11]

MULTI-SITE ORGANIZATIONS

Another challenge facing large nonprofit organizations is marketing through multiple sites in a single country. This is the case where an organization like the American Cancer Society or the Boys & Girls Clubs of America have individual chapters or clubs in different cities or, in some cases, several within a city. The relationship between these individual units and the central "headquarters" is a crucial component of marketing planning.

There are two important dimensions here. First, a manager must ask this: Should local units be independent and to what degree? In the Boys and Girls Clubs of America, each club is independently run with its own board of directors and its own set of activities. At the American Cancer Society, individual chapters are, in a sense, local offices of a central organization. In comparison to the private sector, BGCA is like General Motors or Ford, whereas ACS is like Macy's. The challenges for each are different.

In the "local office" model, the major challenges are two. First, to what extent should marketing capability be built into the local operation and, second, what should be the relationship with "headquarters." Pushing marketing capacity down the chain of command to the extent possible makes sense to many organizations in that it increases the pervasiveness and acceptance of marketing and it increases the probability that strategies will be more responsive to local idiosyncrasies. Clearly, some local operations will be too small to hire a marketing person. However, it should still be the case that the local CEO be given extensive indoctrination into the marketing mindset and a thorough appreciation of the need to be customer-driven. This will make future coordination easier and will often produce insights from the local level that will improve country-wide performance.

An alternative that some larger organizations have adopted is to establish regional offices with marketing staff. These bring the marketing perspective closer to the field and help ensure local coordination and cooperation. In some cases, campaigns might properly be segmented on these very same regional bases.

The more difficult challenge is when there is local autonomy of some considerable degree. Autonomous local organizations can be very powerful. For example, in the United Way system, local operations in New York, Chicago, and Los Angeles annually have operating budgets in the hundreds of millions of dollars. As a consequence, they are likely to have strong CEOs, powerful local boards, and their own marketing staffs. This, of course, can make for much more potent and customer-centered campaigns and programs at the local level. However, it also can lead to great fragmentation and a lack of coordination when *country-wide* strategies are put in place. This has proven especially troublesome when the organization attempts to mount a new national branding campaign as Volunteers of America has recently attempted (see also Chapter 6).

One approach to this problem is for the central organization to consider its role to be a service arm meeting the needs of the "locals." The alternative route—the one more typically taken—is to seek to manage the organization nationally. The "secret" to coordinating such national efforts in an autonomous multi-site system is simply to apply the marketing principles we have been espousing throughout this book. This is another case where one has a target audience (the local enterprises) and a set of behaviors (say, getting "on board" with a nationwide branding and positioning effort) that needs to be influenced. Headquarters must be sensitive to local needs and wants and to demonstrate the ways in which the desired behavior (cooperation) will meet local interests. This is, of course, oftentimes easier said than done, especially when there is a history of friction and/or where strong personalities are involved. It also can be very troublesome when the national efforts are ineffective or counterproductive. It is not surprising to find large locals concluding that they can do it better.

Of course, friction between headquarters and the field will be especially high if there is any scandal or evidence of malfeasance at the central office. The relationship between autonomous chapters and headquarters is typically where the locals raise funds and submit regular fees (franchise fees in the private sector) to headquarters. Misuse of these funds, as with the United Way in the 1980s, can sunder ties with locals in ways that can take years to repair.

ORGANIZATIONAL DESIGN

As the marketing department in any one unit (e.g., national headquarters) grows in physical size, how it is organized internally becomes a critical question. This will affect not only how the department is run but what kinds of people can be employed. The options typically found in the private sector as design alternatives can be adapted to nonprofit marketing with limited rethinking. These alternatives are (1) functional organization, (2) product/service-centered organization, (3) customer-centered organization, and (4) mixed organization.

Functional Organization

Most growing nonprofit marketing units first take on the appearance of a functional organizational structure as shown in Figure 10-1A.

As the marketing group absorbs once separate functions such as public relations, advertising, and marketing research, it is natural to keep them as separate functional units within marketing. Each function may initially be the responsibility of a single employee. As the marketing group grows, the functional units inevitably grow, and each function may well have its own manager.

The organization may choose to retain a functional structure for a long time. One obvious reason for this would be if the subunits never become larger than one or two

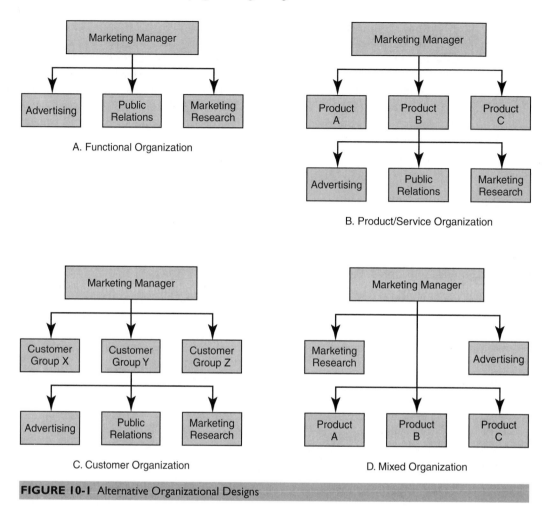

FIGURE 10-1 Alternative Organizational Designs

persons. Even if they did, however, many in the private sector believe that keeping marketing people aligned with their functional specialties has many advantages:

1. *Economies of scale.* A single public relations or advertising group can produce mass communications programs at much less cost or can develop more "clout" with significant outside agencies than can individual advertising or public relations people scattered throughout a complex nonprofit organization.
2. *Functional skill synergies.* Several advertising or public relations people working together in physical proximity will stimulate each other to produce much higher-quality work.
3. *Professional affinities.* A functional organization is consistent with the natural affinities of those it hires. That is, other things being equal, advertising people will feel more comfortable with other advertising people, and public relations people with other public relations people. Even if they are initially located apart, they will gravitate toward each other. Therefore, why not put them together in the first place?

In mature organizations, functional structures are desirable under two conditions. First, the product and customer mix should be relatively homogeneous. Second, the industry to be served should not be particularly dynamic. If the former is not the case, there is serious danger that functionally oriented specialists will ignore product or customer groups that don't interest them. In rapidly changing markets, focusing on individual specialties and not on products or customers may lead functionally oriented departments to miss major changes in consumer behavior, competitor strategies, or both.

The functional approach also has other disadvantages:

1. Informal criteria for performance may become centered on what the *function* values and not on what is good for the nonprofit enterprise. Thus, advertising people working with each other may tend to feel rewarded for "impressive" advertisements. Public relations people may pride themselves on industry awards for their brochures or public education campaigns. Peer accolades may take the place of market performance.

2. Coordination is more cumbersome. If the organization has several products or services, the general marketing manager will have to spend a lot of time running between functional specialists to ensure that campaigns complement each other, that work is done on time and in proper sequence, and so on.

3. Bottom-line responsibility is diffused. If a product or service is unsuccessful or if a major customer group is stolen away by a competitor, functional specialists will blame "the other guy." If, for example, a new adult extension program in a hospital is a flop, the advertising people may blame the public relations people for not getting enough free TV time or news releases in local papers describing the program. For their part, the public relations people may blame the adult education staff for not being customer-oriented enough in actually running the classes. No one person takes final responsibility for the disappointing performance.

Product/Service-Centered Organization

Many of the leading private sector marketers have turned their functional departments into product/service-centered organizations as shown in Figure 10-1B. One person is put in charge of a specific product or service (or a set of relatively similar products and services) and is charged with making them a success. Responsibility is inescapable. If the organization is large enough, each product/service manager would manage his or her own advertising, public relations, and marketing research specialists. In smaller organizations such as those one often encountered in the nonprofit sector, it may be necessary to adopt a mixed form of organization like that in Figure 10-1D which attempts to capture at least the major features of the product/service-centered design. In the mixed format, functional *staff* departments are established along with product/service departments. Each product/service manager then "buys" his or her services, coordinating their use and ensuring that the "purchased" service provider pays strict attention to market performance.

The product/service-centered organization has a number of advantages:

1. Responsibility is clear. If the product or service fails, there is only one person to blame. If it succeeds, one person probably deserves most of the credit (and the rewards that go with it).

2. This single responsibility forces close attention to market dynamics, shifts in customer tastes and preferences, and competitors' current and planned strategies and

tactics. The product/service structure typically is much "faster on its feet" than the functional system.

3. General management skills are developed. Marketing proves to be a good training ground for future top managers. Since all product/service managers have their own little enterprises to manage, they should become very good at overall strategic planning, budgeting, coordination, and personnel management, all skills that should quickly qualify them for higher-level management positions.

4. Small products or services are not neglected.

5. Intraorganizational competition is fostered. Hospital OB/GYN marketing programs could be set in competition with its programs for emergency or outpatient care or for adult education. This internal competitiveness in the private sector seems to keep marketers even more alert and aggressive than do other structural designs.

Despite these important advantages, the product/service manager system can have serious limitations. Some are inherent. Broad general management skills are necessary in this kind of system, but often the product/service managers filling the ranks are young and not yet experienced enough to handle the complex managing job effectively. Further, a product/service emphasis can mean relatively weak skill development in functional areas. Thus, the product/service manager may not be particularly strong in advertising or marketing research or public relations and will need to defer too much operational responsibility to functional specialists. Finally, the product/service structure may encourage top management to assign product/service roles to persons with deep product/service knowledge rather than marketing skills and customer sensitivity. Thus, an older nurse with a large family may be seen as the best person to head up the OB/GYN marketing program. The adult fitness program may be assigned to the hospital "fitness freak," while the outpatient program is assigned to the young woman who dropped out of medical school for a management career.

Clearly, the major disadvantage of the product/service manager approach is that the manager is not given direct line authority over his or her functional specialists. Thus, product/service managers need great persuasive skill to get staff functional specialists to do what is needed *when* it is needed. With other product/service managers competing for the same staff specialists, there is a great chance that programs will be poorly coordinated. Further, where authority does not equal responsibility, product/service managers will feel considerable frustration at being held accountable for things they cannot totally control.

If there is the danger of this frustration occurring, three steps must be taken. First, top management must back up the product/service manager by according him or her an important role in the overall organization and by stressing to functional staff people that their job is to serve the product/service managers and not to decide what should or should not get done. Second, product/service managers should be chosen partly for their interpersonal and persuasive skills. Third, reward systems should explicitly make allowances for situational factors the product/service manager cannot control.

Customer-Centered Organization

If, as we have argued, successful marketing organizations should be customer centered, then it might reasonably be asked why this shouldn't apply to their marketing systems as well (see Figure 10-1C). Take the case of the YMCA, for example. The Y has many "products"—physical fitness programs, arts and crafts programs, educational programs, and so on. A product management system would call for appointing a person to head each major program. Thus, a physical fitness director would study people's needs and interests in physical fitness and would develop plans for expanding the offerings and attracting more users, as well as for pricing the programs competitively. This person would advise various local Y units on how to make their physical fitness programs stronger.

The Y also serves a variety of markets divided by sex (male, female) and age (teens, young adults, adults, senior citizens) and could organize itself around them. In a marketing system organized by customer group, a person would be appointed to focus on each major market. Thus, the market manager for teens would study teens' needs and develop programs that satisfy these needs. This person would consult local Ys that are having trouble attracting teens and propose new programs that might be offered.

IMPLEMENTING A CUSTOMER ORIENTATION

Establishing the marketing structure appropriate to a particular organization does not necessarily make the organization *customer-oriented*. Nonetheless, it is crucial that the departments and key managers and staff everywhere in the institution have the proper philosophy. Inculcating this philosophy may be the marketing manager's most important task. The marketing manager has a limited influence on how many in the organization think and behave toward customers and other publics. The marketing officer in a college, for example, cannot order professors to show a stronger interest in their students. A marketing vice-president in a hospital cannot require nurses to smile and act promptly to meet patient needs. The marketing manager, instead, must work patiently to build up a market-oriented organization. It is not possible for a nonmarket-oriented organization to be transformed into a fully responsive market-oriented organization overnight. Installing the marketing concept calls for major commitments and changes in the organization. As noted by Edward S. McKay, a long-time marketing consultant:

> It may require drastic and upsetting changes in organization. It usually demands new approaches to planning. It may set in motion a series of appraisals that will disclose surprising weaknesses in performance, distressing needs for modification of operating practices, and unexpected gaps, conflicts, or obsolescence in basic policies. Without doubt, it will call for reorientation of business philosophy and for the reversal of some long-established attitudes. These changes will not be easy to implement. Objectives, obstacles, resistance, and deep-rooted habits will have to be overcome. Frequently, even difficult and painful restaffing programs are necessary before any real progress can be made in implementing the concept.[12]

Any attempt to reorient an organization requires a plan. The plan must be based on sound principles for producing organizational change. Achieving a customer orientation calls for several measures, the sum of which will hopefully produce a market-oriented organization within three to five years. These measures are described below.

Top Management Support

An organization is not likely to develop a strong marketing orientation until its chief executive officer believes in it, understands it, wants it, and wins the support of other high-level executives for building this mindset. The CEO should be the organization's highest "marketing executive" and should create the climate for marketing by talking about it and agitating for it. The CEO of a university, for example, must remind the faculty, bursar, housing director, and others of the importance of serving the students. By setting the tone that the organization must be service minded and responsive, the CEO prepares the groundwork for introducing further changes later.

Effective Organization Design

The CEO cannot do the whole marketing job. Eventually, a marketing manager must be added to the organization, in either a staff or a line position.

As we saw earlier, a staff marketing director essentially operates as a *resource manager* who takes responsibility for building and coordinating marketing resources and activities. A marketing director operates as a high-level *strategy and policy manager,* capable of influencing other top managers to take a market-oriented view of the organization's customers and publics.

In-Company Marketing Training

An early task of the new marketing executive should be to develop a series of workshops to introduce marketing to various groups in the organization. These groups are likely to have incorrect ideas about marketing and limited understanding of its potential benefits.

The first workshop should be presented to top corporate and divisional management. Their understanding and support are absolutely essential if marketing is to work in the organization. The workshop may take place at the organization's headquarters or at a retreat; it may consist of a highly professional presentation of concepts, cases, and marketing planning exercises. From there, further presentations can be made to the operations people, financial people, and others to enlist their understanding. These presentations should cover such topics as market opportunity identification, market segmentation, market targeting and positioning, marketing planning and control, pricing, selling, and marketing communication.

Better Employee Hiring Practices

Training can only go so far in inculcating the right attitudes in employees. If a college faculty has grown accustomed to concentrating on research instead of good teaching, it will be hard to change their attitudes and behavior. However, the college can gradually rectify the imbalance by hiring faculty who are more teaching and student oriented. The first principle in developing a caring organization is to hire caring people. Some people are more naturally service minded than others, and this can be a criterion for hiring. Delta Airlines does much of its flight attendant recruiting from the deep South where there is a tradition of hospitality; it minimizes hiring in large Northern cities because people from these cities tend to be less hospitable. Delta operates on the principle that it is easier to hire friendly people than to train unfriendly people to be friendly.

New employees should go through a training program that emphasizes the importance of creating customer satisfaction. They can be taught how to handle complaining and even abusive customers without getting riled. Skills in listening and customer problem solving would be part of the training.

Rewarding Market-Oriented Employees

One way for top management to convince everyone in the organization of the importance of customer-oriented attitudes is to reward those who demonstrate these attitudes. The organization can make a point of citing employees who have done an outstanding job of serving customers. Many colleges have "best teacher" awards based on student voting. Some hospitals carry a picture in their employees' magazine showing the "nurse of the month" and describing how this person handled a difficult situation. By calling attention to examples of commendable customer-oriented performance through internal marketing, it is hoped that other employees will be motivated to emulate this behavior.

Planning System Improvement

One of the most effective ways to build a demand for strong marketing is to improve the organization's planning system. Suppose the nonprofit organization has neither strong marketing nor strong planning. The organization might first design and install an organization planning system. To make this system work, strong marketing data and analysis are necessary. The planners will see that organization plans must begin with an analysis of the market. This will require strengthening the organization's marketing function. Top management will see that organization planning is largely an empty gesture without good marketing data and analysis.

CUSTOMER-DRIVEN ORGANIZATIONAL CHANGE

Many of the world's best known nonprofit organizations are very large and very bureaucratic and are extremely difficult to change. This resistance to change is often brought about by the success of the organization and by the fact that it is very dominant, if not a monopoly, in its field.

A good example is the United Way of America. In September 1985, one of the authors set forth a "Marketing Challenge for the United Way" arguing that the United Way needed to become much more customer-driven.[13] Among other recommendations, he proposed that United Way agencies significantly increase the range of choice their donors were offered. Although the proposal was adopted by a few local United Ways, generally it was met with considerable resistance. The tide, however, began to turn in the 1990s and, with the scandal involving its long-term president as the catalyst, the agency began to rethink its priorities and its approach to its members and to its donors. Donor choice is now very common in the United Way. In its fall 2001 campaign, the National Capital District (Washington, D.C.) United Way offered its donors over a thousand choices, something unheard of 10 years ago.

Other large organizations with a past resistance to change include the American Automobile Association[14] and the American Cancer Society.[15] The American Cancer Society is the sixth-largest charity fundraiser in the United States. In the 1980s, the American Cancer Society was extremely successful, dominating the field of cancer research and treatment. Gains in donations were double digit every year. However, pressure was building inside and outside the organization. Like the United Way, the American Cancer Society operated with a national office and regional and divisional affiliates. The latter collected funds and remitted 40 percent to the national office which, in turn, supplied services and support to local efforts.

By 1990, regional and local officials were criticizing the central operation. A member of the national board accused the organization of having "a sort of stuffy tradition, and a lot of sacred cows." The biggest complaint was that "national" was *not customer-oriented*. The organization was demanding too much of its local affiliates and not giving them the kind of help they wanted and needed in return. As the executive vice-president of the New Jersey division said, "The national office [would] develop what it wanted to and offer it to us, never really asking what we wanted." It was an excellent example of the kind of *organization-centered* operation we described in Chapter 2. The national American Cancer Society office was selling its offerings to its customers, the regions, and divisions, but not meeting the latter's needs and wants.

In the 1990s, competitive pressures were also rising dramatically from other charities that focused on specific cancers, such as breast, prostate, and so forth. Gains in donations fell to single digits. In response, two dramatic changes in the way the American Cancer Society was organized and operated were initiated. First, it decided to focus its efforts. Rather than try to do everything, the organization decided to emphasize a relatively small number of target areas: eliminate tobacco use, promote early detection of breast cancer, promote school health programs, recruit new volunteers, and promote income development. The society also set specific "measures of success" for each area.

Second, it undertook a bottom-up organizational change process. It was clear that a new organizational structure was needed. However, the American Cancer Society's new CEO, John Seffrin, decided to let the employees and volunteers design the new organization rather than imposing a new order from the top down. This bottom-up approach involved a committee of 20 staff members and volunteers who met over the course of eight months and came up with solutions that were enthusiastically received by Seffrin and the board of directors. In the process, the American Cancer Society got the very best ideas from those on the firing line. Employees and volunteers got ownership of the process and the outcome. It was clear that any eventual downsizing and streamlining came from below, not above.

As a result of this change process, national departments such as the Prevention Department were given the task of becoming customer-driven. They were given the responsibility of coming up with the materials and training programs that the divisions needed and liked. Under the new regime, the only way a department could grow would be if it showed that it was meeting its customer's (division) needs.

The result of the process was increased focus and greatly heightened morale that set a course for the American Cancer Society into the next century. As the executive vice president of the Virginia Division noted, "If this fails—and I don't think it will—then we all fail together. It's not something that has been imposed upon us divisions, we bought into it from the very beginning."

Clearly, being customer-responsive applies as much to organizational change as it does to raising funds and changing final consumer behavior.

A description of how these changes have affected the American Cancer Society's marketing efforts is offered by the vice-president for marketing, Cynthia Currence, in Exhibit 10-1.

EXHIBIT 10-1

CYNTHIA CURRENCE, VICE-PRESIDENT FOR MARKETING OF THE AMERICAN CANCER SOCIETY, ON GETTING BEYOND THE RHETORIC AND STIMULATING RAPID MOVEMENT TOWARD AN AGGRESSIVE MARKETING ORIENTATION

Due to market demands, competitive issues, and economic pressures, the American Cancer Society recently shifted the way it does business in some very dramatic ways. First, it moved from addressing all cancer-related issues and activities to doing a few things that promise to save the most lives from cancer and doing those few things with excellence. The organization also moved from measuring success by counting activities to measuring success by progress toward outcome goals like increasing stage 1 diagnosis of breast cancer; it is 85 percent curable if detected at that stage.

Another shift that the organization has embraced is from trying to reach multiple markets at one time (cancer touches one in three people; therefore, those in the organization have long thought that everyone should want to be involved in our cause) to adapting our offerings to specific markets with the greatest potential for demonstrating the behavior we want, be that giving, volunteering, or reduction of cancer-risk behavior. As a part of this heightened market focus, our messages and strategies are derived from research of the markets' unmet needs and analysis of competitive positioning.

These shifts have not come easy and, in fact, we continue to struggle with targeting specific audiences and adapting products and services to their unique needs. It is difficult for an organization such as ours to choose *not* to be all things to all people. For example, there was tremendous debate about the recommendations to focus on poor women over the age of 65 as the primary market for saving lives from breast cancer. Even though 80 percent of all cancer occurs in that age group and the poor have the greatest mortality, it was against our nature to even appear to exclude some women. Volunteers and staff want to focus on markets, but they don't want to leave anyone out.

More information presented on "everyday language" related to the bottom line of saving lives has helped resolve the dilemma and help people "walk the talk" of marketing. The fact is, there are over 40 possible segments of women who could respond to different appeals for action and the American Cancer Society doesn't have the money to effectively reach all women or all segments at the same time. Generic calls for action have effectively reached the middle- to upper-class white woman. A 1992 study by the Jacob's Institute tracked a 10 percent increase in mid- to upper-income white women getting mammograms for the first time, while rates for minority and poor women barely changed.

This dilemma is not restricted to the program side of operations. Income development folks also have difficulty with this and may feel that they are "leaving out" some very good prospects rather than focusing in for better overall results with defined market groups. Again, more information presented in terms related to their bottom line (demonstrating potential dollar increases) was pivotal to getting fundraisers to seriously entertain a different way of conducting business.

continued

A recent study of the American Cancer Society donors revealed that there are certain types of people who are more prone to give to the American Cancer Society than others. Further investigation and use of the Claritas target marketing software system has shown us what they like to do, read, and watch, and describes their basic lifestyle. Combined with attitudinal information, we can create strong strategies for researching these markets. Our fundraisers were very excited about this information, but still were hesitant to "exclude" anyone who might support the cause. It wasn't until we could project a positive and concrete impact on the bottom line of income development that they were interested enough to actually change the way they did business.

Through measuring market penetration, we were able to identify market potentials for fundraising based on local area market make-up and fundraising tactics. For example, in one county in New Jersey, we were able to determine that the county organization could raise $150,000 over its previous year's income by maintaining current operations and increasing penetration in one market cluster to the state average. This would be a significant double-digit income increase for this county which is something that hasn't been seen in income for the area in several years.

In essence, the American Cancer Society's movement toward a marketing orientation is directly linked to the effective communication of concrete successes or opportunities for success related to departmental "bottom lines." We had to address their fears and show results before they could believe that these changes would have an impact worth the effort of change in how business was normally done. Until marketing becomes real and not academic, it will not cause people to change the way they conduct business. In that sense, we need to "market marketing." The unmet need for American Cancer Society staff and volunteers, which was necessary in order for them to truly embrace marketing, was in the area of belief that marketing would make a significant difference. We had to prove it and then turn our success stories into internal news and grapevine news for the organization.

The American Cancer Society's Mission 2000 goals challenged its staff and volunteers as well as the cancer-fighting community at large to create specific changes that will save 12 million lives from cancer by the year 2000. Mission 2000 was a very different way of doing business for the American Cancer Society. In the past, the organization addressed a wide spectrum of cancer-related issues and needs. Mission 2000 focused the organization strategically on a few things that promised the most impact on saving lives. In essence, the organization would do fewer things, but would do more of those few things and do them extremely well.

SUMMARY

When marketing is first introduced in a nonprofit organization it is either *pushed* by one or more key individuals who have been exposed to it elsewhere or *pulled* by environmental forces that make marketing essential to survival and success. Marketing may begin as a staff function coordinating programs and providing advice. It may then move on to be a line function. Only when it is fully accepted as a top-level management function will marketing achieve its maximum effectiveness.

The first choice for organizations is whether marketing should be a line or a staff function. Many think a staff function is preferable because it is less threatening to other organization members. Marketing is much more likely to come to the attention of, and influence, top management when it is a line function; that is, when it has full control over specific resources, which it must use to achieve specific objectives.

The twenty-first century brings new organizational challenges to large, complex nonprofits. They are often multinational and/or multi-site. Thus, they must choose among structures that have either strong central control and consistent positioning and branding or allow local autonomy and the ability to effectively adopt global programs to meet local needs to a great extent.

The choice of initial projects can have an important effect on the acceptance of marketing. These projects should have high economic impact yet be relatively easy to implement. They should be completed in a short period of time and be given high visibility if successful.

Once marketing is well established, a critical question is what organizational structure is best. The major alternatives are a functional orientation, a product/service orientation, a customer orientation, or some mixture. Although the specific form chosen should depend on the experience, market conditions, and mission of the organization, the customer-centered form most explicitly incorporates the philosophy emphasized in this book. And even when the customer-centered form is not chosen, it is essential that the organization adopt a customer perspective. This can be accomplished by careful hiring and training, explicit top management support, and a reward structure that reinforces customer-centered behavior.

Customer-driven approaches can also ensure effective organizational change, especially for large nonprofits whose national offices have regional divisions as their customers.

QUESTIONS

1. You are the CEO of a fast-growing nonprofit organization. You have just hired your first formal marketing manager, a superb marketer from the private sector who is certain to do a good job. What can you do to help keep this person satisfied with his or her career decision? Identify monetary and non-monetary influences.
2. You have just been appointed the first-ever marketing director for a nonprofit organization. You want to ensure that your first project is a success so that you gain personal credibility as well as respect for your function. What four characteristics should your first project have? Identify those characteristics for a project undertaken by a new marketing manager at the community YMCA.
3. Design a customer-centered marketing organization for a retirement home. What are the key customer groups that must be satisfied? What marketing activities must be done for each of these customer groups?
4. Assume you have been appointed as the marketing director of a large hospital. What other internal departments are critical to your success as a marketer? Identify potential sources of conflict between your agenda and that of other departments. How might you mitigate the conflict in each case?
5. Comment on the following statement: A customer orientation is always the foundation of an effective marketing strategy and organization. Is this always true, or can you think of any exceptions? At what level of the organization must this orientation begin?

Notes

1. Francine D. Blau and Marianne A. Ferber, "Occupations and Earnings of Women Workers," in Karen Shallcross Koziara, Michael H. Moskow, and Lecretia Dewey Tanner (eds.), *Working Women: Past, Present and Future* (Washington, D.C.: The Bureau of National Affairs, Inc., 1987), pp. 37–68.

2. Marianne G. Briscoe, "The Politics of Cheap: Are Low Salaries Damaging Nonprofits?" *The Nonprofit Times,* September 1994, p. 12.

3. Debra E. Blum and Domenica Marchetti, "Fund Raisers Find For-Profit Jobs Give Them Best of Both Worlds," *The Chronicle of Philanthropy,* November 16, 2000, p. 24.

4. Sonya Freeman Cohen, "Working in Europe: A Nonprofit Perspective," *The Nonprofit Times,* February 1993, pp. 33–34.

5. Alan R. Andreasen, Ronald C. Goodstein, and Joan Wilson, "Facilitators and Impediments of Cross-Sector Transfer of Marketing Knowledge," Presentation to 2002 Marketing and Public Policy Conference, Atlanta, Ga., May 2002.

6. Christine W. Letts, William P. Ryan, and Allen Grossman, *High Performance Nonprofit Organizations* (New York: John Wiley and Sons, Inc., 1999).

7. George S. Yip, "Global Strategies . . . in a World of Nations," *Harvard Business Review,* Fall 1989, pp. 29–41.

8. Terry Clark, "International Marketing and National Character: A Review and Proposal for an Integrative Theory," *Journal of Marketing,* 54 (October 1990), pp. 66–79.

9. See also Dennis Young, Bonnie Koenig, Adil Najam, and Julie Fisher, "Strategy and Structure in Managing Global Associations," *Voluntas,* Vol. 10, No. 4, (December 1999) pp. 323–344.

10. Sonya Freeman Cohen, "Working in Europe."

11. Saeed Samind and Kendall Roth, "The Influence of Global Marketing Standardization Performance," *Journal of Marketing,* April 1992, pp. 1–17.

12. Edward S. McKay, *The Marketing Mystique* (New York: American Management Association, 1972), p. 22.

13. Alan R. Andreasen, "Marketing Challenge for the United Way," *Community,* 4, 4 (September 1985), pp. 14–16.

14. James S. Hirsch, "Hired to Rev Up AAA, This Outsider Discovers Changing It Is Tough," *Wall Street Journal,* August 30, 1994.

15. Much of the material in this section is drawn from Grant Williams, "A Cure for the Cancer Society," *The Chronicle of Therapy,* July 12, 1994, pp. 32–34.

CHAPTER 11

Planning and Budgeting the Marketing Mix

In the planning of nonprofit campaigns, managers are constantly seeking scientific bases for their decisions about how to allocate limited resources. This was the challenge faced by a major campaign to promote the use of female condoms in Tanzania in the late 1990s. In this project, Population Services International (PSI) employed several key marketing tactics. First, the product was branded as *"Care"* and a positioning strategy was established emphasizing couples and joint decisions to use the product.

Communication was placed in mass media, particularly radio stations and newspapers. In addition, community-based peer educators and health care workers were trained to counsel potential users. Pharmacies were the focus of distribution and doctors were expected to also provide patient counseling and recommendations.

To assess the effectiveness of various program elements, PSI carried out a survey of 3,013 men and women aged 15 to 49 just leaving 33 outlets where the female condoms were sold. Detailed questions were asked on knowledge, use, cross-couple discussions, and intentions to use the new product, as well as standard demographic information.

The large database was subjected to sophisticated structural equation modeling that revealed several valuable insights for planning. For women, mass media proved not to have a direct effect on intentions to use the product. Rather, it had its effect through promoting discussion between the woman and her partner. These discussions turned out to be an important predictor of intentions. Provider explanations had a small direct effect on intentions and also an indirect effect through discussions. By contrast, peer education had no effect on discussions but a direct effect on intentions. Age and education had little or no impact, but single women were more likely to be eventual users.

For men, discussion was a much more powerful predictor of intentions to use. Mass media again had an indirect effect but it appeared to be much more powerful in provoking cross-couple discussions. Peer education affected both discussion and intentions directly. Single men and older men were more likely to use *"Care."*

These insights were important ingredients in the next round of Population Services International planning.

Source: Adapted from Sohail Agha and Ronan Van Rossem, "The Impact of Mass Media Campaigns on Intentions to Use the Female Condom in Tanzania," Population Services International Research Division Working Paper No. 44, Washington, D.C., 2001.

At this point, we assume that the core marketing strategy has been developed in light of the manager's analysis of target customers, probable future environmental changes, potential competition, the organization's strengths and weaknesses, and the appropriate organization structure, and that organization-wide resources have been put in place. The next critical strategic planning task is choosing and developing cost-effective marketing programs. This chapter examines the planning and budgeting tools available to marketing managers in the nonprofit sector to make such determinations. Later chapters examine specific marketing mix elements—products, price, place, and promotion.

There are two broad classes of budgeting decisions that a marketing manager will have to undertake. We refer to these as structural and programmatic. The latter involve specific target efforts to influence the behavior of a target audience. The target audience could be potential donors (for fundraising), volunteers, the media, clients, or legislators (for advocacy programs). It is this set of marketing activities that will be our primary concern in this and succeeding chapters.

However, programmatic activities cannot take place without a significant support structure. In full-fledged marketing operations, there will be a marketing research capability, a new product–new services group, Web site development and management, perhaps a print shop, and a video production capability. None of these support centers are designed for specific programs (although some may be used in some program areas more than others). However, the marketing budget needs to be sufficient to ensure that all support centers have the necessary scope and competence to make the programs effective.

What these levels of support should be is difficult to determine. There are data available on some of these functions in national sources. For example, the American Marketing Association collects data from time to time on the size of marketing research departments. Budgets for other operations can be estimated from suppliers or from friendly businesses likely to have similar needs. The nonprofit's board of directors can often be a good source of leads for this kind of information.

We focus here not on basic infrastructure but on program planning and budgeting.

PROGRAM BUDGETING

A sensible starting point for program budgeting is to ask a set of simple questions: What are the possible programs we could undertake and what could be the scale of each chosen operation? How much can we achieve and what will it cost to get there? This will then allow the manager to go on to choose among the potential programs. To answer these questions, the organization must address the following issues:

1. What is the size of the current market demand for each possible program (e.g., how many potential donors or volunteers are there out there whom we might attract to our cause or how many homeless people are there we might reach with our soup kitchen or our job skills training program)?

2. How can the organization forecast future demand for each of these programs (since it is the future in which these programs will be expected to operate)?

3. How can the organization choose among competing marketing programs (benefit/cost analysis)?

4. How much should the organization spend on marketing them (optimal marketing expenditure level)?

MEASURING CURRENT MARKET DEMAND

Ideally, planning should start by attempting to estimate current market demand for each of the market offerings that the organization might undertake. An offering can be a product (condoms for AIDS prevention, T-shirts in a catalogue), service (a performance of *La Boheme,* vaccinations for polio, participation in a boys or girls organization), or the opportunity to change behavior (stop smoking, wear seat belts). The market can be any target audience including potential clients (college entrants, homeless people, mothers in India with children under two years), volunteers, donors, or the media. There are three types of estimates than an organization will want to make: *total market demand, total industry demand,* and *organization market share.*

Estimating Total Market Demand

A critical starting point is to estimate the size of the total market at the present time — how much potential there is today for the offerings the organization currently markets or is considering marketing. The size of the market is called *total market demand,* which is defined as follows:

Total market demand is the total volume of exchanges with all marketers that would be made by a defined consumer group in a defined geographical area in a defined time period in a defined marketing environment under a set of defined marketing programs.

The most important thing to realize about total market demand is that it is not a fixed number but a function of the specified conditions. One of these conditions, for example, is the marketing programs product features, (proposed psychological and economic cost, promotional expenditure level, and so on) of all marketers. For example, if the federal government is planning a massive campaign to raise public awareness of Sudden Infant Death Syndrome (SIDS), the market for a local well baby program will be much bigger than if the environment features sporadic campaigns and a few magazine articles. The dependence of total market demand on total market effort by all "players" is illustrated in the response curve in Figure 11-1. The horizontal axis shows different possible levels of marketing effort by relevant industry organizations in a given time period. On the vertical axis is shown the resulting demand level. The curve represents the estimated level of market demand associated with different marketing expenditure levels by the industry organizations. Note that it does not begin at zero and it is not a straight line. We see that some base volume (called the *market minimum*) would take place without any demand-stimulating efforts. Positive marketing expenditures would yield higher levels of demand, first at an increasing rate, then at a decreasing rate. Marketing expenditures higher than a certain level would not stimulate much further demand, thus suggesting an upper limit to this year's market demand, called the *market potential.*

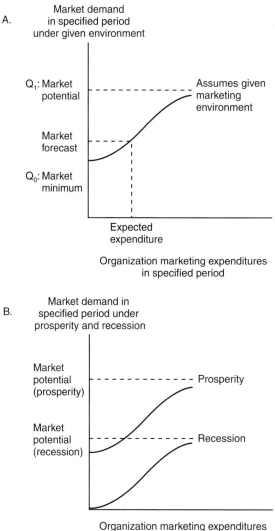

A.

Market demand
in specified period
under given environment

Q_1: Market potential

Assumes given
marketing
environment

Market forecast

Q_0: Market minimum

Expected
expenditure

Organization marketing expenditures
in specified period

B.

Market demand in
specified period under
prosperity and recession

Market potential (prosperity)

Prosperity

Market potential (recession)

Recession

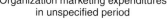

Organization marketing expenditures
in unspecified period

FIGURE 11-1 Market Demand

A. Market Demand as a Function of Marketing Expenditure (assumes particular marketing environment); B. Market Demand as a Function of Marketing Expenditure (two different environments assumed)

The distance between the market minimum and the market potential shows the overall *marketing sensitivity of demand.* We can think of two extreme types of markets, the *expansible* and the *nonexpansible.* An expansible market, such as a market for a new approach to treating H. pylori ulcers, is quite affected in its total size by the level of marketing expenditures. In terms of Figure 11-1, the distance between Q_0 and Q_1 is relatively large. A less expansible market, such as the market for opera, is not much affected by the level of marketing expenditures; the distance between Q_0 and Q_1 is relatively small. The organization operating in a low-expansible market can take the market's size (the level of *primary demand*) for granted and concentrate its marketing resources on getting a desired market share (the level of *selective demand*). In an expansible market, the organization should consider seriously the possibility of joining with several other market entities to "grow" the entire market.

Only one of the many possible levels of marketing expenditure will turn out to be the case in a given year. The market demand corresponding to this expenditure level is called the *market forecast.* The market forecast shows the expected level of market demand for the expected level of organizational marketing expenditures in the given environment. If a different environment is assumed, the market demand function would have to be freshly estimated. The market for theatergoing, for example, is higher during prosperity than recession because market demand is income-elastic.

The main point is that the marketer should carefully define the situation for which market demand is being estimated. The marketer can use a method known as the *chain ratio method* to form the estimate. The chain ratio method involves multiplying a base number by a succession of percentages that lead to an estimation of the defined consumer demand. Here is an example:

The U.S. Navy seeks to attract 112,000 new male recruits each year from American high schools. The question is whether this is a high or low target in relation to the market potential. The market potential has been estimated by the chain ratio method as follows:

Total number of male high school graduating students	10,000,000
Percentage who are militarily qualified (no physical, emotional, or mental handicaps)	× .50
Percentage of those qualified who are potentially interested in military service	× .50
Percentage of those qualified and interested in military service who consider the Navy the preferred service	× .30

This chain of numbers shows the market potential to be 750,000 recruits. Since this exceeds the target number of recruits sought, the U.S. Navy should not have much trouble meeting its target, if it does a reasonable job of marketing. But many of the potential recruits are lost somehow. They are not contacted; their parents talk them out of military service; they hear negative things from friends; or they form a bad impression at the recruiting office. The result is that the Navy barely manages to recruit the targeted number. Knowing the market potential, therefore, provides the Navy with a basis for knowing whether it is doing well or poorly in comparison to what *it could* do.

Estimating Current Total Industry Demand

Another approach to estimating demand is to start with existing levels of sales, donations, or volunteers by aggregating the volume for each competitor. How can this information be obtained? In some situations, secondary databases may already exist, often as the result of mandated government reports. A second approach is to visit each organization's Web site where they may have sections on "who we are" and annual financial reports or "reports to our stakeholders." The next easiest way is to contact each competitor and offer to exchange information. A benefit to competitors of doing this is that each organization can measure its own performance against every other organization and against the total volume for the industry. However, this solution is not always available. Particular competitors may not be willing to divulge this information. In the latter case, the organization can still compare its performance to that of the cooperating organizations.

Another solution calls for a trade association to collect the data and publish the results of each organization, the industry total, or both. If such a trade association does not exist, nonprofit competitors may see the need for comparative data as the very reason to create a trade association or to contact a university research center.

If these solutions are not available, the organization must estimate the volume of one or more competitors through indirect methods. Inova Fairfax Hospital, for example, might infer the number of AIDS patients treated at a particular competitive hospital by knowing the number of beds, the size of the staff, or other clues.

Estimating Organization Market Share

The organization's own volume does not tell the whole story of how well it is doing. Suppose the organization's volume is increasing at 5 percent a year and its competitor's volume is increasing at 10 percent. This organization is actually losing its relative standing in the industry. Organizations will therefore want to compare their volume with that of competitors.

Organizations can estimate at least three market share figures. Ideally, the organization should know its (1) share of the total market, (2) share of the target market, and (3) share relative to the leading competitor or leading three competitors. Each of these measures yields useful information about the organization's market performance and potential.

FORECASTING FUTURE MARKET DEMAND

Of course, understanding today's demand and market share is sometimes not as critical as estimating future demand and market share. Obviously, contemplated strategies will play out in future years; therefore, it is this environment that is most critical for planning. In relatively stable or slow-moving markets, this year's data with some modest increment may be adequate for planning. Such cases generally involve a product or service whose absolute level or trend is fairly constant and whose competition is nonexistent or stable. In the vast majority of markets, total market demand and specific organization demand are not stable from year to year, and good forecasting becomes a key factor in effective performance. This is particularly true for nonprofits in which these problems are compounded by a lack of good historical data. In such cases, poor forecasting can lead to excess or insufficient personnel and supplies. The more unstable the demand, the more critical is forecast accuracy, and the more elaborate is forecasting procedure.

In approaching forecasting, one should list all the factors that might affect future demand and predict each factor's likely future level and effect on demand. Consistent with the OMPP (Chapter 3), the factors affecting demand might be classified into three categories: (1) *noncontrollable macroenvironmental factors* such as the state of the economy, new technologies, and legal developments; (2) *competitive factors* such as competitors' prices, new products, and promotional expenditures; and (3) *controllable organizational factors* such as the organization's prices, new products, and promotional expenditures.

In view of the many factors that might be involved, organizations have turned to various approximation methods to forecast future demand. Each approach involves one of three information bases for building a forecast. A forecast can be based on *what people say, what people do,* or *what people have done.* The first basis—what people say—

involves systematic determination of the opinions of the target market or of those close to them, such as outside experts. It encompasses these methods: target intention surveys and expert forecasts. Building a forecast on what people do involves another method: market testing. The final basis—what people have done—involves using statistical tools to analyze records of past behavior, using either time-series analysis or statistical demand analysis. Each of these methods is described and illustrated later in this chapter.

Target Intention Surveys

Forecasting is particularly difficult when one is dealing with new offerings or markets that have dramatically changed. One way to form an estimate of future demand is to ask a sample of target market members either individually or in focus groups to state their intentions for the forthcoming period. Suppose Georgetown University is trying to estimate the number of majors to expect next year in each of its disciplines. The objective is to schedule enough courses and faculty to service the level of demand for the various majors. A small number of sophomores can be asked to indicate their intended major next year. If 20 percent say that they intend to make economics their major, the college can multiply this against the size of the sophomore class and infer the number of actual students who plan to major in economics.

The reliability of forecasts of target market intentions depends on (1) individuals having clear intentions, (2) individuals being likely to carry out their intentions, (3) individuals being willing to describe their intentions to interviewers, and (4) little time elapsing between the forecast and the behavior. To the extent that these assumptions are weak, the results must be used with caution.

Expert Forecasts

Target market intentions or intermediary predictions may be helpful for near-term forecasting, especially for new offerings. When carrying out long-term forecasting, however, these groups may not have sufficient perspective, experience, or wisdom to be able to see the forest for the trees. In new areas, past experience also will not be very valuable. In such cases, one approach is to ask experts who have studied the industry. These can include university professors, those at industry associations, magazine writers, or members of "think tanks" like the Heritage Foundation or the Brookings Institution. In some areas, there are specific consultants who have made a career of advising organizations in the industry and may well be on top of current trends. Their advice, however, will not be free.

Another possibility is to use what might be called "scenario analysis." This technique, championed by the Hudson Institute, takes past and present developments and offers several pathways into the future. Thus, to help predict demand for future Georgetown executive MBA programs, they may propose these possibilities:

Scenario 1: General demand for executive MBA programs will rise through 2015 as managers who are promoted to senior ranks continue to have formal undergraduate training only in areas other than business (e.g., engineering) and need MBAs. At the same time, competition for this executive market will accelerate even faster, resulting in a decline in Georgetown's market share toward the end of this period. After 2015, industry demand will drop sharply, competitors will be slow to leave the market, and Georgetown's enrollment will drop sharply.

Scenario 2: Industry demand will increase through 2015 but competitors will not increase as fast as the industry, particularly competitors at Georgetown's quality level. After 2015, declining demand will encourage other high-quality competitors to leave the market rapidly, leaving Georgetown with a growing market share in a declining market.

Scenario 3: Industry demand will increase up to 2015 and then drop as far as senior executives are concerned because more senior executives will enter the top ranks after 2015 with business training. However, this will put even greater pressure on these remaining managers who lack MBAs, which will sustain the upward trend in the industry well into the twenty-first century.

Managers and the scenario writers may then apply probability estimates to each scenario (and others that could emerge) to serve as their forecast. A major virtue of this technique is that it forces the nonprofit manager to think about contingency plans should the most likely scenario not take place.

A competing technique called the *Delphi method* permits interaction among diverse experts, who can be widely separated geographically.[1] The Delphi approach is based on a forecast–feedback–reforecast process as follows:

1. In the first round, experts are asked to (a) extrapolate past trends to some distant future point, and (b) write down the major environmental factors they considered in making their extrapolations.
2. The results of the expert forecasts are then pooled, the key environmental factors summarized, and the findings reported back to the original survey group.
3. The experts are then asked to revise their forecasts if they wish and to indicate any new considerations they have introduced.

This pattern may be repeated over additional cycles until a consensus is reached and the variance around the group's estimates is reduced considerably. The technique is costly and time-consuming but can yield important insights because of the time it gives participants for reflection.

Market Tests

In the case where target market members do not plan their future behavior carefully or are very erratic in carrying out their intentions and where experts are not likely to make very good guessers, a more direct market test of probable behavior is desirable. A direct market test is especially desirable in forecasting the sales of a new product or the probable response to a new method of promotion such as the use of Web marketing. Where a short-run forecast of likely market response is desired, a small-scale market test is usually a highly accurate and reliable method.

Time-Series Analysis

As an alternative to costly surveys or market tests, many organizations prepare their forecasts on the basis of a statistical analysis of past data. The underlying logic is that past time series reflect causal relations that can be uncovered through statistical analysis. The findings can be used to predict future demand.

A time series of past performance can be analyzed into four major components. The first component, *trend* (T), reflects the basic level and rate of change in the size of the market. It is found by fitting a straight or curved line through the time-series data. The past trend can be extrapolated to estimate next year's trend level.

A second component, *cycle* (C), might also be observed in a time series. Many behaviors, such as the need for poverty-related programs, are affected by periodic swings in general economic activity. If the stage of the business cycle can be predicted for the next period, this would be used to adjust the trend value up or down.

The third component, *season* (S), would capture any consistent pattern of movements within the year. The term "season" is used to describe any recurrent hourly, daily, weekly, monthly, or quarterly pattern. The seasonal component may be related to weather factors, holidays, and so on. The researcher would adjust the estimate for, say, a particular month by the known seasonal level for that month. Seasonal effects are especially important in predicting likely blood collections. Holiday periods are particularly difficult times.

The fourth component, *erratic events* (E), includes strikes, blizzards, fads, riots, fires, war scares, price wars, and other disturbances. This erratic component has the effect of obscuring the more systematic components. It represents everything that remains unanalyzed in the time series and cannot be predicted in the future. It shows the average size of the error that is likely to characterize time-series forecasting. If it is very large, it may suggest that other forecasting methods, such as statistical demand analysis, should be preferred.

Statistical Demand Analysis

Numerous real factors affect the demand for anything. *Statistical demand analysis* is a set of statistical procedures designed to discover the most important real factors affecting behaviors and their relative influence. The factors most commonly analyzed are economic conditions, household composition and income, population, and promotion.

Statistical demand analysis consists of expressing relevant behaviors such as sales (Q) as a dependent variable and trying to explain variations as a result of variations in a number of independent predictor variables $X_1, X_2 \ldots, X_n$. Such a structural model was used by Hanssens and Levien to study the effects of environmental and marketer-controlled factors on U.S. Navy recruitment.[2] Using measures for 30 variables collected at 43 Navy recruiting districts between January 1976 and December 1978, the researchers constructed and estimated a multiplicative (log-linear) model to explain the number of advertising leads secured, and delayed-entry and direct-shipment recruitment contracts achieved. They concluded the following:

> Overall, changes in the environment have a more dramatic impact on recruiting performance than changes in marketing efforts. . . . [I]ncreased marketing spending does not fully compensate for a much more difficult recruiting environment (e.g., a declining unemployment rate). At the district level, differences in youth attitudes toward the Navy, degree of urbanization, proportion of high school seniors and blacks in the target market are primarily responsible for the variability in recruiting performance across NRDs [Navy Recruiting Districts], in spite of the fact that poorly performing NRDs have received more recruiters, local advertising and recruiter aid support on a per capita basis.[3]

CHOOSING AMONG COMPETING PROGRAMS THROUGH BENEFIT/COST ANALYSIS

Given an overall budget and a forecast of future demand for various existing and possible programs, the nonprofit organization must choose between alternative programs that all fall within the scope of the organization's objectives. Consider the following situations:

- The American Cancer Society is trying to decide between sponsoring a national cervical cancer detection program or a national breast cancer detection program.
- A public school system is trying to decide between establishing a gifted children program or a retarded children program.
- A police department is trying to decide between a campaign to educate people against pickpockets or adding a few more permanent police officers to the force.
- An art museum is trying to decide between establishing an arts library within the museum or adding a few more major paintings to its collection.
- A university is trying to decide between building some badly needed dormitories and building a badly needed parking garage.
- A public library is trying to decide between adding a bookmobile to bring books into neighborhoods or using the same funds to permit opening the library on Sundays.

These examples involve organizations facing a choice between two programs. They can choose one of the programs or allocate funds to both programs and operate them on a smaller scale than planned. In principle, in such cases the nonprofit organization can proceed as a for-profit organization would by attempting to measure the benefits and costs expected from each program. The benefits are all the contributions that the particular program will make to the organization's objectives. These include benefits to target customers and society as a whole, as well as to the organization itself. The costs are all the deductions that the particular program will require from alternative organization objectives. A particular program is considered worthwhile when its benefits exceed its costs. However, several programs may all have positive benefit/cost ratios and thus choices among them will have to be made.

Theory of Benefit/Cost Analysis

Suppose a nonprofit organization is considering a choice between three programs, X, Y, and Z. All programs are estimated to cost about the same—say, 10 (in tens of thousands of dollars). The programs, however, are estimated to yield different levels of benefits. The data on the three programs are shown in the top half of Table 11-1.

All three programs show a positive net benefit (B-C) as well as a benefit/cost ratio (B/C) greater than 1. On both criteria, the best program is X, the next Y, and the last Z. If the organization has funds of only 10, it should invest in program X. If the organization has funds of 20, it should invest in programs X and Y. If the organization has funds of 30, it should invest in all three programs, because in all programs the benefits exceed the costs.

TABLE 11-1 Examples of Benefit/Cost Comparisons

A. Equal Costs

Program	B Benefits	C Costs	B-C New Benefits	B/C Benefit/Cost Ratio
X	60	10	50	6
Y	30	10	20	3
Z	20	10	10	2

B. Unequal Costs

Program	B Benefits	C Costs	B-C New Benefits	B/C Benefit/Cost Ratio
X	60	30	30	2
Y	30	10	20	3
Z	20	5	15	4

Now consider the data in part B of the table, where the three programs differ in costs as well as benefits. In this case, the net benefits and the benefit/cost ratios do not show the same rank order. Program X stands highest in the net benefit but lowest in benefit/cost ratio. Which criterion should dominate? Generally, the benefit/cost ratio is the more rational criterion because it shows the productivity of the funds. If funds of 5 are available, they should be spent on Z because they will yield four times the benefit per dollar of cost. If funds of 15 are available, they should be spent on Y and Z to yield total benefits of 50, which is an average benefit/cost ratio of $3\frac{1}{3}$ per dollar of cost. Notice that program X, although yielding net benefits of 30, only shows a benefit/cost ratio of 2. The only time program X would be preferred would be if the three programs were mutually exclusive, funds of 30 were available, and the objective was to maximize the net benefit. We will now ask how these benefits and costs can be quantified in the first place.

The organization is usually in a position to quantify the dollar costs of a program. If the program leads to some social costs, these are harder to estimate. A city government, for example, typically looks at the cost of building a crosstown expressway in financial terms. But an expressway often destroys specific neighborhoods and increases local pollution and noise. These social costs should be included in the total evaluation of costs.

Evaluating benefits poses many tough problems. Identified benefits tend to fall into three groups. They are:

1. *Monetary quantifiable benefits*—benefits whose total value can be expressed in dollars.
2. *Nonmonetary quantifiable benefits*—benefits whose total value can be expressed in some specific nonmonetary but numerical measure, such as "lives saved."
3. *Nonquantifiable benefits*—benefits whose total value cannot be expressed quantitatively, such as the amount of happiness created, fear relieved, or beauty produced.

If a certain program is estimated to have several benefits, all of which can be measured in dollars, this is the easiest case to handle.

A second possibility occurs when all the benefits can be measured in terms of a common nonmonetary value, such as "lives saved." In this case, we sum up the lives saved as a result of each program. (If one assigned a dollar value to each of those lives, then the problem could be considered under the first category.)

A third possibility occurs when the various benefits do not all share a common value. Some analysts prefer to make a two-stage analysis, the first stage including only the quantifiable benefits and costs. If the benefit/cost ratio in quantifiable terms exceeds one, the program is considered good unless there is a conviction that the non-quantifiable costs substantially exceed the nonquantifiable benefits. If the quantifiable benefit/cost is less than one, the program may nevertheless be good if the nonquantifiable benefits substantially exceed the nonquantifiable costs.

The value of trying to quantify the benefits in dollars or some other common denominator is readily apparent. It makes programming decision making more rational. This has led to a number of ingenious ways to try to determine the dollar value of a hard-to-quantify benefit. The first approach is to try to find an existing market price for this benefit. If a school dropout prevention program persuades a certain number of students to stay in school, the present value of their increased lifetime earnings can be used as a measure of the value of the program. If a fertilizer-education program increases farm output, the expected market value of the additional crops attributable to the educational program could be used as the monetary value of this benefit.

The second approach is used when there is no existing market price for the type of benefit being created by the program. Here people can be asked how much they would be willing to pay for that benefit. If a tennis court is being considered for a local park, local residents could be asked how much they would pay per hour to use it or how much additional taxes they would accept. If the National Aeronautics and Space Administration is contemplating a 10-year program to send astronauts to Mars, it might ask people how much they would be willing to pay personally over a 10-year period to achieve a successful mission.

Problems in Benefit/Cost Analysis

Some of the problems in putting benefit/cost analysis to practical use should now be apparent. Even if one manages to devise dollar values for the various benefits and costs, the technique makes certain assumptions that should be stated clearly.

First, the technique assumes that the program, if adopted, would not yield outputs sufficient to change the market prices that were used to estimate the benefits of the program. If school dropout prevention programs are introduced throughout the country, for example, they will increase the skill level of the population and probably result in a fall in the market price of skilled workers. Therefore, the life earnings calculation based on today's earnings of skilled workers overstates the market value of the benefit.

Second, the technique makes no allowance for redistributional benefits caused by the program. A vocational education program and a gifted children program, for example, may both improve lifetime incomes to the same extent. But the vocational education program may improve the incomes of the poor and a gifted children program may improve the incomes of the well-off. Some analysts believe the technique should give weight to desirable redistribution effects.

Third, the technique assumes that economic value should be given the main weight in deciding among programs. Critics resent the notion that everything worthwhile can be measured in dollars or that the growth of the GNP is the major goal. They see the value of a school dropout prevention program not so much in increased dollars of earnings but in terms of increased self-esteem and improved social attitudes.

The technique also assumes that the rank ordering of projects is insensitive to the particular measure of benefit used. In one study of the net benefit of investing in different disease control programs, the ailment of arthritis did not seem important when the criterion "lives saved" was used because arthritis does not kill people. However, arthritis rates as a high-priority research problem when the criterion "dollars saved through avoiding medical treatment" is used.[4] Thus, various programs may rank differently depending on the benefit measure used.

These difficulties are not created by the technique but exist because the world is complex. The technique was never intended to replace judgment, but to systematize and quantify it where possible. Benefit/cost analysis suggests which important factors should be considered and what information is needed. It introduces relevant data into what otherwise would be a wholly subjective art of decision making. It rests on the premise that organized ignorance is preferable to disorganized ignorance in making decisions.

Finally, it has the advantage that it can be used to make programming decisions and also to evaluate programs once they are completed.

Deciding on the Optimal Level of Marketing Expenditures

When many nonprofit organizations first turn to formal marketing planning, they inevitably ask "What is the proper amount to spend on marketing?" Alternatively, a manager may ask "How many marketing dollars should we budget to increase our demand by 10 percent?" Unfortunately, the answers are not simple. We describe the five major approaches available to organizations to establish their marketing budgets.

Affordable Method

Many organizations set the marketing budget on the basis of what they think they can afford. Thus, a museum manager will assess all the competing claims for funds and arrive at an arbitrary residual amount that can be spent on audience development, retail sales, publicity, and fundraising efforts. Setting budgets in this way is tantamount to saying that the relationship between marketing expenditures and sales is unknown and unknowable. As long as the organization can spare some funds for marketing, this will be done as a form of insurance. The basic weakness is that this approach leads to a changing level of marketing expenditure each year, making it difficult to attain consistent long-run results.

Percentage-of-Revenues Method

Many organizations prefer to set their marketing budget as a specified proportion of revenues (either current or anticipated). Thus, a private college might decide to spend 5 percent of the average annual tuition per recruited student to cover admissions office salaries, advertising, and brochure preparation. If the college aims to recruit 2,000 freshmen and 5 percent of the average tuition of $15,000 is $750, then the admissions office would receive a budget of $1,500,000.

The main advantage of the percentage-of-revenues method is that it leads to a predictable budget each year, once the revenue goal is set. It also keeps marketing costs within reasonable control. Nevertheless, the method has little else to recommend it. It does not provide a logical basis for the choice of a specific percentage, except what has been done in the past or what competitors are doing. Most important, it is countercyclical since if revenues are down, by this method marketing expenditures would decline also. Yet, this is often when one should be spending *more* on marketing.

Competitive-Based Method

Some organizations set their marketing budgets specifically in relation to competitors' outlays. Thus, an opera company may decide on its marketing budget by investigating what a major theater company or museum is spending on marketing. The opera may decide to spend more, less, or the same. Assuming that other arts organizations are roughly the same size, it would spend more if it wants to overtake or surpass them. It would spend less if it believes that it can use its funds more efficiently or influentially. It would spend the same if it believes that the competitors have figured out the proper amount to spend or if it believes that maintaining competitive parity would avoid an aggressive reaction by the competitors.

Knowing what the competition is spending on marketing is undoubtedly useful information. Basing one's spending on this information alone is not warranted, however. Marketing objectives, resources, and opportunities are likely to differ so much among organizations that the budget of one organization is hardly a guide for others to follow.

Objective-and-Task Method

The objective-and-task method calls upon marketers to develop their budgets by (1) defining their marketing objectives as specifically as possible, (2) determining the tasks that must be performed to achieve these objectives, and (3) estimating the costs of performing these tasks. The sum of these costs is the proposed marketing budget.

As an example, consider the private college that seeks to recruit 2,000 freshmen. The admissions office might estimate, on the basis of past experience, that the college would have to mail 20,000 letters to select high school seniors, which would result in approximately 8,000 inquiries, which would produce 4,000 applications, 3,000 admissions, and finally 2,000 acceptances. Each step requires a specific set of activities, the cost of each of which can be estimated. Table 11-2 shows a hypothetical estimate of the

TABLE 11-2 Hypothetical Budget for College Recruiting

20,000 leads	Purchase of names	$4,000
	Mailing cost	20,000
	Office processing	6,000
	Staff costs, including travel	50,000
	Advertising	33,000
8,000 inquiries	Staff cost	16,000
	Mailing cost	24,000
4,000 applications	Staff cost	40,000
	Mailing cost	2,000
2,000 acceptances	Staff cost	4,000
	Mailing cost	1,000
		$200,000

Note: Cost per recruited student = $200,000 / 2,000 = $100.

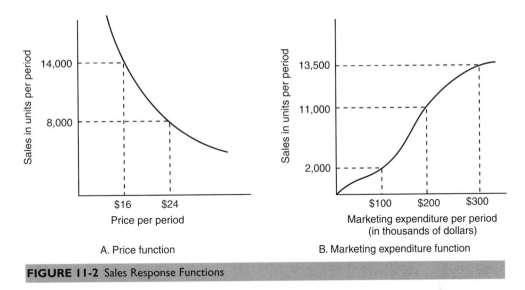

FIGURE 11-2 Sales Response Functions

costs involved in recruiting 2,000 freshmen. The admissions director builds the marketing budget by defining the objectives, identifying the required tasks, and costing them.

This method of setting the marketing budget is superior to the preceding methods. It requires management to think through its objectives and marketing activities. Its major limitation is its failure to consider alternative marketing objectives and marketing budgets in the search for the optimal course of action. We now turn to what is theoretically the soundest method for setting the marketing budget.

Response Optimization Method

Response optimization requires that the manager estimate the relation between a market's response and alternative levels of the marketing budget. The estimate is captured in the *response function,* which is defined as follows:

A response function forecasts the likely response of a market during a specified time period associated with different possible levels of a marketing element.

The best-known response function is the economic demand function where price is the only variable of interest, illustrated in Figure 11-2A. This function shows that the lower the price, the higher sales are in any given period. In the illustration, a price of $24 leads to sales of 8,000 units in that period, but a price of $16 would have led to sales of 14,000 units in that period. The illustrated demand curve is curvilinear, although other shapes are possible.

Suppose that the marketing variable is not price but total marketing dollars spent on customer contact staff, advertising, and other marketing activities. In this case, the sales response function is likely to resemble Figure 11-2B. This function states that the more the organization spends in a given period on marketing effort, the higher the sales are likely to be. The particular function is S-shaped, although other shapes are possible. The S-shaped function says that low levels of marketing expenditure are not likely to produce many sales. The reason is that in most competitive markets a minimal level of marketing effort is necessary merely to attract notice. Higher levels of marketing expenditures per period produce much higher levels of response. Very high expenditures per period, however, may not add much more and would represent "marketing overkill." Thus, at the high end of the curve, responses would again flatten out.

The occurrence of eventually diminishing returns in response to increases in marketing expenditures is plausible for a number of reasons. First, there is an upper limit to the total potential demand for any particular offering. The easier prospects are attracted early; the more recalcitrant prospects remain. As the upper limit is approached, it becomes increasingly expensive to stimulate further responses. Second, as the organization steps up its marketing effort, competitors are likely to do the same, with the net result that each organization experiences increasing resistance. Third, if responses were to increase at an increasing rate throughout, natural monopolies would result. A single organization would tend to take over in each industry because of the greater level of its marketing effort. Yet this is contrary to what we observe in the private sector.

How can a marketing manager estimate the response function? Essentially, three methods are available. The first is the *statistical method* described earlier, in which the manager gathers data on past responses and levels of marketing mix variables and estimates the response functions using statistical estimation procedures.[5] Despite its apparent attractiveness, there are a number of problems with this method. First, a relatively large amount of data is required for the estimation to be reliable. Second, it requires enough variation in the marketing mix variables that a significant range of the response function is covered. Third, it requires that each historical data point represent a glimpse of the same response function and not the results of, say, two or three significantly different functions changing over time. The latter situation, however, may not be a serious problem if industry and competitive conditions have remained relatively stable over the analysis period.

The second method is the *experimental method* described ealier, which calls for deliberately varying the marketing expenditure levels in matched samples of geographical or other units and noting the resulting volume.[6] The third is the *judgmental method,* in which experts are asked to estimate the probable response.[7]

Once the response function is estimated, how is it used to set an optimal marketing budget? We would have to define the organization's objective. Suppose the organization wants to maximize its surplus. Graphically, we must introduce some further curves to find the point of optimal marketing expenditure. The analysis is shown in Figure 11-3. The key function that we start with is the response function. It resembles the S-shaped sales response function in the earlier Figure 11-2B except for two differences. First, response is expressed in terms of dollars of revenue instead of sales units, so that we can find the surplus-maximizing marketing expenditure. Second, the response function is shown as starting above zero sales on the argument that some revenue might be generated even in the absence of marketing expenditures.

To find the optimal marketing expenditure, the marketing manager subtracts all nonmarketing costs from the *revenue response function* to derive the *gross surplus curve.* Next, marketing expenditures are drawn in such a way that a dollar on one axis is projected as a dollar on the other axis. This amounts to a 45° line when the axes are scaled in identical dollar intervals. The *marketing expenditures curve* is then subtracted from the *gross surplus curve* to derive the *net surplus curve.* The net surplus curve

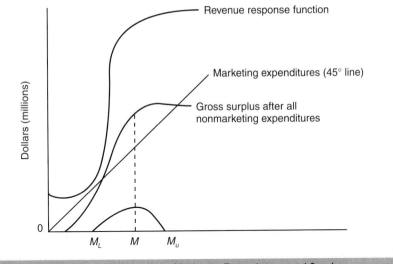

FIGURE 11-3 Relationship Between Volume, Marketing Expenditures, and Surplus

shows positive net surplus with marketing expenditures between M_L and M_U, which could be defined as the rational range of marketing expenditure. The net surplus curve reaches a maximum at M. Therefore, the marketing expenditure that would maximize net surplus in $\$M$.

Additional Factors Influencing the Choice of the Marketing Mix

We have examined the total marketing mix in terms of response functions. We will now go behind those response functions to see what real factors influence the appropriate mix. The appropriate marketing mix is influenced by the following four factors: (1) the type of market target—donors, households, clients, legislators, (2) the marketing task to be accomplished, (3) the stage of the offer life cycle, and (4) the economic outlook.

The Type of Consumer—Household versus Organization

Clearly, there will be differences in the marketing mix depending on whom one is trying to influence. Reaching news directors or legislators across the country involves a different mix from one aimed at getting high-asset businesspeople to give large donations. Some markets expect to be reached in a certain way. Legislators expect to see position papers and direct mail and be contacted personally. High-asset businesspeople disdain direct mail and are likely only to respond to a personal contact, preferably through a respected friend or colleague.

The Marketing Task

Recalling our discussion of stages of change in Chapter 4, it is clear that the optimal marketing mix depends on the stage of readiness of the target market—or where the target market segment is presumed to be.[8] Advertising, sales promotion, and publicity are the most cost-effective tools when target markets in the precontemplation or early contemplation stages are at the initial stage of building market awareness and interest; these tools are better than "cold calls" from sales representatives. Advertising is highly cost-effective in producing comprehension at the late contemplation stage, with communications via the Web increasing in potency in developed countries, especially in reaching young people.

In later stages, personal interaction may be more important and yield occasions to build self-confidence (e.g., media stories or demonstration seminars) may be more effective.[9] Finally, if the target audience is in the maintenance stage, then expenditures on incentive programs may be needed and various formal and personal reminder interventions put in place.

The Stage of the Offer Life Cycle

The effectiveness of marketing expenditures varies at different stages of an offer's life cycle, as will be discussed in greater detail in Chapter 14. The typical offer life cycle has four stages: introduction, growth, maturity, and decline. For many years—many say too long—the AIDS issue was in the introductory stage. It is now in a growth stage in many parts of the world.

Advertising and promotion are important in the introduction stage because market targets are almost all in precontemplation. In the growth stage, word-of-mouth processes begin to work for solutions and these can partially replace or supplement the organization's promotion efforts. If the organization wants to build its market share, it should continue to promote vigorously during the growth stage.

The maturity stage is marked by intensified promotional expenditures to meet competition and to advertise new alternatives. There is generally an increase in sales promotion effort relative to advertising effort. In the decline stage, many organizations reduce their promotion expenditures to improve their profit margins and where possible turn their offerings into "cash cows." Publicity is cut down, and advertising is reduced to a reminder level.

The Economic Outlook

Organizations would do well to revise their marketing mixes with shifts in the economic outlook. During economic downturns, for example, target markets may more often shun behaviors that are personally costly. They look for value. Risky new opportunities will be shunned. In prosperous times, target markets may be more daring and, assuming their economic lives to be secure, move on to new ventures. In the latter cases, vigorous promotional efforts may prove very cost-effective.

SUMMARY

This chapter deals with four tasks in developing and choosing cost-effective marketing mixes.

The first task is to estimate the size of current demand. Total current demand can be estimated through the chain ratio method, which involves multiplying a base number by a succession of appropriate percentages to arrive at the defined market. Estimating actual industry demand requires identifying the relevant competitors and using some method of estimating the sales of each. Finally, the organization should compare its sales to industry sales to find whether its market share is improving or declining.

For estimating future demand, the second task, the organization can use one or any combination of six forecasting methods: target intentions survey, expert forecasts, market tests, time-series analysis, or statistical demand analysis. These methods vary in their appropriateness with the purpose of the forecast, the type of product, and the availability and reliability of data.

The third task is to choose between alternative products or programs. Here cost/benefit analysis is helpful. The programs with the highest benefit/cost ratio are preferred. To calculate benefits and cost, monetary and quantitative measures are preferred, although ultimately nonquantifiable benefits should be taken into account.

The fourth task is to decide on the marketing expenditure level. Organizations decide on their expenditure level using one of five methods: affordable method, percentage-of-sales method, competitive-based methods, objective-and-task method, and the response optimization method.

QUESTIONS

1. Design an experiment that would estimate the likely response of a target audience to changes in expenditures on direct mail for a charity with which you are familiar. The results will only apply to the factors manipulated in the experiment. How would you assess the applicability of the experimental findings to other kinds of manipulation?
2. Describe a Delphi study that you could conduct to assess the likely future demand for a prenatal program in a poor Hispanic community in southern California. Would this approach be preferable to a market intention study? Why or why not?
3. One of the intermediaries involved in many international social marketing programs is the public health department of the local government. You would like to estimate future demand for a new measles immunization pill and are considering using health clinic personnel at the local level to help develop an estimate. How would you use their input? What instructions would you give the local people so that they would not bias the results?
4. Refer to question 3. Suppose you intended to market the measles immunization pills at a low price through pharmacies and health clinics. You do not know what the demand curve looks like (e.g., what demand exists at a given price). What factors should you control across test sites to make the results applicable to the future market for the pills? What might cause the estimates to be wrong?
5. You have just been appointed marketing director at an art museum. Describe how you would develop a marketing budget with the primary goal of attracting more elderly people to the museum.

NOTES

1. See Philip Kotler, "A Guide to Gathering Expert Estimates," *Business Horizons,* October 1970, pp. 79–87.
2. Dominique M. Hanssens and Henry A. Levien, "An Econometric Study of Recruitment Marketing in the U.S. Navy," *Management Science,* Vol. 29, No. 10 (October 1983), pp. 1,167–1,184.
3. Ibid. Quotation reprinted by permission of *Management Science* © The Institute of Management Sciences.
4. "Benefit/Cost Analyses for Health Care Systems," *Annals of the American Academy of Political and Social Science,* January 1972, pp. 90–99, especially p. 94.
5. As an example of this method, see David B. Montgomery and Alvin J. Silk, "Estimating

Dynamic Effects of Market Communications Expenditures," *Management Science,* June 1972, pp. 485–501.

6. As an example, see Russell Ackoff and James R. Emshoff, "Advertising Research at Anheuser-Busch," *Sloan Management Review,* Winter 1975, pp. 1–15.

7. See Philip Kotler, "A Guide to Gathering Expert Estimates," *Business Horizons,* October 1970, pp. 79–87.

8. "What IBM Found About Ways to Influence Selling," *Business Week,* December 5, 1959, pp. 69–70; and Harold C. Cash and William J. Crissy, "Comparison of Advertising and Selling," in *The Psychology of Selling,* Vol.

12 (Flushing, N.Y.: Personnel Development Associates, 1965).

9. Swinyard and Ray have challenged the finding that advertising is more effective when it precedes the sales call. They found that female household residents who were contacted by a Red Cross volunteer followed by some mailings expressed a higher intention to donate blood than a similar group who first received the mailings and then received the sales call. See William R. Swinyard and Michael L. Ray, "Advertising–Selling Interactions: An Attribution Theory Experiment," *Journal of Marketing Research,* November 1977, pp. 509–516.

SECTION IV

Designing the Marketing Mix

CHAPTER 12

Managing the Organization's Offerings

CHAPTER 13

Social Marketing

CHAPTER 14

Developing and Launching New Offerings

CHAPTER 15

Managing Perceived Costs

CHAPTER 16

Facilitating Marketing Behaviors

CHAPTER 17

Formulating Communications Strategies

CHAPTER 18

Managing Communications: Advertising and Personal Persuasion

CHAPTER 19

Managing Public Media and Public Advocacy

CHAPTER 12

Managing the Organization's Offerings

A key issue for nonprofits in settling upon the package of benefits that comprises their "offering" is its assessing both what those benefits have been and what they might be. The Girl Scouts of the USA has explored this issue by carrying out a number of studies seeking to identify possible connections between participation in their programs and personal and professional success later in life. The most recent study was of 1,904 women made up of three groups: 565 Women of Professional Achievement, 57 Women of Distinction (i.e., women who held prominent positions in various sectors of the economy), and 1,339 women who represented a cross-section of America. The study explored factors that the respondents judged to be important in contributing to their success and personal, work, and life satisfaction.

A range of factors were identified as important contributors to success for all groups. These included a positive self-image, good health, children and positive personal relations, religion and spirituality, and individual effort and ability. Surprisingly, role models and mentors were not listed as important by the majority of respondents, although they were relatively more important for Black and Hispanic women.

Most critically for the Girl Scouts was the respondents' indication that their experiences in childhood and adolescence had a critical influence on success later in life. Of those who had been members of Girl Scouts, 61 percent said that their membership influenced their success "a great deal" (27 percent) or "somewhat" (34 percent). The combined figure was even higher (82 percent) for Women of Professional Achievement. The women cited these major positive experiences from their time in the Girl Scouts: trying new things, working with a group to achieve a common goal, setting and achieving goals, and volunteering.

When asked what the major impacts were of the Girl Scouts experience, the respondents indicated that it helped them in five areas:

- The ability to work with others
- Developing strong moral values
- Building self-confidence
- The ability to make friends
- Serving the community

The study concluded with the caution that the findings do not prove that Girl Scouts membership *caused* these outcomes. However, the study does provide a rich picture of what can be promoted as comprising the Girl Scout "product."

Source: Drawn from *Defining Success: American Women, Achievement and the Girl Scouts* (Executive Summary) (New York: Girl Scouts of the USA, 1999).

The singlemost important element of the organization's marketing mix is *its offer*. Marketing's ultimate objective is to influence the behavior of target audiences by offering an attractive bundle of benefits and minimal costs in exchange for a desired behavior. Nonprofit organizations promote these exchanges largely to benefit the target audience and/or the society at large, and only secondarily to meet the organization's own needs for survival and growth. Nonprofits do not have stockholders with paramount claims.

Most organizations, for profit and nonprofit, cannot survive for very long if they do not offer something fundamentally attractive—or, as the current private sector mantra has it, "provide exceptional value." Further, they cannot grow if they cannot distinguish their offerings in significant ways from the competition, even when the "competition" is inaction or the status quo. Even the most creative and dramatic advertising cannot sell a fundamentally weak offering. The latter is a marketing verity learned the hard way by such diverse marketers as Coca-Cola ("New Coke"), IBM ("PCjr Personal Computer"), and Federal Express ("Zap Electronic Mail").

One of the ways organizations remain healthy and vibrant is to introduce new products and services. Such ventures can often be the source of important new revenue streams. Here are some examples:

- The Guthrie Theater in Minneapolis began to offer acting lessons and storytelling sessions for local citizens and brought in $200,000 in 1992.[1]

- Many nonprofit organizations rent out their properties and services in off-peak times. Many colleges, outdoor park theaters, and camps do this routinely. The New York PBS TV station WNET has offered post-production and production services to corporate clients for a fee.[2]

- Adding more high-markup services to existing offerings has been attempted by many service organizations as a new revenue generator. For example, Houston's Methodist Hospital has offered patients (for an increased charge) luxury amenities including gourmet French food, masseuses, and in-room barber and beautician services.[3]

- Zoos have been adding new, dramatic exhibits as a way to lure more customers to their traditional services by helping them learn about their environment. The National Zoo in Washington, D.C., added a new "Amazonia" rain forest exhibit. The Philadelphia Zoo has a giant fiberglass honeycomb and a bee's head big enough to climb into in order to help children learn about bees. The Riverbanks Zoo in South Carolina has had school groups and Scouts hold sleepovers in the zoo to help them explore the natural world more. And the St. Louis Zoo has the Monsanto Insectarium.

In this chapter, we discuss the problems of designing and managing an organization's offer mix. We pay particular attention to the differences involved when the central benefit of the offer involves a product or a service provided by the marketer.

However, a great deal of what nonprofit marketers do is promote what might be called "behavior opportunities"—stopping smoking, volunteering, and donating where "products and services" in the commercial sense are not involved. We discussed volunteering and fundraising in earlier chapters and will consider social marketing in the next chapter. In Chapter 14, we consider the problems of developing and launching *new* offerings that can enhance the organization's societal contribution and its own growth.

DEFINING THE OFFER

Because nonprofits are involved in a wide range of behavioral challenges, a broad definition of an offer is therefore needed. The key to our definition is rooted in our view of the nature of the influence process. As we outlined in Chapter 4, we believe that much of the behavior that nonprofit marketers wish to influence is undertaken because the target audience believes, consciously or unconsciously, that the consequences of the proposed action or actions will be positive on balance and will exceed the consequences of taking any other action (or maintaining a no-action status quo). We therefore define a marketing offer as follows:

A marketing offer is a proposal by a marketer to make available to a target customer a desirable combination of positive and negative consequences if, and only if, the customer undertakes a desired action.

One could also call the marketing offer the "proposed exchange."

Positive consequences, or benefits, may flow from the acquisition of a physical product or a set of products from the marketer, as in the case of condoms sold as part of an AIDS prevention program or food or gift items sold in a museum. They may also result from a contract for a service from a person (social worker, teacher) or a place (museum, zoo). Finally, the benefits may result from the target customer's *own* actions, as when a donor simply feels proud to have given a few dollars to a Salvation Army captain standing on a snowy corner at Christmastime.

Negative consequences are, of course, the costs the target audience has to pay. These costs will be discussed in Chapter 15 and can comprise monetary, psychological, and social elements.

The tripartite distinction among products, services, and other behaviors is artificial in two important ways. First, what is significant about all three is that they are really alternative vehicles for *the delivery of consequences.* Indeed, we would argue that, at bottom, what target audiences are looking for is the set of positive consequences and they only evaluate the delivery mechanism in terms of its ability to provide those consequences at a reasonable cost. In many cases, all three alternatives are available. Thus, a homeless person in a cold climate seeking to become warmer at night (the consequence) could (1) purchase a product, say a Hibachi, at a swap meet for a few cents and heat scraps of wood in it at night, (2) acquire a service such as a bed in a "rescue mission" (for which "payment" might be attendance at a daily religious service), or (3) provide for his or her own needs by sleeping in an area that provides more shelter (e.g., an abandoned building or storm duct) or more natural heat (e.g., over a grating or in an underground subway station).

The tripartite distinction is also arbitrary in that a great many offers are really *combinations* of products, services, and other behaviors. For example, an indigent elderly person on Medicare with a health problem may go to a clinic and see a doctor who gives advice (a service), purchase some antibiotics at the clinic's pharmacy (a product), and improve her eating and exercise patterns (self-help behavior).

Even in the private sector, a product purchase is seldom pure. For example, a new car is a product, but it also comes with certain free services for the first few thousand miles and warranty provisions providing for free service later. Further, if the buyer is seeking as a major consequence of this "product" purchase that the car deliver its transportation benefits for a very long time, he or she must contribute certain personal actions such as nonabusive driving and regular maintenance.

A great many nonprofit organizations simultaneously engage in marketing in all three categories, as the following examples show:

- Population Development Associates in Thailand sells condoms, T-shirts, and aspirins; rents hotel rooms; provides day care services; and lobbies to get legislators to pass a law creating a new form of nonprofit (and nontaxed) private organization.
- The Krannert Center for the Performing Arts at the University of Illinois sells cream cakes and espresso; rents seats to concert attendees; and sponsors arts awareness programs for schoolchildren.
- The U.S. Postal Service sells commemorative stamps to collectors; "rents" its mail service to corporate and private subscribers; and from time to time tries to induce oversight committees to allow it to raise prices.
- The American Marketing Association sells publications; offers members conferences; provides a professional "credentialing" opportunity; and tries to improve the public's perception of the field of marketing.

Different challenges face the marketing manager designing an offer strategy when the core benefit is delivered by a product, a service, or the target audience member himself or herself. In this chapter, we examine the challenges involving products and services. We begin with the problems of managing product offerings, although we will give this topic somewhat less attention. There are three reasons for this. First, product marketing is typically not central to the mission of most nonprofits. Organizations in the major nonprofit categories of education, health care, politics, social service, religion, and the arts are all basically service or self-help enterprises. For most, product marketing either is supplementary to their primary mission (e.g., drugs for hospitals, uniforms for the Girl Scouts) or is part of fundraising (e.g., Girl Scout cookies, WAMU T-shirts, sweatshirts, and tote bags).

Second, excessive focus on products as *things* whose attributes must be promoted ("highest-quality ingredients"; "tested by experts") encourages the unwary marketer to practice organization-centered marketing rather than the customer-centered approach we advocate here. It is tempting to any marketer to want to brag about the fine qualities of his or her products (service marketers are known to brag about their services as well) in his or her own terms ("We're great"). The point missed is that, fundamentally, customers acquire products *for what these products can do for them*—that is, for the positive consequences they deliver. Customers do not want highest-quality ingredients; they want something that will taste good or perform well, will impress their friends, or will not have to be replaced very often. They do not want a product tested by experts because it certifies how great the product is, but because it is an indicator that the product will meet their own high performance standards, will incur low maintenance costs, or will last a long time.

Products should be thought of as only "consequence-delivery" objects as far as the target audience is concerned. Marketers must keep this at the center of their offer management strategies.

The third reason for minimizing the focus on products is because we wish to emphasize the role that the target audience plays in creating successful exchanges. It is the target audience that must think about the offer and construe physical objects and marketer communications into potential costs and benefits. The target audience must actually take the action to make the exchange happen, which in many cases (such as stopping smoking or desisting from child or spousal abuse) may be very hard for the target audience to bring themselves to do. Finally, in many situations, it is the target audience member who must deliver the benefits to themselves after the exchange takes place—for example, by mentally rewarding themselves for sticking to an exercise routine or giving an anonymous donation to a charity.

PRODUCT MARKETING

Marketers offer products as individual items, product lines, and product mixes. For clarity, we use the following definitions:

A product is anything that can be offered in tangible form to a market to satisfy a need.

A product mix is the set of all product lines and items that a particular organization makes available to consumers.

A product line is a group of products within a product mix that are closely related, either because they function in a similar manner, are made available to the same consumers, or are marketed through the same channels.

A product item is a distinct unit within a product line that is distinguishable by size, appearance, price, or some other attribute.

Product Item Decisions

In developing a product to offer to a market, the product planner has to distinguish three levels of the concept of a product: the core, tangible, and augmented levels.

Core Product

At the most fundamental level stands the core product, which answers these questions: What benefits are the consumers really seeking? What need is the product really satisfying? The Georgetown University bookstore markets textbooks, but students seek future earning power. The Sierra Club sells calendars, but purchasers are buying an organizing tool, aesthetic pleasure, and feelings of helping a "good cause." The marketer's job is to uncover the essential needs hiding under every product so that product benefits, not just product features, can be described. The core product stands at the center of the total product, as illustrated in Figure 12-1.

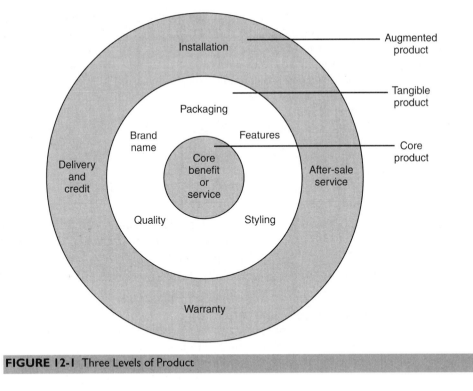

FIGURE 12-1 Three Levels of Product

Tangible Product

The core product is always made available to the buyer in some tangible form. A tangible product can be described as having up to five characteristics. First, it has certain *features;* for example, a birth control pill has high or low hormone levels or does or does not contain iron. Second, it has certain *styling;* some birth control pills are brightly colored and monogrammed, others are drab and featureless. The tangible product also has a certain *quality level;* it is made well or badly. Fourth, it has a certain *packaging.* Birth control pills come in various kinds of blister packs and purse-size compacts designed to make the product appealing and method of use straightforward. An attractive compact case for a birth control pill may increase its appeal; by contrast, an inconspicuous but high-quality package may be just right for a condom. Fifth, the tangible product can have a unique *brand name.*

Features   Features represent individual components of the tangible product that could be added or subtracted without changing the product's style or quality. Consider a nonprofit calendar marketer seeking to expand sales to international travelers. He or she might offer the following feature improvements:

1. Reference materials on the back of the calendar (U.S. and International time zones, foreign currency values)
2. Days and months in several languages
3. Dates of major foreign holidays

The use of features has many advantages. Features are a tool for achieving product differentiation vis-à-vis competitors. The organization can go after specific market segments by selecting features that would appeal to these segments. They have the advantage of being easy to add or drop, or they can be made optional at little expense. They are often newsworthy and can attract free media publicity.

Styling   Styling means giving a product or service a distinctive look or "feel." Much of the competition in durable goods, such as automobiles, watches, and electronic products, is style competition. The style of a product can be established before or after the target market is identified. An American low-cost housing manufacturer can try to sell one style of shelter without modification in every country in which it works. Or the manufacturer could adopt a market-oriented view and design a style of home for each intended audience.

Quality   Quality is the perceived level of performance in a product. Products that have a service component in particular are tremendously variable in quality, depending upon who is providing the service and how much control the organization exercises over its service providers. A basic issue is how sales response varies with the level of quality in a particular market.

Packaging   Good packaging can add significant value to many core products. It can make the product easier to use, as is the case with single-serving oral rehydration packages containing just the right quantity of chemicals for a suffering child's dehydrated system. It can keep the product safe or fresh for a long time, as is the case for foil-wrapped lubricated condoms. It can add psychological value to a product, as in the case of the attractive packages for drug products, differentiating them from products available at government clinics. Many women in developing countries will pay a little more for something that is tastefully packaged and not identified with "poor people's clinics."

Branding   Most products are branded (that is, given a name, term, sign, symbol, design, or some combination of these), which identifies them as the marketer's and differentiates them from competitors' offerings. Branding can also benefit the user, helping the user recognize a product, know its quality in advance, and so on. The seller might also gain. The Family of the Future (FOF) repackaged its basic condom in a new gold-and-white wrapper and branded the new offering as "Golden Tops." Although the tangible product was unchanged, the image of quality permitted FOF to reap a one-third higher price per unit with no loss in sales. (Indeed, the higher price itself probably added to the "quality" image.)

The brand name can also help define the product. We are offered Girl Scout cookies and "Instant Lottery" tickets. The brand name or trademark can tie together a line of items and indicate a general standard of quality, as when all Girl Scout cookies are marked with the organization's official symbol.

Augmented Product

The marketer can offer to the target market additional services and benefits that go beyond the tangible product, thereby producing an augmented product. Thus, a nonprofit that sells used business attire to poor people looking for work could also provide videotape instruction on how to take a job interview and a take-away checklist about workplace etiquette. Organizations augment their tangible products to meet additional target audience wants, to differentiate their products from the competition, or both. Success often depends as much or more on the augmented benefits as on the tangible product. Inducing a news director to run a nonprofit's TV clip may involve hand-delivering it and re-editing the content to permit the insertion of commentary by the local newscaster.

Product Mix Decisions

An organization's product mix can be described in terms of its length, width, and depth. These concepts can be illustrated in a hypothetical example. Figure 12-2 shows a simplified product mix of a museum cafeteria. We see that the product mix, in terms of its length, consists of three product lines: main courses, desserts, and beverages. Each product line has a certain width. Thus, the dessert line includes ice cream and pastries. Finally, each product item has a certain depth: There are 18 ice cream flavors and 10 pastries.

Suppose the museum's cafeteria operated at a profit and the museum wanted to attract more sales. It could choose any of three alternatives. It could lengthen its product mix by adding a line of appetizers or breakfast combinations. Or it could widen one or more of its product lines, perhaps adding Italian or French entrees to its main course line, fruit or cheese offerings to the dessert line, or mineral water or fruit juices to its beverages. Finally, it could deepen any of its present 10 product items—for example, by adding 10 foreign beer brands, three imported wines, another sandwich variety, or six new ice cream flavors. The museum would have to assess which of these product mix choices would increase volume, patronage, or profit the most, depending on its objective.

However, the museum may want or need to prune the product mix in order to save money, free management time and energy, or focus its image better. Again it has three alternatives. It could make some product items "shallower." A more serious move would be to cut out an item altogether. Most radical, of course, would be to eliminate an entire line.

In reviewing the product mix, we should recognize that the products differ in their roles and contributions to the enterprise. Some are the enterprise's core products and others are its ancillary products. Furthermore, certain products play a major role in attracting patrons. They are called *product leaders* or *flagship products*. Often an organization seeks to add a star product to its mix. The museum restaurant may offer a well-publicized torte from a famous Vienna restaurant for which customers save up their calories for weeks. An organization can showcase its flagship product as a symbol in its literature and promotion. The high cost of acquiring one crown jewel is often well repaid by the public relations value it produces.

	← Product Mix Length →		
	Main Courses	**Desserts**	**Beverages**
↑ Product Line Width ↓	Egg Dishes (4)	Ice Cream (18)	Soft Drinks (4)
	Mexican Dishes (3)	Pastries (10)	Coffee/Tea (2)
	Sandwiches (5)		Beer (3)
	Salads (6)		Wine (3)

FIGURE 12-2 Length, Width, and Depth of a Museum Cafeteria's Product Mix

SERVICES MARKETING

A substantial majority of nonprofit organizations are basically in the services business. People enter into exchanges with them because the exchanges provide (1) *people* who educate, conduct art museum tours, or perform surgery; (2) *places* where customers can play golf in a national park, see exotic animals in the city zoo, sunbathe on county beaches; and/or (3) *the use of objects or equipment* so that customers can read a library book, view the distant stars through a high-powered university telescope, or travel across a continent on a government-owned train system. We define a service as follows:

*A **service** is any activity or benefit that one party can offer to another that is essentially intangible and does not result in the ownership of anything. Its production may or may not be tied to a physical product.*

Services are of a great many types. Christopher Lovelock has pointed out that services have at least nine dimensions that affect how they should be marketed. These dimensions are outlined in Figure 12-3. Although there is high diversity in the nature of services, they tend to exhibit five important characteristics. A service is typically:

- Intangible
- Inseparable from its producer
- Variable in its characteristics
- Perishable
- Dependent on the involvement of the customer in its production

Intangibility

Services are intangible; that is, they typically cannot be seen, tasted, felt, heard, or smelled before they are bought. Thus, a patient getting plastic surgery cannot see the result before the purchase; a patient walking into a psychiatrist's office cannot know the content or value of the service in advance since there is no tangible product involved. Under the circumstances, one makes a purchase on the basis of secondary cues and one's confidence in the service provider.

Inseparability

A service is inseparable from the source that provides it. The very act of creating the service requires that the source, whether a person or a machine, be present. Thus, production and consumption often occur simultaneously with services. This is in contrast to products, which continue to exist whether or not their source is present. Consider going to a U2 concert performance to benefit AIDS programs in Africa. The emotional impact is inseparable from the performer. It is not the same service if an announcer tells the audience that U2 is indisposed and that the group's latest videos will be played instead, or that a local rock group will substitute. What this means is that the number of people who can experience a U2 benefit is limited by the amount of time U2 is willing to give to performances.

Services can differ along the following dimensions:

1. Recipient:
   a. Done to people (like health care)
   b. Done to things (like plumbing repair)
2. Tangibility:
   a. Tangible (like a physical examination)
   b. Intangible (like psychotherapy)
3. Length of the service relationship:
   a. One-time (like a tire repair)
   b. Continuing (like telephone service)
4. Connection to customer:
   a. Subscriber (like telephone service)
   b. Nonsubscriber (like a police service)
5. Extent of possible customization:
   a. Low (like movies or public transportation)
   b. Medium (like education)
   c. High (like plumbing or health care services)
6. Stability of demand:
   a. High fluctuation (like hotel or police service)
   b. Low fluctuation (like insurance)
7. Adjustability of supply:
   a. High (like utilities)
   b. Low (like movie theaters)
8. Location of delivery:
   a. Customer comes to the service (like most banking)
   b. Service comes to the customer (like plumbing)
   c. Service is provided at a distance (like TV programming)
9. Role of products versus people:
   a. Mostly products and equipment (like car leasing)
   b. Mostly people (like haircutting)
   c. A mix of products and people (like hospitals)

FIGURE 12-3 Types of Services

Source: Christopher H. Lovelock, "Classifying Services to Gain Marketing Insights," *Journal of Marketing,* Vol. 47 (Summer 1983), pp. 9–20.

Variability

Since a service is so closely linked to its source, it can be highly variable, depending on who is providing it and when it is being provided. A pro bono master class by Luciano Pavarotti is likely to be of higher quality than the same class given by a high school chorus master. In addition, Mr. Pavarotti's quality can vary depending on his energy and mental state at the time of the class. Purchasers of services are aware of this high variability and, when there is a good deal at stake, will engage in extensive risk-reducing behavior such as talking to others and trying to learn who is the best provider.

Perishability

Services cannot be stored. A car can be kept in inventory until it is sold, but the revenue from an unoccupied theater seat is lost forever. The reason many hotels charge customers for missed reservations is that the service value only existed at that point when the guest did not show up. The perishability of services is not a problem when demand is steady, because it is easy to staff the services in advance. When demand fluctuates heavily, however, service firms have difficult problems. Public transportation companies, for example, have to use much more equipment during rush hours because of peak demand than they would if public transportation needs were steady during the day.

Customer Involvement

Service exchanges are one area of nonprofit marketing that has extensive involvement of the target audience as an integral part in the production of the service itself. The target audience therefore plays a crucial role in the ultimate nature and quality of the experience. At one extreme is client-centered psychological counseling, in which much of the value of the experience depends on the patient. Another example is the patient in the foreign hospital who cannot understand the staff, cannot figure out the telephone system, and cannot make his or her food preferences known and so considers foreign hospitals inferior and unpleasant, a judgment that can easily be projected onto the quality of care.

Each of these characteristics poses a special problem for the management of service offerings. Most fundamentally, they make the traditional distinctions between production and marketing and production and consumption extremely fuzzy. A plumber repairing your faucet, a clerk renting you a car or a motel room, and Itzhak Perlman playing a Brahms violin concerto are not just delivering some fixed commodity; rather, they are creating the offering on the spot. They are both producers and marketers. At the same time, the way the customer advises the plumber about the nature of the plumbing problem, uses the rental car or motel room, or experiences the concert will affect the quality of the outcome of the service encounter. They are both (partial) producers and consumers.

We focus on these five major challenges in the design of service offerings.

Making the Intangible Tangible

Services are difficult to evaluate because they do not involve products and are not made in advance. Consumers, therefore, look to other signs of potential quality. Diplomas can signify the quality of a job training instructor. Plaques and awards are signs that a charity or museum is especially noteworthy. "Brand names" like the American Red Cross or the YMCA can make a service more memorable and concrete.

Special attention must be paid to "atmospherics."[4] The way a service clerk is dressed, the quality of the brochures used to describe the offerings, and the character of the external architecture and interiors of the marketer's building can all affect the way the customer expects the service to be delivered. Soup kitchens that are clean and well-maintained are likely to be seen by the homeless as providing healthful meals and by donors as institutions that will use funds wisely. A church or synagogue building that is modern in style will create a different set of expectations from one that is traditional and fitted with antiques and ornate decorations. A college building made of steel and glass will be suitable for an engineering school or an art department, while a granite structure with one or two fireplaces will be ideal for English or philosophy.

Service marketers can also make their offerings tangible by leaving behind concrete signs of their efforts. Charity races typically offer T-shirts to those completing the event. Many customer-oriented service marketers follow up a service encounter with a handwritten note or a telephone call to check on customer satisfaction and to demonstrate continuing interest in the customer.

Making a Virtue of Inseparability

Services are typically produced by people; therefore, the service is often indistinguishable from the person delivering it. Unfortunately, this can have very negative effects. A pleasant and medically successful hospital stay can be fatally marred by a surly clerk demanding (not asking for) payment or the completion of more forms on the last day of the hospitalization. Initially pleasant museum visits can be sabotaged by the guard who is unresponsive to a simple question. The teacher who is always suspicious of student excuses makes job training unpleasant. Damaging also is the social worker who makes clients feel like they are ruining his or her day by mentioning problems, the librarian who makes it clear that interlibrary loans are "difficult," and even the telephone operator at the local chapter who transfers a call and never checks to see that the calling party has reached someone who can help.

The basic cause of these negative experiences is that nonprofit marketers have not trained key customer-contact personnel in the need for a customer orientation. "Problem" service personnel do not see themselves as being there to meet customer needs and wants—and this is often especially true of volunteers. They put themselves and their organization's needs first and usually give the impression that they would prefer it if the customers would just go away so that they could get their jobs done. As an academic colleague once said somewhat facetiously, "This university would run a lot more efficiently and I could get done a lot more of what I am paid to do if only there weren't all these darned students!"

The solution is *internal marketing* (see Figure 12-4). The entire organization must come to realize that every encounter with a customer is what Jan Carlzon of Scandinavian Airlines calls "a moment of truth."[5] A moment of truth is any occasion in which a customer comes into contact with some aspect of the organization and has a chance to form an impression. As Albrecht and Zemke note in their book *Service America! Doing Business in the New Economy,*

> The problem and the challenge, from this point of view, are that most moments of truth take place far beyond the immediate line of sight of the management. Since managers cannot be there to influence the quality of so many moments of truth, they must learn to manage them indirectly, that is, by creating a customer-oriented organization, a customer-friendly system as well as a work environment that reinforces the idea of putting the customer first.[6]

The authors then cite a number of what they call "shining moments" when an organization shows that it is truly customer-oriented in its service delivery. Here are three:

1. A Memphis hospital has a doorman meet surgery patients at curbside and lead them to a special desk for "check-in," and then has a bellman take the "guests" to their rooms. Only then does someone come by to have the guests fill out the necessary admissions records.
2. A policeman in Japan accompanied a tourist back to his motel to inspect the passport the tourist claimed to have forgotten. Having satisfied the legal necessities,

Get the most out of your Day Camp advertising budget with this exciting campaign. Helps you promote learning and fun at the same time. With a unique look that appeals to parents, the Day Camp campaign is designed to trigger responses quickly. Each element was created with the needs of the local YMCA in mind, and have been proven successful at local Ys. Materials are provided on a CD-ROM in template form to allow for customization.

FIGURE 12-4 YMCA Day Camp

Source: YMCA. Reproduced with permission.

the policeman went far out of his way to take the tourist to the restaurant he was originally seeking, introduced him to the restaurant manager, and only then went back to his business of policing.

3. A college in Florida handles all the registration for enrollees in its professional extension programs, sends them course outlines, and even buys their textbooks for them. They feel that busy executives do not have the time for such busywork and would attend a school that recognized that need.[7]

Going to great lengths to satisfy customer needs and wants is the secret to success for many organizations in both the private and nonprofit sectors. An obsession with customers[8] is being adopted by more forward-looking nonprofit marketers as a critical element for achieving high performance. Such a mindset is especially important in service areas in which customers have a great many alternatives and where the real objective of the nonprofit is to build long-term relationships with the target audience and not just one-time exchanges. A good case in point is the plight of classical music. The traditional audience for symphony orchestras is aging rapidly, and symphony and concert hall marketers are trying many approaches to add more customers, especially from among infrequent patrons such as young professionals and families.

"User-friendliness" has become an important ingredient for bringing customers to the symphony and for getting them to come back. A case in point is the Dallas Symphony Orchestra (DSO). The story is told of two elderly people who had come to buy season tickets on a Sunday morning. The DSO's marketing director was there to handle their order; however, when the couple returned to their car, they found that the garage had closed. The appropriate action for the marketing manager was crystal clear: He drove them home! The director made the DSO's new marketing mindset transparent: "We abandoned the whole concept of selling tickets and started building relationships with our customers instead."[9]

Managing Variability

Quality is the greatest concern of service marketers: how to deliver it and how to keep it consistent. The major step is to develop good personnel selection and a training program. Airlines, banks, and hotels, for example, spend substantial sums of money to train their personnel to provide uniform and friendly service. Far too many nonprofit museums and hospitals rely on untrained volunteers and do very little to train their paid staffs to provide consistently high-quality service. They apparently do not appreciate how a few bad experiences can permanently damage a service provider's position. A second step is to routinize or even automate many parts of the service. A third step for controlling variability is to develop adequate customer satisfaction monitoring systems. The main tools are suggestions and complaint systems, customer surveys, and comparison shopping.[10]

Managing Perishability

Service organizations are, in a sense, associations of individuals, facilities, and/or products brought together to form services as customers demand them. They represent *organized capacities to serve*. These capacities can be as simple as a renowned educator sitting at the end of a log awaiting a student or as complex as a grand opera production of *Aïda* complete with elephants and camels awaiting opening night. These capacities are, on the one hand, wasted if demand is too low and, on the other hand, difficult to expand if demand is too high. Service managers must try to bring supply and demand into balance. Sasser has described several strategies for managing demand and supply.[11] On the demand side, the strategies include the following:

1. *Differential pricing* can be used to shift some demand from peak to off-peak periods. An example would be lower fares for riding city buses in off-peak hours.
2. *Nonpeak demand can be developed* through marketing campaigns. The Miami Beach Chamber of Commerce has attempted to convince people to vacation in Miami Beach during the summer months.

3. *Complementary services* can be developed during peak time to provide diversions or alternatives to waiting customers. Physician's offices provide magazines for patients to read while waiting.
4. *Reservation systems* are a way to presell service, know how much service is needed, and reduce consumer waiting. Some hospitals, for example, assign patient beds by requiring physicians to make reservations.

On the supply side, these strategies may be used:

1. *Part-time employees* can be used to serve peak demand. Colleges add part-time teachers when enrollment goes up.
2. *Peak-time efficiency routines* can be introduced. Some academic computer centers do not permit large data sets to be loaded during peak periods.
3. *Consumer participation* in the tasks can be increased. New patients may be asked to fill out their own medical histories before seeing a physician during busy periods.
4. *Shared services* can be developed. Several hospitals can agree to shift patients among themselves, depending on load.
5. *Expandable facilities can be planned.* A nursing home can make arrangements with a nearby motel for extra beds during periods of excess demand.

Helping Consumers Consume

Many services require the active participation of consumers. If consumers misuse the service or do not get as many benefits from it as they could, then (1) the service is de facto of lower quality than would otherwise be the case and (2) the chance of the consumer being dissatisfied is significantly greater. There are several approaches service marketers may adopt for this problem. However, they primarily focus on either changing the marketer or changing the customer.

The most manageable approach is for the marketer to adapt his or her own service as much as possible to the individual customer's ability to consume and appreciate it. Thus, a library designing an online computer-based information retrieval system may wish to design an idiot-proof system with which everyone except the most computer-traumatized or inexperienced user can cope. Art museums could take a number of steps to make the experience that they and the customer *jointly produce* more meaningful:

- Study the types of visitors coming to the museum and what they are looking for. According to Andreasen, the types include *aesthetes,* those interested in the artistic merits of specific works; *historians,* those interested in where the work fits in the stream of art history; and *romantics,* those who want to know about the artist behind the work.[12] Visitors also differ in other respects. There are those who are willing to read the needed information and those who want to be talked to; those who will visit for a brief period and those who stay longer; and those who are visiting for the first time and those who are familiar with the museum.
- Provide separate suggested itineraries through the museum for each type of visitor.
- Provide guidebooks, wall posters, tape-recorded guides, and docent tours for the different types of visitors.

The alternative route is to try to teach the consumer to be a better consumer. This is routinely done in many nonprofit areas. Museums offer art appreciation classes to potential viewers. Symphonies offer before-concert lectures. Colleges offer how-to-study seminars for new students. There are other steps even these organizations could take. One goal would be to make service users' expectations more realistic. A major source of dissatisfaction on the part of many service customers is not inferior service but *exaggerated expectations*. Psychiatric patients often expect instant improvement for serious problems. Playgoers often expect not to be emotionally traumatized or made uncomfortable. Students at many job training courses expect instant career advancement and high salaries. Nonprofits should routinely ask themselves this: What are potential customers being led to expect from this organization and can the organization deliver?

A second goal should be to take every opportunity to make consumers more discriminating. If the organization is proud of its offer mix and if it has effectively differentiated itself from its competitors, it should have little to fear from teaching consumers to be more discerning. Thus, charities could routinely hand out guides to evaluating charities, or point people to the relevant Web sites like the one maintained by the Better Business Bureau. Consultants, museum directors, and psychologists could have booklets available and give introductory "lectures" to new patients on "how to get the most from your consultant/museum/therapy." Nursing homes could teach their residents to hold high (but reasonable) standards. In all cases, a discriminating clientele cannot help but make a caring organization an even better provider of service.

A third approach is to remember that customer contact should be a continuing activity. Good service organizations do not focus on transactions as individual events—for example, as one-time sales. They see their task to be building long-term *relationships* with their customer base.[13] A loyal customer may spend hundreds and thousands of dollars over a decade at a restaurant or performing arts center. Recognizing this, good service marketers are quite willing to take short-term losses and make extra personalized "customer-training" efforts to build a solid relationship that will have a long-term payoff.

This position is sometimes taken to extremes. Danny Newman, former publicist for the Chicago Lyric Opera, has argued that performing arts organizations ought to *ignore* fickle individual customers and seek to presell virtually all seats for all performances to subscribers before the start of each season.[14] Newman says that selling all seats in advance would have three benefits:

1. Subscriptions would provide a secure financial platform for all activities.
2. Subscribers would guarantee a basic audience for even the most adventurous productions.
3. Marketing activities could be concentrated in one period of the year and thereby minimize costs.

Beginning in the early 1960s, Newman developed a "Dynamic Subscription Package" to build continuing relationships with a loyal group of target audience members who support the organization, grow with it, and learn to appreciate its special qualities. Many banks and department stores, such as Nordstrom, today pay the same degree of attention to building enduring customer relationships. They treat customers not as targets to be manipulated but as partners in satisfying service experiences.

SUMMARY

Its mix of offerings in many ways defines an organization and establishes its position against competition. While, traditionally, offerings are categorized as products or services, a broader definition focuses on the fact that, from the customer's standpoint, an offer is simply a set of potential positive and negative consequences (benefits and costs). Consequences can be delivered by products or services or by the customer's own actions (e.g., dieting or exercising). Many nonprofit organizations promote all three kinds of offerings.

Three levels of the concept of a product offering can be distinguished. The core product defines the needs the product is really meeting. The tangible product is the form in which the product exists. It is comprised of the product's features, styling, quality, packaging, and brand name. The augmented product consists of the tangible product and the additional services and benefits such as installation, after-sale service, delivery, credit, and warranty. As competition increases, organizations must carefully manage the length, width, and depth of their product offerings to compete.

Most nonprofit organizations are primarily in the service business. Services can be delivered by people, places, and objects or equipment. Services are especially difficult to manage because they are typically intangible, inseparable from the producer, variable in characteristics, perishable, and involve the customer in their production. Service marketers, therefore, must develop ways of making the intangible tangible, such as using brand names and atmospherics.

Inseparability means that services are often synonymous with the people who deliver them. Service marketers must vigorously pursue internal marketing to ensure that key frontline people have a customer-first attitude and must have internal systems to empower frontline people to take the actions necessary to meet customer needs and wants.

Variability in service quality can be managed by good personnel selection and careful training along with as much routinization of the service itself as is possible without diminishing the service itself. Perishability requires attention to service demand and supply, which can be altered to some extent through creative pricing, marketing campaigns, adjustment of personnel and facilities, and sharing services with other organizations during peak periods. Finally, customer involvement in service delivery can enhance demand and satisfaction if marketers design services so that they are as easy as possible to use and "train" customers themselves to be effective and appreciative co-producers.

QUESTIONS

1. Identify the products offered by a public (city) library. Organize the products into product lines. What are the core benefits that consumers derive from the respective product lines?
2. What is being exchanged by Mothers Against Drunk Driving (MADD) and its donor base? Does MADD have more than one product/service? How might MADD extend its product line?
3. The chapter identified four ways to manage demand for products/services. Use this framework to identify four ways a museum can manage demand to its benefit.

4. If given the choice between having a longer product line, or a wider product line, which should a marketer choose? Justify your answer with specific examples.

5. If demand outstrips supply for a service (e.g., zoo tours), how can a marketer bring better balance to supply and demand?

NOTES

1. Cynthia A. Massarsky, "The Strategies of Enterprise," *The NonProfit Times,* November 1993, pp. 54–55.

2. Ibid.

3. Dana Rubin, "You've Seen the Game, Now Buy the Underwear," *New York Times,* September 11, 1994, p. 5.

4. Philip Kotler, "Atmospherics as a Marketing Tool," *Journal of Retailing,* Winter 1973–1974, pp. 48–64.

5. Jan Carlzon, *Moments of Truth* (Boston: Ballinger, 1987).

6. Karl Albrecht and Ron Zemke, *Service America! Doing Business in the New Economy* (Homewood, Ill.: Dow Jones–Irwin, 1985), p. 27.

7. Ibid., pp. 123–128.

8. James L. Heskett, W. Earl Sasser, Jr., and Christopher W. L. Heart, *Service Breakthroughs* (New York: The Free Press, 1990).

9. Michael Walsh, "Is the Symphony Orchestra Dying?" *Time,* July 22, 1993, pp. 52–53.

10. See, for example, G. M. Hostage, "Quality Control in a Service Business," *Harvard Business Review,* July–August 1975, pp. 98–106; and James L. Heskett, *Managing in the Service Economy* (Boston: Harvard Business School Press, 1986).

11. W. Earl Sasser, "Match Supply and Demand in Service Industries," *Harvard Business Review,* November–December 1976, pp. 133–140.

12. Alan R. Andreasen, "Non-Profits: Check Your Attention to Customers," *Harvard Business Review,* May–June 1982, pp. 105–110.

13. Sean Mehegan, "Keeping Members: The New Priority," *The NonProfit Times,* April 1993, pp. 21–23.

14. Danny Newman, *Subscribe Now!* (New York: Publishing Center for Cultural Resources, 1977).

CHAPTER 13

Social Marketing

"You're giving me an ulcer!" is an expression used for decades by victims of verbal harassment. For these same decades, real ulcers were a painful condition treated by heavy consumption of milk and Pepto-Bismol or, as a last resort, surgery. In the 1990s, however, the National Institutes of Health concluded that the ulcers that affect 25 million Americans were not the result of genetic predisposition, too much spicy food, or a life filled with stress, but in 90 percent of the cases were caused by a bacterium called *Helicobacter pylori* or *H. pylori* and that the condition was curable by antibiotics.

This was a wonderful discovery for sufferers, and one would think they would all rush for the cure. The problem was that in 1997 only 27 percent knew of the bacterial linkage and, indeed, many were incredulous at the news. But an equally serious problem was the medical community. Research in 1994 and 1996 showed that primary care physicians were treating half of first-time ulcer sufferers without ever testing for *H. pylori*. Therefore, the Centers for Disease Control and Prevention and their consultants, Prospect Associates, faced two behavioral challenges that seemed to require what were not unlike "push and pull" strategies in the private sector. On the one hand, they had to get more physicians pushing antibiotic treatment on their patients and, on the other hand, had to get more patients to pull the treatment from the doctors by asking about it—or insisting on it.

The resulting campaign focused on doctors and ulcer sufferers 35 to 60+ years of age with some extra emphasis on African American and Hispanic groups. The campaign started with a briefing for the media and the production of a week-long radio series aimed at "Cuidando Su Salud," a syndicated Hispanic health series. Public service announcements for the campaign focused on the new good news about ulcers and featured a "Happy Ulcer Sufferers" approach. A second series of messages featured ulcer sufferers talking about getting information from their doctors—a key part of the effort to "pull" the behavior change through the health care system. This was paralleled with mailings of waiting room posters and other information for doctors to pass along to ulcer patients. Pharmaceutical manufacturers helped the Centers for Disease Control and Prevention by having their field staffs deliver the materials during their physician office visits.

The campaign recognized the importance of reaching patients at the moment—the "aperture"—at which they would be most receptive to *H. pylori* messages. The decision was made to emphasize promotion in pharmacies by having pharmacists place information on counters and provide knowledgeable advice.

The campaign estimates that over 200 million consumers have been reached by the campaign to date. More than 16,000 called the campaign hotline and three times that number contacted its Web site. Focus groups and other follow-up studies showed that the PSAs were on target and motivational. Doctors said that patients were asking for information, and patients indicated that they were motivated to see their doctors about the new miracle cure.

Source: "Success Stories," Social Marketing Institute Web site (www.socialmarketing.org).

One of the most dramatic developments of nonprofit marketing in the twenty-first century is the widening acceptance of *social marketing* among governmental agencies and nonprofit organizations both in the United States and around the world as an approach to changing important problematic social behaviors. Social marketing has proven to be an immensely powerful tool for affecting massive behavior change. It has saved U.S. taxpayers over $20 billion in losses due to forest fires through the Smokey the Bear campaign. In the field of health care, social marketing has helped many communities and international agencies recruit blood donors to meet growing hospital and research needs, helped to reduce infant mortality from diarrheal dehydration in Egypt and Honduras, contributed to major declines in smoking among U.S. teenagers, and made family planning products and services more accessible than ever in Mexico, the Dominican Republic, Thailand, Ghana, and Bangladesh.

DEFINING SOCIAL MARKETING

Despite the wide evidence of success of social marketing, many public policy makers and managers are still uncertain as to what extent marketing should be encouraged and implemented outside its traditional economic boundaries.[1] Unfortunately, consideration of the proper role of what has come to be called "social marketing" is hampered by the fact that there is great confusion about what the term really *means*, what social marketing *can* do, and what it *ought* to do. There is also a legitimate concern that, without careful training and monitoring, those adopting social marketing will employ some of the more unsavory persuasive strategies that have helped create economic successes of a number of socially dubious products and services. As with many powerful technologies, social marketing can be abused if its proper function and use are not clearly understood.

We make a distinction here between *generic marketing* and *social marketing*.

Generic Marketing

Social marketing is, in the first instance, simply the application of generic marketing to a specific class of problems. In this sense, it is similar to retail marketing, political marketing, or industrial marketing. Generic marketing can be defined in two ways: (1) descriptively as merely another activity, like voting and learning, that members of a society do, or (2) prescriptively as something those members *ought to do* to achieve certain ends. It is the latter perspective that is appropriate here.

All marketers are in the profession of creating, building, and maintaining *exchanges.* For example, a customer pays $1.99 and gets a slice of pizza; a driver buckles up a seat belt and gets peace of mind; or a mother in Bangladesh attends a workshop on diarrhea management and learns how to save her children from dying of dehydration. Because exchanges only take place when a target audience member *takes an action,* the ultimate objective of generic marketing is to influence behavior.

This definition means that generic marketing—and, by extension, social marketing—is not designed ultimately either to educate or to change values or attitudes. It may seek to do so as *a means* of influencing behavior. However, if someone has as a final goal imparting information or knowledge, that person is in the education profession, not marketing. Further, if someone has as a final goal changing attitudes or values, that person may be described as a propagandist, a lobbyist, or perhaps an artist, but not a marketer. While marketing may use the tools of the educator or the propagandist, its critical distinguishing feature is that its ultimate goal is to influence behavior (either changing it or keeping it the same in the face of other pressures).

Social Marketing

What, then, distinguishes social marketing from other types of marketing? Social marketing differs from other areas of marketing *only* with respect to the *objectives* of the marketer and his or her organization. Social marketing seeks to influence *social behaviors* not to benefit the marketer but *to benefit the target audience and the general society.* Social marketing programs, then, by definition are generic marketing programs carried out to change behaviors that are in the individual's or society's interests.

Social marketing can be carried out by anyone: individuals, informal groups, or formal organizations. It can be carried out by nonprofits and for-profits. Its goal is not to market a product or service *per se* but to influence a social behavior (e.g., induce someone to stop smoking or drive 55 mph). Its sponsors simply wish to make the society a better place, not merely benefit themselves or their organization.

Finally, in stating that social marketing involves customer behavior that the marketer thinks is socially desirable, we make no judgments about whether in any given circumstances they are right. Sound marketing approaches and techniques can be used as easily by a Hitler or a Charles Manson as by someone like Mother Teresa or Nelson Mandela. Our purpose is to show social behavior marketers how to do strategic marketing, not to debate whether they should use it in certain cases and not in others. Our hope is to make social marketing technology available to everyone. Whether one helps a particular cause is a personal ethical decision.[2]

THE DOMAIN OF SOCIAL MARKETING

Given these defining characteristics, it is clear that the outer bounds of social marketing's legitimate domain are potentially extremely broad. They comprise *any planned effort to influence any human behavior* where the change agent's motives are, on balance, more selfless than selfish. Further, since *anyone* can carry out social marketing, not just organizations, it includes efforts ranging all the way from personal and relatively trivial, such as a parent's attempt to get a teenager to clean up his or her room, all the way to the global and extremely important, such as the U.S. government's attempts to get Israel and Palestine to sign a peace treaty.

Social marketing can involve influencing individuals to use products or services such as blood pressure pills in high blood pressure social marketing programs. But these are only a means to the end of social behavior change.

Thus, the domain of *potential applications* of social marketing is very broad. In practical terms, at any point the real potential domain is only where members of society will sanction its application. At the present time, for example, most private-sector physicians, many lawyers, and even a few politicians do not feel it is "appropriate" for certain programs to use marketing techniques.[3]

To some extent, overcoming these reservations becomes a social marketing task itself. Only when social marketing is implemented where it has a clear differential advantage and is implemented with the type of customer-centered philosophy, structure, and systems outlined elsewhere in this book will it come to be seen in its proper role as one of many potentially effective social change techniques.

To understand what the conditions are for appropriate and effective use of social marketing, it is necessary to restate basic tenets from earlier chapters. Before proceeding, however, it is desirable to answer the objection that social behavior marketing provides Machiavellian guidance on how to get people to do what they do not want to do, or not do what they want to do—that is, it provides a means of social manipulation and control. In the first place, it is very difficult to change people's behavior with respect to issues that are important to them. Those who work face to face with individual clients and have their trust, such as psychiatrists, social workers, physicians, or relatives, know how difficult it is to change another person. It is even more difficult to change a whole group of people when the means are mass media ads that appear infrequently and are seen as coming from a biased source. Although social behavior marketing attempts to harness the insights of behavioral science and exchange theory to the task of social change, its power to bring about actual change, or bring it about in a reasonable amount of time, is very limited. The greater the target group's investment in an existing value or behavioral pattern, the more resistant it is to change. Social behavior marketing works best where the type of change is one in which people do not have large vested interests.

Distinctions Among Types of Social Behavior Change Programs

Social marketing aims to produce an optimal plan for bringing about a desired social change. The fact that the plan is optimal, however, does not guarantee that the target change will be achieved. It depends on how easy or difficult the target social change is. Without social marketing thinking, it may be that the desired social change has only a 10 percent chance of being achieved; the best social marketing plan may only increase this probability to 15 percent. In other words, some social changes are relatively easy to bring about, even without social marketing; others are supremely difficult to bring about, even with social marketing.

Three major dimensions determine the difficulty of successfully changing social behavior. Here, we need to make a distinction between exchanges that were (1) low involvement or high involvement, (2) one-time or continuing, and (3) by individuals or groups. Examples of social behavior change programs in each of the six categories produced by these dimensions are indicated in Table 13-1.

TABLE 13-1 A Taxonomy of Social Behavior Change Programs	Low Involvement	High Involvement
One-Time Behavior		
• **Individual**	Donating money to a charity Registering to vote Signing up for Medicaid	Donating blood
• **Group**	Voting for a change in a state constitution	Voting out restrictive membership rules in a club
Continuing Behavior		
• **Individual**	Not smoking in elevators	Stopping smoking or drug intake Practicing family planning
• **Group**	Driving 55 mph Driving on the right side of the road	Supporting the concept of an all-volunteer army

Other things being equal, it is more difficult to change behaviors that are (1) high involvement, (2) group decisions, (3) continuing, or some combination of these. We shall discuss some of the problems of marketing one-time and continuous behavior changes.

One-Time Behavior Changes

One-time behavior changes require that the target market comprehend something and take a specific action based on this comprehension. Action involves a cost to the actors. Even if their attitude toward the action is favorable, their carrying it out may be impeded by such factors as distance, time, expense, or plain inertia. For this reason, the marketer has to arrange factors that make it easy for target persons to carry out the one-time action, that is, increase self-efficacy.

Consider mass-immunization campaigns. Medical teams in Africa visit villages in the hope of inoculating everyone. Over the years, medical teams have evolved a procedure to increase the number of villagers they attract. A marketing team is sent to each village a few weeks before the appearance of the medical team. The marketers meet the village leaders to describe the importance and benefits of the program so that the leaders in turn will ask their people to cooperate. The marketers offer monetary or other incentives to the village leaders. They drive a sound truck around the village announcing the date and occasion. They promise rewards to those who show up. Posters are placed in various locations. The medical team arrives when scheduled and uses inoculation equipment that is relatively fast and painless. The whole effect is an orchestration of product, price, place, and promotion factors calculated to achieve the maximum possible turnout.

Another example from the early days of social marketing involved Medicaid sign-ups. When Medicare was enacted into law to provide medical benefits for the elderly, the following year, Medicaid was enacted to provide medical benefits for the indigent and handicapped. In the state of New York, persons and families earning under $6,000 were eligible for Medicaid. One year after Medicaid was enacted, only 1 million of the 3 million eligible persons in New York City were enrolled. A survey revealed three factors behind the low enrollment rate:

1. A widespread lack of knowledge of Medicaid and its benefits.
2. Confusion of Medicaid with Medicare by elderly indigents who failed to realize the additional benefits available from Medicaid.
3. A mistaken belief that one had to be literally on the welfare rolls to be eligible.

The city of New York decided to launch a one-month campaign to increase the number of eligible persons who signed up for Medicaid. The plan for the social marketing of Medicaid included the following elements:

1. The mayor declared the month of June as Medicaid Month.
2. Health educators in 30 health districts went into the community to organize public support. They enlisted the support of professional leaders, active lay leaders, informal leaders, volunteers from the police auxiliary, and persons from anti-poverty programs.
3. Personnel and sound trucks appeared at busy locations on different days to answer questions.
4. Information tables were placed in three department stores in Brooklyn to reach shoppers who might be eligible for Medicaid.
5. Literature was distributed in the streets and through department stores, banks, post offices, supermarkets, and schools.
6. Publicity was placed in newspapers, radio, and television.
7. Car cards were placed in the city subway system.
8. Posters were distributed at hospital outpatient clinics, health centers, and anti-poverty offices.

This campaign was so successful that it was extended by a month and, in the two months, a total of 450,000 additional persons were enrolled in Medicaid.[4]

Continuing Behavior Change

Getting individuals or groups to change their behavior permanently (i.e., to move to the Maintenance Stage described in Chapter 4) is harder than getting them to make one-shot action changes. People must unlearn old habits, learn new habits, and freeze the new pattern of behavior. To prevent AIDS, for example, partners have to learn how to use condoms and get into the habit of using them regularly without anyone being around to help them or to reinforce the behavior. In the area of safer driving, drivers who have a tendency to drink heavily at social gatherings must learn either to drink less or to know when they are not fit to drive their own car. Various campaigns have been directed at problem drivers to condition them to be aware of the problem and the penalties and to delegate driving to "designated drivers."

Low-involvement Continuing Behavior Change   Change agents rely primarily on mass communication to influence permanent changes in low-involvement behavior such as getting the Swedish motoring public to change from driving on the left to driving on the right. In some cases, mass communication can be counterproductive. In the 1970s, when many young people were experimenting with hard drugs, advertising agencies, social agencies, and legislators felt that advertising could be a powerful weapon for discouraging hard drug usage among nonusers. Much effort was designated privately and by the government, with donations of time by advertising agencies and media organizations. Fear appeals were first tried, followed by more informational advertising. Soon some people began to voice doubts about the good that this was doing. The UN Secretary–General, presenting a drug evaluation study to the United Nations in 1972, cautioned, "Special care must be exercised in this connection not to arouse undue curiosity and unwittingly encourage experimentation."[5] Anti-drug messages, especially on television, reach a lot of young persons who may never have thought about drugs. These young persons do not necessarily perceive the message negatively and might in fact develop a strong curiosity about the subject. The worry is that this will be accompanied by the feeling that if the older generation is spending that much money to talk them out of something, there must be something good in it. They start discussing drugs with their friends and soon learn where to obtain illegal drugs, how to use them, and that their peers think the drugs are not dangerous if used carefully. Thus, mass advertising might provoke initial curiosity more than fear and lead the person into exploration and experimentation.[6] The main point is that nonprofit organizations often resort to advertising with insufficient knowledge of the audience or testing of the probable effects of their message upon the audience,[7] and they fail to create mechanisms that enable people to translate their motivation into appropriate actions.

High-involvement Continuing Behavior Change   The most difficult kind of behavior to change is that which first requires a major change in perceptions and values. For example, many individuals do not think they need to worry about their weight or physical condition—despite the fact that a huge and growing proportion of the population is overweight (if not obese) and out of shape. In such cases, individuals have to be taken through all of the *Stages of Change* described in Chapter 4. They first have to be moved from the Precontemplation Stage to the Contemplation Stage— that is, from thinking that the appropriate behaviors do not apply to them to thinking that, reluctantly, yes they do. They must then move to the point where they see the benefits exceeding the costs, think that others important to them want them to do the behavior, and that they can actually make it happen. This should move them to the Preparation and Action Stage. Once there, the social marketer's task is not complete. Far too many individuals who are initially doing "the right behavior" drop out in the Maintenance Stage in part because they are not getting sufficient rewards for sticking to it. Oftentimes, the marketer's challenge is to help individuals reward themselves!

BASIC CONCEPTS

As noted throughout this book, good social marketing begins with a philosophy deeply rooted in a customer or audience orientation. However, when developing specific programs and strategies based on this philosophy, a social marketer brings to bear central concepts and processes outlined elsewhere in this book that further differentiate their specific orientation. Among these are the following:

1. *Exchange Is Accorded a Central Role.* Marketing management involves influencing exchanges. Marketers conceive of decisions consumers make as choices among alternative behaviors that vary in the benefits and costs they will provide. For each alternative, the individual is contemplating giving up—that is, *exchanging*—costs for benefits. In social marketing situations, these exchanges are *complex, personal,* and *anticipatory.*

2. *There Is a Willingness to Change the Offer.* A customer-oriented social marketer, while convinced of the desirability of the behavior being promoted, is totally open to the possibility that many customers may not agree. The social marketer realizes that the behavior being promoted, the "offer," is not an objective reality but *what the customer thinks it is.* Changing the "offer" to the marketer then means changing these perceptions.

Sometimes the perceptions of reluctant or antagonistic customers are deadly accurate, and changing the offer requires that the marketer make fundamental, *real* changes. If seat belts really are uncomfortable and consumers are not just using this as an excuse for personal bravado, then seat belts must be redesigned. If oral rehydration solution (ORS) cannot safely be prepared by typical households in poor countries in one-liter volumes, then ORS packets must be modified to accommodate the best local measure (e.g., a Coke or Pepsi bottle) available. Efforts to convince consumers that their perceptions are wrong will be ill considered.

There are also times when consumer perceptions do not reflect reality and it is the marketer's challenge to understand what has led to the misconception and how to alter it. Many mothers feel ORS can induce vomiting so that two spoonfuls are enough for a small sick child.

It should be noted that good social marketers do not assume that it is the mother's ignorance or apathy that is "at fault" when she does not take action. They do not see their own problem as just having to convince the target audience that they are wrong and that the behavior promoted is *really* highly desirable. Rather, they assume that it is more likely that the marketer has inadequately understood the target market's perceptions and their needs and wants. Mothers want to avoid any chance of vomiting, so marketers must make it clear that ORS must be given slowly with a spoon. Mothers believe two spoonfuls are enough because they've been told that ORS is a "medicine." If marketers "repositioned" it as a "tonic," perhaps this would change their understanding of the product and its benefits and, ultimately, their behavior. It is much easier for marketers to change their own behavior than try to change the target customer.[8]

3. *There Is a Focus on Coordinated Programs.* Target customers fail to respond to a marketer's program because they see too few benefits or too many costs. Usually, the truth is a complex mixture. Effective marketing therefore requires a *coordinated* attack on *all* the major benefits and costs.

4. *Market Research Is Given a Central Role.* Placing customer needs and wants at the center of marketing strategy puts a heavy reliance on the "listening" stage of planning. Good marketers recognize that such research must be carried out at the very start of the strategy development process to find out where target customers are "coming from" and then, as program elements are put in place (e.g., specific positioning platforms, packaging, advertising, and so forth), they must continue to "check these out" with target audience members. Since the challenge in high-involvement behaviors is to influence *perceptions,* research must constantly check what those perceptions are and how they are being affected.

Simultaneously, marketers recognize the need for research to make sure other elements of the marketing mix are working well. This can mean audits of intermediaries to see that they are playing their roles, package testing to make sure products are easy to use, checks on the attitudes of significant outside "publics" to ensure they understand and support the program, and so on. Sophisticated social marketers frequently experiment with alternative strategies to learn which will be the most effective. Exhibit 13-1 describes an

EXHIBIT 13-1

CONDUCTING A SOCIAL MARKETING EXPERIMENT

Although contraceptive prevalence is high along the Mexico–U.S. border, more Mexican-American women in the United States use family planning than do Mexican women in the Mexican border states. Since 65 percent of the maquiladora (assembly plant) labor force are young females, MIPFAC (Materno Infantil y de Planificación Familiar), a private, nonprofit, family planning organization in Ciudad Juárez, thought that a significant unmet need for family planning services existed among young workers at the border.

Two strategies were tested for providing services to factory workers. A clinic-based program used medical and paramedical personnel at the plant clinics to distribute methods in the factories. The promoter-based program drew upon factory workers to work as volunteer family planning promoters in the factory and distribute contraceptives. Training was offered to personnel involved in both interventions.

Data were collected on user characteristics, methods distributed, acceptability of services, and cost of service delivery.

The results indicated that the promoter program distributed 430.6 couple-years-of-projection (CYP) over the 18-month study period, compared with 264.7 CYP distributed by the clinic program. Additionally, the promoters were more successful in attracting male users; 18 percent of users in the promoter program were males, compared to 4 percent in the clinic program.

Promoters were more effective in reaching workers. Over the 18-month period, the promoters distributed an average of .74 CYP per worker, and clinic staff provided .39 CYP per worker. Although there were generally more promoters than clinic staff, the promot-

ers provided almost twice as many CYP on a per capita basis to plant workers. Among the reasons thought to contribute to the promoters' more effective performance were more confidence with co-workers than with clinic staff and fewer workers per promoter.

There was also greater distribution in factories with low worker turnover. Among the 23 factories, the average monthly employee turnover was 8.5 percent. Among the group with less than 8.5 percent employee turnover, an average of 0.65 CYP per worker were distributed during the study; the group with high turnover accepted an average of .47 CYP per worker during the study. This statistically significant difference indicates that plants with low employee turnover may yield greater success in promoting family planning methods.

Workers want more information on family planning and sex education. Focus groups indicated that users in the factories had a need for more in-factory talks on family planning and sex education. Additionally, the males indicated that they felt more comfortable obtaining family planning methods from promoters than from clinic staff.

The promoter program was also more cost effective. Because the promoter program involved more people and required more supervision, it was a marginally more expensive program to operate. However, the greater volume of CYP distributed by the promoters offset the additional cost, making the promoter strategy a more cost-effective means of providing family planning methods.

The promoter program cost $16.37 per CYP and the clinic program cost $20.29 per CYP. However, these costs are higher than found in most community-based distribution programs.

Source: Adapted from "MIPFAC: Family Planning Services Can Successfully Be Provided in the Work Place Through the Use of Promoters," *Alternatives,* March 1989, pp. 6, 9. Reproduced with permission.

experiment by a Mexican family planning program to learn which was the best approach to promoting family planning within factories—working through traditional medical personnel in factory clinics or through volunteer workers who would promote family planning on their own. The volunteer promoters turned out to be both better at reaching workers and more cost-effective.

5.   *There Is a Predilection for Segmentation.* Marketers who constantly keep attuned to their target audiences are confronted again and again by the market's diversity. As a consequence, they assume markets almost always must be segmented with strategies fine-tuned to the needs and wants of each subpopulation. Closeness to consumers also leads to recognition that traditional demographic approaches are seldom adequate to capture the rich diversity in the target audience's needs, wants, lifestyles, perceptions, and preferences.

6.   *There Is a Bottom-Line Orientation.* Good marketers are constantly mindful that their goal is to *influence behavior.* They also recognize that they have limited resources to do so. These two features give them a sometimes brutal yardstick against which to evaluate many of the things they and others would like to do: cost-effectiveness. They ask the following: Does this research study, this advertising campaign, or this cooperative project with another group help me to do a better job of influencing behavior, and is it a good way to expend our limited economic, personnel, and intellectual resources? This bottom-line approach means constant attention to the *efficiency* and *effectiveness* of everything they do.

7.   *There Is a Commitment to Planning.* As part of their sense of responsibility for "the bottom line," good marketers believe very strongly in the need to take reasoned action. This encourages them to think systematically through major steps they undertake, both in determining long-range strategy and in making specific tactical decisions.

8.   *There Is a Willingness to Take "Reasoned Risks."* Marketers recognize that they are operating in a battleground for target audiences' minds. And, while they attempt to use research as much as possible to understand where those "minds" are now and/or how they might respond to a course of action under consideration, they recognize that minds are imperfectly knowable. This is especially so when one is dealing with important social behaviors about which consumers have complex, sometimes guilty feelings.

This recognition has two consequences. First, marketers realize that some proportion of their actions will fail. Good marketers are rarely immobilized by that prospect, unlike those less accustomed to living with day-to-day risk. Marketers routinely take "reasoned risks," often incorporating some formal calculation of inherent risk into their decision-making processes.

Second, because they know their environment is in many ways unknowable or at least unpredictable, good marketers are by nature *experimental.* They do not always go ahead and make major irrevocable commitments to "one best strategy." When they do select a course of action, their bottom-line and research orientations make them vigilant for any signs of failure. And, because they have anticipated this risk, good marketers will have designed contingency plans.

DIFFERENCES IN SOCIAL MARKETING

We have previously argued that generic marketing has the *potential* to bring a unique and proven approach to the challenges facing social change agencies. However, social marketing is not the same as generic marketing. If one is to understand marketing's potential, one must understand the principal ways in which generic and social marketing are different. Social marketers have the following unique responsibilities:

1. *They Face Intense Public Scrutiny.* Since social marketers have as their goal the improvement of the target audience's or general society's welfare, it is typical that some form of formal or informal public scrutiny is accorded the social marketer's performance. This scrutiny may be by the government, a funding source, and/or the general public as represented by the press or academic researcher/critics. This scrutiny, among other effects, makes risk taking more difficult in social marketing and increases the importance of "politics" and "public relations" in the social marketing mix.

2. *They Must Meet Extravagant Expectations.* In commercial markets, marketers are often given responsibility for improving market shares a few percentage points or launching a new product or brand that will yield to a firm a reasonable return on investment. In social marketing, the challenges may be for complete eradication of a problem or the universal adoption of some desirable behavior. Social marketers must spend at least some of their time *reducing* the expectations of key oversight publics.

3. *They Are Often Asked to Influence Nonexistent Demand.* Many of the attitudes and behaviors social marketers are attempting to influence may be entirely new to their target audiences. Households who think that children come "naturally" or as "part of God's plan" need to learn that children are not inevitable. This must take place long before any behavior change marketing can be done about child spacing, particular contraception methods, distribution points, and so on.

4. *They Are Often Asked to Influence Negative Demand.* It is sometimes the case that social marketers must attempt to promote a behavior for which the target audience has a clear distaste. For example, driving 55 mph or wearing a seat belt is restricting to most people. Exercising is not anticipated positively by those who have never done it. Drug or alcohol addicts often are afraid to quit their habits. Conserving water, turning down the thermostat, and separating garbage for recycling are all "costly" behaviors that most consumers would rather avoid. Private-sector marketers are rarely challenged to promote a product or service that consumers consciously or unconsciously detest.

5. *They Often Target Nonliterate Audiences.* Many social marketing programs take place in developing countries and/or with populations with limited reading skills. This restricts the kind of media and messages that can be used and creates major creative challenges for social marketers. In some markets, cartoon characters are used to achieve identification among nonliterate audiences. Special problems are presented when complex information must be communicated.

6. *They Must Understand Highly Sensitive Issues.* Most of the behaviors that social marketers are asked to influence are much more highly involving than most of those found in the private sector. Asking a rural mother to regularly weigh her child and expose the fact that her family has little food is much more personal than asking someone to buy a Toyota or new furniture. One consequence of this very high level of involvement is that it often makes it very hard for social marketers to carry out the customer research that they stress is essential to their approach.[9] One imaginative approach is described in Exhibit 13-2.

7. *The Behaviors to Be Influenced Often Have Invisible Benefits.* Whereas in the private sector, it is usually relatively clear what benefits one is likely to get with a Hilton Hotel room or a new Xerox machine, social marketers are often encouraging behaviors where *nothing happens.* Immunization is supposed to prevent disease "in the future." Individuals with high blood pressure are told it will be lowered if only they take their pills. Mothers are told that ORS will prevent dehydration, a relationship many do not comprehend. The trouble is that the consumer has difficulty knowing whether the behavior worked! Often the consumer who agrees to the behavior has the nagging feeling that the same outcome would have occurred if they *hadn't* taken the recommended course of action. It is much harder to market behaviors without visible consequences than behaviors with them.

8. *The Behaviors to Be Influenced Often Have Benefits Only to Third Parties.* Some behaviors advocated by social marketers have payoffs for third parties such as poor people or society in general and not to the person undertaking the behavior. This is the case, for example, for energy conservation and obedience to speed laws. In these cases, most individuals consider slowing down or turning down the heat to be personal inconveniences, but many still do so because they feel it is in the society's interests. It is much more difficult to motivate people to take actions where they do not personally benefit (even invisibly) than when they or their immediate families are the direct beneficiary.

9. *The Behaviors Often Involve Self-Rewards.* As noted in the previous chapter, marketers of products and services have major control over the benefits offered their consumers. They can manipulate the qualities of their offerings and change the benefit bundles they provide. However, in social marketing, managers often must try to encourage behaviors like dieting or exercise where the marketer can only hold out promises. It is the consumers' own actions that ultimately generate the benefits. Thus, the nature and quality of those benefits are largely out of the marketer's control and very difficult to manipulate.

10. *The Behaviors Often Involve Intangibles that Are Difficult to Portray.* Because the consequences of social behavior change are often invisible, long term, self-generated, and/or apply only to others, they are much more difficult to portray in promotional messages. Marketers must be highly creative to develop advertising indicating the benefits to families of something like growth monitoring. Because symbols in communications became highly central to success, there is often the risk of sending the wrong signals, as when rural consumers in developing countries are alienated by promotions that seem too "Western."

11. *Long-Term Changes Are Central.* Because many of the proposed behavior changes are highly involving and/or entail changing individuals from negative to positive demand, the process for achieving behavior change can take a very long time. This will be because (1) often very large amounts of basic information will have to be

EXHIBIT 13-2

WILLIAM SMITH OF THE ACADEMY FOR EDUCATIONAL DEVELOPMENT ON CONDUCTING DELICATE RESEARCH ON CONDOM USAGE

At the Academy for Educational Development, a nonprofit international assistance agency, marketing is a problem with cross-cultural dimensions. Being so distant from our target audience's daily experience (we work in African villages, Latin American suburbs, and crowded Asian cities) has forced us to rely on very "participatory" tactics. Traditional research in which target groups answer questions is being replaced by more active research involving audience segments in the actual design of materials.

Working with the government of the Dominican Republic (D.R.) in the spring of 1989, our team was faced with helping female sex workers (FSWs) protect themselves and their clients from AIDS. Intercept interviews and street audits had suggested that these women already knew about condoms, carried condoms with them regularly, but complained that condoms were unreliable and often broke. We didn't know if these were exaggerated rumors, product defects, or poor usage.

We put together a research process that tested each hypothesis. The toughest job was measuring condom use skills—do FSWs know how to use condoms properly? Using a rubber dildo as a surrogate, we asked 91 women to place and remove a condom just the way they did in real life. Two surprises! First, 69 percent of the women unrolled the condom like they unroll a stocking while placing it over the dildo; needless stretching, stress, and in some cases small tears from their long fingernails were common. Surprise two: Women reported over and over again, *"We don't put condoms on the man—that's his job."* Further interviews showed that many of these women felt insecure talking about or touching condoms. We noticed that the more at ease a woman felt with the condom, the more clever and willing she seemed to be in convincing her partner to use one. Conclusion: Most FSWs don't put condoms on men in the D.R., but familiarity with condoms, particularly specific condom skills, might give them added confidence to persuade men to use condoms properly. But how could we help increase confidence on a scale large enough to make a difference?

We turned to participatory research. We organized several design groups of female sex workers, brought in a quick-sketch artist, and posed this question: *What will help you convince your client to use condoms?* Our idea was a condom insert. But the women quickly nixed that idea: *"It's too dark, and the men are in a hurry. . . . They're not going to read a condom insert. We need a wall sticker maybe—but it's got to be good looking and realistic."* Hours of working with the women, discussing each facial expression, article of clothing, and background element on the sticker paid off.

Building on segmentation needs, we were pleased when the women suggested creating modifications in the stickers for two different kinds of FSWs. In one wall sticker they created, the man meets a woman at a house and leaves her at the door; in the other, a couple meets on the street, goes to a house, and leaves together. These represent two very different kinds of FSW segments (brothel versus street walker), which the women insisted needed separate visual identities.

The contribution of FSWs to the program continued as we tested where to distribute and place the stickers for maximum effectiveness.

Source: William Smith, Executive Vice President, Academy for Educational Development, private correspondence, December 1989.

communicated, (2) basic values will have to be changed, and (3) a great many outside opinion leaders and/or support agencies will have to be "brought on board." For example, to create widespread use of oral rehydration therapy (ORT), target consumers must learn that dehydration per se is life-threatening, that some "modern" remedies are better than some folk remedies and can be trusted, and that packaged, branded products are safe and reliable. Simultaneously, physicians, pharmacists, and public health workers must be educated about the problem and given/sold supplies to distribute. Marketers accustomed to shorter-term objectives such as those found in consumer packaged goods markets can find the complications and length of time involved in social marketing very frustrating.

12. *There Are Fewer Opportunities to Modify Offerings.* If businesspeople or consumers want a faster, more flexible computer, Apple will invent a better Macintosh. If a commercial marketer cannot satisfy a customer with one product, he or she simply creates another. But if women want a diarrhea remedy that stops the diarrhea as well as prevents dehydration, it does not exist. Years of research are needed to develop such a product. The responsiveness of many social marketers to consumer demand regarding health care is limited by science. Products such as ORS, which meets important public health criteria for effectiveness, must be "marketed" despite inherent disadvantages or obstacles from the consumer's point of view.

13. *There Are Severely Limited Budgets.* Traditional marketers are accustomed to working with relatively generous budgets to meet a given challenge (although they do not always think so) or to being able to convince superiors of the justice of enlarged budgets and the need to take economic risks to achieve clearly defined goals. Social marketers typically have severely restricted budgets, in part because there is not enough to go around and in part because of an implicit understanding that a project that is too well funded is somehow not being frugal with donated or taxpayers' money. As a consequence, social marketers must spend much time and effort *leveraging* their meager budgets by adding the assistance of distributors, advertising agencies, broadcast or print media, business firms, unions, and so forth to carry out their programs.

14. *Social Marketers Often Need to Work with Those with a Suspicion of Marketing.* Social marketers almost always work with those trained in other disciplines. It is not uncommon for such individuals to have a mistrust of marketing and, often, of what they see (negatively) as the "business mentality" in general.

RELATIONSHIP TO OTHER DISCIPLINES

The tools that social marketers use to achieve their ends are adapted from a wide range of other social science disciplines.[10] Rothschild has recently suggested that there are three approaches to social change: education, marketing and the law. Education is appropriate when people are ignorant but will be motivated once they are knowledgeable. Law is appropriate when people who are knowledgeable refuse to act, and social marketing is appropriate for all other cases.[11]

An alternative way of conceiving social marketing is as *applied social science* in the same sense that engineering may be considered applied physics. Among the many fields from which social marketing adopts its tools, four have been found to be particularly helpful. These are social anthropology, education, mass communications, and behavioral psychology. Each of these disciplines has a specific role to play at different stages of the social marketing process.

Social Anthropology

As suggested throughout this book, the hallmark of a modern social marketing program is that it is fully centered on a clear understanding of the customers it must influence. In most conventional economic transactions, the level of subtlety this understanding must achieve is limited to behaviors that are relatively inconsequential. This is decidedly not the case in social marketing where one often seeks to change very fundamental values, beliefs, and patterns of family and social interaction. The level of understanding that one must achieve to bring these about must be exceptionally deep and discriminating. The concepts and tools of social anthropology are particularly valuable in achieving this more profound level of understanding.

Social anthropologists can help social marketers to anticipate the resistances they will face and to tailor programs as closely as possible to the customs, norms, and values of the culture or subculture they seek to influence.[12] The insights of the trained social anthropologist can also help social marketers in the design of effective programs in other ways by:

1. Helping identify likely "early adopters" of specific new behaviors.
2. Learning how the behavior change can best be constructed to maximize adoption (as when oral rehydration programs in The Gambia were designed around the use of readily available soft drink bottles and bottle caps).
3. Showing what words, phrases, and images are appropriate to describe the behavior change so that its benefits are clearly understood and the change advocated is as non-threatening as possible.
4. Helping to select and train change agents who can be most empathetic and effective in a given "foreign" culture.

Education and Mass Communication

Once the cultural context is understood in depth, the next two tasks facing the social marketer involve (1) creating a supportive climate of values and beliefs that make it "okay" for *individuals* to change behavior, that is, to move them from precontemplation to contemplation, and (2) actually to change the behavior of specific individuals and households in specific ways. These tasks can be seen as overcoming four problems:

1. The new behavior must be seen as socially desirable ("for people like us"); this is *the value-change problem.*
2. The new behavior must be seen as personally desirable ("for our family"); this is *the motivation problem.*
3. The new behavior must be understood; this is *the education problem.*
4. The new behavior must be practiced (i.e., begun and repeated); this is *the behavior modification problem.*

Mass communication and education techniques are particularly relevant to the first three of these problems. Mass communication principles can be used to inculcate new values and change norms and show large numbers of target consumers how the new behavior can improve their lives or the lives of their children. Mass media, such as radio and simple posters, can be used to modify the general climate and to explain and legitimize the new behavior. Until this is accomplished, any social marketing efforts devoted to *personal* motivation and behavior change will prove largely fruitless.

Mass communication and education can also be helpful in the motivation phase if marketers choose to focus on a *persuasion* strategy of behavior change. This approach rests upon the assumption that the best (perhaps, only) way to get someone to change behavior in the long run is to convince him or her that this is a good thing to do. This obviously requires that, for example, mothers (1) understand the role vitamins play in their children's diet or how immunization helps prevent disease (an education problem), (2) agree that the new behavior is something that is good to do (a motivation problem), and (3) know where to go and what to do to actually begin the new practice (another education problem). The assumption here is that a properly informed consumer will act in his or her (or the child's) best interests.

If the persuasive approach is adopted, mass communication and education concepts can help to:

1. Develop memorable themes for promotion campaigns.
2. Choose spokespeople for mass education and advertising campaigns.
3. Discover and employ the best channels of communication (usually in combination) to reach the target audience.
4. Develop curricular materials, including effective audiovisual aids, for classroom and lecture presentations.
5. Develop instructive and motivating presentations for face-to-face "sales" presentations.

Behavioral Analysis

A major alternative to the persuasion approach may be called the *behavioral modification* approach. This approach is based on the assumption that people act in certain ways because they learn to appreciate the rewards such actions produce. To secure behavior change from this perspective, then, requires that the social marketer understand the behavior-reward systems to be modified and then restructure these systems to bring about the desired new behaviors. Under the behavior modification approach, little attention is paid to convincing people that the new actions are good things. Instead, the focus is on getting people started on the behavior by some means or other and then ensuring effective *reinforcement* of the desired behavior (see also Chapter 17).[13]

In Honduras, behavioral reinforcement was considered crucial to the success of a tuberculosis treatment program. It was found that many patients were stopping treatment because their families and communities were not supportive and, in fact, treated patients as outcasts. As a result, the social marketing program was designed in part to teach family members about tuberculosis and about their crucial role in encouraging the patient to complete the necessary treatment. At the same time, radio was used to praise tuberculosis patients who had completed their treatments.[14]

Marketing's Coordinating Role

As an eclectic, applied discipline, marketing seeks to employ whatever tools are most appropriate to a given change issue. Social marketers have no vested interest in any one of the four approaches previously described. They blend anthropology, education, mass communication, and behavior modification approaches as appropriate, usually shifting both their content and role as the campaign progresses. Social marketers' commitment to market research ensures that there is continual, careful monitoring of each program element. Particular attention is paid to making program adjustments, both major and minor, in the relative emphasis on persuasion versus behavior modification strategies as the campaign progresses.

DOES IT WORK?

Social marketing can be extremely effective. For example, a review of eight field programs in developing countries shows just how effective it can be in improving child survival:

- In Honduras after two years of broadcasting specific messages, 60 percent of rural women interviewed had used the government's new oral rehydration salts and some 35 percent of all cases of infant diarrhea had been treated with oral therapy.
- In The Gambia after two years, 70 percent of rural women interviewed had correctly learned how to mix a new sugar, salt, and water rehydration solution, and home treatment of diarrhea rose from 17 percent to 50 percent of cases.
- In Egypt the percentage of women who correctly mixed the government's new oral rehydration solution rose from 25 percent in 1983 to 60 percent in 1984. A study of death registrations in Alexandria suggested that during the diarrheal season, overall mortality in children under one year dropped by about 30 percent between 1982 and 1984.
- In Bangladesh 1.3 million households were taught to prepare and use oral rehydration solution in a 2.5 year period. The program evaluation showed that 90 percent of the women interviewed remembered the ORS lessons up to six months after the household visit.
- In Colombia some 800,000 children were immunized during a single three-day massive campaign.
- In Indonesia the Nutrition Communication and Behavior Change Project showed that by 24 months of age, 40 percent of the project infants were better nourished than infants in the comparison group.
- In Swaziland clinic data show that after only three months of a communications campaign, mothers reporting use of ORS made in the home rose from 43 percent to 60 percent.[15]
- In Baltimore, techniques of social marketing developed by the Agency for International Development in Mali, Egypt, and Bangladesh are being tested for their applications to domestic problems of illiteracy, immunization, and population control.[16]

Other success stories can be found on the Web site for the Social Marketing Institute at www.social-marketing.org. Broad overviews of the effectiveness of many social marketing approaches are found in recent compilations by Hornik[17] and by Carroll, Craypo, and Samuels.[18]

SUSTAINABILITY AND INSTITUTIONALIZATION

A large majority of social marketing programs, particularly those in developing countries, are temporary in nature. They are often heavily subsidized by "outside" organizations such as the U.S. Agency for International Development or the World Bank and rely extensively on consulting help from specialists, usually from the United States. As a consequence, both those funding social marketing programs and those who manage them are increasingly concerned about two issues, *sustainability* and *institutionalization.*

Sustainability refers to maintaining the behavior change the social marketers is seeking to influence and is extensively studied by McKenzie-Mohr and Smith.[19] It is often *relatively* easy to get a target consumer to begin a behavior change process, such as stopping smoking, wearing a seat belt, or practicing contraception. But, as noted earlier, many of the behaviors to be influenced (like these) are continuing behaviors. It has been estimated that 70 to 80 percent of those who quit smoking begin again. As a consequence, marketers have become much more sensitive to approaches that will increase the probability that the changes are sustainable. William Smith of the Academy for Educational Development suggests a number of catchphrases he believes can guide efforts at sustainability.[20] For child survival behavior changes, they are:

"Make It Rewarding In Their Terms." Give people something they really want; don't fool yourself about what they "should" want.

"Make It Easy to Succeed." Make everything about it easy—easy to open, easy to find, easy to use, and easy to understand.

"Catch People Doing Things Right." Look for ways to reward success. Train health care workers to give mothers a pat on the back.

"Make It Communal." Make it part of the local fabric of life—normal, respectable. Tie it to broader values, the family, and the community.

"Keep Pace with the Audience." Audiences change. They often leave us behind. Don't work on awareness when they're already aware and need greater access or new benefits.

"Keep the Safety Net Intact." Your distributors, sales force, and health educators are your safety net. Don't let them down. Keep them motivated and informed.

"Monitor the Whole Marketing Mix." Sustainability means people want it, but they also must be able to find it, afford it, and use it. All four elements of the marketing mix are needed, so they must all be monitored regularly to avoid mistakes.

"Be Prepared for the Long Haul." Make people aware that there are few shortcuts to sustained behavior change. Be prepared for long-term commitment.

Institutionalization refers to the task of inducing "local" organizations to take over the social marketing process itself so that, when outside financial and intellectual support is no longer forthcoming, the project neither loses momentum nor expires completely.

Thus, in most social marketing programs, conscientious steps are taken to train local staff in critical marketing skills such as strategic planning, marketing research, recruiting and training sales forces, and developing effective advertising. Turnkey systems are developed, handbooks written, and seminars held, all to the end of making outsiders superfluous.

Institutionalization is a frustrating process in part because of inertia and in part because of local staff fears of taking on risks and responsibilities. This is particularly the case where the local coordinating agency is a government department. As a consequence, in some programs, alternative efforts are made to induce local private-sector marketers to substitute for the imported skills or to take over some or all of the social marketing activities directly. When it has been feasible, these steps have generally proved highly effective.

William Smith also has several catchphrases to guide the institutionalization process.[21] For health care programs, these are:

"Fight the Big Battles." Keep a policy perspective. Work for the big changes in staffing, budgets, and norms. Don't fight over things that are short term.

"Build Bridges to the Future." Invest in training, curricula, and institutions that train young people. Don't ignore the long-term payoff for short-term victories.

"Show That It Works." Demonstrate clear results in terms physicians and public health professionals understand.

"Don't Let the Organization Chart Get in the Way." Work from both ends; build friends and supporters at all levels at the same time.

"Psych Out the Local Communication System." Tie into the real way information moves around an institution. Find out who is listened to and how they communicate, then follow their lead.

"Write the Dictionary Together." Every new movement has a dictionary—a set of key words that helps define it. Write those words with your counterparts; don't impose vocabulary—give them the ownership.

"Keep It Simple." If you can't explain it in a sentence, it's too complicated. Keep the big ideas few, simple, and straightforward.

"Don't Stand Out in the Crowd." Let the program speak for itself. Don't establish a separate identity and garner personal credit.

"Make the Institution a Solid Hero." Publicize success. Make success credible by giving credentials to the winners. Build a solid basis of seriousness (courses, degrees, titles, budgets) under the visible trappings of success.

"Pay Attention to the Wounded." Every new idea produces a cadre of wounded people in other organizations who don't agree or understand, or who feel threatened. Don't dismiss them—keep working to persuade the toughest cases (the resisters). Try to understand their points of view.

SUMMARY

Social marketing is one of the fastest-growing sectors of nonprofit marketing. Social marketing is the application of generic marketing to a specific class of problems where the object of the marketer is to change social behavior primarily to benefit the target audience and the general society. Social marketing can seek to influence behavior that is low or high involvement, individual or group, and one time or continuing. Continuing high-involvement behavior of groups or individuals is the most difficult to influence and often requires legal measures to achieve any major, long-term effect.

Good social marketers accord exchange a central role in their planning, are willing to change their offer (or consumer perceptions of it), seek to develop coordinated programs, make extensive use of marketing research, segment their markets, have a "bottom-line" orientation, are committed to planning, and are willing to take reasoned risks. Social marketing differs from generic marketing in that it is subject to public scrutiny and extravagant expectations and often must seek to influence nonexistent or negative demands of nonliterate target audiences. It deals with sensitive, hard-to-research issues, invisible benefits, or benefits to third parties that are difficult to portray and that are supposed to lead to long-term change. Social marketers, however, have less freedom to change their offerings, more limited budgets, and need to work with others who are often suspicious of marketing.

Social marketers make use of other disciplines, particularly social anthropology, education and mass communication, and behavioral analysis. Marketing is accorded the coordinating role.

While social marketing can now document a significant number of successes, social marketers recognize that they must continue to give attention to the problems of sustaining the behavior they have attempted to influence and of institutionalizing the process of social marketing itself.

QUESTIONS

1. Most social marketing programs have had their success in developing countries where the target populations were often illiterate, isolated, and strongly influenced by local religions and traditional health practices. What are the risks and potential benefits of importing experiences from developing countries to more advanced countries such as the United States?
2. The concept of exchange is central to social marketing efforts, and marketers need to increase the benefits and lower costs of particular recommended behaviors. Make thorough lists of the benefits and costs involved when a social marketing non-violence program seeks to influence a young, urban male to avoid violence and physical conflict. For each benefit, suggest a way to enhance it. For each cost, suggest a way to reduce it.
3. You have just hired a top marketing prospect from Procter & Gamble to join your international social marketing program. Your program's objective is to get young men in Africa to use condoms regularly to control the population and prevent the spread of AIDS. What would you tell the marketing manager on her first day about the nature of her job, and its external and internal environments? What will she likely find to be the same as, and different from, where she came from?

4. Should the marketing mix change as an offering moves from introduction to a more mature phase? Consider an example such as a rape counseling clinic expanding into a new geography. How would the marketing mix for this offering change from the time of introduction to three years after introduction?

5. How would a social marketing strategy differ when the beneficiary is not the person doing the behavior? What are some examples of this situation? Are costs of the behavior more important here? What about communications: What messages should be featured? Is behavior change in these situations likely to be less permanent? Why? If so, what does this imply for strategy?

NOTES

1. Material in this section is drawn from Alan R. Andreasen, "Social Marketing and Child Survival," Working Paper, Academy for Educational Development, Washington, D.C., 1989. See also Alan R. Andreasen, "Social Marketing: Its Definition and Domain," *Journal of Public Policy and Marketing,* Spring 1994, pp. 108–114; Alan R. Andreasen, *Marketing Social Change* (San Francisco, Ca.: Jossey-Bass Publisher, 1995) and Philip Kotter, Ned Roberto and Nancy Lee, *Social Marketing: Improving the Quality of Life* (Thousand Oaks, Ca.: Sage Publications 2002).

2. For a discussion of ethical issues posed by social marketing, see Gene R. Laszniak, Robert F. Lusch, and Patrick Murphy, "Social Marketing: Its Ethical Dimensions," *Journal of Marketing,* Spring 1979, pp. 29–36 and Alan R. Andreasen (Ed.), *Ethics in Social Marketing* (Washington, D.C.: Georgetown University Press, 2001).

3. Charles T. Clotfelter and Philip J. Cook, "The Unseemly 'Hard Sell' of Lotteries," *New York Times,* August 20, 1987, p. 21.

4. Raymond S. Alexander and Simon Podair, "Educating New York City Residents to Benefits of Medicaid," *Public Health Reports,* September 1969, pp. 767–772.

5. "Wrong Publicity May Push Drug Use: UN Chief," *Chicago Sun-Times,* May 8, 1972, p. 30.

6. See "Drug Ed a Bummer," *Behavior Today,* November 13, 1972, p. 2.

7. See Michael L. Ray, Scott Ward, and Gerald Lesser, *Experimentation to Improve Pretesting of Drug Abuse Education and Information Campaigns: A Summary* (Cambridge, Mass.: Marketing Science Institute, September 1973).

8. Mark R. Rasmuson, Renata E. Seidel, William A. Smith, and Elizabeth Mills Booth, *Communication for Child Survival* (Washington, D.C.: Academy of Educational Development, June 1988).

9. N. Ferencic, "Guidelines for Carrying Out In-Depth Interviews about Health in Developing Countries," Working Paper #107, Annenberg School of Communications, University of Pennsylvania, 1989.

10. For an overview, see Michael Rothschild, "Carrots, Sticks and Promises: A Conceptual Framework for the Management of Public Health and Social Issue Behaviors," *Journal of Marketing,* 63, 4 (1999), pp. 24–37.

11. Ibid.

12. See, for example, *Anthropological Perspectives on AIDS in Africa: Priorities for Intervention and Research* (Research Triangle Park, N.C.: AIDSTECH Project, January, 1988), and Claire Monod Cassidy, Robert W. Porter, and Douglas Feldman, "Ethnographic Survey of Nonpenetrative Sexual Activity," Working Paper, AIDSCOM Project, Academy for Educational Development, 1989.

13. Albert Bandura, *Principles of Behavior Modification* (New York: Holt, Rinehart, and Winston, 1969). Also B. Springer, T. Brown, and P. K. Duncan, "Current Measurement in Applied Behavioral Analysis," *The Behavior Analyst,* Vol. 4 (1981), pp. 19–31.

14. Carl Kendall, Dennis Foote, and Reynaldo Martorell, "Anthropology, Communications, and Health: The Mass Media and Health Practices Program in Honduras," *Human Organization,* Vol. 42, No. 4 (Winter 1983), pp. 353–360.

15. HealthCom, *A Consumer Strategy for Health, Nutrition, and Population* (Washington, D.C.: Academy for Educational Development, n.d.).

16. Thomas L. Friedman, "Foreign-Aid Agency Shifts to Problems Back Home," *New York Times,* June 26, 1994, pp. 1, 18.

17. Robert C. Hornik (ed.), *Public Health Communication: Evidence for Behavior Change* (Mahwah, N.J.: Lawrence Erlbaum Associates, Publishers, 2002).

18. Amy Carroll, Lisa Craypo, and Sarah Samuels, *Evaluating Nutrition and Physical Activity Social Marketing Campaigns: A Review of the Literature for Use in Community Campaigns* (Sacramento, Ca.: University of California Davis Center for Advanced Studies in Nutrition and Social Marketing, 2000).

19. Douglas McKenzie-Mohr and William Smith, *Fostering Sustainable Behavior—An Introduction to Community-Based Social Marketing* (Gabriola Island, BC: New Society Publishers, 1999).

20. William Smith, *Communication and Marketing for Child Survival* (Washington, D.C.: Academy for Educational Development, August 8, 1989), p. 5.

21. Ibid.

CHAPTER 14

Developing and Launching New Offerings

Tobacco consumption is a major threat to health everywhere in the world. However, the penetration of tobacco varies greatly by country and the variation follows a traditional product life cycle. While the tobacco industry would like to just follow this life cycle to sales success and profits, a broad coalition of groups from the World Health Organization (WHO) to the U.S. Campaign for Tobacco-Free Kids would like to abort it.

The four stages of the tobacco life cycle are quite straightforward. In Stage 1, countries are too poor for their populations to afford cigarettes and rates are low. This pattern describes countries of sub-Saharan Africa. Stage 2 is marked by rapid economic growth where the population can now afford to smoke and rates rapidly rise to as high as 50 percent for men and 40 percent for women. This is the pattern now seen in China, India, and many other developing nations. Stage 3, the "maturity" phase, is when the negative impact of smoking begins to sink in. People see their heavy-smoking friends and neighbors dying and the warnings of health officials begin to sink in. But this can lag up to 40 years after the beginnings of Stage 2—it takes a long time before the effects are felt. Fortunately, this now appears to be the case in Eastern Europe and Japan. Stage 4 is evidenced in the leading industrial countries like the United States, Canada, Australia, and Western Europe, where rates are declining—albeit not necessarily in a smooth progression.

The World Health Organization would like to galvanize countries and their governments to take action before millions of their citizens die unnecessarily. In particular, they would like to intervene in Stage 2 countries like China where there are already 320 million smokers. WHO's principal focus is on achieving widespread support for a global treaty called the Framework Convention on Tobacco Control (FCTC). This framework would make it easier for governments to impose advertising controls, package and distribution regulations, bans for smoking in places like government buildings and airplanes, and increases in tobacco taxation.

However, they face challenges from both expected and unexpected quarters. Of course, the tobacco industry continues its efforts to attract new smokers every day. Major tobacco companies hand out free samples routinely in Third World countries and continue to portray smoking as attractive and sophisticated. And they argue that regulations on them will just lead to more counterfeiting and roll-your-own activity which will promote crime and drastically cut tax revenues.

In addition, some governments themselves are potential problems. The governments of China and Turkey are tobacco producers. Even in the United States, the government still provides support to tobacco farmers. WHO has its work cut out for it. It can at least point to dramatic programs like Canada's that require vivid images of bleeding brains and diseased lungs on cigarette packages. Canada has seen smoking rates decline 2 percent a year for the last 20 years. Another success story is South Africa, which ought to be in Stages 2 or 3 but, because of actions by Nelson Mandela and his health officials, found its smoking rates falling after apartheid by 22 percent by 2000.

Source: Drawn from Eryn Brown, "The World Health Organization Takes on Big Tobacco (But Don't Hold Your Breath)," *Fortune,* September 1, 2001, pp. 117–124.

As we have indicated throughout this volume, the market environment facing nonprofits in the twenty-first century is one marked by extremely aggressive competition in a large number of sectors, including health care, charitable contributions, the arts, welfare reform, and education. This increased competition means that nonprofits continually run the risk that their existing offer mix will become obsolete—or at least suboptimal. For a vibrant organization to remain on top of its market, it must produce a continuing stream of new offerings simply to "stay in place." Producing such new offerings is even more critical if the organization wishes to grow.

New offerings, of course, can come about by chance insight (the "eureka" of discovery). However, a well-managed organization cannot survive merely on chance or insight. New offerings must *continually* be generated. This requires that a *system* be put in place for developing and launching new offerings. This is the focus of this chapter. We describe how one systematically generates, evaluates, and brings to market new ideas and then launches and (sometimes) modifies them through the introductory and growth phases of their offer life cycles.

OFFER DEVELOPMENT—A PROBLEM OF STRATEGIC PLANNING

The choice of offer development strategies is one of the most important that any manager faces. What an organization offers very much determines what the organization actually is and how it is seen by its customers, competitors, staff, volunteers, donors and the general public. Choices of new offerings will significantly affect the future of every organization and, therefore, must be carefully thought through and not left to chance or personal preferences.

The nonprofit organization has available to it nine basic growth strategies (see Table 14-1). These strategies differ by the extent to which the marketer wishes to emphasize development of markets or offerings. First, the organization can decide to focus on its existing offerings and existing markets (cell 1). For this strategy, it can choose among three substrategies. It can seek to grow by more actively penetrating its existing market either through market expansion or through inducing patronage switching by those already in the market. It can decide not to grow significantly but to become more efficient at marketing to its present clients. Or it can choose to maintain

TABLE 14-1   Offer Strategy Options for Nonprofit Organizations

	Existing Offerings	*New Offerings: Similar*	*New Offerings: Dissimilar*
Existing markets	1. a. Market penetration b. Cost reduction c. Share maintenance	4. Offer extension	7. Offer development
New markets: Similar	2. Market extension	5. Continuous diversification	8. Offer diversification
New markets: Dissimilar	3. Market development	6. Market diversification	9. Radical diversification

the status quo. While it may seem that neither of the last two strategic postures would appeal to many organizations, there are two situations in which they make sense:

- *Declining markets.* If the market demand is declining, as in the need for funding for polio research and treatment, the marketer might want to treat the program as a "cash cow," pull out resources, or become more efficient, thus producing a surplus to be used elsewhere.
- *New competition.* A market leader always faces possible challenges from new competitors. Thus, a major hospital may consider it a great success if it can simply maintain its present level of emergency room volume after a new emergency care center enters the market.

The second posture the organization can take is to seek out new markets for its existing offerings (cells 2 and 3). Firms can add market segments that are similar to their present markets, as when AIDS social marketers seek to take programs that worked in Bangladesh and introduce them in nearby countries like India or Nepal (cell 2, market extension). More daring, and therefore more challenging, would be an attempt to adapt AIDS programs to more dissimilar markets, such as West or East Africa, Tibet, or aboriginal tribes in New Guinea (cell 3, market development).

Carrying out these strategies does not require major changes in the organization's offerings. Rather, it requires more attention to other marketing mix variables like advertising, distribution channels, personal contact, and price and cost management. It can also involve minor changes in the offer such as packaging changes, redesign of features, and so on.

In this chapter, our attention turns to the six remaining strategies suggested in Table 14-1 that involve new offerings. The nonprofit organization can add new offerings that are relatively similar or relatively dissimilar to their present offerings. In either case, they can focus on existing markets (cells 4 and 7), similar new markets (cells 5 and 8), or dissimilar new markets (cells 6 and 9). Clearly, the riskiest stance of all is cell 9, where entirely new offerings (especially offerings new to the world) are brought to radically different markets. Getting very young children to learn to read by speaking into a voice-reading computer would be an example of such a venture. A system of this type has been explored by Educational Development Associates of Newton, Massachusetts.

One organization that has explored offerings in all six of the new offering cells in Table 14-1 is Mechai Varvaiyadia's Population Development Associates (PDA), Thailand's major social marketing organization:

1. *Offer Extension (cell 4)*. PDA has added new *types* of contraceptives (that is, new oral pill formulations) to serve its existing customer markets.
2. *Continuous Diversification (cell 5)*. PDA has added health care services in its family planning clinics, to which any person can come.
3. *Market Diversification (cell 6)*. PDA has developed a program for providing health tests in schools and hospitals, using excess capacity among its full-time medical staff.
4. *Offer Development (cell 7)*. It has developed extensive AIDS campaigns in existing markets.
5. *Offer Diversification (cell 8)*. PDA began helping households in the villages it serves with procedures and funding for building much needed water tanks for storing rain water.
6. *Radical Diversification (cell 9)*. PDA has promoted its TBIRD program to entice major businesses into forming community development partnerships.

These new ventures are a common result of the natural enthusiasm of young organizations still in their growth phase. The remainder of this chapter concerns itself with the question of how a *mature* nonprofit organization ought to develop new offerings.

Every nonprofit sector contains organizations that can be called "innovators." However, a will to innovate is not enough. Many organizations launch new services that fail:

> A 300-bed hospital in southern Illinois got the bright idea of establishing an Adult Day Care Program as a solution to its underutilized space. It designed a whole floor to serve senior citizens who required personal care and services in an ambulatory setting during the day, but who would return home each evening. The cost was $16 a day to the patient's family, and transportation was to be provided or paid for by the patient's family. About the only research that was done on this concept was to note that a lot of elderly people lived within a three-mile radius. The Adult Care Center was opened with a capacity to handle 30 patients. Only 2 signed up!

There are many reasons why this and similar new programs can fail:

1. A top administrator pushes the idea through in spite of the lack of supporting research.
2. There are poor organizational systems for evaluating and implementing ideas for new offerings (poor criteria, poor procedures, poor coordination of departments).
3. There is poor market size measurement, forecasting, and market research.
4. There is poor marketing planning—that is, poor positioning, poor segmentation, underbudgeting, and overpricing.
5. The distinctiveness of the offer of consumer benefits is not sufficiently clear.

6. The offer is poorly designed.
7. Development costs are unexpectedly high.
8. The competitive response is unexpectedly intense.
9. Promotion is inadequate.

A Warning — Beware of Mission Creep

Of course, a good reason for not undertaking new offerings is that they will fail. However, another, more serious problem can stem from offerings that are successful! While it is important for organizations to continually evaluate new ideas to keep the organization growing and employees excited and motivated, there is the real danger that projects will be taken on that are not good fits for organizations. A major source of program innovation for many nonprofits is simply the availability of grant support from government agencies or foundations. Organizations become "grant-chasers" responding to these availabilities without careful thought as to mission fit.[1]

This process can cause a serious distortion of the organization. "Mission creep" can lead the organization into realms and interests that are far removed from its original undertakings. The portrait of the organization begins to look very "lumpy." This has many serious negative consequences. New staff for these new ventures must be acquired and they may be hard to digest organizationally. New skills may be needed that have little synergy with central programs. The organization may be harder to describe to potential donors, and venture philanthropists may shun the enterprise as being ill-focused. Attention may be diverted from remediation needs in the core operations.

Thus, it is very important that a prime criterion for every new venture be this: Is it consistent with the mission? This criterion should also be invoked in annual reviews of past undertakings to ascertain whether they have suffered from "program drift" that imperils the mission.

A PROCESS FOR DEVELOPING NEW OFFERINGS

New offerings should not be left to whim or chance. An organization that wishes to be entrepreneurial must set up systems that will develop and launch successful new offerings. There is an effective methodology for introducing new offerings which, while it does not guarantee success, usually raises the probability of success. Figure 14-1 shows the overall steps involved in new product development. These steps are described in the following sections.

Idea Generation

Organizations differ in their need for new ideas. Some organizations are quite busy carrying out their current activities and do not need new things to do. They may be prohibited by their incorporation documents or by their boards from doing certain things. A hospital, for example, is mandated to carry out certain procedures and is not interested, or even legally able, to consider undertaking new ventures not related to its main business. Other organizations need one or two big new ideas because their main business is taking a turn for the worse. In the early 1970s, the March of Dimes

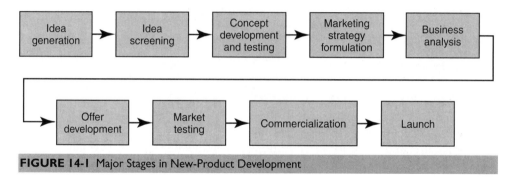

FIGURE 14-1 Major Stages in New-Product Development

had to come up with an entirely new focus when polio was effectively controlled. Now, again, after shifting to a focus on birth defects over the succeeding 30 years, the March of Dimes is again thinking through a new redirection. The organization believes that an emphasis on "defects" is too restrictive and negative and it is repositioning its focus as being about "Helping You Have a Healthy Pregnancy and a Healthy Baby" (www.modimes.org). This refocusing throws open the door to all sorts of new enterprises.

The idea generation stage is most relevant to organizations that need one or more ideas to maintain or expand their services. Indeed, it is our position that, given the high failure rate of many new ideas, the *more* ideas an organization generates—and the more diverse they are—the more chance there will be of finding *successful* ideas. Ideas can occur spontaneously from the following "natural" sources:

- Personal inspiration of one or more members of the organization.
- Serendipitous stimuli from the environment—for example, learning of a new idea from a competitor or in discussion with nonprofit managers from other parts of the country or the world.
- Client or donor requests for new offerings or modification of existing offerings.

Such sources have two major shortcomings. First, relying on them requires a chance combination of an idea appearing *and* management's alertness in recognizing it. Reliance on these approaches may be acceptable for a fledgling nonprofit with a limited budget. However, they are definitely not the type of approaches a mature nonprofit organization ought to adopt. These casual approaches have a second problem. As noted by Crompton, "There is a great deal of evidence which suggests that many efforts to produce new programs which meet client needs are incestuous. That is, there is a tendency to reach for prior experiences, prior approaches, or moderate distortions of old answers, as opposed to really searching for new ideas. We become victimized by habit."[2]

If an organization is to be both systematic and creative in its idea generation, four steps must be taken:

1. A *commitment* must be made to seek new ideas routinely and formally.
2. *Responsibility* for this task must be specifically assigned to someone or some group.

3. A *procedure* must be put in place for *systematically* seeking new ideas.

4. The procedure must contain a *creative* component if truly new ideas are sought.

Procedures for Gathering New Ideas

Establishing an idea generation *procedure* involves the organization in outlining all possible sources for new ideas and then a strategy for generating or collecting ideas routinely from each source. Major sources and procedures for mining them are listed here:

1. *Similar organizations*

   a. A jointly funded clearinghouse could be established to share new ideas.

   b. Routine visits or telephone conversations with similar organizations on *specific dates* (for example, the first week of every February and every July) should be scheduled.

   c. Their Web sites should be visited regularly.

2. *Competitors*

   a. If the competitor has public meetings, for example, with community leaders, these should be attended to learn their development ideas.

   b. If board meetings are open to the public, someone should be assigned to attend them.

   c. Their Web sites should be visited regularly.

3. *Grantmakers*

   a. Foundations and government agency RFPs (requests for proposals) should be regularly scanned.

   b. Reports of recent grants should also be scanned in sources like *The Chronicle of Philanthropy*.

4. *Journals, newspapers, magazines, the Web*

   a. Potential sources of ideas should be identified, subscriptions should be acquired, and someone (or several people) should be assigned to peruse these sources routinely.

   b. A clipping service can be subscribed to.

   c. A librarian can be hired and assigned these tasks.

   d. Regular Web searches can be conducted on key words.

   e. Internet service providers like AOL can be requested to automatically e-mail relevant articles.

5. *Conferences, trade shows, lectures*

   a. People should be routinely assigned to attend important gatherings to collect ideas and useful literature.

6. *Customers and middlemen*

   a. The organization should *solicit* final customers and distributors for their ideas rather than wait until they spontaneously offer them. Many organizations obtain most of their best new ideas by actively listening to customers.

7. *Employees and staff*

   a. The organization should *solicit* employees for suggestions and reward them monetarily or in some other way when these ideas are fruitful.

Specific dates and responsibilities should be set for carrying out each of the previous information-gathering techniques. Further, a formal reporting and assessment mechanism should be developed to ensure that each idea will be formally considered. Finally, the system should be *unblocked*. Lower-level managers should not be able to sabotage the idea generation process by labeling ideas from underlings or outsiders as "too outrageous" or "not really appropriate for us right now." Such judgments must be top management's.

One technique for improving the likelihood that new ideas will emerge is to assign responsibilities to someone who might be called an *idea manager*.[3] The idea manager would serve as a receiving station for the good ideas spotted by others. He or she would do a preliminary analysis and evaluation of the ideas that flow in and make an effort to identify the really good ones, those that help the target customers and the organization. Finally, the idea manager would shepherd new ideas through the organization and serve as their champion.

The idea manager function *should be assigned to someone who has some power and stature in the organization*. Two good candidates are the managers of strategic planning and marketing. Both managers must produce new ideas that will ensure a future for their institution. It is essential, however, that the nonprofit organization's CEO "buy" the idea of assigning idea management to one of these people.

Idea Screening

Once the idea-generating system has accumulated a significant array of ideas, some of them patently outlandish, some attempt must be made to winnow the set to the most promising ideas. The purpose of idea screening is to take a preliminary look at the new ideas and eliminate those that do not warrant further attention. There is some chance that screening might result in an excellent idea being dropped prematurely (a drop error). What might be worse, however, is accepting a bad idea for further development (a go error) as a result of not screening. Each idea that is developed takes substantial management time and money. The purpose of screening is, therefore, to eliminate all but the most promising ideas.

As an example, assume a university is looking for ideas for new programs to expand its educational services in the greater metropolitan area. Among the new program ideas are (1) a new program of women's studies, (2) a new program of black studies, (3) a school of dentistry, (4) a new adult degree program, and (5) a weekend executive master's degree program in business. The university does not have the resources to launch more than one of these new programs, and so it needs a way to identify the most attractive program.

Several steps are necessary to ensure effective idea screening for the organization:

1. A formal screening committee should be established to evaluate new ideas. The committee should include representatives of each key functional department that has expertise that bears on one or more of the proposed undertakings.
2. Regular meetings should be scheduled to evaluate new ideas.
3. Criteria should be developed against which the ideas are to be evaluated. The criteria would be applied consistently over many evaluation sessions. Examples of such criteria include the following:
   a. Size of potential target audience
   b. Size of financial investment necessary

   c. Probable demand on management's time and energy

   d. Newness of the idea to the target audience and organization

   e. Consequences for the organization's desired public image

   f. Extent of probable competition

   g. Likelihood of outside funding assistance

   h. "Downside" consequences if the venture fails.

4. Weights for the criteria should be developed prior to *each* evaluation session. These weights should be set by top management since they will directly affect where the organization wishes to go in the future. Giving a heavy weight to "newness of the idea to the organization" (a negative trait), for example, inevitably means that the organization will accept more ideas nearer to its present offerings. Alternatively, giving a low weight to this factor implies that the organization is more likely to undertake relatively bold innovations.

5. Prior to the committee evaluation meeting, one or more staff members should prepare briefs on each idea as a basis for group discussion. Each brief should present data that are relevant to each of the major criteria.

6. The group should meet and discuss each idea. Afterwards they should rate each idea either individually or collectively on each criterion. (A form should be devised for this purpose.) Each evaluator (or the group as a whole) should also indicate how confident he or she is of the rating on each criterion.

7. A weighted value rating for each new idea should be computed along with a weighted certainty rating.

8. Candidate ideas should then be arranged by value and certainty ratings, as illustrated in Figure 14-2.

9. The best ideas should be moved on to the next stage. These choices will involve management trade-offs between value and certainty ratings. These trade-offs are shown by the F equivalence curves in Figure 14-2. Thus, F_1 shows that management feels that a new venture with a value rating of 50 and a certainty rating of 25 is just as acceptable as an idea with a value rating of 25 and a certainty rating of 50. Management would then decide how many projects it would fund by using F_1 or F_2, and so on, as the feasible frontier. If it chose F_5, for example, management would only consider the adult degree program; if it chose the more generous frontier F_3, it would also consider the executive MBA and the school of dentistry.[4]

Concept Development and Testing

Those ideas that survive screening must undergo further development into full concepts. It is important to distinguish between an idea, a concept, and an image. An *idea* is something the organization can see itself offering to the market. The idea must be developed into a *concept* that is an elaborated version of the idea expressed in meaningful consumer terms. An *image* is the particular picture that consumers acquire of an actual or potential innovation.

Concept Development

Suppose, as a result of screening the various new program ideas, the university described earlier decides the best one is a new adult degree program. This is an offer *idea*. The university's task is to turn this idea into an appealing concept. Every idea can

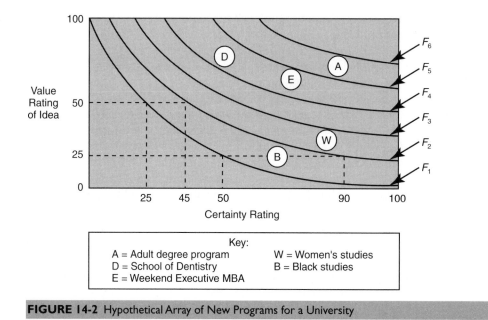

FIGURE 14-2 Hypothetical Array of New Programs for a University

be turned into several concepts, not all of them equally attractive. Among the concepts that might be created around this idea are:

- *Concept 1.* An evening program with a liberal arts orientation, mostly required courses, and no credit for past experience.
- *Concept 2.* An evening program with a career development orientation, much latitude in the courses that could be taken, and credit for past experience.
- *Concept 3.* An evening program with a general education orientation for people over 50 years of age who want a bachelor's degree.

Concept Testing

Concept testing calls for gathering the reactions of target consumers to each concept. Each concept should be presented in written form in enough detail to allow the respondent to understand it and express his or her level of interest. Here is an example of Concept 2 in a more elaborate form:

> We are proposing to offer an evening program, called the School for New Learning, with a career development orientation and much latitude in the courses that can be taken. The program would be open to persons over 24 years of age, lead to a bachelor's degree, give course credit for past experiences and skills that the individual has acquired, give only pass–fail grades, and involve a "learning contract" between the student and the school.

Target consumers are identified and interviewed about their reactions to this concept. One approach is to use questions like those in Table 14-2. The last question in Table 14-2,

TABLE 14-2 Major Questions in a Concept Test for a New Educational Program

1. Is the concept of this adult degree evening program with its various features clear to you?
2. What do you see as reasons why you might enroll in this program?
3. What expectations would you have about the program's quality?
4. Does this program meet a real need of yours?
5. What improvements can you suggest in various features of this program?
6. Who would be involved in your decision about whether to enroll in this program?
7. How do you feel about the tuition cost of this program?
8. What competitive programs come to mind and which appeal to you the most?
9. Would you enroll in this program?

for example, assesses the consumer's *intention to act* and usually reads, "Would you definitely, probably, probably not, definitely not enroll in this program?" Suppose that 10 percent of the target consumers said "definitely will enroll" and another 5 percent said "probably will enroll." The university would apply these percentages (or slightly lower ones) to the corresponding size of the target market to estimate whether the number of enrollees would be sufficient. Even then, the estimate is at best tentative because people often do not carry out their stated intentions. Nevertheless, by ranking the alternative concepts with target consumers in this way, the university would learn which concept has the best market potential.

An alternative approach would involve the technique of conjoint analysis described in Chapter 4. Suppose the university identified key dimensions of the program offer and levels of each as follows:

1. Orientation: (a) liberal arts, (b) general education, (c) career development
2. Credit for past experience: (a) yes, (b) no
3. Student body: (a) mostly under 35, (b) mostly 35 to 50, (c) mostly over 50
4. Cost per semester: (a) $800, (b) $950, (c) $1,200
5. Nightly attendance per week: (a) 4 or 5 times, (b) 2 or 3 times, (c) once

The target audience could then be offered combinations of these dimensions described in some detail as a large number of potential program offerings (that is, concepts) and asked to rank them. This technique would then not only suggest which alternative is rated highest overall, but would indicate the implicit weights the target audience was assigning to each dimension.

Marketing Strategy Formulation

Once a concept has been chosen, the organization should develop a preliminary outline of the marketing strategy it would use to introduce the new program to the target audience. This is necessary so that the full revenue and cost implications of the new program can be evaluated in the next stage of business analysis.

The core marketing strategy should be spelled out in a statement consisting of three parts. The first part describes the size, structure, and behavior of the target market, the intended positioning of the new offering in this market, and the volume and impact goals for the first few years. For the hypothetical university, this might be as follows:

The target market is adults over age 24 living in the greater metropolitan area who have never attained a bachelor's degree but have the skills and motivation to seek one. This program will be differentiated from other programs by offering course credit for relevant past experience, as well as in its career development emphasis. The school will seek a first-year enrollment of 60 students with a net loss not to exceed $300,000. The second year will aim for an enrollment of 200 persons and a net profit of at least $100,000.

The second part of the marketing strategy statement outlines the offering's intended price (if any), distribution strategy, and marketing budget for the first year:

The new program will be offered at the downtown location of the university. All courses will take place once a week in the evening from 6:00 to 9:00 P.M. Tuition will be $800 per course. The first year's promotion budget will be $100,000, $50,000 of which will be spent on advertising materials and media and the remainder on personal contact activities. Another $20,000 will be spent on marketing research to analyze and monitor the market.

The third part of the marketing strategy statement describes the intended long-run goals and marketing mix strategy over time:

The university ultimately hopes to achieve a steady enrollment of 400 students in this degree program. When it is built up to this level, a permanent administration will be appointed. Tuition will be raised each year in line with the rate of inflation. The promotion budget will stay at a steady level of $70,000. Marketing research will be budgeted at $10,000 annually. The long-run target profit level for this program is $200,000 a year, and the money will be used to support other programs that are not self-paying.

Business Analysis

As soon as a satisfactory offer concept and marketing strategy have been developed, the organization is in a position to do a hardheaded business analysis of the attractiveness of the proposal. The university, for example, must estimate the possible revenues and costs of the program for different possible enrollment levels. *Break-even analysis* is the tool most frequently used in this connection. Suppose the university learns that it needs an enrollment of 160 students to break even. If the university manages to attract more than 160 students, this program will produce a net income that could be used to support other programs; if there is a student shortfall, the university will lose money on this new program.

Offer Development

If the organization is satisfied that the concept is financially viable, it can begin giving the program concept concrete form. The person in charge of the concept can begin to develop brochures, schedules, ads, sales plans, and other materials to implement the program. Each of the developed materials should be *consumer tested* before being printed and issued. A sample of prospects in the target audience, for example, might be asked to respond to a mock-up of the brochure describing the new program. This usually results in very valuable suggestions leading to an improved positioning.

Market Testing

When the organization is satisfied with the initial materials and schedules, it can set up a market test to see if the concept is really going to be successful. Market testing is the stage at which the offer and marketing program are introduced into an authentic consumer setting to learn how many consumers are really interested in the program. Thus, the university might decide to mail 10,000 brochures to strong prospects in the area during the month of November to see whether at least 30 students can be attracted. If more than 30 students sign up, the market test will be regarded as successful and full-scale promotion can be launched. Otherwise, the program can be reformulated or dropped.

Test markets are the ultimate form of testing the target market's reaction to a new product. The organization can use one or more sites to measure the new program's viability without installing it wholesale throughout the system. The market test can serve an important second function—determining which of the several alternative marketing strategies is best. Suppose that the State University of New York (SUNY) was considering the same new program as our hypothetical university. SUNY consists of over 60 campuses, not just one campus. SUNY could develop the concept and test it at one of the campuses to see how well it works, or it could test it at several campuses. One campus could emphasize direct mail to alumni, a second could purchase a mailing list of non-alumni who might be interested, a third could use primarily the Internet, and a fourth could advertise in regional editions of national magazines like *Time* or *Newsweek*. As a result, SUNY could develop valuable insights into the cost-effectiveness of different promotional approaches. If the new program proved successful in one or all of the test markets, it could then be launched at other campuses where appropriate.

Introduction to Market

Introduction to Market is a set of activities undertaken following the test market's "go" recommendation to actually bring the new offering to market. The first step is to make four crucial decisions about the launch (although not all four will apply in every case):

1. *When* to launch. Factors to consider are (a) whether there is a need to first phase out an old program (for example, use up an existing lease), (b) whether there is a seasonal peak time for introducing the item (for example, a new museum for children at the start of summer or a drunk-driving program just before the Christmas holidays), (c) whether further work on the offer could profitably be carried out, and (d) whether there is any risk that important rivals will reach the market first (or otherwise compromise favorable launch circumstances).

2. *Where* to launch. If the offer is potentially to be marketed in a wide geographic area, the organization must decide whether to tackle the whole market at once or to start slowly, rolling out the offer on a market-by-market basis. A social service program, for example, could be aimed at the entire city or state or tried out neighborhood by neighborhood. The "whole market" approach has the advantages of scale economies, of preempting competitors, and of achieving significant advertising and

public relations impact. It does, however, assume that the program has pretty well been finalized and that its chances of ultimate success are excellent. The advantages of the roll-out introduction, which can well compensate for its slower speed and greater total cost, are that (a) one can learn as one goes, and (b) if optimistic projections are not realized, the project can be aborted or "sent back to the drawing boards" at lower economic cost and with less embarrassment to the organization.

3. *To whom* to aim the launch. Even in a local roll-out, the program manager must decide whether to aim at all eventual target audience members or to focus at first on (a) those most likely to respond to the offer, (b) those most likely to have an important leadership role for others, or (c) both of these groups.

4. *How* to launch. Tactical decisions must be made about how to achieve the maximum impact at launch date and thereafter. Included are decisions about teaser ads, degree of secrecy, amount and type of media coverage, and so on.

A second step in the commercialization process is to assign responsibility for the launch and introductory period to some individual or group. Here, management must decide whether to have a separate venture management group (or individual) for the new offer, to have a separate new venture *department* to launch *all* new ventures, or to fold the new venture in with the responsibilities of an existing individual or departments.

The last step is to set up a formal scheduling procedure to ensure that all the needed tasks are (1) done in the right order, (2) done on schedule, and (3) done at the least possible cost. There are a number of valuable scheduling tools, such as PERT, CPM, and so on, for this task.[5] Most of them provide (1) directions for individuals who must accomplish each step, (2) a forecast of probable launch dates, (3) the critical series of steps (called *the critical path*) whose delay will mean postponing the launch date, (4) a monitoring tool with checkpoints to ensure that the process is on schedule, and (5) a decision-making capability that would permit the launch manager to decide which activities along the critical path to speed up if the project falls behind schedule.

LAUNCHING THE NEW OFFERING

Once an offering has passed through the Introduction to Market stage of the development process previously described, it must be launched and managed carefully. The performance of a new offering launched into the marketplace typically follows an S-shaped pattern known as the *offer life cycle* (OLC) (Figure 14-3). The S-shaped curve is marked by the following four stages:

1. *Introduction* is a period of slow growth as the offering is introduced into the market.
2. *Growth* is a period of rapid market acceptance.
3. *Maturity* is a period of slowdown in growth because the offering has achieved acceptance by most of the potential buyers.
4. *Decline* is the period when performance shows a strong downward drift.

The offer life cycle can be defined further according to whether it describes an offer *class* (mental health service), an offer *form* (psychoanalysis), or a *brand* (Menninger Clinic). The OLC concept has a different degree of applicability in each case. Offer classes have

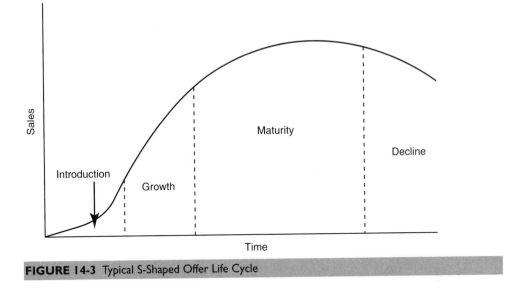

FIGURE 14-3 Typical S-Shaped Offer Life Cycle

the longest life cycles. The performance of many offer classes can be expected to continue in the mature stage for an indefinite duration. Thus, "mental health services" began centuries ago with organized religion and can be expected to continue in the mature state for an indefinite duration. Offer forms, however, tend to exhibit more standard OLC histories than offer classes. Thus, mental health services are dispensed in such forms as psychoanalysis, bioenergetics, group therapy, and so on, some of which are beginning to show signs of maturity, while others, such as "Rolfing," may well be in their decline stage. As for brands, they are the most likely to have finite histories. Thus, the Menninger Clinic is a well-known psychoanalytically oriented clinic that had a period of rapid growth and is now mature. It may pass out of existence or absorbed by new corners.

Not all offerings exhibit an S-shaped life cycle. Three other common patterns are these:

1. *Scalloped pattern.* (Figure 14-4A) In this case, the offer, during the mature stage, suddenly breaks into a new life cycle. The new life is triggered by modifications, new uses, new users, changing tastes, or other factors. The market for psychotherapy, for example, reached maturity at one point, and then the emergence of group therapy gave it a whole new market. At the brand level, interest in the March of Dimes was waning until the organization shifted its focus to birth defects and later to well babies.
2. *Cyclical pattern.* (Figure 14-4B) The performance of some offerings shows a cyclical pattern. Engineering schools, for example, go through alternating periods of high enrollment and low enrollment, reflecting changes in demand and supply in the marketplace. Preferences for political parties also seem to follow this pattern. The decline stage is not a time to eliminate the offer, but to maintain as much of it as possible, while waiting for the next up cycle.
3. *Fad pattern.* (Figure 14-4C) Here, a new offer comes on the market, attracts quick attention, is adopted with great zeal, peaks early, and declines rapidly. The acceptance cycle is short and the offer tends to attract only a limited following of people

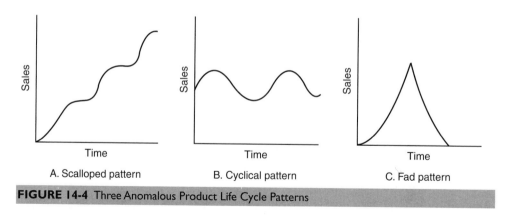

A. Scalloped pattern   B. Cyclical pattern   C. Fad pattern

FIGURE 14-4 Three Anomalous Product Life Cycle Patterns

who are looking for excitement or diversion. Some art and therapy forms exhibit the pattern of a fad.

While the fact that offers have life cycles may at first seem like just common sense, it turns out to be a very useful strategic planning device because it alerts management to the fact that they need to adjust the focus of their marketing thinking depending on the OLC stage they are currently in. The next part of this chapter describes marketing strategies for the introduction and growth stages.

INTRODUCTION AND GROWTH STAGES

One way to characterize the changes sought by all marketers is to distinguish between first-time and repeat acceptance of the marketer's offering. Obviously, the strategic problems of getting people to take an action initially are very different from those of getting them to repeat or continue a given behavior. Thus, getting someone to give blood the first time, begin going to the theater, or even vote Democratic for the first time can be very difficult. Once over this hurdle, the marketing task is infinitely easier, especially if the initial experience is satisfying.

Following this line of reasoning, the offer life cycle can be divided into the two parts shown in Figure 14-5. For some nonprofit offerings, the OLC may *only* involve first-time use (i.e., innovation adoption). Thus, a male only needs to have one small pox shot; there (usually) is no need to repeat the operation. This, however, is relatively rare. Most strategies involve trial followed by repeat exchanges. Repeat exchanges may differ, however, as to whether we mean *repeating* an action like giving blood or attending an opera or whether we mean *continuing* a newly adopted behavior pattern like not smoking.

Innovation Adoption

Many social science disciplines have studied the process by which target audiences begin something new. Cultural anthropologists have researched how ancient cultures adopted new metals, new pot-glazing techniques, and new crops. Rural sociologists

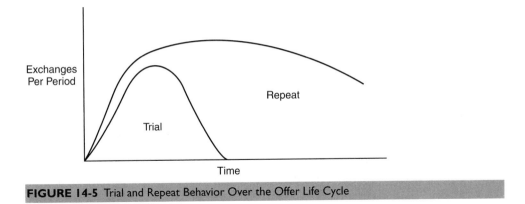

FIGURE 14-5 Trial and Repeat Behavior Over the Offer Life Cycle

have studied how farmers have adopted new fertilizing and farm management practices and new types of seeds. Economists have investigated how firms adopt new manufacturing technologies like oxygen lancing in steel making, while educators have studied the dynamics of adopting teaching innovations, such as the "new math" or "new English." Social psychologists have studied the processes by which individuals acquire smoking, drug, and drinking addictions. And marketers, of course, have long studied new product and service adoptions.

The findings from these studies can help nonprofit managers understand how to induce first-time behaviors. First, they provide insights into the characteristics of those who adopt an innovation at different points during its introduction, growth, and maturity phases and into the interactions among these characteristics. Second, they describe the typical stages that individuals go through to adopt a given innovation. Finally, they identify the characteristics of offerings that will be relatively easy to introduce as compared to those that will not.

Finding Potential Innovators

A *mass market approach* to launching a new innovation typically does not make sense for a new nonprofit venture. It has two drawbacks: (1) It requires heavy marketing expenditures, and (2) it involves a substantial number of wasted exposures to nonpotential and low-potential target audience members. These drawbacks lead to a second approach, *target marketing,* in which the offer is directed to the groups that are likely to be most interested. It turns out that persons (or organizations) differ in how much interest they show in new ideas and in how fast they will move through the Stages of Change and try them. These people (or organizations) are early adopters, and the marketer of an innovation ought to direct marketing efforts to them. *Innovation-adoption theory* holds that:

1. Persons within a target market differ in the amount of time that passes between their exposure to a new offering and their trial of it.
2. Early adopters are likely to share some traits that differentiate them from late adopters.

3. There exist efficient media for reaching early adopter types.
4. Early adopter types are likely to be high on opinion leadership and therefore help-ful in "advertising" the new offer to potential buyers.

Individual differences in response to new ideas is called their *innovativeness.* Specifically, innovativeness is the degree to which an individual or organization is rela-tively earlier in adopting new ideas than the other members of the social system. On the basis of their innovativeness, individuals or organizations can be classified into dif-ferent *adopter categories.* In each product area, there are apt to be "consumption pio-neers" and early adopters. Some women are the first to adopt new clothing fashions or new appliances, such as the microwave oven; some doctors are the first to prescribe new medicines;[6] and some farmers are the first to adopt new farming methods.[7]

Other individuals, however, tend to adopt innovations much later. This has led to a classification of people into the adopter categories shown in Figure 14-6.

The adoption process is represented as following a normal (or near-normal) distri-bution when plotted over time. After a slow start, an increasing number of people adopt the innovation, the number reaches a peak, and then it diminishes as fewer per-sons remain in the nonadopter category.

Convenient breaks in the distribution are used to establish adopter categories. Thus innovators are defined as the first 2.5 percent of the individuals to adopt a new idea; the early adopters are the next 13.5 percent who adopt the new idea, and so forth.

Rogers has characterized the five adopter groups in terms of their central val-ues.[8] The dominant value of the small group of Innovators who are the very earliest in the process is *venturesomeness;* they like to try new ideas, even at some risk, and are cosmopolitan in orientation. The dominant value of the next group, the Early Adopters, is *respect;* they enjoy a position in the community or in an industry as opin-ion leaders and adopt new ideas early with an eye to whether the adoption will enhance their status as trendsetters. This group contains a subset called the Opinion Leaders who are often looked to by others for leads on new ideas. The dominant value of the next group, the Early Majority, is *deliberateness;* these people like to

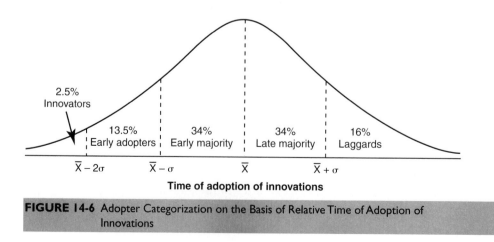

FIGURE 14-6 Adopter Categorization on the Basis of Relative Time of Adoption of Innovations

adopt new ideas before the average member of the social system, although they are rarely leaders. Indeed, this group more often comprises the followers who pay attention to the advice given or the example set by the opinion leaders who preceded them. The dominant value of the Late Majority is *skepticism;* they do not adopt an innovation until the weight of majority opinion seems to legitimate its utility. They typically pay little attention to the opinion leaders, relying more on market cues of general acceptance. Finally, the dominant value of the Laggards is *tradition;* they are suspicious of any changes, and adopt the innovation only because it has now taken on a measure of tradition itself.

Rogers has characterized the traits of the key Earlier Adopters as follows:

> The relatively earlier adopters in a social system tend to be younger in age, have higher social status, a more favorable financial position, more specialized operations, and a different type of mental ability from later adopters. Earlier adopters utilize information sources that are more impersonal and cosmopolite than later adopters and that are in closer contact with the origin of new ideas. Earlier adopters utilize a greater number of different information sources than do later adopters. The social relationship of earlier adopters are more cosmopolite than for later adopters, and earlier adopters have more opinion leadership.[9]

These findings have obvious implications for the kind of strategy one should adopt as one moves through the introductory and growth phases.

Innovators

This group enters the market during the introductory phase of OLC. The marketer can largely ignore the group, however, for three reasons. First, they are a relatively small group. Second, because of their venturesomeness, they are likely to discover the innovation even without the marketer's help. Finally, they have little or no influence on those who follow later. Since the early adopters and early majority tend to look upon the innovators as "try-anything-once" oddballs, the marketer runs a severe risk of cutting off further adoption by identifying too closely with this group.

Early Adopters

Early Adopters are the key to the success of most innovations. If one does not win them over, the introductory period will be prolonged, or the innovation may totally fail. Thus, an important first step in any marketing program involving an innovation is to identify the Opinion Leaders. Unfortunately, opinion leadership is not a generalized trait. Particular consumers or households may be innovators in one area but not in another. The fraternity or sorority fashion leader may not be the first to give blood or attend the latest movies. Furthermore, the notion that innovations "trickle down" from the upper to the lower classes has been found to have limited application. Past research has shown that Opinion Leaders are not necessarily the elite of a society; they can be found in all social strata. Indeed, in recent years many innovations in fashion, music, sports, and the media have received their early push "on the streets" in poorer and ethnic neighborhoods. However, there is some evidence that the same opinion leaders may be found for *similar* innovations. Thus, the early adopters of protective car seats for their babies might be good prospects as opinion leaders supporting airbag legislation. Yet, these assumptions should be tested. Three approaches to identifying opinion leaders are possible:[10]

- *Self-reporting.* Individuals can be asked directly whether they would classify themselves as Opinion Leaders either in general or in ways related to the innovation in question.
- *Reputational.* Individuals may be asked to identify others to whom they might go for information or advice in this particular category. They can be asked to describe the most salient characteristic of these significant others.
- *Sociometric.* The researcher could directly map the interaction among members of a population and use this to determine the most influential members. Thus, Coleman, Katz, and Menzel found that by asking physicians in a particular community whom they would contact (a) to refer a patient, (b) to secure advice on a medical problem, and (c) to socialize with, they could rather accurately predict who would be the Early Adopters of a new drug and who would be likely to follow them when they did.[11]

Early Majority

Some time will elapse before the marketer's strategy of attracting Opinion Leaders has its effect. The marketer should then make it clear to the Early Majority that the Opinion Leaders have already adopted—and, therefore, legitimized—the innovation. This can be accomplished by testimonials, editorials, and news and feature items. A good example of the use of opinion leadership has been the role of former First Lady Betty Ford in trying to get others to follow her lead in the detection of breast cancer and in the treatment of drug abuse, or Bono from U2 setting an example in speaking out against Third World debt.

The Late Majority and Laggards

Once the Early Majority has been heavily penetrated, tactics should shift from securing trial to emphasizing repeat behavior. This is desirable on two grounds. First, if a good trial rate has been achieved, competitors will enter the market and attention must shift to providing superior offers. Second, the emergence of more suppliers and offers will send a clear signal to the late majority that the innovation is accepted. By changing a campaign that says "Try this" to one that says "Try ours, not theirs," the marketer can make the late majority realize that the innovation is no longer risky. Whether such tactics will have an effect on the laggards is unclear.

Stages in the Innovation Adoption Process

Rogers and Shoemaker[12] have identified four steps that individuals typically go through in adopting some new pattern of behavior. These steps exactly parallel the Stages of Change we have been using throughout the book:

1. *Knowledge* (Precontemplation Stage). First, the target consumer must (a) become aware of the innovation and (b) learn enough about it to deduce that it has some relevance to his or her needs, wants, and lifestyle.

2. *Persuasion* (Contemplation Stage). Next, the target consumer must move from simple awareness and vague interest to being motivated to take action. This is primarily a matter of attitude change, although it is also possible that a behavioral response could be achieved through *incentivization* or *coercion* with relatively little attitude change.

3. *Decision* (Preparation/Action Stage). At some point, the target consumer thinks through the probable consequences of the proposed behavior change and makes a decision to adopt or reject it. This stage might well involve a vicarious or personal trial. Thus, a person suffering from hypertension might reduce salt intake for a few days or quiz others who have tried this approach.

4. *Confirmation* (Maintenance Stage). After the initial decision, it is hoped that the target consumer will continue the behavior. This can be a major problem for social change agents.

The value of the Stages of Change model in launching new offerings is threefold. First, it points out that there is a *sequence* of tasks necessary to move a given target segment to adopt. Thus, early messages must create awareness and interest, subsequent messages must persuade, and later messages and other marketing interventions must secure and reinforce behaviors.

Second, it provides a monitoring framework to help detect and identify reasons for a slow rate of acceptance. Thus, if research on quitting smoking shows that many smokers are blocked at the Preparation/Action Stage, persuasion attempts are no longer necessary and effort should focus on inducing a decision and action.

Finally, the model can be used to develop a segmentation strategy. Suppose that research has identified three target segments for a new health program: males working in blue-collar jobs, pregnant women, and senior citizens. Suppose that various proportions of the target audience members have reached the stages of the adoption process as listed in Table 14-3. Obviously, strategies aimed at the blue-collar male sample (Contemplators) should seek to produce decisions and action. As for pregnant women, some messages should create greater interest in the health program (for Precontemplators); other messages should reinforce the behavior of those who have already acted and are in the Maintenance Stage. (Further research differentiating

TABLE 14-3 Distribution of Target Audience Members Across Adoption Categories

Stage of Change	*Blue-Collar Male*	*Pregnant Women*	*Senior Citizens*
Precontemplation (No awareness)	4%	12%	53%
Precontemplation (No knowledge)	26	51	35
Contemplation	61	14	6
Preparation/Action	2	23	4
Maintenance	7	0	2
	100%	100%	100%

these two subpopulations could lead to finer tuning of strategy.) Finally, the majority of senior citizens are not being reached by current messages (Precontemplators). New messages, better execution, or better media are warranted.

Innovation Characteristics

The innovation's characteristics will affect the rate of adoption.[13] Five characteristics have an especially important influence on the adoption rate. The first is the innovation's *relative advantage,* the degree to which it is perceived to be superior to previous ideas. The greater the perceived relative advantage (higher quality, lower cost, and so on), the more quickly the innovation will be adopted. Thus, a five-day smoking cessation program that has a 35 percent initial success rate will be adopted faster than a three-month program that has a 20 percent initial success rate—even though both programs may have the same *long-term* effectiveness.

The second characteristic is the innovation's *compatibility,* the degree to which it is consistent with the values and experiences of the individuals in the target social system. Thus, persuading Muslim women to practice birth control when they believe that their number of children is "in God's hands" will take more time than persuading them to boil water before drinking it, because the latter has no religious significance.

In the first year it attempted to establish opera in Los Angeles, the Los Angeles Music Center Opera organization portrayed a popular movie star, Dudley Moore, dressed in a modern suit on its promotional materials rather than traditional scenes from older operas. This strategy made opera attendance more compatible with Los Angeles's contemporary lifestyles and its identification with the movie industry.

The third characteristic is the innovation's *complexity,* the degree to which it is relatively difficult to understand or use. More complex innovations take a longer time to diffuse, other things being equal. Introducing dietary changes is much more difficult than introducing carpooling.

The fourth characteristic is the innovation's *divisibility,* the degree to which it may be tried on a limited basis. The evidence of many studies indicates that divisibility helps increase adoption. Thus, a severely hypertensive person will be more ready to adopt a self-restricted diet than corrective heart surgery, since the latter is an all-or-nothing proposition.

The fifth characteristic is the innovation's *communicability,* the degree to which the intended results are observable or describable to others. Innovations whose advantages are more observable will diffuse faster in the social system. Thus, obese people will adopt new eating and exercise habits faster than hypertensives because the former will observe their weight loss, whereas hypertensives will not observe any changes unless they use a blood pressure gauge.

The marketing strategist should research how any proposed innovation is perceived by the target market in terms of these five characteristics before developing the marketing plan. Preliminary studies of the potential for injectable, longer-term contraceptives in developing countries, for example, have brought to light the following characteristics:

1. *Relative advantage.* Three advantages are clear. First, the technique puts less of a burden on the woman in terms of memory and possible interferences with sex

(real or perceived). Second, it is a technique that can be adopted easily and in private. Thus, it permits women to secure protection without their parents, friends, and sometimes their husbands or boyfriends knowing about it. Third, depending on the formulation, protection from one injection lasts one to three months.

2. *Compatibility.* Women are accustomed to taking injections for other purposes so that the concept is not as "strange" as some alternatives.

3. *Complexity.* There is an understandable problem for women in that the physical side effects are diverse and sometimes quite pronounced in early months. The problem is also complex for physicians because the U.S. Food and Drug Administration has banned the product because of a very, very small risk that it might produce breast cancer. Doctors face a tough ethical choice between endangering the mother due to the product and endangering her health from too frequent pregnancies.

4. *Divisibility.* Divisibility exists because the product can be stopped and another technique substituted. Several months have to elapse, however, before the women can become pregnant again.

5. *Communicability.* The product's effectiveness in preventing pregnancies can be easily communicated. However, there are problems at the confirmation stage in convincing women that the strong side effects are not serious and will disappear soon.

After learning how the innovation is perceived by the target audience, the marketer can then proceed to make the innovation relatively more advantageous, more compatible, more divisible, less complex, and more communicable.

SUMMARY

To be successful in today's nonprofit environment, organizations must learn to effectively and efficiently develop and launch new offerings. These may involve new or existing offerings in combination with new or existing markets. Extensions into new offerings or markets may involve undertakings that are similar or dissimilar to present marketing programs.

To be successful in developing new offerings, the organization must be both creative and systematic. The first stage of the process is to generate ideas for new offerings. This can involve careful searching of available information or attempts to create new ideas through artificial idea-generation techniques. Once the ideas have been produced, it becomes necessary to screen them to eliminate those that do not meet established organization goals.

The next stage involves elaborating the idea into a concrete concept that can be subjected to formal testing. The concept, if successful, must then generate a specific marketing strategy which, in turn, must survive a rigorous business analysis. The final stages of the development process then involve specific offer development and market testing, followed by a carefully orchestrated and timed commercialization process.

New offerings follow an S-shaped pattern over their life cycle. They move through introductory, growth, maturity, and decline stages. The strategic issues facing the nonprofit marketing manager differ across these stages.

In the introductory and growth stages, the manager must first be concerned with securing trials of the new offering. Five customer groups may be identified on the basis of when they are likely to enter the innovation adoption process. First are the Innovators, who will try almost anything that is new and who are often considered odd by the rest of the population. They can usually be ignored by the new offer manager. The second group, the Early Adopters, cannot be ignored because they are the opinion leaders who influence the next large group, the Early Majority. The Late Majority, which enters next, pays less attention to others in making their decisions to adopt and must be convinced that the new offering is not a fad. The last group, the Laggards, can typically also be ignored because they are very tradition oriented and very slow to try anything new.

There is a clear set of stages through which anyone goes in adopting an innovation, from knowledge to persuasion to decision and confirmation. Innovations that have significant relative advantages over old approaches, that are compatible with the culture, and that are not complex and can be communicated easily and tried out before full adoption will diffuse faster than other innovations.

QUESTIONS

1. Using Table 14-1 as a framework, identify possible new offerings for the Red Cross. What evaluation criteria should the marketer use to determine whether he or she should actually launch any of these offerings?
2. Assume you were appointed as marketing director of a new offering that was about to be launched. There has never been a similar offering like this in the market. How would you go about estimating demand for this offering?
3. Identify various techniques for innovating new offerings for a nursing marketer—list at least three techniques. What are the advantages and disadvantages of each technique? Which technique would be most useful for influencing a group of senior citizens living alone in assisted-living residence? Why?
4. Suppose you are concept testing a new service that a library is considering launching. This service is targeted at kids ages 6 to 10, and is meant to help them collect background research for school projects. How would you assess the likelihood of success for this service? How can you be most assured that your conclusions are valid?
5. Suppose you have just opened a new wing to the museum, with new exhibits, at which you are marketing director. How would you measure the likely success of this offering? How would you determine if the investment in this offering was warranted?

NOTES

1. Mark R. Kramer, "Donors Too Often Support Visionaries Who Don't Have Management Skills," *The Chronicle of Philanthropy,* January 11, 2001, p. 48.
2. John Crompton, "Developing New Recreation and Park Programs," *Recreation Canada,* July 1983, p. 29.
3. Philip Kotler, "Idea Management: A Way to Increase Health Services' Marketing Effectiveness," Presentation to Academy of Health Services Marketing, Las Vegas, Nevada, March 11, 1985.
4. See also Barry M. Richman, "A Rating Scale for Product Innovation," *Business Horizons,* Summer 1962, pp. 37–44; and John T. O'Meara, Jr., "Selecting Profitable Products," *Harvard Business Review,* January–February 1961, pp. 83–89.
5. For example, see Yoram J. Wind, *Product Policy: Concepts, Methods and Strategy*

(Reading, Mass.: Addison-Wesley, 1982), pp. 237–239; and, Glenn L. Urban and John Hauser, *Design and Marketing of New Products* (Englewood Cliffs, N.J.: Prentice-Hall, 1980), p. 469.

6. See James Coleman, Elihu Katz, and Herbert Menzel, "The Diffusion of an Innovation Among Physicians," *Sociometry,* December 1957, pp. 253–270.

7. See J. Bohlen and G. Beal, *How Farm People Accept New Ideas,* Special Report No. 15 (Ames: Iowa State College Agricultural Extension Services, November 1955).

8. Everett M. Rogers, *Diffusion of Innovations,* 4th ed. (New York: The Free Press, 1995).

9. Ibid., p. 192.

10. Everett M. Rogers and David G. Cartano, "Methods of Measuring Opinion Leadership," *Public Opinion Quarterly,* Fall 1962, pp. 43–45; and George Booker and Michael J. Houston, "An Evaluation of Measures of Opinion Leadership," in Kenneth L. Bernhardt (ed.), *Marketing 1776–1976 and Beyond* (Chicago: American Marketing Association, 1976), pp. 562–564.

11. Coleman, Katz, and Menzel, "The Diffusion of Innovation."

12. Everett M. Rogers with F. Floyd Shoemaker, *Communication of Innovations* (New York: The Free Press, 1971).

13. Ibid.

CHAPTER 15

Managing Perceived Costs

A recent survey of studies of women in 50 countries by the Center for Health and Gender Equity at Johns Hopkins University found that from 10 percent to 50 percent of women reported being physically harmed by a male partner sometime in their lives. These cases almost always involved psychological abuse and frequently sexual abuse.

In many cultures, this abuse is the product of cultural norms. Husbands are "allowed" to abuse their wives as a means of control and women should not protest this treatment. Thus, an episode of violence may be provoked if a woman does not obey the man or simply talks back to him. She may not question his use of money or possible infidelity. Some societies set bounds on how far a man may go in "disciplining" his wife, but there is considerable evidence that, even when men are given wide latitude, they still exceed cultural bounds.

Abused women are not always passive and many take actions to minimize or to escape their situation. But many stay in abusive relationships because they see the costs of an exit strategy to be too great. That is, they fear retribution, worry about the fate of their children, lack any means of economic support, and expect little or no support from relatives or neighbors. In many developing countries, unmarried or divorced women are highly stigmatized.

Of course, abusive men are also often very manipulative. They cause many women in abusive relationships to believe that it is the woman's fault she is beaten. Husbands also may hold out the prospect that they will reform. They may turn friends and family against the woman or so intimidate her that she dare not speak out to learn if there is any support for leaving him.

But many women do leave. Often they leave when the children are grown, before the children have come, or before they are old enough to be greatly harmed by what they experience. It may be that the woman finally realizes that the man will not change his behavior or she learns of others who will be supportive of her both emotionally and logistically. Safety is important. A woman's greatest risk of being murdered is right after a separation.

Violence against women has many physiological effects as well as emotional ones. Women in abusive relationships are more likely to have sexually transmitted diseases, high-risk pregnancies, HIV/AIDS, unwanted pregnancies, other gynecological problems, and, of course, physical injury.

A great many programs have been put in place to combat this problem. It has been found that the best, long-term strategy is to empower women and girls in their own societies. A second approach is to raise the cost of abusive behavior to the perpetrator. Third, systems can be put in place that will detect abuse (e.g., in health clinics) and/or that will offer women a safe environment to reveal their torment. These steps must be accompanied by mechanisms and support services so that a woman can extricate herself from an abusive relationship, including help in planning the break, temporary safe housing, and longer-term economic help. Finally, it is very important to continue psychological help after the break. A woman may be fearful of being caught by her husband or partner, may worry that she has done the wrong thing, and may feel that she has damaged her future and that of her children. She will have emotional scars on her sense of self-worth that can last a lifetime. It is not enough to help her escape—programs must also help her heal.

Source: Drawn from Lori Heise, Mary Ellsberg, and Megan Gottemoller, *Ending Violence Against Women,* Population Reports, Series L. No. 11. Baltimore: Johns Hopkins University School of Public Health, Population Information Program, December 1999.

Our view of the marketing task is that it starts with target audience members and their perceptions of the costs and benefits to be derived from undertaking the behavior the marketer wants. In the preceding three chapters, we considered some of the tactics a manager might use to increase the real and perceived benefits that flow from a product, service, or social behavior. In the present chapter, we look at the other side of the exchange equation: its costs. The reader will note that we said "costs," not "cost." This distinction is crucial to the manager's understanding of this component of the marketing task.

THE NATURE AND ROLE OF COSTS

In the Contemplation Stage, target audience members balance the expected benefits from an action against the expected costs. Money payment might be only one of these costs or sacrifices—a price in the traditional economic sense. Sometimes it might be absent altogether. Consider the case of a woman who is deciding whether to go to a doctor's office to have a breast examination because she has a history of breast cancer in her family. She has been exposed to social behavior marketing urging her to have regular examinations and to learn self-examination techniques. The visit to the doctor will cost her money. She will have to pay the doctor (or make a co-payment along with her insurance company). If she is an hourly worker and has no automobile, she will have to pay money for transportation and lose perhaps three hours of wages. If she is at home with a young child and drives, she may have to pay for a baby-sitter, an expressway toll, gasoline, and a parking fee.

Getting to and from the doctor involves nonmonetary costs in terms of physical energy or effort. For many, this may not be an important cost. For an elderly person, however, such a cost can be very dramatic. There are also a number of psychic costs, including these:

- Awkwardness at having to ask for time off from work.
- Embarrassment at having to explain to co-workers where you are going (or lying to them).

- Aggravation at having to find a taxi and find one quickly so as not to wait long (or if she drives, aggravation at traffic delays and wasting time looking for a parking space).
- Worry that the doctor will be late in seeing her.
- Potential embarrassment that she will be criticized for delaying the examination.
- Embarrassment at having her breasts examined.
- Fear that the examination might hurt (for example, if a biopsy has to be done).
- Fear that something will be found.
- Worries that, if something is found, treatment will be costly, consume even more time, and be painful.
- Worries that treatment might involve breast removal, which can cause 'disfigurement' problems for her marriage, and embarrassment with her husband, children, and friends.

All of these "perceived costs" will run through her mind. A marketer who focuses primarily on promoting the *benefits* of having a periodic breast examination will probably fail to motivate many women. But many women already know the benefits. *It is the vast array of perceived costs that keep them from completing the action the marketer wants.* This is particularly true in the latter part of the Contemplation Stage. In a great many of the exchanges a nonprofit marketer seeks, managing the perceived costs is often much more important than managing the benefits. Furthermore, the nominal *money* price tag on the exchange may be the least important of the perceived costs the target audience member is concerned about; in social behavior exchanges, there usually is no price tag at all. We define perceived costs as follows:

*A **perceived cost** is any expected negative consequence of a proposed exchange perceived by a target audience member.*

The Duality of Costs

In an exchange, what is a benefit for one side of the exchange is typically a cost for the other. Thus, a marketer who provides benefits to the consumer in the form of high-quality service, nice surroundings, and a satisfaction guarantee does so at a cost to the marketer's own organization. These are the economic costs *the marketer* has to pay. However, a consumer paying money in exchange for these benefits provides a benefit for the marketer. Therefore, where an exchange involves a money price tag, the marketer is faced with an odd dilemma. There are many nonmoney costs the marketer will work hard to *minimize* so as to secure more exchanges. At the same time, there is at least one cost (the economic price) the marketer would like to *maximize* so the organization can stay in business and grow. To complicate matters even further, there may be occasions when the marketer may not want to minimize nonmoney costs and, indeed, may want to *increase* them. Often a marketer wishes to increase a nonmoney cost because the marketer will enjoy economic savings, which, in turn, will mean more profits from the exchange that could be used to reduce costs elsewhere or permit lower prices overall. Thus, a transit authority may reduce the frequency of its service in a high-income area (thus increasing waiting time and frustration for this market) so as to provide more service in a low-income area, invest in a subway system, or reduce the subsidy required from city or county revenues. Or, a hospital may require a patient to walk in for simple outpatient surgery and bear some of the physical, economic, and psychic costs of managing his or her own convalescence in order to keep all patients' out-of-pocket costs as low as possible.

COST MANAGEMENT

This dual nature of cost management presents a delicate problem for the nonprofit marketer. An optimal cost management strategy from the marketer's standpoint is one that maximizes the number of exchanges (or revenue) for a given cost to the marketer. How can such a strategy be developed? The marketer must begin by researching audience perceptions of the costs they must pay. Otherwise, marketers may miss crucial but subtle barriers affecting particular audience segments. Consider the following examples:

- The National Cancer Institute only realized within the last 25 years that a perceived cost keeping many people from trying to quit smoking was the fear of failure.
- In rural villages in many countries, women who personally want to practice contraception do not do so because all the methods they know require that someone (or many people) become aware of their behavior.
- Some potential attenders of symphony concerts won't go because they believe they have to "dress up."
- Many elderly people do not attend theater in downtown areas because they believe they will be mugged or robbed.
- Many elderly people will not accept nursing home care because this involves admitting that they are old.
- Many alcoholics avoid treatment because they don't want to admit to themselves that they are alcoholics.
- Some males do not take medication for high blood pressure because they believe it will make them sterile or impotent.
- Some organizations won't hire consultants because to do so would be an admission that they lack certain competencies.
- Sanitary water systems are resisted in some villages because they disrupt established social intercourse systems (for example, the twice-daily congregation at the village well).
- Many potential theater, ballet, opera, and symphony attenders avoid going because they don't want to feel ignorant about what's being presented.

Once these costs are understood, the marketer can consider the following questions: Are there strategies that can be used to reduce the perceived costs? What is the cost to the marketer of reducing a perceived cost to the customer? What is the probable responsiveness of the audience to given levels of perceived cost reduction expenditure by the marketer?

While there are many factors to the pricing challenge, we shall adopt a practical perspective.

Practical Management of the Cost Bundle

The difficulty of precisely estimating the theoretical audience response function should not discourage the marketer. If there is a single clearly important cost that drives audience demand (for example, money price), then a formal analysis of the single response curve may well be justified. As noted in Chapter 4, audience responses to offers, however, are usually a reaction to a *bundle* of costs (and, of course, a bundle of benefits). The problem in managing *costs* rather than *a cost* (singular) is to figure out *which* of many costs to reduce and *how much* to reduce them. For these decisions, the marketing manager needs to know *relative responses.* That is, for a given amount of the marketer's expenditure, which cost or costs should be impacted to yield the largest net gain in the number of exchanges?

Suppose a nonprofit clinic is considering reducing one of several customer costs. Suppose further that preliminary research indicates that four nonmoney costs keep potential patients from coming in more often (for example, for checkups) or drives them to other clinics or doctors. These costs are parking costs and the accompanying frustrations; waiting time in the office; inconvenience in filling out forms (for example, for insurance); and the generally unpleasant experience of waiting in unattractive facilities.

The marketer should first determine ways to reduce each cost. Assume that the marketer can spend increments of $5,000 to bring about improvements in each area. For $5,000, the clinic could improve its appearance (for example, the waiting and other rooms could be painted and new curtains installed). For $10,000, the clinic could also acquire new waiting room furniture. Fifteen thousand dollars would also allow recarpeting, and so on. What the marketer now needs is a set of response functions for each of the four areas where costs can be reduced, as in Figure 15-1.

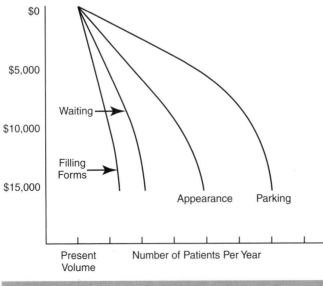

FIGURE 15-1 Responses to Expenditures on Reducing Consumer Costs

As we can see, the best place to put the first $5,000 is toward improving parking. This yields the largest gain in exchanges. The next $5,000 should also go for parking. At that point, assuming that the cost functions are independent, a further $5,000 should be spent on appearance. Given that the marketer can estimate the economic value of the extra exchanges generated by each expenditure increment beyond those indicated in Figure 15-1, he or she can expend $5,000 amounts until the gain in value from the added number of patients is no greater than the last expenditure.

The level of precision the marketer needs for this task is not great. It may be adequate simply to secure intentions data from a representative sample of current and past clinic customers.

SETTING MONEY PRICES

Since a major determinant of the demand for many of the offerings of nonprofit organizations is money price, we shall devote more attention to this part of the bundle.

In handling the complex issues in money pricing, an organization should proceed through two stages. First, it should determine the *pricing objective,* whether it is to maximize profit, usage, fairness, or some other objective. Second, it should determine the *pricing strategy,* whether it should be cost based, demand based, or competition based. Marketers may also wish to use promotional pricing on a short-term basis.

Setting the Pricing Objectives

The first thing an organization must decide in developing a price or pricing policy is the objectives that it wants to achieve. Often the objectives are in conflict, and a choice must be made. Consider the following statement made by a camp director: "I want to keep my camp tuition fees as low as possible to enable more people to enjoy a summer camping experience, but I also must keep the price high enough to ensure that the camp will not lose money in the long run."[1] In this case, the camp director is in conflict over the two opposing goals of *audience size maximization* and *cost recovery maximization.*

However, these are only two of several possibilities. Five different pricing objectives can be distinguished: surplus maximization, cost recovery, market size maximization, social equity, and market disincentivization. Returning to the camp illustration, the camp may aim for surplus maximization on conferences, full cost recovery on weekend retreats, market size maximization for its summer camp program, and lower prices for all events for low-income families to increase social equity.

Surplus Maximization

One would think that nonprofit organizations never use the principle of profit or surplus maximization. This is not so. There are many situations in which a nonprofit organization will want to set its price to yield the largest possible surplus. Thus, a charity organization will set the price for attending a major benefit dinner with the objective of maximizing its receipts over its costs. A university whose faculty has developed patented inventions will price these inventions to maximize its profits. And, of course, the myriad nonprofits with extensive catalogue and retail operations will clearly seek surplus maximization.

Surplus-maximizing pricing requires the organization to estimate two functions, the response (demand) function and the cost function. These two functions are sufficient for deriving the theoretical best price. The demand function describes the expected quantity demanded per period (Q) at various prices (P) that might be charged. Suppose the firm is able to determine through demand analysis that its demand equation is

$$Q = 1{,}000 - 4P \qquad (15\text{-}1)$$

This says that demand is forecasted to be at most 1,000 units (i.e., $P = 0$), and for every $1 increase in price, there will be four fewer units sold. Thus, the number of units purchased at a price of, say, $150, would be 400 units [$Q = 1{,}000 - 4(150)$].

The cost function describes the expected total cost (C) for various quantities per period (Q) that might be produced. Suppose the company derived the following cost equation for its product:

$$C = 6{,}000 + 50Q \qquad (15\text{-}2)$$

With the preceding demand and cost equation, the organization is in a position to determine the surplus maximization price. Two more equations are needed, both definitional in nature. First, total revenue (R) is equal to price times quantity sold:

$$R = PQ \qquad (15\text{-}3)$$

Second, total surplus ($\$$) is the difference between total revenue and total cost:

$$\$ = R - C \qquad (15\text{-}4)$$

With these four equations, the organization is in a position to find the surplus maximizing price. The surplus equation (15-4) can be turned into a pure function of the price charged:

$$\begin{aligned}
\$ &= R - C \qquad (15\text{-}5)\\
\$ &= PQ - C\\
\$ &= PQ - (6{,}000 + 50Q)\\
\$ &= P(1{,}000 - 4P) - 6{,}000 - 50(1{,}000 - 4P)\\
\$ &= -56{,}000 + 1{,}200P - 4P^2
\end{aligned}$$

Equation 15-5 shows total surplus expressed as a function of the price that will be charged. The surplus maximizing price can be found in one of two ways. The researcher could use trial and error, trying out different prices to determine the shape of the profit function and the location of the maximum price. The surplus function turns out to be a parabola or hatlike figure, and surplus reaches its highest point ($34,000) at a price of $150. At this price, the organization sells 400 units that produce a total revenue of $60,000.

The objective of seeking the surplus maximizing price, in spite of its theoretical elegance, is subject to five practical limitations:

1. The model shows how to find the price that maximizes short-run surplus rather than long-run surplus. There may be a trade-off between short-run and long-run surplus

maximization, as when clients get angry at high prices they must pay in the short run (e.g., for a special opera) and eventually switch to other sellers (e.g., go to the theater in the future).

2. There are other parties to consider in setting a price. The model only considers the ultimate audience's response to alternative prices. Other groups that may respond are competitors, suppliers, intermediaries, and the general public. A high price might lead competitors to raise their prices, in which case the demand would be different from that suggested by the demand function if it assumed no competitive reaction. Various suppliers, employees, banks, and raw material producers may take the price to reflect the organization's ability to pay and may raise their prices accordingly, in which case the cost function would be different from that assumed with no supplier reaction. Intermediaries who handle the product may have some strong feelings about the proper price. Finally, the general public might complain about the organization if its price appears to be too high.

3. The government, acting in the interests of the public, might establish a price ceiling, and this may exclude the surplus maximizing price.

4. This pricing model assumes that price can be set independently of the other elements in the marketing mix. But the other elements of the marketing mix affect demand and must be part of the demand function in searching for the optimal price. Thus, a ballet company can charge a higher price if it advertises extensively and builds up audience interest.

5. This pricing model assumes that the demand and cost functions can be accurately estimated. In the case of a new service, there will be no experience upon which to base these estimates. Unless data are available on a similar service, estimates are likely to be highly subjective. Because the demand and cost equations are estimated with an unknown degree of error, the criterion of maximizing surplus may have to be replaced with the criterion of maximizing *expected* surplus where various demand levels for each price are weighted by their likelihood of occurrence. In any situation of risk and uncertainty, the pricing decision maker will want to see how sensitive the theoretically calculated optimal price is to alternative estimates of the demand and cost functions.

Cost Recovery

Many nonprofit organizations seek a price that would help them recover a "reasonable" part of their costs. This is the idea behind the pricing of toll roads, postal services, and public mass transit services. Although the organizations could conceivably charge higher prices and increase their revenue (because of their monopolistic position), they do not want to incite an adverse reaction from the public or legislature.

How much cost should the organization try to recover through its pricing? Some organizations—such as universities and public mass transit organizations—aim at recovery of their *operating costs*. This would not provide money for expansion; they would have to rely on gifts or bond issues to raise the needed capital for these endeavors. Other organizations aim for *full cost recovery,* because they cannot rely on raising sufficient funds from other sources.

Market Size Maximization

Some nonprofit organizations (public libraries and museums, for example) want to maximize the total number of users of their services. These organizations feel that the users and society profit from their services. In this case, a zero price will attract the greatest number of users. Even here there can be exceptions. Consider the following situation:[2]

> Health marketers in India initially believed the distribution of free oral rehy-dration solution for the control of diarrhea would lead to the greatest level of usage. However, they discovered two flaws in the reasoning. Some potential target audience members interpreted the zero price to signify low quality and avoided the free brand. In addition, many retailers would not carry it or dis-play it prominently because it did not yield them profit, with the result that fewer units were ultimately available to target audience members.

In most situations, a low price normally stimulates higher usage *and* may produce more revenue in the long run. Weinberg advocates that theaters should set low ticket prices because this attracts a larger audience, many of whom would eventually make dona-tions to the theaters that would more than make up for the lower ticket prices.[3]

Social Equity

Organizations may wish to price their services in a way that contributes to social equity. In a study of who pays for library services, Weaver and Weaver concluded that "public libraries actually distribute income from the poorest to the more affluent strata of the community."[4]

One of the principal arguments leading to this conclusion is that because the poor rarely use the public library and because public libraries are often supported out of general tax revenues, the working poor are paying for the nonpoor's libraries. Admittedly, there are other situations, such as city parks and welfare services, where the reverse is true. Our concepts of social equity hold that, wherever possible, public (and by extension, nonprofit) services should not operate to transfer wealth from the poor to the rich. In the public library case, the goal of social equity might be achieved by charging users for library services, perhaps charging even more for services (such as videocassette rentals) that the upper classes use relatively more often.

Market Disincentivization

Pricing might be undertaken for the objective of discouraging as many people as possible from purchasing a particular product or service. There are many reasons an organization might want to do this. It might consider the product to be bad for people; it might want to discourage people from overtaxing a facility; it might be trying to ration demand to solve a temporary shortage; or it might want to discourage certain classes of buyers.

The purpose of the high government tax on cigarettes and liquor is to discourage the use of these products and it is considered one of the best tools for reducing teen smoking. But the price is never raised high enough because the government has come to rely on the substantial revenue produced by these taxes. A tax that is truly disincentiviz-ing would yield the government no revenue and possibly create a large black market.

The Golden Gate Authority of San Francisco resorted to disincentive pricing when it learned that the famous bridge structure was overtaxed with traffic. A motorist was charged according to how many passengers were in the car, with the highest fee charged to cars with only the driver. This led to the formation of more driving car pools, although not as many as the authority had hoped.

Public mass transit companies frequently use disincentive pricing to discourage commuting during rush hours. These companies are in a weak financial situation because they have to finance the purchase of enough equipment to cover their needs during the rush hours while the equipment sits idle the rest of the time. The Metro system of Washington, D.C., raises fares during morning and evening rush hours and offers lower fares at off hours.

CHOOSING A PRICING STRATEGY

After the organization has defined its pricing objective, it can consider the appropriate strategy for setting a specific price. Pricing strategies tend to be cost oriented, value based, or competition oriented.

Cost-Oriented Pricing

Cost-oriented pricing refers to setting prices largely on the basis of costs, either marginal costs or total costs including overhead. Two examples are markup pricing and cost-plus pricing. They are similar in that the price is determined by adding some fixed percentage to the unit cost. *Markup pricing* is commonly found in the retail trades where the retailer adds predetermined but different markups to various goods. Museum gift shops use markup pricing in pricing their various items. *Cost-plus pricing* is used to describe the pricing of jobs that are nonroutine and difficult to "cost" in advance, such as some kinds of marketing research and many services.

Nonprofit organizations vary in where they peg their prices relative to their costs. The American Red Cross charges a price for its blood that covers the "irreducible cost of recruiting, processing, collecting, and distributing the blood to the hospitals." However, several nonprofit organizations have historically charged less than their costs (called cost-minus pricing). Tuitions at private colleges and ticket prices for symphony orchestras often cover less than 50 percent of the total cost of these services; the remaining costs are covered by donations, grants, and interest on endowment funds.

The most popular form of cost-oriented pricing uses *break-even analysis*. The purpose of break-even analysis is to determine, for any proposed price, how many units of an item would have to be sold to cover fully the costs; this is known as the *break-even volume*. To illustrate, the director of a summer camp wants to set a tuition for an eight-week summer session that would cover the total costs of operating the camp. Suppose the annual fixed costs of the camp—real estate taxes, interest charges, physical property, insurance, building maintenance, vehicle expense, and so on—are $200,000. This is shown on the break-even chart in Figure 15-2 as a horizontal line at the level of $200,000. The variable cost for serving each camper—food, handicraft supplies, camper insurance, and so on—is $500 per camper. This is shown on the total cost line, starting at $200,000 and rising $500 for each camper. Finally, the camp director initially considers charging $1,000 tuition per camper. This is shown on the total revenue line, which begins at $0 and rises $1,000 per camper. The number of campers needed to break even

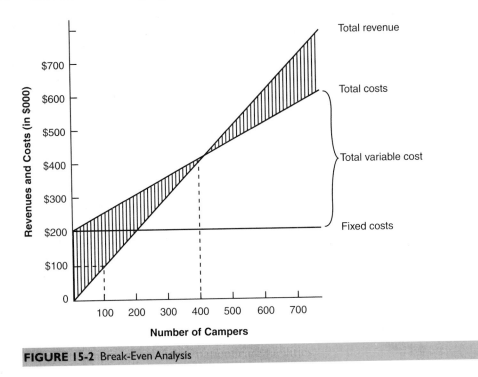

FIGURE 15-2 Break-Even Analysis

is determined by the intersection of the total revenue and the total cost curves, here 400 campers. If the camp fails to attract at least 400 campers at $1,000 each, it will suffer a loss varying with the number of campers attracted. If the camp attracts more than 400 campers at $1,000 each, it will generate profits. The camp director's task is to estimate whether it will be easy or difficult to attract 400 campers at a tuition of $1,000.

The break-even volume can be readily calculated for any proposed price by using the following formula:

$$\text{Break-even volume} = \frac{\text{fixed cost}}{\text{price} - \text{variable cost}} \qquad (15\text{-}6)$$

Using the numbers in the previous example, we get

$$\text{Break-even volume} = \frac{\$200,000}{\$1,000 - \$500} = 400$$

However, if the camp director thought of charging $700 tuition, he would have to attract 1,000 campers to break even (equation 15-6).

Cost-oriented pricing is popular for a number of reasons. First, there is generally less uncertainty about costs than about demand. By basing the price on cost, the seller simplifies the pricing task considerably; there is no need to make frequent adjustments as demand conditions change. Cost-plus pricing is also easier to implement for organizations that have a great many items to price, such as museum bookstores or Boy Scout equipment centers. Second, when all organizations in the industry use this pricing approach, their prices are similar if their costs and markups are similar. Price competition is therefore minimized, which would not be the case if competitors paid attention to demand variations. Third, there is the feeling that cost-markup pricing is socially more fair to buyers and sellers. Sellers do not take advantage of buyers when the demand becomes acute, yet sellers earn a fair return on their investment. It is also seen as socially fair when different prices must be charged to different users (i.e., everyone pays 20 percent over costs). Thus, the popularity of cost-oriented pricing rests on its administrative simplicity, competitive harmony, and social fairness.

Value-Based Pricing

The problem with cost-oriented pricing is that it ignores how valuable the offering is to target customers. Value-based pricing looks at the strength and nature of demand rather than the level of costs to set the price. Value-based approaches estimate how much value buyers see in the market offer, and then price accordingly. Thus, a fine arts organization might set a ticket price of $100 for a YoYo Ma concert and $45 for a cello concert by a less well-known performer. The premise is that price should reflect the *perceived value* in the audience's head. A corollary is that an organization should invest in building up the perceived value of the offer if it wants to charge a higher price. Thus, a private college that builds a reputation for excellence in teaching and research can charge a higher tuition than can an average private college.

There are two difficulties in employing value-based pricing. As mentioned earlier, it is often very difficult to learn what target audience members would pay for a given product or service. This is especially true if the offering is one that is very new to the world or the target market and if it involves outcomes that are hard to describe or predict. If a nonprofit in Latin America decides to offer a weight reduction program based on hypnotism to overweight rural men as a way of improving their longevity, establishing a price may be very difficult because (1) it may be hard for the target audience to envision what benefits they might get from participating—and, indeed, what participating itself might actually involve, and (2) it may be hard for the nonprofit to be very confident about the success rates it claims for the service. Nevertheless, presenting target customers with the concept and seeking their reactions to different pricing strategies may reveal the most acceptable price and perhaps the upper limit.

The other difficulty for the nonprofit is an ethical one. Many nonprofit offerings are very valuable to target audiences. Pills to reduce hypertension can be *extremely* desirable to persons who have lost relatives to high blood pressure. AIDS "cocktails" are critical to the long-term survival of those with the disease. And sugar/salt solutions can be *extremely* valuable to families who have lost children to diarrhea. In such cases, it is possible for the nonprofit to secure very high prices if it were to look only at the perceived value to the audience. However, it will typically choose a price that will be substantially less than what the traffic will bear because of the organization's broader ethical responsibilities to its society.

Competition-Oriented Pricing

When an organization sets its prices chiefly on the basis of what its competitors are charging, its pricing policy can be described as competition oriented. This competition may be very close in nature, such as a rival museum. Alternatively, the museum's competition may be broadened to include movies or dining out for audiences who see museum-going as a relaxing break from routine. In such cases, the nonprofit marketer may choose to charge the same as the competition, a higher price, or a lower price. The distinguishing characteristic is that the organization does *not* seek to maintain a rigid relation between its price and its own costs or demand. Its own costs or demand may change, but the organization maintains its price because competitors maintain their prices. Conversely, the same organization will change its prices when competitors change theirs, even if its own costs or demand have not altered.

VARYING COSTS ACROSS SEGMENTS

Price discrimination goes on in nonprofit organizations all the time. For example, theaters and concert halls discriminate very often on the basis of (1) time of purchase (early ticket purchasers pay less than those who pay at the door); (2) location (close-up seats cost more than seats in the rear balcony); (3) method of payment (purchasers through Ticketmaster will pay a premium over those who come to the box office to purchase); (4) time of performance (those wanting to go on a Saturday night will pay more than those going to a Sunday matinee); and (5) quantity and timing of purchase (those who buy season's tickets will pay less than those who buy at the door).

Each of these tactics represents an attempt by a nonprofit marketing manager to achieve one of the following goals:

- Match the price to the cost of providing the product or service: Ticketmaster charges premiums to help pay for extra paperwork, credit card processing fees, and so forth.
- Match the price to the value received: Closer seats are more valuable.
- Regulate demand: Lower prices for matinees are, in part, an attempt to shift demand to "off-peak" hours of service.
- Capture the most a customer will pay.

The latter is an important point. Customers who will pay a premium for Ticketmaster service or to attend on a Saturday night is doing so because this is what he or she really wants. They are willing to pay more in order to get what they really want. A Rolls Royce Silver Cloud does not cost 10 to 15 times more than a Honda Civic to build, but customers are willing to pay that much more because that is what they want, and they can afford to pay it. Much so-called discriminatory pricing is designed to capture that "consumer surplus" (i.e., what some potential customers would be willing to pay over and above a simple cost-plus price).

PROMOTIONAL PRICING

Often a nonprofit organization will maintain its list price but introduce "price specials" in order to stimulate increased buying. Promotional pricing can take many forms. Consider a theater performance group that wants to attract a larger audience to its performances. Here are some promotional pricing options:

1. The theater group can promote a series subscription that represents a savings over buying individual tickets to all of the performances. A popular way to express the savings is "See five plays for the price of four." Newman strongly favors discounts for subscription series on the grounds that the savings are a prime motivator for buying a subscription.[5] But Ryans and Weinberg, in a survey of subscription buyers for the American Conservatory Theater (ACT) in San Francisco, found that subscribers reported that the main reason for buying subscription series was not the savings but to make sure they went to the theater more often and were sured a good seat. ACT abandoned the discount in the next season with no palpable impact on subscription sales.[6]

2.   The theater group can offer an "early bird" discount on the series subscription to those subscribing up to two months in advance of the first performance.

3.   The theater group can offer second tickets at half price. Andreasen and Belk found potential theatergoers reacting extremely favorably to this proposal, reacting even more positively than to percentage discounts ("40 percent off") that were better bargains.[7] It apparently taps into the notion of bringing a friend or a date to the theater.

4.   The theater group can offer unsold tickets at half price on the day of the performance. This method is used successfully by the ticket kiosks in New York City, Boston, London, San Francisco, and Washington, D.C. The theater gets not only the extra seat revenue it would have lost, but also the revenue from the sale of drinks and candy during intermission.[8]

SUMMARY

Nonprofit marketers seek to influence exchanges. From the target audience's perspective, these exchanges involve trading bundles of benefits for bundles of costs. Costs are the prices the customers perceive they must pay to participate. They can be monetary, nonmonetary, or mixed. Nonmonetary costs include psychic pain, the need to change old habits or ideas, expenditures of time and energy, and dislocations of social arrangements.

The nonprofit manager has a dual task in managing these costs. Some costs must be kept reasonably high to ensure continuing revenues to the organization. Other costs must be reduced as much as possible to lower barriers to customer action. Since it will cost the organization to reduce each of these costs, it needs to know the relative responsiveness of target customers to each of these reductions.

In developing a strategy for monetary prices, the organization must first establish objectives. It could seek surplus maximization, cost recovery, market size maximization, social equity, or market disincentivization. Its specific strategy to meet these objectives may be primarily cost oriented, demand oriented, or competition oriented.

QUESTIONS

1. Identify the major costs that one incurs when giving blood. If you managed a blood bank in an urban area, which costs would you select to try and reduce? Why? What steps could you actually take to reduce the costs you identified?
2. How would you rank the relative price elasticity for the following nonprofit products and services: free condom distribution in the United States, vitamin distribution in rural China, YMCA tennis court fees, uniform costs for the Boy Scouts, and an executive education program at a major university? Support your conclusions.
3. Does it always make sense for a marketer to price an offering based on costs? Why? Identify an example where a marketer would be severely misled by developing a pricing schedule based on costs.

4. What forms of price discrimination could a YMCA manager utilize if his goal were to maximize revenues? Explain your reasoning for each form you identified.
5. Do all customers have the same cost for a given offering (consider blood donation)? Using segmentation, identify the costs (differences) for donating blood for a university student, a stay-at-home father, and a female CEO. Is it possible to equally reduce costs effectively for each segment? How does this impact strategy?

NOTES

1. Quoted from an article by Ben F. Doddridge, "Toward the Development of a Practical Approach for a Solution of the Pricing Dilemma," *Christian Camping International,* January-February 1978, pp. 19–22.
2. See T. R. L. Black and John Farley, "Retailers in Social Program Strategy: The Case of Family Planning," *Columbia Journal of World Business,* Winter 1977, pp. 33–43.
3. Charles Weinberg, "Marketing Mix Decision Rules for Nonprofit Organizations," in Jagdish Sheth (ed.), *Research in Marketing,* Vol. 3 (Greenwich, Conn.: JAI Press, 1980), pp. 191–234.
4. Frederick S. Weaver and Serena A. Weaver, "For Public Libraries the Poor Pay More," *Library Journal,* February 1, 1979, pp. 325–355.
5. Danny Newman, *Subscribe Now!* (New York: Publishing Center for Cultural Resources, 1977).
6. Adrian B. Ryans and Charles B. Weinberg, "Consumer Dynamics in Nonprofit Organizations," *Journal of Consumer Research,* September 1978, pp. 89–95.
7. Alan R. Andreasen and Russell W. Belk, "Consumer Response to Arts Offerings: A Study of Theater and Symphony in Four Southern Cities," in Edward McCracken (ed.), *Research in the Arts* (Baltimore: Walters Art Gallery, 1979), pp. 13–19.
8. "New York City Opera Rolls Back Prices," *The Cultural Post,* Vol. 7, March–April 1982, p. 9.

CHAPTER 16

Facilitating Marketing Behaviors

Twenty-five percent of the world's population lives in substandard housing or has no home at all. Habitat for Humanity International (HFHI) has developed a powerful and imaginative program to address this problem. The idea began in the United States in 1976 when Millard and Linda Fuller developed a way to build and market low-cost housing in a small, interracial farming community near Americus, Georgia. The concept was simple: Those in need of the housing would work with volunteers to build "simple, decent homes." These would be built and sold with no profit added and no interest charged. The homes were not charity: Financing from Habitat's Fund for Humanity would have to be repaid by each owner—and in almost every case, it has been!

The Habitat concept is one that has been spread around the world by the establishment of local "franchises" or affiliates. Affiliates are grass roots organizations that may be associated with a specific organization like a church, a town, a state, or some other geographic entity. There are more than 1,600 affiliates in the United States and more outside the United States. The number of countries in which Habitat now builds has grown to 79.

Habitat for Humanity International does not go into a country and start building houses—even when the need is obviously great. It must be invited by a local group that will both legitimize HFHI's involvement and make certain there is follow-through and control. The affiliates in the United States are responsible for both fundraising and building. Internationally, local Habitat organizations are beginning to raise their own funds, but most money for house building still comes from U.S. donors. While the local affiliate is ultimately responsible for operations, HFHI zealously guards the brand and its use by local affiliates. The principal vehicle for this control is the Habitat Affiliate Covenant that spells out the principles to which the local "franchise" must adhere. Constant publicity and feedback are also used to motivate affiliates and implicitly indicate standards and goals.

The system has been extremely successful. Habitat has built over 100,000 "simple, decent homes" worldwide, producing over 17,500 in 2000 alone. In a few cases, Habitat operations have moved beyond home building to disaster relief and working with refugees and other nongovernmental organizations (NGOs) in rebuilding damaged communities. However,

Habitat leadership never forgets that its ultimate goal is to produce stories like this reported in a recent issue of *Habitat World:*

> Goiania, Brazil: Ademar de Souza and his wife, Valderene, for years paid almost half their income for low-quality housing. Two years ago, the rent went up and the increase was more than they could handle. So they built a shack, 12 feet by 9 feet, made of scrap wood, cardboard and plastic to live in with their 7-year-old daughter, Samara. A nearby latrine enclosed with black plastic wrapped around saplings served as the family's "private" bathroom. Then they found HFHI and began work on their own dream home. Each family member held their own dream about moving into their Habitat house: Ademar, who works nights, dreamt of a house cool enough to sleep in during the day; Valderene dreamt of an indoor bathroom, a kitchen with a sink and space to care for her children; and Samara envisioned a bedroom decorated with flowers. The de Souza family's dreams became reality in January of 2001, just weeks after the birth of their new baby.

Source: Drawn from the Habitat for Humanity International Web site at www.habitat.org.

In this chapter, we focus primarily on the challenges involved in getting target audience members through the Preparation/Action Stage. As we have said repeatedly, the bottom line of nonprofit marketing is influencing behaviors. And behaviors take place on specific occasions at specific times and places. Making behavior easy to accomplish—even pleasant to accomplish—is a key component of the marketing mix. In the case of products, this means that the goods must be made available and physically delivered to target audiences. This can be through retail outlets, catalogues, or over the Internet. For services, it means making the services available when and where the consumer can use them and, preferably, in an attractive, welcoming environment that encourages repeat visits and/or strong word-of-mouth promotion. For social behaviors where a product or service is not involved, it means arranging stress-free, convenient means for target audience members to do what the marketer hopes that he or she will do.

In the private sector, this is often referred to as the "place" component of the marketing mix. Here, we refer to it as "Facilitation."[1]

Consider the challenge of getting a TV news director to cover a nonprofit event. Assume she has become aware of the event through effective communications and has thought about it enough to be inclined toward covering it. However, she is still reluctant. It is at this point that the nonprofit marketer needs to think very hard about what can be done to make the event feasible, easy, and (hopefully) pleasant and rewarding. The marketing director should also be thinking not only of this one-time event but also of ways to use the occasion to build a relationship that will lead to future transactions (i.e., future coverage). Among the facilitation options the marketer may employ are these:

- Scheduling the event when it is best for the director's "news cycle."
- Providing convenient VIP parking and easy access for the film crew and their equipment.
- Having attractive, articulate interviewees ready for the TV crew when they arrive.

- Making sure that the event itself has a lot of visual elements that would look good on TV.
- Making sure the event (or the interview) is completed in time for the news director to get the tape edited and onto the evening newscast.

In this situation, the creation of the "event strategy" may be a highly interactive process whereby the marketer and the target audience member (the news director) work together to complete the transaction and presumably build a pleasant and mutually rewarding long-term relationship. The marketer's task is to create *time and place utility* for the target audience member.

THE NATURE AND ROLE OF FACILITATION PLANNING

Creating time and place utilities is *facilitation*. There are two principal dimensions to the facilitation process. One involves the set of activities that need to take place on the marketer's side to bring the exchange opportunity to the target audience member. We refer to this component as the *channel strategy*. The second dimension is the content of behavioral event itself, its characteristics and choreography. We refer to this component as the *occasion strategy*.

CHANNEL STRATEGY

We define a channel as follows:

A channel is a conduit for bringing together a marketer and a target audience member at some place and time for the purpose of facilitating behavioral opportunities.

Among the channels a marketer can use are specific buildings (i.e., stores, offices, clinics, and showrooms); paid or volunteer staffers; independent intermediaries such as transportation companies, wholesalers, and retailers; telephones; direct mail; and the Internet. In the future, there may also be interactive television.

A host of other organizations face the problem of locating a set of facilities to serve optimally a spatially distributed population. This can be characterized in the following terms:

> Hospitals must be located . . . to serve the people with complete medical care, and we must build schools close to the children who have to learn. Fire stations must be located to give rapid access to potential conflagrations, and voting booths must be placed so that people can cast their ballots without expending unreasonable amounts of time, effort, or money to reach the polling stations. Many of our states face the problem of locating branch campuses to serve a burgeoning and increasingly well-educated population. In the cities we must create and locate playgrounds for the children. Many overpopulated countries must assign birth control clinics to reach the people with contraceptive and family planning information.[2]

An example of the set of channels in the health care industry is given in Exhibit 16-1.

EXHIBIT 16-1

HEALTH CARE DELIVERY SYSTEMS IN THE UNITED STATES

Health care delivery systems are institutions that deliver preventative and curative health services to the public. In the past, Americans obtained health care services in two ways: by visiting a private physician or an emergency room of a local hospital. Some target audience members sought out their pharmacists for advice on minor problems such as the common cold.

Today's health care services are available through several channels.

1. *Health maintenance organizations.* A growing number of people obtain their medical care through health maintenance organizations. By joining and paying a monthly fee, they can see staff doctors at any time and also get their hospitalization costs covered.

2. *Neighborhood health clinics.* Target audience members in poorer neighborhoods often go to neighborhood health clinics for help. The clinic charges no fee or a low fee and has doctors ready to examine sick patients. The clinic is supported by public money, private money, or both.

3. *Hospital-based ambulatory care units.* Many hospitals have opened clinics in shopping areas or apartment buildings where people pay a fee for service. Since some of these patients need hospital care, these clinics serve as feeder operations to the hospital.

4. *Group practices.* The vast majority of physicians now belong to private group practices, which give them the opportunity to structure their hours better and gain the advantages of having expert colleagues. Patients pay a fee for service every time they visit their physicians.

5. *Freestanding specialized service units.* Target audience members can directly obtain specific services such as X-rays, blood tests, and minor surgery in specialized units set up for these purposes. They pay fees that in most cases are reimbursed by their health insurance plans.

6. *The Internet.* The Internet is a great source of information and advice about health matters. Highly useful Web sites are managed by government agencies like the Centers for Disease Control and Prevention, nonprofits like the American Cancer Society, and for-profits like DrKoop.com. Sites like Medscape exist for finding the latest medical news and research.

Careful planning of channel strategy can have important positive payoffs, but there are also important resource challenges. Nonprofit organizations are typically deficient in resources, both financial and personnel. They typically cannot put in place all elements of the channel strategy and will need the help of other individuals and organizations to bring their offerings to the public. The careful use of independent channels can make marketing programs more *efficient* by sharing costs, achieving economies of scale, and so on, and make them more *effective* by leveraging meager resources, small staffs, cramped facilities, and so on. The National Cancer Institute's (NCI) anti-smoking program, for example, was able to have a significant impact with a relatively small budget by enlisting the help of physicians to distribute how-to-quit materials and to carry out "personal selling" with patients who had a history of smoking. NCI was able to obtain the same kind of leveraging for its breast self-examination program by securing the help of major corporations to serve as intermediaries for its awareness and training programs.

Some nonprofit organizations are not fully aware of their channel problems and possibilities. Organized religion, for example, can be thought of as operating a religion distribution system. Consider the following example of the Evangelical Covenant Church of America.

> The central church office can be seen as the *manufacturer* or originator of the church's product; the regional offices throughout the country can be viewed as the *wholesaler;* and the individual churches, such as Faith Evangelical Covenant Church in Wheaton, might be viewed as the *retail outlets* for the church's services and products. Faith Covenant Church is the part of the organization that comes face to face with the target audience member or members of the church and potential members. It is the individual "outlet" that can perform many of the critical functions needed to maintain members of the church and in fact, to increase its membership rolls.[3]

COMPONENTS OF A CHANNEL STRATEGY

All marketers need conduits to their target audience members, and target audience members need access to the marketer's offerings. The kinds of channels a marketer might use will vary depending on whether goods, services, or communications are the major flows within the channel. There are a number of strategic problems, however, that apply to all channel decisions:

1. *Direct versus indirect marketing.* The nonprofit must decide whether to carry out channel services within its own organization or with outsiders and, if so, which ones. An example of using an outside but critical delivery system is described by Richard Delano and David Lange in Exhibit 16-2.
2. *Length and breadth of the channel structure.* The nonprofit must decide on (a) the number of levels to be interposed between the production of the offer and its eventual exchange with target audience members (length decisions) and (b) the total number of different channels or the number of elements to be included at each level of the channel (breadth decisions).
3. *Allocation of functions.* The nonprofit needs to decide who will handle the several channel flows (for example, information, goods, and money) in the channel.
4. *Recruiting channel members.* The nonprofit needs to know how to recruit and help motivate channel members.
5. *Coordination and control.* The nonprofit must develop systems for coordinating and controlling various channel members in the system.[4]

In considering these issues, we use *efficiency* and *effectiveness* as our principal criteria. We define these as follows:

Efficiency is the extent to which a system achieves a given level of performance at the least possible cost in financial, time, and personnel resources.

Effectiveness is the extent to which a system achieves the maximum performance for a given level of resources.

EXHIBIT 16-2

RICHARD K. DELANO OF SOCIAL MARKETING SERVICES AND DAVID LANGE OF SCHOLASTIC MARKETING PARTNERS ON MOBILIZING CHILDREN AND TEENS FOR CENSUS 2000 THROUGH THE "SCHOOL MARKETING CHANNEL"

Census bureau staff had observed a steady decline in the mail response to the 1970, 1980, and 1990 decennial mail outs (78% in '70 to 65% in '90). Prior to the 2000 Census, the National Academy of Sciences projected a mail response rate below 60 percent. The Census bureau estimates that each percentage point decline in mail response translates into about a $25 million cost increase due largely to the follow-up activity that must take place to gather information not provided on the first mail out. Advertising and publicity were traditionally accomplished through the Advertising Council on a pro bono basis. Bureau staff made the case to Congress that a paid advertising (social marketing) campaign was needed to boost participation. Congress agreed. Incremental funds were allocated to the "dress rehearsal" process in April 1998 so all Census advertising and promotional materials could be evaluated. Dress rehearsals are "live" tests held two years prior to each decennial.

Bureau staff were also concerned about the net "undercount" of approximately 4.7 million in the 1990 Census. They estimated that children accounted for about half of the undercounted population. This undercount of children in 2000 would mean that programs that serve children and their families were less likely to be adequately funded throughout the 2000 to 2010 decade.

Recognizing that an undercount in a decennial census can have a long-term impact on the well-being of children, the Census Bureau decided to implement the *Census in Schools* program for Census 2000. The short-term goal of the *Census in*

Schools program was to help students understand the Census and its importance to them, their families, and their community. The program was designed to increase participation in Census 2000 by engaging parents through schools and through the active involvement of children and teens. (Adult voting rates are known to rise in communities where schoolchildren hold "mock elections".) In the longer term, Census staff believe adults who learned about the Census as children are more likely to participate in future decennials.

To engage the education community, the *Census in Schools* project would provide educators with teaching tools to bring the Census to life for students and to explain to them and to their parents the importance of Census participation. The U.S. Census Bureau and Young & Rubicam (Y & R) contracted with Scholastic Inc. who helped to develop the messages, packaging, and distribution strategy that would be most effective in reaching U.S. educators, motivating them to involve their students and the parents of those students. All Y&R design, slogan and strategic targeting decisions were integrated into the Census in Schools materials.

Census in Schools was tested, along with advertising from Young & Rubicam, in the three "dress rehearsal" communities in April 1998. The post–dress rehearsal research helped Census 2000 planners determine how best to deploy their communication budget to reach targeted audiences, including parents. Modifications were made as necessary for the rollout of Census 2000.

Scholastic's Social Marketing Solutions, part of the company's custom publishing unit, helped the Census Bureau and Y&R design this part of the larger program. Scholastic Inc. generates over $2 billion in sales annually through book clubs, book fairs, and classroom magazines because of its unique understanding of how to market through what is sometimes referred to as the "school marketing channel." This commercial "know-how" on how to motivate teachers, parents, and students through schools is significant and desirable from a social marketing perspective.

Scholastic recommended to Census staff that all education materials and their distribution should be modeled on successful commercial marketing strategies and commercially viable products. For instance, elementary school teachers in targeted low-response Census tracks (correlated to percentage of students receiving free or reduced school meals) received take-home materials similar in design to book club "kits." Over 1 million (out of 3 million total) U.S. teachers are Scholastic agents for book clubs. By modeling this part of the *Census in Schools* program on this familiar product (a four-page teacher wraparound and 32 identical four-page parent take-home fliers), we believe the performance of this communication activity was enhanced.

Similarly, a pre–K program called *Everybody Counts* was modeled on a best-selling Scholastic Early Childhood product. Head Start centers receive a "Big Book" that the instructor use before the assembled class and 30 identical but smaller individual "Little Books" that each child could take home to read with a parent. Scholastic's research suggested that the process of first reading the big book in class stimulates a "nag" factor compelling parents to read the lap book at home.

Similar modeling provided the formative design of many other materials and the distribution of those materials including *Making Sense of Census 2000* teaching kits, principal materials, American Indian maps, materials for Puerto Rico and the Island Areas, as well as special materials for Adult Literacy programs.

Census in Schools partners included 23 national education associations and government agencies that helped spread Census 2000 messages and information about the *Census in Schools* materials.

The Census Bureau promoted *Teach Census Week* (March 13–17, 2000) as a prime time to teach about Census 2000. It coincided with the week when the questionnaires were delivered to most homes. Other school activities were organized by other partner organizations throughout the country.

By April 2000 nearly 2 million *Making Sense of Census 2000* kits had been distributed to educators in public, private, and parochial schools in the United States, Puerto Rico, and the Island Areas. These kits were offered to all schools and were available on the Internet. About 35,000 sets of *Everybody Counts* were sent to Head Start Centers and 200,000 Adult ESL/Literacy teaching kits were mailed to instructors of adult education nationwide. In addition, 45 million copies of the take-home activities were distributed for K–8 students to share with their families. Of the $167 million Census 2000 advertising and publicity budget, approximately $20 million was provided for the *Census in Schools* promotion.

The Census Bureau has funded extensive research designed to determine, among other things, how adults across the country learned about Census 2000. We expect that the results of this research will help us better understand the role that the "school marketing channel" can play in large-scale social marketing programs.

Direct versus Indirect Channels

Other things being equal, organizations normally prefer to deal with their target audience members directly and not use intermediaries. There are a number of advantages to such an approach:

1. Any organizational benefits (e.g., revenue, brand building, media attention) from the transaction do not have to be shared with other organizations or individuals.
2. All channel activities are controlled by the marketer.
3. Direct contact with target audience members provides the marketer with a better understanding of their needs and wants.
4. Direct contact with target audience members means quicker awareness of any problems with programs and products.
5. Responses to changes in the marketplace (e.g., to new competitor initiatives) can be more rapid.
6. Opportunities for experimentation with alternative ways of reaching target audience members are available.
7. More attention can be given to the marketer's offering than would be possible if it were only one of many carried by an intermediary.
8. Strategies aimed at various target audience segments can be precisely tailored.

Given all of these advantages, why would an organization give up control at all? One reason we have already noted is that many organizations lack the financial resources to carry out a full program of direct marketing themselves.

Even if an organization has the funds to build its own channel to the target audiences, it might not be able to do so as cheaply as through using an existing system. The cost of distributing nonprofit health care products throughout India is low because the commercial intermediaries carry many other products that share in the cost of the distribution network. In a one-product distribution system, all the costs would be borne by that product. The same reasoning applies to services. In the developing world, child-care services are provided through existing community organizations (private clinics, schools, community centers) rather than through new duplicative facilities.

Nor should the organization build its own distribution system if it can put its funds to better use. Thus, the number of infant deaths averted might be higher if Indonesian nonprofit organizations spent their funds to advertise the advantages of oral rehydration or Vitamin A nationwide rather than using all their money to set up their own distribution systems or their own health care clinics.

The case for using intermediaries often rests on their superior efficiency and effectiveness in the performance of basic marketing tasks and functions. Marketing intermediaries, through their experience, specialization, contacts, and scale, offer the producing organization more than it can usually achieve on its own.

Length versus Breadth

Whether or not a nonprofit decides that it would be efficient to use intermediaries, decisions must be made as to how many levels of distribution to have and how many units to have at each level. These are often referred to as length and breadth decisions, and they usually are not independent decisions. Consider first the breadth decision.

The most economical decision is to work with a single outlet. By having one large library in a major city, duplication of books, staff, and building costs are avoided. Citizens gain in that they will find an extensive collection of reading material. They pay the price, however, of having to travel a longer distance. A system consisting of many smaller libraries would attract more users. Most major cities compromise by building a central library and several branch libraries for the convenience of target audience members. Some go further and operate bookmobiles, which are mobile libraries that park in different neighborhoods on different days and make books available to target audience members. The same problem applies in health care where a nonprofit could create one large central clinic or operate though many, many local centers and mobile health units.

At the local level, breadth decisions are often dictated by target audience members. Certain offerings must be mass distributed because target audience members will not go out of their way to come in contact with them. In commercial marketing, these offerings are called *convenience goods and services.* In retailing, they usually involve offerings that are not particularly distinctive. For example, men will normally not go far out of their way to acquire condoms for the prevention of AIDS. As a consequence, many AIDS prevention strategies feature the installation of condom vending machines in men's rooms and the provision of goblets of free condoms near the exits in gay bars.

Not all behavior opportunities must be made maximally convenient for target audience members. There are some offerings for which target audience members will undertake some effort to find and evaluate—they need not be exceptionally convenient. In retailing, these are referred to as *shopping goods and services,* since target audience members believe they would gain something by looking around and finding the best option. Thus, target audience members will go a moderate distance to secure the best emergency care service or smoking-cessation clinic. They will go some distance to see a good museum or watch a good play. In such cases, channel breadth becomes less important.

The final class of offerings is usually referred to as *specialty goods and services.* These are offers that target audience members find so special that they will make a strong effort to seek them out, often at considerable cost. Further, these offerings are perceived to be sufficiently unique that target audience members will typically not accept substitutes. This status of being a specialty offering is one that many nonprofit marketers covet. The Mayo Clinic, for example, is clearly a "specialty institution" for well-off target audience members with unusual afflictions. Art Museums have found that a number of high-profile traveling art exhibits have proved to be "specialty goods" that target audience members would go long distances and endure long lines to see.

If a nonprofit organization determines that its target audience members require a broad distribution system, the next channel strategy question is "How long should the channel be?" For nonprofits that manufacture a product (like the Sierra Club or the U.S. Treasury), two-, three-, and four-level channels are possible, as suggested in Figure 16-1. In general, the *broader* the distribution at the local level, the *longer* the channel has to be. That is, if a nonprofit marketer wanted only *exclusive distribution* in a few major locations, a two-step channel (manufacturer to supplier to consumer) would be perfectly adequate. However, if a *selective distribution* system is chosen, with, say, half a dozen outlets

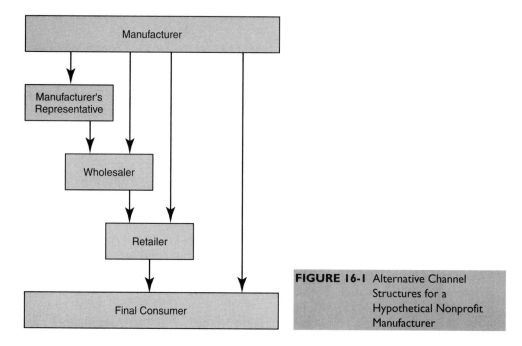

FIGURE 16-1 Alternative Channel Structures for a Hypothetical Nonprofit Manufacturer

handling the nonprofit's line in each of the 50 largest metropolitan areas in the United States, then several regional wholesalers may be needed to provide coverage. In addition, if the nonprofit wishes to have *mass distribution* in every nook and cranny of the country, then a manufacturer's representative may be needed to contact the hundreds of wholesalers required to service such a broad market.

Finally, note that strategic decisions about the length and breadth of a channel and whether the channel should be owned by the nonprofit marketer are independent decisions. That is, a marketer could choose a three-tiered system but set up its own wholesaling functions. This tactic would be known as *forward integration.* An environmental lobbying organization that produced its own books and calendars, for example, initially could use wholesalers to market them to recreation areas, book chains, university bookstores, and the like. But later, it could decide that recreation areas were underserved and that it could do better by handling its own product lines and even those of other manufacturers seeking better representation in recreation areas.

Nonprofit organizations can also undertake *backward integration.* A growing number of nonprofit organizations such as museums and hospitals have active retail operations for which they contract with one or more wholesalers for merchandise. Many service-based nonprofits, such as nursing homes and religious institutions, acquire substantial amounts of supplies from wholesalers to carry out their operations. Some of these organizations could use available investment capital to integrate backward in their channel by buying out or setting up a wholesale operation of their own, possibly serving other outlets as well. Again, the prime consideration in such a move should be whether it would result in important efficiencies, better service, or new revenues.

ACHIEVING COORDINATION AND CONTROL

Whether a nonprofit marketer is the "captain" of a channel system or a member of someone else's system, a crucial set of issues involves day-to-day management. In a mature marketing system, it is usually extremely important not only to have the right intermediaries performing the right function, but to make sure that they are carrying out those functions *when* and exactly in the *form* that is in the best interests of the overall system (e. g. maximizing customer "delight.")

For many reasons, coordination and cooperation are difficult to achieve in nonprofit organizations. Among the impediments are the following:

- Competition among nonprofits for limited funds from either federal sources or third-sector agencies like the United Way may make some nonprofits reluctant to help out present or future rivals. Cooperation may be viewed as helping another agency grow, possibly at the expense of one's own operations.
- Nonprofit leaders or staff may perceive cooperation as potential meddling, as a waste of time, or as a distraction from a job with low security.
- Territoriality can be a problem if one agency is unwilling to be subservient to another in an area in which the first agency believes it should be in charge.
- Differences in goals and values can often raise problems when marketing "rears its ugly head." Those who have a social service orientation (Chapter 3) may feel that involvement with another agency that is an aggressive marketer will be "unprofessional" or will otherwise taint the potential channel member.
- Excessive time and energy costs may occur. If the channel is not well managed, much time may be spent in meeting, planning, and "coordinating." Besides delaying action, this can drive away more action-oriented participants. It has discouraged more than one private-sector marketer from cooperating in a nonprofit program.
- Personality clashes are not unusual. Early in their organizational life cycle, many nonprofits are small and dominated by strong-willed, charismatic executives. In the struggling years of the enterprise, rivalries with other equally strong-willed leaders may develop. These can be very acrimonious and for many years stand in the way of needed cooperation.

The Basic Problem

The fundamental difficulty in achieving coordination and control is that another, separate organization with different perceptions, goals, and skills must undertake tasks that will help your organization achieve its goals.[5] Yet the "channel cooperation problem" is not really different from the problem involved in marketing to final target audience members. The problem is still one of *influencing the behavior of target markets,* in this case, key independent intermediaries. As such, the steps involved in developing an effective intermediary marketing strategy are clear.

1. Identify all potential intermediary segments.
2. Evaluate potential segments and select the best subset for detailed investigation.
3. Identify the basic BCOS factors that are likely to influence these target intermediaries; for example:
   a. What benefits are they likely to see?

    b. What costs are likely to hold them back?

    c. What groups of others might influence them positively or negatively?

    d. What barriers do they see that would cause them to believe that they cannot make the partnership work?

4. Develop strategies to increase the perceived benefits and reduce the perceived costs of participation, bring the pressure of "important others" to bear, and remove any important barriers that diminish the intermediary's sense of self-efficacy.

5. Evaluate the probable costs and payoffs of each strategy and select, for the given planning period, those that will best achieve the organization's objectives.

6. Determine optimal strategies for *maintaining* the desired relationships.

Implicit in this approach are a number of marketing principles that we have already emphasized:

- The best marketing strategy *begins with the target audience member* (the intermediary) rather than the nonprofit organization.

- It is the target audience member's needs, wants, and perceptions that are crucial to success, not those of the nonprofit organization.

- Since these needs, wants, and perceptions are subjective phenomena, the marketer cannot *know* them and so must resort to formal or informal research to ascertain them.

- The number of exchanges *increases* if and only if the cost/benefit ratios perceived by selected target audiences are *changed* in a favorable direction.

- Since *change* in cost/benefit ratios is crucial, the key research issue is how will target audience perceptions *change* as a result of alternative marketing strategy choices?

- Strategies must be developed not only to create first-time trials, but also to ensure *continued* usage by trial participants, to *increase* usage by present or trial participants, or both. That is, the Maintenance Stage is particularly important here.

- Finally, the selection of optimum short- and long-run strategies is not merely a matter of increasing *effectiveness* in creating exchanges; the selection must also take into account the costs to the organization of creating exchanges (the *efficiency* issue).

Developing Intermediary Coordination Strategies

The nonprofit marketer must choose influence strategies that will secure intermediary participation and cooperation in particular programs. The choice should be based on an analysis of the marketer's power bases. While the choice often yields a mixed strategy, the options can be grouped into three broad strategic categories. These categories can be described as follows:

1. *Requiring* intermediary cooperation through the use of coercive, or legal power, often in the framework of specific contracts.

2. *Rewarding* intermediary cooperation through the manipulation of rewards.

3. *Persuading* intermediaries to cooperate through the use of experts and information (although persuasion, in a sense, is implicit in *all* of these alternatives).

Requiring Cooperation

Requiring cooperation is a common form of channel control in both the private and public sectors. It is carried out through the use of formal contracts, which specify in greater or lesser degree the rights and duties of each party. These contracts can cover specific functions, as when an advertising agency agrees to provide copy and execution for a series of ads, place the ads in media, and perhaps evaluate the advertising's effects.

Such contracts can be very beneficial to the nonprofit because they benefit from the skills and economies of others while maintaining the contract power to insist on performance. An issue here is how tightly to word the contract. In the private sector, contracts sometimes involve voluntary assistance by the contractee at or below market prices. In such cases, the temptation is to write the contract loosely so that the pro bono subcontractor (e.g., a research or advertising agency or a broadcasting medium) is not "offended" by "meddling" in its delegated area of responsibility. This loose wording is generally unsatisfactory to both sides. Subcontractors may not know what is expected of them. They may exaggerate their independence and feel abused when the contractor tries to impose its will upon them. Ethical issues may arise. The contractor, however, may feel that it has no clear grounds for making criticisms, and that it has lost control of the subcontracted operation. And, of course, if legitimate disputes do arise, the ensuing bickering can destroy a channel relationship that may be the *only* way for a nonprofit contractor to get its job done.

A channel control technique that has become increasingly common in the private sector is *franchising*. For years, there have been territorial agreements in the automobile and beverage industries whereby the number of dealers in an area is regulated. In return for this local partial monopoly, the franchisee is expected to meet certain performance standards (e.g., quotas) and to carry on the enterprise in a particular fashion (e.g., use certain signs, charge certain prices, engage in so much cooperative advertising, and so on). Recent growth, however, has been in franchise systems with much stronger central control. In chain franchises like McDonald's, Burger King, and Midas Muffler, among others, virtually the entire operation of the franchise may be specified by the franchisor down to the size of the dollop of catsup to go on a hamburger or the number of straws in a soft drink. Usually, the franchise is based upon some distinctive trade name or style such that the franchisee is willing to pay for both the expertise and the extra marketplace competitive edge.

The contractual approach ultimately relies on legal authority and the potential imposition of penalties as a means of achieving the nonprofit marketer's ends. As long as the terms are carefully described, are fair to both sides, and there is a sense of shared responsibility for desired social outcomes, a contractual approach can work well, and the use of formal power by the contractor need only be a subtle background issue. However, if the contractual relationship is unclear and the interaction between the parties discordant, power may be used by the contractor to coerce the contractee into performing the needed channel functions. To the extent that such formal coercive power has to be used, the long-term potential for the channel relationship is not promising.

Rewarding and Persuading Cooperation

Rather than base channel cooperation on negative incentives, many organizations simply make it worthwhile for others to help them out. They offer specific economic rewards such as commissions or noneconomic rewards such as increased prestige through cooperating with a major social program. In both cases, extensive persuasion may still be needed to convince potential target intermediaries that cooperation will benefit both parties.

The building of strong nonprofit brands can significantly increase the reward potential for a potential partner. It is a strong incentive for the cause-related marketing partnerships described in Chapter 10. It can be equally strong when inducing cooperation by organizations that are needed to deliver the organization's offerings.

OCCASION STRATEGIES

A component of nonprofit marketing mixes that has seen limited attention is the management of behavioral occasions. The behaviors that a marketer wants will take place in a specific time and place—or, for a behavior like exercising that is continuing, in several places over time. If an organization is going to maximize the number of behaviors, it needs to consciously plan and implement attractive, convenient occasions to ensure that the behavior is:

- Easy to accomplish in a physical sense.
- An emotionally positive experience.
- Rewarding and reinforcing.

Making Behavior Easy

There are a number of factors that can have major effects on the ease in which a behavior can be performed which the marketer can potentially control—or at least influence:

- *Convenience in time*—for example, making blood donations possible after midnight for shift workers, holding job training at night, offering instructions for various health behaviors on the Web or on videotapes, DVDs, or CD-ROMs (and loaning VCR or DVD players if necessary), minimizing paperwork.
- *Convenience in location*—for example, bringing the product or service to the community or to someone's home through mobile vans, videos, or traveling trainers; providing transportation to remote sites; offering opportunities in the workplace or at airport terminals or train stations; allowing behavior (e.g., donations or volunteering) through the Web or by telephone.
- *Minimal distractions*—for example, providing play areas or child care for accompanying kids.
- *Complete availability of any tools, equipment, or advice that might be needed*—for example, having multiple sets of necessary gear, and providing instructions in simple terms and in multiple languages.

However, providing maximum ease is not without cost. The marketer must determine the level and quality of service to offer to the target market. Each organization can visualize a maximum level of service that could be offered. Following are some examples:

- A public welfare department must distribute thousands of checks a year to people on public relief. The maximum level of service would be to mail checks daily to their homes or even to deliver the checks personally to avoid mail theft.

- A public library could render the maximum amount of service if it stood ready to receive calls for books and deliver them within a few hours to the person's home.
- A city health department could dispatch doctors to the homes of sick patients upon call.
- A university could send a lecturer to any home or dorm room upon request.

These solutions are oriented toward maximum consumer convenience. But, they are not practical because target audience members would probably not pay for the extra convenience and the supplying organization could not afford the cost. Organizations have to find solutions that offer less consumer convenience in order to keep down the cost of distribution. Libraries and health departments, for example, can bring down their costs by offering services in only a few locations and leaving the cost of travel to the target audience members. They can cut down their costs further by running an efficient organization in which waiting time is borne mainly by target audience members instead of becoming idle time borne by the staff. If a health clinic had five doctors instead of ten, the doctors would be continually busy while the patients would absorb the cost of waiting. Finally, they could reduce their costs by using other media for delivery, such as when a university offers interactive TV lectures over the Web or on pay cable for those who wish to pay for it.

Making the Behavior Occasion an Emotional "High"

Behavioral occasions can be mundane or they can be charged with very positive emotions. Opportunities abound:

- 10K races or walk-a-thons can be made exciting occasions to donate.
- Walking up stairs (for exercise) at work can be made fun by providing videos or office-related cartoons on the landings.
- Exercise classes can be enlivened by upbeat music (think "Jazzercise").
- Scary or painful health procedures like blood donation can be made positive experiences by warm, enthusiastic staff members.

One of the important contributors to an emotionally satisfying encounter is what private sector marketers call "atmospherics."[6] *Atmospherics* describes the conscious designing of the place of delivery to create or reinforce specific effects on buyers, such as feelings of well-being, safety, intimacy, or awe. Where the nonprofit organization provides the service in some location, the marketing manager needs to make decisions on the "look" of the facilities, because the look can affect target audience members' attitudes, behavior, and level of satisfaction. Consider how the "atmosphere" of a hospital can affect patients. Many older hospitals have an institutional look, with long narrow corridors, drab wall colors, and badly worn furniture, all of which contribute a depressed feeling to patients who are already depressed about their own conditions. Newer hospitals are designed with colors, textures, furnishings, and layouts that reinforce positive patient feelings. They have circular or rectangular layouts with the nursing station in the center, permitting nurses to monitor patients better. Single-care units are replacing the traditional semi-private rooms, based on the overwhelming preference of both patients and physicians. Waiting areas are like hotel lobbies.

An organization that is designing a service facility for the first time faces four major design decisions that will affect the atmosphere. Suppose a city wishes to build a public art museum. The four decisions are as follows:

1. *What should the building look like on the outside?* The building can look like a Greek temple (as many museums have looked in the past), a villa, or a glass sky-scraper (Frank Gehry's Bilbao museum). It can look awe inspiring, ordinary, or in-timate. The decision will be influenced by the type of art collection and the message that the museum wants to convey about art in general.

2. *What should be the functional and flow characteristics of the building?* The plan-ners have to consider whether the museum should consist of a few large rooms or many small ones. (Many museums compromise by having large rooms with many movable walls.) They also have to consider whether the major exhibits and best-known artworks should be located near the entrance or at the other end of the building. The rooms and corridors must be designed in a way to handle capacity crowds so that people do not have to wait in long lines and experience congestion.

3. *What should the museum feel like on the inside?* Every building conveys a feeling, whether intended or unplanned. The planners have to consider whether the museum should feel awesome and somber, bright and modern, or warm and inti-mate. Each feeling will have a different effect on the visitors and their overall satis-faction with the museum.

4. *What materials would best support the desired feeling of the building?* The feeling of a building is conveyed by visual cues (color, brightness, size, shapes), aural cues (vol-ume, pitch), olfactory cues (scent, freshness), and tactile cues (softness, smoothness, temperature). The museum's planners have to choose colors, fabrics, and furnish-ings that create or reinforce the desired feeling.

MAKING THE BEHAVIOR OCCASION REWARDING AND REINFORCING

Target audience members are likely to repeat an important behavior and to spread positive word of mouth if they come away from the experience feeling that their expec-tations were met and that they received the kind and level of benefits—and minimal costs—they anticipated. This points out the importance of *expectations management.* As we note in Chapter 20, research has shown that individuals rate their experiences (e.g., the purchase of a product or an encounter with a service provider) by comparing expectations with experience. A given level of experience may lead to satisfaction if expectations are met or exceeded or dissatisfaction if expectations are not met. (Sometimes the latter can be mitigated if the target audience members are given a chance to complain and/or receive some remediation.)

Thus, it is important to keep expectations at or below what the nonprofit can deliver. If waiting time can be as high as an hour, do not promise "quick service." If there is high turnover of staff, do not promise high levels of personal care and a client-centered mentality. On the other hand, whenever possible, the nonprofit should con-sider an approach many commercial marketers have adopted, which is to plan not just to *satisfy* target audience members but to *delight* them! These cutting-edge marketers ask what they can do to make the behavior occasion significantly better than people expected. Premier service providers are especially good at this. The Ritz-Carlton knows that a request by a guest for some missing item can be remedied just by having a replacement item delivered but that the guest may be delighted if the manager leaves a phone message offering regrets or a letter is sent later to his or her home apologizing for the oversight and offering an upgrade on the next visit.

Many of these tactics do not cost very much, but they do require planning and training on the part of nonprofit marketers. Their payoff in repeat behaviors can be significant—and therefore highly cost-effective.

Reinforcing behavior is, of course, a standard principle of behavioral psychology. It is well known that people will repeat behaviors when they are rewarded.[7] Hotels give "frequent guest rewards." There is no reason that a nonprofit clinic could not offer the same reinforcement.

Marketers often use unexpected material rewards as reinforcers. Nonprofit marketers can offer these, also. Indeed, fundraising organizations are masters at this. However, we emphasize that it is the *unexpected* reward that can have the most reinforcing effect. Personal letters from the CEO (or maybe a celebrity board member) to a donor who just increased his or her giving or to a volunteer who performed extra services can be powerful reinforcers. Sometimes such rewards can be social as well as psychological, as when high-volume blood donors are portrayed in a poster on a factory wall or a great volunteer or donor is praised at an annual banquet or in the organization newsletter.

Finally, we must recognize that, while rewards can be administered by the nonprofit in many instances, oftentimes the only—or perhaps major—rewards and reinforcements will come from the target audience members *rewarding themselves*. Thus, nonprofit marketers need to think about tactics that could help audiences reinforce themselves. For example, dieters or blood donors could be provided with score sheets that allow them to tell how well they are doing. Alternatively, if means can be found to have them record progress through the Web, then their progress can be given direct praise from the unseen Web correspondent—and, where relevant, the progress can be posted (perhaps in disguised form) for others to see and admire. This can be very reinforcing.

SUMMARY

Making behaviors happen requires facilitation. Marketers must find ways to make behavioral opportunities convenient and personally pleasant and rewarding. This involves developing channel strategies to bring behavioral opportunities to the target audience and "occasion strategies" to make the actual encounter entirely reinforcing

Channel strategies ensure that offers are made available at a particular time and in a particular place. Often, this requires the services of other agencies (who can provide warehouse and transportation facilities) and careful coordination of complex interacting systems. Although channels may simply be a means to facilitate target audience members' time and place utilities, they have the potential to either significantly augment or effectively sabotage carefully designed marketing programs.

To achieve an effective and efficient channel strategy, the nonprofit marketer must decide what quality of service to offer and whether marketing will be direct or indirect. Then, the marketer must determine the length and breadth of the channel, recruit channel members, and assign functions. Finally, the marketer should put systems in place for effective coordination and control among the channel members.

The other major facilitation challenge is making occasions easy, emotionally satisfying, and rewarding. This requires attention to atmospherics and to customer reinforcement. Often target audiences need to be taught how to reward themselves.

QUESTIONS

1. Assume that your hospital has set up franchise health clinics in neighboring rural areas using the hospital brand name. How would you set up a monitoring system to control the performance of the satellite clinics? What performance measures would you use?

2. The U.S. Treasury had problems in getting channel intermediaries to accept the $2 bill in the 1970s. How could the Treasury department re-launch the $2 bill more successfully post-2000? What sorts of efforts would be needed to secure channel cooperation and coordination?

3. Many nonprofit programs enlist for-profit enterprises to achieve their objectives. For example, a private company now markets condoms for the family planning and AIDS social marketing programs in Pakistan. What would be the objectives for the for-profit organization in becoming involved in this effort? Would these objectives be a source of conflict with the nonprofit? If so, how can the nonprofit manager reduce conflict and ensure goal coordination?

4. An AIDS program manager determines that bars and hotels would be a good place to make condoms available. How could the manager further segment these markets? Based on the segmentation differences, how would the marketing strategies be different?

5. Many nonprofits now sell products on their premises (e.g., t-shirts) as a way of generating extra revenue. In the United States, the IRS has become alarmed that these sales are becoming more like for-profit marketing, and should therefore be taxed. How should a nonprofit distribution plan be set up to minimize the risk of taxation by the IRS?

NOTES

1. Early intimations of this approach are found in Sidney J. Levy and Philip Kotler, "Beyond Marketing: The Furthering Concept," *California Management Review,* 12 (Winter 1969), pp. 67–73.

2. Ronald Abler, John S. Adams, and Peter Gould, *Spatial Organization* (Englewood Cliffs, N.J.: Prentice-Hall, 1971), pp. 531–532.

3. Quoted from an unpublished term paper on the Faith Covenant Church of Wheaton written by Mark F. Pufundt at Northwestern University, 1980.

4. An excellent introduction to these issues is found in Louis W. Stern and Adel I. Ansary, *Marketing Channels,* 2nd ed. (Englewood Cliffs, N.J.: Prentice-Hall, 1982).

5. The material in the following section is adapted from Alan R. Andreasen, "A Power Potential Approach to Middlemen Strategies in Social Marketing," *European Journal of Marketing,* Vol. 18, No. 4 (1984), pp. 56–71. See also John R. French and Bertram Raven, "The Bases of Social Power," in D. Cartwright (ed.), *Studies in Social Power* (Ann Arbor: University of Michigan Press, 1959); Jack Kasulis and Robert Spekman, "A Framework for the Use of Power," *European Journal of Marketing,* October 1980, pp. 70–78.

6. For more details, see Philip Kotler, "Atmospherics as a Marketing Tool," *Journal of Retailing,* Winter 1973–1974, pp. 48–64.

7. Michael Rothschild and William C. Gaidis, "Behavioral Learning Theory: Its Relevance to Marketing and Promotions," *Journal of Marketing,* Spring 1981, pp. 70–78.

CHAPTER 17

Formulating Communication Strategies

I t is hard to believe that a social marketing project could lead to a top 10 record. Yet, the Mexican nonprofit Fuentes y Fommento Intercontinentales (FFI) succeeded in doing just that. FFI worked with Patrick Coleman of Johns Hopkins University's Center for Communications Programs. The planners set out to develop a piece of music (or several pieces of music) that would get across a message of sexual responsibility to young people. They realized that it was critical to not only create attractive records but to get them played.

They began by asking 32 composers and writers throughout Latin America to create two songs each. These were then narrowed to six options through a series of focus groups. Once two of the six songs were chosen, they sought out recording artists and settled on two up-and-coming young artists known as "Tatiana and Johnny" to record the songs. One song was a very upbeat dance tune called *Cuando Estamos Juntos* and the other was *Détente*, a piece that was slower and more romantic.

As Vice President Rogelio Villareal of FFI points out, the production was very international. The composers were Argentinean and Mexican. Johnny was Puerto Rican and Tatiana was Mexican. The music was recorded in Spain and the video was filmed in Mexico. Mixing was done in Los Angeles.

The campaign began by releasing the music first with no indication that it was part of some nonprofit or governmental campaign. The idea was to overcome the natural suspicions of young people about anything "institutional." Once the music reached its peak on the charts, the campaign sprang to life with follow-up media work repeating the messages and urging young people to contact youth service centers for advice and counseling. The music video was played on "Siempre en Domingo" on the Televisa network and reached a potential 180 million viewers all over the world. Requests for the song came from many countries other than Mexico and, in such cases, FFI referred callers to local country agencies.

The music and videos received an estimated $1 million in free radio and TV time and many broadcasters followed the records with other programming around youth, family planning, and responsibility. Best of all, both songs became top 10 hits!

Source: Adapted from Rogelio Villareal, "Marketing a Successful Enter-Educate Music Project," in Patrick L. Coleman and Rita C. Meyer (eds.), *Proceedings of The Enter-Educate Conference: Entertainment for Social Change* (Baltimore, Md.: The Johns Hopkins University Center for Communications Programs, 1990), pp. 30–31.

In Chapter 1, we defined marketing as a philosophy, process, and set of concepts and theories for influencing behavior—either changing behavior or preventing it from changing (e.g., keeping teenagers from taking up smoking). In the immediately preceding chapters, we considered the offer, price, and facilitation components of the marketing mix and saw that these components must be put in place before any program can be successful. We have also seen that these components can influence behaviors directly by providing incentives for action (benefits) or reducing disincentives (costs). However, in the vast majority of nonprofit marketing strategies, influencing behavior involves significant amounts of *communication*. It is a matter of:

1. *Informing* target audiences in the Precontemplation Stage about the alternatives for action and getting them interested.
2. Telling those in the Contemplation Stage of the positive consequences of choosing a particular option and of the positive approval of role models.
3. Providing motivations for acting at a particular time and place and teaching any needed skills for acting to those in the Preparation/Action Stage.
4. Offering rewards for *continuing* to act for those in the Maintenance Stage.

Although too many nonprofits overemphasize communication in their marketing mix and outside observers often think that communication is *all* marketing is about, this element is typically very important.

Communication is not something that nonprofits can ignore. Everything about an organization—its products, employees, facilities, and actions—communicates something. Each organization must examine its communication style, needs, and opportunities and develop a communication program that is influential and cost-effective. The organization's communication responsibilities go beyond communicating to target consumers. The organization must communicate effectively with all of its external publics such as the press, government agencies, and potential donors. It also must communicate effectively with its internal publics, particularly its board members, middle management, and professional clerical employees, as well as any volunteers it uses. The organization must know how to communicate about itself to various groups in order to gain their support and goodwill.

An organization may use a great many communication vehicles to inform and motivate target publics. These include:

TV and radio advertising	Word of mouth; viral marketing	Packaging
Print ads	Posters and show cards	Books and articles
Web site messages	Point-of-sales	Endorsements
Web banner ads	Displays	Special events
Mailings	Catalogs	Giveaways
Speeches; community meetings	Soap operas or movie scripts	Public service
Brochures and annual reports	Conference exhibits	announcements
Demonstrations		

These are only the more conventional vehicles. Nonprofit marketers in Thailand have painted logos on water buffalo. Buses and Volkswagens have been painted with prevention messages. And celebrities have appeared at Congressional Hearings to support their favorite causes (and gain some personal publicity).

Decisions on which of these vehicles to use, when to use them, and how must follow from a clear understanding of the communication process.

THE COMMUNICATION PROCESS

Any communication process involves a message *sender* and a message *receiver* (a target audience).[1] The sender has an *intended message,* but whether the *received message* is in most respects identical to it is determined by the extent to which the communication process is relatively noise free and the sender and receiver share the same *cultural codes.* This process is outlined in Figure 17-1.

A *sender* (the National Symphony Orchestra in Washington, D.C., for example) formulates an *intended message* ("A new conductor, Leonard Slatkin, brings fresh, new excitement to National Symphony concerts"). The *encoder* (an advertising agency) translates this intended message into an *encoded message* (a picture of an energetic Leonard Slatkin, a headline: "Musical Excitement Comes to D.C.," and four paragraphs describing Slatkin's past connections with the city and his rave reviews as guest conductor of other major orchestras. The paragraphs also describe the diversity of his background and his own thoughts on his plans for the National Symphony).

This message gets transmitted through such *media* as regional editions of *Time* and *Newsweek* magazines, which the ad agency believes will add an aura of "seriousness" to the encoded message. The *decoders* may be a young couple glancing at a magazine in a doctor's office, discussing between themselves the direct and implied content of the ad ("He's an American. Aren't all the really good conductors from Europe?"). Finally, each *receiver* in the couple retains traces of the memorable parts of the message and associations (e.g., Slatkin's nationality and his quotes about the orchestra), which can be assessed by a market *researcher* checking for *feedback* in a post-campaign telephone survey.

In many actual situations, the roles portrayed in Figure 17-1 may be combined. For example, there can be two-party communication involving (1) the sender–encoder–medium–researcher and (2) the decoder–receiver. This would be the case in many kinds of personal influence situations, such as a fundraising presentation to a potential major donor. The fundraiser would decide what message to get across, encode it into a "prospect pitch," transmit it verbally, and watch for or inquire about

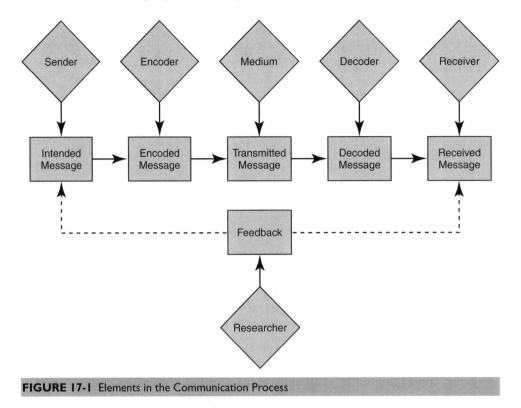

FIGURE 17-1 Elements in the Communication Process

the potential donor's response. The donor would decode the fundraiser's pitch and store whatever was personally meaningful in it.

Even in this relatively simple two-party situation, a number of kinds of "noise" can creep in:

1. *Encoding.* The fundraiser may choose the wrong wording to convey key concepts. He or she, for example, may intend to make it clear that the donor can be anonymous, but by making frequent references to *possible* forms of recognition, leave the overall impression that the donor cannot escape publicity.

2. *Transmitting.* Vocal inflections or body language in the delivery of the message can change its meaning. For example, if a person seeking a donation for a hospital adopts too "serious" a tone of voice when speaking about the scientific quality of the research work being done at the hospital, he or she may unintentionally convey the impression that the scientists are pessimistic about possible breakthroughs. In another example, if a flip chart is used to outline the possible types of funding sought and possible uses of those funds, the speed with which pages of the chart are physically "flipped" may unintentionally tell a potential donor which areas the hospital *really* thinks are important.

3. *Decoding.* The target audience can mishear what is said. A 70 percent success rate for a health care facility may be heard as 17 percent. A distracted decoder may miss important benefits. The meaning given to heard statements can also vary greatly, depending on what experiences the decoder brings to the message. A

potential donor with queasy personal reactions to the sight of blood may not really "see" flip chart pictures or slides showing or implying "bloody" events. A biased potential donor may "decide" that an agency is not well run if "too many" female or 20-something staff members are portrayed. The target audience member may not like the fundraiser and so tend to discount his or her opinions or assertions.

4. *Researching.* Individuals vary greatly in their ability to read the responses of target customers. Thus, noise is added to the communication process if the fundraiser interprets a potential donor's silence as signaling a lack of interest when it actually means that the donor is reflecting carefully on the merits of a proposal. Alternatively, the fundraiser might decide that the cause of a potential donor's indifference is stinginess when in fact it is caused by the donor's irritation at the fundraiser's manner of presentation. Finally, it is possible that the target consumer may encode his or her own feelings with some distortion. Indeed, feedback is really another communication process with the target consumer as the sender and the marketing organization as the receiver.

Of course, in a great many communication situations, the process involves several agencies or individuals acting in one or more of the roles indicated in Figure 17-1. In these cases, the potential for "noise" is enhanced:

1. *Encoding.* Celebrity spokespeople may be designated as agents for communicating top management's sense of mission for the nonprofit organization, and they can get the message wrong or distort it. Alternatively, an advertising agency or public relations firm may be given the task of encoding the organization's *intended* message but may produce words or images that distort or inflate management's intentions. For example, too-slick graphics or a "cool" ad layout for a symphony orchestra may suggest that the orchestra is not a solid, well-trained ensemble or that its repertoire is too avant-garde for most tastes. Every time another participant is added to the communication process, he or she brings to it his or her own interests, values, goals, and perceptions. Some advertising or public relations agencies working pro bono or for reduced fees may direct their messages at least partly toward their fellow advertising or PR colleagues whom they want to impress. Sometimes their main goal seems to be to attempt to dazzle their peers with the style and drama of a message's "encoding." The advertising community is replete with stories of campaigns that secured very high recall scores but did not "move the product." Early Pepsi ads featuring Shaquille O'Neal scored very high in ad tests while actual Pepsi sales declined 1.6 percent.

2. *Transmitting.* The vehicle through which you say something can enhance or distort a message. Many advertisers believe that putting an ad in a particular medium (e.g., *The New Yorker* or *Town and Country*) can add a sense of "class" to their presentation. Or they may choose a spokesperson (a Denzel Washington, Julia Roberts, or Martin Sheen) who will bring his or her own prestige or charisma to the nonprofit agency's message. Sometimes, however, the spokesperson can be inappropriate, can be seen as "doing it for the money," or as having little in common with the target audience.

Certain media can be inappropriate. Radio ads on a rock station may be wrong for a "serious" hospital, and a classical music station may be wrong for a hospital trying to position itself as being "for everyone." Print ads in *Maxim* may get high readership but convey the wrong impression about a clinic's exercise therapy program. A symphony orchestra that wants to seem less elite should avoid *U.S. News and World Report*, whereas a political candidate might find this magazine a very appropriate vehicle for adding to his or her "stature."

3. *Decoding.* Depending on how they are viewed by potential customers, channel members and their agents may serve as decoders for consumers. Thus, a physician may be asked by a patient to interpret the latest publicity release on smoking or high blood pressure, or by an older woman to explain what a new calcium pill will do for osteoporosis. In a similar fashion, newspaper or TV critics may "decode" a symphony or theater's offering. The Consumers Union may evaluate products, services, and even advertising themes. Reporters and political analysts play the same role for voters. In all of these cases, what the marketer wants to say may take on very different meaning once it is filtered through these "helpful" role players.

4. *Researching.* Outside agencies can be hired by the marketer to assess directly the target audience's present moods, opinions, or specific responses to the marketer's messages. To the extent that this intervention involves the perceptions, judgments, empathy, *and* communication skills of these other agents, there is significant potential for distortion.

Most problematic is the case where "independent" third parties take on the role of providing feedback to the marketer. Examples include the self-appointed spokesperson for the oppressed who tells marketers "the truth" about how the group has been mistreated and the opinion polls from trade associations that purport to tell the government how the public is reacting to particular ongoing programs or new proposals. Nonetheless, there are also many respected associations that offer accurate feedback about what their members think and feel as well as thoughtful newspaper, magazine, and television commentators who are well attuned to the public opinions of special subgroups.

Strategic Implications

The major implication of this view of the communication process is that in any given situation the probability is very high that the *received message* will be different from the *intended message.* Two corollaries of this conclusion are these:

1. The more role players there are in the communication process, the greater the chance for distortion.
2. The less control the marketer has over the role players in the communication process, the greater the chance for distortion.

These concerns have several implications for marketing strategy:

1. The nonprofit communicator should *never* assume that the target audience will "receive" what the communicator thinks is being "sent."
2. If communication strategy is to be improved, it is essential that the marketer know what is likely to be received (through pretesting) and actually received (through posttesting monitoring).
3. If knowing what is received is crucial, careful attention must be paid to the quality of the *feedback* link in the system (i.e., the research).

4. If formal feedback research is carried out before the launch of the message or a message campaign, pretesting should simulate the *entire* communication process. For example, if a program of patient hypertension education is to be conducted with PowerPoint presentations and through brochures that physicians pass along to patients, simply testing physicians' responses or patients' responses to the materials alone would be inadequate. The marketer must test *both* steps in either a laboratory or a test market setting to see (a) how the physicians perceive the materials, (b) how often and with what advice they pass them on to the patients, and (c) how patients decode and store what the physicians tell them.

5. If communications are distorted at the receiving end, it is important to trace the source of the distortion to its roots. In the preceding example, the hypertension message could be inaccurately received for a variety of reasons, including these:

   a. It was poorly encoded by the marketer in the first place (that is, the brochures and slides were poorly designed).

   b. It was well encoded, but physicians often added their own embellishments, verbal cues, or body language, which changed the content.

   c. The typical receiver was sufficiently misinformed about the disease *before* hearing the message that parts which seemed frightening were simply not "heard" at any important level.

The changes needed in the communication program would vary significantly depending on which of these problems was the primary source of message noise.

1. If a message *must* be received undistorted (for example, instructions about what a mother should do when her child is in a life-threatening situation), and it must be the same for all targeted customers, perfectly clear written communications directly delivered to the consumer are obviously superior.

2. However, if a message must be carefully adjusted to individual consumers (e.g., how a person should change personal diet and exercise patterns), then a flexible, personally delivered message strategy is preferable because of its potential for ongoing feedback. (The one proviso here is that the personal spokesperson be one who is naturally empathetic or is carefully trained in *undistorted listening* techniques.)

MAJOR STEPS IN DEVELOPING EFFECTIVE COMMUNICATIONS

We shall now consider the major steps in developing strategies to use these processes. The steps include (1) setting communication objectives, (2) generating possible messages, (3) overcoming selective attention, (4) overcoming perceptual distortion, (5) choosing a medium, and (6) evaluating and selecting messages. We turn later to the possibilities of modifying behavior directly.

Setting Communication Objectives

The first step calls for the marketer to define carefully the objective or objectives of the communication program. Possible objectives include these:

1. Making target consumers aware of a product, service, or social behavior.
2. Educating consumers about the offer or changes in the offer.

3. Changing beliefs about the negative and positive consequences of taking a particular action.
4. Changing the relative importance of particular consequences.
5. Communicating wide social support for an action.
6. Teaching skills needed to carry out the behavior.
7. Enlisting the support of intermediary agencies (e.g., securing shelf space).
8. Recruiting, motivating, or rewarding employees or volunteers.
9. Changing perceptions about the sponsoring organization.
10. Influencing governing agencies, review boards, commissions, and the like.
11. Preventing discontinuation of behaviors.
12. "Proving" superiority over competitors.
13. Combating injurious rumors.
14. Influencing funding agencies.

Generating Possible Messages

Once the nonprofit marketer has determined a broad objective or set of objectives for a communication campaign, the next step is to encode it in *specific* messages. Message generation involves developing a number of alternative messages (appeals, themes, motifs, ideas) from which the best one can be chosen.

Messages can be generated in a number of ways. One approach is to talk with members of the target market and other influential parties (for example, in focus groups) to determine how they see the product or service or behavior, talk about it, and express their desires about it. A second approach is to hold a brainstorming meeting with key personnel in the organization to generate several ideas. A third method is to use some formal deductive framework to tease out possible communication messages. We discuss two of the many possible deductive frameworks below.

Rational, Emotional, and Moral Framework

One framework identifies three types of messages that can be generated: rational, emotional, and moral.

1. *Rational messages* aim at passing on information, serving the audience's self-interest, or both. They attempt to show that the service will yield the expected functional benefits. Examples are messages discussing a service's quality, economy, value, or performance or messages spelling out the long-term health consequences of exercise or increasing calcium intake.
2. *Emotional messages* are designed to stir up some negative or positive emotion that will motivate the desired behavior. Communicators have worked with fear, guilt, and shame appeals, especially in connection with getting people to start doing things they should do (e.g., brush their teeth, have an annual health checkup) or stop doing things they shouldn't do (e.g., smoke, drink and drive, abuse drugs, overeat, or bring illegal fruit across the border) (see Figure 17-2.). Advertisers have found that fear appeals work up to a point, but if there is too much fear the audience may ignore the message. Communicators have also used positive emotional appeals such as love, humor, pride, and joy. Evidence has not, however, established that a humorous message, for example, is necessarily more effective than a straight version of the same message.

FIGURE 17-2 Example of "Shame" Appeal

Source: Foote Cone & Belding, Chicago, Il. Reproduced with permission.

3. *Moral messages* are directed to the audience's sense of what is right and proper. They are often used in messages exhorting people to support such social causes as a cleaner environment, better race relations, equal rights for women, and aiding the disadvantaged. An example is this March of Dimes appeal: "God made you whole. Give to help those He didn't."

The BCOS Theory Framework

A second way to generate possible messages is to work through the BCOS framework, particularly if the target audience is in the Contemplation Stage or in the Preparation/Action Stage. Here, one would use audience research to ascertain the potential impact of messages around perceived benefits, costs, the wishes of others, and self-efficacy.

Consider the communication problem of the marketing director of St. Anthony's Hospital, Axel Arneson, who is seeking to persuade a specific physician, Dr. Laura Goldman, to admit more of her patients to the hospital's oncology ward instead of to a competitor, the Downtown Medical Center (DMC). Suppose that from conversations with Dr. Goldman, Mr. Arneson has determined that there are four key potentially positive consequences (benefits) that Dr. Goldman considers when deciding where to admit a patient—the behavior that is the bottom line of this potential influence process. These are the consequences:

1. The extent to which the nursing staff is well trained enough to competently administer Dr. Goldman's treatment plan and to make sensible judgments on occasions when the plan doesn't apply and Dr. Goldman is unavailable for consultation.
2. The extent to which other physicians affiliated with the hospital (especially those in oncology) can provide good advice and share in patient treatment.
3. The extent to which Dr. Goldman will have access to the latest testing and treatment equipment and other patient care facilities.
4. The extent to which Dr. Goldman will have her wishes respected and carried out regarding admissions, treatment, office space, fees, and billing.

Mr. Arneson has estimated Dr. Goldman's beliefs about the likelihood of achieving these positive consequences if she takes the behavior of affiliating with each of the rival hospitals as follows:

	St. Anthony's	Downtown Medical Center	Importance
Good nursing care	.8	.7	20%
Access to knowledgeable colleagues	.9	.6	30
Access to best facilities	.5	.7	30
Have my wishes respected	.4	.8	20

Note that Mr. Arneson is *not* interested in Dr. Goldman's perceptions of the *organizations* but of her perceptions of the consequences of a *behavior* toward them. It is the behavior that Mr. Arneson knows he has to influence and so he is resolutely focused on this.

From his conversation, Mr. Arneson also judges that Dr. Goldman gives weightings of 20 percent, 30 percent, 30 percent, and 20 percent, respectively, to the four benefits of the alternative behaviors. Mr. Arneson further believes that Dr. Goldman's perceptions of the likely outcomes are very similar to those of a sizable contingent of other physicians in the area. Finally, Mr. Arneson believes that his hospital's low ratings on the "facilities" and "respect" consequences stem from the relative age and overcrowded appearance of his physical plant.

There are three ways that the overall evaluation of the benefits of taking action can be changed: (1) changing the importance of one or more consequences, (2) changing beliefs about one or more consequences, or (3) adding new (presumably positive) consequences.

Changing Importance Weights   The first possibility open to Mr. Arneson is to attempt to change the importance weightings that Dr. Goldman and those like her attach to the four behavioral consequences. Thus, he might attempt to increase the weighting given to "access to knowledgeable colleagues" (on which his hospital scores well) and reduce that given to "access to best facilities" by arguing as follows:

> Many physicians think that the kind of hospital they want to work in is the one with the very best equipment and testing facilities. We know that's important. But the best equipment is only as good as the people who make it work and who help draw the most from its results. It is one thing to have the latest CT scanner, quite another to be around colleagues who know just when to use it and how to wring the last ounce of meaning from its readouts. We think that is *really* the kind of institution you want to be affiliated with, one that has the most up-to-date facilities but, even more, that has the staff and colleagues who are on the leading edge of research and diagnoses using these new technical wonders.

Notice that this attempt at changes in perspectives made no mention of St. Anthony's or its rivals. Mr. Arneson knew that St. Anthony's scored well on "knowledgeable colleagues" and not so well on "facilities." He knows that if he can switch the weightings from 30 to 40 percent on "colleagues" and 30 to 20 percent on "facilities," St. Anthony's would be the favored institution, not Downtown Medical Center.

Changing Beliefs   Should Arneson decide that changing the weightings is too difficult or too risky to attempt, he has another option, trying to change beliefs. Here he can make use of suggestive social science frameworks, such as dissonance and assimilation/contrast theories.

Dissonance theory.   One characteristic of human beings is that we prefer order and meaning. We like things to fit well together. We don't take kindly to messages that run counter to our present cognitions. When we encounter such dissonant messages, if the issue is involving, we will attempt to reassert order in our cognitive structure (our view of the world). That is, we will attempt to restore consonance.[2] We adopt several strategies to cope with dissonance.

Suppose that Dr. Goldman heard a rumor that two Downtown Medical Center laboratory technicians had drug abuse problems. This would be dissonant with her view that Downtown had reasonably good colleagues for her to work with (and, of course, with any interest in sending her patients there). Dr. Goldman could restore consonance in several ways:

1. *Denial.* She could convince herself that the rumors "couldn't be true" (e.g., that they were the work of "enemies" of DMC).
2. *Search for disconfirmation.* She could seek information from administrators at DMC that would counter the rumors.

3. *Reduce the importance of the issue.* We can all live with some amount of dissonance provided it isn't perceived to be related to an issue in which we are highly involved. Thus, Dr. Goldman might decide that although the rumor may be true, it isn't really a very serious matter because (a) the people in question probably don't work in highly technical areas like hers, (b) even if they did, she could personally spot them and avoid them, (c) hospital administrators would certainly take care of the problem, or (d) even if the problem can't be entirely dealt with, it would be no better anywhere else (e.g., at St. Anthony's).
4. *Change prior beliefs.* Dr. Goldman may judge the rumors to be true and change her belief about DMC's staff and her own decision to send patients there.

The last mentioned is, of course, an instance of *changed beliefs.* It is a case in which new information caused a negative result from DMC's standpoint but a positive one where St. Anthony's is concerned. While one would not expect Mr. Arneson to resort to spreading unsubstantiated rumors about a rival institution, one can see that the introduction of dissonant information can change beliefs. Thus, Mr. Arneson could seek to offer facts about St. Anthony's or about Downtown Medical Center that he believed Dr. Goldman would find dissonant. It is crucial that the facts chosen (1) be so convincing that they cannot easily be denied, (2) concern some highly involving area not likely to be minimized by Dr. Goldman, and (3) be difficult to counter by other facts.

Assimilation/contrast theory. A danger that Mr. Arneson risks in presenting potential dissonant information is that it may fail a plausibility test even before Dr. Goldman considers it. Sherif, Sherif, and Nebergill have proposed that an individual's perspective about a consequence can be seen as a position on a given belief dimension.[3] Thus, we noted that Dr. Goldman's best estimate of the likelihood that she will receive respectful treatment at St. Anthony's is currently .4. If one were to probe Dr. Goldman's beliefs further, we might discover that, given additional information, she might revise this probability downward as low as .2 or upward as high as .7. Sherif, Sherif, and Nebergill refer to this range as Dr. Goldman's *latitude of acceptance.* By contrast, if for some reason Mr. Arneson tried to maximize Dr. Goldman's dissonance by suggesting that the true probability would be almost certain at .9 or 1.0 (in sharpest contrast with .4), Dr. Goldman would find the assertion implausible. In such a case, dissonance would *not* occur and no attitude change would ensue. The region in which implausible statements would fall is labeled by Sherif et al. as the *latitude of rejection.* (Beliefs falling into neither range are said to be in the *latitude of indifference.*)

To get the maximum change in perceptions of consequences, Sherif et al. would recommend that Mr. Arneson try to bring information to bear that would seem likely to bring Dr. Goldman's belief to the .7 level, the upper end of the latitude of acceptance. Thus, he should *not* promise her a large, immaculately furnished office and instant response to requests for laboratory tests. Rather, he should indicate, for example, that she would have a recently redecorated, if modest-size, office equal to that of other senior staff members and that her laboratory requests would be given rapid attention as befits a senior staffer (providing she was judicious in the number of rush requests). That is, he should suggest that the "respect" and "facilities" consequences of affiliating with St. Anthony's would be at the believable level of .7 rather than the unbelievable 1.0 level. In general, as suggested in Figure 17-3, it is best to bring individuals to the furthest and most desirable point *within* their latitude of acceptance.

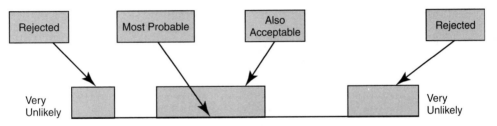

A. "Increasing industrial pollution controls will cause many jobs to be lost."

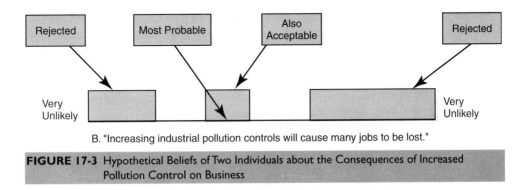

B. "Increasing industrial pollution controls will cause many jobs to be lost."

FIGURE 17-3 Hypothetical Beliefs of Two Individuals about the Consequences of Increased Pollution Control on Business

Further, the theory suggests that, as the target audience adjusts to this new belief, its latitude of acceptance will also shift and new communication strategies can be designed to move them along even further. By this process, they may eventually be brought to the point advocated by the dissonance theorists in the first case.

Of course, not everyone will have either the same beginning beliefs or the same range of acceptable positions. Indeed, one measure of the firmness of a person's beliefs is the ratio of the latitude of acceptance to the latitude of rejection. The individual in Figure 17-3B is clearly much more fixed in beliefs than the individual in Figure 17-3A. The former is described as being much more *dogmatic* or narrow minded.

Adding Consequences A third alternative available to Mr. Arneson is to add one or more new, positive beliefs. Indeed, this is a common strategy in the commercial sector for differentiating a brand in a highly competitive market environment or resuscitating a brand in the decline phase of its life cycle. Potential customers are told about a new consequence of using the product or service or engaging in a behavior. Sometimes, these new consequences only require imagination and not a fundamental change in the offering. Thus, a marketer may point out to those not swayed by arguments about the positive health consequences of participating in a stop-smoking clinic that participation may also lead to making new friends. Or new parents may be encouraged to use a library not only for information about parenting, but also to learn about library services that their new child could appreciate or learn to use, such as weekly storytelling hours or children's CD rentals.

In Mr. Arneson's case, he may discover additional "perks" that might appeal to Dr. Goldman. This could be an augmentation to the basic offering such as a special parking location, an advanced dictation system for patient reports, or first perusal of the library's copies of key journals in her field. Alternatively (or in addition), Mr. Arneson may simply point out additional existing features of St. Anthony's and its staff, such as the publication record of attending physicians, which would indicate that both secretarial facilities and knowledgeable colleagues would be available for whatever writing ambitions Dr. Goldman might harbor.

Introducing Other Components of the BCOS Model

Mr. Arneson must recognize that perceived benefits and costs are not the only factors likely to drive Dr. Goldman's behavior. She may be influenced by important groups of "others." For example, she may perceive a strong positive benefit/cost ratio for St. Anthony's in terms of consequences important to her but still not choose to affiliate because some important patients of hers object or because her clinic partners think it is a mistake. Arneson's challenge then may be to mount a mini-campaign aimed to change the views of these *other* voices that can influence Dr. Goldman. Alternatively, he can add additional voices that he knows Dr. Goldman respects (for example, having a prestigious doctor make a personal telephone call urging her to affiliate).

Finally, there may be matters of self-efficacy that could "kill" the campaign even if the other BCOS elements are positive. If for some reason Dr. Goldman thinks that it is just not *possible* to affiliate with St. Anthony's, she will not do so. Subtle probing may lead Mr. Arneson to discover that Dr. Goldman views the prospect of switching her records over to the sophisticated info-tech system at St. Anthony's to be too complicated and challenging, especially since her long-time assistant just went on a six-month maternity leave. Arneson may raise her sense of personal self-efficacy by offering to loan her a part-time staffer knowledgeable in info-tech systems for the six-month transition period.

Overcoming Selective Attention

Change in beliefs is only possible if the audience member perceives the message. Mr. Arneson must recognize that people are constantly bombarded with promotional messages. Some estimates suggest that we are exposed to as many as 1,400 messages in a day. But, of course, we *perceive* far fewer. We selectively attend to the information environment around us. This is often called "the cocktail party effect."[4] It helps us simplify and manage our lives. We attend to subjects, themes, or images that interest us and ignore others that don't. Thus, older people will notice ads for extended vacations. Hypochondriacs catch ads for over-the-counter drugs, teens pay attention to rock stars, and business people seldom ignore computer ads.

In contrast, we tend to avoid messages that don't interest us or that in some way frighten us. This is a particular problem with fear appeals. Many nonprofit organizations involved in social or health issues find it tempting to use fear appeals (see Figure 17-4). For example, the Metropolitan Energy Council, a group of New York fuel dealers, tried to compete with gas suppliers with an ad in the *New York Times* that depicted a young mother saying, "Gas comes from a big utility. They don't know my family. If you need prompt service from them, you have to say, 'I smell gas.' That's what scares me most. I think gas heat is dangerous—too dangerous for my home, my kids."[5]

Fear is not always effective. Researchers in Ontario, Canada, reviewed past studies of seat belt use and determined that an appeal based on the fear of being injured *but not killed* in a car crash could be potentially quite powerful. A test set of six messages

USING IT WON'T KILL YOU. NOT USING IT MIGHT.

Maybe you don't like using condoms. But if you're going to have sex, a latex condom with a spermicide is your best protection against the AIDS virus.

Use them every time, from start to finish, according to the manufacturers' directions. Because no one has ever been cured of AIDS. More than 40,000 Americans have already died from it.

And even if you don't like condoms, using them is definitely better than that.

HELP STOP AIDS. USE A CONDOM.

Photo: Jerry Friedman   ©1988, The Ad Council.

AIDS CAMPAIGN
NEWSPAPER AD NO. AIDS-88-1382—2 COL.
TABLOID SIZE (9⅜" x 14") AD NO. AIDS-88-1381

FIGURE 17-4 Example of Fear Appeal

Source: The Advertising Council. Reproduced with permission.

was constructed (see Table 17-1) and run 943 times over nine consecutive months on one cable network of a dual cable system in Ontario. Seat belt use of a random sample of drivers was unobtrusively observed before, during, and after the study by using license plates to learn which cable network each driver was exposed to. After correcting for the effects of weather (seat belts are less often used with bulky clothes in Canadian winters), the researchers concluded that the television campaign was a failure and that

TABLE 17-1 **Examples of Fear Appeals in a Seat Belt Use Campaign**

1. A father is shown lifting his teenage son from a wheelchair into a car. As they ride along, safety belts obviously fastened, the father's thoughts are voiced off camera intermixed with the son's on-camera expressions of excitement at going to a football game. The father expresses guilt for not having encouraged his son to use safety belts before the crash in which he was injured. An analogy is drawn to the protection that the son wore when he played football.
2. A teenage girl is shown sitting in a rocking chair while looking out a window. She says, "I'm not sick or anything. I could go out more but since the car crash, I just don't. . . . The crash wasn't Dad's fault. I go for walks with my father after dark . . . that way I don't get, you know, stared at." She turns enough to reveal a large scar on what was the hidden side of her face. She continues, "It doesn't hurt anymore." An announcer says off camera, "Car crashes kill two ways: right away and little by little. Wear your safety belts and live!"
3. A woman whose face cannot be seen is shown applying makeup in front of a mirror. A full-face picture on her dressing table shows her as a beautiful woman. Her husband enters the scene and suggests that they go to a party. She asks him not to look at her without makeup as she turns to reveal a scarred face. An off-camera announcer describes a crash in which the wife was driving slowly and carefully. The announcer continues, as the picture on the table is shown, "Terry would still look like this if she had been wearing seat belts." Safety belts are shown through a shattered windshield. Announcer: "It's much easier to wear safety belts than to hear your husband say, 'Honey, I love you anyway.' "
4. A father and mother are shown riding in the front seat of a car, their eight-year-old daughter seated between them. The father must brake hard to avoid another car entering from a side road. The daughter bumps her head as she is thrown into the dashboard and begins to cry. A policeman walks up to the car and the father angrily says, "Did you see what that guy just did? That jerk. I had to jam on my brakes. My little girl hit her head." The policeman asks the father why the child wasn't wearing a seat belt. Over the father's protestations about the other driver, the policeman emphasizes the father's responsibility to protect his child. The scene closes with the policeman walking away saying, "When are people gonna learn?" and the announcer following with "It doesn't take brains to wear safety belts. But it sure is stupid not to."

Source: Leon S. Robertson, Albert B. Kelley, Brian O'Neill, Charles W. Wixom, Richard S. Eiswirth, and William Haddon, Jr., "A Controlled Study of the Effect of Television Messages on Safety Belt Use," *American Journal of Public Health,* Vol. 64, November 1974, p. 1,074. Reprinted with permission of the American Public Health Association.

only coercion would work, either laws or mandatory passive restraint systems like air bags or automatic seat belting systems.[6]

The use of emotional appeals will continue to be a controversial topic in nonprofit marketing.[7] Experimental research by Bagozzi and Moore demonstrated that emotional anti–child-abuse ads were more effective than rational ads in generating negative emotions, empathy for victims, and the decision to help.[8] The researchers recognized that nonprofit marketers have to create powerful impacts with limited budgets. They conclude that "high-impact ads that evoke strong emotions and stimulate empathy could require fewer exposures, yet be successful in influencing attitude formation and decision making." They, however, note that ads that evoke strong negative emotions could have rapid wear-out with repeated exposure. They think that, in situations such as those they studied involving the stopping of child abuse, nonprofit marketers will have more effect than private sector marketers because target audience members will not mentally counterargue the message as they might with a commercial sector ad.

Message Execution

Overcoming the selective attention problem is the responsibility of the creative specialists on the nonprofit communication team (in-house or at the advertising or public relations agency). These specialists have several variables at their command in designing an effective message. They need to find a *style, tone, wording, order,* and *format* to make the message effective.

Any message can be put across in different *execution styles.* Suppose the YMCAs around the country are planning to launch an early morning jogging program (6:30 A.M.) and want to develop a 30-second television commercial to motivate people to sign up for this program. Here are some major advertising execution styles they can consider:

1. *Slice-of-life.* A husband says to his tired wife that she might enjoy jogging at the Y in the early morning. She agrees, and the next frame shows her coming home at 7:45 A.M. feeling refreshed and invigorated.
2. *Lifestyle.* A 30-year-old man pops out of bed when his alarm rings at 6:00 A.M., races to the bathroom, races to the closet, races to his car, races to the Y, and then starts racing with his companions with a "big kid" look on his face.
3. *Fantasy.* A jogger with a YMCA T-shirt runs along a path and suddenly imagines seeing her friends on the sidelines cheering her on.
4. *Mood.* A jogger runs in a residential neighborhood on a beautiful spring day, passing nice homes, noticing flowers beginning to bloom and neighbors waving to her. This ad creates a mood of beauty and harmony between the jogger and her world.
5. *Musical.* Four young joggers run side by side wearing YMCA T-shirts. Specially written pulsating rock music fills the background.
6. *Personality symbol.* A well-known sports hero is shown jogging at the Y with a smile on her face.
7. *Technical expertise.* Several Y athletic directors are shown discussing the best time, place, and running style that will give the greatest benefit to joggers.
8. *Scientific evidence.* A physician tells about a study of two matched groups of men, one following a jogging program and the other not, and the greater health and energy felt by the jogging group after a few weeks.
9. *Testimonial evidence.* The ad shows three members of the Y jogging group telling how beneficial the program has been to them.

The communicator must also choose a *tone* for the message. The message could be deadly serious (as in an anti-smoking ad), chatty (as in a message on weight control), humorous (as in a zoo ad), and so on. The tone must be appropriate to the target audience and target response desired.

Words that are memorable and elicit attention must be found. This is nowhere more apparent than in the development of headlines and slogans to lead the reader into the message. There are six basic types of headlines:

- *news* ("United Way Offers New Giving Options")
- *questions* ("How Many Calories in This Health Shake?")
- *narrative* ("In the September 11 Terrorist Attack in New York, the Middle Classes Became the American Red Cross's Newest Victims")

- *command* ("Save Water—Shower with a Friend")
- *1-2-3 Ways* ("12 Ways to Enjoy the High Cs at the Long Beach Opera")
- *how—what—why* ("You Can't Get AIDS from a Door Knob, a Public Swimming Pool, or a Handshake")

Once the headline and the themes are determined, the communicator must consider the ordering of the ideas. There are three issues: conclusion drawing, one- or two-sided arguments, and order of presentation.

The first is the question of *conclusion drawing,* the extent to which the message should draw a definite conclusion for the audience, such as telling them to give five hours a week to volunteering. Experimental research seems to indicate that explicit conclusion drawing is more persuasive than leaving it to the audience to draw their own conclusions. There are exceptions, however, such as when the communicator is seen as untrustworthy or the audience is highly intelligent and annoyed at the attempt to influence them.

The second issue is the question of the *one-* or *two-sided argument*—that is, whether the message will be more effective if one side or both sides of the argument are presented. Two-sided arguments are of two types. First, there is the approach that admits that the offering has some costs. The classic example of this approach is the early series of ads for the Volkswagen Beetle that admitted it was homely and that it didn't change its looks every model year but that otherwise it was a marvelously sensible purchase! In the nonprofit sector, there are many situations in which the target audience will *know* there is a negative side to a requested behavior:

- Potential blood donors *know* the needle will hurt and that they may feel a little faint.
- Alcoholics, smokers, and drug addicts *know* that quitting or cutting down will be agonizing and require very strong willpower.
- Older persons *know* that investigating a retirement home means admitting negative things about their own competence.
- Young people *know* that not drinking or smoking in some cases may subject them to the teasing of friends and classmates.
- Symphony, theater, and museum goers *know* that a great many of the events they could attend will have elements they don't understand.

A two-sided message would recognize these counterarguments or perceived costs and, where possible, directly address them.

The other kind of two-sided argument recognizes the fact that there are other alternatives. The burger and cola "wars" are message campaigns fully recognizing that there are tough competitors "out there." In the nonprofit sector, there are many parallel situations:

- Going to the theater or symphony means not going to a movie or nightclub or just staying home to watch TV.
- Having a medical checkup or practicing breast self-examination means giving up the "bliss of ignorance."
- Giving to the United Way may mean not giving to the American Cancer Society or a university's alumni fund.

- Choosing UCLA means not choosing Stanford, Northwestern, and Georgetown.
- Choosing to vacation in Jamaica or Southeast Asia means not vacationing in Sun Valley or Paris.
- Practicing birth control means not having the potential long-run economic benefits of another income producer and immediate psychic pleasures of an additional child.

One-sided presentations are common in the nonprofit sector in part because of the "mindset problem" described in Chapter 2. Nonprofit staffers often see the target audience as "the problem" and their ignorance as a barrier to their undertaking an obviously desirable behavior. The tendency is to want to harangue the audience with virtues of the behavior. In the private sector, this is called a "hard-sell" approach. Yet social science research suggests that one-sided approaches may be relatively more effective in three situations: (1) when the audience is less educated, (2) when the audience already favors the message's central proposition, and (3) when the audience is not likely to be exposed later to counterpropaganda. Two-sided messages are said to be more effective when the opposite is true.

There is another, perhaps more compelling, factor that should influence whether two-sided messages are used: It is the degree of the audience's involvement in the behavior that the marketer is attempting to influence. In general, we argue the following: The higher the audience's involvement in the behavior, the more frequently the nonprofit marketer should use two-sided messages.

There are several reasons for this. As the BCOS model emphasizes, in high-involvement situations, target audience members are more likely to be very concerned about the *costs* of the behavior (see Chapter 15); be opposed to the action advocated, if it means change; and be aware of very attractive alternatives. In high-involvement situations, the target audience will engage in extensive internal cognitive activity, which will include considering costs and alternatives. They will engage in an extensive external search that will make available to them the "other side" of the argument. The marketer should seize the initiative and deal with the other side of the issue rather than leave it to the individual or to competitors. A useful concept in this regard is what is called *inoculation theory*. If a communicator knows that a target audience member will *later* be exposed to counterpropaganda (the "other side"), a more favorable outcome will be achieved if the marketer deals with the counterarguments in advance (in effect "inoculating" the target audience against the later influence attempts).

Finally, it must be reemphasized that in situations in which a two-sided strategy would be appropriate, the nonprofit communicator must go to great lengths to understand what *the target audience* perceives to be the key costs of the behavior and what *they* consider to be the reasonable alternatives. Only with a solid research base can an effective two-sided strategy be developed.

In the case of St. Anthony's Hospital, Mr. Arneson should recognize that Dr. Goldman will be exposed to counterpropaganda from DMC at some later point. Thus, the two-sided inoculation concept indicates that Arneson must say things like "I know you'll hear people say that St. Anthony's is overcrowded. Let me set the record straight right now." If at all possible, Arneson should seek to have Dr. Goldman agree with St. Anthony's arguments. Internalizing a position makes it more likely that an individual will adhere to it even after other information is received.

A third issue for the marketer in cases where several ideas are to be conveyed is the best *order of presentation*. Social scientists have found that, other things being equal, people tend to remember the items in a message stream presented first (the primacy effect) and last (the recency effect). There are arguments for Mr. Arneson putting his strongest statements in either position.

Format elements can make a difference in a message's impact, as well as in its cost. If the message is to be carried in a print ad, the communicator has to develop the elements of headline, copy, illustration, and color. Communication specialists are adept at using such attention-getting devices as *novelty, contrast, arresting pictures,* and *movement.* In magazines or on Web sites, large ads, for example, gain more attention, and so do four-color ads, and this must be weighed against their higher costs. If the message is to be carried over the radio, the communicator carefully has to choose words, voice qualities (speech rate, rhythm, pitch articulation), and vocalizations (pauses, sighs, yawns). If the message is to be carried on television or given in person, then all of these elements plus body language (nonverbal cues) have to be planned. Presenters have to pay attention to their facial expressions, gestures, dress, posture, and hairstyles.

Overcoming Perceptual Distortion

As we have already noted, individuals have a substantial background of experiences, categorization schemes, prejudices, associations, needs, wants, and fears that can markedly affect what they "see" or "hear" in the message. Thus, poor children will imagine foreign coins that they have seen larger than will children who are economically better off. Pessimists will see half-empty glasses, optimists half-full ones.

This potential for distortion can work to the communicator's advantage. Messages can be relatively economical in what they say by using associations that they know people will bring to a symbol, a word, or an example. For example, readers need to see only *one* of the following symbols depicted in an ad to know that a restaurant is *not* a fast-food outlet: a tablecloth, flowers on the table, silverware, a waiter taking an order, candles, subdued lighting, upholstered chairs, wine glasses, or china. Someone sipping wine is assumed to be of a higher social class than someone holding a beer mug. Someone wearing eyeglasses is supposed to be smarter than someone without them. Colors have symbolism. In the United States, white is pure, gold is rich, blue is soothing, pastels are "modern," and so on.[9]

Symbolism, however, varies significantly both within and across cultures. In Norway, an advertisement showing a female flight attendant fluffing a pillow and offering a brandy to a tired businessman was considered offensive to the consumer ombudsman as depicting women as merely servants to men.[10] The airline company, Singapore Airlines, viewed the scene very differently, of course, since its cultural norms were very different. Similarly, showing wives making the decisions about the couple's social life would be perfectly appropriate in upper-class white American social settings but less appropriate for many immigrant groups.

Symbols can help or hurt communicators. The problem, of course, is to choose the right symbols and to be assured that your audience sees them as you do. Mr. Arneson may make an important mistake by assuming, for example, that Dr. Goldman would associate stainless steel furnishings with high-quality office decor. While Mr. Arneson should carefully plan his choice of associations, one advantage of personal communication is that a sensitive communicator can secure feedback on how the message is actually perceived and fine-tune it so that it is perceived as intended.

Even if a message is perceived in an appropriate fashion, this does not guarantee that it will be retained or, more importantly, recalled at the moment it is "needed" to influence a particular behavior. One technique to reduce this possibility is, of course, repetition. Krugman and others have suggested that up to three repetitions will improve the probability of retention under high-involvement conditions.[11] Thus, Mr. Arneson might mention the hospital's superior accounting and scheduling services several times in a conversation or over a series of conversations to increase the likelihood that the information will be permanently retained. Another technique is to link the new information to existing cognitions. Individuals are more likely to recall things that they can assimilate well.

Choosing a Medium

The message the marketer decides to use will be transmitted to the target consumer through some medium or a combination of media. The medium chosen can be *personal,* as when the organization's own spokesperson is used, or *impersonal,* as when a poster, a brochure, a magazine or newspaper advertisement, a product container, a shopping bag, a Web site, or a banner ad on the side of a truck is used. The medium can be perceived by the customer as an *advocate* for the offering or as *independent.* Thus, there are four possibilities, as suggested in Table 17-2.

In the twenty-first century, an important new medium for reaching audiences is the Web. The Web is particularly powerful with young audiences, especially teenagers. A recent study commissioned by Craver, Matthews, Smith, and Company suggests that the Web may also be a preferred vehicle for reaching "social activists."[12] The Office of National Drug Control Policy has used this medium very effectively in its teen anti-drug campaign (www.freevibe.com). In Exhibit 17-1, Beverly Schwartz and Ann Hardison of Fleishman Hillard describe their approach using a conceptual framework employing four stages parallel to those described through this book. The home page of their Web site is shown in Figure 6-6.

Choosing a Spokesperson

Choosing a spokesperson is also an important challenge. In many situations involving either paid or unpaid advocacy of a nonprofit organization, its product, service, or cause, the marketing manager will wish to use some person to deliver the message. Whom to choose and what to have the person say are crucial questions.

TABLE 17-2 Alternative Media

	Personal	**Impersonal**
Advocate	Salesperson Political supporter "Friend of the Arts"	Brochure Advertisement Billboard
Independent	Newscaster Independent researcher Noted physician	*Wall Street Journal* Government Study *Consumer Reports*

EXHIBIT 17-1

BEVERLY SCHWARTZ, ANN HARDISON, FLEISHMAN HILLARD INTERNATIONAL COMMUNICATIONS, ON USING THE WEB TO "ENGAGE" AUDIENCES

As the power and reach of the Internet have evolved, social marketers have gained an invaluable new tool for use in behavior change campaigns. While social marketers may sometimes envy product marketers for their ability to implement large-scale marketing programs to finely segment, reach and influence audience groups, the Web offers us a new tool to achieve these objectives.

The Online Integration Model to Promote Behavior Change was developed by Fleishman Hillard to generate a paradigm for online activities—something that could be used as a guide to develop a Web-based program that delivered four elements. It needed to be as strategic as it was sustainable; as informative as it was behav-

ioral; as cohesive as it was dynamic; and could transport the individual user from being a lone entity facing an inanimate computer screen—to being a part of a community. We realized that it was imperative to not only "know" our audience, but to critically examine the nexus of the audience, the market, and the technology and to understand how the interplay of those dynamics determine our approach to the development of Web components. Our objective was to create an online communication strategy that went beyond building well designed and attractive Web sites to building sites that encouraged the development of online communities with individuals personally adopting and advocating a campaign's messages.

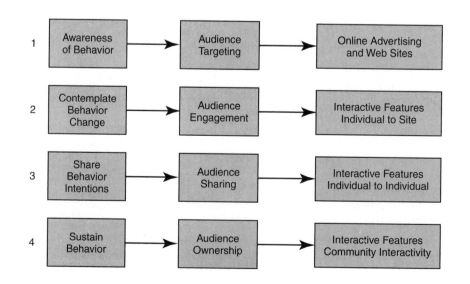

The model was developed and tested as part of the Office of National Drug Control Policy's National Youth Anti-Drug Media Campaign targeting both adolescents and parents. Since Internet-based components were determined to be vital to integrating the advertising and non-advertising activities within this campaign, we needed to extend and support the active involvement of youth and adults to the Web components, thereby ensuring a more balanced and behaviorally oriented integrated approach.

To achieve behavior change, at some point along the behavioral continuum, passivity—e.g., uni-directional intake—must be transformed into multi-directional activity. Therefore, as our interactive strategy evolved, two behavioral models—the transtheoretical model and the diffusion of innovation model—were utilized as the foundational underpinnings for the model.

The initial results of this application indicate a high degree of success in using the Internet to encourage adolescents along the behavior change continuum and, although more challenging, a real potential for success with parent audiences. Engaging partners—online and offline—has also emerged as critical to the success of the interactive strategy.

The continually evolving interactive programs in this campaign have clearly moved this social marketing campaign from a traditional "information out" approach to a revolving door where the target audiences have first become partners and then advocates for the campaign's message within their own social networks.

Spokespersons tend to be viewed positively for one of two reasons.[13] First, they may be respected as *credible experts* on a particular topic. This would be the case where a teenage former drug user or a noted medical expert is the spokesperson for an anti-drug program. The other case is where the person is not an expert but is considered by the target audience to be highly *trustworthy*. Thus, the nonprofit might use Michael Jordan or Tom Brokaw to advocate a drug-free life. The target audience may reason that although the spokesperson doesn't necessarily know anything about the subject, he or she can be counted on to tell the truth or advise one wisely. Betty Ford, when speaking about drugs, is presumably both a credible and a trustworthy person. The same can be said of Denzel Washington or baseball's Alex Rodriguez when they speak for the Boys & Girls Clubs of America (to which they once belonged).

Choosing the ideal spokesperson is not easy. Of course, the appropriate choice will depend on both the topic and the issue. One possibility is to hedge one's bets by using multiple spokespeople, as has New York City in the wake of the September 11, 2001, terrorist attacks. In all cases, it is important that the nonprofit marketer research the credibility and trustworthiness of the proposed spokespersons with the target audience. It is seldom a good idea to use someone who is very famous but who may seem to be so lacking in expertise that his or her credibility is low. Nonetheless, the right match of person and message can be very powerful (see Figure 17-5).

Once the spokesperson is chosen, the audience must believe he or she is telling the truth. Half the battle will be won if the right spokesperson is chosen. Still, alternative messages must be carefully pretested to ensure that there is little possibility that the target audience could believe that the spokesperson somehow really didn't mean it.

FIGURE 17-5 Robert Gates of the CIA Speaks for the Boy Scouts of America

Source: Boy Scouts of America. Reproduced with permission.

Message Evaluation and Selection

The marketer must select the best message from the set of alternatives, preferably with some form of formal pretesting. This calls for evaluation criteria. Twedt has suggested that contending messages be rated on three scales: *desirability, exclusiveness,* and *believability.*[14] He believes that the communication potency of a message is the product of these three factors because if any of the three has a low rating, the message's communication potency is greatly reduced.

The message must first say something desirable or interesting about the product, service, or behavior. This is not enough, however, since many competitors may be making the same claim. Therefore the message must also say something exclusive or distinctive that does not apply to every alternative. Finally, the message must be believable or provable. By asking consumers to rate different messages on desirability, exclusiveness, and believability, these messages can be evaluated for their communication potency.

For example, at one time, the March of Dimes was searching for an advertising theme to raise money for a fight against birth defects.[15] A brainstorming session led to over 20 possible messages. A group of young parents were asked to rate each message for interest, distinctiveness, and believability, assigning up to 100 points for each. The message "Seven hundred children are born each day with a birth defect," for example, scored 70, 60, and 80 on interest, distinctiveness, and believability, while "Your next baby could be born with a birth defect" scored, 58, 50, and 70 (see Figure 17-6). The first message outperforms the second and would be preferred for advertising purposes. The best overall message was "The March of Dimes has given you the polio vaccine, German measles vaccine, 110 birth defects counseling centers" (scoring 70, 80, and 90).

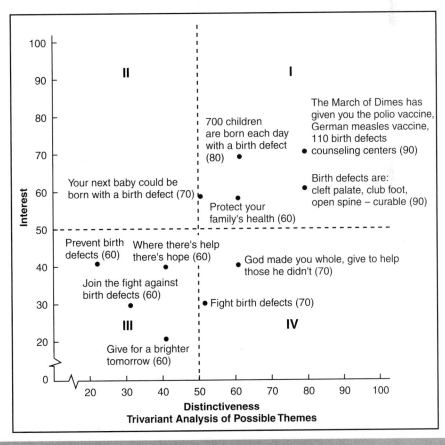

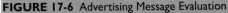

FIGURE 17-6 Advertising Message Evaluation

Source: William A. Mindak and H. Malcolm Bybee, "Marketing's Application to Fund Raising," *Journal of Marketing,* July 1971, pp. 13–18.

COMMUNICATION IN THE PREPARATION/ ACTION STAGE

Persuading target audience members to become predisposed toward acting is not the same as getting them to actually undertake the act (i.e., to move from the Contemplation Stage to the Preparation/Action Stage). A set of models around the concept of "shaping" can be useful here. This concept recognizes that there are some behavioral outcomes that a marketer wishes to have repeated that can be approached, not in one step, but by successive approximations. This is known as "shaping" behavior. Shaping can take place directly by the manipulation of the "size" of the requested behavior or indirectly by *modeling* the desired behavior either in person (e.g., in demonstration seminars) or through the media. Marketers using the media, however, lack direct feedback from the people they are trying to influence. Thus, they need to conduct research to learn whether they are having the effects they desire. Exhibit 17-2 shows how the Academy for Educational Development learned that it was modeling the wrong immunization behavior.

One of the areas in which shaping is used as a behavior change technique is in securing smoking cessation. The smoker is asked to observe his or her own smoking behavior, noting two things: the occasions on which a cigarette is smoked, and the relative importance of smoking behavior on each occasion. The smoker then determines his or her own schedule of cutting down (shaping) the smoking behavior. In a sense, the smoker slowly increases the psychological "size" of the behavioral challenge. The smoker starts by eliminating the least important smoking occasions and then works up to the most important. Smokers are trained to either reward themselves directly or to report their successes to a smoking cessation group or an individual therapist for attention, praise, and affectional reinforcement.

COMMUNICATION IN THE MAINTENANCE STAGE

The approaches offered to this point for communication strategies have been based on a model of behavior change that assumes that the BCOS factors for a particular target audience and behavior must be understood *before* the behavior change. As a consequence they are appropriate for the Precontemplation, Contemplation, and Preparation/Action Stages. In the Maintenance Stage our interest is in securing repeat behavior. Here, another communication approach is needed, known variously as *instrumental conditioning* or *behavioral modification* and is most closely associated with the name of B. F. Skinner.[16]

The approach is still grounded in the view of consumer behavior that we have used throughout this volume, namely that one of the important sets of reasons why target audience members take particular courses of action is because of the anticipated positive consequences. The BCOS approach to behavior change seeks to modify consumer's *anticipations* about possible consequences. Behavior modification attempts *to modify the consequences themselves.* By teaching the target individual that a particular action will lead to a desired reward, the probability of the action is increased. Thus, if a blood donor gets an unanticipated award certificate or a free promotional gift after being dragged by co-workers to give blood, behavior modification theory predicts that the chances are increased that the donor will return. Further, his or her attitudes toward the behavior will become more positive. The rewards after the behavior are

---

EXHIBIT 17-2

WILLIAM SMITH OF THE ACADEMY FOR EDUCATIONAL DEVELOPMENT ON MODELING IMMUNIZATION BEHAVIOR IN ECUADOR

The Academy for Educational Development works with governments around the world helping develop social marketing strategies to save infants from diarrhea, protect adults from AIDS, and help couples space their children. Immunization of children is a big priority, and the problem in many developing countries is that mothers just don't realize or believe that more than one shot is needed to protect their child fully from polio, diphtheria, or tetanus.

Working in Ecuador from 1985 to 1988, AED staff helped the government's massive program of immunization draw thousands of women for their child's first shot. But by the end of year 1, most children over one year old were still not fully immunized (three shots plus one for measles were needed).

The campaign had popularized two children, the PREMI kids, as the major theme. Focus groups and intercepts conducted after phases 1 and 2 of the campaign dis-covered the kids looked two to three years old to most mothers. We'd found the problem! The campaign's biggest visual cue modeled the wrong behavior.

The answer was a birth in the family. The PREMI kids had a baby brother, Carlitos, who became the hook to tie all our messages to "get your Carlitos" immunized by age one. A special gold star was added to a diploma women received if their child was immunized by age one. A "crystal bell" radio and TV campaign was tied into the Carlitos program to remind mothers each week, at the sound of the bell, "ask yourself—does your child need his next shot?"

Research, the right cues, and simple incentives made a difference. Full immunization coverage rose from 14 percent to 32 percent over the course of the program. Carlitos became widely known, and the certificate with a gold star became a prized possession.

Source: William Smith, Senior Vice President, Academy for Educational Development, private correspondence, December 1989.

---

referred to as *reinforcers.* Cracker Jack candied popcorn has successfully used modest prizes for years as just such reinforcers. Most commercial marketers using the Web are quick to send "Thank You" e-mails confirming orders and urging repeat patronage—often with the further inducement of a discount coupon.

There are many kinds of reinforcers, including these:

- *Economic:* Coupons, trading stamps, prizes, rebates, chances in a contest, free goods.
- *Social:* Praise, commendation, affection, conversation, attention.
- *Other:* Certificates, feedback on achievement.

The American Cancer Society makes significant use of social reinforcers in its work (see Figure 17-7).

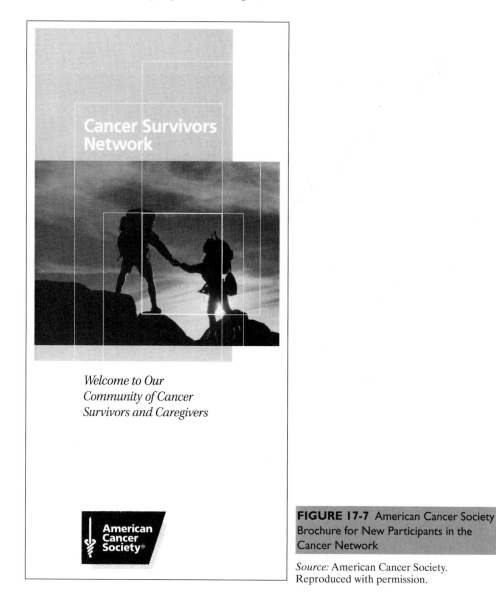

FIGURE 17-7 American Cancer Society Brochure for New Participants in the Cancer Network

Source: American Cancer Society. Reproduced with permission.

Social scientists have documented that children who are given more attention and praise after eating unfamiliar foods are more likely to repeat this behavior (and subsequently to "like" the foods) than those who are not. Simple feedback on household energy consumption has led to a reduction in energy use. Reductions in home oil use, for example, were induced by rewarding householders with a window sticker saying "We Are Saving Oil."

A great many companies have used economic rewards to get their employees to take better care of their health. At one time at Johnson & Johnson, for example, employees could earn "Live-for-Life Dollars" to be exchanged for sweat suits, socks, or fire extinguishers for attending smoking or stress workshops, exercising for 20 minutes, wearing seat belts, or installing home smoke detectors. Intermatic, Inc. gave employees who quit cigarettes for a year a trip for two to Las Vegas. Hospital Corporation of America paid workers 24 cents for each mile walked or run, each quarter mile swum, or each four miles bicycled. The government of Bellevue, Washington, and firms like the Berol Corporation and King Broadcasting in Seattle gave rewards negatively related to the amount of health insurance claims an employee filed. Speedcall Corporation gave a $7 bonus for each week an employee didn't smoke on the job. In four years, the number of smokers in the company fell 65 percent and the number of health insurance claims by quitters fell 50 percent.[17]

There is some controversy about what patterns of reinforcement should be used. In general, *constant reinforcement* (rewarding every instance of the desired behavior) yields the fastest rate of learning but also the fastest extinction of the behavior when the reinforcements are stopped. However, *variable or random reinforcement* yields slower rates of initial learning but also slower extinction. The reasons offered for this finding are that during the reinforcement period, the subject is initially not sure which behavior (if any) is being rewarded. This accounts for the slower rate of initial learning. Then, when rewards *are* linked to the behavior, the subject must interpolate his or her own rewards on those occasions when the externally provided rewards are absent.

In a study, Deslauriers and Everett found that offering 10-cent tokens to bus riders had a positive effect on bus usage. However, they found that variable reinforcement (every third passenger) was just as effective as continuing reinforcement and, of course, much more economical.[18]

For this type of behavioral modification to work, certain simple conditions must be present:

1. The desired behavior must be under the individual's control (thus, it is not particularly effective with physical drug dependency).
2. There must be a clear link between the behavior and the reinforcement, although this need not always be apparent to the subject; the closer the reward is in time to the behavior, the greater the effect (thus, praising someone two days after a desired behavior—for example, cutting out certain smoking occasions—is less effective than immediate praise).
3. The reinforcer must constitute a reward for the individual (thus, praise from a feared autocratic schoolteacher would not be as reinforcing for a schoolchild as praise from a peer).

In our continuing example, once Dr. Goldman begins to send patients to St. Anthony's, Mr. Arneson should not consider his marketing task completed. He should find opportunities to reward Dr. Goldman for her behavior. Options could include taking her to lunch, having other staffers come around to say "Glad you're here," and/or paying especially close attention to the patients she refers and rewarding *them* for their patronage.

INTEGRATION

It is critical that all elements of the communication program be integrated. Themes should be consistent. The "look" should be similar. Spokespeople in one medium should be carried over into others. Where relevant, one communication component (e.g., a Web site) can replicate another component (an advertisement) and lead the audience to a third (an 800 number) that sends out a final component (a brochure that repeats the themes and look of the ads and Web site).

Such integration creates opportunities to build repeat impressions that increase the likelihood of the desired effects in knowledge, perceptions, and behavior. However, in complex, large nonprofit organizations (and even some smaller ones with multiple locations), ensuring an integrated communication strategy across chapters and divisions requires extensive training and constant reinforcement. One of the central roles of complex nonprofits like the United Way and the YMCA is providing other organizational units with communication templates that can be adapted to local needs but that maintain a carefully crafted integrated campaign (see Figure 17-8).

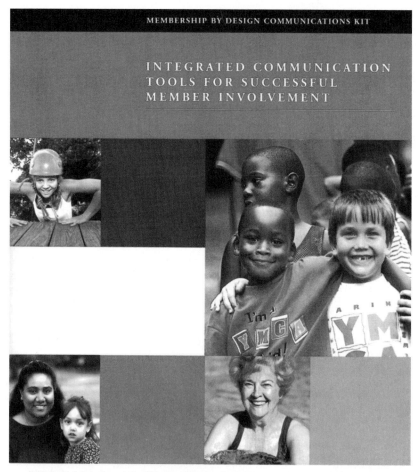

FIGURE 17-8 Integrated Communications Kit for YMCA

Source: YMCA. Reproduced with permission.

SUMMARY

Every contact a nonprofit has with its many publics directly or indirectly is an occasion for communication and influence. These contacts may be carried out by many different departments or people using diverse vehicles ranging all the way from standard paid and unpaid media to package designs, corporate publicity releases, personal sales presentations, and even promotional "gimmicks" like shopping bags and T-shirts. For programs to be effective, however, they must be grounded in a clear understanding of communication processes.

Communication typically involves persuasion. This requires the preparation and transmittal of specific messages. Messages must be encoded by the marketer, communicated through media, and then decoded by the receiver. At each of these stages, considerable noise can be introduced into the communication process such that the accumulated effect of the received message is very different from what was intended. In general, the more parties involved in the communication system and the less control the marketer has over them, the greater the chance of miscommunication. Marketers use formal and informal feedback to track these effects. Where communication is face to face, feedback can be easily obtained. Where it is not, as in media campaigns, pre- and posttests of message strategies must always be carried out.

Six steps are involved in developing effective messages. First, the communication objectives must be determined. Second, messages must be generated. These can be rational, emotional, or moral, or they can be generated from the BCOS framework. Third, thought must be given to how these communications can overcome consumers' tendencies to selectively expose themselves or attend to messages in which they are interested. The style, tone, wording, order, and format of the messages are all critical to getting a message noticed. Fourth, thought must be given to constructing the communications to overcome perceptual distortion, the tendency to add to and reinterpret what is actually in the message based on the audience member's own past experience, motives, and biases. Fifth, a medium must be chosen to convey the message to achieve maximum impact. Often, in the nonprofit sector, this means choosing a spokesperson. If a spokesperson is used, the marketer must ensure that he or she is credible and trustworthy and that the message is so clear that it cannot be distorted by a target audience. Sixth, the marketers must evaluate all the possible messages and select the ones that are most desirable, exclusive, and believable. The BCOS model developed in Chapter 4 is a useful framework guiding this set of decisions.

The marketer must recognize that strategies to influence behavior need not rely only on advanced communication—that is, on first changing cognitions in order to change behavior. Other strategies, such as behavior modification, can simply manipulate rewards. These strategies rely on a different model, in which it is assumed that changing behavior is an adequate goal in itself and that, once behavior is changed, perception may also change.

QUESTIONS

1. Referring to the communication process model in Figure 17-1, identify the steps in communicating the benefits of a public (city) library to public school students. Identify the possible sources/types of noise that might affect the communications to students. How can the marketer minimize those noises?

2. Outline the possible emotions that a marketer could leverage to generate a greater enrollment in organ donation programs. In each case, give an example of a message or advertisement that would embody the emotion and some of the risks that might go along with its use.

3. Refer to the assimilation/contrast theory of Sherif et al. as presented in the chapter, and consider the use of stem cell research to improve science and medical treatment. Devise a range of statements that would comprise a continuum from *strongly for* to *strongly against* the use of stem cell research. Interview five people and ask them which statements are (a) their present position; (b) positions they might accept; or (c) positions they would reject. Develop a message strategy based on this research.

4. List 10 spokespeople who might be considered for a safe driving campaign targeted at suburban professionals. Develop a set of criteria which can be used to evaluate these spokespeople. Rate the candidates on the criteria and select a spokesperson. Develop a short message that the spokesperson would deliver to influence the target.

5. Behavior can often be influenced by merely showing individuals how to act and then rewarding them once they comply. How might this principle be used to get middle-class adults to attend operas? What types of rewards might be used to encourage repeat patronage?

NOTES

1. See, for example, Peter L. Wright, "The Cognitive Process Mediating Acceptance of Advertising," *Journal of Marketing Research*, February 1973, pp. 53–62.

2. The classic work in this field is Leon Festinger, *A Theory of Cognitive Dissonance* (Evanston, Ill.: Row, Peterson, 1957). See also J. W. Brehm and A. R. Cohen, *Explorations in Cognitive Dissonance* (New York: John Wiley, 1962). For an example showing consumers' willingness to live with dissonance in a nonprofit context, see M. T. O'Keefe, "The Anti-Smoking Commercials: A Study of Television's Impact on Behavior," *Public Opinion Quarterly*, 1971, pp. 242–248.

3. Carolyn W. Sherif, Muzafer Sherif, and Ronald Nebergill, *Attitude and Attitude Change* (New Haven, Conn.: Yale University Press, 1961).

4. See J. T. Bertrand, "Selective Avoidance on Health Topics: A Field Test," *Communications Research*, July 1979, pp. 271–294. See also Wolfgang Schaefer, "Selective Perception in Operation," *Journal of Advertising Research*, February 1979, pp. 59–60.

5. "Death Turns Up the Thermostat," *Newsweek*, October 15, 1984.

6. Leon S. Robertson, Albert G. Kelley, Brian O'Neill, Charles W. Wixom, Richard S. Eiswirth, and William Haddon, Jr., "A Controlled Study of the Effect of Television Messages on Safety Belt Use," *American Journal of Public Health*, November 1974, p. 1077 ff.

7. See Michael L. Ray and William L. Wilkie, "Fear, The Potential of an Appeal Neglected by Marketing," *Journal of Marketing*, January 1970, pp. 55–56; Brian Sternthal and

C. Samuel Craig, "Fear Appeals Revisited and Revised," *Journal of Consumer Research,* December 1974, pp. 22–34; John J. Burnett and Robert E. Wilkes, "Fear Appeals to Segments Only," *Journal of Advertising Research,* Vol. 20, No. 5, October 1980, pp. 21–24.

8. Richard P. Bagozzi and David J. Moore, "Public Service Advertisements: Emotions and Empathy Guide Prosocial Behavior," *Journal of Marketing,* 58 (January 1994), pp. 56–70.

9. Edward T. Hall, *The Silent Language* (Garden City, N.J.: Doubleday, 1973).

10. John Karevoll, "Singapore Girl Nixed in Norway," *Advertising Age,* March 23, 1981, pp. m-2–3.

11. Herbert E. Krugman, "Why Three Exposures May Be Enough," *Journal of Advertising Research,* December 1972, pp. 11–15.

12. *Socially Engaged Internet Users: Prospects for Online Philanthropy and Activism* (Arlington, VA: CMS and The Mellman Group, 1999).

13. See Brian Sternthal, R. R. Dholakia, and Clark Leavitt, "The Persuasive Effect of Source Credibility: Test of Cognitive Response," *Journal of Consumer Research,* Vol. 4 (1978), pp. 252–250; and C. Samuel Craig and John M. McCann, "Assessing Communications Effects on Energy Conservation," *Journal of Consumer Research,* Vol. 5, September 1978, pp. 82–88.

14. Dik Warren Twedt, "How to Plan New Products, Improve Old Ones, and Create Better Advertising," *Journal of Marketing,* January 1969, pp. 53–57.

15. See William A. Mindak and H. Malcolm Bybee, "Marketing's Application to Fund Raising," *Journal of Marketing,* July 1971, pp. 13–18.

16. Michael Rothschild and William C. Gaidis, "Behavioral Learning Theory: Its Relevance to Marketing and Promotions," *Journal of Marketing,* Spring 1981, pp. 70–78.

17. "Giving Goodies to the Good," *Time,* November 18, 1985, p. 98.

18. Brian C. Deslauriers and Peter B. Everett, "Effects of Intermittent and Continuing Token Reinforcement on Bus Ridership," *Journal of Applied Psychology,* Vol. 62, No. 4, 1977, pp. 369–375.

CHAPTER 18

Managing Communications: Advertising and Personal Persuasion

Organ donations are a high-priority need in any society. This is especially so in industrialized countries where increasingly sophisticated surgical techniques and other life-prolonging interventions make the availability of viable organs even more likely to have major long-term benefits. Yet in a typical year, more than 65,000 men, women, and children in the United States wait for organs that are not there.

Advertising agency Arnold Communications decided to take on the challenge of filling this important gap in our health infrastructure as part of a campaign adopted by the Advertising Council. The client for the campaign was the Coalition on Organ & Tissue Donation, and was launched during National Organ and Tissue Donor Awareness Week in April 2000.

Formative research leading up to the creative development for the campaign identified a crucial piece of information that subsequently constituted the major campaign theme. Contrary to what many believed, the majority of Americans were already aware of the need for organs. So, "awareness" was not the need (the target audience is not in the Precontemplation Stage). Further, over one-half of American adults had signed a donor card or indicated on their driver's licenses that they wanted to donate in the event of death. So, clearly the target audience had thought about the issue and was well through the Contemplation Stage.

The roadblock was at the Preparation/Action Stage. What the formative research discovered was that the actual donation of an organ was too often thwarted at the point at which a relative had to sign a consent form for organ donation after the death of a loved one. It turned out that a great many people who wanted to donate their organs never had a serious conversation with their loved ones about that desire. And so, in the traumatic moment of death when these loved ones were naturally distraught and grief-stricken, a significant number of them did not grant the necessary permission.

Therefore, the Arnold Communications campaign focused on generating conversations about the permission behavior with the tagline "Talk to Your Family About Donating Life." The ad emphasized that this conversation should be undertaken with simplicity and openness and that it really is about extending "life," not about dying.

Source: Drawn from *The Public Service Advertising Bulletin*, March/April 2000.

The nonprofit marketer has a large number of tools available for carrying a message to a target audience. There are six main tools, and each differs in the coding and encoding problems (discussed in the previous chapter) it presents to managers.[1]

- *Paid advertising: Any paid form of nonpersonal presentation and promotion of an offer by an identified sponsor through a formal communication medium.* Paid advertising permits total control over encoded message content and over the nature of the medium, plus substantial control of the scheduling of the message (and therefore its specific environment). However, paid advertising permits no control over message decoding by the audience and little (or, at best, lagged) feedback on the received message.

- *Unpaid (public service) advertising: Any form of advertising in which space or time for the placement of the advertisement is free.* Marketer control is similar to that with paid advertising except that there is very little control over the scheduling of the message and therefore the audiences reached. Many public service radio or television advertisements appear after midnight or on Sunday mornings when the audience is small and the media have unsold spots.

- *Joint advertising: Any form of advertising where a partner pays for the message placement often as part of the partner's own advertisement.* Many Internet banner ads for nonprofits are on the Web sites of other organizations, often corporations, that consider the ads as either good strategy for themselves or part of their public service. Depending on the partnership agreement, the nonprofit may have great or limited control over the message content. The audience is obviously whomever the partner normally reaches.

- *Promotions: Short-term incentives to encourage purchase or sales of a product or service or the performance of a behavior.* Marketer control is substantial, although the decoding of specific promotions by the receiver is not controllable.

- *Publicity: Nonpersonal stimulation of behavior for an offering by securing the reporting of significant news about the offer in a published medium or on radio, television, the Web, or the stage that is not paid for by the sponsor.* Here, the marketer's control over message encoding and the medium varies depending on whether journalists or scriptwriters will use and revise the message. Some feedback is possible from journalists or from selected target audiences.

- *Personal persuasion: Oral presentation of information about an offering in a conversation with one or more prospective target audience members for the purpose of securing a desired transaction.* In personal persuasion, the organization has less control over encoding, that is, what the individual actually says. The individual, however, has excellent opportunities to secure feedback on how the message is being received.

In this chapter, we consider specific issues relevant to using two principal forms of paid communication: advertising and personal persuasion. The next chapter deals with unpaid or "earned" communication. We begin with a cautionary note.

EXCESSIVE RELIANCE ON ADVERTISING

One of the characteristics of the organization-centered nonprofit organizations described in Chapter 2 is that they rely excessively on advertising and promotion to achieve their objectives. As we noted, this is partly because they have a distorted view of what it takes to change people's behavior, but it is also partly due to what might be called "client pressure." A great many nonprofit CEOs and general managers equate marketing with advertising. When they want better marketing, they *think* they want more advertising.

Therefore, when considering advertising and promotion, nonprofit marketing specialists must be vigilant to make sure of the following:

1. Advertising and promotion are not relied upon as the only way—or even the primary way—to achieve behavioral objectives. Almost always, advertising can only get consumers aware and interested in a new behavior. It is much less effective at achieving final action. That is, it is useful in the first two of the Stages of Change but not the last two.

2. The objectives for advertising and promotion are within the nonprofit's reach. A great many naive general managers think that a good dose of advertising is all that is needed to solve performance problems for the organization. They also expect advertising to make dramatic changes when only modest goals are more realistic.

3. There is a careful consideration of the ethical implications of advertising. Because advertising must simply convey messages and because they often use symbols to imply absent traits, there is a significant potential to deceive. As we discussed earlier in this book, those with the public trust that nonprofits and government agencies have should be especially diligent that they do not abuse this trust. Those who want to achieve "good" must *do* good.

ADVERTISING

Advertising consists of nonpersonal forms of communication conducted through paid media under clear sponsorship. It involves such varied media as magazines and newspapers, radio and television, outdoor media (posters, signs, and skywriting), novelties (matchboxes, calendars), cards (car, bus), catalogues, directories and references, programs and menus, circulars, Internet Web sites and messages, and direct mail. It can be carried out for such diverse purposes as long-term buildup of the organization's name (institutional advertising); long-term buildup of a particular offering (product or service advertising) or brand (brand advertising); information dissemination about a sale, service, or event (classified advertising); and so on.

Total media advertising spending in the United States aimed at both consumers and business was estimated to be $191.6 billion in 2000.[2] Advertising is coming into increasing use by public and private nonprofit organizations. The major categories of nonprofit organization advertising are as follows:

1. *Political advertising.* Political advertising has skyrocketed in recent elections. Total campaign expenditures (much of it advertising) in the 2000 U.S. presidential race alone were over $342 billion.[3]

2. *Social cause advertising.* For many years, the Advertising Council, Inc., a nonprofit organization financed by American industry, has used advertising to promote social causes such as brotherhood, safe driving, aid to education, religious faith, forest fire prevention, and so on. It accepts a number of causes each year and solicits donated services from advertising agencies and media to prepare and broadcast this advertising. The estimated value of the space and time for this advertising was $1.5 billion in 2001. It tends to avoid controversial causes. Social cause organiza-

tions such as ecology groups, advocacy groups, and health care agencies have also stepped up their advertising budgets to get their messages out to the public.[4]

3. *Charitable advertising.* Charitable advertising is specifically directed toward raising donations on a regular or emergency basis; the money is used to help the needy, unfortunate, or sick. Examples include the paid or donated advertising done by the Red Cross, United Way, Easter Seal Society, and so on.

4. *Government advertising.* Various government units are frequent advertisers. Municipalities, states, and counties spend considerable sums to attract new residents, tourists, and industrial developers. Park and recreation departments advertise outdoor recreational facilities. Police departments issue messages to the general public on safety issues. The federal government has used paid advertising to sell products (U.S. postage stamps), services (veterans' hospitals), and behaviors (energy conservation).[5]

5. *Private nonprofit advertising.* Colleges, museums, symphonies, hospitals, and religious organizations all have strong communication programs and develop annual reports, direct mailings, classified ads, broadcast messages, and other forms of advertising. Various professionals whose ethical codes formerly banned advertising (social workers, psychologists, and so on) have been free to advertise ever since the Federal Trade Commission ruled that the American Medical Association could not prevent physician members from advertising.

6. *Association advertising.* Professional and trade associations have substantially increased their use of paid advertising. The American Bankers Association, the American Dental Association, and the National Association of Realtors spend several million dollars annually on television and print advertising and on their Web sites. Their common objective is to improve their public image and also the public's knowledge of their services. Public service advertising programs have recently been undertaken by associations representing lawyers, accountants, engineers, and nurses.

In developing an advertising program, marketing management must make five major decisions (see Figure 18-1). We considered message issues in the preceding chapter and discuss the remaining four decisions in the following sections.

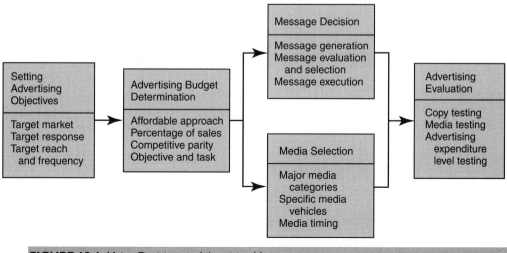

FIGURE 18-1 Major Decisions in Advertising Management

SETTING ADVERTISING OBJECTIVES

Before an advertising program and budget can be developed, advertising objectives must be set. These objectives must flow from prior decisions about the target market, market positioning, and marketing mix. The marketing strategy defines advertising's job in the total marketing mix.

Developing advertising objectives calls for defining the target market, target response, and target reach and frequency.

Target Market Selection

A marketing communicator must start with a clear target audience (or, in well-segmented programs, audiences, plural) in mind. The audience may be potential future targets, current participants, and those who might influence them. The audience may consist of individuals, groups, particular publics, or the general public. The target audience has a crucial influence on the communicator's decisions on *what* to say, *how* to say it, *when* to say it, *where* to say it, and *who* should say it.

Consider this in terms of a small private college in Iowa called Pottsville. Suppose it is seeking applicants from Nebraska, and it estimates that there are 30,000 graduating high school seniors in Nebraska who might be interested in Pottsville College. The college must decide whether to aim its communications primarily at high school counselors in Nebraska high schools or at the high school students themselves. Beyond this, it may want to develop communications to reach parents and other people who are influential in the college decision process. Each target market would warrant a different advertising campaign.

Target Response

Once the target audience is identified, the marketing communicator must define the target response that is sought. The ultimate response, of course, is behavior. In highly involving and infrequent decisions, however, behavior is the end result of the target audience going through all of the Stages of Change. The marketing communicator needs to know the current stage of the decision process of the target audience and which stage it should be moved to next. Two important values of the Stages of Change model are that it suggests obvious segmentation possibilities and it can be used to track progress.

It is also a framework that can encompass more extensive lists of specific communication objectives for advertising. Colley distinguished 52 possible advertising objectives in his *Defining Advertising Goals for Measured Advertising Results* (DAGMAR). The various advertising objectives can be categorized on the basis of whether their aim is to inform (Precontemplation Stage), persuade (Contemplation Stage and Preparation/Action Stage), or remind (Maintenance Stage).[6]

Target Reach and Frequency

The third objective a nonprofit manager must set is the optimal *target reach and frequency* of the advertising. Funds for advertising are rarely so abundant that everyone in the target audience can be reached, and reached with sufficient frequency. Marketing management must decide what percentage of the audience to reach with what exposure frequency per period. Pottsville College, for example, might decide to use local newspapers and buy 20,000 advertising exposures. This leaves a wide choice available concerning target reach and frequency. Pottsville could place an advertisement in one paper in a large city and reach 20,000 different students, or it could place two different ads a week apart in five smaller papers and reach 10,000 students twice, and so on. The issue is how many exposures are needed to create the desired response, given the market's state of readiness. One exposure could be enough to convert students from being unaware to being aware. It would not be enough to convert students from awareness to preference.

ADVERTISING BUDGET DETERMINATION

We assume that Pottsville College is using the preferred objective-and-task approach to setting advertising budgets (see Chapter 11). Suppose that Pottsville wants to place two ads in five papers to reach 10,000 students twice. The gross number of exposures would be 20,000. Supposing the average ad in each paper costs $2,000 and design costs for the two ads are $5,000, Pottsville will need a rough advertising budget of $25,000.

In addition to estimating the total size of the required advertising budget, a determination must be made about how the budget should be allocated over different market segments, geographical areas, and time periods. In practice, advertising budgets are allocated to segments of demand according to their respective populations or sales levels or in accordance with some other indicator of market potential. It is common to spend twice as much advertising money in segment B as in segment A if segment B has twice the level of response potential. In principle, the budget should be allocated to different segments according to their expected marginal response to advertising. A budget is well allocated when it is not possible to shift dollars from one segment to another and increase total market response.

MEDIA SELECTION

Once the advertising budget is set for a given market segment, region, and time period, the next step is to allocate this budget across media categories and vehicles. Presumably some thought will already have been given to this problem, since the selection of a target segment inevitably leads to the use of media to which the segment is most frequently exposed. Also, the media considered will affect one's thinking about the size of the overall budget; a television campaign is much more costly than a radio campaign. Finally, the choice of media will affect the kind of messages one can use.

There are three basic steps in the media selection process: choosing among major media categories, choosing among specific media vehicles, and timing. An important consideration here is finding the *aperture* (opening) when the target audience is likely to be most receptive to a campaign's message. If the target audience is in the Precontemplation Stage, the marketer wants an opening where the target audience would not be defensive or dismissive of the message. For those who are at the Contemplation Stage, the marketer would want to know where the target audience expects to see useful information or where he or she goes to look for it. A viewer of the network evening news is more likely to see a lot of ads for prescription drugs and investment services. This is in part because the audience is proven to be upscale but is also likely to be in a thoughtful, concerned mood—and therefore receptive to messages about their health and finances.

Choosing Among Major Media Categories

The first step calls for allocating the advertising budget to the major *media categories*. These categories must be examined for their capacity to deliver reach, frequency, and impact. In order of their advertising volume, they are newspapers, television, radio, magazines, cinema, and outdoor advertising, although Internet expenditures are catching up. Advertising expenditures in the four largest world ad markets in 2000 are shown in Table 18-1, showing, for example, the greater importance of television and outdoor advertising in Japan and newspapers and magazines in Germany and the United Kingdom:[7]

Marketers choose among media categories by considering the following variables:

1. *Target audience media habits.* For example, radio, television, and the Internet are the most effective media for reaching teenagers.
2. *Product, service, or behavior.* Media categories have different potentialities for demonstration, visualization, explanation, believability, and color. Television, for example, is the most effective medium for demonstrating how a product or service works or for creating an emotional effect, while magazines are ideal for accurately reproducing the appearance of a social scene or the victim of some crime.
3. *Message.* A message announcing an emergency blood drive tomorrow requires radio, the Internet, newspapers, or posters. A message containing a great deal of technical data might require specialized magazines or direct mailings. Messages that would benefit from consumers adding their own images and fantasies might be most effective on the radio.
4. *Cost.* Television is very expensive, and newspaper advertising, the Internet, and billboards are relatively inexpensive. What counts, of course, is the cost per thousand exposures rather than the total cost. In developing countries, posters are often highly cost-effective.

The advantages and disadvantages of the major media are summarized in Table 18-2.

On the basis of these characteristics, the marketer has to decide how to allocate the given budget to the major media categories. The U.S. Army Recruiting Command, for example, might decide to allocate $14 million to evening television spots, $4 million to male-oriented magazines, and $2 million to daily newspapers.

TABLE 18-1   Advertising Expenditures by Media, Top Four Countries, 2000

	United States	*Japan*	*Germany*	*United Kingdom*
Total Spending (in $billions)	*$134.3*	*$33.2*	*$21.6*	*$15.8*
Television	38.7%	45.1%	23.1%	33.5%
Newspapers	34.3%	26.8%	45.1%	39.2%
Radio	13.0%	5.0%	3.6%	4.7%
Magazines	12.2%	9.9%	24.0%	17.3%
Outdoor	1.8%	13.2%	3.2%	4.3%
Cinema	—	—	0.9%	1.0%

Source: Advertising Age Dataplace at adage.com/dataplace/topmarkets.

TABLE 18-2	Strengths and Weaknesses of Alternative Media for Nonprofits

Strengths	Weaknesses
Television	
High impact	High production costs
Audience selectivity	Uneven delivery by market
Schedule when needed	Upfront commitments required
Fast awareness	
Sponsorship availabilities	
Merchandising possible	
Radio	
Low cost per contact	Nonintrusive medium
Audience selectivity	Audience per spot small
Schedule when needed	No visual impact
Length can vary	High total cost for good reach
Personalities available	Clutter within spot markets
Tailor weight to market	
Magazines	
Audience selectivity	Long lead time needed
Editorial association	Readership accumulates slowly
Long life	Uneven delivery by market
Large audience per insert	Cost premiums for regional or demographic editions
Excellent color	
Minimal waste	
Merchandising possible	
Newspapers	
Large audience	Difficult to target narrowly
Immediate reach	Highest waste
Short lead time	High cost for national use
Market flexibility	Minimum positioning control
Good upscale coverage	Cluttered
Posters, Billboards	
High reach	No depth of message
High frequency of exposure	High cost for national use
Minimal waste	Best positions already taken
Can localize	No audience selectivity
Immediate registration	Poor coverage in some areas
Flexible scheduling	Minimum one-month purchase

Source: A Program Manager's Guide to Media Planning (Washington, D.C.: SOMARC, The Futures Group, no date). Reproduced with permission.

However, in developing countries, the preferred medium is radio, because it is ubiquitous and does not require literacy. Many social marketers combine advertising on radio with "social" soap operas that are heard by millions. Airtime for the latter is typically provided free, although the scripts must be paid for. Soap opera subjects have included family planning, immunization, and AIDS prevention. Some social marketing programs have even given away radios run by hand-cranked batteries so that poor people in remote areas can have access to social messages as well as the news.

Direct Mail

A medium increasingly being used by nonprofits, particularly for fundraising and the promotion of events, is direct mail. The Direct Marketing Association estimates that direct mail expenditures were $44.6 billion in 2000 split about three-fifths to consumer campaigns and two-fifths to business-to-business direct mail.[8] Bill Novelli, now CEO of AARP, has suggested that direct mail has seven important advantages for nonprofit marketers (and these advantages also apply to the Web):[9]

1. It tends to be very focused: It can achieve maximum impact on a specific target market.
2. It can be private and confidential, a major advantage for charities and programs dealing with venereal disease, child abuse, and AIDS.
3. Purchase of direct-mail services is not forbidden to government agencies, whereas purchase of broadcast, newspaper, magazine, outdoor, and other media sometimes is forbidden.
4. Cost per contact and cost per response can often be very low, which is an important appeal to impoverished nonprofits.
5. Results are quite often clearly measurable, and this can help make nonprofit marketing programs more accountable. The American Heart Association may not know its effect on cholesterol levels, but it can calculate how many responded to a specific mail promotion of a low-cholesterol cookbook and what cost it incurred per inquiry.
6. Small-scale tests of proposed strategies are very feasible with direct mail. In fact, direct mail is an ideal field-test vehicle. A number of marketing factors can be varied over several mailings and the results compared to baseline measures. In tests of other media, it is often difficult to link a specific surge in sales to, say, a flight of radio advertisements. By contrast, if more cookbook requests come in from those who receive a mailing with a message about cholesterol involving a medium level of fear than from those who get a high-fear or low-fear treatment, it is hard not to conclude that a medium-fear message works best.
7. The effectiveness of direct mail can be assessed directly in terms of *behavior* (e.g., orders, requests, and inquiries), whereas other media assessments usually require attitude and awareness indicators that are fraught with measurement problems.

The Internet

In developed countries, a vehicle more and more often considered in the promotional mix is the Web. The figures in Table 18-1 do not include the Internet. In 2001 there were over 70 million subscribers to Internet connections via dial-up, DSL, cable modem, Internet TV, and satellite. Advertising spending was about $5.7 billion in 2001 and is expected by Jupiter Media Research to rise to $15.4 billion by 2006.[10] Many nonprofits have found this vehicle a powerful tool for reaching upscale markets and young people. The potential for interactive "conversations" with those one wishes to influence are immense. However, it is still a medium about which much is still experimental. For example, despite early enthusiasm, there is now much skepticism in the commercial sector about the value of banner ads.

Web advertising has four additional advantages important to nonprofit marketers:

1. It is possible to track performance (Web site hits) minute by minute (for example, if an advertisement is changed or a new offer is made available).
2. Messages can be changed more or less whenever the marketer wants. Underperforming ads can be quickly replaced with better options.
3. Messages can potentially be tailored to "segments of one" if the marketer is able to obtain any incoming clues about the person visiting the Web site.
4. Messages can be inexpensively rotated on a random schedule to keep a campaign fresh and reduce target market fatigue.

The latter is exemplified in Figure 18-2, which shows a Web page for the anti-drug campaign of the Office of National Drug Control Policy through Fleishman Hillard. A key feature of the campaign is to get young people to substitute some other activity or interest for doing drugs—the "anti-Drug." On this page, the target audience has a chance to "talk back" to the site and, indirectly, to others who might visit it in the future.

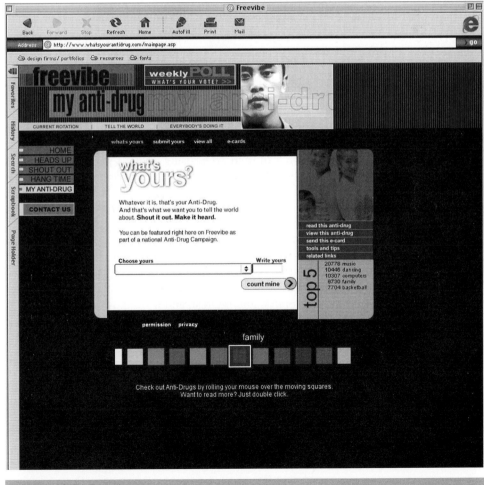

FIGURE 18-2 Freevibe.com

Selecting Specific Media Vehicles

The next step is to choose the specific media vehicles within each media category that would produce the desired response in the most cost-effective way. Consider the category of male-oriented magazines, which includes *Playboy, GQ, Esquire, Motorcycle,* and so on. The media planner in the United States can turn to several volumes put out by Standard Rate and Data that provide circulation and cost data for different ad sizes, color options, ad positions, and quantities of insertions. Beyond this, the media planner evaluates the different magazines on qualitative characteristics such as credibility, prestige, availability of geographical or occupational editions, reproduction quality, editorial climate, lead time, and psychological impact. The media planner makes a final judgment as to which specific vehicles will deliver the best reach, frequency, and impact for the money.

Of course, media choice in part depends on the nature of the message. For example, when the Partnership for a Drug-Free America creates a message featuring Andy MacDonald, one of the world's best skateboarders, for a TV ad aimed at kids (Figure 18-3), it will seek placement in programming watched by what psychologists call "sensation seekers," a segment found to be particularly prone to experiment with—and use—drugs.

Deciding on Media Timing

The third step in media selection is *timing.* It breaks down into a macro problem and a micro problem. The macro problem is that of *cyclical* or *seasonal timing.* For most products and services, audience size and interest vary at different times of the year. There is not much interest in Senator X until her reelection comes up or much interest in university affairs during the summer. Most marketers do not advertise when there is little interest, spending the bulk of their advertising budgets just as natural interest in the product or service class begins to increase and when it peaks. Counter-seasonal or counter-cyclical advertising is still rare in practice. The concept of aperture is relevant here. The marketer seeks to reach the target audience members that are most likely to be interested and receptive to the intended messages.

The other problem is more of a micro problem, that of the *short-run timing* of advertising. How should advertising be spaced during a short period of, say, one week? Consider three possible patterns. The first is called *burst advertising* and consists of concentrating all the exposures in a very short period of time, say, all in one day. Presumably, this will attract maximum attention and interest, and if recall is good, the effect will last for a while. The second pattern is *continuous advertising,* in which the exposures appear evenly throughout the period. This may be most effective when the audience buys or uses the product frequently and needs to be continuously reminded. The third pattern is *intermittent advertising,* in which intermittent small bursts of advertising appear with no advertising in between. This pattern is able to create a little more attention than continuous advertising, yet it has some of the reminder advantage of continuous advertising.

Timing decisions should take three factors into consideration. *Audience turnover* is the rate at which the target audience changes between two periods. The greater the turnover, the more continuous the advertising should be. *Behavior frequency* is the number of times the target audience takes the action one is trying to influence (e.g., smoking, not wearing seat belts). The more frequent the behavior, the more the adver-

Partnership for a Drug-Free America

"ANDY MACDONALD" :30

DETV-1005

7/27/99

FIGURE 18-3 Partnership for a Drug-Free America

Source: Partnership for a Drug-Free America. Reproduced with permission.

tising should be continuous. The *forgetting rate* is the rate at which a given message will be forgotten or a given behavior change extinguished. Again, the faster the forgetting, the more continuous the advertising should be.

A related issue is the sequencing of various types of advertising in an overall strategic program. An example of such a program is shown in Exhibit 18-1.

EXHIBIT 18-1

SEQUENCED STRATEGY AT ROYCE HALL

The performing arts program at UCLA's Royce Hall has been highly successful because it attracts high-quality performers. Attendance has been further enhanced by the careful development of well-thought-out marketing strategies. One feature is the careful *sequencing* of communications for each season. In a recent year, the program carried out the following eight steps:

1. First, announcements were sent to past program subscribers to give them first chance at the best seats for season subscriptions and, not incidentally, to make them feel that they were receiving special attention.

2. After a suitable delay, full-page advertisements in local papers announced the entire program to the general public and solicited season ticket subscriptions.

3. Once season ticket subscription orders plateaued, single ticket availability was announced to past subscribers by mail and then to the general public.

4. At this point, attention was shifted to recapturing past season ticket subscribers who had not renewed through relatively high-cost telephone marketing (telemarketing).

5. Just before the season started, mailers were sent to subscribers, nonsubscribers, and others, and newspaper ads were placed reintroducing the fall portion of the schedule.

6. Radio ads, both paid and public service, and quarter-page newspaper ads then promoted the first (and each subsequent) performance.

7. Flyers were sent to those who subscribed to or bought single tickets for one specific series promoting *other* similar events in which they might be interested.

8. Finally, on the night of the performances, posters were hung on campus, and ads promoting related events were placed in programs, presumably catching concert-goers at the moment when they were most in the spirit of "going out to the theater."

Advertising Evaluation

The final step in the effective use of advertising is *advertising evaluation.* The most important components are copy testing, media testing, and expenditure-level testing.

Copy testing can occur both before an ad is put into actual media (pretesting) and after it has been printed, broadcast, or put on the Web (posttesting). The purpose of *ad pretesting* is to make improvements in the advertising copy to the fullest extent prior to its release. There are several methods of ad pretesting:

1. *Comprehension testing.* A critical prerequisite for any advertisement is that it be comprehensible. This can be a major problem when dealing with less-educated or even illiterate audiences. When words are used in the advertisement, a marketing staff member can apply one or more readability formulas to predict comprehension. These formulas measure the length of sentences and the number of polysyllabic words. One popular measure of comprehensibility called SMOG has been used by the Office of

Cancer Communications of the National Cancer Institute to test public and patient education health materials.

2. *Formal questionnaires.* Here a panel of target consumers or advertising experts is given a set of alternative ads and fills out rating questionnaires—possibly through the mail or over the Web. Sometimes a single question is raised, such as "Which of these ads do you think would influence you most?" Or a more elaborate form consisting of several rating scales may be used, such as the print ad version shown in Table 18-3. Here the person evaluates the ad's attention strength, read-through strength, cognitive strength, affective strength, and behavioral strength, assigning a number of points (up to a maximum) in each case. The underlying theory is that an effective ad must score high on all these properties if it is ultimately to stimulate action. Too often ads are evaluated only for their attention-getting or comprehension-creating abilities. At the same time, direct rating methods are judgmental and less reliable than harder evidence of an ad's actual impact on target audience members. Direct rating scales help primarily to screen out poor ads rather than to identify great ads.

3. *Portfolio recall tests.* Here respondents are exposed to a portfolio of ads. After viewing them, the respondents are asked to recall the ads they saw—unaided or aided by the interviewer—and to describe as much as they can about each ad. The results are taken to indicate an ad's ability to stand out and its intended message's ability to be understood.

4. *Physiological tests.* Some researchers assess the potential effect of an ad by measuring physiological reactions—heartbeat, blood pressure, pupil dilation, perspiration—using such equipment as galvanometers, tachistoscopes, and pupil measuring equipment. These physiological tests at best measure the attention-getting and arousing power of an ad rather than any particular cognition or emotion that the ad might produce.

5. *Focus-group interviews.* Since advertisements are often viewed in a group setting, pretests with groups can often indicate both how a message is perceived and how it might be passed along. As noted in Chapter 5, the focus-group technique also has the advantages that (a) synergism within a group can generate more reactions than a one-on-one session, (b) it is more efficient in that it gathers data from 6 to 12 people at once, and (c) it can yield data relatively quickly.

TABLE 18-3 Rating Sheet for Ads	
Attention: How well does the ad catch the reader's attention?	_____ (20)
Read-through strength: How well does the ad lead the reader to read further?	_____ (20)
Cognitive strength: How clear is the central message or benefit?	_____ (20)
Affective strength: How effective is the particular appeal?	_____ (20)
Behavioral strength: How well does the ad suggest follow-through action?	_____ (20)
	_____ Total

```
|_____|_____|_____|_____|_____|_____|
0      20     40     60     80     100
Poor ad        Average ad          Great ad
```

There are three popular *ad posttesting methods,* whose purpose it is to assess if the desired impact is achieved after transmission or what the possible ad weaknesses are:

1. *Recall tests.* These involve finding persons who are regular users of the media vehicle and asking them to recall advertisers and products contained in the issue or program or on a Web site under study. They are asked to recall or play back everything they can remember. The administrator may or may not aid them in their recall. Recall scores are prepared on the basis of their responses and used to indicate the ad's power to be noted and remembered.

2. *Recognition tests.* Recognition tests call for sampling the audience of a given vehicle, say a magazine, and asking them to point out what they recognize having seen or read before. In one such magazine-rating technique, Starch Readership Services (www.roper.com/products/starch) computes three different readership scores:
   - *Noted.* The percentage of readers of the magazine who say they had previously seen the advertisement in the particular magazine.
   - *Seen/associated.* The percentage of readers who say they have seen or read any part of the ad that clearly indicates the names of the product (or service) of the advertiser.
   - *Read most.* The percentage of readers who not only looked at the advertisement, but who say that they read more than half of the total written material in the ad.

3. *Direct response.* The preceding techniques measure *cognitive outcomes* of advertising. But favorable cognitive outcomes may not translate into *behavioral outcomes.* Behavioral responses can be solicited by a message, however, and the results directly measured. The effectiveness of alternative messages or media in influencing behavior can be tracked as follows:
   - Placing mailback coupons in the advertisement with a code number or P.O. box that varies by message and medium.
   - Asking target audience members to mention, send, or bring in an advertisement in order to receive special treatment (e.g., a price discount or free parking).
   - Setting up an 800 number and asking individuals to call for further information (on which occasion the marketer can ask where they saw or heard the ad, what they remember, and so on).
   - Staggering the placement of ads so that this week's behavior can be attributed to ad A while next week's can be attributed to ad B. This is also an effective method for assessing alternative expenditure levels.
   - On the Web site, tracking frequency of visits before and after ads are introduced and, where relevant, tracking how visitors move around the site. Web tracking can also be used to learn the source of visitors (i.e., from what other Web sites— e.g., ones with your banner ad—did they come?).

One of the most elaborate and careful efforts to research the effectiveness of non-profit advertising was the 1990 study of the American Cancer Society's colon cancer prevention campaign. This is described in Exhibit 18-2.

EXHIBIT 18-2

ASSESSING THE IMPACT OF A PUBLIC SERVICE ADVERTISING CAMPAIGN

One of the most difficult challenges in non-profit marketing is assessing the effectiveness of specific marketing activities. Typically, too many things are going on in a competitive, complicated real world environment to be able to "see" what a specific effort has done. This is especially problematic with advertising, because the intended effects are often not directly observable, but are cognitive and personal. Without measures of effectiveness, however, nonprofit marketers do not know how to spend their limited resources.

To remedy many of these problems, a unique study was carried out by the Advertising Research Foundation and the Advertising Council's Advertising Research Committee in 1989 and 1990 to (1) measure the effects of public service advertising (PSA) on the awareness, beliefs, and actions of a target audience; (2) measure the effects of both average and above-average media schedules over time; and (3) create a research model to aid in evaluating future public service advertising campaigns.

The focus was on a PSA campaign developed for the American Cancer Society's Colon Cancer Early Detection campaign entitled "Don't find out too late in life," developed and placed by Calet, Hirsch & Spector, Inc.

The campaign was run in four U.S. test markets that have been used for private sector marketing research by Information Resources, Inc. (IRI). The campaign targeted adults 40 to 69, particularly men. IRI's Behavior Scan research technology split the households in each of the four markets into two cells and directed average levels of advertising to one cell and above-average levels to the other cell. IRI technology allowed monitoring of actual exposure to the ads (i.e., finding out which sets were on) in 40 percent of the households. The campaign consisted of the same 30-second PSA running one year from July 31, 1989, to July 23, 1990, in a media schedule skewed toward dayparts reaching adults 40 to 69, especially men.

The *average* level was the equivalent of $21.3 million in media time, 53 Gross Rating Points, and the *above average* level was the equivalent of $53.3 million in media time, 143 Gross Rating Points. Research on the campaign's impact was conducted on samples of households contacted in each market on three occasions: before the campaign, after 6 months, and after 12 months.

The major findings of the research were the following:

- Above average spending is not cost-effective. There was a relatively limited increase in effect from spending 2.6 times more advertising effort.

- PSAs can have a significant and continuing impact on awareness. Proven/related levels of awareness of the need to prevent colon cancer increased steadily over the campaign, going from 11 percent before the campaign to 29 percent at 6 months and 40 percent at 12 months.

- Targeting media placements can significantly increase effectiveness. Awareness increased faster for men than for women, reflecting the more careful placement of ads in sports, prime-time, and early news programming.

- PSAs can reinforce existing beliefs. Smaller increases were found in beliefs

(continued)

455

about the curability of colon cancer and the desirability of annual checkups after 40. Both beliefs were already relatively high before the campaign.

- *Actual* exposure should be monitored. Households found to be exposed to 31 or more ads over the year expressed the highest personal concern about colon cancer.

- Advertising wearout can be observed with respect to intentions to act. Peak intention levels occurred with 16 to 30 exposures. After this point, ads appeared to have diminishing returns, although this could be attributable to the fact that

there was only one execution of the advertisement.

- Patience and consistency are necessary. It took one year for there to be significant effects on reported behavior; 7 percent of the sample recalled talking about colon cancer with their doctors during their last visits at both the baseline and 6-month points. However, this figure rose to 10 percent after 12 months. The figure for men rose to 15 percent after 12 months, more than double the baseline figure. This could translate into 2.7 million more men over 40 consulting their doctors about colon cancer as a result of this campaign.

Source: Advertising Council, *A Strategic Research Approach to Measuring Advertising Effectiveness,* n.d.

PERSONAL MARKETING

It has been our experience that the marketing tool about which nonprofit marketers are most ambivalent is exerting personal influence. This reticent posture seems to follow from two attitudes. First, as noted in Chapter 2, nonprofit managers typically believe that their offering is inherently desirable and needs simply to be made available to be happily embraced by a grateful public. Second, they often believe that planned personal influence strategies are synonymous with manipulation and reflect all that is evil about private sector marketing. They are comfortable using personal marketing techniques for fundraising and for promoting events or products in a gift shop, Web site, or catalogue— as long as it is tasteful! However, when it is proposed that the nonprofit's workers should personally persuade people to attend a college, or join a political party, library, or church, resistance to using a planned, vigorous approach is quite common.

Not only is personal selling resisted when clear opportunities exist for its use, it is often neglected in more general situations. The best-run for-profit service organizations and many retailers long ago recognized that *every time* a member of the organization interacts with a member of a key public, there is an opportunity to further or weaken progress toward the organization's marketing goals. How often have our favorable feelings about a hospital or museum been tarnished by the perfunctory or surly attitude of a guard or the cashier? What nonprofit marketers have to recognize is that almost everyone in their organizations is at one point or another a *boundary person.* Their personal communication style will affect the organization's success. It is better to manage these communications than just to let them happen.

We shall use the term *personal marketing* to refer to *attempts by an organization staff member or volunteer to use personal influence to affect target audience behavior.* Personal marketing can be a very effective tool for certain activities such as lobbying, fundraising, and volunteer recruitment. It can play a role at key points in the Stages of Change. Marketers can help people become aware of a needed behavior in the Precontemplation

Stage and feel the behavior might be appropriate for them. Their strongest role can be at the Contemplation Stage where they can argue for the right behavior, pointing out the benefits and minimizing the costs. They can help people move through the Preparation/Action Stage by accompanying them while they take the desired action and, if they are around at the Maintenance Stage, can play an important role in giving the target audience member a verbal and emotional "pat on the back." This is because personal marketing has three distinctive qualities in comparison to advertising:

1. *Personal contact.* Personal marketing involves a living, immediate, and interactive relationship between two or more persons. Each party is able to observe the others' needs and characteristics at close hand and make immediate adjustments.
2. *Cultivation.* Personal marketing permits all kinds of relationships to spring up, ranging from a matter-of-fact selling relationship to a deep personal friendship.
3. *Response.* Personal selling makes the target audience member feel under some obligation for having listened to the suggestions and arguments. He or she has a greater need to attend and respond, even if the response is a polite "thank you."

These distinctive qualities come at a cost. Personal marketing is the organization's most expensive customer contact tool. To be most effective, there must be careful training and constant reinforcement of people who have potential contacts with target audience members, including many who do not think of themselves as key links to the target public.

ESTABLISHING PERSONAL INFLUENCE OBJECTIVES

Personal communication is part of the marketing mix, and as such is capable of achieving certain marketing objectives better than other tools in the marketing mix. Personal contacts can perform as many as five tasks for their organizations:

1. *Prospecting.* Personal representatives can find and cultivate new customers.
2. *Communicating.* Personal representatives can communicate useful information about the organization.
3. *Persuading.* Personal representatives can be effective in the art of "salesmanship"—approaching, presenting, answering objections, and inducing action.
4. *Servicing.* Personal representatives can provide various services to customers—counseling on their problems, rendering technical assistance, and reducing service times.
5. *Information gathering.* Personal representatives can supply the organization with useful market research and intelligence.

The organization has to decide the relative importance of these different tasks and coach their personal representatives accordingly. College recruiters, for example, spend most of their time prospecting, communicating, and persuading. Lobbyists, in contrast, tend to emphasize communicating, servicing, and information gathering. Each organization normally gets its representatives to set specific goals for each of its activities so that its performance against these goals can be measured.

Selecting Personal Communicators

Most nonprofits have at least some individuals whose primary responsibility is to influence target audiences on a person-to-person basis. These include fundraisers, lobbyists, telemarketers, and gift shop sales clerks. Selecting the individuals to serve in these roles would not be such a problem if one knew the characteristics of an ideal personal communicator. If ideal personal communicators were outgoing, aggressive, and energetic, it would not be too difficult to check for these characteristics in applicants. But a review of the most successful personal communicators in any organization is likely to reveal a good number who are introverted, mild-mannered, and far from energetic. The successful group will also include men and women who are tall and short, articulate and inarticulate, well groomed and slovenly.

Nevertheless, the search for the magic combination of traits that spells surefire persuasion ability continues unabated. The number of lists that have been drawn up is countless. Most of them recite the same qualities. McMurry wrote:

> It is my conviction that the possessor of an *effective* sales personality is *a habitual "wooer," an individual who has a compulsive need to win and hold the affection of others.* . . . His wooing, however, is not based on a sincere desire for love because, in my opinion, he is convinced at heart that no one will ever love him. Therefore, his wooing is primarily exploitative . . . his relationships tend to be transient, superficial and evanescent.[11]

McMurry went on to list five additional traits of the super personal communicator: a high level of energy; abounding self-confidence; a chronic hunger for rewards; a well-established habit of industry; and a state of mind that regards each objection, resistance, or obstacle as a challenge.[12]

Mayer and Greenberg offered one of the shortest lists of traits exhibited by effective personal communicators.[13] Their seven years of fieldwork led them to conclude that the effective personal communicator has at least two basic qualities: (1) *empathy,* the ability to feel as the customer does, and (2) *ego drive,* a strong personal need to make the sale. Using these two traits, they were able to make fairly good predictions of the subsequent performance of applicants for sales positions in three different industries.

It may be true that certain basic traits may make a person effective in any line of persuasion. From the viewpoint of a particular organization, however, these basic traits are rarely enough. Each persuasion job is characterized by a unique set of duties and challenges. One only has to think about college recruiting, corporate fundraising, and Congressional lobbying to realize the different educational, intellectual, and personality requirements that would be sought in the respective sales representatives.

How can an organization determine the characteristics that its prospective personal communicators should "ideally" possess? The particular duties of the job suggest some of the characteristics to look for in applicants. Is the job mostly order taking, or must a lot of "influencing" be carried out? Is there a lot of paperwork? Does the job call for much travel? Will the personal communicator confront a high proportion of refusals? Is creativity necessary? Will the personal communicator be closely supervised or be expected to use a lot of initiative? In addition, the traits of the company's most successful sales representatives can suggest additional qualities to look for. Some organizations compare the standing of their best versus their poorest sales representatives to see which characteristics differentiate the two groups.

One of the traits that has proved to be particularly valuable in social marketing settings is empathy with the target audience. In social marketing, one is often dealing with extremely delicate subjects. Finding personal communicators, or *change agents* as they are sometimes called, from among the population to be influenced is usually very effective. They are most likely to know the audience's concerns, the appropriate language and metaphors for discussing problems and possible solutions, and which motivations can be played upon to bring about needed behavior change. In Ethiopia, for example, as outlined in Exhibit 18-3, the Ministry of Health found that former prostitutes were better at asking difficult intimate questions and communicating information about AIDS to other prostitutes than were traditional social workers.

Training Personal Representatives

The training of effective personal communicators today involves expenditures of hundreds of millions of dollars in training programs, books, cassettes, and other materials. Millions of copies of books on selling are purchased every year, bearing such provocative titles as *How to Outsell the Born Salesman, How to Sell Anything to Anybody, The Power of Enthusiastic Selling, How Power Selling Brought Me Success in 6 Hours, Where Do You Go From No. 1,* and *1,000 Ways a Salesman Can Increase His Sales.* One of the most enduring books is Dale Carnegie's *How to Win Friends and Influence People.*

All of these training approaches are designed to convert a personal communicator from being a passive *order taker* to a more active *influencer. Order takers* operate on the following assumptions: (1) Target audience members are aware of their own needs, (2) they cannot be influenced or would resent any attempt at influence, and (3) they prefer personal communicators who are courteous and self-effacing. An example of an order-taking mentality would be a college fundraiser who phones alumni and asks if they would like to give any money.

Nonprofit organizations need effective order takers (in the catalogue telephone center, the gift shop). In addition, *influencers* are often needed. In training personal communicators to be assertive influencers, there are two basic approaches, one desirable and one to be avoided—especially in the nonprofit world. Consistent with our description of many nonprofit organizations in Chapter 2, one can observe either an organization-centered approach or a customer-oriented approach. The first one trains the personal communicator to be adept in the use of *hard-sell techniques* such as those used in selling encyclopedias or military service. The techniques include overstating the offer's merits, criticizing competitive offerings, using a slick canned presentation, selling yourself, and offering some concession to make the "sale" on the spot. The assumptions behind this form of selling are that (1) target audience members are not likely to respond except under pressure, (2) they are influenced by a slick presentation and ingratiating manners, and (3) they won't regret the behavior, or if they do, it doesn't matter.

The other, preferable approach attempts to train personal communicators in *target audience need satisfaction.* Here the personal communicator studies the target audience members' needs and wants and tailors a proposal to meet these needs. An example would be a museum fundraiser who senses that a wealthy shoe manufacturer has a strong ego and need for recognition as a supporter of the arts. The fundraiser could propose building and naming a new room at the art gallery after this person. The assumptions behind this approach are that (1) the customers have latent needs that

EXHIBIT 18-3

USING EMPATHETIC (IF UNORTHODOX) SALESPEOPLE IN ETHIOPIA

In a tin-roofed, shanty-like classroom where primary school students usually struggle to learn math, a smartly dressed prostitute posed her problem to a nurse conducting a seminar on AIDS.

"I don't have a baby and I want one," she said, "But if I use a condom, I won't become pregnant."

The nurse, Etaferahu Kebede, replied that the woman could solve her problem by having only one sex partner. "Then you can have safe sex and you don't need a condom," she said.

The classroom session, during school vacation, was part of an unusual program in the government's efforts to gather more accurate information on the spread of AIDS in Ethiopia and warn prostitutes about the dangers of not protecting themselves.

The nurse's briefing to the 10 prostitutes seated on the classroom's benches was a prelude to the program's focus.

The Ministry of Health hired the former prostitutes and trained them in the art of asking delicate questions in the hope that they can succeed where social workers have failed: in persuading prostitutes to talk frankly. As confidential interviewers, the former prostitutes are more persuasive in selling the virtues of condoms, epidemiologists said. At the conclusion of the interviews, prostitutes are asked to donate blood for testing and given condoms.

As in other African countries, AIDS is largely a heterosexual disease in Ethiopia; primary carriers are prostitutes, truck drivers, and soldiers.

Prostitution has become more endemic in Ethiopian cities because of increasing poverty. Sociologists here say that another result of poverty is promiscuity in general, as young people find it too expensive to marry and so tend to have numerous affairs, increasing their risk of AIDS.

A 20-year-old woman waiting to be interviewed in the dirt schoolyard said she turned to prostitution five months ago. "I'm trying to make a living," said the woman, a kerchief over her head. She knew about AIDS, she said, and was grateful for the seminar. "It is going to help us in prevention."

The Ethiopian medical authorities, confronted with some of the worst public health problems in the world—the rate of child immunization is the second-lowest in the world, according to the United Nations—were prompted to further action on AIDS after a blood survey last year showed an alarming spread of the virus. In one town, Dessie, a major transportation hub, 38 percent of prostitutes and drivers of the Ethiopian Freight Transport Corporation tested positive for the virus.

With money from the World Health Organization, the Ministry of Health started its AIDS program two years ago, focusing mainly on education and tracking the disease.

Source: Excerpted from Jane Perlez, "Ethiopia Uses Unlikely Warriors in Anti-AIDS Effort," *New York Times,* October 10, 1989, p. 14. Copyright © 1989 by the New York Times Company. Reprinted by permission.

constitute opportunities for the personal communicator, (2) they appreciate good suggestions, and (3) they will be responsive to communicators who have their long-term interests at heart. Within a customer-oriented marketing framework, the need satisfier is certainly a more appropriate image for the nonprofit organization than the image of the hard seller or order taker. It is also one with which nonprofit personal communicators will feel comfortable.

Relationship Marketing

A major recent trend in private sector marketing is the shift in selling approaches from transactional marketing to *relationship marketing*[14]—in our terms, shifting from a focus on target audience members in the Contemplation and Preparation/Action Stages to those in the Maintenance Stage. In transaction marketing, the emphasis is on the individual exchange, getting the target audience member to act in some desired way one time (e.g., a visit to a clinic or museum or a one-time donation). In relationship marketing, the focus shifts to building long-term relationships where the target audience member is encouraged to continue his or her involvement with the marketer. Thus, a Nordstrom department store in the United States will often take seemingly foolish steps like giving credit for returned merchandise they never sold in the first place. They argue that, while this might not be a way to maximize immediate profits, it is a very good way to make someone a lifetime customer.

Building strong long-term relationships rather than making transactions is important in many areas of nonprofit marketing and it is one in which personal contact can play a major role. It is critical in fundraising and blood donations. Here, for example, a smart marketer who encounters a reluctant donor will willingly forego securing a direct donation but get the individual to take some small supporting step, like signing a pledge for a future donation or helping stuff envelopes for a half hour. Praise for such help can then make the reluctant target audience member feel like part of the marketer's team.[15] In such circumstances, they are much more likely to want to build long-term commitments, to become part of the Volunteers of America or Memorial Hospital family of supporters.

Relationship marketing means focusing on key target audience members and giving them continuous attention. People who have carried out one transaction with the organization are better sources for future transactions than is someone entirely new. Therefore, relationship marketing is easier and more cost-effective. Smart marketers are always thinking about new ways to promote further interactions with their existing customer base. For example, colleges and universities were once mainly interested in getting students to enroll in their institutions. Now, they realize that these students can be lifetime customers. In future years, former students can be donors of funds and services. They can nominate future students or can serve as advisors or influencers for those who are uncertain about attending. For many individuals today, learning is a lifelong enterprise. Former students are often the best candidates for the money-making seminars, workshops, and advanced degrees that many colleges and universities are now promoting.

A relationship marketer recognizes that attention to target audience members now (i.e., those in the Maintenance Stage)—talking with them from time to time, giving them small rewards for patronage, asking them for new ways they can be of help—may seem costly in the short run; however, these small gestures can have important effects on the target audience member in the long run. This nurturing of customers can also have important payoffs in favorable word of mouth. When one of the authors worked on the West Coast, his students were always regaling him with "Nordstrom Stories." These were tales of the extraordinary lengths Nordstrom sometimes went to in order to make its customers happy. Of course, these gestures helped build tight relationships with Nordstrom's own customers. But they also had impressive ripple effects on the rest of us who heard the tales.

Internal Marketing

As noted earlier, every individual in the nonprofit organization (full-time, part-time, or volunteer) who has contact with target audience members is at that moment a marketer. Thus, it is important that the marketing director not neglect these key influencers: They can have a great positive and negative effect on organizational performance. In developing an internal marketing program, the place to begin is with an audit of the organization and its external relations—what are all the points of contact with "the outside world" and who is involved? The next step is to alert the relevant organization members and make clear to them how important their attitudes and behaviors can be to the mission of the organization.

Probably the most difficult challenge is to get telephone operators, security officers, cleaning staff, and the like to (a) see that customer contact is part of their job and (b) have the right customer mindset when they do pay attention to target audience members. The first problem is relatively easily resolved by carefully crafted job descriptions and initial orientation. The latter is more difficult. There are several approaches that should be implemented:

1. The marketing manager or a marketing staffer should be part of the training program of every potential personal staff communicator.
2. Numerous examples should be collected of what makes for good and bad personal interaction.
3. There should be regular auditing of these key staff members' performance on these dimensions.
4. In-house media and organization-wide meetings should be used routinely to publicize (and reward) exceptional public-friendly acts.

Internal marketing is simply another occasion during which a good marketer can use the concepts and tools in this book. Changing internal staff behaviors is just another marketing challenge and thus one should:

1. Develop approaches to staffers at each point of the Stages of Change:
   a. Emphasize the nature and importance of the moments of public contact for those employees and volunteers in the Precontemplation Stage.
   b. Use the BCOS model in constructing interventions (e.g., communications, training) for those in the Contemplation and Preparation/Action Stages.
   c. Reward, reward, and reward those in the Maintenance Stage.
2. When thinking through the BCOS factors:
   a. Make sure the benefits enunciated are those that are important to the target audience (i.e., the staffers). For example, help them feel that they are an impor-

tant "voice" for the institution and not just another functionary. Talk about growth potential for those who see the "bigger picture" about their role. Talk about the great experiences they can have and the chances to see a great smile on a target audience member who got service with which he or she was *delighted!* By all means, do not emphasize the benefits to the *organization* as the reason for the staffer to act positively.

b. Try to understand the potential costs the staffer might see and seek to minimize them. Many will see efforts at personal persuasion as taking time and focus away from their assigned responsibilities. They themselves need to see that satisfied, happy target audience members can cause less work for the staff—less complaining, less extended explanations, and so forth.

c. Bring the pressure of others to bear. Newsletter stories about exceptional public encounters will tell the laggards that others are participating. Creating group meetings to brainstorm customer-friendly tactics can build team momentum for this mindset and behavior.

d. Remove any self-efficacy concerns that staffers might have that they "don't know how to say the right thing." In training sessions, have them role-play effective approaches. Provide reminder cards or computer screen "pop-ups" that offer concrete suggestions for various situations.

Nonprofit organizations that are especially good at personal persuasion at all contact points are those that do an excellent job of building a strong sense of teamwork across the entire enterprise where everyone is focused on maximizing the number of positive responses from a range of target audiences. They see marketing as a challenge not just for those with a marketing title but for everyone on the team.

Internal marketing is extremely important at the American Cancer Society. The organization maintains a National Cancer Information Center and has 130 operators available all day, every day to talk with people about cancer issues. In 1999, they also opened a second center to take "inbound" calls only, including calls with donations. By early 2000, the two centers were handling 120,000 calls a month. The two centers are used to build databases on each caller and to seek to develop long-term relationships with them. E-mail addresses are solicited as both a way to ship information instantaneously to them and a way to begin a longer-term dialogue. Well-trained operators secure useful information from each caller that goes directly into the American Cancer Society's Atlanta database and is used to craft future communications around the caller's needs and situations. The society also maintains an "outbound" call center for telemarketing to present or past donors only and to alert supporters to upcoming events and advocacy needs (i.e., time for a letter-writing campaign on some issue).

A major payoff for the society has been the number and amount of donations that have resulted. It collected $4.5 million via this route and found that, without any promotion, the average first-time gift to the call center was $47.25 compared to $25.60 from other forms of fundraising.[16]

Recruiting Allies in Personal Persuasion: The Role of External "Others" in the BCOS Model

Many nonprofit programs can only succeed if others help carry their message to the right audiences. Some potential target audiences can *only* be reached through others. For example, people with eating disorders or depression may not know they need help. Thus, any campaign aimed directly at them will have no impact. This is where others can be very influential in bringing the problem up and getting victims in the Precontemplation Stage into treatment situations, or at least thinking about treatment.

Others must play a role sometimes because they are part of the problem. Many child abuse or drug abuse programs recognize that the abuser or the user is not the whole problem. The problem may be with a dysfunctional family or a renegade brother or father. Solutions must be at the family level, not at the individual level. Everyone needs to work on solutions.

Other individuals can also play a role in helping someone starting a new behavior to keep it up at the Maintenance Stage. Quitting smokers and dieters need a lot of willpower and support to achieve their objectives. The family member or co-worker who praises the weight loss of a friend will do wonders to keep him or her going. The ex-smoker who tells the target member how he or she was able to quit may serve as an influential role model, and the in-law who talks to the smoker who keeps failing in his or her attempts to quit (as most do) and urges them to try something else can be more influential than any direct advertising campaign. Advertising messages can stress the important role of others, as in the Ad Council campaign that tells people that "Friends Don't Let Friends Drive Drunk" (see Figure 18-4). Other types of communication, such as soap operas and movies, can show desired behaviors (for instance, modeling the farmer talking to his friend about new environmentally friendly land use and fertilization practices).

An analysis of some of the results of nonprofit behavior change programs in Africa suggests the power of "others." It has been noticed that once the rate of adoption of some new practices passes a certain point in terms of percentage of adopting households, then the influence of external nonprofit marketers diminishes significantly. What this suggests is that, although nonprofit programs are very important in promoting behavior change at early stages of a diffusion process, after some time the process becomes self-sustaining. The reason for this is that when many people in a close-knit community are doing a new activity, three things happen: (1) There are many more people to pass along information about the new behavior, (2) there are many more people who are demonstrating the behavior to nonadopters, and, perhaps most important, (3) the new behavior replaces the old as the community norm. This is akin to what private sector marketers call "viral marketing."[17]

These findings again demonstrate the enormous power that the influence of friends, neighbors, co-workers, and relatives can have on the behavior of target audiences—the importance of the "O" component of the BCOS model. Unfortunately, this power can also work against programs. Many social marketing efforts to get young mothers in developing countries to adopt new practices in the preparation of more nutritious meals, the treatment of diarrhea, or the practice of breast-feeding can run afoul of mothers-in-law. Tradition in many such countries requires that new brides move in with the husband's family immediately after the wedding. While in her birth home, the bride was influenced by her own family; after marriage she comes under the not inconsiderable influence of her mother-in-law. Programs aimed directly at the new "more modern" mothers often simply cannot overcome the power of the mother-in-law. The latter must be won over first.

Sometimes, to get the proper social support, entire villages or even countries must be changed. A recent program to get parents in a Southeast Asian country to allow their daughters to go on to secondary school as the boys did found that it had to work first at convincing the entire country that educating girls was not a waste of valuable resources.[18]

FIGURE 18-4 Advertisement Promoting Personal Influence

SUMMARY

Advertising, nonpersonal communication conducted through paid media under clear sponsorship, must be planned strategically like any other element of the marketing mix. Objectives must be set, budgets determined, messages defined, media selected, and a system of evaluation established. Marketers should not make grand promises of what advertising can do and should be alert to ethical issues.

Advertising objectives must fit with prior decisions about the target market, offer positioning, and the nature of the remainder of the marketing mix. It must be clear what response is sought from the target audience. Typically, the response is movement forward through the stages of change described in Chapter 4.

Budgets can be set by affordable, percentage-of-sales, or competitive methods, but the objective-and-task method is best. Budgets must be both set in total and allocated among different market segments, geographical areas, and time periods. Budgets must also be allocated across media categories and to specific media vehicles. Choices here depend on the marketer's objectives, the intended target audience, the planned message, and media costs.

Managers must also decide on media timing. Ads should be scheduled seasonally or cyclically to parallel changes in audience interest. Within seasons, decisions must be made on short-run timing. The major options are to advertise continuously, intermittently, or in preplanned bursts. These choices should be based on audience turnover, the frequency of the behavior to be influenced, and forgetting rates.

Evaluation schemes involve pretesting and posttesting advertising. Pretesting can incorporate comprehension studies, mailed questionnaires, portfolio recall tests, physiological tests, focus-group interviews, or self-administered questionnaires. Posttests are usually based on recall, recognition, or some direct behavioral response such as inquiries or sales.

Personal interventions are critical to many behaviors. They are essential in fundraising and volunteer recruitment. Care must be taken in selecting personal persuaders with the right traits. Personal interventions can build long-term relationships. They can be carried out by many people in the organization who might not normally think of themselves in this role. Internal marketing to this group is important.

QUESTIONS

1. Assume you are the marketing director for a stop-smoking campaign and that you have the budget to place 25 30-second television advertisements during prime-time programming in the next six months. Identify the criteria that you would use to choose among prime-time television programs to air your advertisements. Rank the current leading prime-time shows against your criteria and select the spots.

2. Assume that you are the marketing director for the city zoo and that you are responsible for increasing gate revenue by 25 percent through direct mail only. What kinds of mailing lists would you seek to obtain? How would you select the best lists from those available? In other words, what would your selection criteria be?

3. In developing countries, two of the most commonly used promotion vehicles are radio and posters. Design a study to measure the effectiveness of these two vehicles. What measure of effect would you use?

4. Incentives are frequently used as a way to generate repeat behavior. However, there is the risk that the effects are temporary. How should a marketer use incentives to ensure that the effects remain long after the incentives are taken away?

5. Assume you are the marketing manager for Habitat for Humanity. Consider a university and its general schedule (e.g., semester beginning and ending, vacations, summer holiday, and so on). How would these events affect the promotions you use to recruit volunteers? How would your message change during the course of the school year?

NOTES

1. See Figure 17-1.
2. Advertising Age Dataplace at adage.com/ dataplace/topmarkets/us.html.
3. Federal Election Commission at www.fec.gov/finance/precm8.htm.
4. See John A. Zeigler, "Social Change Through Issue Advertising," *Sociological Inquiry,* Winter 1970, pp. 159–165.
5. Janet Meyers, "Pentagon to Cut Ad Ammunition?" *Advertising Age,* December 18, 1989, p. 3.
6. See Russell H. Colley, *Defining Advertising Goals for Measured Advertising Results* (New York: Association of National Advertisers, 1961).
7. Advertising Age Dataplace at adage.com/dataplace/topmarkets/us.html.
8. Direct Marketing Association Web site at www.the-dma.org/library/publications/charts/dmexp_med_market.shtml.
9. William D. Novelli, "Social Issues and Direct Marketing: What's the Connection?" presentation to the Annual Conference of the Direct Mail/Marketing Association, Los Angeles, Calif., March 12, 1981.
10. http://www.jup.com/sps/research/reportoverview.jsp?doc=dcn01-v04.
11. Robert N. McMurry, "The Mystique of Super-Salesmanship," *Harvard Business Review,* March–April 1961, p. 117.
12. Ibid., p. 118.
13. David Mayer and Herbert M. Greenberg, "What Makes a Good Salesman?" *Harvard Business Review,* July–August 1964, pp. 119–125.
14. Jagdish Sheth and Atul Parvatiyar (eds.), *Handbook of Relationship Marketing* (Thousand Oaks, Ca.: Sage Publications, 2000); Mary Jo Bitner, "Building Service Relationships: It's All about Promises," *Journal of the Academy of Marketing Science,* Fall 1995, pp. 246–251.
15. Carol A. Scott, "Modifying Socially Conscious Behavior: The Foot-in-the-Door Technique," *Journal of Consumer Research,* 1977, pp. 156–164.
16. Clint Carpenter, "Call Centers Nearly Double ACS's Average Gift," *Nonprofit Times,* January 15, 2000, pp. 1, 4.
17. Emanuel Rosen, *The Anatomy of Buzz— How to Create Word-of-Mouth Marketing* (New York: Doubleday & Company, 2000).
18. Susan E. Middlestadt, Beverly Schwartz, and Jaraid Kaiser, Cecilia Verzosa, and Achintya Das Gupta, "Promoting Secondary Education for Women in Bangladesh: Using a Theory-Based Behavioral Elicitation Technique to Identify Salient Consequences for Enrolling Daughters," *1997 Innovations in Social Marketing Conference Proceedings,* pp. 41–44.

CHAPTER 19

Managing Public Media and Public Advocacy

U.S. Savings Bonds are not glamorous products. They are not easy to distinguish from other investment vehicles and they have fallen out of favor since their heyday during World War II. They have lost sales and market share in the last decade as companies and banks have focused on other investment instruments. Savings bond sales fell from the $6–8 billion range in the 1980s to $4.9 billion in 1999.

The U.S. Savings Bond Marketing Office (SBMO) engaged the Ball Group to conduct formative research and build a campaign to reposition the bonds. Research showed that people thought the bonds were old-fashioned and were not for people like them—no matter what their demographics and income. Nonetheless, research showed that women could be a prime market for the new I-Bonds, which had significant inflation and tax benefits.

The first step in the new campaign was to redesign the product, eliminating the drawings of signers of the Declaration of Independence and replacing them with "inspirational leaders" like Helen Keller. Next, given the small marketing budget, the SBMO decided to put a heavy emphasis on public relations. Vice President Al Gore and Treasury Secretary Robert Rubin announced the launch in 1999, taking advantage of Rubin's record as head of a major investment firm prior to his appointment as Treasury Secretary. This was followed by largely positive recommendations in the financial columns of major magazines and journals.

The creative component of the public service announcement media campaign threw out the old historical iconography and featured a young woman arguing with her broker about the pros and cons of the new bond. Next, the campaign directors focused on the distribution component of the marketing mix, creating simple payroll and bank deduction systems for automatic purchases. They also allowed purchase through their Web site—www.savingsbond.gov.

Initial sales were very promising. Bond sales were estimated to rise to $5 billion or more in the twenty-first century largely driven by the newly repositioned I-Bond.

Source: Adapted from Dana James, "Marketing Bonded New Life to 'I' Series," *Marketing News*, November 6, 2000, pp. 7–8.

Paid promotion through advertising or the personal persuasion of staffers is only one of the ways in which nonprofit organizations seek to achieve their behavior change objectives through communications with target audiences. A second major approach is through media that are not controlled by the organization, the earned media. We define earned media very broadly:

Earned media comprise any form of communication not under the control of the nonprofit marketing organization through which the organization must earn coverage.

In the twenty-first century, earned media can be extremely important vehicles for promoting, or retarding, the nonprofit organization's objectives.

- Appearances on key talk shows can do more to further a nonprofit marketing cause than can tens of thousands of dollars in media advertising. The President of the United States can often do much more for his legislative agenda by appearing on Larry King Live than he can by individual arm twisting with senators and representatives.
- Articles in major newspapers can sway thousands toward a particular course of action. If former Surgeon General David Satcher holds a press conference and is quoted in the *New York Times* or in the *Washington Post,* he can have a great effect on people's awareness of the risks of cigarette smoking or of AIDS.
- Op-ed pieces are now a major vehicle for trying to influence public opinion. Advocates on both sides of the school voucher issue regularly pen op-ed pieces, hoping to sway citizens to take action for or against school voucher funding.

Thus, public media can be an extremely positive force in achieving a nonprofit organization's goals; however, they can also be a thorn in the side of many organizations. Vigorous investigative reporting by the press and such television newsmagazines as *60 Minutes, 20/20,* and *Dateline* have uncovered a number of dark corners in the nonprofit world, bringing to light financial scandals involving John Bennett and the Foundation for New Era Philanthropy and United Way CEO William Aramony, charges that the Girl Scouts were exploiting the cookie-selling capabilities of their girls, and reports of child molestation in Catholic dioceses.

Because they recognize the power of the public media to influence, or inhibit, their marketing programs, sophisticated nonprofits typically assign specific individuals to the task of working with these media. In many organizations, this person's title is public relations manager. Traditionally, public relations managers have been responsible for protecting and enhancing the *organization's* image. The public relations manager's job was to seek out opportunities to plant positive stories about the organization and its activities in the media. He or she also was the one responsible for extricating the organization or one or more of its staff when some whiff of impropriety hit the public airwaves and pressrooms or the Web. This traditional approach can be challenged by those who think that the public media have a broader role to play in nonprofit organization strategy.

Recently, the role of public relations has been expanded to encompass strategies and tasks related to nonprofits' basic missions. This new role, which we call "public advocacy," involves efforts to change the societal structure of norms and values surrounding controversial individual behaviors (often referred to as "public agenda setting" or as "changing social norms"). It also involves attempting to change the way debates on issues of importance to nonprofits are carried out and to pressure actors in those debates to take particular positions. One kind of public advocacy is lobbying, but there are many others.

In this chapter we consider both the traditional and the more modern, expanded conception of public relations in the nonprofit organization. We begin with traditional public relations before looking at how public relations might fit directly into an aggressive behavior change program.

TRADITIONAL PUBLIC RELATIONS

The traditional *public relations manager* is usually responsible for maintaining and enhancing the reputation of the organization among key publics.[1] While the principal focus of this effort is on support publics, it is quite clearly recognized that an organization's image has important effects on its own employees, its donors and volunteers, and its clients. By employing a public relations manager, the organization can gain several advantages: (1) better anticipation of potential problems, (2) better handling of these problems, (3) consistent public-oriented policies and strategies, and (4) more professional written and oral communications.

The public relations function can be accorded high or low influence in the organization, depending on the board's and chief executive officer's attitude toward the function. In some organizations, the public relations manager is a vice president and sits in on all meetings involving information and actions that might affect public perceptions of the organization. He or she not only puts out fires but also counsels management on actions that will avoid starting fires. In other organizations, public relations is a middle-management function charged with getting out publications and handling news and special events. The public relations people are not involved in policy or strategy formulation, only in tactics.

The emergence of marketing as a "hot topic" in nonprofit circles has raised a major question in the minds of chief administrators and public relations managers as to the relationship between marketing and public relations in a nonprofit organization. Clearly, the two functions work well together in business firms with marketing focusing on the development of plans to market the company's products to consumers, while public relations takes care of relations with other publics. In nonprofit organizations, however, the relationship between the public relations and marketing departments has often been marked by tension and lack of clearly defined areas of responsibility.

The tension is mainly an historical artifact.[2] In many institutions, the public relations function was already well established when marketing was introduced. In such cases, three factors tended to create friction between the two areas. First, the marketing department was often assigned functions that were "taken away" from public relations. Second, public relations directors often felt that they should have been given the new, often more prestigious and better-paying position of marketing director in the new organization. Third, many public relations executives felt that marketing ought to be a division within their departments or that marketing as a separate function was not needed at all.

These frictions were often exacerbated by the lack of clearly specified separate roles for the two functions and a clear understanding of how they were to be coordinated with each other. Both are boundary functions concerned with achieving certain results with various internal and external publics. Are the two functions redundant? Is one more important or comprehensive than the other? Do they play equal but different roles?

This chapter advances the thesis that public relations is most effective when viewed and conducted as part of the marketing mix being used by the organization to pursue its marketing objectives.

THE RELATIONSHIP BETWEEN PUBLIC RELATIONS AND MARKETING

Traditional public relations (PR) is often confused with one of its subfunctions, such as press agentry, company publications, lobbying, fire fighting, and so forth. Yet it is a more inclusive concept. The most frequently quoted definition of PR is the following:

Public relations is the management function that evaluates the attitudes of important publics, identifies the policies and procedures of an individual or an organization with the public interest, and executes a program of action to earn understanding and acceptance by these publics.[3]

Sometimes a short definition is given, which says that PR stands for *performance* (P) plus *recognition* (R).

We see the following differences between public relations and marketing:

1. Public relations is primarily a communication tool, whereas marketing also includes other elements of the marketing mix.
2. Public relations seeks to influence awareness and attitudes, whereas marketing tries to influence specific behaviors, such as purchasing, joining, voting, donating, and so on. Public relations focuses on the first two steps of the Stages of Change while marketing focuses on all four.
3. Public relations does not define the goals of the organization, whereas marketing is intimately involved in defining the business's mission, target audiences, positioning, and interventions.

Nonetheless, the mission of public relations is one that can benefit from the kind of strategic marketing planning that we have stressed throughout this book. For the public relations function, we have simplified the strategic planning process to the seven steps outlined in Figure 19-1.

THE PUBLIC RELATIONS STRATEGIC PLANNING PROCESS

We cannot emphasize strongly enough the need for careful long-range and annual planning of the public relations function. It has been our experience that in many organizations, public relations is mainly (or only) *reactive*. It gets out press releases as

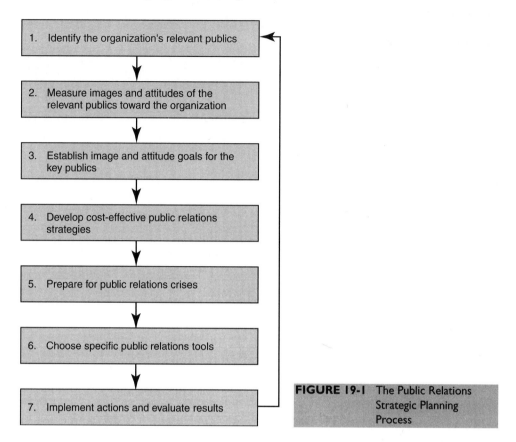

1. Identify the organization's relevant publics

2. Measure images and attitudes of the relevant publics toward the organization

3. Establish image and attitude goals for the key publics

4. Develop cost-effective public relations strategies

5. Prepare for public relations crises

6. Choose specific public relations tools

7. Implement actions and evaluate results

FIGURE 19-1 The Public Relations Strategic Planning Process

needed, fights "brush fires" as they emerge, and copes with individual and group complaints. This reactive stance has many negative consequences including these:

1. The environment rather than the organization sets the public relations agenda.
2. The organization's image is defined only by its response to special situations rather than by the creation of a set of carefully designed messages over a long period of time.
3. The organization's responses to crises are not guided by a long-term strategy.

The *active* public relations stance avoids these problems and ensures that the organization has control over how others see it.

Identify the Organization's Relevant Publics

As we noted in Chapter 3, major nonprofit organizations can have a great many publics with which it must interact. (We noted 16 for the American Cancer Society.) An organization would like to have the goodwill of every public that is affected by, or affects, it. Given limited public relations resources, however, the organization will have to concentrate more of its attention on some publics than others. An organization has primary, secondary, and tertiary publics.

An organization's primary publics are those that it relates to actively and continuously, such as clients, employees, directors, and the general community. Secondary publics are those it must monitor and relate to less frequently but on a fairly continuous basis—suppliers, agents, government officials, and competitors. Tertiary groups are those that do not have any present impact on the organization but whose support and goodwill may be helpful in the future. Tertiary publics may also include groups to whom the organization might like to market in the future.

The various publics are related not only to the organization, but also to each other in many important ways. A particular public may have great influence on other publics. Consider a college whose students are highly satisfied. Their enthusiasm will be transmitted to their parents and to friends back home who might be potential students. Their enthusiasm will have a reinforcing effect on the faculty, who will feel that their teaching is effective. Their enthusiasm will affect the future level of support they give to the school as alumni. Finally, the good "buzz" will potentially improve the university's public perceptions and standing, which can have unknown payoffs in future years.

Measure Images and Attitudes of the Relevant Publics

Once the organization has identified its key publics, it needs to find out how each public thinks and feels about the organization. Management will have some ideas of each public's attitude simply through its regular contacts with that public. However, impressions based on casual contact cannot necessarily be trusted. At one time, a college wanted to rent its stadium facilities to a professional football team for five Sundays as a way of raising more revenue. The college's administrators thought that most local residents and city council members would approve. When it sought a favorable city council vote, however, a group of local citizens attacked the college, calling it insensitive and arrogant. They complained that the football crowd would use up parking spaces, leave litter, walk on lawns, and be rowdy. A large number of citizens, including city council members, revealed deep-seated hostile attitudes toward the college that only needed an issue like this to bring out their animosity. Even in this case, the college's administration dismissed the community spokesman as a minority voice. Needless to say, the vote went against the college, to its surprise.

To know a public's attitudes well enough to use them as a solid basis for its strategic planning, the organization needs to undertake the kind of formal "listening" marketing research we discussed in Chapter 5. A good start is to organize focus groups of publics annually to probe their knowledge and feelings about the organization. While the observations of these focus groups are not necessarily representative, they normally contribute perspectives and raise interesting questions that the organization will want to explore more systematically. Most importantly, they will alert management to key problems as they emerge. Eventually, the organization may find it worthwhile to conduct formal field surveys on a regular basis. It can track awareness, knowledge, interest, and attitudes toward the organization.

Establish Image and Attitude Goals for Key Publics

By periodically researching its key publics, the organization develops hard data on how these publics view the organization. To translate this information into a strategic plan, the organization must evaluate each key public in terms of whether each has a negative, neutral, or positive attitude toward the organization and the degree of impact its members can have on the organization if they act on their attitude.

Suppose the public relations manager for St. Anthony's Hospital rates 20 key publics in terms of these two factors (see Table 19-1). She concludes that there are five groups that are unfavorably disposed toward the hospital (bottom row). However, the competitive nature of the hospital market and the relatively weak position of unions in this particular state have led her to conclude that the negative reactions of two of these publics, competitors and labor unions, will have little impact on the hospital. Local politicians are seen as hostile, but no legislation is presently pending. If politicians do decide to act, however, they can be troublesome, so the hospital must pay some attention to them. Technicians and insurers (lower right corner) are a more serious problem. Technicians are upset about the hospital's recent decision not to buy certain state-of-the-art equipment to replace older equipment. Insurers are rankled by the hospital's antiquated billing procedures and higher-than-average charges for certain exotic surgical procedures. Both groups should receive considerable attention in the upcoming year.

Physicians, patients, and media should also receive close attention. Although the present attitude of these groups is not negative, it is not positive and can have a major impact on the organization. All of these groups are concerned about a recent scandal at the hospital in which two physicians were discovered abusing drugs. The same issue has caused a potential problem for the other groups in the other two "neutral" cells of the matrix. Informal soundings indicate that all four publics in these two cells are concerned about the hospital's medical staff and control systems. Medical schools and research foundations must be satisfied, since future negative attitudes could have the potential for affecting future recruitment of physicians and winning of research grants.

Those with positive attitudes (top row) would seem not to merit immediate attention. The upper right cell is a discretionary target. Some attention may be devoted to the board, nurses, regional health agencies, and charitable organizations. Their interest and concerns, however, might be met by programs directed at other target publics. However, to the extent that their positive attitude might bleed through to some of the

TABLE 19-1 A Portfolio of Publics for St. Anthony's Hospital

Probability of Negative Reaction	*Potential Impact*		
	Low	*Medium*	*High*
Low	Suppliers	Nursing Schools Volunteers	Board Nurses Regional Health Agency Charities
Medium	General Public Nonmedical Staff	Medical Schools Research Foundations	Physicians TV/Radio Newspapers Patients
High	Competitors Labor Unions	Local Politicians	Technicians Insurers

neutral and negative publics, they must not be ignored. They may well be some of the organization's most useful (and one hopes vocal) supporters.

As for the three remaining cells of the matrix, the analysis suggests that the public relations manager with a finite budget can pay relatively little attention to suppliers, nursing schools, volunteers, the general public, and nonmedical staff in the upcoming year. She should continue, however, to monitor their attitudes over the year to make sure that her initial assessment of a favorable attitude is correct and that they do not "migrate" to other, more potentially damaging cells.

Once the public relations manager has determined the amount of effort to direct to each key public in the matrix, specific communication goals must be set for each segment. The manager might set a goal, for example, that "Ninety percent of TV and radio news directors and city newspaper editors within a 50-mile radius of the hospital should know within six months the full details of the hospital's internal policing system. Seventy-five percent should have full confidence in the hospital by the end of that period." These specific goals naturally suggest the means for their achievement and indicate what results should be measured later to evaluate the success of the strategic plan.

Develop Cost-Effective Public Relations Strategies

An organization usually has many options in trying to improve the attitudes of a particular public. Its first task is to understand why negative attitudes have arisen so that the causal factors can be appropriately addressed. It is especially important to establish whether the attitudes are problems of perception or reality. Clearly, if the problem is perception, then the challenge is really one of communications and positioning. However, if there are aspects of the organization and its performance that need to be fixed, this must come first. Credibility is probably the single most important attribute that a public relations professional must carry into the field. Nothing will damage that credibility as much as lying. Presumably, a public relations professional would never commit an outright lie, but attempts to put a positive spin on a basically flawed situation is not only hard to do but risks seriously the organization's credibility and the likelihood it will be believed in the future. Our crusading press very often will ferret out underlying weaknesses—it makes for great headlines, especially for a local issue.

Consider the case of the college that found it had weak community support when it wanted to rent its stadium to the professional football team. In digging deeper into the negative citizen attitudes, the college discovered that many citizens harbored a history of resentment against the college for various reasons, including the opinion that (1) the college never consults citizen groups before taking actions, (2) the college discriminates against local high school students, preferring to draw students from other parts of the country, (3) the college does not actively inform the local community about campus events and programs, and (4) the college owns local property that goes tax free and thereby raises the taxes of the citizens. Essentially, the community feels neglected and exploited by the college.

The diagnosis suggests that the college first needs to make real changes in the ways it relates to the community and thus establish stronger ties with that community. It needs to develop a *community relations program* as part of its public relations strategy.

Here are some of the steps it might take to build ties once it makes the needed fundamental changes in the way it operates:

1. Identify the local opinion leaders (prominent businesspeople, news editors, city council members, heads of civic organizations, school officials) and build better relationships by inviting them to campus events, consulting with them on college issues that will affect the community, and sponsoring luncheons and dinners.
2. Encourage the college's faculty and staff to join local organizations and participate in community campaigns such as the United Way and American Red Cross Blood Bank programs.
3. Develop a speakers' bureau to provide speakers to local groups such as the Kiwanis, Rotary, and so on.
4. Make the college's facilities and programs more available to the community. Classrooms and halls can be offered to local organizations for meetings.
5. Arrange open houses and campus tours for the local community.
6. Participate in community special events such as parades, holiday observances, and so on.
7. Establish an advisory board of community leaders to act as a sounding board for issues facing the college and the community.
8. Put links to university Web sites on the Web pages of the Chamber of Commerce and other "booster" organizations.

Each project involves money and time. The organization will need to estimate the amount of expected attitude improvement for each project to arrive at the best mix of cost-effective actions.

Prepare for Public Relations Crises

Every nonprofit organization more than a few years old has "horror stories" of organizational oversights, executive improprieties, volunteer excesses, and so on that were for many days and weeks the focus of dramatic and potentially damaging stories in the press. A month seldom passes without a story of malfeasance in the popular press or in *The Chronicle of Philanthropy*. Major crises in the last 15 years have affected such organizations as the United Way of America, the American Medical Association, the American Red Cross, and Covenant House. A strategically oriented public relations program must manage such crises and not let the crises manage them.

Crises are not always the result of steps an organization takes for which it is embarrassed. It may be that they are just very controversial. For example, in the first years of the new millennium, the Boy Scouts of America faced a significant amount of negative press as a result of dismissing a former Eagle Scout who was a troop leader because he was gay and, in the Boy Scout organization's view, not of "strong moral character."[4] The troop leader, James Dale, sued and eventually the U.S. Supreme Court ruled that, as a private organization, the Scouts did not have to abide by state anti-discrimination laws. The Scouts believed they did the right thing. Many gay rights groups and many in the general public criticized the organization and urged schools to stop allowing Boy Scout meetings on their premises and individuals to stop donating. Internal constituencies were also affected with some regional Boy Scout councils, such as one in New England, adopting more tolerant "Don't ask, don't tell" policies.

There are two approaches to crisis management: long term and short term. In the long term, the public relations manager must actively prepare for the inevitable unexpected disaster or controversy. This means, first of all, cultivating strong media relations. If the public relations staff truly has a customer-centered approach to its relationships with the media, it will have established itself as having *the media's interests* at the center of its public relations program. This should lead to key media people giving the organization the benefit of any doubts and a clear opportunity to get its story across.

The other long-term approach is to prepare key managers to deal with the media in crisis situations. This means, first, creating an attitude on the managers' part that regards members of the media not as the enemy, but rather as individuals like the managers themselves attempting to do their jobs as thoroughly and professionally as possible. Second, it means giving managers advanced training in holding press conferences and being part of high-stress interviews with the media.

In the short run, public relations experts must have clear guidelines as to how to handle each individual crisis event. The Foundation for American Communications, which has as its mission improving the quality of information reaching the American public through the media, offers a number of suggestions, as outlined in Exhibit 19-1.

One of the keys to any response from a marketing standpoint is to remember that the organization ultimately relies on the goodwill of the public. Thus, in any crisis the interests of the public should always come before the interests of the organization. A simple example of the proper response is offered by David Gunn, general manager of the Washington, D.C., Metro. During a morning rush hour in the second week of May 1993, service on the Metro's Red Line was delayed two hours because a woman was struck by a train. Rather than ignoring the issue or treating it as just an unfortunate random occurrence over which Metro had no control, Gunn issued a *written apology* to Red Line riders. Gunn said, "We're selling a product, and if we don't deliver it—and we didn't big-time that morning—we owe the people an apology."[5]

Choosing Specific Public Relations Tools

Here, we want to examine in more detail the major public relations media and tools that can be used in implementation. They are (1) written material, (2) audiovisual material, (3) organization identity media, (4) news, (5) interviews and speeches, (6) public service announcements, (7) events, and (8) the organization's Web site.

Written Material

Organizations rely extensively on written material to communicate with their target publics. Boys and Girls Clubs of America and the Volunteers of America, for example, use such written material as an annual report, catalogues, employee newsletters, informational flyers, and posters. Many nonprofits now have very extensive publication programs, including their own magazines. The AARP magazine, *AARP Modern Maturity,* has the largest circulation of any magazine in the United States at 21 million, far outstripping *Reader's Digest* at 12 million.

In preparing each publication, the public relations department must consider *function, aesthetics,* and *cost.* The function of an annual report, for example, is to inform interested publics about the organization's accomplishments during the year and about its financial status, with the ultimate purpose of generating confidence in the organization and its leaders. Aesthetics enter in because the annual report should be readable,

EXHIBIT 19-1

HOW TO HANDLE BAD NEWS

Accidents happen. Acts of nature cut wide swaths of destruction. Fire damages property and injures people. You may discover that your agency or an individual associated with it is the victim of a crime. Or an individual who is part of your organization may be identified as the suspect in a crime. Accusations are made, complaints are raised, and you are not immune.

There is also the possibility of a hard news story developing elsewhere that concerns an agency like yours, or involves people like your clients. Just as many nonprofit organizations "piggyback" on news from other places, thoughtful editors will see a problem reported in another community and wonder if that problem could happen in yours.

Reporters and editors tend to think of hard news stories as "real news" and are keen on obtaining all available information when such stories come along.

How can you prepare to survive a crisis, should it take place?

There are three points to keep in mind:

1. Do nothing to make things worse.
2. Get the story over with and behind you.
3. Remember that you will be dealing with many of the same news organizations long after this story is over.

What makes things worse? Wasting time searching for someone to blame. Pretending things are okay when they are not. Stalling, stonewalling, or getting in the way of reporters. Telling lies. Speculating. Showing what looks like indifference to suffering. Attempting to cover up a problem. And panicking.

How do you end coverage of a story? Disclosure is the fastest way. Gather information and release it as soon as you can. If information is not available or must be held up for some reason, assure reporters that it will be provided as soon as possible. Reporters get nervous when they think they may miss out on information available to others. Be even-handed.

Fact-finding is one of the regular public relations jobs. When there is a potentially damaging or difficult story in the works, fact-finding is more difficult, but also more necessary.

And finally, carry out your media responsibilities in professional and self-respecting ways. Every editor has stories to tell about the swarm of public relations people who come around looking for coverage of positive news and disappear at the first hint of controversy or trouble.

Source: Media Resource Guide, 5th ed. (Los Angeles: Foundation for American Communications, 1987), p. 21. Reproduced with permission.

interesting, and professional. If the annual report is published with a dull design, it suggests a poor, amateur-type organization. At the other extreme, if the annual report is too fancy, the public may raise questions as to why a nonprofit organization is spending so much money on graphics instead of needed services. Cost acts as a constraint in that the organization will allocate a limited amount of money to each publication. The public relations department has to reconcile considerations of function, aesthetics, and cost in developing each publication.

Audiovisual Material

Audiovisual materials such as films, slides, audio and video cassettes, and CD-ROMs are coming into increasing use as communication tools. In former days, college recruiters would visit different campuses and present a talk, answer questions, and pass out some written materials to the high school seniors gathered to hear about the college. The students had to concentrate hard on the recruiter's words. Today's recruiter, in contrast, delivers a high-impact audiovisual presentation about the college. Many avant garde programs use CD-ROMs. Larry Abeln, former associate dean at the McDonough School of Business at Georgetown University, developed a mini-CD-ROM describing the Georgetown MBA for everyone making an inquiry about the school's program.

Organization Identity Media

Normally, an organization's various visual and print materials lack a uniform look, which not only creates confusion but also misses an opportunity to create and reinforce an *organization identity* or *brand.* In an overcommunicated society, organizations compete for attention. This has led to efforts at organizational branding on the part of institutions like the Centers for Disease Control and Prevention, the Girl Scouts, and Volunteers of America (as described in Chapter 6). The objective is to create a visual identity that the public immediately recognizes. Visual identity is conveyed through logos, stationery, Web sites, brochures, signs, business forms, call cards, buildings, uniforms, and rolling stock. There is now a rather well-defined brand-building process and a number of consulting organizations, to help nonprofit organizations with this process.

News

One of the major tasks of a public relations department is to find or create favorable news about the organization and market it to the appropriate media. The appeal of publicity to many organizations is that it is "earned advertising"—that is, it represents exposures at no financial cost. As someone once said, "Publicity is sent to a medium and *prayed for* while advertising is sent to a medium and *paid for.*" Publicity is far from free, however, because special skills are required to write good publicity and to "reach" the press. Good publicists cost money.

Publicity has three qualities that make it a worthwhile investment. First, it may have *higher veracity* than advertising because it appears as normal news and not as sponsored information. Second, it tends to catch people off guard who might otherwise avoid sponsored messages. Third, it has high potential for dramatization in that it arouses attention, coming as it does in the guise of a noteworthy event.

Among the audiovisual public relations tools being used much more frequently in the twenty-first century are video news releases. These releases are, in effect, TV news stories prepared by the nonprofit organization to look like a regular news report. Harried TV stations can then use all or part of the material in their local newscasts. Viewers are unaware of the source. The technique was used by *Glamour* magazine and Hanes Hosiery in introducing their Hand-in-Hand breast awareness program in 1992. Video news releases containing remarks by Bernadine Healy, then Director of the National Institutes of Health, discussing the program were made available and were run on a wide range of stations as well as network news programs.[6]

Getting news items in the local press or on television or radio is itself a marketing task. As such, the publicist must start with the immediate audience. One must understand what *the media* are looking for in a news story. Among the prime characteristics they will have in mind are these:

1. The interest of the subject to their audience.
2. The possibility for dramatization through pictures, live interviews, and so forth.
3. The clarity and exhaustiveness of any press release (e.g., including supporting materials, statistics, and so on).
4. Limited need for further "digging."
5. The possibility of exclusive coverage—for either the entire story or for a specific angle.

Interviews and Speeches

Increasingly effective vehicles for publicity are the media interview, Web "chat rooms" and the TV and radio talk shows.[7] Often guests on news and talk shows are not celebrities or especially newsworthy individuals. They are simply experts on some subject or people with a simple story to tell. Nonprofits can usually provide to the media a number of subjects and guests over a year's time to meet the voracious need for program material. An attractive, articulate veterinarian from a zoo can tell of the special problems of dealing with large animals. A college recruitment director can talk about the new competition for students or offer advice on how to get one's son or daughter into their college of choice. Visiting artists at theaters or music performances are always in demand. Anything offbeat generally has a much better chance of getting time or space to tell the organization's story than a subject that has already been worn out in the media. The new public access channels on TV are particularly eager to find and use such guests.

Public Service Announcements

In addition to their need for guests, TV and radio stations (and networks) are usually quite willing, even eager, to give air time to public service announcements (PSAs). There was a time when they were required to do so by the Federal Communications Commission. They no longer are subject to such a requirement, but most still wish to include PSAs as some part of their programming. This is in part because they need to fill otherwise empty air time with interesting material, but more so because the stations simply wish to be seen as good community citizens (especially when license renewal time comes about). At the same time, many local and national advertising agencies and production houses are willing to donate some or all of their services to developing such PSAs. The program of the Advertising Council is perhaps the most prominent in this regard.

A study by the Health Message Testing Service showed that effective PSAs on health issues had the following characteristics:

- They emphasized both the health problem and the solution in the PSA.
- They used a person typical of the target audience when presenting a testimonial.
- They visualized a reward from practicing the recommended healthful behavior.
- They communicated the psychological benefits of practicing the healthful behavior.
- They used an approach other than humor.
- They demonstrated the healthful behavior (if possible).
- They used a high or moderate emotional appeal.[8]

The major disadvantage of PSAs is the lack of control the nonprofit organization has in their timing and placement. A recent study of both paid and unpaid PSAs on 10 TV channels by the Henry J. Kaiser Family Foundation found that nearly half were run between midnight and 6:00 A.M. Less than half of 1 percent of air time was given to PSAs compared to 25 percent given to paid ads and other promotions. Seventeen seconds of each hour comprised PSAs compared to over 17 minutes of other non-program content. Even this figure overstates the value of PSAs. The study also revealed that about 25 percent of the broadcast PSAs involved the networks' own stars giving vague upbeat social statements not crafted for specific social campaigns or specific nonprofit organizations.[9]

Events

A nonprofit organization can increase its newsworthiness by creating events that attract the attention of target publics. Thus, a hospital seeking more public attention can host major research symposia, feature well-known speakers and celebrities, celebrate anniversaries of important events in the history of the institution, create birthday parties for special patients, and hold news conferences. Each well-run event not only impresses the immediate participants, but also serves as an opportunity to develop a multitude of stories directed to relevant media vehicles and audiences.

Event creation and management comprise a particularly important skill in running fundraising drives for nonprofit organizations. Fundraisers have developed a large repertoire of special events, including anniversary celebrations, art exhibits, auctions, benefit evenings, bingo games, book sales, 10K races, contests, dances, dinners, fairs, fashion shows, parties in unusual places, phonathons, rummage sales, tours, and walkathons. The American Cancer Society, for example, distributes a brochure to local units in which it outlines the following ideas for special events:

> Dramatic special events attract attention to the American Cancer Society. They bring color, excitement, and glamour to the program. Well planned, they will get excellent coverage in newspapers, on radio and TV, and in newsreels. . . . A Lights-on-Drive, a one-afternoon or one-night House-to-House program have such dramatic appeal that they stir excitement and enthusiasm . . . keep in mind the value of bursts of sound such as fire sirens sounding, loudspeaker trucks, fife and drum corps. . . . A most useful special event is the ringing of church bells to add a solemn, dedicated note to the launching of a drive or education project. This should be organized on a division or community basis, and the church bell ringing may be the signal to begin a House-to-House canvass. Rehearsals of bell ringing, community leaders tugging at ropes, offer good picture possibilities.[10]

The Web Site

In the new millennium, an extremely important source of information and insight about the nonprofit organization is its Web site. Web sites can present facts about the organization, recent press releases, examples of advertisements and programs, all designed to give visitors a sense of the organizations and what they do. Web sites are places where one can learn about crises. They are places where one can go to volunteer or to donate. If they are well designed, they will have ways for visitors to follow up with personal contacts. There will be links to other sites visitors might find helpful and perhaps chat rooms where they can "meet" and discuss common concerns, such as the

American Cancer Society's Web site area, "The Cancer Survivors Network." Discussion topics in chat rooms on the very diverse AARP Web site in mid-2001 included these:

BookTalk	Grandparenting	Heroes & Leaders
Computers & Technology	Health & Wellness	History Matters
I Remember	My Generation	Today's AARP
Legislative Issues	Online Learning	Trips N Travel
Messages to the Next Generation	Spiritual Journey	What I'm Most Proud Of
	The Volunteer	Working Options
Modern Maturity	Experience	Your Life

The "look" of the Web site and the ease of interacting with it can affect visitors' reactions to the organization. Young publics will appreciate highly visual fast-moving sites, preferably with moving images, whereas older groups may prefer more text-based appearances. It is extremely important to keep the site fresh and change its content from time to time to keep people coming back. The latter is most likely to happen if the visitor gets the sense the Webmaster is someone who is always looking for ways to serve the visitors' needs better. Webmasters can be very important members of the public relations and marketing team.

Implementing Actions and Evaluating Effects

Public relations actions to be taken have to be assigned to responsible individuals within the organization along with concrete objectives, time frames, and budgets. The public relations department should oversee the results. Evaluating the results of public relations activities, however, is not easy, since it occurs in conjunction with other marketing activities and its contribution is hard to separate.

Consider the problem of measuring the value of the organization's publicity efforts. Publicity is designed with certain audience-response objectives in mind, and these objectives form the basis of what is measured. The major response measures are exposure, awareness, comprehension, attitude change, and specific behaviors.

The easiest and most common measure of publicity effectiveness is the number of *exposures* created in the media. Most professional publicists supply the client with a "clippings book" or reports of Web searches showing all the media that carried news about the organization and a summary statement such as the following:

Media coverage included 3,500 column inches of news and photographs in 350 publications with a combined circulation of 79.4 million; 2,500 minutes of air time on 290 radio stations and an estimated audience of 65 million; and 660 minutes of air time on 160 television stations with an estimated audience of 91 million. If this time and space had been purchased at advertising rates, it would have amounted to $1,047,000.

The purpose of citing the equivalent advertising cost is to make a case for publicity's cost-effectiveness, since the total publicity effort must have cost less than $1,047,000. Furthermore, publicity usually creates more reading and believing than ads.

Still, this exposure measure is not very satisfying. There is no indication of how many people actually read, saw, or heard the message, and what they thought afterward. Furthermore, there is no information on the net audience reached, since publications have overlapping readership. Indeed, there is the very real danger that the organization will attempt to maximize *what it can measure.* It is easy and satisfying to measure success by brochures passed out, articles written, and so on. Distributing more brochures in 2003 than in 2002 can be considered great progress.

A better measure calls for finding out what change in public *awareness, comprehension,* or *attitudes* occurred as a result of the publicity campaign (after allowing for the impact of other promotional tools). This requires the use of survey methodology to measure the before and after levels of these variables.

CUSTOMER-CENTERED TRADITIONAL PUBLIC RELATIONS

Marketing is simply an approach to changing behavior.[11] As we have emphasized, just as it can be applied to getting donors to give money and clients to consume services, so too can it be applied to the task of inducing journalists or news editors to run a story or, in general, to communicate accurately about a given organization, individual, or idea.

To illustrate the use of the principles outlined in Chapter 2, let us take the case of a hypothetical public relations specialist for a gun owners' association and consider, first, how an *organization-centered* specialist would approach the problem of getting favorable press coverage of a story of importance to the organization:

1. The organization-centered PR specialist would begin by assuming that he or she has a basically interesting story in which the general public would really be interested *if only* the journalist would cover it.
2. If journalists are reluctant to run the story, then it is assumed to be either because they do not fully appreciate how truly interesting it is and how much their audience would like to be exposed to it or because they have the usual liberal bias against gun owners and want to run as little as possible that is positive about them.
3. The PR specialist reflects on his or her years of experience with journalists and takes pride in knowing how they think. There will be little need really to explore *in advance* how journalists will react to this kind of story opportunity. The specialist will prepare the necessary press releases and rely on his or her well-tested ability to be really persuasive on the telephone or through imaginative direct mailings.
4. Getting coverage will be seen mainly as a matter of convincing journalists of the fact that it is a great story. This means pushing the story hard to make sure that the journalist comes to see the PR specialist's view of its great merit.
5. Different materials will be prepared for print, radio, and television journalists, but one or two treatments for each broad category ought to do it.

What would a *customer-oriented* approach look like? This PR specialist would proceed in a very different way:

1. He or she would not assume that the likely reactions of target journalists are known or that they are likely to be the same as the PR specialist's. Further, he or she will assume that there may be major differences both *within* as well as among media.
2. If time permits, when planning the strategy for securing news coverage, the PR specialist would begin with calls to a few key newspeople to get initial reactions to

the proposed story and to learn which features seem to resonate with the interests of which kind of journalists.

3. The PR specialist would recognize that getting the story covered means that it must meet the journalists' near-term needs and wants. These needs will differ by journalist and may include one or more of the following concerns:

   a. How long will the story need to be?
   b. How well will the story appeal to the journalists' audiences?
   c. How well will the story appeal to the journalists' editors or news directors?
   d. What opportunities are there for a journalist to contribute his or her own "spin" to the story?
   e. Will the journalist have to dig further to cover the story well (some may want a lot of opportunities for digging, others none)?

4. Persuasion is not the heart of the strategy. The PR specialist would recognize that the "product" to be offered has to be right in the first place. The journalist should be presented with not only the facts of the story but a range of peripheral material that may respond to specific needs and wants of theirs. This peripheral material could include photos or photo opportunities, profiles of key figures in the story, names of follow-up sources both inside and *outside* the association, lists of reference materials, floppy disks with news release materials in each journalist's own word processing language, and so forth.

5. The PR specialist would recognize that the story is only one of many he or she will want to have covered over the years by target journalists. Thus, each particular story is to be marketed as a part of a longer-term strategy of building *relationships* with the journalists. This often means sacrificing near-term gain for a long-run benefit. For example, selling-oriented PR specialists are usually reluctant to help journalists dig up critical (or even objective) material about the organization for the particular story. This would be seen as just getting in the way of "making the sale." A customer-oriented PR specialist providing journalists the names of one or more independent outside sources of follow-up information will recognize that this may cause short-run problems but (a) the journalist in all likelihood will find sources anyway (often more hostile ones), (b) providing outside sources will increase the credibility of the present message, and (c) most importantly, the PR specialist will more likely be seen (except by the most cynical journalists) as someone who is basically concerned about meeting the *journalist's* needs—not just selling a story. The customer-oriented news source is someone who tries to help.

Alternatives

There are a great many alternatives available for free or low-cost publicity for nonprofits. Sometimes creativity can be stimulated by the use of outside consultants. Rhoda Weiss, a California–based marketing and public relations consultant, has developed a number of tips which she passes along to her nonprofit clients. Several of these are listed in Exhibit 19-2.

EXHIBIT 19-2

RHODA WEISS'S PUBLIC RELATIONS TIPS FOR NONPROFIT ORGANIZATIONS

Talk Shows

Hundreds of hours of free time on television and radio public affairs programs and cable systems can be used to educate the public, raise money, alter attitudes, and make a name for an organization. The key to successfully pitching a story to a talk show producer or guest coordinator is to mix timelines with consumer interest.

- Keep pitch letters to one page.
- Use national, regional, or local statistics and background information to show how and why your suggestion is important to the audience.
- Suggest a few thought-provoking questions to be asked during the interview.
- Provide brochures and related news clippings that help sell the idea as timely and provocative.
- Follow up your letter with a phone call to the producer or coordinator and be prepared to sell your idea.
- Bring along visual aids or props to help enliven a television segment.
- Make sure your representative has seen or heard the show prior to the day of his or her appearance.
- Send stations a list of possible discussion topics and experts to deal with each one. Routinely remind the talk show contact that you exist and that your people are available.

Identify Yourself

If you work in a large city, it's easy to get lost in the shuffle with other community nonprofit groups. Even in smaller communities you have to remind the news contact that you exist. Some people are in the news every day, but most of us need to work on setting up and maintaining contact with newspeople.

- Send a yearly letter to reporters and editors in your service area, listing your name and address with a short description of your services, including daytime and evening contacts and phone numbers.
- Print your agency's interest on Rolodex cards, and send them to reporters and editors in your area. This makes it easier for them to find you and identify your interests.
- Consider letters to the editor or opinion articles. Ask for editorials on your area of concern.
- Identify all procedures and deadlines for calendar listings, club listings, and other regular sections of newspapers or broadcasts where you can list activities and meetings.
- Ask to participate in editorial board meetings with news executives to provide them with your firsthand impressions of current issues.
- Schedule events to take advantage of slow news days such as holidays.
- Encourage supporters to write complimentary letters to the editor about all community activities, not just your own organization's.
- Attend programs where reporters are present to get to know them.

The Other Media

Before modern newspapers and broadcasting, we communicated with flyers, broadsides, and by word of mouth. It's useful today to look beyond the standard news media.

- Consider asking for mention in telephone books, souvenir programs for cultural or sporting events, bus benches, bus shelters, taxi panels, marquees at schools and private or public buildings, community bulletin boards, grocery bags, milk cartons, restaurant placemats, bowling alley score sheets, balloons, buttons, caps, even T-shirts.

(continued)

- Send your news releases to church bulletins, chamber of commerce publications, service club newsletters, and employee newsletters published by major employers in your service area.

- Leaflets can be inserted in billing envelopes by major employers.

- You might find places for leaflets in doctors' offices, building lobbies, health clubs, libraries, YMCAs and YWCAs, museums, or even grocery checkout stands.

Speakers' Bureau

You can generate many firsthand contacts with the public in your area by providing your volunteers, staff, or members as public speakers through your own speakers' bureau.

- Identify the potential audiences in your area such as service clubs, social clubs, churches, business associations, schools, or cultural associations. Chambers of commerce may have listings of such organizations in your area.

- Develop a list of speakers in your organization.

- Determine how many speakers you might be able to provide.

- Send a notice of your speakers' bureau to program coordinators at stations aimed at your potential audiences.

- Develop a comprehensive checklist or worksheet for each speaking assignment covering the date, exact location, specific start time, whether to expect questions and answers, audience size, program length, and the name of the contact person.

- Provide backup information, materials and support for your speakers, including audio-visuals, handouts, and transportation if needed.

- Don't forget to use your speakers' bureau mailing list for publicizing your programs, fundraisers, and for other direct-mail purposes.

Celebrities

Well-known people can spread the word about your cause in public service announcements, publications, and personal appearances. They are instantly recognizable and newsworthy and will frequently donate time if they believe in the cause being promoted.

- Many celebrities maintain contact with their hometown or college alma mater—you don't have to live in Hollywood or New York to think about celebrity endorsements. Jack Benny's hometown of Waukegan, Illinois, and many other communities have benefited from celebrity endorsements.

- The Screen Actors Guild in Los Angeles provides information about members' agents or publicists. Directories of actors, such as the Academy Players Directory, are available from the Academy of Motion Picture Arts and Sciences.

- The television networks will forward letters, but will handle them as fan mail, which underscores the value of direct contact.

- Consider local sports, news, television, or radio personalities or professional athletes in your community as celebrity spokespeople.

- When a celebrity performs in your community, request a personal appearance on your agency's behalf or participation in a public service announcement.

Source: Media Resource Guide, 5th ed. (Los Angeles: Foundation for American Communication, 1987), pp. 39–41. Reproduced with permission.

PUBLIC ADVOCACY

Traditionally, the central role for public relations specialists has been to maintain and enhance the image a nonprofit organization, its programs, and its staff have with important external publics. In recent years, many nonprofits have recognized that the expertise of public relations professionals could be extended to play a major role in furthering the organization's central behavior change mission, particularly for behaviors where the vast majority of target audience members are in the Precontemplation Stage. In this section, we discuss this expanded role.

Expanded Role for Public Relations: Institutional Effects on Behavior

Much of the focus in this book is on *individual* behavior change. We argue that if a nonprofit marketer is to get someone to change to a socially desirable behavior such as wearing seat belts, volunteering for the Red Cross, or giving to the United Way, the best approach is to focus on what the individual thinks are the costs and benefits of the action, to emphasize what he or she thinks important others want him or her to do, and to help him or her acquire any capabilities needed to carry out the action.

There are a number of scholars and nonprofit managers who argue that the focus on the individual ignores the larger social conditions that *lead* to undesirable behaviors. These observers argue that interventions aimed at these broader institutional factors can be more effective for creating social change than programs that try to influence one individual at a time. Wallack argues that "upstream" decisions that a society makes about its basic values and their relative rankings, how controversial issues are to be argued, what priorities are given to various participants in such arguments, and so on can have profound impacts on what individuals can and will do "downstream."[12] Wallack and others argue that, in many cases, it may be better to tackle important social problems upstream than downstream.

A case in point is cigarette smoking. For many years, smoking was generally perceived as an acceptable, even desirable, activity by mainstream society. Advertisements everywhere portrayed the pleasures of smoking. Movies made smoking seem the epitome of sophistication. Even doctors promoted the use of specific brands in advertising. Efforts by a few vocal health practitioners and activists to get cigarette advertising banned and warnings put on package labels were branded as the work of radicals who wanted to trample on individual freedoms. The cigarette industry carefully portrayed the quitting issue as one of individual choice, and anyone opposing smoking as someone who was against the most fundamental American rights.

Beginning in the 1970s, however, the framing of the debate on smoking changed. Partly as a result of overwhelming medical evidence on the negative effects of smoking on smokers and, later, on nonsmokers, and partly as a result of the Surgeon General's willingness to take a tough stand on the issue, the cigarette smoking debate changed from one in which anti-smokers were the "bad guys" trampling on individual freedoms to one in which the cigarette marketers were the "bad guys" selling death. One can characterize public health battles as between defenders of health and profit seekers or between health scientists and paid propagandists.

As a result of efforts of these public and private advocates, cigarette advertising disappeared from television, package labeling became blunter, restrictions on smoking in the workplace grew dramatically, and more managers of public spaces such as restaurants became willing to voluntarily ban smoking. The presidents of the leading tobacco manufacturers were called before a congressional committee to listen to charges that they had known all along that cigarettes were addictive yet kept this information secret from the public. And, finally, just before the turn of the century the tobacco industry agreed to settle suits brought by dozens of state attorneys general for $100s of millions to be used to compensate for the damage they have done and for future anti-smoking marketing efforts. These settlements led to the formation of the American Legacy Foundation, now leading massive efforts to further reduce smoking. Similar efforts are now being mobilized internationally (www.americanlegacy.org).

An Upstream Role for Public Relations

Many nonprofit organizations have recognized both the potential and the need for efforts to change the institutional and social environment in which undesirable behaviors take place. Thus, various groups see the need to effect such reforms as these:

1. Changing tax legislation so that willing donors can give more property to nonprofits.
2. Bringing pressure on manufacturers and retailers to package goods in degradable containers rather than just encourage individuals to recycle.
3. Ending the informal ban that TV networks in the United States have on advertising of condoms on television.
4. Changing the perception of rape victims from "deserving it" to being true victims.
5. Changing the nutrition issue from one of helping people eat better and lose weight to one of getting food producers to reduce saturated fats in their products and provide better nutrition labeling.
6. Bringing pressure to bear on the U.S. Congress to reduce tobacco farm subsidies and/or increase tobacco taxes so that higher prices will reduce tobacco consumption.
7. Urging more advertisers to include disabled people in their advertisements so that society will consider it normal to make accommodations for them.[13]

Achieving these reforms is increasingly being given a central role in nonprofit marketing strategies. Those who once were called traditional public relations specialists are now being given the challenge, usually in cooperation with many other individuals and organizations, of changing the social and institutional structure surrounding social problems.

We propose that this new role for public relations specialists be called *nonprofit public advocacy.*

Tools and Tactics

The task of the nonprofit public advocate can be broadly defined as public education and public pressure. The targets of their advocacy may be legislators, regulators, media gatekeepers, business executives, potential advocate–allies, and the general public. When focused on legislators and regulators, their advocacy is typically called lobbying.

There are a great many tools and tactics that a nonprofit public advocate can use to achieve its twin aims. We describe the main ones.

Reframing the Issues

Whichever organization or institution determines the labels and symbols that are used in any important debate has an important advantage in determining the outcome. Early in the abortion debate, one side framed the issue as between those who were pro-abortion and those who were pro-life. Put on the defensive, the pro-abortionists attempted to recreate the debate as *really* between those who were anti-abortion and those who were pro-choice. Being first to state the issue is always the preferred strategy. But, if the advocate is not first, at least the debate should never be argued on the opponent's terms without a challenge.

Conducting Public Education Campaigns

Before people would consider taking precautions to prevent AIDS, they had to know that there was a problem and that the problem is one that could affect them personally unless they changed their behavior. The role of public education campaigns in such Precontemplation Stage cases is to influence awareness and social norms. They say to college students, "AIDS is a killer; it is more prevalent than you think; and it is not just a problem for somebody else."[14]

Encouraging Media Advocacy

Pertchuck describes media advocacy as "the strategic use of mass media to advance a public policy initiative"[15] Wallack describes it as follows:

> Media advocacy promotes a range of strategies to stimulate broad-based media coverage in order to reframe public debate to increase public support for more effective policy-level approaches. . . . It does not attempt to change individual risk behavior directly but focuses attention on changing the way the problem is understood.[16]

One powerful media advocacy technique Wallack proposes in the field of health is what he calls "creative epidemiology." This approach uses good, hard science to bring the media's attention to an issue that they should cover and to frame the data in such a way that the media cannot afford to ignore it. He cites the example of an American Cancer Society videotape on smoking that says that "1,000 people quit smoking everyday—by dying. That is equivalent to two fully loaded jumbo jets crashing every day, with no survivors."[17] Such vivid use of the facts not only makes the point clear but also gives the media gatekeepers a graphic word-bite they can instantly use in the next edition or next newscast.

Creating Pseudo-events

Daniel Boorstin first described the pseudo-event in 1961 as a "newsworthy" event artificially created by advocates to bring media attention and coverage to an issue of importance to those advocates.[18] Examples of pseudo-events are press conferences, ribbon-cutting ceremonies, televised legislative bill signings, and most "photo opportunities" in a political campaign. A classic example of the pseudo-event is the tactic of advocates in the early part of the century to bring the public's attention to the degree to which unregulated food products contained toxic substances. The advocates set up a press conference in which reporters faced a table on which were piled powders in several colors. After the reporters arrived, various people at the head table silently proceeded to spoon the substances into their mouths. The point made to the assembled reporters was that the piles represented the amount of formaldehyde, arsenic, and so on that a typical consumer ingested every year. Such an event got more coverage than any dry report and set of statistics could ever achieve.

Producing Influential Books

The debates on a number of major social issues have been dramatically changed by the publication of a landmark book by a committed advocate. Upton Sinclair's *The Jungle* upset the meatpacking industry forever. Betty Friedan's *The Feminine Mystique* changed the way women thought about themselves and gave major impetus to the women's movement. Ralph Nader's *Unsafe at Any Speed* first brought America's attention to serious safety deficiencies in the way most automobiles were designed and resulted in major safety legislation in the 1970s. And Rachel Carson's *Silent Spring* profoundly changed the level of concern about the environment shared by people all over the world.

Enlisting the Help of the Entertainment Media

It is well understood that movies and television have a great deal of influence on what citizens consider normal or acceptable behavior, what goals they seek, what people they treat as authorities, and so on. Many argue that the casual and sensational attitude of these two media toward sex and drug use has made a major contribution to the problems we have in both areas today, especially among young people. Teen smoking patterns often seem to rise and fall depending on what is shown in the movies.

However, television and the movies can also be instruments of positive change. Sometimes, it is simply a matter of bringing an issue to the attention of the broadcast or movie industry. For example, for many years no one in a movie or television episode, including police officers, ever put on a seat belt before driving off. Once they became aware of their neglect, many directors incorporated regular seat belt use in their filming. Their actions made an important contribution toward defining seat belt usage as expected and routine.[19]

In the first years of the twenty-first century, the NBC program *The West Wing* has done a great deal to educate the public about important public policy issues. Many social observers believe that this program has done more to explain the issues of the day (the nature of terrorism, the use of sampling in the Census) than has any other public discussion or media coverage. (Observers have also noted that the program has also done a great deal to counteract the widespread notion that federal government leaders were immoral, self-serving egotists—an unanticipated public relations coup.)

Just as television and movies can be powerful influencers, social marketers in developing countries have found that radio soap operas are very effective unobtrusive vehicles for changing norms and behaviors around nutrition and AIDS.[20]

Lobbying

Volumes have been written about the importance of lobbyists in the legislative and regulatory process. Many nonprofits hire organizations whose sole responsibility is to get to know legislators, key aids, committee members, and other major players in any public policy debate that can affect the nonprofit's future and the success of its various missions. The lobbyist's job is to make sure that the nonprofit's position is clear to ultimate decision makers. Often, this means ensuring that nonprofit spokespeople have access to important people in order to present their case. As Fred Kroger notes in Exhibit 19-3, sometimes the important people can be inside your own team.

Working Through the Educational System

Many social change initiatives expressly target school systems as a way to influence future consumers and future decision makers and the way an issue is debated.[21] School programs can also have direct effects. In many developing countries, it has been discovered that one of the best ways to influence parents is to influence their children first in school and have them carry the message home. In other programs, the preparation of class syllabi, handouts, audiovisual aids, and quizzes can be effective in changing the way people think about good eating or the value of the union movement.[22]

Using the Fax Machine and the Web

The accelerated growth of sophisticated communication technologies creates new approaches for advocacy. Twenty years ago, the fax machine was a critical communication vehicle for revolutionaries in Eastern Europe to document what was happening inside their countries for the rest of world, especially foreign media,. Today, viral marketing through the Internet has proven to be very powerful (www.viralmarketing.com). For example, Amnesty International has created an advocacy network called FAST (Fast Action Stops Torture), linking a wide range of individuals and organizations who can speak out when a major human rights problem emerges around the world. In October 2000, it urged net members to contact Turkish authorities about Sehmuz Temel, a Kurd in custody who had previously been tortured by authorities. The campaign prompted 2,200 e-mails and Temel was released, quite possibly because of this campaign.[23]

Being Audience-Centered

Of course, the objective of most of the efforts of the nonprofit public advocate is to influence the behavior of key target individuals whether they be educators, media gatekeepers, legislators, or business executives. Clearly, this is really just another marketing task. Therefore, many of the principles elucidated elsewhere in this book are perfectly appropriate for the task of public advocacy. Probably the most important of these principles is to make sure that the advocate's attempts to influence focus on the needs and wants of the target audience, not the nonprofit organization or its cause. The danger is always that the nonprofit public advocate will be so immersed in seeking his or her "noble" behavioral goal that it is inevitable the persuasive argument put to the legislator or news director to get them to act is in terms of how this will benefit the advocate and his or her cause. This would be a major tactical mistake.

The key point is to show the targets how the recommended action is in *their* interests. We discussed earlier how this approach would apply to reporters and others in the

EXHIBIT 19-3

FRED KROGER OF THE CENTERS FOR DISEASE CONTROL AND PREVENTION ON POLITICS—THE FIFTH "P" OF SOCIAL MARKETING

The Centers for Disease Control and Prevention (CDC) described the first cases of what became known as AIDS in June 1981. American scientists were instrumental in unraveling many mysteries surrounding the disease in short order. U.S. efforts to inform the public about AIDS and its causative agent, HIV, were slow to develop, a problem often attributed to political indifference.

The federal government's information campaign, "America Responds to AIDS," was launched in October 1987, more than six years and 40,000 deaths after the first cases were reported. A brochure, which was to accompany the launch as a mailing to every U.S. household, needed clearance from the White House Domestic Policy Council. The brochure was neither approved nor disapproved, so it was never sent.

Subsequently, Congress passed legislation for a national mailout of AIDS information and authorized CDC to approve the content. In June 1988, the United States became the seventh country to mail an AIDS brochure to its residents. The brochure, "Understanding AIDS," carried a cover message from Surgeon General C. Everett Koop. Consumer testing had shown Dr. Koop to be the only widely recognized government official who was considered credible on the AIDS issue. According to various public opinion surveys, this was the most widely read publication in America for June and July of that year, with an estimated 86 million adults claiming to have read all or parts of it. The brochure was also praised by the National Academy of Sciences in *AIDS: Sexual Behavior and Intravenous Drug*

Use for communicating "in a value-free manner with simple and explicit language that avoids moralizing." Much of the brochure's acceptance can be attributed to the extensive review and consumer testing that it underwent to ensure that it communicated relevant information that could be understood by adults with a sixth-grade level of literacy.

A second report on HIV and AIDS that carried a message from Dr. Koop's successor, Dr. Antonia Novello, was released to the public in June 1993 at a press conference in Berlin, Germany, in conjunction with the Sixth International AIDS Conference. This comprehensive update on AIDS included information on medical advances and on the efficacy of condoms in preventing HIV and sexually transmitted disease (STD) transmission, and had been slated for domestic distribution on December 1, 1991, World AIDS Day. The Surgeon General's update was to have been the communication centerpiece to the sixth phase of the "America Responds to AIDS" campaign. Consumer testing had shown that the report produced dramatic improvements in what readers understood to be true about the disease. Like its predecessor publication, early drafts of the report were neither approved nor disapproved by administration officials, this time in the Office of the Assistant Secretary for Health.

When the Clinton administration took office and sought to replace Surgeon General Novello with then Arkansas Health Commissioner Dr. Joycelyn Elders, Dr. Novello agreed to resign her post before her term had expired with one proviso—that she be allowed to publish and distribute her report to the American public on AIDS before she left office. Administration officials agreed, the report was resurrected by CDC staffers, revised to reflect additional medical advances, and announced to the American public from a foreign platform.

As a government agency attempting to apply marketing principles to the "selling" of HIV prevention, CDC has learned the importance of social marketing's big "Ps." Along with product, price, place, and promotion, governmental marketing efforts must take into account the overriding principle of politics.

Source: Personal correspondence.

media. In the case of legislators, a key need is always going to be reelection. As a consequence, the nonprofit public advocate needs ultimately to demonstrate how the proposed action will aid reelection or at least not harm it. One of the ways many lobbyists, such as those for the National Rifle Association, seek to demonstrate positive electoral impact is by orchestrating phone calls and letters from constituents telling the senator or representative that a certain position would certainly please the voters. This is just sound marketing that can apply equally to other advocate targets.

SUMMARY

Public relations is a well-established function in profit and nonprofit organizations. Traditionally, public relations has been responsible for maintaining and enhancing the organization's public image. More recently, the role of public relations has been expanded to include public advocacy.

Traditionally, the task of public relations is to form, maintain, or change public attitudes toward the nonprofit organization, its programs, and its personnel. The process of public relations consists of seven steps: (1) identifying the organization's relevant publics, (2) measuring the images and attitudes held by these publics, (3) establishing image and attitude goals for the key publics, (4) developing cost-effective public relations strategies, (5) preparing for public relations crises, (6) carefully choosing specific public relations tools, such as written material, audiovisual material, organization identity media, news, events, speeches, Web messages and telephone information services, and (7) implementing actions and evaluating results. Just as elsewhere in the organization, a customer orientation is the best philosophy to apply to both long-term and short-term public relations strategies.

In their new role as public advocates, nonprofit public relations specialists are increasingly being asked to influence the "upstream" social structures, norms, and values that have profound effects on individual behaviors "downstream." There are a number of tools and tactics the advocate can use to achieve these goals, including reframing the nature of public debate, conducting public education, encouraging media advocacy, creating pseudo-events, writing influential books, enlisting the help of the entertainment media, lobbying, and working through the educational system.

QUESTIONS

1. Reporters have linked recent announcements by your nonprofit organization to a conspiracy. They call you as the marketing director and recount a series of events including large payments made to your organization by private companies. They allege that your organization's CEO is improperly spending funds, including the use of organization funds for his personal use. How do you respond to these allegations?

2. How would you organize and execute a public advocacy campaign to get the FCC and major television networks to permit condom advertising on television?

3. Create a list of pseudo-events that you would execute in the United States to draw attention to the fact that children are starving in East Africa. What would you like the target audience response to be? How would you measure the effectiveness of these events?

4. If you were asked to create a public image campaign for the U.S. Department of Defense, how would you first measure that image and then what approaches would you utilize to improve it?

5. What are the major publics for which the campaign described in question 4 is relevant? What are the image goals that you would set for each and why? How would you rank those publics in terms of their importance to the Department of Defense and why?

NOTES

1. Some of the material is this chapter is adapted from Philip Kotler and William Mindak, "Marketing and Public Relations," *Journal of Marketing,* October 1978, pp. 13–20.

2. Scott M. Cutlip, "The Beginning of PR Counseling," *Editor and Publisher,* November 26, 1950, p. 16.

3. *Public Relations News,* October 27, 1947.

4. Robert Hanley, "New Jersey Court Overturns Ouster of Gay Boy Scout," *New York Times,* August 5, 1999, p. A–1.

5. Robert F. Howe, "Metro Apologizes for Delays," *Washington Post,* May 14, 1993, p. C4.

6. Joel Bleifuss, "New Angles from the Spin Doctors," *New York Times,* November 20, 1994, p. F13.

7. Timothy G. Manners, "TV Talk Show Tour Extends Marketing Reach," *Marketing News,* August 16, 1985, p. 1.

8. "Study Identifies Qualities of Effective Health Public Service Announcements," *Marketing News,* April 3, 1981, p. 7.

9. Lisa de Moraes, "The TV Column," *Washington Post,* February 22, 2002, p. C7.

10. *Public Information Guide* (New York: American Cancer Society, 1965), p. 19.

11. Material in this section is taken from Alan R. Andreasen, "Communicating by Listening," *Issues & Opportunities,* Vol. 1, No. 5 (August 1989).

12. Lawrence Wallack, "Media Advocacy: Promoting Health Through Mass Communication," in K. Glanz, F. M. Lewis, and B. K. Rimer (eds.), *Health Behavior and Health Education* (San Francisco: Jossey-Bass Publisher, 1990), pp. 370–386. See also Charles T. Salmon, *Information Campaigns: Balancing Social Values and Social Change* (Newbury Park, CA: Sage Publications, 1989).

13. Richard W. Pollay, "The Distorted Mirror: Reflections on the Unintended Consequences of Advertising," *Journal of Marketing,* 50 (1986), pp. 18–36.

14. Jeffrey D. Fisher and William A. Fisher, "Changing AIDS-Risk Behavior," *Psychological Bulletin,* 1992, Vol. 111, No. 3, pp. 455–474.

15. Advocacy Institute, *Smoking Control Media Advocacy Guidelines* (Bethesda, Md.:

National Cancer Institute, National Institutes of Health, 1989).

16. Wallack, "Media Advocacy," p. 376.

17. Ibid. p. 377.

18. Daniel Boorstin, *The Image or What Happened to the American Dream* (New York: Atheneum, 1961).

19. E. Scott Geller, "Using Television to Promote Safety Belt Usage," in Ronald E. Rice and Charles K. Atkin (eds.), *Public Communications Campaigns,* 2nd ed. (Newbury Park, Ca.: Sage Publications, 1989), pp. 201–203.

20. Phyllis T. Piotrow and P. L. Coleman, "The Enter-Educate Approach," *Integration,* 31 (March 1992), pp. 4–6.

21. M. B. Mittelmark et al., "Community-wide Prevention of Cardiovascular Disease: Education Strategies of the Minnesota Heart Health Program," *Preventive Medicine,* 15 (1986), pp. 1–17.

22. Charles T. Salmon, "Campaigns for Social 'Improvement': An Overview of Values, Rationales, and Impacts," in Charles T. Salmon, *Information Campaigns: Balancing Social Values and Social Change* (Newbury Park, Ca.: Sage Publications, 1989), p. 45.

23. Nicole Wallace, "Activists Use E-Mail to Combat Torture," *The Chronicle of Philanthropy,* November 16, 2000, p. 33.

SECTION V: CONTROLLING MARKETING STRATEGIES

CHAPTER 20

Marketing Evaluation, Monitoring, and Control

CHAPTER 20

Marketing Evaluation, Monitoring, and Control

Celebrities and charitable causes can have a marvelously symbiotic relationship. Nonprofits recruit spokespeople like Denzel Washington for the Boys & Girls Clubs of America who personify the values of the organization, who can get them public attention for issues they wish to raise, and who can be a potent draw in fundraising activities. For celebrities, involvement with a charitable cause provides the chance to use their status to have an impact on causes for which they have a personal connection, like Michael J. Fox and Parkinson's disease. It can also provide valuable publicity when one's career is at a low ebb. And, it can add depth and dimension to a personal profile which society may expect to be shallow and single-minded.

But these potentially synergistic partnerships can have major negative effects if either side does not evaluate the proposed relationship they are anticipating. One major nonprofit seeking a new spokesperson evaluated a range of candidates, made a choice, built a launch campaign, and was about to go national. At almost the last moment, a "guardian angel" at a major magazine called up to report something he just heard on the radio and to suggest that it seemed sensible not to launch the campaign introducing the new spokesperson, O. J. Simpson!

Celebrities can find themselves embarrassed, too. Author Tom Clancy had to shut down a foundation to aid children with cancer because he said that his administrator spent $5 million in seven years and never set up the Web site for sick kids she was supposed to do. Similarly, baseball player Sammy Sosa found that the charity he set up to help the Dominican Republic's hurricane victims was under investigation and questions were being raised about Sosa's own use of the foundation's money (apparently taking funds and putting them in his business account in the Dominican Republic).

These and other celebrities have realized the importance of careful monitoring as essential to maintaining the integrity of their personal foundations. Garth Brooks and his advisors set up the Touch 'em All Foundation with an experienced manager and installed someone whose specific title is "executive vice president for finance." All funds collected (much from major league ballplayers) are deposited in a fund managed by Merrill Lynch. Touch 'em All's finance vice president notes, "We deal in the image of Garth [Brooks]. You don't screw up when you're dealing with people's reputations."

Source: Drawn from Bridget Rosenberg and Richard Williamson, "Celebs Find that Good Causes Can Lead to Bad Blood," *Nonprofit Times*, September 200, pp. 1, 6.

Strategic planning in marketing is crucial in setting the nonprofit organization off in the proper direction, whether for a year's activities or for a specific campaign. But pushing an enterprise into the stream of behavior change by no means ensures that it will either get to its desired goal or get there as quickly and efficiently as possible. To ensure that strategic marketing achieves its goals in a timely and efficient manner, the nonprofit manager must develop and put in place effective control systems for strategic plans and specific campaigns and, where necessary, prepare to take corrective action. There are two types of control that management needs: strategic control and program control.

Strategic control focuses on larger issues and requires tracking changes in the broad environment, competitors' actions and plans, perceptions of the organization held by the general public, organization strengths and weaknesses, and broad trends in organization performance. This information then becomes input into subsequent rounds of the organization's strategic marketing planning process (OMPP) described in Chapter 3.

Program control requires the development of systems for more or less continual monitoring of program performance for purposes of day-to-day fine-tuning of the strategic plan to correct for undesirable performance. In this chapter, we shall focus primarily on such systems for regular monitoring and corrective action. We investigate several considerations in designing such systems and look at several measures that could be used by specific institutions. We look at various approaches to measuring behavioral outcomes and to tracking target audience satisfaction. The latter is particularly important since (1) target audience satisfaction is—or ought to be—the goal of most nonprofit organizations, and (2) behavior measures may be either inappropriate at a given stage of a program or unavailable.

Throughout this chapter it should be remembered that not all evaluation research need be expensive or time-consuming. As we noted in Chapter 5, there are many techniques available for doing inexpensive *but good* marketing research. A good example was reported by Peter Drucker, the well-known management consultant and teacher. Drucker noted that he had been teaching for over 60 years. Once a year, he takes a few days to telephone a random sample of 50 or 60 students who graduated 10 years earlier. He asks, "Looking back, what did we contribute in this school? What is still important to you?" He follows this by asking "What should we do better? What should we stop doing?" He reports that "This feedback has been absolutely essential in those areas where I had some leadership responsibility."[1]

MONITORING AND CONTROL

When we described the process of developing campaign plans, we emphasized the need to use the target audience member as the touchstone for every element of the campaign. And we emphasized the need for *listening* at the outset, *pretesting* before going into the field, and *monitoring* to keep track of progress. Monitoring is critical to help campaign managers know such things as these:

1. Is the campaign on schedule?
2. Are we reaching all of the target segments?
3. Are we having the desired impact on each segment?
4. What elements of the campaign are working well and which ones are not?
5. What's missing from the campaign?
6. Has the competitive or social environment changed in important ways that would recommend campaign changes?
7. How are our partners (if any) responding; is their participation likely to change?
8. What do the funders (e.g., the government, a venture philanthropist, or a foundation) think of the campaign and its progress?

Many surprises are likely to occur during any campaign's execution that will call for new responses or adjustments. Some things will work and some won't. Marketing monitoring and control systems are an intrinsic part of the campaign planning and implementation process since they permit such crucial and timely adjustments.

As indicated in Figure 20-1, the control process is in reality a cybernetic system that will ideally function not unlike a thermostat regulating a building's temperature. Management sets a goal (the desired temperature) and puts in place a device or system for detecting deviations from the goal (a thermometer) and ascertaining causes of the deviations (above or below ideal temperature because the space has warmed or cooled). The loop in the system is then closed by a device or subsystem that makes the necessary corrections (a trip-switch that restarts the furnace or turns on the air conditioning).

Control systems in nonprofit organizations, of course, can differ greatly in complexity, timeliness, and precision. For example, a library can simply monitor its total circulation and periodically smooth out irregularities or stimulate increased book use through radio ads, newspaper articles, Web site promotions, or direct mail. Or it can look periodically at the circulation of each of its departments during different parts of the day or week and seek corrective actions that would boost lagging departments or increase patronage in particular departments during off-peak hours or days. At a more complex level, it could attempt to look, not just at circulation, but at *who* was taking out books and develop program elements that would, say, bring the number of elderly or teenagers coming to the library up to goal levels.

Monitoring systems can also vary as to timeliness. The library can measure its performance daily, weekly, monthly, quarterly, or even annually. Obviously, the faster an

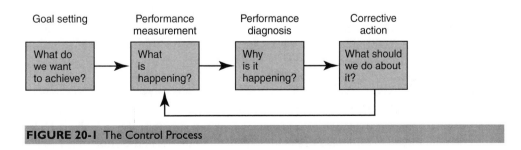

FIGURE 20-1 The Control Process

organization's environment changes and the more competitive the activity that takes place, the more frequently the system should be "read." Thus, libraries can get by with relatively infrequent measures compared to hospitals in major urban centers. In very volatile situations, daily monitoring may be necessary.

Finally, the distinction between monitoring and evaluation must be emphasized. In the nonprofit world—especially that part of it that relies heavily on grants or government funding—there is usually a requirement that a program be evaluated. Typically, this is interpreted to mean "show us at the end what you have achieved." This gets translated into a before-and-after evaluation protocol where a baseline measure is taken before the program is started and then the same measures are taken at the end. Differences are then submitted as evidence that the program worked (or didn't) and the money was well spent. There are two related problems with this approach. First, it very often means that defects in the program are discovered too late to do anything about them. Second, the funder never really knows how effective the program *could* have been if adjustments were made along the way.

Monitoring systems are designed to avoid these occurrences by providing managers with along-the-way measures that provide timely adjustments and maximize program cost-effectiveness.

A Caution

It is important to note that some observers of nonprofit programs argue that measures ought to go *beyond* specific behaviors to assess their broader social impact. To illustrate the point, assume that a multiyear program that increases the number of immunizations of children under two in Ghana can be monitored by counting the number of children showing up for the immunizations. From a marketer's standpoint, this should be the major benchmark for his or her performance because the marketer's "job" is to bring about these desired behaviors. However, social critics or funders might ask (1) does an increase in child immunizations lead to better health and longer lives for the target children and (2) is it possible that immunizations would rise while general morbidity and mortality also rise? Is it possible that (1) the immunizations made the children healthier; (2) because they were healthier, parents sent them out to work at a much younger age; and therefore (3) they were getting sick and dying more often—and at a younger age—from work-related causes?! In the latter case, from the country's standpoint, the marketing campaign was a success but the *real* objective—what the society really sought (healthier children)—was not achieved; in fact, it was made worse.

It is not the marketer's responsibility to decide what the goal of a specific behavior-influence program should be. This is the responsibility of the program sponsor or the nonprofit organization's strategic planning committee. The marketer's task is to bring about the assigned behavior in an effective and efficient manner.[2] However, as the participant in of the program who will be most in touch with the target audience, the marketer must from time to time ask whether the campaign is really designed to achieve the social change outcome everyone really wants.[3]

Types of Monitoring Tools

A monitoring system like that described in Figure 20-1 is driven by an approach called *management by objectives*. Top management starts the process by developing aggregate goals for each program (or the entire enterprise) for the planning period, (for example, number of people reached, messages delivered, trial behaviors taken, relationships created, and so on). These goals can then be assigned to individual managers or supervisors.

What are the monitoring indicia that might be used by management to check on the progress of their programs in reaching their goals? Given the marketing framework of this book, it is clear that the starting point must be (1) a clear specification of *behavioral* objectives—even if they are long run and (2) an explicit road map of how the organization proposes to get there. The monitoring process then is simply a set of tracking devices for measuring progress along the road. A thorough tracking process also has the advantage of allowing complex ex post facto analyses and modeling of cause-and-effect relationships that allow managers to confirm, revise, or abandon their mental models of what it takes to achieve the behavioral outcome in future campaigns

While the monitoring system must emphasize behavioral outcomes and the steps necessary to achieve them, it is also critical to track marketing costs. Marketing managers must be tasked not only with achieving—or at least moving toward—key behavioral objectives, as we pointed out in Chapter 11, he or she must also be charged with doing so in a cost-effective manner. While we do not discuss this component here, it is important that marketing management be able to answer the following questions:

1. Are we over- or under-spending the budget allocated (or the one the manager asked for)?
2. Are all of the program elements cost effective—what are the benefit/cost ratios of various outlays? Was the big kickoff banquet worth it? Are we spending too much on Web site development? Should we keep renting this equipment or buy it ourselves?
3. Is the budget adequate to the task? Is it excessive (few will conclude this!)?
4. Is the budget appropriately allocated—are we getting equivalent performance from a dollar spent in each program component?
5. How are our marketing staff members using the money entrusted to them—are some more wasteful than others?

We begin where all good nonprofit programs ought to end—with behavior.

Tracking Target Audience Behavior

The single most important kind of measure for any nonprofit should be a measure of *behavior*. As we noted in the very first chapters, the ultimate objective of any marketing effort is influencing behavior. In retail and catalogue ventures, the behavior is captured in sales. In other cases, marketers might look at such behaviors as (1) membership applications, (2) votes, (3) volunteering, (4) donations, (5) attendance, (6) trash recycled, or (7) letters written to legislators. In social marketing cases, they might look at the number of people in the target audience stopping smoking or immunizing their children, the number of child abuse cases reported, or the number of missing children found. In each of these cases, the experienced marketer would like to develop a tracking system to measure success both at any point in time and over time.

Non-Behavioral Measures

Of course, any program will want to measure other outcomes and activities in addition to behavior impacts, especially for campaigns expected to take a long time to achieve their goals. In such cases, interim measures of progress along the Stages of Change will be important. Measures of knowledge and attitudes of individuals toward considering the behavior (for example, reducing energy consumption) will indicate the size of the audience still in the Precontemplation Stage. Measures of the number of people who have formed perceptions of benefits and costs of proposed actions will give a sense of the size of the group in the Contemplation Stage. These measures will also give valuable insights into what might need to be done to change these perceptions — for example, alerting management to the need to add new benefits.

It will also be useful to find out how many people are trying to change (in the Preparation/Action Stage) and the number already doing the new behavior (in the Maintenance Stage). Studies of those in these two stages should be designed to not only estimate the size of the groups but also to identify barriers that seem problematic for the first group and rewards that seem to be working for those in Maintenance.

Simple bar charts tracking the number of people in major segments who are at each stage can be an excellent visual device for seeing progress and communicating it to those stakeholders inside and outside the organization.

Measuring Change

Monitoring involves the measurement of change. To measure change, one must have the right instruments. Researchers who wish to monitor the performance of a target market over time can choose among four basic types of change measures. For example, they can study changes in target audience behavior in these ways:

1. *Retrospectively,* by asking a single sample of target audience members what they are doing now and what they did at some past point in time.
2. *Cross-sectionally,* by comparing behaviors of a single sample of target audience members presumed to be earlier or later in a process (e.g., comparing seat-belt use of 21- to 30-year-olds with that of 31- to 40-year-olds, or those never exposed to a particular campaign with those exposed for two, four, and six months).
3. *Cross-sectionally over time,* by asking about behaviors of different samples at two points in time (e.g., as in traditional polling).
4. *Longitudinally over time,* by taking behavioral measures of the same panel of target audience members at different points over time.

The value of the last approach, panel studies, as compared to cross-sectional polls, is suggested in the following hypothetical but realistic example. Suppose AARP creates a detailed report on the impact of Internet health insurance fraud on the elderly, as part of a campaign to get the U.S. Congress to pass a federal statute regulating insurers who are seeking target audience members over the Web. The report is filled with dramatic examples of elderly people who have been duped into unneeded expenditures. AARP distributes the report to Congressional offices and to the media. Further, suppose that small surveys of 100 Congressional staffers and several reporters were taken before and after the report was issued using *different* samples and that these samples showed that the proportion of individuals supporting the legislation rose from 40 to 50 percent.

Understandably, AARP would be pleased with such results. But this pleasure is based on a belief that if one studied the *same* target audience members before and after the report, the shifting of their positions over time would look like the figures shown in Table 20-1a. The true result in a worst-case scenario, however, could be like that in Table 20-1b.

As shown in Table 20-1a, the AARP report added nicely to its present core of supporters. However, as Table 20-1b shows, the report alienated three-quarters of its core supporters and attracted a third of those opposing the legislation and *all* those previously undecided. Under the Table 20-1b scenario, AARP would realize it had to move fast to win back "its people" while at the same time trying to hold on to the possibly fickle "undecideds" who have just switched over to supporting AARP. Learning this crucial information is *only* possible with panel data. Only panel data can show *who* changed. Such data may be absolutely crucial to an organization that wishes to move quickly and correctly in a volatile marketplace.

Panel data, however, have their problems. First, there is a serious danger that prior measures will influence later measures or interact with the intervention to foul up the results. In the previous example, people contacted before the AARP report may have been stimulated to pay more attention to the topic (and the report) and so the intervention would appear to be *more* effective than it really was. A second problem is dropouts. The example above assumed that the panel stayed intact. But if some people drop out between waves and they are the ones indifferent to the topic, measures of those still in the panel will again overstate the effects.

The way around these problems, of course, is to use different cross-sections each time. One gives up the ability to understand who changed for (presumably) a more accurate measure of gross effects.

Tracking Target Audience Satisfaction

Even when a significant number of target audience members are in the Maintenance Stage, many marketing managers will want measures that indicate the likelihood of repeat transactions (i.e., regular recycling, revisits to the symphony or museum, or repeat participation in exercise programs). A key measure used in the commercial sector for this purpose is a measure of target audience satisfaction. Thus, target audience member satisfaction data often should be included as a major indicator of organizational success. We define the term "satisfaction" as follows:

TABLE 20-1 Hypothetical Panel Study Results

	a		b		
	After Speech		*After Speech*		
Before Report	*Support Legislation*	*Oppose Legislation*	*Support Legislation*	*Oppose Legislation*	*Total*
Support Legislation	40%	0%	10%	30%	40%
Oppose Legislation	10%	20%	10%	20%	30%
No preference	0%	30%	30%	0%	30%
Total	50%	50%	50%	50%	100%

Satisfaction is the state felt by a person who has experienced a performance (or out-come) that has fulfilled his or her expectations.

Thus, as we noted earlier, satisfaction is a function of the relative levels of expectations and perceived performance.[4] A person will experience one of three states of satisfaction. If the results exceed the person's expectations, the person is highly satisfied — even delighted. If the results match the expectations, the person is satisfied. If the results fall short of the expectations, the person is dissatisfied.

In this last case, the amount of dissatisfaction depends upon the target audience member's method of handling the gap between expectations and performance. Some target audience members will try to *minimize* the felt dissonance by imagining that performance was really better than they first thought or by thinking that they set their expectations too high. Other target audience members will exaggerate the perceived performance gap because of their disappointment. These will be more of a problem for the marketer because they are more prone to reduce or end their contact with the organization and/or complain to friends and co-workers.

Thus, to understand satisfaction, we must also understand how people form their expectations. Expectations are formed to some extent on the basis of people's past experience with the same or similar situations and statements made by friends and associates. Statements made by the marketer also affect them. The marketer, therefore, needs to monitor both the performance of its offerings and also the expectations it raises. If it raises expectations too high, it is likely to create subsequent dissatisfaction; if it sets them low enough, it might create high satisfaction—although it risks lowering the number of transactions by suggesting that its offerings promise only limited benefits.

Monitoring target audience member satisfaction can be extremely helpful to management, especially if "total quality" is a major part of a strategy—for example, in hospital or education settings or in various participation programs (stop smoking, dieting, exercise). In Cleveland, local hospitals banded together to produce a twice-yearly target audience member attitude study. Patrick McTigue, President of Corbett Health Connect, noted that the research "has become a major quality-driving effort on the part of Cleveland's hospitals that are not doing well."[5]

Still, target audience member satisfaction, in spite of its central importance, is difficult to measure. Organizations use various methods to infer how much target audience member satisfaction they are creating.

Complaint and Suggestion Systems

One possible approach is to establish complaint and suggestion systems. A responsive organization makes it easy for its clients to complain if they are disappointed in some ways with the service they have received. Management will want complaints to surface on the theory that clients who are not given an opportunity to complain might reduce their relationship with the organization, spread negative word of mouth, or abandon it completely. Indeed, it has been found that dissatisfied target audience members are likely to tell 9 to 12 other target audience members, whereas satisfied target audience members speak to only 2 or 3.[6] However, the likelihood of negative effects will be reduced substantially if dissatisfied target audience members are encouraged to voice their complaints to the marketer. They are more likely to continue to patronize the organization, *even if* the marketer does not respond to the complaint to the target audience member's satisfaction. Further, it has been found that the faster the marketer responds to a voiced complaint, the more likely it will lead to a favorable attitude on the part of the target audience member.

How can complaints be facilitated? The first step is for management to accept the seemingly contrary notion that more complaining is *better* and to communicate this position up and down the organization. Complaints should be seen as audience-volunteered marketing research data to be actively sought, not as information to be squelched for fear that complaints will lead only to reprimands. Once this crucial atmosphere is established, the organization can set up systems that make it easy for dissatisfied target audience members (or satisfied target audience members) to express their feelings to the organization. Several devices can be used in this connection. A hospital, for example, could place suggestion boxes in the corridors. It could supply exiting patients with a card on which comments can be easily checked off. It could establish a patient advocate or ombudsman system to hear patients' grievances and seek remedies. It could establish a nurse grievance committee to review nurse complaints.

An organization can then identify the major categories of complaints. It should then focus its corrective actions on those categories showing high frequency, high seriousness, and high remediability.

Target Audience Satisfaction Surveys

A major problem with volunteered complaints, as noted in a 1977 Andreasen and Best study, is that they are unrepresentative of both the types of complaints and the types of complainers.[7] The study found that target audience members are more likely to volunteer complaints about problems in which high costs (economic, social, and psychological) are involved or by which they are seriously inconvenienced. Further, they are more likely to complain if they think the nonprofit organization is to blame and they themselves did not contribute to the problem. Finally, they are more likely to complain if the nature of the problem and its source are manifest—that is, if the existence of a problem is not really a matter of individual judgment. For these reasons, a nonprofit is more likely to receive complaints about issues involving large monetary and time costs on the part of clients. Problems involving broken items, delayed services, and discourteous employees are more likely to surface than problems in which, say, medical care is just a bit impersonal or in which the staff of an educational seminar seems underprepared and the seminar is not taught very well. Yet it is just these more minor kinds of unreported feelings of dissatisfaction that management would like to know about. The obvious bad features of any program usually quickly become apparent without much management research. The subtle things that can truly sink a basically good program or institution through poor word of mouth, lack of repeat behavior, and, perhaps worse still, just plain apathy are the very things that don't get volunteered by dissatisfied target audience members. People must be asked.

People must also be asked because not all of them will speak up. To voice a complaint, one must not only have a problem or a dissatisfaction, but one has to understand where and how to complain and have the skills to do so and the gumption to speak up. Not everyone has these qualities. Indeed, research has consistently shown that vocal complainers are much more likely to be socially upscale and have higher incomes and better educations. They are also likely to be relatively young. Yet many nonprofit programs, such as those in social work or those requiring long-term behavioral change, like stopping smoking or exercising regularly, have downscale audiences as their primary targets. Hearing from these people is essential to program success, yet they are the least likely to volunteer information about their dissatisfaction.

Finally, the voicing of complaints is sometimes inhibited by the institution itself. Unless the circumstances are right and the nonprofit marketer sets the right tone, people are relatively unlikely to complain about their church, their doctor, or even their lawyer or accountant. The Andreasen and Best study reported the following dissatisfaction experience rates for medical and dental services compared with rates for all services and all products.[8]

	Medical/Dental	All Services	All Products
Percentage reporting problems	14.9%	20.9%	20.0%
Percentage with problem voicing a complaint to marketer	32.7%	42.3%	40.2%
Percentage who complained who were not satisfied with marketer response	46.4%	28.7%	23.6%

While patients perceived fewer problems with their medical and dental care than with other services or products, they were significantly less likely to speak up about them. And when they did, they found the medical and dental community much less responsive than other product and service marketers in resolving their complaints. Only one in six of those who had a serious dissatisfaction felt bold enough to speak up about it and were lucky enough to have it handled satisfactorily.

As a result of these types of factors, the better, more responsive nonprofits supplement the devices described earlier with direct periodic surveys of target audience member satisfaction. They send questionnaires or make telephone calls to a random sample of past users to find out how much they like the service. Some organizations also survey clients of competitors or of marketers of unrelated products and services to identify potential market opportunities on which they might capitalize. Through direct surveys, they avoid the several biases of complaint monitoring systems.

Target audience member satisfaction can be measured in a number of ways; consider the following approaches:

Directly Reported Satisfaction   A university can distribute a questionnaire to a representative sample of students, asking them to state their satisfaction with the university as a whole and with specific components. The questionnaire would be distributed on a periodic basis either in person, in the mail, through the Internet, or through a telephone inquiry.

The questionnaire would contain questions of the following form:

Indicate how satisfied you are with _____ *on the following scale:*

1	2	3	4	5
Highly dissatisfied	Dissatisfied	Indifferent	Satisfied	Highly satisfied

Here, five values are used, although some scales use only three values and others use as many as eleven.

When the results are in, a histogram can be prepared showing the percentage of students who fall into each group. Of course, students within any group—such as the highly dissatisfied group—may have quite different intensities of dissatisfaction ranging from mild feelings of disappointment with the university to intense feelings of anger. Unfortunately, there is no way to make interpersonal comparisons of intensity and we can only rely on the self-reported feelings of the respondents.

If the histogram shows more answers to the left, then the university is in deep trouble. If the histogram is bell shaped, then it has the usual number of dissatisfied, indifferent, and satisfied students. If the histogram shows more answers to the right, the university can be very satisfied that it is a responsive organization meeting its goal of delivering high satisfaction to the majority of its target audience members.[9] Finally, if the distribution is bimodal (i.e., two peaks), the organization may need to develop a second offering to meet the needs of the dissatisfied market while retaining the present offering to serve the satisfied group.

Derived Dissatisfaction   The second method of satisfaction measurement is based on the premise stated earlier that a particular student's satisfaction is influenced by the perceived performance and his expectations. He is asked two questions about each component of the university's offering, for example:

The accessibility and availability of the faculty:

a. How much is there now?
   (min)   1   2   3   4   5   6   7   (max)
b. How much did you expect?
   (min)   1   2   3   4   5   6   7   (max)

Suppose the student circles 2 for part (a) and 5 for part (b). We can then derive a "performance deficiency" score by subtracting the answer for part (a) from part (b), here 3. The greater the performance of deficiency score, the greater his degree of dissatisfaction (or the smaller his degree of satisfaction).

This method provides more useful information than the previous method. By averaging the scores of all the respondents to part (a), the researcher learns the average perceived performance. The dispersion around the average shows how much agreement there is. If all students see the academic program of the university at approximately 2 on a 7-point scale, this means the program is pretty bad. If students hold widely differing perceptions of the program's actual quality, further analysis is needed of why the perceptions differ so much and what individual or group factors it might be related to.

It is also useful to average the scores of all the respondents to part (b). This reveals the average student's view of how much quality is expected in the academic program. The measure of dispersion shows how much spread there is in student opinion about the desirable level of quality. This is, in effect, a good measure of how clear the institution's brand image is.

Problem Rates   A third approach is simply to ask respondents three major questions: (1) Have you engaged in some transaction with us in the last 12 months? (2) If yes, did you experience any problems with it? (3) If no problems are mentioned, was there any way in which it could have been better for you? There are several advantages to this approach. First, specific problems or deficiencies can be identified, including many that management may not have anticipated. These can then be the subject of immediate corrective action, especially if respondents indicate how serious a problem it was for them.

Second, respondents reporting problems can be asked about their subsequent actions, including whether they complained to the marketer, spoke with friends, or took other actions. This would yield data on how well the organization's complaint-generation system was working. Those who complained to the organization could also be asked how this process turned out so that management could monitor the effectiveness of its complaint-handling operation.

Relation Between Target Audience Member Satisfaction and Other Goals of the Organization

Many people believe that the marketing concept calls upon an organization to *maximize* the satisfaction of its target audience members. This, however, is not realistic, and it would be better to interpret the marketing concept as saying that the organization should strive to create a high level of satisfaction in its target audience members about recommended behaviors, though not necessarily the maximum level. The reasons are several.

First, target audience member satisfaction can always be increased by accepting additional cost. Thus, a university might hire better faculty, build better facilities, and charge lower tuition to increase the satisfaction of its students. Obviously, however, a university faces a cost constraint in trying to maximize the satisfaction of a particular public.

Second, the organization has to satisfy many publics. Increasing the satisfaction of one public might reduce the satisfaction available to another public. The organization owes each of its publics some specific level of satisfaction. Ultimately, the organization must operate on the philosophy that it is trying to satisfy the needs of different groups at levels that are acceptable to these groups within the constraints of its total resources. This is why the organization must systematically measure the levels of satisfaction expected by its different constituent publics and the current amounts they are, in fact, receiving.

The organization hopes to derive a number of benefits as a result of creating high satisfaction in its publics. First, the staff of the organization will work with a better sense of purpose and pride. Second, the organization creates loyal publics and this reduces the costs of market turnover. Third, the loyal publics say good things to others about the organization, which attracts new target audience members without requiring as much direct effort on the part of the organization.

EXTERNAL SURVEILLANCE AND INTERNAL ETHICS

A growing phenomenon in the nonprofit sector is the amount of public monitoring of the organizations in the field.[10] This is partly a result of the recent scandals in the sector, but it is also a result of more and more outside organizations and philanthropists demanding measures of performance of both effectiveness and efficiency. Formal regulation is exercised by the Exempt Organizations Division of the Internal Revenue Service. Outside the government, the Better Business Bureau's measuring system (found at its Web site www.give.org) is perhaps the most extensive. A portion of their standards for charitable solicitations is reproduced in Exhibit 20-1.

EXHIBIT 20-1

CBBB STANDARDS FOR CHARITABLE SOLICITATIONS

These standards apply to publicly soliciting organizations that are tax exempt under section 501(c)(3) of the Internal Revenue Code, and to other organizations conducting charitable solicitations. While the Council of Better Business Bureaus and its member Better Business Bureaus generally do not report on schools, colleges, or churches soliciting within their congregations, they encourage all soliciting organizations to adhere to these standards. These standards were developed with professional and technical assistance from representatives of soliciting organizations, professional fund raising firms and associations, the accounting profession, corporate contributions officers, regulatory agencies, and the Better Business Bureau system. The Council of Better Business Bureaus is solely responsible for the contents of these standards.

For The Purposes of These Standards:

1. "Charitable solicitations" (or "solicitation") is any direct or indirect request for money, property, credit, volunteer service or other thing of value, to be given now or on a deferred basis, on the representation that it will be used for charitable, educational, religious, benevolent, patriotic, civic, or other philanthropic purposes. Solicitations include invitations to voting membership and appeals to voting members, when a contribution is a principal requirement for membership.

2. "Soliciting organizations" (or "organizations") is any corporation, trust, group, partnership or individual engaged in a charitable solicitation; a "solicitor" is anyone engaged in a charitable solicitation.

3. The "public" includes individuals, groups, associations, corporations, foundations, institutions, and/or government agencies.

4. "Fund raising" includes a charitable solicitation; the activities, representations and materials which are an integral part of the planning, creation, production and communication of the solicitation; and the collection of the money, property, or other thing of value requested. Fund raising includes but is not limited to donor acquisition and renewal, development, fund or resource development, member or membership development, and contract or grant procurement.

Public Accountability

A1. Soliciting organizations shall provide on request an annual report.

The annual report, an annually-updated written account, shall present the organization's purposes: descriptions of the overall programs, activities and accomplishments: eligibility to receive deductible contributions; information about the governing body and structure; and information about financial activities and financial position.

A2. Soliciting organizations shall provide on request complete annual financial statements.

The financial statements shall present the overall financial activities and financial position of the organization,shall be prepared in accordance with generally accepted accounting principles and reporting practices, and shall include the auditor's and treasurer's report, notes and any supplementary schdules. When total income exceeds $100,000, the financial statements shall be audited in accordance with generally accepted auditing standards.

A3. Soliciting organizations' financial statements shall present adequate information to serve as a basis for informed decisions.

Information needed as a basis for informed decisions generally includes but is not limited to: a) significant categories of contributions and other income; b) expenses

(continued)

reported in categories corresponding to the descriptions of major programs and activities contained in the annual report, solicitations, and other informational materials; c) a detailed schedule of expenses by natural classification (e.g. salaries, employee benefits, occupancy, postage, etc.), presenting the natural expenses incurred for each major program and supporting activity; d) accurate presentation of all fund raising and administrative costs; and e) when a significant activity combines fund raising and one or more other purposes (e.g. door-to-door canvassing combining fund raising and social advocacy, or television broadcasts combining fund raising and religious ministry, or a direct mail compaign combining fund raising and public education), the financial statement shall specify the total cost of the multi-purpose activity and the basis for allocating its costs.

A4. Organizations receiving a substantial portion of their income through the fund raising activities of controlled or affiliated entities shall provide on request an accounting of all income received by and fund raising costs incurred by such entities.

Such entities include committees, branches or chapters which are controlled by or affiliated with the benefiting organization, and for which a primary activity is raising funds to support the programs of the benefiting organization.

Use of Funds

B1. A reasonable percentage of total income from all sources shall be applied to programs and activities directly related to the purposes for which the organization exists.

A reasonable percentage requires that at least 50% of total income from all sources be spent on programs and activities directly related to the organization's purposes.

B2. A reasonable percentage of public contributions shall be applied to the programs and activities described in solicitations, in accordance with donor expectations.

A reasonable percentage requires that at least 50% of public contributions be spent on the programs and activities

described in solicitations, in accordance with donor expectations.

B3. Fund raising costs shall be reasonable.

A reasonable use of funds requires that fund raising costs not exceed 35% of related contributions.

B4. Total fund raising and administrative costs shall be reasonable.

A reasonable use of funds requires that total fund raising and administrative costs not exceed 50% of total income.

An organization which does not meet one or more of these percentages limitations (B1, B2, B3, and/or B4) may provide evidence to demonstrate that its use of funds is reasonable. The higher fund raising and administrative costs of a newly created organization, donor restrictions on the use of funds, exceptional bequests, a stigma associated with a cause, and environment or political events beyond an organization's control are among the factors which may result in costs that are reasonable although they do meet these percentage limitations.

B5. Soliciting organizations shall substantiate on request their application of funds, in accordance with donor expectations, to the programs and activities described in solicitations.

B6. Soliciting organizations shall establish and exercise adequate controls over disbursements.

Solicitations and Informational Materials

C1. Solicitations and informational materials, distributed by any means, shall be accurate, truthful and not misleading, both in whole and in part.

C2. Soliciting organizations shall substantiate on request that solicitations and informational materials, distributed by any means, are accurate, truthful and not misleading, both in whole and in part.

C3. Solicitations shall include a clear description of the programs and activities for which funds are requested. Solicitations which describe an issue, problem, need or event, but which do not clearly describe the programs or activities for which funds are requested will not meet this standard. Solicitations in which time or space restrictions apply shall identify a source from which written information is available.

C4. Direct contact solicitations, including personal and telephone appeals, shall identify a) the solicitor and his/her relationship to the benefiting organization, b) the benefiting organization or cause and c) the programs and activities for which funds are requested.

C5. Solicitations in conjunction with the sale of goods, services or admissions shall identify at the point of solicitation a) the benefiting organization, b) a source from which written information is available and c) the actual or anticipated portion of the sales or admission price to benefit the charitable organization or cause.

Fund Raising Practices

D1. Soliciting organizations shall establish and exercise controls over fund raising activities conducted for their benefit by staff, volunteers, consultants, contractors, and controlled or affiliated entities, including commitment to writing of all fund raising contracts and agreements.

D2. Soliciting organizations shall establish and exercise adequate controls over contributions.

D3. Soliciting organizations shall honor donor requests for confidentiality and shall not publicize the identity of donors without prior written permission.

Donor requests for confidentiality include but are not limited to requests that one's name not be used, exchanged, rented or sold.

D4. Fund raising shall be conducted without excessive pressure.

Excessive pressure in fund raising includes, but is not limited to, solicitations in the guise of invoices; harassment; intimidation or coercion, such as threats of public disclosure or economic retaliation; failure to inform recipients of unordered items that

they are under no obligation to pay for or return; and strongly emotional appeals which distort the organization's activities or beneficiaries.

Governance

E1. Soliciting organizations shall have an adequate governing structure.

Soliciting organizations shall have and operate in accordance with governing instruments (charter, articles of incorporation, bylaws, etc.) which set forth the organization's basic goals and purposes, and which define the organizational structure. The governing instruments shall define the body having final responsibility for and authority over the organization's policies and programs (including authority to amend the governing instuments), as well as any subordinate bodies to which specific responsibilities may be delegated.

An organization's governing structure shall be inadequate if any policy-making decisions of the governing body (board) or committee of board members having interim policy-making authority (executive committee) are made by fewer than three persons.

E2. Soliciting organizations shall have an active governing body.

An active governing body (board) exercises responsibility in establishing policies, retaining qualified executive leadership, and overseeing that leadership.

An active board meets formally at least three times annually, with meetings evenly spaced over the course of the year, and with a majority of the members in attendance (in person or by proxy) on average.

Because the public reasonably expects board members to participate personally in policy decisions, the governing body is not active, and a roster of board members may be misleading, if a majority of the board members attend no formal meetins in person over the course of a year.

If the full board meets only once annually, there shall be a least two additional, evenly spaced meetings during the year of an executive committee of board members having interim policy-making

(continued)

authority, with a majority of its members present in person, on average.

E3. Soliciting organizations shall have an independent governing body.

Organizations whose directly and/or indirectly compensated board members constitute more than one-fifth (20%) of the total voting membership of the board or of the executive committee will not meet this standard. (The ordained clergy of a publicly soliciting church's policy-making governing body are excepted from this limitation, although they may be salaried by or receive support or sustenance from the church.)

E4. Soliciting organizations shall have an independent governing body.

Organizations engaged in transactions in which board members have material conflicting interests resulting from any relationship or business affiliation will not meet this standard.

Source: Reprinted with permission. Copyright 1982. Council of Better Business Bureaus. At the time this text went to press, the Better Business Bureau Wise Giving Alliance, the national charity watchdog affiliated with the Better Business Bureau system, was in the process of completing a 2-year project to revise these standards. New charity standards will be finalized in the fall of 2002. To obtain a copy of the revised standards visit *www.give.org* or contact the Alliance at: 4200 Wilson Blvd., Suite 800, Arlington, VA 22203.

SUMMARY

Nonprofit managers must have in place carefully designed measurement systems in order to track organizational performance and make appropriate adjustments. There are two broad categories of control systems. Strategic control systems monitor the organization's environment, competitors, publics, strengths and weaknesses, and performance. Tactical control systems monitor day-to-day performance for the purposes of fine-tuning current marketing efforts.

Two types of tactical control systems are those that measure organization influence on behavior and those that measure target audience member satisfaction. Tracking of behavior requires formal monitoring of systems. Panel studies are useful vehicles for accomplishing this.

Target audience member satisfaction should also be a major objective of all nonprofits. Complaint tracking systems provide one way of assessing this satisfaction over time. However, complaint measures are typically biased both as to the types of complaints and persons affected. Periodic direct surveys of target audience members do not suffer from these biases. They can measure satisfaction directly as simple ratings, indirectly as derived dissatisfaction, or as problems. Studies of problems can be particularly helpful if they also track performance of the organization's complaint-handling activities.

External evaluation is a growing concern for nonprofits in the 1990s. As the result of recent scandals involving charitable organizations, many media watchdogs, and citizens groups are asking whether nonprofits are meeting their social responsibilities. One outgrowth of this increased scrutiny has been the rise of codes of ethical conduct. The Better Business Bureau has produced an extensive code that can serve as a model for many nonprofit organizations.

QUESTIONS

1. Develop a code of ethical conduct for an undergraduate university in your home state. Restrict the code to the university's marketing activities. What are the implications of this code on the university?
2. In some nonprofit categories, satisfaction data are more important than other categories. What are the characteristics of nonprofits for which target audience member satisfaction is especially important? Knowing that satisfaction data are costly to collect, could some direct behavioral outcomes serve as substitutes? What are the dangers in using behavioral outcomes?
3. Suppose that satisfaction data indicate that your chapter of your organization severely underperforms sister chapters. Identify an approach to close the gap in performance. How would you ensure that such performance gaps do not arise in the future?
4. When would it be valuable for a nonprofit to collect competitive intelligence? What are the characteristics of sectors in which these nonprofits are involved? Being that all nonprofits are supposed to be doing "good" for society, is spending money on monitoring competitors a waste? Why?
5. Consider an episode of unethical behavior within a nonprofit with which you are familiar. Describe alternative approaches that could be taken to reduce the future incidence of such behavior. Be sure to include legal action, target audience member self-help, industry self-policing, and company codes of ethics as responses. Which approach do you think is best? Why?

NOTES

1. Peter F. Drucker, "The Nonprofit Bottom Line," *The NonProfit Times*, February 1994, pp. 44–45. See also Kevin P. Kearns, "The Strategic Management of Accountability in Nonprofit Organizations. An Analytical Framework," *Public Administration Review*, March/April 1994, pp. 185–192.
2. It is, of course, a personal ethical decision for the nonprofit marketing professional as to whether he or she wishes to use his or her skills to bring about behaviors with questionable social outcomes. Marketing is a powerful set of tools. The nonprofit marketer must be careful to use them for good ends.
3. Alan R. Andreasen (ed.), *Ethics in Social Marketing* (Washington, D.C.: Georgetown University Press, 2001).
4. See Ralph E. Anderson, "Target Audience Member Dissatisfaction: The Effect of Disconfirmed Expectancy on Perceived Product Performance," *Journal of Marketing Research*, February 1973, pp. 38–44.
5. Kim Cleland, "Patient Power Over Hospitals Grows," *Advertising Age*, October 24, 1994, p. 46.
6. Technical Advisory Research Program (TARP), *Target Audience Member Complaint Handling in America: Final Report* (Washington, D.C.: U.S. Department of Health, Education and Welfare, 1979).
7. See Alan R. Andreasen and Arthur Best, "Target Audience Members Complain— Does Business Respond?" *Harvard Business Review*, July–August 1977, pp. 93–101.
8. Ibid.
9. It is, however, not uncommon for the typical pattern of responses to be more positive than negative or indifferent (the "yea saying" bias).
10. Robert O. Bothwell, "Trends in Self-Regulation and Transparency of Nonprofits in the U.S.," *The International Journal of Not-for-Profit Law*, Vol. 2, No. 3 (March 2000); Joel L. Fleishman, "Public Trust in Not-for-Profit Organizations and the Need for Regulatory Reform," in Charles Clotfelter and Thomas Ehrlich (eds.), *Philanthropy and the Nonprofit Sector in a Changing America* (Bloomington: Indiana University Press, 1999); Regina E. Hertzlinger, "Can Public Trust in Nonprofits and Governments Be Restored?" *Harvard Business Review*, 74, 2 (March–April 1996), pp. 97–107.

Index